Insurance Operations, Regulation, and Statutory Accounting

Insurance Operations, Regulation, and Statutory Accounting

Ann E. Myhr, CPCU, AIM, ARM
Director of Curriculum
American Institute for CPCU/Insurance Institute of America

James J. Markham, JD, CPCU, AIC

Second Edition • Fifth Printing

American Institute for Chartered Property Casualty
Underwriters/Insurance Institute of America
720 Providence Road, Suite 100
Malvern, Pennsylvania 19355-3433

Second Edition · Fifth Printing · April 2009

Library of Congress Control Number: 2004109463

ISBN 978-0-89463-161-0

Foreword

The American Institute for Chartered Property Casualty Underwriters and the Insurance Institute of America (the Institutes) are not-for-profit organizations committed to meeting the evolving educational needs of the risk management and insurance community. The Institutes strive to provide current, relevant educational programs in formats that meet the needs of risk management and insurance professionals and the organizations that employ them.

The American Institute for CPCU (AICPCU) was founded in 1942 through a collaborative effort between industry professionals and academics, led by faculty members at The Wharton School of the University of Pennsylvania. In 1953, AICPCU coordinated operations with the Insurance Institute of America (IIA), which was founded in 1909 and remains the oldest continuously functioning national organization offering educational programs for the property-casualty insurance sector.

The Insurance Research Council (IRC), founded in 1977, is a division of AICPCU supported by industry members. This not-for-profit research organization examines public policy issues of interest to property-casualty insurers, insurance customers, and the general public. IRC research reports are distributed widely to insurance-related organizations, public policy authorities, and the media.

The Institutes' new customer- and solution-focused business model allows us to better serve the risk management and insurance communities. Customer-centricity defines our business philosophy and shapes our priorities. The Institutes' innovation arises from our commitment to finding solutions that meet customer needs and deliver results. Our business process is shaped by our commitment to efficiency, strategy, and responsible asset management.

The Institutes believe that professionalism is grounded in education, experience, and ethical behavior. The Chartered Property Casualty Underwriter (CPCU) professional designation offered by the Institutes is designed to provide a broad understanding of the property-casualty insurance industry. Depending on professional needs, CPCU students may select either a commercial or a personal risk management and insurance focus. The CPCU designation is conferred annually by the AICPCU Board of Trustees.

In addition, the Institutes offer designations and certificate programs in a variety of disciplines, including the following:

- Claims
- Commercial underwriting
- Fidelity and surety bonding
- General insurance
- Insurance accounting and finance
- Insurance information technology
- Insurance production and agency management
- Insurance regulation and compliance

- Management
- Marine insurance
- Personal insurance
- Premium auditing
- Quality insurance services
- Reinsurance
- Risk management
- Surplus lines

You can complete a program leading to a designation, take a single course to fill a knowledge gap, or take multiple courses and programs throughout your career. The practical and technical knowledge gained from Institute courses enhances your qualifications and contributes to your professional growth. Most Institute courses carry college credit recommendations from the American Council on Education. A variety of courses qualify for credits toward certain associate, bachelor's, and master's degrees at several prestigious colleges and universities.

Our Knowledge Resources Department, in conjunction with industry experts and members of the academic community, develops our trusted course and program content, including Institute study materials. These materials provide practical career and performance-enhancing knowledge and skills.

We welcome comments from our students and course leaders. Your feedback helps us continue to improve the quality of our study materials.

Peter L. Miller, CPCU
President and CEO
American Institute for CPCU
Insurance Institute of America

Preface

Insurance Operations, Regulation, and Statutory Accounting is the textbook for CPCU 520, one of the five foundation courses required of students pursuing the CPCU designation. If you are planning to take the CPCU 520 examination, you should make sure that you have the current CPCU 520 study materials by checking the Institutes' Web site or calling the Institutes' Customer Service Department.

This edition of CPCU 520 replaces the previous text, *Insurance Operations and Regulation*. The current text includes three new chapters covering insurance financial statements, statutory accounting, and insurer financial management. Also new in this edition is a chapter on insurer business strategy and global operations.

The fifteen chapters in *Insurance Operations, Regulation, and Statutory Accounting* can be summarized as follows:

Chapter 1 provides an overview of insurance operations, including classifications and types of insurers and their major goals.

Chapter 2 discusses the insurance regulatory environment.

Chapter 3 describes the unique characteristics of insurance marketing and the three marketing systems and five alternative distribution channels that insurers use.

Chapters 4, 5, and 6 explain the underwriting process and illustrate how this process applies to property insurance and liability insurance. These chapters also include a discussion of the loss control and premium audit functions.

Chapter 7 introduces the ratemaking process, describes ratemaking methods, and explains how ratemaking data are developed.

Chapters 8, 9, and 10 describe the claim adjusting process and discuss the challenges of adjusting different types of property and liability claims.

Chapter 11 discusses the functions performed by reinsurance, the categories and types of reinsurance agreements, and the considerations related to administering a reinsurance program.

Chapters 12, 13, and 14 review the financial statements used by insurers, explain how to interpret the information contained in these statements, describe the differences between statutory accounting principles (SAP) and generally accepted accounting principles (GAAP), and discuss insurer financial management.

Chapter 15 describes the strategic management process and the global environment for insurance operations.

This text is designed to provide an overview of property-casualty insurance operations and to acquaint you with how the insurance mechanism operates. Through increased knowledge of the concepts covered in this text, you will be able to better understand the challenges facing both the insurance industry as a whole and your specific organization.

The Institutes are deeply indebted to the following individuals who reviewed one or more chapters of the manuscript:

Elizabeth L. Brinkman, CPCU, AIM, ARe
Salvatore V. Fazio, AIM, AIAF
Robert S. Fleming, CPCU, AIM, ALCM
William R. Gawne, CPCU
Nancee A. James, CPCU
Linda B. Mendenhall, CPCU, AU
James A. Sherlock, CPCU, CLU, ARM
Valerie Ullman-Katz, CPCU, AIM, ARM
Lawrence White, CPCU, ACAS, MAAA
Barbara A. Zielinski, CPCU, ARM

Their thoughtful review of the material has contributed to making this text accurate and relevant to current industry conditions. The Institutes remain equally thankful to individuals who contributed to the development of earlier texts for this course, although they are too numerous to name here. The current updated and revised text still reflects the valuable insight of these insurance professionals.

For more information about the Institutes' programs, please call our Customer Service Department at (800) 644-2101, e-mail us at customerservice@cpcuiia.org, or visit our Web site at www.aicpcu.org.

Ann E. Myhr

Contributing Authors

The American Institute for CPCU, the Insurance Institute of America, and the authors of this text acknowledge, with deep appreciation, the work of the following contributing authors:

Mary Ann Cook, CPCU, AU, AAI

Arthur L. Flitner, CPCU, ARM, AIC

Connor M. Harrison, CPCU, AU, ARe

Bernard L. Webb, CPCU, FCAS, MAAA

Eric A. Wiening, CPCU, ARM, AU

Contents

Chapter 1

Direct Your Learning

Overview of Insurance Operations

After learning the content of this chapter, you should be able to:

- Describe the risk management process.

- Explain how insurers have organized to provide property-casualty insurance.

- Describe insurers' major goals and the constraints that impede insurers from achieving them.

- Describe and calculate the measurements used to evaluate insurer performance.

- Explain how the principal functions within an insurer operate and how they interrelate.

Develop Your Perspective

What are the main topics covered in the chapter?

The chapter addresses the risk management process, the types of insurers, the methods insurers use to measure their financial results, departments or functions within insurance organizations, and the interactions among those departments.

Categorize insurers by their structure and form of ownership.

- What activities are restricted based on the form of ownership?

- What pressure might an insurer's executives feel from stockholders or policyholders?

Why is it important to learn about these topics?

An insurer's financial results are monitored continually to make sure the insurer is on track with its goals. An insurer might make adjustments that seem arbitrary on the surface, but these adjustments help an insurer align its performance with its goals. An insurer's actions will also be restricted by internal and external constraints.

Consider how an insurer's activities are affected by its ownership and the constraints on its activities.

- Which departments within an insurer are responsible for making decisions?

- How do constraints and the division of responsibilities affect how the organization does business?

How can you use what you will learn?

Interpret an insurer's activities:

- How has its ownership and structure affected its goals?

- How do departments interact, and who are the decision-makers?

Chapter 1

Overview of Insurance Operations

PROPERTY-CASUALTY MARKET

The financial services sector is vast, and the property-casualty industry constitutes a large part of that sector in the United States. The property-casualty industry has 624,000 employees and had total net written premiums for the year 2001 of $323.4 billion.[1] This chapter provides an overview of property-casualty operations and starts by explaining the insurance mechanism and the risk management process. The remaining sections of the chapter examine types of insurers and their goals as well as factors that constrain insurers from meeting established goals. The chapter's final section discusses the functions found in most insurance operations. The discussion of these topics is expanded in later chapters of this text.

The Insurance Mechanism

The insurance mechanism focuses primarily on uncertainty about the chance that a particular loss will occur. This uncertainty is referred to as risk. The costs associated with risk can discourage business growth, investment in research and development, or expansion into new technologies or industries. From a customer standpoint, uncertainty over the financial consequences of loss to homes or autos can affect spending levels. By transferring the potential financial consequences of their loss exposures to an insurer, businesses and individuals reduce their uncertainty. The risk transfer process does not eliminate the possibility that a loss will occur, but it does reimburse the costs associated with that loss. In return for this transfer, an insurer receives a premium.

As an example, a young couple is completing the purchase of their first house. They are concerned about a wide range of possible losses, including damage to the house or its contents by fire, natural causes, theft, or vandalism. They might also be worried about being unable to make mortgage payments because of an illness or a job loss. The house is also subject to increases or decreases in value over time. Will they be able to sell the house for a profit at some point in the future? All of these situations involve uncertainty about the outcome of various events related to house ownership. These situations provide opportunities for loss, for no loss, or, regarding the house's eventual market value, for gain. This book focuses only on risk involving uncertainty over either loss or no loss. This type of uncertainty is called pure risk, which indicates only a chance for either financial loss or no financial loss. Insurance policies cover only pure risk loss exposures. In this example, the house will be damaged by fire or some other cause of loss, or it will remain undamaged. This couple will most likely purchase an insurance policy with a deductible and pay a premium to an insurer for the coverage provided. Consequently, the couple minimizes its concern over the financial consequences of a loss and also shares its loss exposures with many other policyholders. This sharing of loss exposures is an important part of the **insurance** mechanism. The premiums of many policyholders contribute to the payment of losses suffered by relatively few policyholders.

Insurance
Insurance is a risk management technique that transfers some or all of the potential financial consequences (liability) for certain loss exposures from the insured to the insurer.

RISK MANAGEMENT PROCESS

A business would go through a process similar to that followed by the new homeowners. However, because a business has a much broader range of possible loss exposures, the risk or uncertainty related to the potential for loss is also much greater than for the homeowners. To minimize the negative effect of risk, an individual or a business must thoroughly identify all potential loss exposures. This is the first step in the risk management process; the second step is to thoroughly analyze a business's loss exposures. The third step is to investigate the various techniques to address the loss exposures that have been identified. These techniques generally fall into three broad categories: risk control, risk financing techniques, and loss exposure avoidance. Risk control techniques are designed to eliminate or reduce the chance or amount of loss. Risk financing techniques provide a means to pay for losses that do occur. The risk management process recognizes that some losses are unavoidable and reinforces the importance of identifying as many loss exposures as possible. Uncovering all loss exposures is important, because the unintended assumption of loss exposures can be costly to any business. Avoidance occurs when the entity decides not to incur a loss exposure in the first place or to eliminate one that already exists. For example, the prospective homeowners could avoid all of the loss exposures related to property ownership by not purchasing the house. However, this is usually neither desirable nor practical. Therefore, purchasing insurance is generally a more suitable option. Once the potential for loss has been recognized, the risk associated with that potential can be managed by selecting (the fourth step) and implementing (the fifth step) the most appropriate risk management technique. The final step in the risk management process is to monitor the results and make changes as needed.

Steps in the Risk Management Process

1. Identify loss exposures.

2. Analyze loss exposures.

3. Examine the feasibility of risk management techniques.

4. Select the most appropriate techniques.

5. Implement the risk management techniques.

6. Monitor results and make changes as needed.

Risk control methods either prevent the occurrence of a loss or reduce the severity of losses that occur despite attempts at prevention. In a residence, a risk control might be as simple as installing smoke detectors or door locks. In a business, risk control might include installing a sprinkler system or implementing a driver-safety training program. Because the risk of loss can rarely be eliminated entirely, risk financing techniques are also required. If a loss does occur, a means must exist for responding to the financial consequences. Purchasing insurance is one example of a risk financing technique called risk transfer. Buying insurance transfers the uncertainty about the expense of losses to the insurer for a premium payment. Consequently, a small, certain expense—the premium or fee—is substituted for an unknown loss amount that might be large. A loss might still occur, but the risk, or uncertainty, is reduced because a financing mechanism exists to pay for the financial consequences of the loss. Insurers determine appropriate premiums based partly on a projection of probable future loss payments for a given number of exposure units using the **law of large numbers**. This theory states that when the number of similar, independent exposure units increases, the relative accuracy of projections of future outcomes based on these exposure units increases. The law of large numbers is the foundation for ratemaking and pricing insurance products.

Law of large numbers
A mathematical principle stating that as the number of similar but independent exposure units increases, the relative accuracy of predictions about future outcomes (losses) also increases.

Not all loss exposures can be insured. Some coverage for those loss exposures might not be available, or the cost might not be affordable. However, risk can also be transferred contractually to a third party; for example, a landlord might hold tenants responsible for damage to the premises in a lease agreement. From the landlord's perspective, the uncertainty about paying particular losses arising from the ownership of his or her building has been transferred to the tenants. The chance of loss has not been reduced, but the responsibility for any resulting loss payment has shifted from the landlord to the tenant.

Alternative Risk Financing Techniques

During the past decade, a move away from insurance as a risk financing technique has occurred. This move was motivated to some extent by concerns about pricing, coverage availability, and legal or regulatory changes. Large commercial operations decided to retain more of their loss exposures, which allows them to spend less money on insurance. Funding arrangements for future losses can be made, and certain insurance services such as loss settlement or loss control can be purchased separately from the insurer. Doing this frees up funds that would have been used to pay a large premium and that can now be used to invest in the business. Examples of this type of alternative risk financing technique include self-insurance programs, captives, risk retention programs, and others. The term "alternative risk financing" refers to any number of risk management techniques other than insurance. According to A.M. Best, almost half of the risks in the U.S. commercial market would be placed in the alternative market by 2003.[2]

CLASSIFICATIONS AND TYPES OF INSURERS

United States property-casualty insurers can be classified in the following four ways:

1. Legal form of ownership
2. Place of incorporation
3. Licensing status
4. Marketing systems used

Exhibit 1-1 shows the general classifications and types of insurers to be discussed. An insurer might be further classified by what types of insurance it writes or its specialty.

Form of Ownership

The first classification of insurers is by legal form of ownership. The two major types of insurers in this classification are proprietary and cooperative insurers.

Proprietary Insurers

Proprietary insurers
Insurers formed to earn a profit for their owners.

Proprietary insurers are the first type of insurer in the legal form of ownership classification. These insurers are formed for the purpose of earning a profit for their owners. Stock insurance companies, Lloyd's, and insurance exchanges are all types of proprietary insurers.

Stock Insurance Companies

Stock insurance companies are the most prevalent type of proprietary insurer in the United States. These companies are owned by their stockholders, who elect a board of directors to oversee the company's operations. This board then appoints officers who make the day-to-day decisions and hire employees to operate the company.

EXHIBIT 1-1

Classifications and Types of Insurers

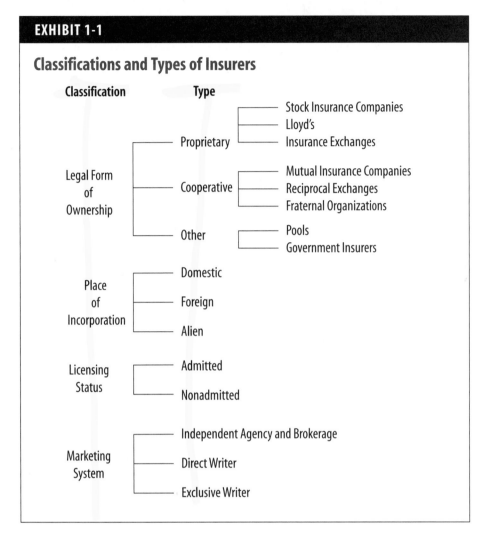

Lloyd's

Another type of proprietary insurer is Lloyd's, which consists of Lloyd's of London and American Lloyds organizations. Lloyd's of London is not an insurance company, but a marketplace such as a stock exchange. All of the insurance written at Lloyd's is written by or on behalf of individual members, and the insurance each member writes is backed by his or her personal fortune. The liability of each member is limited to the amount that member agrees to write. Individual members are not liable for the obligations assumed by any other member. Each member belongs to one or more of over fifty syndicates, with the day-to-day management delegated to the syndicate manager. Lloyd's provides coverage for many unusual or difficult loss exposures and underwrites much of the global marine and aviation insurance.

American Lloyds account for a very small amount of U.S. premiums, with most companies domiciled in Texas. Currently, fewer than 100 American Lloyds companies are licensed under Texas law. These were originally formed because of the favorable regulatory climate in Texas. These companies are usually reinsured 100 percent by their parent companies.

Insurance Exchanges

An insurance exchange is a proprietary insurer similar to Lloyd's because it acts as an insurance marketplace. Exchange members underwrite any insurance or reinsurance purchased on the exchange. Members can be individuals, partnerships, or corporations, and they have limited liability. Members belong to syndicates and delegate day-to-day operations to the syndicate manager.

The only existing exchange is INEX (formerly the Illinois Insurance Exchange), which was formed in 1979. This exchange serves as an excess and surplus lines market writing various types of insurance. Member syndicates operate as separate businesses that focus on a particular group of loss exposures.

Cooperative Insurers

Cooperative insurers are the second type of insurer in the legal form of ownership classification. This type of insurer is formed to provide insurance at a minimum cost to policyholders, who own the insurer. Cooperative insurers include the following:

- Mutual insurance companies
- Reciprocal exchanges
- Fraternal organizations
- Other cooperatives

Cooperative insurers
Insurers owned by their policyholders and usually formed to provide insurance protection to their policyholders at minimum cost. Mutual insurance companies, reciprocal exchanges, and fraternal organizations are examples of cooperative insurers.

Mutual Insurance Companies

Mutual insurance companies constitute the largest number of cooperative insurers. Mutuals are corporations owned by their policyholders and formed to provide low-cost insurance to those policyholders. The policyholders elect a board of directors that appoints officers to manage the company. Some profit is retained to increase surplus, and excess profit is usually returned to policyholders as dividends.

Most mutuals are advance premium mutuals. Policyholders pay a premium at policy inception and renewal to cover expenses and losses during the policy period. Some mutuals retain the right to assess policyholders for additional premiums if more funds are needed. Most of the large mutual companies, however, issue nonassessable policies, and policyholders are not subject to any type of assessment.

Reciprocal Exchanges

Reciprocal exchanges (also called interinsurance exchanges), like mutuals, are usually formed to provide insurance at a lower cost to members and are owned by their members. However, mutuals and reciprocals differ significantly. When insurance is purchased from a mutual insurer, the potential financial consequences (liability) for certain loss exposures are transferred to the insurer. In a reciprocal exchange, the liability is transferred to the other members of the exchange. Also, a reciprocal is managed by an attorney-in-fact, not officers elected by a board of directors. A reciprocal is a nonprofit organization, but the attorney-in-fact can be formed for profit.

Fraternal Organizations

Fraternal organizations resemble mutual companies, but they combine a lodge or social function with their insurance function. They write primarily life and health insurance.

Other Cooperative Insurers

Cooperative insurers include captive insurers, risk retention groups, and purchasing groups. Captive insurers can take several forms, but, regardless, they are formed to insure the loss exposures of the captives' owners. The ultimate purpose of the captive is to fund the losses of its owners; this arrangement has sometimes been referred to as "formalized self-insurance." Several states, such as Vermont, have enacted legislation to facilitate the formation and operation of captive insurers within their jurisdictions. However, only 38 percent of states permit captives.[3]

Legislation has also allowed risk retention groups and purchasing groups to form. These cooperatives can be stock companies, mutuals, or reciprocal exchanges. They are usually organized so that a limited group or type of insured is eligible to purchase insurance from them. These types of insurers are becoming more important in the evolving insurance marketplace.

Other Insurers

Other insurers are the third type of insurer in the legal form of ownership classification. Insurers that fall into this classification include pools and government insurers.

Pools

A **pool** consists of several insurers, not otherwise related, that join together to insure loss exposures that individual insurers are unwilling to insure. These loss exposures present the potential for losses that either occur too frequently or are too severe (catastrophic). A major airline crash illustrates such a catastrophic loss.

Another example of loss exposures that insurers might be unwilling to insure individually are those associated with a large nuclear power plant, whose losses could amount to billions of dollars for property and liability damage. Because no single insurer was willing to assume such tremendous liability, nuclear energy pools were formed. They allow many member insurers to spread any losses among members. Additionally, the pools buy reinsurance from nonmembers to increase their capacity.

Pools can be formed either voluntarily or to meet statutory requirements. They operate either as a syndicate or through reinsurance. A syndicate pool issues a joint (or syndicate) policy to the insured, listing all pool members and specifying the part of the insurance for which each member is responsible. Under such policies, the insured has a contractual relationship with each pool member and can sue any or all of them directly if a disagreement arises.

Pool
An association of persons or organizations that combines its resources to economically finance recovery from accidental losses.

Under a reinsurance pool, one member of the pool issues the policy to the insured, and the other pool members reinsure an agreed proportion of the policy's insured loss exposures. The insured has a contractual relationship only with the member that issued the policy. The policyholder has no legal rights against the other members of the pool and might not even know that they exist.

Many pools are required by law. Virtually all states require some kind of pooling arrangement to provide auto liability insurance for drivers who cannot obtain such insurance in the standard market. Similar pools are required for workers' compensation coverage in most states. **Fair Access to Insurance Requirements (FAIR) plans** are required by law in twenty-eight states. These pools provide property insurance to qualified property owners who are unable to obtain coverage in the standard market. Many states in the southeastern U.S., such as Florida, have pools that provide windstorm coverage for residents in storm-prone areas who cannot obtain coverage in the standard market. As of 1995, pools were in operation in seven states, writing $53 billion of coverage. Similar statutory pools for other types of insurance are required by state law. The protection that these pools provide is underwritten by private insurers and not by state governments, although state and federal governments do act as insurers in some situations.

Fair Access to Insurance Requirements (FAIR) plans
An insurance pool through which private insurers collectively address an unmet need for property insurance on urban properties, especially those susceptible to loss by riot or civil commotion.

Government Insurers

A number of states have government insurance operations. One-third of the states have state insurance funds that provide workers' compensation insurance for some or all employers in the state. Most of the funds compete with private insurers. Several others are, by law, the only source of workers' compensation in their states.

The U.S. federal government has many insurance operations. The largest federal insurance program is the Social Security system, which provides life insurance, annuities, disability income coverage, and medical expense coverage for millions of U.S. residents. One of the largest property insurance programs is the National Flood Insurance Program (NFIP) administered by the Federal Insurance Administration (FIA) under the Federal Emergency Management Agency (FEMA). Federal insurance programs also include deposit insurance for banks and other financial institutions, crop insurance, and crime insurance.

Place of Incorporation

The second classification of insurers is by place of incorporation as domestic, foreign, or alien insurers. Insurance is regulated at the state level. Therefore, a domestic insurer is incorporated within a specific state or, if not incorporated, is formed under the laws of that state. Reciprocal exchanges are the only unincorporated insurers permitted in most states. Insurance exchanges and Lloyd's organizations are permitted under law in only a few states. A foreign insurer is a domestic insurer that is licensed to do business in states other than its domiciled state. Alien insurers are incorporated or formed in another country. The formation and licensing of insurers is discussed in more detail in a subsequent chapter.

Licensing Status

The third classification of insurers is by licensing status. A **licensed** (or an **admitted**) **insurer** is an insurer that has been granted a license to operate in a particular state. An **unlicensed** (or a **nonadmitted**) **insurer** has not been granted a license to operate. Producers for primary insurance (except excess and surplus lines producers) are licensed to place business only with admitted insurers. Excess and surplus lines producers are licensed to place business with nonadmitted insurers, but only after licensed insurers have declined to write it. Licensing status is also important for reinsurance purposes.

Licensed insurer, or admitted insurer
An insurer authorized by the state insurance department to transact business within a particular state.

Unlicensed insurer, or nonadmitted insurer
An insurer not authorized by the state insurance department to transact business in the insured's state.

Marketing Systems

The fourth classification of insurers is by marketing system—that is, the system used to deliver insurance products to the marketplace. Three types of insurers fall into the classification:

1. Independent agencies and brokerages
2. Direct writers
3. Exclusive writers

These systems are discussed in detail in a subsequent chapter.

INSURER GOALS

Senior managers of insurers seek to meet the goals established by the insurer's owners, as do all senior managers. An insurer's overall goals are not really different from those of any other organization. What is different is how an insurer meets these goals and the conflicts that exist among competing goals. Insurers' major goals are to:

-   Earn a profit.
-   Meet customer needs.
-   Comply with legal requirements.
-   Fulfill duty to society.

Earn a Profit

The profit goal is most commonly associated with proprietary, or for-profit, insurers. Cooperative insurers should also earn a profit, but doing so is not the primary goal for which they are formed.

A proprietary insurer must earn a profit to provide a return on the investment made by the individuals and institutions that purchased the insurer's stock. A proprietary insurer can attract capital only as long as its profits are comparable to or better than similar insurers. If investors do not believe that they will receive an acceptable rate of return on their investment, they will seek opportunity elsewhere. The insurer is then unable to raise the capital needed to run the business.

Funds from policyholders are one source of capital for cooperative insurers. Growth of surplus derived from underwriting operations is another. Funds in excess of those used to pay losses and operating expenses, generally considered profits, are contributed to surplus or returned to policyholders in the form of dividends. Surplus accumulation ensures continued solvency and protects against unforeseen catastrophic losses.

Under certain circumstances, a cooperative insurer can obtain additional capital by borrowing funds by using surplus notes. These notes can usually be repaid only from profits, so funds from additional capital are also likely to depend on the insurer's anticipated profitability.

Meet Customers' Needs

To attract customers, an insurer must provide the products and services those customers are seeking. This involves determining what customers need and then finding the best way to satisfy those needs. Insurance is an intangible product; the customer receives an insurance policy, but what the customer actually purchases is a transfer mechanism. The customer pays a premium to transfer some or all of the potential financial consequences of certain loss exposures to the insurer.

Customers also expect prompt service and timely responses to inquiries. When customers suffer a loss, they can be upset or under considerable stress. Consequently, the insurer must provide quick and professional assistance, which requires well-trained personnel and automated support systems.

Meeting customers' needs can often conflict with the profit goal. Offering high-quality insurance at a price that the customer can afford might not generate the profit that the insurer needs to attract and retain capital. Providing training, operating automated call centers, and maintaining current information technology can also conflict with achieving the profit goal.

Comply With Legal Requirements

Insurers, like other businesses, must meet all of their legal obligations. Legal compliance is part of being a responsible corporate citizen. Additionally, legal compliance promotes the insurer's good reputation in the business community and the insurer's ability to attract capital and customers. Lack of compliance can lead to fines and penalties.

One of an insurer's greatest responsibilities is compliance with state regulations. The insurance industry is highly regulated, and the expense associated with compliance can be substantial. Insurers incur expenses for filings, recordkeeping and accounting, and legal activities. Additional expenses are incurred for participation in assigned risk plans, FAIR plans, and insolvency funds. To the extent that these expenses increase the cost of insurance, they create a conflict between the profit goal and the customer needs goal.

Fulfill Duty to Society

All corporations are obligated to promote the well-being of society. At the minimum, this obligation means that the insurer should avoid causing any public harm. Many insurers go well beyond the minimum by contributing to medical, educational, and other public service organizations and by establishing employee benefit plans. Such activities create conflicts with the customer needs and the profit goals.

CONSTRAINTS ON ACHIEVING GOALS

Conflicts among goals are not the only reasons that insurers do not always achieve their goals. Several other constraints exist, both inside the insurer's operation and in the external environment.

Internal Constraints

Several internal constraints might prevent an insurer from meeting all of its goals, including the following:

- Efficiency
- Expertise
- Size
- Financial resources
- Other internal constraints

Fortunately, not all of these constraints apply to all insurers.

Efficiency

Some insurers operate more efficiently than others. An insurer's lack of efficiency might be caused by poor management, insufficient capital, lack of information technology, an inability to adapt to change, or other causes. Inefficient insurers are at a disadvantage in competing with efficient ones. This competitive weakness might prevent them from meeting their profit goals, which can lead, in turn, to the inability to meet humanitarian or societal goals. Inefficiency, particularly in information technology and customer service, can prevent an insurer from adequately meeting its customers' needs. In extreme cases, inefficiency can lead to insolvency and a consequent failure to meet legal and regulatory goals.

Expertise

The insurance business is complex, and a considerable amount of expertise is required to successfully operate an insurer. This is particularly true as insurers move into niche or specialty markets, both of which require expertise in underwriting, pricing, and claim settlement for unusual losses. Lack of expertise could prevent the insurer from making a profit or meeting customers' needs or eventually cause the insurer to fail to meet any of its goals. As with efficiency, in extreme cases, lack of expertise could ultimately lead to insolvency.

Size

An insurer's size affects its ability to meet its goals. A small insurer has more challenges than a large insurer in terms of available resources. Large insurers can take advantage of economies of scale and might have more financial resources to update technology or reach additional markets. Large insurers can invest more in market research and product development than small insurers can. One advantage for a small insurer is that it can be more nimble, allowing it to respond quickly to an emerging trend. The limited resources of a small insurer might still be a disadvantage, however.

A recent Conning Research study, however, indicates that growth rates for small insurers outpaced those of large insurers. Further analysis is required to determine whether these results are accurate or whether mitigating factors apply.[4]

Financial Resources

Insufficient financial resources can pose a serious threat to an insurer. When financial resources become strained, insurers are unable to effectively train staff, make new capital investments, or reach new markets. Management must make difficult decisions about allocating scarce resources among competing priorities. In recent years, some insurers have had their financial resources reduced by underwriting losses, investment losses, or both. Financial constraints can further affect insurers' ability to achieve profit and/or societal goals.

Other Internal Constraints

Other internal constraints can interfere with achieving goals. A newly established insurer might lack the name recognition necessary to achieve its profit goals even if it has the expertise and financial resources to do so. Many established banks experienced this difficulty when they entered the insurance industry. Banks are well known in the financial services area but lack the brand recognition of established insurers.

Another internal constraint is a reputation damaged by past problems. Even if past problems have been corrected and the insurer is operating flawlessly, it can have ongoing difficulty overcoming its poor reputation.

External Constraints

In addition to internal constraints, insurers face the following external constraints that might prevent them from meeting their goals:

- Regulation
- Public opinion
- Competition
- Economic conditions
- Marketing systems
- Other external constraints

Regulation

Insurance operations are closely regulated, extending from incorporation to liquidation and encompassing most activities in between.

Insurance regulators monitor insurers' solvency to protect the insurer's policyholders and members of the public who benefit from the existence of insurance.

Regulation can also extend to the insurance rates and forms insurers use. If filed rate increases are not approved by the applicable regulator, an insurer might not meet its profit goals. Policy form approval and the time constraints related to the filing process might keep an insurer from fully meeting customers' needs.

Insurance regulation is complex and extensive. Regulation varies by state, and federal regulation adds another layer of complexity. Consequently, regulation imposes a major constraint on insurers, requiring significant personnel and financial resources that can inhibit the insurer's ability to achieve its profit goals.

Public Opinion

Public opinion toward the insurance industry as a whole can act as a constraint for individual insurers in meeting goals. While many customers are satisfied with their insurers, several high-profile issues can lead to a negative perception of the insurance industry. For example, affordability and lack of availability of personal auto insurance in some states have been highly publicized and overshadow the overall satisfaction customers have with their insurers. Dissatisfaction with insurers can also lead to the involvement of legislators and regulators. Corrective action, such as California's Proposition 103 mandating rate rollbacks, can seriously constrain individual insurers from meeting profit goals.

Additionally, such actions can also constrain insurers from meeting societal goals. When the insurance industry is viewed negatively by the public, it contradicts the idea of serving in the public's best interests.

Competition

Insurance industry market cycles are referred to as either hard markets or soft markets. Hard markets are characterized by decreasing competition and rising prices. Soft market cycles are characterized by increasing competition and decreasing prices. The industry entered a protracted soft market in the late 1980s that continued throughout the 1990s. This soft market resulted in many mergers and the consolidation of major insurers because of decreasing premium levels. Many insurers that existed in 1990 either no longer existed in 2000 or had significantly changed their operations because of acquisitions or mergers with competitors.

Despite the decline in the number of insurers, so many insurers remain in the market that competition is great. Competition is further fueled in personal insurance by highly standardized products that customers view as commodities.

In soft markets, competitive pressure to decrease prices makes it difficult for insurers to achieve their profit goals. Low profits can affect insurers' ability to meet societal goals. Excessive competition can entice some insurers to bend the rules, making insurers unable to meet their legal and regulatory goals.

Economic Conditions

Insurers' investment operations can be affected severely by economic downturns. The investment income of most insurers grew substantially during the economic expansion throughout the 1990s. These investment gains quickly declined with the market downturn that began late in 2000.

Insurers can be adversely affected during inflationary cycles as well. Inflation affects the cost of insurance losses through increased medical costs, construction costs, and other loss-related costs. Inflation also affects insurance premiums, but the effect on losses is felt more quickly than the effect on premiums. This difference in timing makes it difficult for insurers to achieve their profit goals during periods of rapid inflation.

Marketing Systems

The system an insurer chooses to distribute its products can affect the insurer's ability to meet its goals. Insurers distribute their products through systems using different types of sales and service personnel called producers. Each distribution system meets the needs of some customers, and each fails to meet the needs of others. For example, the independent agency system, which uses agents and brokers, seems to successfully meet the needs of commercial insurance customers. This system, however, has been less effective in meeting the needs of personal insurance customers, and other marketing systems now dominate personal insurance. Conversely, some insurers using the exclusive agency or the direct writer marketing system have difficulty reaching personal insurance customers in rural areas. Some insurers in those areas have begun using independent agents and brokers.

Likewise, other insurers have tried to overcome the limitations of a given marketing system by using more than one system.

Other External Constraints

Other external constraints can hinder an insurer's ability to reach its goals. Some of these constraints are natural or man-made catastrophe losses, the breakdown of law and order, and legal changes that affect liability claims.

MEASURING INSURER PERFORMANCE

Measuring the performance of an insurer involves determining how successful the insurer is at meeting established goals. As with any assessment, some measurements are objective, while others may be subjective. Financial measurements are based on statistical evidence and are considered to be more objective. Measurements of customer satisfaction or how well an insurer fulfills its duties to society are more subjective and therefore difficult to obtain.

Measuring Profit

Several financial figures must be considered in measuring the profitability of an insurer. These include premiums, expense ratio, loss ratio, combined ratio, investment income, and operating profit or loss.

Premiums

An insurer's profits depend heavily on the premium revenue the insurer generates. Consequently, a review of an insurer's success in meeting its profit goals must consider the volume of premium the insurer writes. Investment profit also depends, in part, on premium revenue that creates the funds used for investment. Premium growth must also be sustained over time. An insurer should achieve premium growth by writing new policies rather than depending solely on insurance rate increases or inflation. Rapid premium growth, however, may be undesirable and could indicate lax underwriting standards or inadequate premium levels. Inappropriate premium growth can eventually lead to reduced profits as losses begin to exceed premiums collected for loss exposures. Of course, premium growth, or the lack thereof, must be evaluated in light of current market conditions. During periods of intense competition, significant premium growth is difficult to achieve.

Establishing reasonable rules with which to measure the adequacy, inadequacy, or excessiveness of premium growth is also difficult. Growth that is slower than the industry average usually indicates a problem. Likewise, a growth rate substantially higher than the industry average might indicate changes that might be unfavorable in the long term. Did growth result from a competitive advantage, relaxed underwriting, inadequate insurance rates, or a combination of these factors?

Exhibit 1-2 shows the total net written premiums (gross written premiums less ceded reinsurance premiums) for the property-casualty insurance industry for 1991 through 2000. Growth, in current dollars, varied from 1.8 percent in 1998 to 6.2 percent in 1993, reflecting competitive conditions in the market. When measured in constant 1991 dollars, the industry's net written premium growth was flat or declined in six of the ten years during this period.

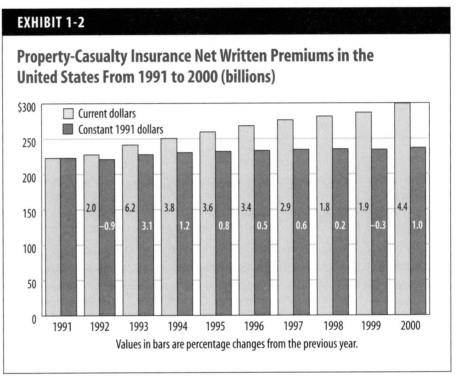

EXHIBIT 1-2

Property-Casualty Insurance Net Written Premiums in the United States From 1991 to 2000 (billions)

Values in bars are percentage changes from the previous year.

Data for net written premiums in current dollars are used with permission from © A.M. Best Company, *Best's Aggregates and Averages, Property-Casualty, United States,* 2001 Edition, p. 299. The U.S. Bureau of Labor Statistics Consumer Price Index for all urban consumers was used in the calculation of the real rate of premium growth (constant dollars).

Expense Ratio

Expense ratio
An insurer's incurred underwriting expenses for a specific period divided by its written premiums for the same period.

Insurer expenses are most commonly measured by the **expense ratio**, the ratio of expenses to premiums. Exhibit 1-3 shows the property-casualty insurance expense ratios for the years 1997 through 2001. The loss adjustment expense ratio shown is the ratio of loss adjustment expenses to earned premiums. The commission and other expense ratios are to net written premiums. As indicated in the exhibit, the total underwriting expense ratio excludes loss adjustment expenses. The expense ratio varies widely by type of insurance.

As shown in Exhibit 1-3, the expense ratio also varies over time. When rates are rising rapidly, the expense ratio tends to decline because expenses do not rise as rapidly as losses. When competition or regulation holds insurance rates down, the expense ratio tends to increase because expenses, in dollar terms, continue to rise with inflation. This relationship is seen by comparing the total underwriting expense ratio from Exhibit 1-3 with the change in net written premiums in current dollars from Exhibit 1-2.

EXHIBIT 1-3

Property-Casualty Insurance Expense Ratios in the United States From 1997 to 2001

Year	Loss Adjustment Expense (LAE) Ratio	Commission Expense Ratio	Other Expense Ratio	Total Underwriting Expense Ratio (excluding LAE)
1997	12.5	11.4	15.5	26.9
1998	13.1	11.3	16.3	27.6
1999	13.3	11.1	16.7	27.8
2000	12.9	11.1	16.4	27.5
2001	13.1	10.7	15.8	26.6
5-year average	13.0	11.1	16.1	27.3

Note: Rounding of underlying data prevents the total underwriting expense ratio from summing in the year 2001.

© A.M. Best Company. Used with permission, *Best's Aggregates and Averages, Property-Casualty, United States,* 2002 Edition, p. 107.

Loss Ratio

The **loss ratio,** the ratio of incurred losses to earned premiums, measures how well an insurer controls the amount of insured losses. This ratio can be calculated with or without loss adjustment expenses. It is important to know whether loss adjustment expenses have been included, because they can constitute a significant percentage of losses. For example, in 2000, losses alone were 74.4 percent of earned premiums for medical malpractice insurance, and loss adjustment expenses were 36.0 percent.[5] For 2001, the loss ratio before adding loss adjustment expenses for medical malpractice had jumped more than 20 percentage points to 97.4 percent.[6] Loss ratios are usually calculated with loss adjustment expenses included so that all costs related to losses are contained within one statistic.

An insurer's loss ratio must be evaluated in light of its expense ratio. An insurer with an expense ratio lower than the industry average can afford a loss ratio higher than the industry average while still earning an acceptable profit. Exhibit 1-4 shows property-casualty insurance industry loss ratios for the years 1995 through 2001.

Loss ratio
An insurer's incurred losses (including loss adjustment expenses) for a specific period divided by its earned premiums for the same period.

EXHIBIT 1-4

Property-Casualty Insurance Loss Ratios in the United States From 1995 to 2001

Year	Pure Loss Ratio	Loss Adjustment Expense (LAE) Ratio	Loss and LAE Ratio
1995	65.8	13.2	**79.0**
1996	65.7	13.0	**78.7**
1997	60.6	12.5	**73.1**
1998	63.4	13.2	**76.5**
1999	65.4	13.3	**78.8**
2000	68.5	12.9	**81.4**
2001	75.4	13.1	**88.5**

Note: Rounding of underlying data prevents the pure loss ratio and the loss adjustment expense ratio from summing to the loss and LAE ratio in 1999.

© A.M. Best Company. Used with permission, *Best's Aggregates and Averages, Property-Casualty, United States,* 1999 Edition, p. 103; 2002 Edition, p. 107.

Combined Ratio

Combined ratio
The sum of an insurer's loss ratio and its expense ratio.

Because the loss ratio and the expense ratio each must be interpreted in light of the other, combining them is convenient. The sum of the loss ratio and the underwriting expense ratio is known as the **combined ratio**. A combined ratio of less than 100 percent indicates that the insurer earned a profit on its insurance operations (often referred to as an underwriting profit), not including any investment profit or loss. A combined ratio in excess of 100 percent indicates a loss on insurance operations.

Financial basis combined ratio
A profitability ratio calculated by dividing incurred losses and incurred expenses by earned premiums.

Two combined ratios are used in the insurance industry: the financial basis combined ratio and the trade basis combined ratio. The **financial basis combined ratio** is calculated by dividing the sum of incurred losses, loss adjustment expenses, and incurred expenses by earned premiums. For a growing insurer, earned premiums lag behind net written premiums. Because most underwriting expenses are closely related to net written premiums, the financial basis combined ratio tends to understate the profitability of a growing insurer. On the other hand, it tends to overstate profit for an insurer with a shrinking premium volume.

Trade basis combined ratio
A profitability ratio calculated by dividing incurred losses and loss adjustment expenses by earned premiums and then adding the result of dividing incurred underwriting expenses by net written premiums.

The **trade basis combined ratio** was developed in an effort to avoid the weaknesses of the financial basis combined ratio. In calculating the trade basis combined ratio, incurred losses and loss adjustment expenses are divided by earned premiums, and the incurred underwriting expenses are divided by net written premiums.

An example will clarify the difference. Assume that Insurance Company reported the financial data for last year as shown in Exhibit 1-5.

Insurance Company's premium volume grew rapidly last year, as shown by net written premiums 25 percent greater than earned premiums. Consequently, its trade basis combined ratio was lower than its statutory basis combined ratio.

EXHIBIT 1-5

Combined Ratio Calculation—Insurance Company

Incurred underwriting expenses	$ 5,000,000
Incurred losses and loss adjustment expenses	14,000,000
Net written premiums	25,000,000
Earned premiums	20,000,000

Insurance Company's *financial basis* combined ratio would be:

$$\frac{\text{Incurred losses and loss adjustment expenses}}{\text{Earned premiums}} + \frac{\text{Incurred underwriting expenses}}{\text{Earned premiums}}$$

$$= \frac{14,000,000 + 5,000,000}{20,000,000}$$

$$= 0.95 \text{ or } 95\%.$$

Insurance Company's *trade basis* combined ratio would be:

$$\frac{\text{Incurred losses and loss adjustment expenses}}{\text{Earned premiums}} + \frac{\text{Incurred underwriting expenses}}{\text{Net written premiums}}$$

$$= \frac{14,000,000}{20,000,000} + \frac{5,000,000}{25,000,000}$$

$$= 0.70 + 0.20 = 0.90 \text{ or } 90\%.$$

Exhibit 1-6 shows the trade basis combined ratio for property-casualty insurance for the years 1996 through 2001. The industry sustained an underwriting loss in all years of the period, with the combined ratio reaching its peak of 115.1 percent in 2001. The 2001 figures reflect the influence of catastrophes in that year, particularly those losses related to the September 11 terrorist attacks.

Like the expense ratio and loss ratio, an insurer's combined ratio must be evaluated with due consideration to competitive conditions within the industry. Also, the combined ratio for a single year might be adversely affected by catastrophic events. The overall results for the insurer might, however, indicate profitable operations over the long term. It is essential to consider these factors in determining insurer profitability levels.

Investment Income

To this point, the discussion of insurer profitability has dealt only with underwriting profit or loss, without any consideration of the insurer's investment operations. Insurance operations generate substantial amounts of investable funds, primarily from loss reserves, loss adjustment expense reserves, and unearned premium reserves. Loss and loss expense reserves are especially significant in insurers that write liability insurance. This is because of the long delay inherent in the liability loss adjustment process that generates very large loss reserves. The rise in returns on the equity market during the 1990s contributed to large investment returns for insurers. In January 1990, the Dow Jones Industrial Average stood at 1,900. By January 2000, the index had risen to over 11,000.[7] While investments in stocks represent only a portion of the total investments insurers make, the growth of the stock market during that decade led to substantial investment income. Although the market has declined since January 2000 and interest rates have held steady, investment income is the sole source of profit for many insurers.

EXHIBIT 1-6

Property-Casualty Insurance Trade Basis Combined Ratio in the United States From 1996 to 2001

Year	Combined Ratio Before Policyholder Dividends	Policyholder Dividends	Combined Ratio After Policyholder Dividends
1996	104.9	1.2	**106.1**
1997	100.1	1.8	**101.9**
1998	104.1	1.9	**106.0**
1999	106.5	1.3	**107.8**
2000	108.8	1.5	110.3
2001	115.1	0.8	115.9

© A.M. Best Company. Used with permission, *Best's Aggregates and Averages, Property-Casualty, United States,* 1999 Edition, p. 103; 2002 Edition, p. 107.

Operating Profit or Loss

Operating profit or loss
The sum of underwriting profit or loss and investment profit or loss.

Operating profit or loss is the sum of underwriting profit or loss and investment profit or loss. Insurers realize investment profit or loss from three sources. The first is investment income, consisting of interest, dividends, and rents derived from bonds, stocks, real estate, and other assets held for investment purposes. The second source is realized capital gains, which result when an investment asset is sold for more than its original cost. The third source is unrealized capital gains, resulting when the market value of an asset rises above its original cost, but the asset is not sold. Exhibit 1-7 shows the industry's combined ratio after policyholder dividends, the net investment ratio, and the operating ratio for the years 1992 through 2001. The operating ratio is calculated by subtracting the net investment ratio from the combined ratio.

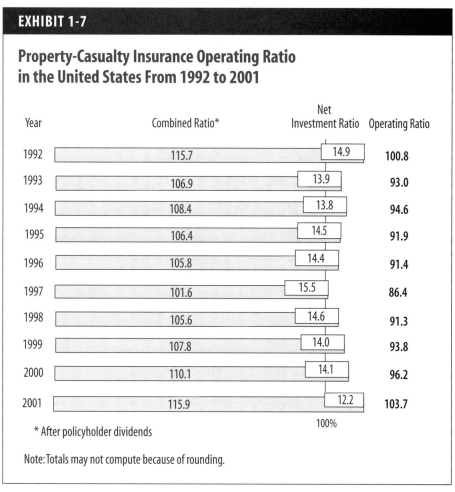

EXHIBIT 1-7

Property-Casualty Insurance Operating Ratio in the United States From 1992 to 2001

Year	Combined Ratio*	Net Investment Ratio	Operating Ratio
1992	115.7	14.9	**100.8**
1993	106.9	13.9	**93.0**
1994	108.4	13.8	**94.6**
1995	106.4	14.5	**91.9**
1996	105.8	14.4	**91.4**
1997	101.6	15.5	**86.4**
1998	105.6	14.6	**91.3**
1999	107.8	14.0	**93.8**
2000	110.1	14.1	**96.2**
2001	115.9	12.2	103.7

100%

* After policyholder dividends

Note: Totals may not compute because of rounding.

Problems in Measuring Profitability

One of the biggest problems in measuring insurer profitability arises from the indefinite nature of loss reserves. Insurers establish reserves for losses that have occurred but that have not yet been paid. These reserves include an amount for losses that have already happened but that have not yet been reported to the insurer, known as incurred but not reported (IBNR) losses. IBNR reserves are essentially estimates of ultimate loss payments, because the exact amount that will eventually be paid out for such losses is unknown. Errors in these estimates are common, and insurers must adjust these amounts as more concrete information becomes known. These errors in estimating outstanding loss amounts lead to distortions in insurers' reported profits. This is true for both the year in which inaccurate estimates were originally made and the year in which corrections are made to the estimates.

Meeting Customers' Needs

Determining how well insurers meet customers' needs is difficult because insurers are more likely to hear from customers who believe they have not been treated fairly. All insurers receive complaints, and each one should be evaluated. In some instances, a real problem exists that the insurer should address. In other instances, customers hold expectations that the insurer had not intended to fulfill.

Insurance producers can also be a source of information for evaluating an insurer's success in this area, as they are in frequent contact with customers and hear their complaints and praise of insurers. Producers seldom keep formal records of such customer reactions, so their evaluations are likely to be subjective.

Many insurers emphasize a customer focus to maintain and raise levels of customer satisfaction with the insurer's products and services. Insurers often use response cards and phone surveys to determine whether customers feel properly treated after a transaction, particularly following a claim. Insurers can also conduct customer focus groups or interviews to determine how well a new or an existing product meets customers' needs.

Insurers that market products through independent agents and brokers usually view this network of producers as their customers in addition to the ultimate insurance customer. These insurers recognize that many insurers are available to producers and that a competitive marketplace exists within their offices. Being responsive to producer requests and permitting access to insurer policy data and information systems are examples of how insurers maintain and strengthen the insurer-producer relationship. As with customers, insurers can survey or meet with producers to measure their satisfaction with the insurer or to reveal unserved needs the insurer might be able to meet.

Several state insurance departments tabulate complaints they receive and publish lists showing the number of complaints received for each insurer. The number of complaints might indicate one insurer's customer relations success or failure relative to other insurers in the industry.

Consumers Union periodically surveys its membership to determine their level of satisfaction with the performance of auto and homeowners insurers. The results are published in that organization's magazine, *Consumer Reports*, including a list of the most satisfactory and least satisfactory insurers as indicated by the survey responses. Only a few of the largest insurers are included in the list, because smaller insurers are not mentioned in the responses with sufficient frequency to evaluate their performance fairly.

Meeting Legal Requirements

An insurer's success or failure in meeting legal requirements is indicated by the number of criminal, civil, and regulatory actions taken against the insurer. These actions are automatically brought to the attention of management and should be evaluated carefully to see whether they result from a consistent disregard of legal requirements.

State insurance departments monitor the treatment of insureds, applicants for insurance, and claimants, as well as oversee four insurer operational areas: sales and advertising, underwriting, ratemaking, and claim settlement. This regulatory oversight, called market conduct regulation, exists in addition to state insurance regulation's role in solvency surveillance.

Most states publish a listing of regulatory actions against insurers. This information can be useful in showing how one insurer's performance in this area compares to that of its competitors.

Meeting Social Responsibilities

Meeting social responsibilities is the most difficult of the major goals to evaluate. No standards exist for judging an insurer's performance in this area, and little information on an individual insurer's performance is publicly available. Of course, an insurer can get information from its own records to show its own performance, but comparisons with competing insurers are difficult to make because of the lack of available information. Many insurers use their Web sites to indicate their participation in home and workplace safety programs, support of community projects, and other social programs.

Another possible indicator of social responsibility is the benefits that an insurer provides for its employees. Some insurers have also begun to promote family-friendly policies within their organization to assist employees with balancing work and family responsibilities. Comparative information for employee benefits is available from the United States Chamber of Commerce and from various insurer trade associations. Companies that promote family-friendly workplaces are listed annually in publications such as *Working Mother*, which ranks companies according to their programs.[8] Although generous employee benefit plans can be construed as merely another method of competing for good employees, they can also indicate an insurer's concern for the welfare of its employees. Expenditures on loss control activities may also indicate an insurer's level of humanitarian concern; some insurers go beyond typical efforts in loss control to improve safety conditions for their policyholders. Many insurers contribute to associations that do research and raise public concern for safety. Contributions to medical, welfare, and educational institutions and programs are another indication of humanitarian efforts and social responsibility.

INSURANCE FUNCTIONS

Insurers perform three core functions to meet their goals:

1. Marketing
2. Underwriting
3. Claims

Insurers perform the following nine additional functions that support the core functions:

1. Loss control
2. Reinsurance
3. Actuarial
4. Investments
5. Information technology
6. Premium audit
7. Human resources
8. Legal services
9. Accounting

This section provides an overview of these insurer functions. Some insurers might perform only some of these functions, some might combine functions, and some might use a different name for these functions. Although each function operates individually, each contributes to the insurer's overall effectiveness. The interaction of these functions is vital to the survival and continued success of the organization involved.

Marketing

Marketing involves determining what products or services customers want and need and delivering them to those customers. The marketing function contributes significantly to an insurer's profit goals and goals of meeting customers' needs. The insurer cannot make a profit if it does not provide products and services the customer needs.

Many insurers market insurance through independent agents and brokers, who are independent businesspeople representing several otherwise unrelated insurers. Some market through exclusive agents, who represent only one insurer or group of insurers under common ownership and management. Others rely on the marketing efforts of their own employees, using a marketing system called "direct writer."

A successful marketing program is likely to include the following elements:

1. Market research to determine the needs of potential buyers and segment markets
2. Advertising and public relations programs to inform customers about the insurer's products and services

3. Training programs to prepare the sales force (either insurer employees or independent or exclusive agents called producers) to meet the public's needs

4. Setting production goals and strategies for achieving them

5. Motivating and managing producers

Underwriting

The underwriting department's responsibility is to determine whether the applications received meet the guidelines established by the insurer. The goal of the underwriting department is to write a profitable book of business for the insurer, which supports the insurer's profit goal. Underwriters work with the marketing department to accept those accounts most likely to produce a profit for the insurer.

Claims

When customers purchase insurance, they are buying protection for the potential financial consequences of their loss exposures. The insurer promises to make payments to or on behalf of the policyholder for a covered loss. The claim function is responsible for keeping this promise to the policyholder by providing prompt and professional loss adjustment services.

In many cases, claim professionals act in a public relations role for the insurer. The interactions during the loss adjusting process might be the only contact that a policyholder or claimant has with the insurer outside the initial sales transaction. The claim function supports marketing by promptly and fairly paying claims, which promotes policy renewal and referrals for new business.

The purpose of the loss adjusting process is to achieve a fair, equitable settlement based on the circumstances of the loss. Loss settlements that are too high increase the cost of insurance for everybody. Loss settlements that are too low deprive the policyholder of the full benefits of the insurance policy. Consistently inadequate loss settlements might lead to litigation and regulatory actions against the insurer. Paying inadequate loss settlements also diminishes the insurer's business reputation and can negatively affect future marketing efforts.

Loss Control

The primary responsibility of an insurer's loss control department is to prevent losses if possible and to minimize any losses that do occur. Loss control has always been an important insurer function, and it continues to grow in importance as policyholder loss exposures become more complex.

From an economic viewpoint, preventing and reducing losses is preferable to transferring the financial consequences of loss exposures because it reduces the waste of valuable resources, both human and material. As a practical matter, both transferring financial consequences and controlling losses are likely to be used jointly for most large loss exposures, because preventing all losses is seldom possible.

Reinsurance

Reinsurance transfers to the reinsurer some or all of the potential financial consequences of certain loss exposures covered by the policies of another insurer. Consequently, reinsurance protects the financial solvency of insurers by enabling them to meet their obligations to policyholders and claimants. Reinsurance departments can be of two types. The first type of reinsurance department establishes and negotiates reinsurance programs with reinsurers or reinsurance intermediaries. This reinsurance department establishes guidelines for reinsurance procedures, usually in conjunction with staff underwriters. The department also supports any administrative, accounting, and claim-processing tasks related to reinsurance. The second type of reinsurance department provides reinsurance for other primary insurers.

Actuarial

The actuarial function supplies all of the information required to calculate insurance rates, develop rating plans, and estimate loss reserves. Actuaries are highly trained specialists who perform all of the mathematical functions underlying insurance operations. On a corporate level, actuaries might assist with corporate planning and with establishing corporate goals by compiling and analyzing statistics and producing reports. Actuaries might also be involved in assessing the insurer's success in meeting these goals.

The actuarial function is also responsible for providing ratemaking information to regulators. Insurers' actuaries develop factors to reflect individual insurer expenses and anticipated profits. These factors are applied to loss costs to obtain final insurance rates.

Investments

The investment function is key in any insurance operation because of the nature of the risk transfer mechanism. Policyholders pay premiums at policy inception, but losses, if any, are paid at a later date. The insurer invests premiums until they are needed to pay losses. Any funds not used to pay losses or expenses are considered profit. Many insurers lose money on their operations because losses and expenses exceed the premiums received.

The positive effect of interest rates and investment returns was illustrated in Exhibit 1-7, which showed that, in many years, returns from investments helped to offset underwriting losses. The investment function is essential in any insurance operation because insurers invest premium and loss reserve funds to provide cash flow to pay future losses.

Information Technology

The information technology function provides the infrastructure that supports all of the insurer's internal and external communications and many of the rating, statistical, claim payment, and other automated functions. To provide state-of-the-art claim services, insurers depend on evolving technology to improve interactions between office and field staff and interactions with customers and claimants. As customers depend more on the Internet as a source of information on products, services, and pricing, technological experts are required to find ways to respond to these customers in an efficient and timely manner.

Other Functions

Insurer operations also involve a number of other important functions that are not discussed in detail here. These include premium audit, human resources, legal services, and accounting. Each of these areas contributes to an insurer's overall effective operation.

Although insurers serve society in many ways, their principal function is to facilitate the transfer of the financial consequences of loss exposures. All of the preceding departments must work together to serve this principal function and to meet other insurer goals.

INTERDEPENDENCE AMONG FUNCTIONS

Although each function within an insurer must have some autonomy to perform its work, those functions are far from completely independent. They must interact constantly if the insurer is to operate efficiently.

Marketing and Underwriting

While the underwriting department decides which insurance applications to accept, those applications are generated based on marketing activities. Clear communication must occur between these departments to ensure that acceptability guidelines are clearly understood and that the insurer's products and services are viable in the marketplace.

In addition, the underwriting department should cooperate with the marketing department to find ways to make marginal applications acceptable.

Also, the marketing and sales departments are in regular contact with customers and receive feedback on the products and services the insurer provides. This information can be shared with the underwriting department for use in product development. In addition, the marketing department might acquire information about the policyholder that is relevant to the underwriting process.

Underwriting and Loss Control

The loss control department is sometimes called the eyes and ears of the underwriting department. An underwriter who is considering an insurance application can ask the loss control department to inspect the premises and survey the loss exposures involved in the application. This survey would assist the underwriter in determining acceptability and in pricing the coverage based on the applicant's loss exposures. In providing continuing loss control services to existing policyholders, the loss control department might also obtain information that is important to the underwriting process.

Loss Control and Marketing

The loss control department might also be able to assist with marketing. Some insurers feature their loss control activities as a selling point in their advertising and sales presentations. Loss control personnel might accompany marketing personnel on sales calls to prospective policyholders who are especially concerned about loss control issues. Finally, loss control personnel might be able to offer suggestions to improve a loss exposure to make it acceptable to the underwriting department.

Claim and Other Departments

The claim department interacts with the underwriting, marketing, and loss control departments. It can assist the underwriting department by conveying important underwriting information that arises during claim adjusting. The underwriting department might be asked to provide information about its intent in providing specific coverage provisions. The claim department also generates loss-history information on policyholders that both the underwriting and marketing departments can use.

The claim department can assist with marketing by notifying the marketing and underwriting departments when it denies claims that are not covered under existing policies. Marketing might need to refocus advertising materials, and underwriting might need to reconsider coverages offered.

In the course of the claim adjusting process, the claim department might discover aspects of the policyholder's operations that need loss control attention. Such information should be conveyed to the loss control department. Conversely, the loss control department might be able to provide information about a policyholder's operations that would assist the claim department in claim settlement.

Actuarial and Other Departments

The actuarial department interacts primarily with underwriting and marketing. It determines most of the insurance rates and rating plans used by the underwriting department, and it prepares the statistical information used to evaluate the underwriting department's performance. In determining rates and rating plans, the actuarial department must also consider the views of the marketing department about the acceptability of the rates in the marketplace.

The actuarial department is responsible for developing loss reserves for the insurer's Annual Statement. Consequently, it must maintain contact with the claim department, because the case reserves that the claim department establishes are an important element in establishing statement reserves.

Information Technology and Other Departments

The information technology department interacts with all of the other insurer functions and facilitates exchanges of information among them all. The information technology department collects and stores data that are used by internal departments as well as customers and producers. The information technology department must work closely with underwriting, claims, and marketing to provide the computer applications needed to ensure efficient insurer operations.

SUMMARY

Insurance operations have many facets. In the insurance mechanism, the insured transfers some or all of the potential financial consequence for certain loss exposures to an insurer. This transfer reduces insureds' uncertainty. Consequently, capital is made available for investment in homes or businesses, or for the expansion of commercial ventures. The insurance mechanism is also a means of sharing expenses associated with certain losses that do occur among a group of policyholders.

The risk management process is a method for thoroughly examining the operations of a given entity to determine the potential for loss. Based on this examination, the loss exposures can be managed using risk control and risk financing techniques or using avoidance.

Insurers can be classified in several ways. Typical categories for doing so are the legal form of ownership, place of incorporation, licensing status, and marketing system. The primary reason for which an insurer operates—for example, to return a profit to its owners or to provide insurance protection at a minimum cost for its members—directly relates to the overall set of goals that guide the insurer's daily operations. The insurer's goals and the obstacles to achieving them need to be understood by its management and staff so that the insurer's strengths can be exploited and weaknesses, minimized.

As many businesses do, insurers pursue their goals by segmenting operations into functional areas or departments. These departments must cooperate to serve the primary function of risk transfer and to meet other insurer goals. An insurer's core functions are marketing, underwriting, and claims. Loss control, reinsurance, actuarial, investments, information technology, and other functions support the core functions. Each department must have some autonomy to perform its responsibilities; however, each department must interact effectively with other departments for the insurer to achieve its goals. Subsequent chapters discuss many of these functions in greater detail.

The next chapter deals with insurance regulation. It discusses the regulatory issues that insurance professionals face as they work toward meeting their organizations' goals.

CHAPTER NOTES

1. Insurance Information Institute, *The Fact Book 2003* (New York: Insurance Information Institute, 2003), pp. 7 and 9.

2. A.M. Best Company, "New Alternatives," *Best's Review*, June 2002, p. 58.

3. A.M. Best Company, "New Alternatives," *Best's Review*, June 2002, p. 58.

4. "Surprise! Small Insurers Prosper," *National Underwriter*, Property & Casualty, Risk & Benefits Management Edition Online, September 16, 2002, http://www.nationalunderwriter.com/pandc/hotnews/viewspc.asp?article= 9_16_02_6535.xml (accessed September 17, 2002).

5. A.M. Best Company, *Best's Aggregates and Averages, Property-Casualty*, United States, 2001 edition, p. 276.

6. A.M. Best Company, *Best's Aggregates and Averages, Property-Casualty*, United States, 2002 edition, p. 276.

7. "Dow Jones Industrial Average Milestones," http://www.djindexes.com/jsp/ avgStatistics.jsp (accessed October 8, 2002).

8. "The 100 Best Companies for Working Mothers List 2002," http://www.working mother.com/list/shtml (accessed October 8, 2002).

Chapter 2

Direct Your Learning

Insurance Regulation

After learning the content of this chapter, you should be able to:

■ Identify three recurring issues in insurance regulation.

■ Describe the effect each of the following had on insurance regulation:
  a. *Paul v. Virginia*
  b. Sherman Antitrust Act
  c. South-Eastern Underwriters Association Decision
  d. McCarran-Ferguson Act
  e. Insurance Services Office (ISO) and the Attorneys General Lawsuit
  f. Gramm-Leach-Bliley Act

■ Explain how insurance regulation protects consumers, contributes to maintaining insurer solvency, and assists in preventing destructive competition.

■ Identify the regulatory activities of state insurance departments and the duties typically performed by state insurance commissioners.

■ Describe the arguments for and against federal regulation of insurance.

■ Describe how insurers are formed and the licensing requirements for insurers and insurance personnel.

■ Describe the methods that regulators use to ensure the solvency of insurers and identify the challenges of insurer solvency regulation.

■ Describe the process used to regulate insurance rates.
  • Identify the goals of insurance rate regulation.
  • Describe the major types of state rating laws and discuss the advantages and disadvantages of these laws.

■ Explain how insurance policies are regulated.

■ Describe the market conduct areas in insurance that are regulated, and explain how these regulations operate.

■ Identify organizations that act as unofficial regulators in insurance, and explain how these organizations affect insurance activities.

Develop Your Perspective

What are the main topics covered in the chapter?

The business of insurance is regulated by the states, with a few important exceptions. Regulation of insurance protects consumers, helps insurers maintain solvency, and deters destructive competition.

Contrast the jurisdiction of state and federal regulation of insurers.

- What is uniquely state regulated?
- What is the purpose of the federal regulations that have authority over insurance operations?

Why is it important to learn about these topics?

By understanding how insurance is regulated, you can recognize the restrictions within which your own insurance organization operates. As a consumer of insurance products, you can also appreciate how you are protected against an insurer's insolvency or unfair dealings.

Assess how your organization's activities are directed by state and federal regulations.

- How is competition affected by regulation?
- What activity occurs within your organization to ensure compliance with insurance regulations?

How can you use what you will learn?

Consider possible changes in insurance regulations.

- How would the market and competition change if insurance were regulated by the federal government rather than by the states?
- How might increasing federal control of insurance regulation change how your organization operates?

Chapter 2

Insurance Regulation

This chapter explains how and why insurance regulation evolved and discusses how state insurance departments and other government and private organizations operate to meet regulatory goals. The chapter deals with the following three issues and related questions that have been addressed repeatedly throughout the evolution of insurance regulation. These issues might never be resolved completely. Some of them had been resolved at one time and have reemerged as issues.

1. Locus of regulatory control

    • Should insurance be regulated by state governments or the federal government?

    • Does the unique nature of the insurance business require regulatory standards different from those for other businesses?

2. Extent of regulation

    • Should regulators control the insurance rates that insurers charge?

    • Should a competitive market allow the laws of supply and demand to determine insurance rates?

3. Collaboration among insurers

    • Should collaboration be required?

    • Should collaboration be encouraged?

    • Should collaboration be prohibited?

Insurance regulation in the United States began when the Constitution gave Congress the right to regulate commerce among the states. The following six subsequent legal events significantly influenced the three issues discussed in this chapter.

1. *Paul v. Virginia.*[1] This 1869 legal decision determined that insurance was not interstate commerce and became the basis for a long-standing belief that insurance is exempt from federal regulation.

2. *Sherman Antitrust Act.* This 1890 Congressional act prohibited collusion to gain a monopoly. The act prevented insurers from banding together to control insurance rates and coverages.

3. *South-Eastern Underwriters Association Decision.*[2] This 1944 legal decision turned the U.S. insurance world upside down by making insurance subject to federal regulation. This decision eliminated the role of state

insurance regulators and made insurance subject to federal regulation that prohibits many collaborative activities that the states had previously approved and encouraged.

4. *McCarran-Ferguson Act*. This 1945 Congressional act restored most insurance regulatory responsibility to the states. However, federal regulation that applies to boycott, coercion, and intimidation and federal regulation that deals only with insurance (and not business in general) supersedes state regulation.

5. *Insurance Services Office (ISO) and the Attorneys General Lawsuit*. This 1988 lawsuit alleged that insurers and industry associations conspired to draft restrictive policy language that created a liability crisis in the late 1980s. One result of this lawsuit, which was settled out of court, was to restrict how insurance rates were developed.

6. *Gramm-Leach-Bliley Act*. This 1999 Congressional act, also known as the Financial Services Modernization Act, facilitated affiliations among banks, insurers, and other financial service providers. The act reaffirmed the McCarran-Ferguson Act, making it clear that states would continue to have primary regulatory authority for all insurance activities.

EVOLUTION OF INSURANCE REGULATION

The Constitution, which gives Congress the right to regulate commerce among the states, marks the beginning of the history of insurance regulation in the U.S.

Commerce Clause of the United States Constitution

The Commerce Clause of Section 8 of the United States Constitution provides that "The Congress shall have power to…regulate commerce with foreign nations, and among the several states, and with the Indian tribes."

Until the 1850s, insurance regulation was overseen by state legislatures and various offices within state governments. In 1851, New Hampshire became the first state to establish an insurance board.

Most other states had established boards of insurance regulation by 1859, when New York created the first state insurance department. Eventually, the other states followed suit, and insurance boards were replaced by insurance commissioners.

Paul v. Virginia

Insurance regulation received its first legal test in 1869. Samuel B. Paul, a Petersburg, Virginia, insurance agent, wanted to be licensed in his home state of Virginia, but he wanted to represent New York insurers. According to

Virginia law, insurers domiciled in another state were required to deposit a bond with the Virginia state treasurer, but the insurers Paul represented had not met this requirement. The state of Virginia therefore denied Paul's application for a license. Paul nevertheless continued to sell insurance for the New York insurers. He was indicted, convicted, and fined $50 by the Circuit Court of Virginia, and that decision was upheld by the Virginia Court of Appeals.

Paul continued to fight the charge and, in 1869, the U.S. Supreme Court reviewed the decision. Paul argued that the Virginia licensure law was unconstitutional because only Congress could regulate interstate commerce under the United States Constitution. The U.S. Supreme Court disagreed and upheld the lower court's ruling.

The Supreme Court determined that insurance was not interstate commerce; insurance was a contract that was delivered locally. The Court's unanimous opinion against Paul concluded by saying:

> Issuing a policy of insurance is not a transaction of commerce. The policies are simple contracts of indemnity against loss by fire…. They are not commodities to be shipped or forwarded from one State to another, and then put up for sale. They are like other personal contracts between parties which are completed by their signature and the transfer of the consideration…. The policies do not take effect—are not executed contracts—until delivered by the agent in Virginia. They are, then, local transactions, governed by local law.[3]

Therefore, the U.S. Supreme Court upheld state regulation of insurance, and Virginia could continue to regulate its insurance market.

Insurers were not happy with the Paul decision. By 1869, many insurers were operating in more than one state, and they found it difficult to meet the states' varying demands. In a long line of subsequent cases, usually involving an insurer seeking to defeat state legislation, *Paul v. Virginia* was cited as the ground for upholding state regulation. By implication, despite few explicit judicial statements, this decision came to be relied on as supporting the premise that the federal government had no authority over insurance.

Meanwhile, the states had problems determining what areas of the insurance business needed to be regulated and how. In 1871, New York's insurance commissioner met with regulatory representatives from nineteen other states to address their common problems. By 1872, thirty states had become members of this initial regulators' association, known as the National Insurance Convention (NIC).

Sherman Antitrust Act

Before the end of the nineteenth century, insurance was considered a private, negotiated contract. Any party who did not like the price of insurance did not make the contract. The free market, not the government, determined prices.

Pricing attitudes in U.S. society changed fundamentally starting in the late 1800s and continuing through the early 1900s. During that time period, major federal legislation reflected a new business climate in the U.S. and a new role for the government.

The Sherman Antitrust Act (1890)—Excerpts

Section 1. Trusts, etc., in restraint of trade illegal; penalty

Every contract, combination in the form of trust or otherwise, or conspiracy, in restraint of trade or commerce among the several States, or with foreign nations, is declared to be illegal. Every person who shall make any contract or engage in any combination or conspiracy hereby declared to be illegal shall be deemed guilty of a felony, and, on conviction thereof, shall be punished by fine not exceeding $10,000,000 if a corporation, or, if any other person, $350,000, or by imprisonment not exceeding three years, or by both said punishments, in the discretion of the court.

Section 2. Monopolizing trade a felony; penalty

Every person who shall monopolize, or attempt to monopolize, or combine or conspire with any other person or persons, to monopolize any part of the trade or commerce among the several States, or with foreign nations, shall be deemed guilty of a felony, and, on conviction thereof, shall be punished by fine not exceeding $10,000,000 if a corporation, or, if any other person, $350,000, or by imprisonment not exceeding three years, or by both said punishments, in the discretion of the court....

Section 7. "Person" or "persons" defined

The word "person", or "persons", wherever used in sections 1 to 7 of this title shall be deemed to include corporations and associations existing under or authorized by the laws of either the United States, the laws of any of the Territories, the laws of any State, or the laws of any foreign country.

A fundamental political question of the time was what to do about the "trusts." Trusts were combinations of business firms that attempted to dominate the market and control prices. The market power resulting from such combinations prompted consumer rebellions that spilled over into politics. Many believed these combinations to be an abuse of economic power.

One apparent remedy for the abuse of economic power was to outlaw collusion or conspiracy in restraint of trade. Several states passed antitrust laws. In 1890, Congress enacted the Sherman Antitrust Act (Sherman Act), which prohibits contracts, combinations, and conspiracies in restraint of trade and other attempts to monopolize the market. The Sherman Act applies to more than collusive pricing activities, and it remains in effect today.

Insurance consumers hoped that these state and federal antitrust laws would limit the ability of insurers to raise rates, but applying antitrust laws to insurance was complicated because of the nature of insurance operations. In periods of intense competition, insurers cut prices to levels that could not support severe losses, and catastrophes had the potential to cause many insurer insolvencies. Insurers often tried to organize the market to control rates and break this devastating cycle.

One way to organize the market was to devise a rate "tariff" listing the prescribed rates for different types of loss exposures. Insurers agreed to abide by the tariff. In time, loss statistics helped to refine the tariffs to reflect the degree of risk inherent in the various classes of business.

By 1912, twenty-three states had passed legislation to prohibit insurer compacts or associations from controlling rates. Such associations were viewed as deterrents to open and free competition—and, in effect, they were. However, they also helped to prevent insurer insolvency.

Eventually, however, states came to support insurance industry control of insurance rates through rating bureaus (see box).

A Brief History of Insurance Rating Bureaus

Early rating bureaus were privately owned, often by only one person, to avoid state antitrust laws.

Eventually, state restrictions were removed, and a fire insurance rating bureau was established in every state. The need for uniform approaches to ratemaking and policy language led to regional advisory organizations, which eventually took control of the local bureaus in their regions.

In 1960, these organizations were consolidated into the Inter-Regional Insurance Conference (later the Fire Insurance Research and Actuarial Association), and they eventually became part of Insurance Services Office (ISO), formed in 1971.

In addition to the fire rating bureaus, rating bureaus started for inland marine, casualty, surety, workers' compensation, and multiple-lines insurance.

Although at one time they were known as rating bureaus that promulgated insurance rates, their successor organizations became known as advisory organizations that provide statistical data in the form of loss costs for insurers to use in developing their own insurance rates.

In 1923, the National Convention of Insurance Commissioners (NCIC, the renamed NIC) passed a resolution to repeal state anticompact laws. Insurance regulators had concluded that rating bureaus and insurer compacts or associations were necessary if insurers were to develop and maintain adequate rates and to prevent unfair discrimination. By 1925, most insurance regulators were actively pursuing the repeal of their states' anticompact laws.

In a 1925 noninsurance case, the U.S. Supreme Court affirmed that, sometimes, public policy favors exchanging cost and pricing information in a competitive environment. With this affirmation, states continued to expand their regulation of insurance rates, and rating bureaus became the preferred way to gather the necessary information.

South-Eastern Underwriters Association Decision

As state anticompact laws were repealed, insurer compacts—often subject to state regulation—once again began to take hold. Among these compacts was the South-Eastern Underwriters Association (SEUA), which comprised nearly 200 private stock insurers that controlled about 90 percent of the fire and allied lines insurance market in six southeastern states: Alabama, Florida, Georgia, North Carolina, South Carolina, and Virginia.

The state of Missouri wanted the federal government to challenge rating bureaus, and the SEUA seemed like an ideal target. Even though Missouri had no connection with SEUA, Missouri's attorney general tried to stop the SEUA's rate fixing and filed a complaint with the Antitrust Division of the United States Department of Justice. A federal investigation ensued, and criminal indictments were brought against the SEUA, twenty-seven of its officers, and all of its members for the following activities:

- Continuing agreement and concerted action to control 90 percent of the fire and allied lines insurance market

- Fixing insurance rates and agents' commissions

- Using boycott and other forms of coercion and intimidation to force non-SEUA members to comply with SEUA insurance rates

- Withdrawing the rights of agents to represent SEUA members if the agents also represented non-SEUA insurers

- Threatening insurance consumers with boycott and loss of patronage if they did not purchase their insurance from SEUA members

The District Court of the United States for the Northern District of Georgia dismissed the case based on the U.S. Supreme Court's decision in *Paul v. Virginia*. On appeal, the U.S. Supreme Court agreed to hear the SEUA case in 1944. The Court noted that each of the activities, if performed by companies that were not insurers, would have been subject to prosecution under the Sherman Act. The SEUA was not denying this but contended that it was not subject to the Sherman Act because of the *Paul v. Virginia* decision.

The Court decided that the Sherman Act was intended to prohibit the kinds of conduct exhibited by the interstate fire insurers and SEUA. Consequently, insurance was commerce and, as such, was subject to Congressional regulation. As part of its decision, the Court indicated the following:

- Insurance is not a business that is distinct in each state, but it is interrelated, interdependent, and integrated across states. Individuals in different states can obtain insurance from the same insurer. The decisions insurers make consider not only the environment of the state of domicile but also of the states in which insurance is sold.

- Both before and after the *Paul v. Virginia* decision, intangible products, such as electrical impulses of telegraph transmissions, were subject to Congressional regulation.

- Other businesses make sales contracts in states where they are not head-quartered, and these businesses are subject to Congressional regulation.

The Court's argument for federal regulation of insurance can be summarized as follows: *No commercial enterprise of any kind that conducts its activities across state lines has been held to be wholly beyond the regulatory powers of Congress under the Commerce Clause. We cannot make an exception for the business of insurance.*

The Court's decision stunned state insurance regulators and insurers. The system of insurance regulation that had existed for years and that regulators and insurers preferred was now in jeopardy.

The immediate effect of the Court's decision was that the following federal acts now applied to insurance:

- *The Sherman Act (1890)*—This act prohibits collusion to gain a monopoly. Any activity that restrains trade or commerce and any attempt to monopolize are illegal. Insurers could no longer band together, as in the SEUA and similar groups, to control insurance rates and coverages.

- *The Clayton Act (1914)*—This act, together with its amendment, the Robinson-Patman Antidiscrimination Act (1936), prohibits activities that lessen competition or create monopoly power, including price discrimination, tying (requiring the purchase of one product when purchasing another product) and exclusive dealing, and mergers between competitors. The Robinson-Patman Act limited price discrimination only to price differentials that could be attributed to differences in operating costs resulting from competing "in good faith." Insurers could no longer reduce insurance rates to eliminate competition unless the insurers could prove that the reduced rates were caused by increased efficiencies in operations.

- *The Federal Trade Commission (FTC) Act (1914)*—This act prohibits unfair methods of competition and unfair or deceptive trade practices and therefore promotes competition and protects consumers.[4]

Together, these federal acts significantly changed how insurers could operate. However, state insurance regulators and insurers believed that some forms of cooperation, especially to establish the statistical base for adequate insurance rates, were necessary for the insurance mechanism to function effectively. The National Association of Insurance Commissioners (NAIC; the NCIC was renamed in the 1930s) worked to eliminate federal regulation of insurance.

McCarran-Ferguson Act

In 1945, Congress passed the McCarran-Ferguson Act (McCarran Act). The McCarran Act essentially gave the NAIC and the insurance business what they wanted. McCarran is reproduced in the appendix at the end of this chapter.

Subject to certain conditions, the McCarran Act returned insurance regulation to the states. Congress justified the legislation on the basis that it was "in the public interest."

One condition of the McCarran Act is extremely important because, if it is not met, Congress resumes the regulation of insurance. The Sherman Act, the Clayton Act, the FTC Act, and the Robinson-Patman Act do not apply to the "business of insurance" *unless* the states are not regulating the activities described in the acts. That condition, however, has an exception: the Sherman Act continues to apply to boycott, coercion, or intimidation by insurers.

In other words, states must have their own antitrust legislation and their own unfair trade practices legislation if they want to prevent the federal government from enforcing these acts. Even then, state legislation does not supersede federal authority regarding boycott, coercion, and intimidation. Also, if Congress passes a law that applies only to the insurance business, not to business in general, the federal law supersedes any state regulation in the areas addressed by the federal legislation.

The McCarran Act did not define what constitutes the "business of insurance." Based on the court decisions that have been rendered so far, the "business of insurance" is defined as any activity that has one or more of the following three characteristics:

1. The risk of the policyholder or insured is shared and underwritten by the insurer.
2. The insurer and the insured have a direct contractual connection.
3. The activity is unique to entities within the insurance business.[5]

The McCarran Act also prohibits states from controlling labor relations. Therefore, insurers are still subject to federal regulation regarding labor relations.

Under the McCarran Act, the states had until 1948 to pass legislation to regulate insurance, thereby limiting federal regulation. Consequently, the NAIC and state legislatures began developing and implementing various insurance laws to allow cooperation in setting rates and to restrict Congressional control of insurance.[6]

In 1946, the NAIC approved two model rate regulation bills—one that applied to liability insurers and another that applied to fire, marine, and inland marine insurers. The two purposes of those bills were as follows:

1. To ensure that insurance rates were not excessive, were not unfairly discriminatory, and were adequate
2. To allow cooperation in setting insurance rates, as long as it did not hinder competition

Most states enacted some form of rate regulation that met the requirements of the McCarran Act and therefore preempted federal legislation on cooperative ratemaking.

In 1947, the NAIC adopted the Act Relating to Unfair Methods of Competition and Unfair Deceptive Acts and Practices in the Business of Insurance.

The NAIC's model act described certain activities that were deemed to be methods of unfair competition or unfair and deceptive practices and actions. Most states enacted laws that were similar to the NAIC model act.[7] By the end of 1947, the NAIC and the states believed that they had succeeded in preempting federal legislation.

ISO and the Attorneys General Lawsuit

In 1971, six separate national service bureaus (then known as rating bureaus) consolidated to form Insurance Services Office (ISO). By the end of 1971, nine local or regional property bureaus also joined ISO.

ISO's role has changed over the years. In 1987, ISO characterized itself as follows:

> A national, non-profit corporation that gathers, stores and disseminates aggregate statistical information to insurance regulators—as required by law—and to insurers for their use. In addition, ISO develops and assists in implementing insurance policy coverage programs that help to define and cover the risks faced by policyholders. ISO also distributes industrywide advisory rate information and, where appropriate, files that information with state insurance regulators.[8]

Major changes, however, were the result of a 1988 lawsuit by seven states' attorneys general that once again raised antitrust issues. These lawsuits, filed in federal District Court in San Francisco, charged that major insurers, domestic and foreign reinsurers, and industry associations—thirty-two defendants in all—had conspired to create a global boycott of certain types of commercial general liability coverages, particularly coverage for environmental damages stemming from pollution. Twelve other states subsequently joined the federal lawsuit.

The lawsuit focused on a narrow aspect of the insurance business: the development of new policy language by ISO. The lawsuit alleged that the defendants engaged in a secret "global conspiracy" to draft restrictive policy language and that the "conspiracy" led to the mid-1980s liability insurance crisis. Six years of litigation ensued.

In 1994, insurers, the attorneys general from twenty states, and several private plaintiffs reached an out-of-court settlement. Under this settlement, the thirty-two defendants were required to pay $36 million to establish the Public Entity Risk Institute (PERI).[9] PERI would provide risk management education, technical services, and a public entity insurance database for local government agencies. Part of the $36 million would be used to reimburse the states and private plaintiffs for legal expenses.[10]

The settlement also reorganized ISO. ISO's board was reconstituted to comprise three insurance company executives, seven executives from noninsurance companies, and ISO's president as chairman. ISO continues its role as a statistical agent for regulators in almost every state. Insurer committees have been dissolved and replaced with insurer advisory panels, whose members make recommendations in their areas of expertise. Rate and form decisions are made not by insurer committees but by ISO staff.

ISO continued to provide insurance products and services to insurers. However, the settlement helped to eliminate a perception that ISO provided a vehicle for insurer collusion.

Currently, ISO is a for-profit corporation, and the rating information it provides involves loss costs rather than advisory rates. Each insurer that subscribes to ISO services can base its insurance rates on its own expenses as well as on ISO's loss cost information. ISO continues to develop insurance policy forms and coverage programs that are adopted by many property-casualty insurers.

Gramm-Leach-Bliley Act

The issue of state versus federal insurance regulation has never been completely resolved. Many times during the last fifty years, it seemed likely to reappear as a major legislative concern. The issue came to the forefront during the 1990s, when affiliations between banks and insurers began to occur and questions arose about who would regulate these "bankassurance" organizations. Banking activities were traditionally regulated by the federal government and, in some cases, by the states, while insurance was regulated only by the states.

The Gramm-Leach-Bliley (GLB) Act of 1999, also called the Financial Services Modernization Act, addressed this issue. However, although the GLB Act answered some questions, it raised many others that have not been answered, at least at the time this was written.

Under the act, each segment of the financial services business is regulated separately. Regarding insurance, the GLB Act makes it clear that states continue to have primary regulatory authority for all insurance activities. However, the act prohibits state actions that would prevent bank-related firms from selling insurance on the same basis as insurance producers. Meanwhile, securities activities are regulated by securities regulators, and banking activities are regulated by banking regulators.

The GLB Act also treats insurance underwriting differently from insurance sales and marketing. National banks are prohibited from underwriting insurance through an operating subsidiary. However, they can arrange for a financial holding company to create an insurance affiliate. This arrangement makes it more difficult for a failing bank to use insurer assets.

Information sharing among banks and insurance affiliates raises privacy concerns. The act addresses these concerns through a provision requiring banks to disclose to customers their information-sharing policies and practices. Because states can have laws that are more restrictive than federal laws, this provision could lead to some inconsistency in practice.

The act also compels states to facilitate insurance producers' ability to operate in more than one state. The GLB Act contains a provision that gave states three years to adopt full reciprocal licensing agreements. If at least twenty-nine states failed to enact reciprocity within this time frame, then the law would establish a National Association of Registered Agents and Brokers (NARAB), under which producers (agents and brokers) could choose to be federally licensed. Because the reciprocity requirement has been met, NARAB will probably not be established. The NAIC also responded to the requirements in the GLB Act by creating a Producer Licensing Model Act that satisfies the NARAB provisions. This licensing act requires states to establish either a system of reciprocal producer licensing or uniform licensing standards. Reciprocity and uniformity issues will continue to evolve as regulators, insurers, and producers try to streamline producer licensing procedures.

A *National Underwriter* editorial noted the following:

> On the horizon is a potentially new world of integrated financial services which, if the optimists are correct, will provide consumers with exciting product innovations and lower costs.[11]

At the same time, the editorial noted, financial services modernization might give rise to a new set of issues, including:

- Privacy of personal financial information
- Ability of state regulation to adequately serve an integrated and global financial services market
- Consumers' want or need for integrated financial services

Commercial Insurance Deregulation

The complexity of the state system of insurance rate and form regulation increased pressure for a simpler regulatory system. In response, states started to deregulate commercial insurance for large corporations that have the expertise necessary to evaluate complex insurance policies and pricing systems.

By September 2000, twenty states had enacted laws deregulating commercial rate and/or form filing requirements, and many others were considering such laws. Regulators also plan to review personal insurance regulation.[12]

Both the extent of deregulation and the eligibility requirements that commercial insureds must meet vary by state. Commercial insureds must generally meet specified requirements regarding their size and sophistication as insurance buyers. These requirements might include a specified minimum insurance premium level, minimum annual net revenues or sales, a minimum number of employees, and a full-time risk manager.

REASONS FOR INSURANCE REGULATION

Insurers are regulated primarily for the following three reasons:

1. To protect consumers
2. To maintain insurer solvency
3. To prevent destructive competition

Although these reasons clearly overlap, each is examined separately.

Protect Consumers

The first reason insurance is regulated is to protect consumers. When consumers buy food, clothing, or furniture, they can usually inspect the products before purchasing them to ensure that the products meet their needs. Even if consumers inspect the insurance policies they purchase, they might not be able to analyze and understand complex legal documents. Regulators help to protect consumers by reviewing insurance policy forms to determine whether they benefit consumers. Regulators can set coverage standards, specify policy language for certain insurance coverages, and disapprove unacceptable policies.

Insurance regulators also protect consumers against fraud and unethical market behavior. Most insurance representatives are honest and ethical, but, unfortunately, exceptions such as the following exist:

- Producers have sold unnecessary insurance.
- Producers have misrepresented the nature of coverage to make a sale.
- Insurers have engaged in unfair claim practices, refusing to pay legitimate claims or unfairly reducing claim payments.
- Insurance managers have contributed to the insolvency of insurers through their dishonesty.

Regulation helps to protect consumers against such abuses.

Regulators try to ensure that insurance is readily available, especially the insurance that is viewed as a necessity. For example, all states now try to ensure that continuous personal auto insurance coverage is available by restricting the rights of insurers to cancel or nonrenew personal auto insurance policies. At the same time, regulators recognize that insurers sometimes must break long-term relationships with policyholders whose loss exposures no longer match those the insurer wants to cover. Cancellation restrictions aimed at promoting availability can therefore lead insurers to reject more new-business applications, which reduces insurance availability.

Insurance regulators also provide consumers with information about insurance matters so that consumers can make more-informed decisions.

Maintain Insurer Solvency

The second reason insurance is regulated is to maintain insurer solvency. Solvency regulation protects policyholders against the risk that insurers will be unable to meet their financial obligations. Consumers and even some sophisticated businesspeople may find it difficult to evaluate insurers' financial ability to keep their promises. Insurance regulators try to maintain and enhance the financial condition of private insurers for several reasons:

- *Insurance provides future protection.* Premiums are paid in advance, but the period of protection extends into the future. If insurers become insolvent, future claims might not be paid, and the insurance protection already paid for might become worthless.

- *Regulation is needed to protect the public interest.* Large numbers of individuals and the community at large are adversely affected when insurers become insolvent.

- *Insurers have a responsibility to policyholders.* Insurers hold substantial funds for the ultimate benefit of policyholders. Government regulation is necessary to safeguard such funds.

Insurers have become insolvent despite regulatory reviews. However, sound regulation minimizes the number of insolvencies. Solvency regulation is covered in more detail later in this chapter.

Prevent Destructive Competition

The third reason insurance is regulated is to prevent destructive competition. Regulators are responsible for determining whether insurance rates are high enough to prevent destructive competition. At times, some insurers underprice their products to increase market share by attracting customers away from higher-priced competitors. This practice drives down price levels in the whole market. When insurance rate levels are inadequate, some insurers can become insolvent, and others might withdraw from the market or stop writing new business. An insurance shortage can then develop, and individuals and firms might be unable to obtain the coverage they need. Certain types of insurance can become unavailable at any price, such as products liability or directors and officers coverage.

INSURANCE REGULATORS

Insurance is regulated primarily by state insurance departments. State regulators, in turn, are members of the National Association of Insurance Commissioners (NAIC), a nonprofit corporation that has no regulatory authority of its own but that plays an important coordinating role. Insurers are also subject to federal regulations that affect noninsurance businesses as well. Although not discussed here, most of the state and local regulations that affect other businesses, such as zoning laws, also apply to insurers.

State Insurance Departments

Every state has three separate and equal branches of government: legislative, judicial, and executive.

- The legislative branch makes the laws.
- The judicial branch (the court system) interprets the laws.
- The executive branch implements the laws.

Day-to-day regulation of the insurance business is performed by state insurance departments, which fall within the executive branch of each state government. State insurance departments enforce insurance laws enacted by the legislature. These laws regulate the formation of insurers, capital and surplus requirements, licensing of producers, investment of funds, financial requirements for maintaining solvency, insurance rates that can be charged, marketing and claim practices, taxation of insurers, and the rehabilitation of financially impaired insurers or the liquidation of insolvent ones.

Under the insurance commissioner's direction, a state insurance department engages in a wide variety of regulatory activities that typically include:

- Approving policy forms
- Holding rate hearings and reviewing rate filings
- Licensing new insurers
- Licensing producers
- Investigating policyholder complaints
- Rehabilitating or liquidating insolvent insurers
- Issuing cease-and-desist orders
- Conducting periodic audits of insurers, including claim and underwriting audits
- Evaluating solvency information
- Performing market conduct examinations
- Fining insurers that violate state law
- Publishing shoppers' guides and other consumer information (in some states)

The Insurance Commissioner

Every state insurance department is headed by an insurance commissioner, superintendent, or director appointed by the governor or elected by the voting public.

The duties of a typical state insurance commissioner include:

- Overseeing the state insurance department's operation
- Promulgating orders, rules, and regulations necessary to administer insurance laws
- Determining whether to issue business licenses to new insurers, producers, and other insurance entities
- Reviewing insurance pricing and coverage
- Conducting financial and market examinations of insurers
- Holding hearings on insurance issues
- Taking action when insurance laws are violated
- Issuing an annual report on the status of the state's insurance market and insurance department
- Maintaining records of insurance department activities

The commissioner does not personally handle most of these duties, but instead delegates them to others in the state insurance department.

Although most commissioners are appointed, some states elect their commissioners. Disagreement exists regarding which selection method better serves the public interest. Proponents of an elective system cite the following reasons:

- An appointed insurance commissioner is subject to dismissal, while an elected commissioner is generally in office for a full term.

- An appointed commissioner might continue regulating in the same manner as his or her predecessor when a different approach is required, but an elected commissioner would more likely change the insurance department's stance.

- An appointed commissioner might not be aware of the public's concerns, but an elected commissioner would be keenly aware of the issues important to the public.

- An appointed commissioner might feel inclined to yield to the interests of those responsible for the appointment, while an elected commissioner is not obligated to any particular group or special interest.

Proponents of an appointing system cite the following reasons:

- An appointed commissioner has no need to campaign or to be unduly influenced by political contributors.

- An appointed commissioner is less likely to be swayed by ill-informed public opinion than an elected one.

- An appointed commissioner is more likely to be perceived as a career government employee interested in regulation than as a politician interested in political advancement.

Many commissioners were employed in the insurance business before they entered public office, and many are employed by insurers or insurance-related organizations after leaving office. The expertise and understanding of insurance operations necessary to regulate effectively are most likely found in a person who has worked in the insurance business. However, some allege that such insurance commissioners have less than an objective relationship with the insurers they regulate. In rebuttal, state insurance commissioners usually deny that they are overly responsive to insurers. Commissioners frequently issue cease-and-desist orders, fine or penalize insurers for infractions of the law, forbid insurers to engage in mass cancellations, limit insurance rate increases, and take numerous other actions that benefit policyholders at insurers' expense.

State Regulation Funding

State insurance departments are partly funded by state premium taxes, audit fees, filing fees, and licensing fees, but premium taxes are the major source of funding. Although state premium taxes are substantial, only a relatively small proportion is spent on insurance regulation. Premium taxes are designed primarily to raise revenues for the state as a whole.

The National Association of Insurance Commissioners (NAIC)

National Association of Insurance Commissioners (NAIC)
An association consisting of the insurance commissioners of each U.S. state, the District of Columbia, and the U.S. territories and possessions that coordinates regulatory activities among the various insurance departments.

The **National Association of Insurance Commissioners (NAIC)** is an association of insurance department commissioners from the fifty U.S. states, the District of Columbia, and U.S. territories and possessions. The NAIC coordinates insurance regulation activities among the insurance departments but has no direct regulatory authority. However, by providing a forum to develop uniform policy when appropriate, the NAIC has a profound effect on the nature and uniformity of state regulation.

The NAIC meets quarterly to discuss important problems and issues in insurance regulation. The NAIC developed uniform financial statement forms that all states require insurers to file. It also assists state insurance departments by sharing financial information about insurers that are potentially insolvent and by developing model laws and regulations.

The insurance laws and regulations of many states incorporate at least the primary concepts of NAIC model laws, resulting in some degree of uniformity among the states. Examples of model laws include model legislation on the regulation of risk retention groups, and a model property and liability insurance rating law.

Model law
A draft bill—the suggested wording of a new law—for consideration by state legislatures. Any state may choose to adopt the model bill or adopt it with modifications.

Laws are passed by the state legislature, while regulations are developed and enforced by a regulatory body such as the state insurance department. A **model law** is a draft bill that state legislatures consider; any state can choose to adopt or to adapt the model bill. A **model regulation** is a draft of a regulation that can be implemented by a state insurance department if the model law is passed.

Model regulation
A draft regulation that may be implemented by a state insurance department if the model law is passed.

In addition to developing model laws, the NAIC, in 1990, implemented an accreditation program to increase the uniformity of insurer solvency regulation across the states. To become accredited, a state insurance department must prove that it has satisfied the minimum solvency regulation standards required by the accreditation program.

State insurance departments must meet three criteria to satisfy the NAIC's Financial Regulation Standards and to be accredited:

1. The state's insurance laws and regulations must meet basic standards of NAIC models.
2. The state's regulatory methods must be acceptable to the NAIC.
3. The state's insurance department practices must be adequate as defined by the NAIC.

As of September 2002, forty-nine state insurance departments had been accredited by the NAIC.[13]

Federal Regulation

The McCarran Act reverses the usual state-federal allocation of regulatory powers only for the business of insurance, and this does not include everything that insurers do. For example:

- As employers, insurers are subject to federal employment laws just like any other business.
- As businesses that sell their stock to the public to raise capital, stock insurers are subject to regulations like any other such business.

Insurance Fraud Protection Act

The Insurance Fraud Protection Act is part of a federal anti-crime bill titled "Violent Crime Control and Law Enforcement Act of 1994."[14] This broad legislation protects consumers and insurers against insolvencies resulting from insurance fraud.

The act prohibits anyone with a felony conviction involving trustworthiness from working in the business of insurance unless he or she secures the written consent of an insurance regulator. Moreover, it is illegal for insurers, reinsurers, producers, and others to employ a person who has a felony conviction involving breach of trust or dishonesty.

The act identifies the following crimes involving the business of insurance:

- Making false statements or reports to insurance regulators—including overvaluing assets—to influence regulatory decisions
- Making false entries in books, reports, or statements to deceive anyone about an insurer's financial condition or solvency
- Embezzling from anyone who is engaged in the business of insurance
- Using threats or force or "any threatening letter or communication to corruptly influence, obstruct, or impede" insurance regulatory proceedings[15]

State Versus Federal Regulation

The question of which level of government—state or federal—should regulate insurance is far from settled. Proponents of federal regulation present the following arguments:

- *Federal regulation would provide regulatory uniformity across the states.* Insurers doing business in more than one state are confronted with differing laws, regulations, and administrative rules. Federal regulation would be uniform.
- *Federal regulation would be more efficient.* Insurers doing business nationally would deal with only one government agency instead of fifty different ones. Also, a federal agency might be less likely to yield to pressure from local or regional insurers. Federal regulation might also be less expensive than state regulation.

- *Federal regulation would attract higher-quality personnel.* If the federal agency were adequately funded under the Federal Budget versus individual state budgets, higher salaries and prestige would likely attract higher-quality personnel who would do a superior job of regulating insurers.

Opponents of federal regulation present the following arguments:

- *State regulation is more responsive to local needs.* Conditions vary widely among states, and state regulators can respond quickly to local problems and needs. In contrast, federal regulation and government bureaucracy would result in considerable delay in solving local problems.

- *Uniformity of state laws can be attained through the NAIC.* As a result of the NAIC's model laws and regulations, current state laws are reasonably uniform, with consideration given to local circumstances and conditions.

- *Greater opportunities for innovation are possible with state regulation.* An individual state can experiment with a new approach to regulation. If that approach fails, only that state is affected. In contrast, if a new approach to federal regulation fails, the entire country might feel its effects.

- *State regulation already exists, and its strengths and weaknesses are known.* In contrast, the benefits and possible adverse consequences of federal regulation on the insurance business and consumers are unknown. Moreover, some local regulation is inevitable; thus, increased federal involvement would result in increased dual regulation.

- *State regulation results in a desirable decentralization of political power.* In contrast, federal regulation would increase the power of the federal government and would dilute states' rights.

The debate over state versus federal insurance regulation will persist. The increasing role of electronic commerce raises challenging questions about the regulation of transactions that occur in cyberspace. And the changing role of banks (traditionally federally regulated) in marketing insurance (traditionally state-regulated) raises additional questions.

Increasingly, large insurers, national or international businesses, and insurance trade associations favor a more centralized insurance regulatory system. The complex, fragmented U.S. insurance regulatory system seems archaic to international businesses now that the European Economic Community is eliminating barriers among European countries. Consequently, the NAIC has taken steps to simplify state regulatory structure, making it less subject to variation while preserving positive state regulation features.

REGULATORY ACTIVITIES

Insurance regulation focuses primarily on the following seven activities:

1. Forming and licensing insurers
2. Licensing insurance personnel
3. Monitoring insurer solvency

4. Regulating insurance rates
5. Regulating insurance policies
6. Monitoring market conduct
7. Ensuring consumer protection

Each area is examined below.

Forming and Licensing Insurers

The first regulatory activity applies to forming and licensing insurers. By issuing a license to an insurer, a state indicates that the insurer meets minimum standards of financial strength, competence, and integrity. If these standards change later, and if the insurer fails to meet the new standards, the insurer's license can be revoked. A license indicates that the insurer has complied with the state's insurance laws and is authorized to write certain types of insurance in the state. The process of obtaining a license can take months or even years for a new insurer. Once licensed, the insurer is subject to all applicable state laws, rules, and regulations.

As explained next, licensing standards vary among admitted domestic, foreign, alien, and nonadmitted insurers. Risk retention groups face yet another set of standards.

Domestic Insurers

An insurer licensed (authorized to transact business) in its home state is called a **domestic insurer**. If a domestic insurer obtains licenses in states other than its state of domicile, it is a **foreign insurer** in those other states. A domestic insurer's license generally has no expiration date. Licenses of foreign insurers and **alien insurers** (domiciled out of the country) generally must be renewed annually.

Domestic insurers usually must meet the conditions imposed on corporations engaged in noninsurance activities as well as some special conditions imposed on insurers. An applicant for an insurer license must apply for a charter, giving the names and addresses of the incorporators, the name of the proposed corporation, the territories and types of insurance it plans to market, the total authorized capital stock (if any), and its surplus. The state insurance commissioner reviews the application to see whether the applicant also meets the state's licensing requirements.

An insurer must be financially sound. State laws require that domestic stock insurers satisfy certain minimum capital and surplus requirements before a license is granted. Traditionally, state capital and surplus requirements were criticized for several reasons:

*   The capital and surplus requirements for stock insurers varied widely by state.
*   Many states had very low minimum capital and surplus requirements.

Domestic insurer
An insurer doing business in its home state.

Foreign insurer
A U.S. insurer doing business in a state that is not its home state.

Alien insurer
An insurer domiciled outside the U.S.

- Some states did not relate the amount of capital and surplus to the premium volume to be written.
- Economic conditions might change the adequacy of fixed-dollar capital and surplus requirements.

During the early 1990s, the NAIC developed model laws that impose risk-based capital requirements. Risk-based capital requirements stipulate that each insurer must have a certain amount of capital based on the level of risk of its insurance and investment operations.

Essentially, the risk-based capital formula requires more capital for property-casualty insurers than for other insurers whose operations are less risky. A similar formula applies to life-health insurers.

Capital and Paid-In Surplus Requirements—Stock Insurers

Domestic stock insurers must meet capital stock and paid-in surplus requirements:

- The *capital stock* is the value of the shares of stock issued to stockholders. If 600,000 shares with a $1 par value are issued and outstanding, the capital stock account would have $600,000.
- *Paid-in surplus* is the amount stockholders paid in excess of the par value of the stock. If 600,000 shares of stock with a $1 par value are sold for $1.50 per share, for a total of $900,000, the paid-in surplus would be $300,000.

Minimum initial capital and paid-in surplus requirements vary widely by state and by amounts and types of insurance written.

Surplus Requirements—Mutual and Reciprocal Insurers

Because a mutual insurer has no capital derived from the sale of stock, the minimum financial requirement applies only to surplus. When a mutual insurer is forming, its initial surplus can be derived from premium deposits paid by prospective policyholders. Also, a portion of the initial surplus can be borrowed. Most states require mutuals to have an initial surplus equal to the minimum capital and paid-in surplus requirement for stock insurers writing the same type of insurance. Some states, however, have set a minimum surplus requirement for mutuals that is lower than the minimum capital and paid-in surplus requirement for stock insurers. In most states, minimum surplus requirements for mutual insurers and reciprocals are the same.

Many states require the organizers of a mutual insurer to have applications and deposit premiums from a stated minimum number of persons for at least a stated number of separate loss exposures with aggregate premiums exceeding a specified amount. These requirements help to guarantee that the insurer has a minimum book of business and hence some stability before it officially begins operations.

Other Requirements

In addition to financial requirements, states impose other requirements on new insurers. For example, the proposed name for a new mutual insurer must include the word "mutual," and the proposed name of a new insurer must not be so similar to that of any existing insurer that it would be misleading. The commissioner might have the authority to refuse a license if he or she believes the insurer's incorporators or directors are not trustworthy. Some states even permit the commissioner to deny a license to an otherwise worthy applicant if the commissioner believes that no additional insurers are needed in the state. Once the license has been issued, it can be revoked if the insurer operates in a manner that is clearly detrimental to the welfare of its policy-holders (for example, consistent failure to pay legitimate claims or fraudulent business conduct).

Foreign Insurers

To be licensed in an additional state (in other words, as a foreign insurer), an insurer first must show that it has satisfied the requirements imposed by its home state (its state of domicile, or the state where it is a domestic insurer). Second, a foreign insurer must generally satisfy the minimum capital, surplus, and other requirements imposed on domestic insurers.

Alien Insurers

Alien insurers (insurers domiciled outside the U.S.) must satisfy the requirements imposed on domestic insurers by the state in which they want to be licensed. Additionally, they must usually establish a branch office in any state and have funds on deposit in the U.S. equal to the minimum capital and surplus required.

Nonadmitted Insurers

An admitted insurer is licensed by a state insurance department to do business in the insured's home state. A nonadmitted insurer is not licensed (not authorized) in the insured's home state; it might be an admitted insurer in other states, and it might even be an alien insurer. A nonadmitted insurer is typically a surplus lines insurer. The surplus lines insurance mechanism allows U.S. consumers to buy property-casualty insurance from nonadmitted insurers when consumers are unable to purchase the insurance they need from admitted insurers. Surplus lines insurers provide a positive and legal supplement to the admitted insurance market. The business that surplus lines insurers generally accept includes distressed risks (those that have underwriting problems), unique risks (those that are difficult to evaluate), and high-capacity risks (those that require very high coverage limits). Surplus lines coverages commonly include products liability, professional liability, employment practices liability, special events, and excess and umbrella policies.

Surplus lines laws
State laws that permit producers with a surplus lines license to write business for an "acceptable" nonadmitted insurer when protection from admitted insurers is not available.

Under **surplus lines laws**, a nonadmitted insurer might be permitted to transact business through a specially licensed surplus lines producer if (1) the insurance is not readily available from admitted insurers, (2) the nonadmitted insurer is "acceptable," and (3) the producer has a special license authorizing him or her to place such insurance. The surplus lines producer usually must be a resident of the state.

An "acceptable" nonadmitted insurer generally must file a financial statement that the insurance commissioner finds satisfactory; supply documentation of transactions to state regulators; obtain a certificate of compliance from its home state or country; and, if an alien insurer, maintain a trust fund in the U.S. Some states leave the determination of acceptability to the producer. A few states permit producers to use other nonadmitted insurers if the desired insurance cannot be obtained from either admitted or "acceptable" nonadmitted insurers.

A nonadmitted insurer writing business in the surplus lines market does not face regulatory constraints on insurance rates and forms. However, premium taxes must be paid by the surplus lines producer on the insurer's behalf. From the insured's perspective, a distinct disadvantage of surplus lines insurance is that it is not usually protected by the state's guaranty fund (discussed later in this chapter).

Risk Retention Groups

A risk retention group is a special type of group captive enabled by the 1986 Liability Risk Retention Act. Once licensed as a liability insurer under the laws of at least one state, a risk retention group can write insurance in all states. However, in a nonchartering state, a risk retention group might be subject to some state laws, such as unfair claim settlement practice laws, and to premium taxes. The risk retention group might also be required to become a member of a joint underwriting association (JUA) or a similar association with which insurers share losses in such areas as assigned-risk auto insurance.

Some state regulators have expressed concerns about the financial security of risk retention groups, particularly when the group providing the insurance is licensed in another state. Congress assisted with addressing these concerns by allowing the licensing state to request and, if necessary, mandate an examination of a group's financial condition even when the commissioner has no reason to believe that the group is financially impaired. However, some state regulators still fear abuses under the Act, and some advocates of risk retention groups remain concerned about the possibility of overregulation.

Licensing Insurance Personnel

The second regulatory activity is licensing insurance personnel. States license many of the people who sell insurance, give insurance advice, or represent insurers, including producers, insurance consultants, and claim adjusters.

Producers

Producers must be licensed in each state in which they do business. To obtain a license to sell a particular type of insurance, a producer must pass a written examination. Insurance producers operating without a license are subject to civil, and sometimes criminal, penalties. Traditionally, lack of uniformity among the states' licensing requirements has been a tremendous source of frustration and expense for producers licensed in more than one state. Provisions in the GLB Act have led to greater licensing reciprocity among states. Regulators' ultimate goal is to move beyond reciprocity and to resolve issues related to uniformity in producer licensing. Meeting this goal will streamline the licensing process while retaining state regulatory authority over it.

States that issue a separate broker's license might use a different set of examinations to test candidates' competence, or they might establish higher standards for the broker's license than for the agent's license. Some states prohibit persons from taking the broker's examination until they have been licensed agents for a specified period, such as two years.

Insurance Consultants

Insurance consultants give advice, counsel, or opinions about insurance policies sold in the state. Some states require insurance consultants to be licensed, and requirements for a consultant's license vary by state. Separate examinations are usually required to be an insurance consultant in both life-health insurance and property-casualty insurance.

Claim Adjusters

Some states license claim adjusters who represent insurers. Licensing claim adjusters is justified because of the complex and technical nature of insurance policies and because claimants must be protected from unfair, unethical, and dishonest claim practices. Licensing also provides some assurance that adjusters are aware of prohibited claim practices, will have minimum technical skills, and will treat policyholders fairly.

Public adjusters, who represent insureds for a fee, are generally required to be licensed to ensure technical competence and to protect the public.

Monitoring Insurer Solvency

The third regulatory activity is monitoring insurer solvency. Monitoring solvency protects policyholders and the public by accomplishing two broad goals:

1. Reducing the insolvency risk
2. Protecting the public against loss when insurers fail

A delicate balance exists between achieving these goals and reducing the total cost of risk for society as a whole. Insurers' costs are raised by requirements that increase the amount of capital they must hold in reserve. Whether directly or indirectly, insurance consumers also pay for the costs of regulation, including regulators' salaries and the costs of collecting and maintaining financial data.

Insurers hold large sums of money for long periods of time. Their financial strength must be carefully monitored to ensure their continued ability to pay covered claims, both now and in the future.

Individual consumers and most businesses are not sophisticated enough to analyze claim-paying ability when selecting an insurer. Therefore, some of the analysis is delegated to others. State regulators, independent rating organizations, and state-sponsored insurance guaranty funds all help to protect consumers. Insurance producers, who have a vested interest in having long-term relationships with consumers, can also help them avoid purchasing insurance from financially unsound insurers. Unfortunately, none of these efforts is foolproof.

Methods To Ensure Solvency

Regulators use the following four methods to ensure solvency:

1. Establish financial requirements
2. Review financial annual statements
3. Administer the Insurance Regulatory Information System (IRIS)
4. Conduct on-site field examinations

The first method to ensure solvency is to set financial requirements. To obtain and keep a license as an admitted insurer, each insurer must meet certain minimum financial requirements, such as capital and surplus requirements. Specific financial requirements vary widely by state. Meeting risk-based capital standards is an example of an ongoing financial requirement. Another financial requirement restricts how insurers can invest loss reserves.

The second method to ensure solvency is to require insurers to submit annual financial statements to state insurance departments in a prescribed format: the NAIC Annual Statement, which requires detailed information on net written premiums, expenses, investments, losses, reserves, and other financial information. These statements are analyzed to assess insurers' financial strength.

The third method to ensure solvency is to administer the Insurance Regulatory Information System (IRIS). This system identifies insurers with potential solvency problems. Diagnostic tests are applied to the data submitted by insurers to allow early detection of insurers that might require closer monitoring.

IRIS has two phases:

*   Phase I uses financial ratios and other reports based on Annual Statement data. Twelve ratios are computed that provide information about (1) leverage—the amount of business an insurer is writing compared to its capital, (2) profitability, (3) liquidity, and (4) loss reserve integrity.

Insurers that do not meet certain criteria in four or more ratios receive additional review.

- Phase II uses experienced state examiners and financial analysts to evaluate the financial ratios and selected Annual Statement data.

Based on these evaluations, certain insurers might receive immediate or targeted regulatory attention. Insurers designated for immediate attention must be investigated by regulatory officials in the state where the insurer is domiciled. Insurers designated for targeted attention are examined on a priority basis. Although helpful in setting regulatory priorities, IRIS has limitations as an early detection tool.

The fourth method to ensure solvency is to conduct on-site examinations. Regulators conduct on-site field examinations to monitor insurers' financial strength. State laws usually require that insurers be examined at least once every three to five years. By dividing the country into four geographic zones to avoid duplicate examination of multi-state insurers, the NAIC coordinates the field examinations of insurers that write business in several states.

Liquidation of Insolvent Insurers

If an insurer is insolvent, the state insurance department places it in receivership. With proper management, successful rehabilitation might be possible. If the insurer cannot be rehabilitated, it is liquidated according to the state's insurance code. Many states now liquidate insolvent insurers according to the Uniform Insurers Liquidation Act drafted by the NAIC. This model act promotes uniformity in liquidating assets and paying claims of a failed insurer. Under this act, creditors in each state in which the insolvent insurer has conducted business are treated equally; creditors in the state where the insurer is domiciled do not receive preferential treatment. Some states prioritize claimants who are entitled to the failed insurer's assets.

State Guaranty Funds

Guaranty funds do not prevent insurer insolvency, but they mitigate its effects. All states have property-casualty insurance guaranty funds that pay unpaid claims of insolvent insurers licensed in the particular state. With the exception of New York, where a pre-assessment system maintains a permanent fund, a post-insolvency assessment method is used to raise the necessary funds to pay claims. Insurers doing business in the state are assessed their share of unpaid claims. Although the amounts involved are not trivial—from 1969 through 1999, state guaranty fund net assessments on behalf of insolvent insurers totaled about $6.6 billion[16]—they still represent a very small percentage of total premiums. Insurers can recoup all or part of the assessments by insurance rate increases, by special premium tax credits, and by refunds from the state guaranty fund.

Guaranty funds
State-established funds that provide for the payment of unpaid claims of insolvent insurers licensed in that state. Although guaranty funds do not prevent insurer insolvency, they mitigate its effects.

State guaranty funds vary by state. However, the following characteristics are common.[17]

- *Assessments are made only when an insurer fails.* As mentioned, New York is the exception. The definition of "failure" varies by state. Some states regard an insolvency order from a state court as evidence of failure. Others require a liquidation order from the state. All states limit the amounts that insurers can be assessed in one year.

- *Policies usually terminate within thirty days after the failure date.* Unpaid claims before termination, however, are still valid and paid from the guaranty fund of the policyholder's state of residence if the insolvent insurer is licensed in the state. Under the NAIC's model act, if the failed insurer is not licensed in the state, a policyholder or claimant cannot file a claim with the guaranty fund but must seek payment by filing a claim against the failed insurer's assets, which are handled by the liquidator.[18]

- *Claim coverage varies by state.* No state fund covers reinsurance or surplus lines insurance (except New Jersey).

- *Claims are subject to maximum limits.* The maximum limit is usually the lesser of $300,000 or the policy limit. Some states have limits under $300,000, and a small number of states have much higher limits, such as $500,000 or $1 million.

- *Most states provide for a refund of unearned premiums.* However, a few states have no unearned premiums claim provision. In these states, a policyholder with a failed insurer is not entitled to a refund of the unearned premiums from the guaranty fund.

- *Most states apply a $100 deductible to unpaid claims.* Many states exempt workers' compensation claims from a deductible.

- *Most states divide their guaranty funds into separate accounts, usually auto, workers' compensation, and other types of insurance.* So, auto or workers' compensation assessments can be limited to insurers that write only that type of insurance.

- *Assessment recovery varies by state.* Thirty-two states permit insurers to recover assessments by an insurance rate increase. The remaining states generally reduce annual state premium taxes, usually over a period of five years. Consequently, taxpayers and the general public, as well as insureds, are subsidizing the unpaid claims of insolvent insurers.

Homeowners and auto insurance claims are covered by all state funds, but some types of insurance, such as annuities, life, disability, accident and health, surety, ocean marine, mortgage guaranty, and title insurance often are not covered. Self-insured groups, including risk retention groups, are not protected by guaranty funds. Only one state has established a special fund for surplus lines.

Reasons for Insolvency

Why do insurers fail? Some insolvencies have occurred when an insurer was overexposed to losses resulting from a major insured catastrophe. Usually, no single event or mistake causes an insurer to become insolvent; rather, poor management and adverse events combine to cause insolvencies. Experts have identified the following factors that frequently contribute to insolvencies:

- Rapid premium growth
- Inadequate insurance rates and reserves
- Excessive expenses
- Lax controls over managing general agents
- Uncollectible reinsurance
- Fraud

Poor management is at the root of most of these factors. A combination of inadequate insurance rates and lax underwriting starts a deterioration in a book of business. If these problems are not detected and corrected promptly, the decay in the quality of the business accelerates.

Rapid premium growth precedes nearly all major insolvencies. Rapid growth by itself is not harmful, but it reduces the margin for error in insurers' operations. Moreover, it usually indicates bargain-basement insurance rates and lax underwriting standards. If insurance rates are inadequate and losses understated, net losses and capital deterioration rise faster than management can handle.

Solvency Regulation Challenges

Solvency regulation presents some significant challenges. Among them are the time lag in obtaining data, inadequate resources, underqualified personnel, and inadequate sharing of information.[19]

- *Time lag in determining problem insurers.* Annual Statements are submitted two months after the end of the accounting year, and insurance department review can take as long as three months. At this point, certain negative financial trends, such as loss reserve development, might be more than a year in progress. This time lag delays detection of a problem and allows insolvent and struggling insurers to continue operating for months. Moreover, most states require field examinations only once every three to five years, and the examinations often take months or years to complete. Meanwhile, problem insurers continue to operate and to write new business.
- *Inadequate resources.* Some state insurance departments are understaffed and have insufficient financial resources for effective monitoring of the solvency of insurers.

- *Lack of professional qualifications for field examiners.* Some field examiners do not meet NAIC qualification standards for examiners who participate in zone examinations.

- *Inadequate sharing of information by the states.* States vary in the amount of information about problem insurers they share with other states. Some states openly share all information. Others are reluctant to do so, even though the interstate operations of many large insurers and state responsibility under a guaranty fund make interstate sharing of solvency information absolutely necessary.

Regulating Insurance Rates

The fourth regulatory activity is regulating insurance rates. Rate regulation might well be the regulatory activity that receives the most public attention. This section covers rate regulation goals, types of rating laws, and arguments for prior approval and open competition rating laws. Ratemaking principles are discussed in a subsequent chapter.

Property-casualty insurance pricing has historically been cyclical. The typical pattern is a few years of low rates, relaxed underwriting, and underwriting losses (soft market) followed by a few years of high rates, restrictive underwriting, and strong underwriting gains (hard market). This pattern is known as the **underwriting cycle**.

Underwriting cycle

A cyclical pattern of insurance pricing in which a soft market (low rates, relaxed underwriting, and underwriting losses) is eventually followed by a hard market (high rates, restrictive underwriting, and underwriting gains) before the pattern again repeats itself.

The underwriting cycle has strong, generally undesirable effects on the market and challenges all aspects of rate regulation. A full discussion of the underwriting cycle is beyond the scope of this text.

Insurance Rate Regulation Goals

The three major goals of rate regulation are to ensure that rates are:

1. Adequate
2. Not excessive
3. Not unfairly discriminatory

Adequate

The first goal of insurance rate regulation is that rates be adequate. Rates for a specific type of insurance should be high enough to pay all claims and expenses related to those rates. This requirement helps maintain insurer solvency. If rates are inadequate, an insurer might fail, and policyholders and third-party claimants would be financially harmed if their claims were not paid.

Several factors complicate the regulatory goal of having adequate rates:

- An insurer usually does not know what its actual expenses will be when the policy is sold. Premiums are paid in advance, but they might be insufficient to pay all related claims and expenses that occur later. An unexpected increase in claim frequency or severity can make the rate inadequate.

- Insurers might charge inadequate rates in response to keen price competition in order not to lose business.
- State rate approval systems might not approve insurers' requests for adequate rates for political reasons or because of disagreement over the level of requested rates.
- Unanticipated events might lead to higher losses than those projected when rates were set.

Although insurance rate adequacy is a goal of insurance regulation, no method of rate regulation guarantees that rates will be adequate.

Not Excessive

A second goal of insurance rate regulation is that rates not be excessive. Insurers should not earn excessive or unreasonable profits. Regulators have considerable latitude and discretion in determining whether rates are excessive for a given type of insurance, and they consider numerous factors. These factors include (1) the number of insurers selling a specific coverage in the rating territory, (2) the relative market share of competing insurers, (3) the degree of rate variation among the competing insurers, (4) past and prospective loss experience for a given type of insurance, (5) possibility of catastrophe losses, (6) margin for underwriting profit and contingencies, (7) marketing expenses for a given type of insurance, and (8) special judgment factors that might apply to a given type of insurance.

Regulators sometimes use the fair rate of return approach in determining whether an insurer's rates are adequate or excessive. An insurer should expect at least some minimum rate of return on the equity invested in its insurance operations. An insurer's fair rate of return presumably should resemble the rate of return applicable to other types of businesses, especially if insurers are to attract investment capital. Many believe that the insurance business, by its nature, involves a higher degree of risk than many other businesses and that higher risks generally should be accompanied by higher returns. To date, little agreement exists as to what constitutes a fair rate of return for insurers.

Not Unfairly Discriminatory

The third goal of insurance rate regulation is that rates not be unfairly discriminatory. The word "discrimination," as usually used, carries negative connotations, but the word itself is neutral, implying only the ability to differentiate among things. Discrimination, in the neutral sense, is essential to insurance rating. However, insurers' discrimination must be fair and consistent. This means that *loss exposures that are roughly similar regarding expected losses and expenses should be charged substantially similar rates*. For example, two drivers age twenty-five operating similar vehicles in the same rating territory who buy the same type and amount of auto insurance from the same insurer should be charged similar rates.

Only unfair discrimination is prohibited, not *fair* discrimination. If loss exposures are substantially different in terms of expected losses and expenses, then different rates can be charged. For example, if a woman age twenty-five and another age sixty-five are in good health and purchase the same type and amount of life insurance from the same insurer, it is not unfair rate discrimination to charge the older woman a higher rate. The higher probability of death for a woman at age sixty-five clearly and fairly justifies a higher rate.

Types of Rating Laws

The rates that property-casualty insurers can charge in any state are affected by that state's rating laws. Generally, the major types of state rating laws are as follows:

- *Mandatory rate law.* Under a **mandatory rate law**, a state agency or rating bureau sets rates, and all licensed insurers are required to use them.

- *Prior approval law.* Under a **prior approval law**, rates must be approved by the state insurance department before they can be used. Insurers have criticized prior approval laws because there is often considerable delay in obtaining a rate increase. Consequently, a rate increase might be inadequate by the time it is approved. Furthermore, the statistical data required by the state insurance department might not be readily available.

- *File-and-use law.* Under a **file-and-use law**, rates have to be filed with the state insurance department, but they can then be used immediately. The department has the authority to disapprove the rates if they cannot be justified or if they violate state law. A file-and-use law overcomes the problems of delay associated with prior approval laws.

- *Use-and-file law.* Under a **use-and-file law**, which is a variation of the file-and-use law, insurers can change rates and later submit filing information that is subject to regulatory review.

- *Flex rating law.* Under a **flex rating law**, prior approval is required only if the new rates exceed a certain percentage above (and sometimes below) the rates filed previously. Insurers are permitted to increase or decrease their rates within the established range without prior approval. Typically, a range of five to ten percent is permitted. Flex rating permits insurers to make rate adjustments quickly in response to changing market conditions and loss experience, but it prohibits wide swings within a short period of time. Flex rating also can restrict insurers from drastically reducing rates to increase market share. The result should be smoother insurance pricing cycles.

- *Open competition.* Under an **open competition system**, rates do not have to be filed with the state insurance department. Market prices driven by the economic laws of supply and demand, rather than the discretionary acts of regulators, determine the rates and availability. However, insurers might be required to furnish rate schedules and supporting statistical data to regulatory officials, and the state insurance department has the

Mandatory rate law
State law under which insurance rates are set by a state agency or rating bureau and all licensed insurers are required to use those rates.

Prior approval law
State law under which insurance rates must be approved by the state insurance department before they can be used.

File-and-use law
State law under which insurance rates must be filed with the state insurance department but can then be used immediately.

Use-and-file law
State law under which insurance rates can be put into effect with filing information subsequently submitted and subject to regulatory review.

Flex rating law
State law under which prior approval is required only if the new rates exceed a certain percentage above (and sometimes below) the rates previously filed.

Open competition system
A system under which rates do not have to be filed with the state insurance department.

authority to monitor competition and to disapprove rates if necessary. The goals of adequate, nonexcessive, and equitable rates still apply.

These laws apply not only to rates for a new type of insurance, but also to rate changes.

Desirability of Strict Rate Regulation

Generally, consumer groups and politicians tend to support prior approval or other forms of strict regulation, while insurers and economists tend to support use-and-file and open competition.

Proponents of prior approval laws offer the following reasons for their position:

- Prior approval laws require insurers to justify their requests for rate increases with supporting actuarial data.

- Prior approval laws tend to promote insurer solvency. Because regulators review rate data, rates can be set at adequate levels to maintain insurer solvency.

- Prior approval laws keep rates reasonable and prevent insurers from charging excessive rates. Many people assume that insurers are earning excessive profits and that rates can be reduced only by direct government action.

Proponents of open competition offer the following reasons for their position:

- Prior approval laws might cause rate increases to be inadequate for writing profitable business. Inadequate rates might force insurers to reduce the amount of new business written or might even force them to withdraw from the market, which could lead to an insurance availability problem.

- Prior approval laws might distort incentives for controlling claim costs. This argument applies largely to auto insurance. To make auto insurance more affordable, regulators might reduce rates for drivers with the highest premiums by increasing rates for other drivers. Regulators might limit the rates insurers can charge drivers who are in a residual market plan or might restrict the use of age, gender, or territory as ratemaking variables. The result is that high-risk drivers are more likely to drive, they are more likely to purchase expensive cars, and they are less likely to exercise caution in preventing accidents and theft losses than if their rates were not subsidized.[20]

- Prior approval laws might lead insurers to abandon the state, increasing the number of drivers in residual market plans. Considerable evidence exists that in states with strict rate suppression, the proportion of drivers in residual market plans is much higher than in states with competitive rating laws. Under open competition, the equilibrium market price is determined by market forces, not by government regulators. Consequently, most drivers can be insured in the voluntary standard market by paying market prices.

- Open competition is less expensive to administer. Regulators are not required to review thousands of rate filings or to hold costly hearings.

Consequently, the state insurance department's limited resources can be devoted to higher-priority areas, such as solvency regulation and consumer affairs.

- Open competition tends to overcome the limitations of prior approval laws. Open competition laws allow rates to be adjusted more quickly in response to changing economic and market conditions. Fewer political pressures are encountered, and the need for supporting actuarial data is reduced.

- Open competition among insurers keeps rates reasonable and equitable. Free market forces, rather than government intervention, curtail excessive rates.

Regulating Insurance Policies

The fifth regulatory activity is regulating insurance policies. This is considered necessary for the following reasons:

- *Insurance policies are complex documents.* Because most insurance policies are difficult to interpret and understand, regulating their structure and content is necessary.

- *Insurance policies are almost always drafted by insurers who sell them to the public on a take-it-or-leave-it basis.* Regulation can protect policyholders from policies that are narrow, restrictive, or deceptive.

Insurance policies are regulated through legislation and insurance departments' rules, regulations, and guidelines. Court decisions can also cause changes in policy language and forms.

Legislation

Insurance policy regulation starts with the state legislature, which can pass laws controlling the structure and content of insurance policies sold in the state. Legislative policy regulation affects the following four areas: standard forms, mandatory provisions, forms approval, or readability standards.

First, legislation might require insurers to use a standard policy to insure property or liability loss exposures. A standard policy is one policy all insurers must use if a coverage is sold in the state.

Second, legislation might also require that certain standard mandatory policy provisions appear in certain types of insurance policies. The required and optional provisions are based on a model bill developed by the NAIC. States usually require that workers' compensation insurance, no-fault auto coverage, and often uninsured motorists coverage, for example, contain mandated policy provisions.

State regulations might require that the mandated policy provisions meet certain minimum standards, providing at least a basic level of protection.

Third, legislation might require that policies be filed and approved by the state to protect policyholders against ambiguous, misleading, or deceptive policies. Many states require that a policy be submitted for approval before it is used. However, if a specified period elapses and the policy has not been disapproved, the policy is considered approved. (Some states permit the state insurance department to extend the review period.) The purpose of such approval is to encourage a prompt review of the policy. However, it can cause a perfunctory review.

The NAIC has recently begun exploring some "speed to market" proposals, designed to reduce the time involved in approving policies, so that innovations can reach the market faster. At this writing, the outcome of these proposals remains uncertain.

Fourth, legislation might require that insurance policies meet a readability test. Legislation also can specify policy style and form as well as the size of print. Readability legislation has influenced the drafting of both personal and commercial insurance policies, but readability tests do not necessarily measure understandability.

Policy Rules, Regulations, and Guidelines

State insurance departments implement specific directives from the legislature or exercise the general authority they have to regulate insurance policies. Administrative rules, regulations, and guidelines can be stated in (1) regulations communicated by the state insurance department to insurers, (2) informal circulars or bulletins from the same source, and (3) precedents set during the approval process. For example, the state insurance department might require specific wording in certain policy provisions or might notify insurers that certain types of policy provisions will be disapproved.

Courts

Although the courts do not directly regulate insurers, they clearly influence them by determining whether insurance laws are constitutional and whether administrative rulings and regulations are consistent with state law. The courts also interpret ambiguous and confusing policy provisions, determine whether certain losses are covered by the policy, and resolve other disputes between insurers and policyholders over policy coverages and provisions.

Court decisions often lead insurers to redraft their policy language and to modify provisions. For example, based on the legal doctrine of concurrent causation, certain courts ruled that if a loss under a risk of direct physical loss (formerly "all-risks") policy is caused by two causes of loss, one of which is excluded, the entire loss is covered. As a result of this doctrine, insurers were required to pay certain flood and earthquake claims they had believed were excluded by their property insurance policies. Subsequent revision of the language in many such property policies explicitly excluded coverage for flood and earthquake losses in cases in which an unexcluded cause of loss contributed to the loss.

Monitoring Market Conduct

The sixth regulatory activity is monitoring market conduct. Unfair trade practices acts prohibit abusive practices. Among market conduct areas that are regulated are sales practices, underwriting practices, claim practices, and bad-faith actions.

Currently, all U.S. jurisdictions but the District of Columbia and Guam have unfair trade practices acts. State **unfair trade practices acts** regulate the trade practices of the business of insurance as required under the McCarran Act.

Unfair trade practices acts
State laws that prohibit an insurer from using unfair methods of competition and engaging in unfair acts or practices as defined in the acts.

Unfair trade practices acts prohibit an insurer from using unfair methods of competition and engaging in unfair practices as defined in the acts. Most acts also authorize the insurance commissioner to decide whether activities not specifically defined in the law might result in unfair competition or might qualify as unfair trade practices.

Unfair trade practices cases can be decided by the commissioner of the state in which the activity occurred. If the insurer violates the unfair trade practices act, the insurer is subject to one or both of the following penalties:

- *Fine per violation.* The fine is often increased significantly if the activity is considered to be flagrant, with conscious disregard for the law.
- *Suspension or revocation of license.* This usually occurs if the insurer's management knew or should have known that the activity was an unfair trade practice.

If an insurer disagrees with the commissioner's findings, generally it can file for judicial review. If the court agrees with the commissioner, the insurer must obey the commissioner's orders.

Sales Practices

Producers are subject to fines, penalties, or license revocation if they engage in certain illegal and unethical activities. A producer might be penalized for engaging in practices, such as those mentioned below, that violate the state's unfair trade practices act.

- *Dishonesty or fraud.* A producer might embezzle premiums paid by policyholders or might misappropriate some claim funds.
- *Misrepresentation.* A producer might misrepresent the losses that are covered by an insurance policy, which might induce a client to purchase that policy under false pretenses.
- *Twisting.* A producer might induce a policyholder to replace one policy (usually life insurance) with another, to the insured's detriment. This is a special form of misrepresentation called "twisting."
- *Unfair discrimination.* A producer might engage in any number of acts that favor one insured unfairly over another.

- *Rebating.* A producer might engage in **rebating**, which is the practice of giving a portion of the producer's commission or some other financial advantage to an individual as an inducement to purchase a policy. Rebating is currently illegal in all but two states. The practice is especially problematic with life insurance policies for which the producer's first year's commission is sizable. If a producer rebates part of the commission to one policyholder but not to another, that act is considered unfair discrimination. If the producer rebates the same percentage of the commission to all policyholders, that act is not unfairly discriminatory, but it is still illegal.

Rebating
The practice of giving a portion of the producer's commission or some other financial advantage to an individual as an inducement to purchase the policy.

Underwriting Practices

Unfair underwriting practices are detailed in Exhibit 2-1. Insurance regulators are concerned that improper underwriting could result in insurer insolvency or unfair discrimination against an insurance consumer. To prevent these problems, insurance regulators do the following:

- *Constrain insurers' ability to accept, modify, or decline applications for insurance.* To increase insurance availability, states often require insurers to provide coverage for some loss exposures they might prefer not to cover.
- *Establish allowable classifications.* Regulators limit the ways in which insurers can divide consumers into rating classifications. For example, unisex rating is required in some states for personal auto insurance. This promotes social equity rather than actuarial equity.
- *Restrict the timing of cancellations and nonrenewals.* All states require insurers to provide insureds with adequate advance notice of policy cancellation or nonrenewal so that insureds can obtain replacement coverage. Insurers are typically allowed to cancel or nonrenew only for specific reasons.

Typical violations that are discovered during market conduct examinations of an insurer's underwriting function include:

- Discriminating unfairly when selecting loss exposures
- Misclassifying loss exposures
- Canceling or nonrenewing policies contrary to statutes, rules, and policy provisions
- Using underwriting rules or rates that are not on file with or approved by the insurance departments in the states in which the insurer does business
- Failing to apply newly implemented underwriting and rating factors to renewals
- Failing to use correct policy forms and insurance rates
- Failing to use rules that are state specific

EXHIBIT 2-1

Unfair Trade Practices With Respect to Underwriting

- Making or permitting unfair discrimination under the following conditions:

  - Among individuals of the same class with equal life expectations in any terms and conditions of a life insurance policy

  - Among individuals of the same class with similar health characteristics in any terms and conditions of an accident or health insurance policy

  - Among individuals or risks of the same class with similar characteristics by refusing to insure or renew or by canceling or limiting the amount of insurance on property-casualty loss exposures solely based on the geographic location of the risk unless such action was necessary for sound underwriting and actuarial principles related to actual or reasonably expected loss experience

  - Among individuals or risks of the same class with similar characteristics by refusing to insure or renew or by canceling or limiting the amount of insurance on residential property, or personal property contained within, solely based on the age of the residential property

- Refusing to insure or to continue to insure or limiting the amount of insurance available to an individual because of his or her sex, marital status, race, religion, or national origin. However, marital status can be considered with respect to eligibility for dependent coverage.

- Terminating, changing, or refusing to issue or renew a property-casualty policy solely based on the applicant's or insured's physical or mental impairment. However, this does not apply to accident and health insurance sold by property-casualty insurers. Furthermore, this provision does not change any other provision of the law with respect to termination, modification, issuance, or renewal of a policy.

- Refusing to insure a risk solely because another insurer has refused to insure or has canceled or nonrenewed an existing policy on the risk. This does not prevent termination of an excess insurance policy due to failure of the insured to maintain underlying coverage.

- Failing to maintain books, records, documents, and other business records so that data is accessible and retrievable by insurance regulators for examinations.

Source: National Association of Insurance Commissioners (NAIC), "Unfair Trade Practices Act," *NAIC Model Laws, Regulations, and Guidelines,* vol. IV, Section 4 (Kansas City, Mo.: NAIC, 1993), pp. 880-4 to 880-6.

Claim Practices

All states prohibit certain claim practices by law. Apart from regulatory penalties, failure to handle claims in good faith can lead to claims for damages, alleging bad faith on the insurer's part.

Unfair Claim Practices Laws

Unfair claim practices laws prohibit unethical and illegal claim practices. The laws generally are patterned after the NAIC Model Unfair Claims Settlement Practices Act (see Exhibit 2-2). Prohibited insurer practices typically include:

EXHIBIT 2-2

Unfair Claims Settlement Practices Defined

Any of the following acts by an insurer, if committed in violation of Section 3 [of the Unfair Claims Settlement Practices Model Act], constitutes an unfair claims practice:

A. Knowingly misrepresenting to claimants and insureds relevant facts or policy provisions relating to coverage at issue;

B. Failing to acknowledge with reasonable promptness pertinent communications with respect to claims arising under its policies;

C. Failing to adopt and implement reasonable standards for the prompt investigation and settlement of claims arising under its policies;

D. Not attempting in good faith to effectuate prompt, fair and equitable settlement of claims submitted in which liability has become reasonably clear;

E. Compelling insureds or beneficiaries to institute suits to recover amounts due under its policies by offering substantially less than the amounts ultimately recovered in suits brought by them;

F. Refusing to pay claims without conducting a reasonable investigation;

G. Failing to affirm or deny coverage of claims within a reasonable time after having completed its investigation related to such claim or claims;

H. Attempting to settle or settling claims for less than the amount that a reasonable person would believe the insured or beneficiary was entitled by reference to written or printed advertising material accompanying or made part of an application;

I. Attempting to settle or settling claims on the basis of an application that was materially altered without notice to, or knowledge or consent of, the insured;

J. Making claims payments to an insured or beneficiary without indicating the coverage under which each payment is being made;

K. Unreasonably delaying the investigation or payment of claims by requiring both a formal proof of loss form and subsequent verification that would result in duplication of information and verification appearing in the formal proof of loss form;

L. Failing in the case of claims denials or offers of compromise settlement to promptly provide a reasonable and accurate explanation of the basis for such actions;

M. Failing to provide forms necessary to present claims within fifteen (15) calendar days of a request with reasonable explanations regarding their use;

N. Failing to adopt and implement reasonable standards to assure that the repairs of a repairer owned by or required to be used by the insurer are performed in a workman-like manner.

Reprinted, with permission, from the NAIC Unfair Claims Settlement Practices Act, copyright 1997, National Association of Insurance Commissioners.

- Misrepresenting important facts or policy provisions
- Failing to make a good faith effort to pay claims when liability is reasonably clear

- Attempting to settle a claim for less than the amount that a reasonable person believes he or she is entitled to receive based on advertising material that accompanies or is made part of the application
- Failing to approve or deny coverage of a claim within a reasonable period after a proof-of-loss statement has been completed

Strict regulatory controls on claim practices protect policyholders. Unfair claim practices tarnish the offending insurer's image and reputation; erode public confidence in the insurance industry; and allow insurers to hide behind the "fine print" of policy provisions to deny claims, to policyholders' detriment.

Fairness in making claim payments requires honesty on both sides. Payment of fraudulent claims submitted by dishonest insureds should be vigorously resisted, and excessive claim settlements should be avoided. Valid and legitimate claims, however, should be paid promptly and fairly with a minimum of legal formality.

Bad-Faith Actions

In some cases, courts have ruled that an insurer's improper claim handling constitutes not only a breach of contract but also an independent tort, the tort of bad faith. An insurer that violates good-faith standards can be required to honor the policy's intent (paying the claim) and to pay extra-contractual damages such as emotional distress and attorney fees. Legal remedies for bad-faith actions can lead to both first-party actions (involving the insured) and third-party actions (involving the claimant). These extracontractual damages—damages above the amount payable under the terms of the insurance policy—are payable by the insurer.

Ensuring Consumer Protection

The seventh regulatory activity is ensuring consumer protection. In a sense, all insurance regulatory activities protect insurance consumers. But some activities are designed specifically to support consumers. For example, state insurance departments respond to consumer complaints, and they also provide much information to consumers.

State insurance departments generally lack direct authority to order insurers to pay claims when facts are disputed; such disputes are generally best resolved through the courts. However, most state insurance departments investigate and follow up on every consumer complaint, at least to the extent of getting a response from the insurer involved.

Many states compute complaint ratios, and some make them readily available to consumers through the Internet. To help make consumers more knowledgeable about the cost of insurance, some states publish shoppers' guides and other forms of consumer information, and much of this information can also be found on the Internet. Consumers can obtain information provided by state insurance departments by linking to each state insurance department's Web site from the NAIC Web site at www.naic.org.

UNOFFICIAL REGULATORS

Only the state and federal governments have authority to regulate insurers. The NAIC plays an influential role, but it has no direct regulatory authority. Other organizations—which can be called "unofficial regulators"—also substantially affect insurer activities. This section briefly examines how the following four "unofficial regulators" influence insurer activity:

1. Financial rating agencies
2. Insurance advisory organizations
3. Insurer trade organizations
4. Consumer organizations

Financial Rating Organizations

Because good financial ratings help to attract and retain customers—and vice versa—insurers try to conduct business in ways that maintain a good rating. Several financial rating agencies provide insurer solvency ratings. The best-known rating agencies are the following:

*   A.M. Best Company
*   Duff and Phelps
*   Moody's
*   Standard and Poor's
*   Weiss Ratings, Inc.

Generally, each organization provides summary information about insurer financial strength in the form of a financial rating, typically a letter grade similar to those appearing on a student's report card. Corporate risk managers, independent insurance producers, consumers, and others consult these ratings when choosing an insurer. Many corporate and public entity risk managers purchase insurance only from insurers whose financial rating meets or exceeds a specific rating. Contractors and other organizations are often required to furnish a certificate of insurance from an insurer with a specified minimum financial rating. Banks and other lending institutions typically require mortgagors to provide evidence of insurance from an insurer with a specified minimum financial rating.

Insurers whose financial ratings have declined can find it very difficult to attract and retain customers, and a decrease in customers often causes financial ratings to decline further. Insurers remain highly aware of the factors that financial rating agencies consider, and they try hard to avoid an adverse rating. When an insurer's financial rating is threatened, the insurer can implement remedial measures such as using more reinsurance; limiting new business; selling a portion of its book of business; selling stock to raise additional capital; or merging with another, more financially secure insurer.

Poor financial ratings are not a widespread problem. Also, a "poor" rating does not mean that an insurer will become insolvent, and a "good" rating does not ensure that the insurer will never become insolvent. Some of the large insurers that recently failed received high solvency ratings until a year or two before they were declared insolvent. The value of financial ratings is limited because they are based on past performance. Despite this limitation, insurers work hard to maintain sound financial ratings.

Insurance Advisory Organizations

Advisory organizations
Independent corporations that work with and on behalf of insurers that purchase or subscribe to their services. Services include prospective loss costs and standard contract forms.

Insurance **advisory organizations** are independent corporations that work with and on behalf of insurers that purchase or subscribe to their services. Advisory organizations primarily develop prospective loss costs and standard insurance policy forms. Sometimes, they also file loss costs and policy forms with the state on behalf of their member and subscribing insurers. They often provide other valuable services to participants in the insurance market and its regulators, such as the following:

- Developing rating systems
- Collecting and tabulating statistics
- Researching important insurance topics
- Providing a forum for discussing issues
- Educating insurers, insurance regulators, and the public about relevant issues
- Monitoring regulatory issues of concern to members

Insurers must pay a fee for the services of insurance advisory organizations. Well-known insurance advisory organizations include Insurance Services Office (ISO), the American Association of Insurance Services (AAIS), and the National Council on Compensation Insurance (NCCI).

Even though insurers that use advisory organizations' services are not required to use specific insurance rates or forms, advisory organizations impose a certain degree of uniformity. Relatively few insurers have the resources to independently develop the statistical data on which to base their own insurance rates or to develop policy forms, endorsements, and rating systems for many different coverages that also comply with many state regulations. Insurance consumers benefit from competition among insurers who base their rates on sound statistical data. Uniformity in insurance policies also makes it easier for consumers to comparison-shop.

Insurance Professional and Trade Associations

Several national property-casualty industry professional associations and trade associations have developed over the years to provide services to their member insurers and producers. Some of these associations are listed in Exhibit 2-3.

EXHIBIT 2-3

Insurance Industry Professional and Trade Associations

Name	Year Founded	Members	Interests
American Insurance Association (AIA), www.aiadc.org	1964, with roots in the National Board of Fire Underwriters established in 1866	Property-casualty insurers	Provides safety and legislative services.
Council of Insurance Agents and Brokers, www.ciab.com	1913	Commercial property-casualty insurance agencies and brokerage firms	Takes an active leadership role in crafting the commercial insurance industry's response to issues that affect members and their customers.
Independent Insurance Agents & Brokers of America (IIABA), www.independentagent.com	1896	Independent insurance agencies handling property, fire, casualty, and surety insurance	Promotes education of agents and promotes regulatory and legislative issues of agents.
Inland Marine Underwriters Association (IMUA), www.imua.org	1930	Member companies representing inland marine insurers	Provides its members with education, research, and communications services that support the inland marine underwriting discipline.
National Association of Mutual Insurance Companies (NAMIC), www.namic.org	1895	Property-casualty insurers	Promotes governmental affairs representation; compiles and analyzes pertinent information.
National Association of Professional Insurance Agents, www.pianet.com	1931	Insurance agents	Provides educational, representative, and service-oriented activities.
National Association of Professional Surplus Lines Offices (NAPSLO), www.napslo.org	1975	Associate and wholesale brokers and agents	Sets standards for surplus lines industry and provides educational seminars and workshops and internships.
Property Casualty Insurers Association of America (PCI), www.pciaa.net	2004, by the merger of the National Association of Independent Insurers and the Alliance of American Insurers	Property-casualty insurers	Provides a voice on public policy issues affecting property-casualty insurers before state and federal regulatory agencies and in the courts; serves as an information and education clearinghouse for consumers and the media.
Reinsurance Association of America (RAA), www.reinsurance.org	1968	Property-casualty reinsurers	Promotes the interests of the property-casualty reinsurance industry to federal and state legislators, regulators, and the public.
Risk and Insurance Management Society (RIMS), www.rims.org	1950	Individuals representing more than 4,000 member companies	Promotes the practice of risk management.

Sources: *Encyclopedia of Associations, 2000*, 36th ed., vol. 1, part 1, Tara E. Sheets, ed. (Detroit, Mich.: Gale Research, Inc., 2000); *The Fact Book 2001* (New York: Insurance Information Institute, 2001); and organizations' Web sites listed above.

Trade associations serve an important function for property-casualty insurers and producers. For a fee, members have timely access to legislative developments and can use association personnel to help them lobby. Trade association members can also participate on trade association committees to draft new legislation or to influence pending legislation. Trade associations also continually watch for new regulations issued by state insurance departments in response to new or modified state insurance laws. Participation in one or more major trade associations can enable insurers to gain information without the expense of a large internal staff. Individual insurers would find it difficult to match the prompt dissemination of information and the scope of coverage that the trade associations provide.

Trade associations do not operate only on the national level. Many state and local associations focus on local issues important to their members. For insurers and producers doing business only in one or two states, membership in these associations can be vital and more cost effective than membership in a national trade association that provides many services the one- or two-state insurer or producer might not need.

Trade associations at the national, state, and local levels influence the NAIC, state and federal legislators, and state insurance regulators. Each trade association has the collective power of its membership behind it. One person speaking on behalf of a major segment of insurers affected by a proposed piece of legislation can have far more influence than the representative of a single insurer expressing the same opinion.

Legislators and state insurance regulators sometimes propose legislation based on incorrect market assumptions and misinformation, or in reaction to crises. Trade associations can often provide accurate information and educate legislators and regulators about critical issues in time to influence the development of legislation, regulations, and rules. Sometimes, trade associations can intervene and convince legislators and regulators that the insurance industry can solve a problem without legislation. This type of intervention provides an important service to association membership and is an example of association influence.

Consumer Organizations

Consumers, through consumer groups, have had a major influence on state insurance departments, state and federal legislators, the NAIC, and insurance consumers themselves. Some consumer groups focus solely on insurance issues, while others tackle a variety of public interest issues. Some have adopted a watchdog approach, carefully monitoring insurers and their actions. Others take a more activist approach to confront issues and to work for change.

One such group, the Consumer Federation of America (CFA),[21] is headquartered in Washington, D.C. CFA is an advocacy organization that provides information to consumers about auto insurance and that has worked to improve the safety of household products.

Complaints made to state insurance departments alert regulators to problems and can trigger market conduct examinations, which, in turn, can lead to actions ranging from insurer warnings to revocation of an insurer's license. Additionally, regulators view many complaints as a signal of financial trouble, which can trigger financial examinations. Frequently, consumers and their groups can focus on such complaints to influence state insurance commissioners to require hearings on problems. Such hearings can lead insurers to take corrective action or regulators to develop legislative proposals.

SUMMARY

As noted at the start of this chapter, the following three issues of insurance regulation continue to reemerge:

1. State versus federal regulation
2. Extent of regulation necessary
3. Extent to which insurers should collaborate

In addition to the U.S. Constitution, six subsequent legal events influenced these regulatory issues:

1. *Paul v. Virginia*
2. Sherman Antitrust Act
3. South-Eastern Underwriters Association Decision
4. McCarran-Ferguson Act
5. ISO and the Attorneys General Lawsuit
6. Gramm-Leach-Bliley Act

Insurance regulation is considered necessary to protect consumers, to maintain insurer solvency, and to avoid destructive competition. Every state has an insurance department, headed by a commissioner, that is responsible for regulating insurance in that state. Insurance regulators belong to a trade association, the National Association of Insurance Commissioners, which has no regulatory authority of its own but has substantial influence in coordinating the activities of various state regulators and developing model acts and regulations, as well as sharing financial information. Federal regulation takes many forms, including the Insurance Fraud Protection Act, and a variety of regulations that affect insurers and other organizations alike. The question of state versus federal regulation is an ongoing issue, with strong arguments on both sides; the debate is likely to continue for many years.

Insurance regulators govern the formation and licensing of insurers, the licensing of insurance personnel, insurer solvency, insurance rates, insurance policies, and market conduct, in addition to providing consumer protection.

Other types of organizations serve as unofficial insurance regulators: financial rating organizations encourage insurers to maintain good solvency ratings;

advisory organizations develop standard policy forms and rating systems; professional and trade associations serve many roles and offer various services; and consumer organizations serve as watchdogs and activists.

The next chapter deals with marketing. Consider the regulatory issues discussed in this chapter and how those issues might affect the marketing functions discussed in the next chapter.

CHAPTER NOTES

1. *Samuel B. Paul v. Commonwealth of Virginia*, S.C., 8 Wall., 168–185 (1869).
2. *United States v. South-Eastern Underwriters Association, et al.*, 322 U.S. 533 (1944).
3. *Paul v. Virginia*, 8 Wall., pp. 183–184 (1869).
4. Daniel F. Spulber, *Regulation and Markets* (Cambridge, Mass.: The MIT Press, 1989), pp. 464–468.
5. A more detailed examination of this question appears in Justin L. Brady, Joyce Hall Mellinger, and Kenneth N. Scoles Jr., *The Regulation of Insurance*, 1st ed. (Malvern, Pa.: Insurance Institute of America, 1995), Chapter 5, on which this discussion is based.
6. Banks McDowell, *Deregulation and Competition in the Insurance Industry* (New York: Quorum Books, 1989), p. 19.
7. National Association of Insurance Commissioners, "Unfair Trade Practices Act," *Model Laws, Regulations and Guidelines*, vol. IV (April 1994), pp. 880-15 to 880-18.
8. Insurance Services Office, *Insurance Services Office in a Competitive Marketplace: ISO's Role Within the Property/Casualty Insurance Industry* (New York: Insurance Services Office, June 1987), p. 3.
9. The Public Entity Risk Institute's Web site address is http://www.riskinstitute.org (accessed July 28, 2003).
10. The foregoing paragraphs under this heading are adapted from Ruth Gastel, CPCU, ed., *Insurance Issues Update* (New York: Insurance Information Institute, November 1994).
11. "S.900 Does Not Mean All The Battles Are Over," *National Underwriter*, Life & Health/Financial Services edition, November 22, 1999, p. 42.
12. Ruth Gastel, CPCU, "Rate Regulation and Other Regulatory Issues," *Insurance Issues Update*, September 2000, p. 3.
13. "Financial Regulation Standards and Accreditation Program," National Association of Insurance Commissioners, September 2002, http://www.naic.org (accessed November 6, 2002).
14. 18 USC Sec. 1033.
15. Ann Monaco Warren, Esq., and John William Simon, Esq., "Dishonesty or Breach of Trust" in 18 U.S.C. § 1033: "Are *You* Criminally Liable on the Basis of an Associate's Record?" *FORC Quarterly Journal of Insurance Law and Regulation*, vol. X, edition III, September 12, 1998.

16. National Conference of Insurance Guaranty Funds, http://www.ncigf.org (accessed August 15, 2001).

17. A.M. Best Company, *Insurer Failures, Property/Casualty Insurer Insolvencies and State Guaranty Funds* (Oldwick, N.J.: A.M. Best Company, 1991), pp. 26–34.

18. A.M. Best Company, *Insurer Failures, Property/Casualty Insurer Insolvencies and State Guaranty Funds*, p. 28.

19. General Accounting Office, Insurance Regulation, Problems in the State Monitoring of Property/Casualty Insurer Solvency (Washington, D.C.: U.S. Government Printing Office, 1989), pp. 2–26.

20. Scott E. Harrington, "Competition and Regulation in the Automobile Insurance Market" (paper prepared for distribution at the ABA National Institute on Insurance Competition and Pricing in the 1990s, Baltimore, Md., June 2–3, 1990), p. 6.

21. Consumer Federation of America, http://www.consumerfed.org (accessed June 5, 2002).

Appendix

McCarran-Ferguson Act (Public Law 15)

McCarran-Ferguson Act 15 U.S.C.

Sections 1011-1015 March 9, 1945
Section 1011.

The Congress hereby declares that the continued regulation and taxation by the several States of the business of insurance is in the public interest, and that silence on the part of the Congress shall not be construed to impose any barrier to the regulation or taxation of such business by the several States.

Section 1012.

(a)   The business of insurance, and every person engaged therein, shall be subject to the laws of the several States which relate to the regulation or taxation of such business.

(b)   No act of Congress shall be construed to invalidate, impair, or supersede any law enacted by any State for the purpose of regulating the business of insurance, or which imposes a fee or a tax upon such business, unless such Act specifically relates to the business of insurance: Provided, that after June 30, 1948, the Act of July 2, 1890, as amended, known as the Sherman Act, and the Act of October 15, 1914, as amended, known as the Clayton Act, and the Act of September 26, 1914, known as the Federal Trade Commission Act, as amended, shall be applicable to the business of insurance to the extent that such business is not regulated by State law.

Section 1013.

(a)   Until July 30, 1948, the Act of July 2, 1890, as amended, known as the Sherman Act, and the Act of October 15, 1914, as amended, known as the Clayton Act, and the Act of September 26, 1914, known as the Federal Trade Commission Act, as amended, and the Act of June 19, 1936, known as the Robinson-Patman Antidiscrimination Act, shall not apply to the business of insurance or to acts in the conduct thereof.

(b)   Nothing contained in this Act shall render the said Sherman Act inapplicable to any agreement to boycott, coerce, or intimidate, or act of boycott, coercion, or intimidation.

Section 1014.

Nothing contained in this Act shall be construed to affect in any manner the application to the business of insurance of the Act of July 5, 1935, as amended, known as the National Labor Relations Act, or the Act of June 25, 1938, as amended, known as the Fair Labor Standards Act of 1938, or the Act of June 5, 1920, known as the Merchant Marine Act, 1920.

Section 1015.

As used in this Act, the term "State" includes the several States, Alaska, Hawaii, Puerto Rico, Guam, and the District of Columbia.

Chapter 3

Direct Your Learning

Insurance Marketing

After learning the content of this chapter, you should be able to:

- Describe the unique characteristics of insurance marketing, including the legal status of agents and the powers and duties of agents.

- Describe the basic elements of an insurance product marketing plan.

- Describe the three types of traditional insurance marketing systems, including the principal characteristics that distinguish one marketing system from another.

- Describe the functions performed by insurance producers.

- Describe the collaborations for marketing insurance products that resulted from the Gramm-Leach-Bliley Act and market convergence.

- Describe the five types of alternative insurance distribution channels.

- Describe the challenges associated with using the Internet as an alternative distribution channel for insurance products and services.

- Describe the key factors an insurer should evaluate during the distribution channel selection process.

- Describe the considerations in combining traditional marketing systems and alternative distribution channels for insurance products.

Develop Your Perspective

What are the main topics covered in the chapter?

Insurers must reach their customers to sell their policies and to deliver services once the policies have been sold. Three traditional marketing systems and five alternative distribution channels facilitate the delivery of insurance products and services.

Consider what systems and channels your insurance organization uses to distribute its products, information, and services.

- How does the system dictate the service that employees must provide directly to customers?

- What are the producers' functions within these systems and channels?

Why is it important to learn about these topics?

Each marketing system and distribution channel provides some benefits and some restrictions.

Understand how the marketing systems and distribution channels your organization has chosen operate.

- What are the limitations and opportunities created by those systems and channels?

How can you use what you will learn?

Analyze the strengths and weaknesses of the various marketing systems and distribution channels.

- How do they affect other decisions made by your organization?

- Can your organization easily increase its market share of desirable policies by using its current systems and channels?

Chapter 3
Insurance Marketing

According to Peter Drucker, in his book *The Practice of Management*, marketing and innovation are the two chief functions of any business. However, successful marketing—that is, gaining new customers—is insufficient for a business to thrive. In fact, Drucker goes so far as to say, "It is not necessary for a business to grow bigger, but it is necessary that it constantly grow better."[1]

The global marketplace has repeatedly proved Drucker right. Businesses that thrive are those that constantly find new ways (1) to produce better products and (2) to provide better service to their customers. As part of the global marketplace, insurance, like all businesses, has been pressured to accomplish both of these things. Consequently, insurance marketing has been reconfigured and reinvented, and marketing innovations have been introduced.

This chapter focuses on insurance marketing and marketing systems. A **marketing system** is the framework that directs and facilitates the design, development, sale, and support of a product or service. A **distribution channel** is the method (or channel) used to sell that product or service to the ultimate consumer. Any firm that sells a product or service must have a marketing system strategy and a distribution channel strategy in place if the firm is to successfully execute its marketing plan and deliver its product or service to the customer. A business can select from a wide variety of possible marketing systems, based on the type of business it conducts, including, for example, a retail outlet, a wholesale outlet, or a direct sales force. The distribution channels from which a firm can select include direct mail, telemarketing, media advertising, or Internet access.

This chapter begins with an overview of the characteristics that are unique to marketing in the insurance industry. Next, it discusses the three traditional marketing systems: the independent agent and brokerage marketing system, the exclusive agency marketing system, and the direct writer marketing system. The chapter then outlines alternative distribution channels, which include the Internet, call centers, direct response, group marketing, and financial institutions. The chapter concludes by presenting the factors to be considered in selecting the most appropriate channel through which to distribute various insurance products.

Marketing system
The system that directs and facilitates the design, development, sale, and support of a product or service.

Distribution channel
The channel used by the producer of a product or service to transfer that product or service to the ultimate customer.

UNIQUE CHARACTERISTICS OF INSURANCE MARKETING

Legal Status of Agents

Most insurance companies are corporations. As such, they can operate only through the activities of agents. An agent is a person or firm authorized to represent another person or firm in the performance of some function. The person or firm an agent represents is called the principal. Legally, an agent can be either an employee of the principal or an independent contractor. Within the insurance industry, the term "agent" is sometimes reserved for independent contractors who represent insurers. The term "broker" is reserved for independent contractors who represent policyholders and prospective policyholders in their dealings with insurers. In effect, a broker acts as an agent of the policyholder, who then becomes the principal in the relationship. However, the laws of agency presume that the principal knows what the agent knows; therefore, at times, such as when a broker accepts payment from a policyholder on behalf of a particular insurer, the broker is deemed an agent of the insurer. Additionally, a broker might have authority to bind coverage on behalf of an insurer, as an agent would.

Another term used frequently in insurance marketing is producer, which refers to a person who sells insurance to customers. Producers can be brokers, agents of the insurer, employees of insurers or of intermediaries, or independent broker-contractors. In this chapter, the term "producer" is used to refer to any of the above.

The powers an agent possesses are limited to those powers conferred by the principal. When an insurer appoints a producer, normally a written contract is executed. The contract usually specifies the powers and duties of the producer. The powers granted typically include the producer's authority to bind coverages, the claim adjusting authority of the producer, the types of insurance the producer is permitted to write, the commissions to be paid, and similar issues. The duties specified normally deal with accounting for policies and other supplies furnished by the insurer; accounting for insurer funds handled by the producer; and adhering to the accounting, administrative, and underwriting rules of the insurer.

Actual authority
Authority (express or implied) conferred by the principal on an agent under an agency contract.

Agency law recognizes two primary types of authority in agent-principal relationships: **actual authority** and **apparent authority**. The agent's actual authority is conferred by the principal under the agency contract. For example, a property-casualty producer might be contractually granted the authority to bind (effect) coverage on behalf of an insurer in fifteen states. Therefore, the producer can bind coverage for a customer in any one of those fifteen states.

Apparent authority
Authority that arises from a third party's reasonable belief based on appearances created by a principal that an agent has authority to act on behalf of that principal.

Apparent authority arises when a principal creates a reasonable belief in a third party that an agent has certain authority, even though the agent does not.

For example, suppose a customer who has just purchased a new vacation home in a neighboring state contacts the same producer who sold the insurance policy for his or her primary home. At this producer's direction, the customer completes an application for coverage with the same insurer that issued the primary homeowners policy. The producer offers the customer a premium quote for the new policy, and the customer pays the premium. The customer can reasonably assume that coverage has been placed into effect, even if the producer did not have binding authority for that specific state. This is true because, from past dealings with this insurer, the customer has been given the impression that the producer in question has authority to bind coverage. In the event of a claim, the customer would be protected on the basis of the apparent authority that was presented to him or her at the time of the transaction.

Duties Producers Owe to Customers

Although insurance producers primarily represent insurers, the law imposes on them certain duties to insurance customers as well. The extent of these duties depends on the relationship established between the producer and the insurance customer. If the producer merely agrees to provide one or more specific insurance policies to the customer, the producer has only two duties to the customer: (1) to provide the agreed-on policies and (2) to place the agreed-on policies with a solvent insurer. If the policies are placed with an insurer licensed in the state where the insured loss exposures are located, the fact that the producer has no knowledge of any information indicating that the insurer is financially impaired is usually sufficient to satisfy the second duty. If insurance is placed with an insurer not licensed in that state, the producer might have a duty to exercise greater care regarding the insurer's financial status.

The liability outlined above is the minimum liability imposed on producers. A producer's liability can be expanded substantially by the types of business activities in which the producer engages or by contract. For instance, if a producer provides risk management services to a policyholder, the producer might be held liable for overlooking certain loss exposures. In this example, the producer could be held liable for failing to advise a business client of the need for fire legal liability coverage at a building the client leases to house its business.

OVERVIEW OF INSURANCE PRODUCT MARKETING

The Marketing Plan

Before introducing a new insurance product or service, the insurer completes a comprehensive marketing plan. The plan identifies the product or service to be promoted and the customers to be targeted, and it details the resources and strategies that will be used to create, price, promote, and sell the product or service. A marketing plan for a typical insurance product or service might include, but is not limited to, the following items:

1. Product proposal and sales goals—A summary of the new product's operation, a description of the unmet need the product is designed to fulfill, and summarized sales projections.

2. Situational analysis—A SWOT (Strengths, Weaknesses, Opportunities, Threats) analysis of the current marketplace, including analyses of the competition; critical factors required for success; resource, technology, and training requirements; and an assessment of the existing legal and regulatory environment.

3. Marketing goals—An outline of the proposed target market, including detailed sales projections and specifics as to how success will be measured.

4. Marketing strategies—Plans and proposals for how the product will be developed, priced, promoted, and sold. These strategies include determining the appropriate distribution channels for products and services.

Marketing plans are also essential for existing products and services. Most of the requirements for new-product marketing plans apply to marketing plans for existing products, including sales goals, SWOT analysis, marketing objectives, and marketing strategies.

Marketing plans are as varied as the products and services they promote. However, all plans serve the same fundamental purpose: they provide the "roadmaps" necessary to profitably and effectively acquaint sellers with potential buyers.

TRADITIONAL MARKETING SYSTEMS FOR INSURANCE

Once the marketing plan has been developed, insurers market their products and services through the insurance marketing systems identified in their plans. Property-casualty insurers market their products and services to customers through traditional marketing systems, alternative distribution channels, or some combination of both. This section discusses the three traditional marketing systems, which are as follows:

1. Independent agency and brokerage system
2. Exclusive agency system
3. Direct writer system

The principal characteristics that distinguish one traditional marketing system from another are the following:

• Contractual relationship between the producer and insurer—The producer can be an employee of the insurer or an independent contractor.

- Ownership of policy expirations—The producer can own the agency expiration list of the policies the producer has placed with the insurer, or the insurer can retain ownership of the list.

- Compensation methods—The methods insurers use to compensate producers can include sales commissions, contingent commissions, salaries, bonuses, fees, or a combination of methods.

Insurers select a marketing system based on organizational structure, business and marketing plans, growth goals, technological capabilities, staffing, and other resources necessary to support the selected system(s).

Independent Agency and Brokerage Marketing System

Independent Agents and Brokers

The first traditional marketing system is the **independent agency and brokerage marketing system**, which uses producers (agents and brokers) who are independent contractors. These producers are not employees of insurers and are usually free to represent as many or as few insurers as they want. Agencies and brokerages that participate in this system have contracts with insurers to produce new business and to renew (and often service) existing business accounts. Independent producers own the policy expirations and can place business with ("broker" business to) any of the insurers they represent or any producers who have access to insurers that the primary producer does not, subject to policyholder approval. This ownership of expirations is usually clearly stated in the agency contract. However, the ownership exists as a matter of custom and law even in the absence of a contract provision. The expirations usually constitute the largest and most marketable asset of an insurance agency.

Independent agency and brokerage marketing system
An insurance marketing system under which producers (agents or brokers), who are independent contractors, sell insurance, usually as representatives of several unrelated insurers.

Compensation under the independent agency and brokerage system is typically in two forms:

1. A flat percent commission on all business submitted
2. A contingent or profit-sharing commission earned by meeting volume or profit goals

Exhibit 3-1 illustrates a contingent commission scale. The contingent commissions shown in Exhibit 3-1 vary only with the agency's loss ratio. However, some insurers base contingent commissions on the amount of business the agency writes with the insurer (earned premiums) and the agency's premium growth, as illustrated in Exhibit 3-2.

Independent producers might also provide risk management advice to their customers, helping them to select the insurance coverages needed and on the most advantageous terms. Many producers also assist their customers in establishing and managing self-insurance programs, implementing loss control measures, and determining alternatives or supplements to insurance.

EXHIBIT 3-1

Contingent Commission Based on Loss Ratio

Loss Ratio	Contingent Commission as Percentage of Earned Premiums
0.00	14.00%
0.05	12.05
0.10	10.35
0.15	8.65
0.20	7.15
0.25	5.65
0.30	4.50
0.35	3.30
0.40	2.25
0.45	1.30
0.50	0.60
0.55	0.00

EXHIBIT 3-2

Contingent Commission Based on Earned Premiums and Premium Growth

Earned Premiums	Percentage Growth in Premium Volume					
	10%	15%	20%	30%	40%	60%
$ 50,000	3.50%	7.00%	10.50%	17.50%	24.50%	38.50%
75,000	4.69	8.50	12.31	19.94	27.56	42.81
100,000	5.87	10.00	14.12	22.38	30.62	47.12
150,000	8.25	13.00	17.75	27.25	36.75	55.75
200,000	10.62	16.00	21.37	28.37	42.87	64.38
250,000	13.00	19.00	25.00	37.00	49.00	73.00
400,000	20.12	28.00	35.87	51.62	67.37	98.87
500,000	24.87	34.00	43.12	61.37	79.62	100.00

The independent agency and brokerage system is flexible and able to meet the needs of many different insurance customers. The system gets its flexibility from the variety of participants that operate within the system, including national and regional brokers, independent agent networks, managing general agents (MGAs), and excess and surplus lines brokers. Each of these participants can meet a different need for customers. These needs are described in the sections that follow.

National and Regional Brokers

Large insurance brokerage firms operate regionally and nationally, and some even operate internationally. These firms meet the needs of large commercial customers who demand sophisticated technical knowledge and comprehensive servicing. They can also meet the need for insurance program business for customers or groups of customers who require a particular type of coverage for multiple locations, which is often specially designed and developed. Examples of such a program are insurance marketed to attorneys, which might include professional liability coverage, or an insurance program for daycare centers including coverages tailored to their needs.

In addition to selling insurance, national and regional brokers are equipped to provide their customers with risk management services and loss control, actuarial, and claim administration services that are typically supported by offices in multiple states. The brokers receive negotiated fees for the services they provide, or they receive fees in addition to commissions, subject to state regulation.

Independent Agent Networks

Independent agent networks, also known as agent groups, agent clusters, or agent alliances, consist of independent agencies and brokerages that join together to gain advantages normally available only to large national and regional brokers. Agent networks operate nationally, regionally, or locally and, in the majority of cases, allow their agent-members to retain individual agency ownership and independence. By combining individual agency forces into a single selling, negotiating, and servicing unit, an agent network can offer many benefits to its agent members, including:

- Obtaining access to an increased number of insurers
- Combining premium volume to meet insurer requirements for profit-sharing
- Generating additional sales income
- Receiving preferred agency contracts
- Facilitating agency succession planning
- Providing expertise in risk management services
- Offering expertise in financial planning services
- Enabling resource sharing and expense reduction
- Increasing market share

Managing General Agents (MGAs)

Managing general agents (MGAs)
Independent business organizations that function almost as branch offices for one or more insurers and that appoint and supervise independent agents and brokers for insurers using the independent agency and brokerage system.

Managing general agents (MGAs) are also part of the independent agency and brokerage system. MGAs serve as intermediaries between insurers and the producers who sell insurance directly to the customer, similar to wholesalers in the marketing system for tangible goods. An MGA operates as an independent business firm that performs, on behalf of insurers, some or all of the services and functions usually performed by an insurer's branch office.

The exact duties and responsibilities of an MGA depend on its contracts with the insurers it represents. MGAs can represent a single insurer, though they more commonly represent several insurers. Some MGAs can be strictly sales operations, appointing and supervising subagents or dealing with brokers within their contractual jurisdiction. That jurisdiction can be specified in terms of geographic boundaries, types of insurance, or both. A few MGAs cover large multi-state territories, though frequently only for specialty insurance.

The advantage to an insurer of operating through an MGA is the low fixed cost; an insurer who writes business through an MGA does not have to staff and support a branch office. The MGA is usually compensated by a commission override on business its subagents sell. The MGA, by writing relatively small amounts of business for each of several insurers, generates enough commissions to cover its expenses and earn a profit. The MGA might also receive a contingent commission based on the profitability or the volume of business it writes.

MGAs develop expertise in particular markets and design insurance programs in collaboration with the insurers they represent. Specialty insurance programs offered by MGAs include those for such diverse risks as petroleum distributors, fire departments, horse farms, employment practices liability, and directors and officers liability.

In addition to insurance program development, full-service MGAs can provide an array of benefits to their subagents and brokers, including claim administration, information management, loss control and risk management services, underwriting and marketing services, policy issuance, and premium collection. Insurers must supervise the MGAs that represent them, and most states regulate the MGAs' activities and contracts.

Excess and Surplus Lines Brokers

Excess and surplus lines (E&S) brokers
Persons or firms that place business with insurers not licensed (nonadmitted) in the state in which the transaction occurs but that are permitted ("eligible") to write insurance because coverage is not available through standard-market insurers.

Excess and surplus lines (E&S) brokers place business with insurers not licensed in the state in which the insurance transaction occurs. These insurers are called E&S insurers. Other producers are usually limited to placing business with licensed (or admitted) insurers. The circumstances under which business can be placed with an unlicensed (or nonadmitted) insurer through a surplus lines broker vary by state. Normally, a reasonable effort to place the coverage with a licensed insurer is required. The producer, who must be licensed to place surplus lines business in that state, might be required to certify that a specified number (often two or three) of licensed insurers have refused to provide the coverage. In some states, brokers must provide letters from the insurers rejecting the coverage. Some state insurance departments maintain lists of coverages that are eligible for surplus lines treatment without first being rejected by licensed insurers. Some states also maintain lists of eligible surplus lines insurers, requiring producers to place business only with financially sound insurers.

When a producer who represents an insurer that operates in the standard market wants to sell a policy, the producer (1) quotes a premium for the coverage requested and issues the policy to the customer or (2) submits an insurance application to the insurer for underwriting review, quoting, and policy issuance. When a producer wants to sell excess and surplus lines insurance, he or she must usually go through an excess and surplus lines broker (also known as a "wholesaler") or another intermediary rather than contacting the insurer directly. Occasionally, some E&S insurers deal directly with the producer.

Using an E&S broker has two advantages. The first advantage is that E&S brokers have access to insurers that have the capacity to provide the needed insurance. In a hard market, standard insurers' capacity, or financial ability to write new business, is diminished. When the producer is unable to obtain coverage from one of the insurers he or she directly represents, coverage might be available from an E&S insurer for a higher premium than is normally charged for the policy. A producer who is rejected by standard insurers might contact an E&S broker if the producer is presented with one or more of the following:

1. An unusual or a unique loss exposure
2. A customer who requires high limits of insurance
3. A customer who requires unusually broad or specialized coverage
4. Loss exposures requiring a tailored insurance program

The second advantage is that the producer can use an E&S broker to place coverage on an unfavorable loss exposure (that is, one that has a poor claim history, difficult-to-treat exposures, etc.). Consequently, the producer preserves the relationships his or her agency has with its standard insurers and prevents loss ratios from deteriorating should a significant loss or losses occur.

E&S brokers work with their producers to ensure that (1) coverage is placed only with eligible nonadmitted insurers, (2) the customer's unique or unusual requirements can be met by the prospective E&S insurer, and (3) the financial security of the E&S insurer is properly evaluated.

However, producers who place coverage with nonadmitted insurers face some risks. For example, the policy forms the E&S insurer uses might be different; the producer might be unfamiliar with the E&S insurer; and, most importantly, state guaranty funds, which provide claim-payment protection to insureds in the event of insurer default, are not available to E&S policyholders, except in New Jersey.[2]

E&S insurers are subject to certain regulations, such as meeting solvency requirements and being licensed in their home state or country. E&S brokers are also subject to insurance regulations and codes, which might differ by state. Among the various regulatory responsibilities of E&S brokers are the following:

- Document maintenance—Documents of each insurance transaction must be maintained, and the E&S broker's records must be made available to state insurance department regulators at their request.

- Bonding—The E&S broker must maintain a surety bond in a required minimum amount, often representing a percentage or portion of insurance transacted annually by the broker.

- Diligent effort or search—The E&S broker must have proof that the application for insurance was rejected by standard insurers; proof is frequently in the form of an affidavit that cites the insurers who rejected the application, the date of rejection, and the name of a contact at each rejecting insurer.

- Notice to insured—This is a disclaimer that must be presented to the insured, often requiring the insured's signature of acceptance of coverage and affirming that the coverage provided by the nonadmitted insurer in question is not subject to guaranty fund protection.

- Report filing and tax collection—The E&S broker must submit periodic reports to the state's E&S insurance regulatory body, indicating the insurance transacted and premiums paid or returned. Taxes and stamping fees (if applicable) must be remitted, based on gross premiums collected.

- Property-casualty licensing—The E&S broker must maintain that state's general property-casualty license in addition to a surplus lines license.

E&S brokers, like independent agents, national or regional brokers, independent networked agents, and MGAs, operate within the independent agency and brokerage system. As such, they maintain their independence, can represent multiple insurers, and are compensated based on a portion of the commissions generated by the business they write.

Exclusive Agency Marketing System

Exclusive agency marketing system
An insurance marketing system under which agents contract to sell insurance exclusively for one insurer (or for an associated group of insurers).

The second traditional marketing system is the **exclusive agency marketing system**, which uses independent contractors called exclusive agents (or captive agents), who are not employees of insurers. Unlike independent agents, exclusive agents are usually restricted by contract to representing a single insurer. Consequently, insurer management can exercise greater control over exclusive agents than over independent agents. Exclusive agents are limited to selling only the policies of the insurer they represent; however, some exclusive agency companies allow their agents to place business with other insurers if the exclusive agency company does not offer the product or service needed.

Exclusive agents are usually compensated by commissions. During initial training, some of them might receive a salary, a guaranteed minimum income, or income from a drawing account. In terms of overall compensation, insurers in the exclusive agency system commonly pay one commission rate for new business and another, lower rate for renewal business. Independent agents and brokers, on the other hand, usually receive the same commission rate for both new and renewal business, because lower renewal commissions might tempt an independent agent to switch business to a different insurer on renewal to get the higher new-business commission. For exclusive agents, the focus is on new-business production, and a reduced renewal commission rate encourages sales and supports growth. Recently, some independent agency and brokerage companies have reduced policy renewal commissions, particularly in personal insurance, to spur new-business growth and control commission expenses.

Exclusive agents typically do not have ownership of expirations as independent producers do. However, some insurers that market through the exclusive agency system do grant limited ownership of expirations to their agents. Usually, such ownership of expirations applies only while the agency contract is in force. When the agency contract is terminated, the ownership of expirations reverts to the insurer. The insurer might be obligated to compensate the agent for the expirations upon termination of the agency contract, but the agent does not have the option of selling the expirations to anyone other than the insurer.

The exclusive agency company handles many administrative functions for the exclusive agent, including policy issuance, premium collection, and claim processing. Exclusive agents might offer loss adjustment services similar to those offered by independent agents and brokers; however, these agents might be restricted in their ability to offer some risk management services to their customers.

Direct Writer Marketing System

The third traditional marketing system is the **direct writer marketing system**, which uses sales agents (also known as sales representatives) who are employees of the insurers they represent. The direct writer producer sells insurance for his or her employer at office locations provided by the direct writer company. Direct writer producers are not independent contractors like independent agents and exclusive agents.

Direct writer marketing system
An insurance marketing system that uses sales agents (or sales representatives) who are direct employees of the insurer.

Producers in the direct writer system might be compensated by salary, by commission, or by both salary and a portion of the commission generated. Because direct writer producers are employees of the insurers they represent, they usually do not have any ownership of expirations and, like exclusive agents, are usually restricted to representing a single insurer or a group of insurers under common ownership and management. Like exclusive agents, direct writer agents are largely relieved of administrative functions by their employers.

Functions of Producers

Generally, the functions that insurance producers are to perform are specified in the agency or brokerage contract. They vary widely from one marketing system to another and also from one producer to another within a given marketing system. Several of a producer's typical activities are discussed subsequently, including prospecting, risk management review, sales, policy issuance, premium collection, customer service, claim handling, and consulting. Some producers perform all of these functions and others, only some of them.

Prospecting

Virtually all producers prospect. Prospecting involves locating persons, businesses, and other entities that might be interested in purchasing the insurance products and services offered by the producer's principals. Prospects can be located using several methods:

- Referrals from present clients
- Referrals from strategic partners (banks, real estate brokers, etc.)
- Advertising of various kinds, including media advertising and direct mail
- Interactive Web sites
- Telephone solicitations
- **Cold canvass**

Cold canvass

Also known as "cold calling," cold canvass is an insurance sales technique involving the solicitation of insurance prospects either by phone or in person, without a prior appointment.

Large agencies and brokerages might have employees who specialize in locating prospective clients. However, the producer is typically responsible for his or her own prospecting. Insurers might also assist with prospecting, especially in the exclusive agent and direct writer marketing systems.

Risk Management Review

Risk management review is the principal method of determining a prospect's insurance needs. For an individual or a family, the risk management review process might be relatively simple, requiring completing an interview or a questionnaire that assists in identifying the prospect's loss exposures and enables the producer to suggest methods—often insurance based—of treating them. The risk management review process for businesses is likely to be more complex. Much time is required to develop and analyze loss exposure information for a large firm with diversified operations.

Sales

Selling insurance products and services is one of the most important activities of an insurance producer because it is essential to sustaining the livelihood of the agency or brokerage. Commission on business sold is the principal source of income for producers, and the ownership of policy expirations applicable to the business sold is the principal asset of an insurance agency. Steps in the sales process include contacting the prospective client, determining the prospect's needs, preparing and presenting a proposal, and closing the sale.

Policy Issuance

Some producers maintain a supply of an insurer's pre-printed policies and forms in their offices and issue them as needed to their customers, while other producers use their own agency management systems to generate computer-issued policies on site. More common is insurers' practice of assembling policies at the producer's request and either mailing them directly to policyholders or sending them to the producer for delivery.

Premium Collection

Producers who issue policies might also prepare policy invoices and collect premiums. After deducting their commissions, they send the net premiums to the insurers, a procedure known as the **agency bill** process. For business that is agency billed, the three widely used methods of transmitting premiums to the insurer are

1. The item basis
2. The statement basis
3. The account current basis

With the item basis, the premium (less commission) is forwarded to the insurer when the producer collects it or when it becomes due. It is the least complex of the three methods.

Under the statement method, the insurer sends a statement to the producer showing the premiums that are due. The producer is obligated to pay the premiums indicated as due or to show that the statement is in error.

Under the account current method, the producer periodically prepares a statement showing the premiums due to the insurer, after deducting appropriate commissions, and transmits that amount to the insurer. The agency contract indicates how often the producer must submit the account current statement. The most common interval is monthly.

With the item basis, the producer is usually not required to pay the insurer until the premium has been collected. Under the other two methods, the producer must pay the insurer when the premium is due, even if the policyholder has not paid the producer. To give the producer some protection against policyholders' late payments, premiums are usually not due to the insurer until thirty or forty-five days after the policy's effective date. This delay also permits the producer to invest the premiums collected until they are due to the insurer. The resulting investment income might be a significant part of the producer's remuneration.

Agency billing may be used for personal insurance policies, but it is more commonly used with large commercial accounts. For small commercial accounts and

Agency bill
A payment procedure in which a producer sends premium bills to the insured, collects the premium, and sends the premium to the insurer, less any applicable commission.

the vast majority of personal insurance, the customer is usually directed to send premium payments to the insurer, bypassing the producer in a procedure known as the **direct bill** process. In this scenario, the insurer (1) sends the premium bill to the policyholder, (2) collects the premium, and (3) sends the commission to the producer, usually on a monthly basis.

Direct bill
A payment procedure in which an insurer sends premium bills to the insured, collects the premium, and sends any commission payable on the premium collected to the producer.

Customer Service

Most producers are involved to some degree in customer service. For independent agents and brokers, value-added services and the personalization of insurance packages are what differentiates them in the marketplace. For the producer of a direct writer, service might consist of taking an endorsement request over the phone, providing coverage quotes, or transferring a policyholder who has had a loss to the claim department.

Additional customer service activities that producers perform can include responding to billing inquiries, performing customer account reviews, and engaging in field underwriting (obtaining loss reports, insurance credit scores, motor vehicle reports, etc.). The producer must be able to respond to questions about policyholders' existing coverage and additional coverage requirements. Finally, producers are expected to facilitate contacts between policyholders and insurer personnel, including premium auditors and loss control representatives.

Claim Handling

All producers are likely to be involved to some extent in handling claims filed by their policyholders. Because the producer is the policyholder's principal contact with the insurer, the insured naturally contacts the producer first when a claim occurs.

In some cases, the producer might simply give the policyholder the telephone number of the claim department and possibly the name of a person to speak with. Alternatively, the producer might obtain some basic information about the claim from the policyholder, relay it to the insurer, and arrange for a claim representative to contact the insured. Frequently, insurers issue their policies with a "claim kit" directing their policyholders in the proper procedures and contacts.

Finally, many producers are authorized by their insurers to adjust some types of claims. Most often, the authorization is limited to small first-party property claims—for example, property losses under $5,000. Less frequently, if they are properly trained to do so, some producers are also authorized to settle small third-party liability claims; usually these claims are for auto property damage liability losses. A few large agencies or brokerages that employ skilled claim personnel might be authorized to settle large, more complex claims. The limitations on the producer's claim-handling authority should be specified in the agency contract.

Claim handling by qualified producers offers two major advantages: quicker service to policyholders and lower loss adjustment expenses to the insurer.

However, if the producer is not properly trained in how to handle claims, overpayment of claims might offset the savings.

Consulting

Many producers offer consulting services, for which they are paid on a fee basis. Such services are usually performed for insureds, but they may also be performed for non-insureds or for prospects. Services might be provided for a fee only, or the producer might set a maximum fee, to be reduced by any commissions received on insurance written because of the consulting contract. Laws in some states prohibit agents from receiving both commission and a fee from the same client. Fees are billed separately from any insurance premiums due, whereas commissions are included in the premium totals billed.

CONVERGENCE OF TRADITIONAL MARKETING SYSTEMS

No one marketing system meets the needs of all insurers and all insurance customers. The independent agency and brokerage system is likely to attract buyers who have complex insurance needs or consider quality of service more important than cost. In addition, independent agents and brokers are also effective at reaching insurance customers living in rural areas and small towns, where "main street" independent agencies are often located.

The exclusive agency and direct writer systems have been most successful in dealing with large volumes of insurance buyers who have relatively simple needs—primarily individuals; families; and small, main-street-type businesses. However, an increasing number of exclusive agency and direct writer companies are making inroads in marketing their products and services to larger businesses and associations.

Exclusive agents and direct writers have also been successful in reaching urban customers, although some have specialized in meeting the needs of customers living on farms and in rural areas. Generally, exclusive agents and direct writers have appealed most successfully to customers who are more concerned with price than with personalized service, but many agents in both groups are well qualified to provide the services needed in their markets.

Insurers are driven by competition, pressure to expand market share, technological advances, and customer preferences. In this environment, insurers find it advantageous to blend marketing systems and to use several sales and distribution channels. Also, the introduction of the Gramm-Leach-Bliley Act lifted the restrictions on bank holding companies that had prevented them from affiliating with securities firms, insurers, and other financial services providers. This act added enormous momentum to the trend toward multiple distribution channels.

The Gramm-Leach-Bliley Act

As discussed in a previous chapter, the Gramm-Leach-Bliley Act (GLB Act), also known as the Financial Services Modernization Act, was long-awaited legislation that revolutionized the ways that providers of goods and services within the financial services industry—including insurers—do business. A bank, an insurer, and a securities firm can now affiliate under common ownership and offer customers a combined array of financial services products.

The most significant result of the GLB Act has been the entry of banking institutions into the insurance industry as sellers and distributors of insurance products. Exhibit 3-3 shows a portion of a 2002 study completed by the American Bankers Insurance Association (ABIA), which highlights the insurance products that banks currently distribute. This example of market convergence is a recurring theme throughout the remainder of this chapter.

The insurance and banking industries have responded to the GLB Act with business alliances and collaborations thought impossible in the marketplace only a decade or two ago. For example, leading insurers such as Allstate, Farmers, and Nationwide supplement their exclusive agency sales forces with independent agents. Increasingly, insurers are venturing outside the traditional insurance and financial services environment to market and distribute their products. In addition to changes in the marketing systems insurers use to distribute products, insurers are also collaborating in new ways with banks and other businesses to uncover additional cross-selling opportunities.

Insurers and the Agency Force

In the aftermath of the GLB Act and market convergence, it has become increasingly difficult to find an insurer that uses only the direct writer, exclusive agent, or independent agency marketing system. Insurers are using multiple marketing systems to complement their selected primary system. Direct writers and exclusive agent companies, in particular, are seeking to access and coexist with the independent agent and broker system. Several insurers have been very successful with using mixed marketing systems, and the use of multiple marketing systems will probably continue to grow in the foreseeable future.

Another recent marketing development in property-casualty insurance is the movement toward vertical integration. Vertical integration occurs when an organization owns several stages in the process of providing a product to the customer. For example, an agent or a broker might own an insurance company, or an insurance company might own an agency or a brokerage firm.

Vertical integration in property-casualty insurance began when large brokerage firms started to acquire insurers. Regulatory authorities have discouraged such acquisitions in recent years because of the insolvency of some broker-owned insurers and because of the apparent conflict between the brokers'

EXHIBIT 3-3

Insurance Products Currently Distributed by Banks

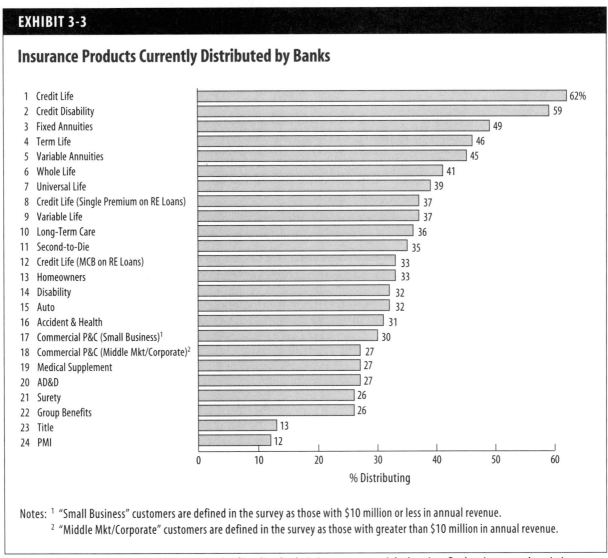

1	Credit Life	62%
2	Credit Disability	59
3	Fixed Annuities	49
4	Term Life	46
5	Variable Annuities	45
6	Whole Life	41
7	Universal Life	39
8	Credit Life (Single Premium on RE Loans)	37
9	Variable Life	37
10	Long-Term Care	36
11	Second-to-Die	35
12	Credit Life (MCB on RE Loans)	33
13	Homeowners	33
14	Disability	32
15	Auto	32
16	Accident & Health	31
17	Commercial P&C (Small Business)[1]	30
18	Commercial P&C (Middle Mkt/Corporate)[2]	27
19	Medical Supplement	27
20	AD&D	27
21	Surety	26
22	Group Benefits	26
23	Title	13
24	PMI	12

% Distributing

Notes: [1] "Small Business" customers are defined in the survey as those with $10 million or less in annual revenue.
[2] "Middle Mkt/Corporate" customers are defined in the survey as those with greater than $10 million in annual revenue.

Reprinted with permission from the 2002 ABIA Study of Leading Banks in Insurance, copyright American Bankers Insurance Association.

duties as representatives of the policyholders and their interest in the profits of the insurers they own. Consequently, several large brokerage firms have sold their subsidiary insurers.

More recently, several large insurance agencies and brokerage firms have been acquired, in whole or in part, by insurers or by holding companies that also own insurers. The acquired agencies or brokerage firms are units of the independent agency system. Company ownership of agencies and brokerage firms closely approximates the exclusive agency system. The relationship differs from the exclusive agency system because the subsidiary agency or brokerage firm is still permitted to deal with other, unrelated insurers. However, some observers question whether the subsidiary agencies and brokerage firms can remain impartial when dealing with unrelated insurers.

Banks and Insurers

Insurers and financial services firms are collaborating to maximize cross-selling opportunities. For insurers, aligning with a bank is a way to access a great number of new prospects. For a bank, distributing insurance products and services to its customers provides an additional source of revenue and solidifies the banking relationship with the customer. Here are a few examples of this type of collaboration:

- A large national bank partners with an insurer to market auto and homeowners insurance to targeted customers by using its current database of customers.
- A prospect visits the Web site of a national insurer and selects from a menu of options including "insurance," "banking," and "mutual funds."
- A financial services conglomerate teams up with a national insurer to offer personal insurance and businessowners coverage to its credit card customers.

Banks and financial services firms commonly use the following four methods to expand into insurance:

1. Organic growth—A firm builds and develops its own insurance operation.
2. Merger or acquisition—A firm merges with or acquires an existing insurer, agency, or brokerage.
3. Outsourcing—A firm contracts with an independently operated insurance provider in order to offer its goods and services to customers.
4. Combinations of methods 1 through 3—A bank, for example, might form a strategic alliance with a national insurer to market commercial insurance to its customers and might acquire outright a regional agency to market insurance to smaller commercial accounts and personal insurance accounts.

Each of these methods has advantages and disadvantages. Organic growth is the most difficult method to employ because it takes time and effort to train and develop internal insurance expertise. Merger or acquisition has the advantage of greatly reducing the time and cost associated with developing internal expertise; however, the firm may have to pay a premium for the merger or acquisition. A firm that prefers to outsource can make the most of its partner's expertise; additionally, the relationship can be initiated easily and, just as important, dissolved easily if it proves unsatisfactory to the parties involved. However, the firm might have little control over the outsourced functions. Exhibit 3-4 summarizes the advantages and disadvantages of these methods.

Various factors influence which of the four methods a bank or financial services firm selects, including (1) the profiles of current and prospective customers; (2) the firm's existing resources, including administrative, information systems, financial, and technical; (3) the congruence of the initiative with the fund's marketing plan; and (4) the ability of the firm to integrate services.

EXHIBIT 3-4

Cross-Selling

Method	Advantages	Disadvantages
Organic growth	Allows company to maintain control of product development process	Takes time and effort to develop internal insurance expertise
Acquisition	Reduces need to develop internal insurance expertise	Incurs costs related to acquisition
Outsourcing	Is easy to initiate; can discontinue arrangement if unsatisfactory	Entails potential loss of control over outsourced functions/operations
Combinations of the above	Varies based on choice of method combination	

Banks already have established relationships with their primary customers. Banks must decide whether a new product would enhance those relationships or damage them (if a new product or service and its price did not meet customer expectations). To preserve customer relationships, many banks prefer outsourcing insurance sales and servicing in return for fees generated. Banks prefer to focus on the fee-based distribution of insurance, whereas insurers opt for the role of insurance "manufacturer."[3]

Insurers and Other Businesses

Rapid technological advances have facilitated information-gathering and the growth of numerous cross-selling systems. Information gathered in one area of a sales operation can now be transferred instantly to an affiliated area and reviewed. The methodology is simple: Turn a primary customer for one product into a referred prospect for another. Customer demand fuels much of the growth in the cross-selling arena; for example, a customer who purchases a new car might expect that the dealer who sold the car can offer the insurance needed to drive it off the lot. A customer might also expect that a bank that provides him or her with a new mortgage can also provide homeowners insurance.

Businesses that typically engage in cross-selling with insurers include:

- Car dealers
- Real estate companies
- Financial services firms
- Certified public accountants
- Risk management firms
- Credit unions

ALTERNATIVE INSURANCE DISTRIBUTION CHANNELS

The convergence of insurance marketing systems has dramatically affected how insurers distribute their products. In addition to using the three traditional marketing systems, insurers as well as producers use the following five **alternative distribution channels** to sell insurance:

Alternative distribution channels
Distribution channels used by insurers that elect not to use an agency force to obtain and service customers; frequently the channels are technology driven (Internet, interactive voice response) and are combined with traditional distribution channels.

1. Internet
2. Call centers
3. Direct response
4. Group marketing
5. Financial institutions

The increasing use of these alternative distribution channels has been driven by technology and customer preference. For example, a customer who, in three days, receives a new book ordered from an Internet wholesaler is increasingly disinclined to wait three weeks for an insurance policy to be quoted and issued. Customers who are familiar with the prompt, efficient delivery and service they obtain from other product providers more frequently expect the same type of response from their insurers.

Most of the alternative distribution channels allow insurers to contact customers directly. No producer is used. One channel, the Internet, allows producers as well as insurers to provide information about insurance products that customers can directly access on their own.

Insurers, and the producers who represent them, are constantly searching for ways to quote and issue policies more quickly, while keeping costs reasonable. At the same time, customers desire competitive pricing, customized insurance products, and high-quality service. Insurers and producers must remain attentive to customer preferences while controlling acquisition expenses and maintaining or increasing market share. The following section examines the primary alternative distribution channels that insurers and producers now use, either independently or with their cross-selling collaborators.

Internet

The emergence of the Internet as a sales and marketing tool has fundamentally affected the business practices of the insurance industry. Insurers and producers must build Web strategies into their marketing budgets or risk being left behind the competition. The long-term effect of the Internet on insurers remains to be seen. However, what cannot be denied is that the customer's ability to access information has increased dramatically, as has the speed of the insurance transaction itself.

Insurers and producers derive a number of benefits from having an Internet presence, including:

• Reduced costs for underwriting and claim processing services because of lower overhead arising from automated operations

- Streamlined business practices—fewer employees are needed to conduct direct sales
- Increased brand awareness
- Broadened marketing potential
- Lead-generation and cross-selling opportunities for all products, not just property-casualty insurance

The Internet can be used at various times to varying degrees by all parties to the insurance transaction: the insurer, the producer, other intermediaries, and the customer. Interaction can occur between the producer and the insurer (often via an Internet-enabled interface), the producer and the customer, and the customer and the insurer. Interactions can range from simple exchanges of e-mail to more complex multiple policy quoting, billing, and policy issuance.

Customers also interact with insurers on the Internet via Internet-based insurance distributors, also known as insurance portals or "aggregators." Examples of insurance aggregators include Insweb.com and Quotesmith.com and, in the banking and financial services area, LendingTree.com. The objective of such Internet portals is to deliver leads to the firms whose products they offer through their sites.

Insurance portals can offer personal insurance, life insurance, or health and disability insurance, as well as limited commercial coverage. For example, a customer interested in obtaining car insurance visits an insurance portal. From an array of insurance products presented, the customer selects "automobile insurance." The customer then responds to a series of underwriting and general questions, much the same as if he or she were being interviewed face to face by an agent. With the click of a button, a series of insurance price quotes with various insurers is presented, based on the prospect's responses. Another example of how an insurance portal operates is when information the consumer enters is forwarded to subscribed insurers, who contact the prospect via e-mail.

The success of insurance portals depends on the speed at which the insurance price quotation is delivered, the number and types of insurance providers and products the portal represents, and the ease of site navigation.

Portals benefit customers by offering the products and services of many insurance providers on one Internet site, in a form of cyberspace one-stop shopping. Although the leads that portals generate must subsequently be screened and fully underwritten by the insurers accepting the coverage, those leads can increase market share and brand awareness.

Challenges of the Internet as a Distribution Channel

Banks and other financial services firms have been online for more than a decade, allowing customers to perform transactions, review accounts, and buy and sell mutual funds. Most insurance customers expect the same transaction ease when they attempt to buy insurance online. Among the challenges for insurers, in terms of their relationships with customers, are:

- Assumed cost advantage—Consumer perceptions that a product bought over the Internet will be less expensive than the same product bought from a producer. These assumptions are not necessarily valid.

- Competitors are only a click away—If customers do not like what they see, they are apt to click to another, more favorable Web site.

- Quoting capabilities—An insurer's ability to quote easily and quickly is critical, because about 50 percent of users will simply move to another Web site if the quoting mechanism is too complicated.[4]

- Availability of information—Many customers do not fully understand insurance products; the Internet largely eliminates intermediaries who would otherwise provide explanations and advice. So, a Web site must maintain a frequently asked questions (FAQ) section and/or a "live contact" or e-mail opt-out.

- Extent of services provided—The insurer or producer must determine whether its Internet presence will be sales only or a combination of sales and service.

- The informed consumer—Information about many insurance products and their prices is available to customers, shifting the customer's focus toward price rather than service.

- Security concerns—Some customers are unwilling to transmit personal and financial information over the Internet.

- Web site content—Information posted on the Web site must be kept fresh, interesting, and accessible.

Those who use the Internet as a distribution channel strive to capture the attention of increasingly sophisticated insurance customers, who research insurance information on the Internet. To that end, the quality of Web site services is critical.

Insurers continually work to enhance their Web sites, refining ways to lower transaction costs while also responding to customer preferences. Insurers' Web sites may allow consumers not only to pay their insurance bills online, but also to engage in "self-service" transactions such as (1) changing address, (2) changing phone number, (3) making e-mail inquiries, (4) reviewing policy billing and order status, and (5) making limited types of coverage changes.

Call Centers

Traditional insurance marketers frequently use call centers as an alternative distribution channel. For example, a large personal insurer operating through the independent agency and brokerage system might make available to its agents, for a percent of commissions earned, a company call center that handles all client-related customer service issues and cross-sells the agents' current customers.

A call center can operate with:

1. Customer service representatives
2. Touch-tone service
3. Speech-enabled service

Options 2 and 3 typically are equipped with an "opt-out" selection, allowing the customer to speak with a customer service representative if desired. The less often the "live opt-out" selection is used, the lower the cost of operating the call center.

The best-equipped call centers can replicate the activities of producers. In addition to making product sales, call center staff can (1) respond to general inquiries, (2) handle claim reporting, (3) answer billing inquiries, and (4) process policy endorsements. In some cases, a customer can begin an inquiry or a transaction on the Internet, then have a customer service representative at the insurer's call center access the Internet activity and answer the inquiry or conclude the transaction.

Direct Response

The **direct response distribution channel** is also referred to as "direct mail," although today, direct response can be in the form of an Internet or a telephone interaction. Direct response relies heavily on advertising and targeting a specific group of affiliated customers, encouraging them to contact the insurer directly with their inquiries. Customers can respond by mail when, for example, they receive an offer to quote their auto insurance in the same envelope with their credit card bill or when they receive an insurance solicitation from their auto club.

Direct response distribution channel
An insurance distribution channel that markets directly to the customer through such distribution channels as mail, telephone, or the Internet.

With direct response, commission costs, if any, are greatly reduced as a result of the disintermediation that is a function of the process. However, a disadvantage is that advertising costs are typically higher. The customer can sometimes "opt out" and speak with a call-center customer service representative or be assigned to a local servicing office.

Group Marketing

Distributing insurance to specifically targeted groups is known by a number of terms, including the following:

1. Affinity marketing
2. Mass marketing or mass merchandising
3. Worksite marketing or payroll deduction

The objective of group marketing is to sell insurance products and services to individual purchasers or businesses that are all members in the same organization.

Affinity marketing
A type of group marketing that targets various groups based on profession, association, interests, hobbies, and attitudes.

Affinity marketing involves targeting various customer groups based on profession, interests, hobbies, or attitudes. For example, the insurer, agent, or broker might decide to market personal insurance products to university alumni groups, chambers of commerce, bar associations, or users of a particular credit card. Coverage is sometimes offered at a discounted premium.

Mass marketing or mass merchandising plans offer an insurer's policies to large numbers of targeted individuals or groups. Coverage is frequently offered at a discounted premium, and the insurer retains the right to underwrite each applicant, with guaranteed policy issuance available as an option.

Employers can contract directly with an insurer or through a producer to offer voluntary insurance coverage as a benefit to their employees. Worksite marketing (or "franchise marketing") of insurance is used frequently to offer personal insurance coverages or optional life, health, and disability coverage to employees. Premiums for employees are usually discounted and are deducted (after tax) from employees' paychecks, with an option available for employees to pay for the coverage in another way.

The success of any marketing program depends on:

1. Having the support of the sponsoring organization or employer
2. Offering discounted premiums
3. Treating the employees as a preferred group for underwriting purposes
4. Facilitating program operation, particularly from the employer's administrative perspective

Although a group marketing program can give an insurer access to large numbers of prospects, it might not generate a significant amount of new business if:

1. The sponsoring organization does not fully support the program.
2. The insurance products and services offered in the program are not competitive.
3. There is an overall lack of group penetration.

Customers who purchase insurance through group marketing might do so through call centers, Web sites, direct mail response, or direct interaction with an insurance agent or broker.

Financial Institutions

Insurers and producers can elect to market their products and services through a bank or another financial services institution, either exclusively or through using additional distribution channels. The collaboration between an insurer and a bank might be as simple as a small insurance agency placing an agent at a desk in a local bank, or as complex as a large insurer forming a strategic alliance with a regional or national financial holding company to solicit its customers.

The prospect of diversifying into new markets appeals to many financial institutions. At the same time, insurers view financial institutions as beneficial strategic partners because of their:

1. Strong customer base
2. Predisposition to product cross-selling
3. Strength at processing "transactions"
4. Efficient use of technology for database mining geared to specific products and services

To sustain distribution relationships with financial institutions, insurers must focus on providing salable products and efficient "back room" service and support while also protecting their professional presence or "shelf space" in financial institutions from competitors.

Distribution Channel Selection

The selection of a distribution channel depends on (1) customer preferences and (2) a firm's operations.

Customer Preferences

The first consideration in selecting an alternative distribution channel is customer preferences. Examples of customer preferences that an insurer or a producer should examine when selecting a distribution channel include the following:

- Can customers navigate easily within the channel? Customers value ease of use and speed.

- Will customers be willing to pay a premium for personalized products and services? The types of products and services to be delivered must fit the marketing channel selected, with "opt-outs" available when offering customers premium services. For some customers, price is more important than service.

- How quickly can inquiries and transactions be processed? Customers routinely experience speedy financial services transactions and increasingly expect the same response from their insurance providers.

- What are customers' expectations regarding accessibility? The selected channel must be consistent with the customer's expectations in this area. For example, a recent study by the Independent Agents and Brokers of America noted that while 59 percent of personal insurance consumers wanted online access to their insurance account information, only 6 percent of agents thought online access was a priority for customers.[5]

Operations

The second consideration in selecting an alternative distribution channel is the firm's operations, including the following:

- Who is the target market? The optimum channel for reaching the target market must be selected.

- Does the selected channel capitalize on the firm's core capabilities? An insurer whose strength is large, complex commercial accounts should not select, for example, a direct mail response channel.

- Is the expertise of current staff adequate? The expertise of current staff and producers must be sufficient to manage the selected channel.

- Is there channel conflict? If multiple channels are selected, they should complement one another.

- Does cost outweigh the benefit? Revenue generated by the selected channel might be outweighed by an increase, rather than a decrease, in cost. For example, salaries for the technical staff required to support the Internet distribution channel might be higher than those for clerical processing staff, and additional advertising costs are associated with the Internet.

- What is the primary goal of the channel: sales or service? Some channels are better than others at sales and service. For example, direct response via mail is not an effective way to service an account, but the channel does promote sales.

- What future acquisitions, strategic alliances, or mergers are planned? A future business partner might already possess expertise in the selected channel.

- Are sufficient resources available to support the selected channel? In today's business environment, marketing relies heavily on technology. Sufficient staffing, training, and economic resources must be in place to support channel operation.

Combining Traditional Marketing Systems and Alternative Distribution Channels

Three considerations in combining traditional marketing systems and alternative distribution channels are:

1. Maintaining consistent customer communications
2. Providing a consistent customer experience
3. Matching the type of insurance with an appropriate marketing system

Consistency of Communication

The first consideration in combining traditional marketing systems and alternative distribution channels is consistency of communication. An insurer must send customers the same clear, consistent message about its products and services across all marketing systems. For example, an insurer risks alienating a potential customer who calls an insurer's local agent to obtain an auto insurance quote and is told that the insurer does not write auto insurance in that state, only to go online and obtain a quote from the insurer's Web site later on. Whether a customer contacts the insurer by meeting with a local agent, by accessing the Internet, or by telephoning a call center, the messages he or she receives must be consistent.

In addition, the insurer's internal communications must be consistent across marketing systems and distribution channels, and workflows, data management, and underwriting standards must be coordinated.

Consistency of the Customer Experience

The second consideration in combining traditional marketing systems and alternative distribution channels is consistency of the customer experience. The experience a customer has when interacting with an insurer must be consistent across all systems and channels. Customers' access to the Internet and its wealth of information has created knowledgeable, demanding insurance customers with distinct preferences and expectations.

For example, a prospect might receive a flyer about a particular insurer with his or her credit card bill. The prospect then goes online and, perhaps after accessing an insurance portal, arrives at the insurer's Web site. There, the prospect obtains product details, enters personal underwriting information, and obtains a quote. At that point, the prospect might opt out of the Web site and contact the insurer's call center. A customer service representative at the call center can access the prospect's Web account and answer any questions. In the end, the prospect seeks a local agency representing the insurer and completes the transaction through the agent. At every step along the way of this marketing process, it is vital that the prospect have a consistent experience—not only before and during the sale, but also in the course of any post-sale servicing.

Type of Insurance

The third consideration in combining traditional marketing systems and alternative distribution channels is matching the type of insurance with the appropriate system.

Some marketing systems are more suitable than others based on the product being sold. Personal insurance and commercial insurance vary in terms of the product's level of complexity and in terms of the expertise insurers, agents, and brokers need to properly sell the product to consumers and service it after the sale.

The combination of systems and channels selected depends on the particular type of insurance to be sold.

Personal Insurance

Personal insurance products are typically considered to be less complex than commercial insurance products. Many customers, incorrectly or not, perceive a "sameness" among personal insurance policies, viewing them as commodities for which price matters more than service.

Because of its simplified, fairly standard format, personal insurance generally requires the least amount of "hands-on" service, while commercial insurance requires more direct involvement from the producer. Consequently, the direct writer and the exclusive agent marketing systems, and the direct response distribution channel, are used most frequently for personal insurance.

At the other extreme, the independent agency and brokerage system probably offers better service than any of the other systems, but at a higher cost. Customers who have significant assets to protect, or who prefer premium services, usually elect to do business with an independent agent or broker. Such customers may own high-value homes or have extensive fine art or other expensive collections.

Commercial Insurance

Generally, because of its complexity, commercial insurance requires greater producer expertise. Some exclusive agency and direct writer producers have been successful at selling commercial insurance, especially to small, main-street-type businesses. However, the independent agency and brokerage system still dominates the medium to large commercial insurance business, especially in specialized areas such as surety bonds and ocean marine insurance.

Customers with complex commercial insurance loss exposures frequently require the assistance of an intermediary in order to fully understand what insurance products are needed. Thus, an insurer that wants to market medium to large commercial accounts should probably use the independent agency and brokerage system rather than the direct response system. Although many producers within the direct writer and exclusive agency systems possess substantial expertise at handling complex insurance products, as a group, independent agents and brokers have an edge, both actual and perceived, in the expertise needed for such products. An Independent Agents and Brokers of America report, based on A.M. Best's 2001 figures, noted that the independent agency system finished 2001 with a 75 percent share of the commercial insurance market, up almost two points from 2000.[6]

Small-business customers, however, are increasingly opting to explore alternative distribution channels, including participating in group coverage offered through associations or choosing insurers that offer multiple points of contact. For example, small- or "select" business customers might call the toll-free phone number of a major insurer that supports the independent agency and brokerage system and deal directly with the insurer's customer service representatives for policy servicing, claim servicing, and new-business placement.

SUMMARY

Insurance marketing systems and alternative distribution channels are the means through which products and services are delivered to targeted customers. While insurance marketing and distribution is similar to marketing and distribution in the general business environment, it also possesses several unique characteristics, including (1) the legal status of insurance agents and (2) the powers and duties of insurance agents. Traditional insurance marketing systems are typically characterized by the presence of a producer or the producer's degree of independence, method of compensation, and the control that producers can exercise over policy expirations. Examples of traditional insurance marketing systems are the (1) independent agency and brokerage system, (2) exclusive agency system, and (3) direct writer system.

The independent agency and brokerage system played a significant role in the development of the U.S. insurance industry, and the scope of the system today includes agents and brokers who (1) operate nationally and regionally, (2) maximize resources and expertise through the formation of independent agent networks, and (3) develop certain underwriting and marketing skills (such as MGAs and excess and surplus lines brokers). Because independent agents and brokers are entrenched as an institution, the newer forms of marketing and distribution are frequently compared to those of independent agents. The exclusive agency and direct writer marketing systems have made substantial inroads into the market once dominated by independent agents. In addition, the entry of financial services institutions into the insurance marketplace has catalyzed a convergence in traditional insurer marketing systems and distribution channels.

The functions that insurance producers perform on behalf of the insurers they represent are generally specified in the agency contract. These functions include prospecting, risk management review, sales, policy issuance, premium collection, customer service, claim handling, and consulting.

In addition to distributing their products through traditional insurance marketing systems, insurers and producers may use alternative channels of distribution, including (1) the Internet, (2) call centers, (3) direct response, (4) group marketing, and (5) financial institutions. If multiple distribution channels are selected, effective channel management is paramount, including consistent communication and a consistent customer experience. Factors that insurers should consider when selecting distribution channels include customer preferences and operations. Additionally, the suitability of any one channel for a particular product may vary based on that product's level of complexity. No one marketing system or distribution channel is best—insurers and producers must select one or a combination based on overall business plans and their core production and service capabilities.

Marketing matches the customer's needs with appropriate insurance products. Underwriting matches appropriate coverage to specific loss exposures with an appropriate price. The next chapter explains how underwriting accomplishes this.

CHAPTER NOTES

1. Peter Drucker, *The Practice of Management* (New York: Harperbusiness, 1993), pp. 37–39.

2. A.M. Best Company, Inc., *Annual Review of the Excess & Surplus Lines Industry* (Oldwick, N.J.: A.M. Best Company, Inc., 2001), p. 8.

3. Hank Lauricella, "Financial Services Convergence Update," Cochran, Caronia Securities LLC, June 5, 2002, p. 10.

4. Lynna Goch, "What Works Online," *Best's Review*, May 2002, p. 25.

5. Lee Ann Gjertsen, "Agents, Clients Cite Different Priorities," *The National Underwriter*, April 17, 2000, p. 16.

6. Madelyn Flannagan and Jeff Yates, "2001 Market Share Numbers Confirm Positive Trend for Independent Agents," Independent Agents and Brokers of America Report, November 6, 2002, p. 1.

Chapter 4

Direct Your Learning

Underwriting

After learning the content of this chapter, you should be able to:

- Describe the purpose of underwriting.
- Describe the six steps in the underwriting process.
- Contrast the responsibilities of staff underwriters with those of line underwriters.
- Explain how underwriting results are measured.

Develop Your Perspective

What are the main topics covered in the chapter?

The underwriting department in an insurer is responsible for developing and maintaining a profitable book of business.

Examine the activities required to achieve the insurer's underwriting profitability objectives.

- What policies must be developed?
- What processes must be in place?

Why is it important to learn about these topics?

Although an underwriting profit is never a certainty, an underwriting department's goal is to select and maintain those policies that are most likely to be profitable for the insurer.

Consider the effort required to achieve and maintain underwriting profitability goals.

- What are the profitability goals for your organization?
- What activity is required by underwriting in your organization to achieve profitability?

How can you use what you will learn?

Examine your own organization's underwriting goals.

- Is your organization's underwriting department achieving its goals? How could line and staff underwriters correct any failure to achieve these goals? How could they be more efficient?
- What activity is required by underwriting to prepare to write policies for a new insurance product?

Chapter 4

Underwriting

Underwriting is the process of determining what loss exposures will be insured, for what amount of insurance, at what price, and under what conditions. Underwriters determine underwriting criteria and apply them to the loss exposures of applicants.

Exactly who has what amount of underwriting authority varies considerably by insurer and by type of insurance. Specialty insurers, such as those offering surety bonds, aviation insurance, and livestock mortality insurance, usually centralize underwriting authority. At the other extreme, some insurers decentralize underwriting authority, which they grant to specific producers or managing general agents (MGAs), believing that doing so capitalizes on producers' and MGAs' familiarity with local conditions. When granted such underwriting authority, the producer or MGA uses an underwriting guide that shows the classes of business that the insurer finds acceptable. The insurer's underwriting guide also indicates which loss exposures the producer or MGA must refer to a higher underwriting authority.

When producers or MGAs have underwriting authority, the compensation for their expense of underwriting, issuing policies, and handling claims is a higher commission rate and a larger percentage of profit sharing (contingent commission). A contingency commission agreement, which provides the producer or MGA with an additional commission based on a favorable loss ratio and on the increase in premium volume, provides an incentive for sound underwriting.

The degree of underwriting authority given to producers and MGAs depends on the insurer's philosophy, the experience and profitability of the producer or MGA, the type of insurance involved, and other factors. For certain types of insurance, the producer might have no underwriting authority, not even binding authority. High limits of insurance, specialized types of insurance, and unusually hazardous classes require the producer to submit every account to an underwriter, who then makes the underwriting decision.

Underwriting serves the same purpose for all insurers, whether underwriting authority is centralized or decentralized. After briefly stating the purpose of underwriting, this chapter discusses each step in the underwriting process. Next, the chapter examines the activities that line and staff underwriters perform to fulfill their responsibilities. Finally, the chapter examines how to measure underwriting results.

Underwriting
The process of determining what loss exposures will be insured, for what amount of insurance, at what price, and under what conditions.

PURPOSE OF UNDERWRITING

Book of business
A group of policies, also called a portfolio, with a common characteristic, such as territory or type of coverage, or all policies written by a particular insurer, producer, or agency.

The purpose of underwriting is to develop and maintain a profitable book of business for the insurer. A **book of business** is all of the policies that an insurer has in force or some subgroup of those policies. For example, a book of business can include all of an insurer's commercial policies or all of its commercial general liability policies. "Book of business" can also refer to business produced in a specific geographic area or by a particular branch office or agency.

Adverse selection
A situation that occurs because people with the greatest probability of loss are the ones most likely to purchase insurance.

For underwriting to achieve its purpose, insurers must minimize the effects of adverse selection. **Adverse selection** occurs because the individuals and businesses with the greatest probability of loss are those most likely to purchase insurance. For example, persons and businesses owning property in a flood plain are generally much more interested in buying flood insurance than applicants who do not own property in a flood plain. Insurers, on the other hand, are not interested in selling insurance to applicants who expect frequent, severe losses. Underwriters minimize the effects of adverse selection by carefully selecting the applicants whose loss exposures they are willing to insure.

UNDERWRITING PROCESS

Underwriting has been defined as determining what loss exposures will be insured, for what amount of insurance, at what price, and under what conditions. To make an underwriting decision, underwriters go through the following six steps:

1. Evaluating loss exposures
2. Determining underwriting alternatives
3. Selecting an underwriting alternative
4. Determining the appropriate premium
5. Implementing the underwriting decision
6. Monitoring the loss exposures

Although experienced underwriters do not always follow each of these steps in strict sequence, the sequence of steps provides a sound framework for underwriters to make decisions. For example, as each piece of information is received, the underwriter considers how that information will affect the available alternatives. Likewise, if the underwriter receives information clearly indicating that the applicant is unacceptable, he or she immediately "implements the decision" to reject the account.

Evaluating Loss Exposures

The first step in the underwriting process is evaluating loss exposures. Underwriters begin this step by gathering information about an applicant's loss exposures. Underwriters must understand the activities, operations, and character of every applicant. However, tradeoffs are necessary to control underwriting expenses and to handle a reasonable number of applications. Underwriters weigh the need for information against the cost to obtain it. For example, an underwriter is likely to investigate a chemical manufacturer extensively. However, the underwriter might require much less information to underwrite a gift shop.

The underwriter compiles information from a number of sources to develop a profile of loss exposures including the applicant's business operations, financial condition, and other characteristics. The underwriter pays close attention to information about hazards, which are conditions that increase the frequency or severity of a loss. Underwriters identify four hazard categories, as follows:

- Physical hazards
- Moral hazards
- Morale hazards or attitudinal hazards
- Legal hazards

A **physical hazard** is a tangible condition of property, persons, or operations to be insured that increases the frequency or severity of loss. An untrained driver, damageability of cargo being shipped, and the quality of public fire protection are all examples of physical hazards.

A **moral hazard** is a condition that increases the likelihood that a person will intentionally cause or exaggerate a loss. Underwriters try to recognize symptoms of moral hazard, such as property that is grossly overinsured. An insured facing serious financial difficulty might present a moral hazard because such difficulty might present an incentive to commit insurance fraud.

A **morale hazard**, sometimes called an attitudinal hazard, is a condition of carelessness or indifference that increases the frequency or severity of loss. Careless driving, failure to lock an unattended building, or failing to clear an icy sidewalk to protect pedestrians are examples of attitudinal hazards.

A **legal hazard** is a condition of the legal environment that increases loss frequency or severity. For example, people in some geographic areas are much more litigious—likely to initiate a lawsuit—than those elsewhere.

The principal sources of underwriting information are the producer, the application, loss control or independent inspection reports, government records, financial rating services, loss data, field marketing personnel, premium auditors, claim files, and production records.

Producers

The producer can be an excellent source of underwriting information about the loss exposures of an insurance applicant. Typically, the producer has personal contact with the applicant, has firsthand knowledge of the applicant's business operations, and knows the applicant's reputation in the community. The producer usually determines the applicant's coverage needs and "pre-qualifies" or field underwrites applicants.

Physical hazard
A tangible condition of property, persons, or operations that increases the frequency or severity of loss.

Moral hazard
A condition that increases the likelihood that a person will intentionally cause or exaggerate a loss.

Morale hazard
A condition of carelessness or indifference that increases the frequency or severity of loss.

Legal hazard
A condition of the legal environment that increases loss frequency or severity.

The degree to which an insurer depends on the producer to evaluate the applicant varies by producer and type of business and might differ based on the insurer's marketing system. Direct writing and exclusive agency insurers are explicit about the characteristics of the ideal applicant. Producers for these insurers screen applicants knowing the criteria that their insurers' underwriters use.

Producers for independent agency insurers face a more complex task, because they must understand the marketing goals and underwriting guidelines of the various insurers they represent. Independent agents must also try to balance the placement of their business among their insurers to maintain good relations and to meet the obligations of their various agency contracts. The ability to match each applicant with an appropriate insurer is an essential skill for independent producers.

Applications

Insurance applications provide general information required to process, rate, and underwrite loss exposures of the applicant. Usually, a different application form exists for each type of insurance. The application requires specific information necessary to evaluate the acceptability of an applicant's loss exposures for that type of insurance. Each insurer develops its own application or uses standard ACORD applications. Industry committees developed ACORD applications to reduce the amount of paperwork producers must handle when working with several insurers.

Even when an application is completed properly, the underwriter usually finds it necessary to obtain additional information about the applicant's loss exposures. This information can be categorized as internal or external and objective or subjective.

Internal information, which comes from the insurer's in-house sources, can usually be accessed quickly and economically. External information, which comes from outside sources, might be expensive to obtain and might delay the processing of the application.

Objective information consists of recorded facts that can be verified. Subjective information consists of opinions or personal impressions. The underwriter must identify subjective information that could influence objective information. For example, a published article about a business applying for insurance might reflect the author's bias. The applicant's product brochure probably emphasizes the product's positive features and minimizes any shortcomings.

Inspection Reports

Independent inspection or loss control reports provide underwriting information about the property's physical condition, the business operations' safety record, and the insured's management.

Most inspection reports in commercial insurance contain mandatory and suggested recommendations. The underwriter could follow up to determine the degree of compliance, which provides insight into management's attitude toward safety.

Government Records

Government records that provide underwriting information include motor vehicle reports; criminal court records; and civil court records, including records of suits filed, mortgages and liens, business licenses, property tax records, and bankruptcy filings.

Motor vehicle records (MVRs) are a fundamental information source for auto underwriting. Some states require insurers to obtain MVRs each year so that drivers' convictions for traffic violations and/or accidents can be incorporated into each policy's rating scheme.

Most underwriters use independent services to obtain civil and criminal information even though they can obtain that information directly from court records. Civil and criminal reports show any previous bankruptcies or judgments that are on record.

Financial Rating Services

An applicant's financial status provides important underwriting information. Dun & Bradstreet (D&B), Standard & Poor's, and TRW are some of the major financial rating services that underwriters use. These services provide data on the credit ratings of individual businesses, together with industry averages for comparison. Using a financial rating service is almost universal in surety bond underwriting, and the services are also used with many other types of commercial insurance. Services can verify an applicant's financial statements and can provide an overall picture of the applicant's financial status. A financially weak business might present an unacceptable hazard. To understand financial rating service data, the underwriter should be familiar with financial ratios used to evaluate a firm's liquidity, profitability, and debt structure. In addition, the 10-K form filed with the Securities and Exchange Commission (SEC) contains a wealth of information on public companies.

Loss Data

Underwriters usually have access to aggregate loss experience by class, type of insurance, and territory, both for the insurer and the industry, as well as loss experience on individual policyholders and producers. Aggregate data might indicate insurance rate inadequacy, causing a modification of underwriting policy pending approval of higher rate levels. The loss experience of a commercial policyholder might be extensive enough to be statistically significant on its own, while the loss experience for the class or territory has more significance in personal insurance.

Loss frequency, loss severity, and the type of loss are all important when analyzing loss data and evaluating loss exposures. Hazards might be reduced through loss control measures, or insured losses might be reduced by adding or increasing a deductible. The cause and date of loss provide further insights into loss exposures. For example, the date of loss provides information on possible seasonality or trends in loss experience.

Field Marketing Personnel

In most insurers, field marketing personnel (such as marketing representatives or special agents) can provide both specific and general underwriting information. Field marketing personnel often obtain information that a producer omitted from an application. In sparsely populated areas or other situations in which qualified loss control personnel are not available, many insurers use field marketing personnel to make simplified inspection reports. The field marketing person can also provide detailed background information on the producer and sometimes on the applicant. Sales managers, MGAs, or the producer might also provide this type of information.

Premium Auditors

The premium auditor can gather information about the policyholders' operations that might have underwriting implications, including moral and morale hazards. The premium auditor examines the policyholders' operations, records, and books of account to determine the actual loss exposure for the coverage already provided.

Claim Files

When renewing existing policies, an underwriter can obtain insights into the policyholder's character by reviewing the policyholder's claim files. Claim adjusters typically accumulate a significant amount of underwriting information during their investigations. For example, an adjuster investigating a small fire loss at a machine shop might uncover evidence of poor housekeeping and the policyholder's disregard for loss control. Some insurers have a formal system for claim adjusters to notify underwriters about pertinent information on hazards.

For personal insurance policies, a claim file review can identify insureds who are making many small claims that most people attribute to normal wear and tear. For a workers' compensation policy, a claim file review might help the underwriter identify dangerous conditions requiring loss control attention.

The claim adjuster is one of the few insurer employees who get a firsthand view of the insured locations. The adjuster's observations are valuable, and every effort should be made to gain them. An example of a checklist that could facilitate communication is shown in Exhibit 4-1.

EXHIBIT 4-1

Claim Report to Underwriter

INSTRUCTIONS TO ADJUSTER: Check applicable blocks below and explain each item checked under "REMARKS."

A. AUTOMOBILE	B. WORKERS COMPENSATION OR GENERAL LIABILITY	C. FIDELITY, OR BURGLARY, OR PLATE GLASS; OR FIRE, MARINE, AND MULTI-LINE
☐ 1. Physical disability	☐ 1. Hazardous physical condition	☐ 1. Inadequate safeguards or training
☐ 2. Vehicle in poor condition	☐ 2. Machinery	☐ 2. Inadequate records
☐ 3. Evidence of drinking	☐ a. Defectively manufactured	☐ 3. Loss frequency
☐ 4. Reckless driving	☐ b. Poorly designed	☐ 4. Possible illegal activities
☐ 5. Uncooperative	☐ c. Does not meet industry standards	☐ 5. Questionable loss
☐ 6. Loss frequency	☐ d. Inadequately labeled	☐ 6. Vacant premises
☐ 7. Poor driving record	☐ 3. Poor location	☐ 7. Underinsured
☐ 8. Driver under age 25*	☐ 4. Uncooperative	☐ 8. Questionable physical condition
☐ 9. Indiscriminate loan of vehicle	☐ 5. Poor management or supervision	☐ 9. Late notice
☐ 10. Driver fell asleep	☐ 6. Inadequate records	☐ 10. Poor housekeeping
☐ 11. Gross negligence	☐ 7. Loss frequency	☐ 11. Uncooperative
☐ 12. Total loss of insured vehicle	☐ 8. Late notice	☐ 12. Possible financial problems
☐ 13. Late notice	☐ 9. Pollution loss	☐ 13. Exposure from adjoining risks
☐ 14. Owned vehicle not on policy	☐ 10. Other	☐ 14. Fire protection/first-aid system impeded
☐ 15. Other		☐ 15. Carelessness
*Personal auto policy not so classified		☐ 16. Other

REMARKS

_____

ADJUSTER'S SIGNATURE   C.R.U. DATE

Note: This checklist would be accompanied by additional loss details.

Production Records

Records on individual producers, indicating loss ratio, premium volume, mix of business, amount of supporting business, length of service, and industry experience, help underwriters make decisions about the quality of the applicants that the producer is submitting. In personal auto underwriting, for example, the mix of business indicates whether a particular producer is submitting an inordinately large percentage of young drivers or drivers with poor driving records. In commercial insurance, production records indicate the producer's familiarity with complex or unusual classes of business. For example, the producer's background and experience might be a concern to the underwriter evaluating a complex manufacturing submission. If the producer's business involves mostly personal insurance, the underwriter might question the producer's familiarity with commercial coverages and his or her ability to service those accounts properly.

With an independent agent, the number and identity of other insurers represented by the agency are also relevant. In all marketing systems, producer results over time (usually three to five years) are a good measure of the producer's capability as a field underwriter.

Determining Underwriting Alternatives

The second step in the underwriting process is determining underwriting alternatives. The underwriter must evaluate each alternative carefully and must choose the optimal one under the circumstances.

The three underwriting alternatives are:

1. Accept the submission as is.
2. Reject the submission.
3. Make a counteroffer to accept the submission subject to certain modifications.

Four major types of modifications, discussed next, are as follows:

1. Require loss control measures.
2. Change insurance rates, rating plans, or policy limits.
3. Amend policy terms and conditions.
4. Use facultative reinsurance.

Require Loss Control Measures

The first type of modification for an unacceptable submission is to require loss control measures to reduce certain hazards. Loss control measures such as installing an automatic fire-extinguishing sprinkler system, adding guard service, and improving housekeeping and maintenance can reduce physical hazards. Likewise, installing machinery guards can reduce the frequency of employee bodily injuries. Some loss control measures are relatively inexpensive and simple to implement, while others, such as sprinklers, require considerable capital investment.

Some applicants welcome an insurer's recommendations to reduce hazards and understand that implementing such recommendations reduces ultimate business costs. Other applicants view loss control requirements unfavorably and consider them to be unnecessary expenses. Therefore, underwriters should make sound recommendations accompanied by well-reasoned and convincing explanations.

Change Insurance Rates, Rating Plans, or Policy Limits

The second type of modification for an unacceptable submission is to change insurance rates, rating plans, or policy limits. A submission that is not acceptable at standard rates might be desirable if the underwriter can charge a different rate, use a different rating plan, or provide a different limit. A rate modification could either increase or decrease the premium. In private passenger auto, for example, an applicant might not be eligible for the requested preferred-risk program but might qualify for another program at higher, standard rates. Alternatively, the underwriter might offer a preferred-risk program to a desirable applicant who applies for coverage at standard rates. By offering a lower price, the underwriter might keep that applicant from buying coverage from a competitor.

Underwriters have greater price discretion in commercial insurance than in personal insurance. For example, in "A-rated" general liability policies, for which no manual loss cost is published, the underwriter can use a range of rates. Good judgment plays an important role in selecting a rate that earns a reasonable profit and is competitive enough to obtain the account. Pricing obviously plays a key role in underwriting judgment-rated insurance such as inland and ocean marine and general liability loss exposures subject to "A-rating."

In addition to changing rates, this type of modification also includes changing rating plans. Several rating plans are available for commercial applicants, including experience rating, schedule rating, and retrospective rating.

Experience rating uses the policyholder's past loss experience to develop a premium modification factor to adjust the manual rate upward or downward. Experience rating is available for general liability submissions that have a specific premium level (varies by insurer) and at least one year of experience.

The experience rating plan uses three years of past loss experience, when available, and a credibility factor based on the size of the policyholder's premium to determine the modification. In comparison to other rating plans, experience rating has a formal methodology that must be applied without discrimination to all submissions that must meet experience-rating eligibility requirements.

Schedule rating awards debits and credits to a submission based on specific categories such as the care and condition of the premises and the training and selection of employees. The underwriter uses debits and credits to appropriately adjust the manual rate upward or downward. Credits and debits vary by insurer,

Experience rating
A ratemaking technique that adjusts the insured's premium for the upcoming policy period based on the insured's experience for the current period.

Schedule rating
A rating plan that awards debits and credits based on specific categories, such as the care and condition of the premises or the training and selection of employees.

are limited by insurance statute (usually between 25 and 40 percent of premium), and reflect the underwriter's estimate of the insured's loss exposure. Insurance statutes require that insurers apply schedule rating plans to all eligible submissions without discrimination and that adequate documentation be kept on file to justify the pricing decision.

Retrospective rating
A ratemaking technique that adjusts the insured's premium for the current policy period based on the insured's loss experience during the current period; paid losses or incurred losses may be used to determine loss experience.

Retrospective rating is an individual experience modification program that uses the current year as the experience period to develop the experience modification factor. Under this rating plan, a provisional premium is charged at the beginning of the policy period. At the end of the policy period, the actual loss experience *for that same period* is determined, and a final premium is calculated. The insured's premium is then adjusted, after the end of the policy period, to reflect the insured's expenses and losses during the policy period. The premium is subject to a specified minimum and maximum. This rating plan has several variations that protect the policyholder from fluctuations in the final premium.

Changing policy limits also falls into this type of modification. An insurer's underwriting guide usually specifies the maximum limits of insurance that an underwriter can approve. The limits usually reflect reinsurance limitations or reinsurance availability and possible catastrophic loss from a single loss exposure. If high policy limits are requested, the underwriter might suggest lower limits within the underwriter's authority or might use facultative reinsurance, discussed later.

For property insurance, the underwriter must be alert for overinsurance that could indicate a moral hazard and might lead to a fraudulent loss. Underinsurance, however, is a more common problem. Adequate insurance limits are essential to collect a premium commensurate with the loss exposure. From the insured's standpoint, adequate limits also meet coinsurance requirements and ensure an adequate loss recovery.

Amend Policy Terms and Conditions

The third type of modification for an unacceptable submission is to amend policy terms and conditions. An unacceptable submission might become acceptable by modifying the policy to exclude certain causes of loss, add or increase a deductible, or make another coverage change. An insurer might be unwilling to provide replacement cost coverage on a run-down home but might be willing to provide a more-limited coverage form. For small commercial accounts in which a large number of small losses might have caused unsatisfactory loss experience in the past, increasing the deductible might make coverage more viable.

The underwriter's flexibility varies by type of insurance. If policies have been approved by state regulators, coverage modifications are seldom possible. When the requested coverage cannot be provided, the underwriter might suggest alternative coverage.

Use Facultative Reinsurance

The fourth type of modification for an unacceptable submission is to use facultative reinsurance. If the applicant is in a class of business that is not covered by the underwriter's reinsurance treaty, or if the amount of insurance needed exceeds net treaty capacity, the underwriter might be able to transfer a portion of the liability for the applicant's loss exposure to a facultative reinsurer. An alternative to purchasing facultative reinsurance is to ask the producer to divide the insurance among several insurers—an approach sometimes called "agency reinsurance."

Selecting an Underwriting Alternative

The third step in the underwriting process is selecting an underwriting alternative. The underwriter must decide whether to accept the submission as offered, accept it with modifications, or reject it. Rejection is sometimes unavoidable; however, rejections produce neither premium nor commission, only expense. Therefore, underwriters try to make the submission acceptable because one of the insurer's goals is to produce profitable business.

Selecting an alternative involves weighing a submission's positive and negative features, including loss exposures contemplated in the insurance rate, loss control measures, and management's commitment to loss prevention. The following additional factors need to be considered before selecting an underwriting alternative:

- Amount of underwriting authority required
- Presence of supporting business
- Mix of business
- Producer relationships
- Regulatory restrictions

Underwriting Authority

Before accepting an application, also called a submission, an underwriter must determine whether he or she has the necessary underwriting authority. If the underwriter lacks authority, the submission must be referred to a higher underwriting authority. Because referral is often time consuming, underwriters should determine as soon as possible whether underwriting authority is likely to be an issue and should notify the producer.

Supporting Business

A submission that is marginal by itself might be acceptable if the other insurance components of the applicant's account—the supporting business—are desirable. However, premium volume alone usually does not make an account acceptable; the premium from five separate marginal components is not five times as desirable as one marginal component. For example, the underwriter might decide to accept a marginal workers' compensation submission if the insurer already provides commercial general liability, commercial property, and automobile policies that are acceptable. If, however, the existing policies were marginal as well, the additional premium volume generated by another marginal component would not be sufficient to offset potential losses from the overall account.

On the other hand, above-average business in other account components might make a marginal component acceptable, provided the supporting business is profitable enough to subsidize the marginal business. In account underwriting, all of the business from a particular applicant can be evaluated as a unit. The account underwriting approach evaluates not only the submission for each type of insurance but also its supporting business.

Mix of Business

The underwriting policy, determined by management and specified in the underwriting guide, frequently indicates the insurer's mix-of-business goals. The mix of business is the distribution of individual policies that constitute the book of business of a producer, territory, state, or region among the various types and classifications. Particular classes, such as youthful drivers in private passenger auto insurance or restaurants in commercial property coverage, might be overrepresented in the book of business. Consequently, the insurer might decide to change the acceptability criteria or prohibit new business in a particular class. When underwriting an individual application, the underwriter must consider whether accepting the application supports the insurer's goals for mix of business.

Producer Relationships

Some producers often pressure underwriters to accept a marginal submission as an accommodation. Usually, the producer assures the underwriter that the producer will deliver some outstanding business later. Underwriters should maintain accommodation files to track requests for accommodations and to determine whether the promised outstanding business materializes.

The relationship between the insurer and the producer should be based on mutual trust and respect. Differences of opinion are common, particularly because some of the goals of producers and underwriters conflict when producers focus on production and underwriters focus on strict adherence to selection standards. Nevertheless, the long-term goals of producers and underwriters are growth and profit. Mutual accommodation and willingness to see the other's viewpoint are essential to building a satisfactory working relationship.

Regulatory Restrictions

State regulations restrict underwriters' ability to accept or renew business. Additionally, federal and state privacy laws restrict the type and the amount of information about an applicant that an underwriter can obtain.

Underwriters must know these restrictions, which are usually codified within the state's unfair trade practices laws. If regulation limits reasons for cancellation or refusal to renew, then new submissions should be evaluated carefully because eliminating undesirable business after it has been written can be difficult. Many states also limit the time within which an underwriter can decline a submission or provide notice of refusal to renew. Therefore, underwriters should make timely decisions to avoid mandatory acceptance or renewal of an otherwise unacceptable submission.

Determining the Appropriate Premium

The fourth step in the underwriting process is determining the appropriate premium. Underwriters must ensure that each loss exposure is properly classified so that it is properly rated. Insurance loss costs are typically based on an elaborate classification system in which similar loss exposures are combined into the same rating classification. Combining loss exposures into rating classifications enables the insurer to appropriately match potential loss costs with an applicant's particular loss exposures. Consequently, the insurer can develop an adequate premium to pay losses and operating expenses and to produce a profit.

Accurate classification ensures a pooling of loss exposures whose expected loss frequency and loss severity are similar. Misclassification can produce adverse results, including insufficient premium to cover losses and expenses, inability to sell policies because prices are higher than competitors' prices, and charges that the insurer has violated regulations prohibiting unfair trade practices.

The appropriate premium must be not only high enough to enable the insurer to continue to write profitable business, but also low enough to compete with other insurers. If an insurer does not price each policy appropriately, some insureds will buy insurance at prices that do not adequately reflect their loss exposures.

For most types of personal insurance, workers' compensation, and some other commercial insurance, proper classification automatically determines the appropriate projected loss costs, which are one premium component. For major types of commercial insurance, such as general liability, the underwriter might have the option of adjusting the premium based on the characteristics of the insured's loss exposures.

Many insurers operate subsidiary insurers with different rating plans that reflect the loss exposures of different groups of insureds. For example, personal insurers typically have subsidiary companies for insureds with loss exposures that fall into the preferred-risk, standard-risk, and high-risk categories. Underwriters can place each applicant with the subsidiary considered most appropriate. The underwriter must be certain in each case that the characteristics of the applicant's loss exposures justify the placement and must document that any adjustment is consistent with the insurer's rating plan if it is filed with regulatory authorities.

Implementing the Underwriting Decision

The fifth step in the underwriting process is implementing the underwriting decision. Implementing underwriting decisions generally involves three steps:

1. Communicating the decision
2. Putting coverage into effect
3. Recording information for accounting, statistical, and monitoring purposes

The first step in implementing the underwriting decision is communicating it to the producer, if necessary, and to other insurer personnel. If the decision is to accept the submission with modifications, the reasons must be clearly communicated to the producer or applicant, and the applicant must agree to accept or implement the modifications. Also, the insurer must establish controls to verify that modifications such as loss control measures are implemented.

If the underwriter decides to reject the application, he or she must communicate the rejection to the producer in a positive way to preserve their long-term relationship. Underwriters must provide clear and logical reasons why the particular applicant does not meet the insurer's underwriting requirements. Effective communication of both positive and negative decisions clarifies the insurer's standards and helps the producer understand what kinds of business the insurer wants to write.

The second step in implementing the underwriting decision is to put coverage into effect. The underwriter might need to issue a binder or send a policy worksheet to the policywriting department. For some types of business, the underwriter might also need to prepare certificates of insurance.

The third step in implementing the underwriting decision is to record information about the policy and the applicant for accounting, statistical, and monitoring purposes. Data entry personnel enter essential information into the insurer's information system. Data about the policyholder include location, limits, coverages, price modifications, and class of business. Those data must be coded so that the insurer and the industry can accumulate information on all accounts for ratemaking, statutory reporting, financial accounting, and book-of-business evaluations. Those data are also used to monitor the account, to trigger renewals, and to flag situations requiring special attention. For example, expiring policies are identified so that updated information can be obtained.

A good policy information system, containing accurate data, also alerts underwriters to claim activity during the policy period, problems, or substantial changes regarding the policyholder. A claim referral system can immediately refer the file to the underwriter if the loss frequency exceeds a predetermined limit or if a severe loss occurs.

Monitoring Loss Exposures

The sixth step in the underwriting process is monitoring loss exposures. After an underwriting decision has been made on a new-business submission or a renewal, the underwriter must monitor activity on the individual policies to ensure that satisfactory results are achieved.

Underwriters must be alert to changes in insureds' loss exposures. Changes in the nature of a policyholder's business operation, for example, could significantly raise or lower the policyholder's loss potential. Underwriters do not have the resources necessary for constant monitoring of all policies and underwrite new submissions. Monitoring existing policies usually occurs only when policy changes or losses are brought to the underwriter's attention. For example, adding a new location to a property policy or a new driver to an auto policy can cause the underwriter to investigate whether the additions significantly change the loss exposures. A notice of loss provides the underwriter with another opportunity to review the account and to determine whether that loss is the type the underwriter expected. Summary information about the claim or a review of the claim file provides valuable information about the nature of the loss and the policyholder's operations.

Other opportunities to review accounts come from loss control and premium audit reports. A loss control and safety inspection might contain recommendations that were requirements for policy issuance. A follow-up investigation could reveal that only some of the requirements were met. Premium audits usually lag behind a renewal policy by several months. The audit report could disclose larger loss exposures than originally contemplated, unacceptable operations, new products, new operations, or financial problems.

Once a claim has been processed or a premium audit has been conducted, the underwriter can contact insurer personnel who have first-hand knowledge of the insured. They can provide information on new loss exposures or uncover additional hazards or operations that help the underwriter reevaluate the account and determine its continued acceptability.

In addition to monitoring individual policies, underwriters must monitor books of business. Monitoring a book of business means evaluating the quality and profitability of all business written for a type of insurance. The evaluation should identify specific problems for each type of insurance, which can be subdivided into class of business, territory, and producer. The insurer is concerned primarily with the loss ratio for each type of insurance. Additionally, the insurer is concerned that premium volume covers fixed costs and overhead expenses.

Underwriters use premium and loss statistics to identify aggregate problems in a deteriorating book of business. Reviewing the book of business can also help determine compliance with underwriting policy and can detect changes in the type, volume, and quality of policies that might require corrective action.

A poor loss ratio in a particular class of business can indicate inadequate pricing or a disproportionate number of high-hazard policyholders relative to the average loss exposure in the classification. Classes with poor or deteriorating loss experience can be identified and corrected through rate increases, coverage restrictions, or more stringent selection standards. Changes in technology, materials, and operations, as well as changes in the social and legal environment, can significantly affect the loss ratio of a class of business.

An insurer can identify territories or geographic areas where the insurer realizes a profit or a loss. A territory can be defined in various ways to reflect an insurer's operations. For example, territory could encompass a single state or the three-state area serviced by a branch office. Territories can also be geographic areas within a state used in pricing policies.

Monitoring territorial underwriting results can help the insurer to target areas for future agency appointments in profitable regions. Poor results could indicate areas from which the insurer might withdraw or in which the insurer might raise rates, if permitted by regulators. The regulatory and legal climate for insurance varies by state. Regulation can have a major effect on the desirability of conducting business in a state and the possibility of achieving a profit. Other factors to consider in monitoring territorial underwriting results include the degree of urbanization, physical differences in terrain, and the potential for natural disasters.

Underwriting results can also be monitored by the producer. Ideally, each producer's book of business should be evaluated annually. The producer's premium volume, policy retention, and loss ratio are evaluated both on an overall basis and by type and class of business. That evaluation should include the balance or mix of business desired between personal and commercial insurance and the projected growth factor. Key considerations are the goals that the insurer and producer established and the progress made toward achieving them.

If the producer has a small premium volume with the insurer, one large loss can distort the loss ratio. A similar situation can occur in a small class of business. For example, a producer might appear to have unprofitable workers' compensation experience based on loss ratio when the producer actually had only one policy with an unsatisfactory loss ratio.

As underwriters monitor underwriting results, and as insurers evaluate an underwriter's performance, both should understand that underwriting decisions and underwriting results are not always related. Underwriting decisions are made under conditions of uncertainty, and a good decision does not always produce a good result. An underwriter can accept an apparently preferred submission only to suffer a major loss. On the other hand, an underwriter might make a poor underwriting decision, such as accepting a substandard submission, and incur no losses. Over the long run, however, the better the quality of the underwriting decisions, the better the results will be.

TYPES OF UNDERWRITERS

Insurers commonly distinguish between **line underwriters** and **staff underwriters**.

- Line underwriters are primarily responsible for implementing the steps in the underwriting process. Line underwriters are generally located in insurers' branch or regional offices.
- Staff underwriters assist underwriting management with making and implementing underwriting policy. Staff underwriters are typically located in an insurer's home office.

Line and staff underwriting activities sometimes overlap. For example, staff underwriters might be directly involved in individual underwriting decisions for large or unusual accounts. Whether to accept a large or an unusual account, and on what terms, sometimes requires a decision by staff underwriters or top management about how that particular account fits with the insurer's overall underwriting goals.

Line Underwriters

In addition to their primary responsibilities in implementing the steps in the underwriting process, line underwriters also engage in the following activities not previously mentioned:

- Assisting with determining appropriate coverage
- Providing service to producers and policyholders

Assisting With Determining Appropriate Coverage

An underwriter can offer valuable technical assistance to the insured's risk manager and the producer who is directly responsible for determining what coverage best meets the insured's needs. For simple or routine submissions, the underwriter verifies that the policy is issued with the appropriate forms and endorsements. For complex or unique submissions, the underwriter might draft manuscript policies and endorsements based on the characteristics of each submission.

An underwriter's knowledge of insurance policy forms and ability to relate policy provisions to the loss exposures of individual policyholders or applicants benefits producers and applicants. For example, suppose an applicant requested a Building and Personal Property Coverage Form (BPP) with the Causes of Loss—Broad Form to insure the loss exposures of a manufacturing location. While reviewing the applicant's operations as described in the inspection report, the underwriter discovers that the applicant has a loss exposure to property in transit that would not be covered adequately by these coverage forms. The underwriter discusses this loss exposure with the producer and offers to provide the coverage in an inland marine policy, thereby broadening the insured's coverage.

Line underwriter
Underwriter who is primarily responsible for implementing the steps in the underwriting process.

Staff underwriter
Underwriter who is usually located in the home office and who assists underwriting management with making and implementing underwriting policy.

Sometimes an underwriter must narrow an insured's coverage. Producers often request broader coverage for the loss exposures of a particular applicant than the insurer is willing to provide. Rather than decline the application, the underwriter might offer a more limited form of coverage involving higher deductibles or covering fewer causes of loss. The producer has an opportunity to provide reduced coverage that might be acceptable to the applicant rather than reject the applicant altogether.

Providing Service to Producers and Policyholders

Line underwriters also provide services to both producers and policyholders. Line underwriters prepare premium quotations and assist producers with proposals. Once a quote has been accepted, the underwriter prepares the file for the policywriting or data entry department.

Line underwriters also answer telephone calls, e-mails, and correspondence promptly; and process cancellations, endorsements, certificates, and renewals in a timely manner. The skill and efficiency with which line underwriters provide technical assistance, prepare quotations, issue policies, and perform routine services contribute to the insurer's success.

Staff Underwriters

Staff underwriters usually work at the insurer's home office, and they engage in the following activities:

- Researching the market
- Researching and developing coverages
- Evaluating underwriting experience
- Reviewing and revising rating plans
- Formulating underwriting policy
- Developing underwriting guides
- Conducting underwriting audits
- Assisting with education and training

Researching the Market

Insurers must continually research fundamental issues such as which markets the insurer should target. Staff underwriters typically share these research responsibilities with actuarial and marketing departments. This research includes an ongoing evaluation of the following:

- Effect of adding or deleting entire types of business
- Effect of expanding into additional states or retiring from states presently serviced

- Optimal product mix (the composition of the book of business, such as the percentage of premium generated by general liability or workers' compensation policies)
- Premium volume goals

Researching and Developing Coverages

Staff underwriters modify the insurer's preprinted policy forms and endorsements to reflect changes in market conditions or state regulations. Staff underwriters might also serve on industry or association committees that study standard policy forms and recommend changes.

Evaluating Underwriting Experience

To discern trends, staff underwriters analyze the loss and premium data of their own companies' books of business and of the insurance industry by type of insurance, class, size of loss exposure, and territory. That analysis is then used to determine whether changes must be made in the insurer's marketing or underwriting strategies. The necessary changes are usually communicated through the underwriting guide, but sometimes underwriting bulletins address special situations.

Reviewing and Revising Rating Plans

Rates and rating plans must be reviewed and updated continually—subject to regulatory constraints—to respond to changes in loss experience, competition, and inflation. The review and update must occur whether the insurer develops rates independently or uses the services of an advisory organization.

Advisory organizations assist insurers with gathering the data necessary to calculate rates. Examples include Insurance Services Office (ISO), the American Association of Insurance Services (AAIS), and the National Council on Compensation Insurance (NCCI). Most advisory organizations develop historical and prospective loss costs that they file with the appropriate regulatory authorities. Each insurer examines its own operational costs and profit requirements and combines them with loss costs to create its final insurance rates.

For those coverages for which advisory organizations do not develop loss costs, the insurer must develop its own rates. In such situations, reviewing and revising rating plans become even more crucial.

Formulating Underwriting Policy

Staff underwriters try to formulate an underwriting policy that effectively translates the goals of an insurer's owners and executive management into rules and procedures that guide individual and aggregate underwriting decisions. Underwriting policy determines the composition of the insurer's book of business. Goals for an insurer's book of business might be established by types of insurance and classes of business to be written; territories to be developed; or forms, insurance rates, and rating plans to be used.

An insurer's underwriting policy is influenced by senior management's desired position in the insurance marketplace. Most insurers see their role as standard insurers—that is, they seek better-than-average accounts. Some insurers, however, see an opportunity to offer coverage in areas that are underserved by the standard market. These nonstandard or specialty insurers might use loss control, more restrictive coverage forms, or higher prices to make a profit insuring accounts considered marginal or unacceptable in the standard market.

Underwriting policy is subject to constant review and periodic change and must consider the following four constraints:

1. Financial capacity
2. Regulation
3. Personnel and physical resources
4. Reinsurance

Exhibit 4-2 depicts these constraints and their effect on the book-of-business characteristics listed earlier. The following sections describe each of these constraining factors and illustrate how they affect underwriting policy changes.

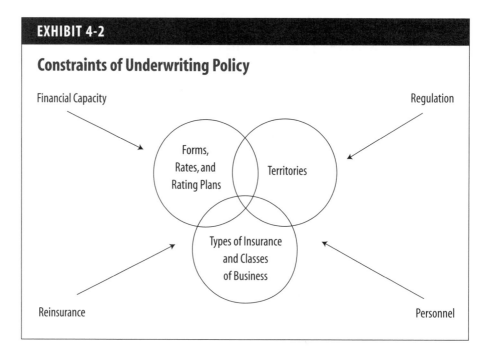

EXHIBIT 4-2

Constraints of Underwriting Policy

Financial Capacity

Regulation

Forms, Rates, and Rating Plans

Territories

Types of Insurance and Classes of Business

Reinsurance

Personnel

Financial Capacity

Insurers must prudently use their limited financial capacity to write business. Sometimes, the insurer might decide to stop writing a type of insurance or to add a type not previously written to optimize its allocation of scarce capacity. For example, a particular class of general liability insureds might be experiencing a level of losses that exceeds the level anticipated by the rate.

Therefore, the insurer might decide to stop pursuing that class of business and, instead, use capacity to increase the volume of commercial property insurance. Alternatively, the insurer might decide to limit its writing of a given type of insurance in a particular territory. In the past, for example, inadequate rate levels and rising benefit levels for claimants in many states led some insurers to develop restrictive acceptance criteria for workers' compensation submissions. In establishing underwriting policy, underwriters must also consider the possible effect of a catastrophic loss simultaneously affecting many types of insurance.

Regulation

The insurance industry is highly regulated, and insurance regulation constrains underwriting policy. Insurers must obtain licenses to write insurance by individual types of insurance within each state. They must file rates, rules, and forms with state regulators. Some states, such as Florida, specifically require underwriting guidelines to be filed.

In response to consumer-group complaints, regulators sometimes focus their attention on insurance availability in geographic areas that consumer groups believe the insurance industry has not adequately served. Regulators perform market conduct examinations to determine whether insurers adhere to the classification and rating plans they have filed. When a market conduct examination discloses deviations from filed forms and rates or improper conduct, the insurer is subject to penalties.

The effect of regulation on underwriting policy varies by state. In some states, insurers might be unable to get rate filings approved, or approval might be granted so slowly that rate levels are inadequate in relation to rising claim costs. Insurers sometimes withdraw from jurisdictions where they believe regulation is too restrictive.

Personnel and Physical Resources

Personnel limitations can also constrain underwriting policy. An insurer must have enough properly trained underwriters to implement its underwriting policy. No insurer, for example, should pursue aviation, equipment breakdown, or ocean marine insurance unless it has enough underwriting specialists experienced in those types of insurance.

In addition to having personnel with the necessary skills, the insurer must have the personnel *where* they are needed. All other things being equal, premiums should be obtained from a broad range of insureds to create the widest possible distribution of loss exposures. However, regulatory expenses and policyholder service requirements make it difficult for small insurers to efficiently handle a small volume of business in many widespread territories.

Even if people are available, an insurer cannot handle business without the necessary physical resources. Information systems are especially important; many growth plans have been scuttled because computer support was not available.

Reinsurance

The availability and cost of adequate reinsurance can constrain underwriting policy. Reinsurance treaties might exclude certain types of insurance or classes of business, or the cost of reinsurance might be prohibitive. Reinsurers are also concerned about the underlying policy forms offered by the insurer. A reinsurer might have no reservations about an insurer's use of forms developed by advisory organizations but might expressly exclude reinsurance coverage for loss exposures covered by manuscript forms developed for a particular insured or covered by forms developed independently.

Developing Underwriting Guides

Staff underwriters communicate an insurer's underwriting policy to line underwriters and others by developing underwriting guides and related bulletins. Underwriting guides describe the practices necessary to implement underwriting policy. Staff underwriters periodically update the guides to reflect changes in policy.

The underwriting guides that staff underwriters prepare identify the major elements that line underwriters should evaluate for each type of insurance. Underwriting guides help to ensure that underwriting policy—and therefore selection decisions—are made uniformly and consistently throughout all geographic regions. These guides also synthesize the insights and experience of seasoned underwriters and help the less experienced ones. Underwriting guides also distinguish routine from nonroutine decisions.

Some underwriting guides include step-by-step instructions for handling particular classes of insureds. Such guides might identify specific hazards to evaluate, alternatives to consider, criteria to use when making the final decision, ways to implement the decision, and methods to monitor the decision. The guides might also provide pricing instructions and reinsurance-related information. An excerpt from an underwriting guide with many of these characteristics is shown in Exhibit 4-3. This particular guide categorizes loss exposures as "below average," "average," or "good." See the comment on these categorizations in the following box.

Average, Better-Than-Average, Worse-Than-Average Loss Exposures

This chapter and the two that follow focus on characteristics and conditions that distinguish the average loss exposure from loss exposures that are better or worse than average. They do not generally refer to loss exposures that are "acceptable" or "unacceptable." The worse-than-average loss exposures might not be desirable to most underwriters in the standard market, but they might still be acceptable to insurers whose underwriting policy reflects a different underwriting philosophy.

EXHIBIT 4-3

Commercial Property Underwriting Guide

UNDERWRITING EVALUATION EXHIBIT

This exhibit presents the most important elements that might categorize a loss exposure as "below average," "average," or "good." Few loss exposures will be totally "below average" or totally "good" for all categories. Most loss exposures will be subject to variations of one degree or another for each of the underwriting elements. The underwriter's final classification will be determined by weighing the relative importance of each characteristic as applied to the loss exposure.

IMPORTANT: IF THE LOSS EXPOSURE CLASSIFIES AS "BELOW AVERAGE" IN RESPECT TO "OWNERSHIP," IT IS UNACCEPTABLE REGARDLESS OF ANY OTHER FAVORABLE CHARACTERISTICS.

	BELOW AVERAGE	AVERAGE	GOOD
O W N E R S H I P	Abnormal loss history or unsatisfactory adjustment record	Loss record satisfactory	Little or no loss history
	Moral instability	Morally sound	Morally above reproach
	Criminal record	No criminal record	No criminal record
	Dishonest	Honest	Unquestionable integrity
	Illegal business	Legitimate business	Legitimate business
M A N A G E M E N T	Poor credit or bankruptcies	Good credit	Excellent credit
	Business unprofitable	Business profitable	Business highly profitable
	New venture and/or lack of experience	In business three to five years	In business five years or more
	Heating, wiring, plumbing more than twenty years old	Heating, wiring, plumbing remodeled within last twenty years	Heating, wiring, plumbing less than ten years old
	Poor control of common hazards	Minor common hazards	Common hazards well safeguarded
	Poor housekeeping/maintenance	Adequate housekeeping/maintenance	Good housekeeping/maintenance
	Usually careless	Reasonably careful	Exceptionally careful

Continued on next page.

	BELOW AVERAGE	AVERAGE	GOOD
C O N S T R U C T I O N	More than twenty-five years old	Less than twenty-five years old	Less than ten years old
	No fire-stops where advisable	Minimum fire-stops	Effective fire-stops
	Poorly suited to occupancy	Basically suitable for occupancy	Especially suitable for occupancy
	Converted buildings	Built for occupancy	Built for occupancy
	Large undivided area	Standard fire divisions	Important hazards cut off
	Poor design	Architecturally sound	Very well designed
	"Short-cut" construction	Good basic construction	Excellent construction and engineering
O C C U P A N C Y	Vacant, unoccupied	Occupied	Occupied
	Contents highly combustible (Cl. C4 & 5)	Contents moderately combustible (Cl. C3)	Contents low combustibility (Cl. C1 & 2)
	Contents highly susceptible (Cl. S4 & 5)	Contents moderately susceptible (Cl. S3)	Contents low susceptibility (Cl. S1 & 2)
	Extra-hazardous process for class	Normal processes for class	Processes well safeguarded
	Ordinary hazards not guarded	Ordinary hazards guarded	All hazards well guarded
	Obsolete merchandise or products	Merchandise and products saleable	Products or merchandise in demand
	Run-down equipment	Good equipment	Excellent equipment
	Undesirable tenancy	All occupants acceptable	Owner occupancy or all desirable tenants
	Susceptible to quick-spreading or flash fires	Quick-spreading fire unlikely	Quick-spreading fire unlikely

	BELOW AVERAGE	AVERAGE	GOOD
P R O T E C T I O N	No first aid	Minimum first aid	Private protection good
	Public protection at risk, deficient	Public protection equal to town protection	Public protection excellent
	No watch service	Ordinary public police patrol	Private watch service
	Delayed alarm probable	Normal alarm expected	Early alarm probable
	Inefficient public fire department	Normal public fire department operations	Very effective public fire department
E X P O S U R E	Severe	Ordinary	Light or none
	Large frame exposures	Frame exposure limited	No frame exposure
	Large concentrated values	No large concentration of values	Values well spread
	Unprotected wall openings or no parapets	Parapets and protection of exposed wall openings inadequate	Exposed wall openings protected and exposed walls adequately parapeted
	Neighborhood declining	Neighborhood stable	Good environment
	Poor location for type of business	Acceptable location for type of business	Especially desirable location for type of business
	Outmoded business location	Stable or good business location	Prime business location economically prosperous
	Shore-front or hurricane exposure	No extraordinary storm exposure	No weather exposure
R A T E	Inadequate	Satisfactory	Satisfactory
I N S U R A N C E T O V A L U E	Less than 80%	At least 80%	At least 80%

Other insurers use underwriting guides that are less comprehensive. For example, they might list all classes of business and indicate their acceptability by type of insurance. Codes are then assigned to indicate the desirability of the loss exposure and the level of authority required to write the class of business. An example of this type of underwriting guide appears in Exhibit 4-4.

Conducting Underwriting Audits

Underwriting audit

A process in which members of an insurer's home office underwriting department examine files to see whether underwriters in branch or regional offices are following underwriting guidelines.

An **underwriting audit** is a management control tool used to determine whether line underwriters are properly implementing underwriting policy. Typically, a staff underwriter or a team of staff underwriters visits a branch or regional office and reviews individual underwriting files. The audit focuses on proper documentation; adherence to procedure, classification, and rating practices; and conformity of selection decisions to the underwriting guide and bulletins.

Staff underwriters also monitor underwriting activity by analyzing statistical results by type of insurance, class of business, size of loss exposure, and territory. Statistical data show the extent to which underwriting goals are met, but they do not conclusively demonstrate whether the results are a product of implementing the insurer's underwriting guidelines. Staff underwriters also conduct field audits to ensure compliance with the insurer's underwriting guidelines.

Assisting With Education and Training

Staff underwriters are usually responsible for determining the educational needs of line underwriters. The training department implements the resulting training program and continuing educational activities. If an educational need involves a technical insurance area, staff underwriters often develop the course and serve as instructors.

UNDERWRITING RESULTS

Underwriting results can be evaluated using two types of measures: financial and non-financial. The most common financial measure of underwriting results over a specific time period—typically one year—is the insurer's combined loss and expense ratio. Proper underwriting should produce an underwriting profit or perhaps a small underwriting loss that is more than offset by investment profits. Certain issues, however, make it difficult to evaluate underwriting success in the short term by using financial measures.

Financial Measures

Sometimes underwriting produces good financial results only because of luck. Other times, underwriters do all the right things, but financial results are unsatisfactory. The factors that can make it difficult to evaluate the financial results of underwriting in the short run include the following:

- Insurance industry trends
- Major catastrophic losses
- Premium volume
- Loss development delays

Insurance Industry Trends

The insurance business as a whole is cyclical. During some periods, most insurers are profitable; during other periods, most are unprofitable. Fairly evaluating the underwriting results of a particular insurer requires measuring them against the performance of other insurers during the same time period. Sometimes underwriting success means incurring a smaller underwriting loss than the competition's.

Investment gains have sometimes, but not always, offset underwriting losses. Certain forces significantly affect the underwriting results: inflation, regulation, competition, and investment results. When the major components of loss costs are increasing rapidly because of inflation, rates tend to increase more slowly because of state regulation or competition among insurers. Competition also affects underwriting results. During periods of seemingly favorable results, insurers might try to increase their premium volume, writing business at less-than-adequate rates. Some managers believe they can write more commercial insurance at an underwriting loss, for which they can compensate with superior investment results, a practice called *cash-flow underwriting*. Although this practice can be effective in the short run when investment conditions are favorable, it has resulted in disastrous operating losses for some insurers.

Residual market programs introduce competitive factors that can affect underwriting results. Automobile insurance plans, joint underwriting associations (JUAs), and similar residual market plans are designed to solve social as well as insurance problems. Once limited to substandard private-passenger auto insurance, residual market plans have expanded to include property, workers' compensation, and medical malpractice insurance.

Major Catastrophic Losses

Underwriting results are usually evaluated annually, but major hurricanes, major earthquakes, and other natural catastrophes occur too irregularly to predict annually. Floods, for example, are typically predicted over a hundred-year period; certain flood plains are predicted to have a flood, on average, once every one hundred years or, in lower-elevation areas, once every ten or twenty years.

EXHIBIT 4-4

Selection Guide

A.   GENERAL:

The Selection Guide is a comprehensive alphabetical listing by class of business showing what the IIA Insurance Companies believe to be the desirability of insuring an average loss exposure in the class. The Guide grades each class for Property, Commercial Automobile, Workers' Compensation, Burglary and Robbery, Fidelity, Premises/Operations Liability, and Products/Completed Operations Liability. In addition, the final column titled "Form" indicates whether the General Liability coverage must be written on a Claims-Made Form (indicated by a "C"), or whether the Occurrence Form is available (indicated by an "O"). Please remember the loss exposure selection guide is only a guide. The company retains final authority regarding the acceptance or rejection of any specific loss exposure.

B.   CLASSIFICATION ACCEPTABILITY RATINGS:

The Selection Guide is being published as a section of this agent's manual to answer the question: "Are loss exposures within a particular class likely to be accepted by the IIA Insurance Companies?" In light of this question, the loss exposure grades as found in the Selection Guide are defined as follows:

E—Excellent

This class of business is considered to have excellent profit potential. Unless a specific loss exposure in this class has unusual hazards, it will rarely present any underwriting problems. The agent may bind loss exposures graded as "E" without prior underwriting consent.

G—Good

This class of business is considered to have good profit potential. Normally this loss exposure may be written before obtaining an inspection or developing additional underwriting information other than that present on the application. The agent may bind loss exposures graded as "G" without prior underwriting consent.

A—Average

Potential for profit is marginal due to high variability of loss exposures within the class. It is understood that the underwriter might think it is necessary to inspect the loss exposure before authorizing binding. In all instances, it is recommended that the agent call the underwriter and discuss the loss exposure before binding.

S—Submit

The account presents little potential for profit. These loss exposures will require a complete written submission before binding. The underwriter *must* obtain a complete inspection and evaluate any other underwriting information deemed necessary before authorizing the binding of this loss exposure.

D—Decline

Because of the lack of potential for profit, this class of loss exposure is prohibited and will not be considered. Under no circumstances may a loss exposure classified as "D" be bound without the prior written approval of the Vice President of Commercial Underwriting.

C.   FOOTNOTES:

Footnotes sometimes are indicated as applying to an individual classification for a specific type of insurance. These footnotes are displayed at the bottom of each page and are designed to make you aware of certain hazards that are unacceptable or need to be addressed in an acceptable manner.

We hope the Selection Guide will be valuable in understanding the types of business our companies want to be writing. However, please call your underwriter if you are unsure about how to classify a particular loss exposure, or if you believe the factors associated with a specific loss exposure make it considerably better or worse than the grading assigned by this guide.

DESCRIPTION	PROPERTY	AUTO	WC	BURG. & ROB.	FIDELITY	PREM & OPS	PROD & CO	FORM
Abrasive wheel manufacturing	S	A	D	A	G	S	D	C
Abrasives or abrasive products manufacturing	S	A	D	A	G	S	D	O
Abrasives or abrasive products manufacturing—Artificial	S	A	D	A	G	S	D	O
Adhesives manufacturing	S	A	S	A	G	A[1]	S[1]	O
Adhesive tape manufacturing	S	A	S	A	G	A[1]	S[1]	O
Advertising sign companies—outdoor	A[2]	G	S[3]	G	G	A[3]	G[3]	O
Aerosol container manufacturing	S	A	D	G	G	A	D	O
Aerosol containers—filling or charging for others	D	A	D	G	G	A	D	C
Agate or enamelware manufacturing—Workers' compensation only			D					
Air conditioning equipment manufacturers	A[2]	A	S	A	G	A[1]	S[1]	O
Air conditioning equipment—dealers or distributors only	G	G	A	G	G	G	G	O
Air conditioning systems or equipment—dealers or distributors and installation, servicing, or repair	G	G	A	G	G	G	G	O
Air pressure or steam gauge manufacturing—Workers' compensation only			D					
Aircraft or aircraft parts manufacturing	A	G	S	A	G	D	D	O
Airport control towers—not operated exclusively by the Federal Aviation Administration	D	A	D	D	D	D	D	O
Airport—lessees of portions of airports engaged in the sale of aircraft or accessories, servicing or repairing of aircraft, or pilot instructions	D	A	D	D	D	D	D	O
Airports—commercial	D	A[4,5]	D	D	D	D	D	O
Airports—private	D	A[4]	D	D	D	D	D	O
Airport runway or warming apron—paving or repaving, surfacing, resurfacing or scraping	A	G	S	G	G	D	D	O
Alarm manufacturing—burglar	A[2]	A	A	A	G	A	D	C

[1] Acceptability will depend on specific nature of the operation and specific types and uses of the products.
[2] The loss exposure is unacceptable if any painting or finishing is done inside without an approved spray booth.
[3] Work done above two stories in height is unacceptable.
[4] No vans, mini-vans, or buses. Any automobile used in public or private livery is unacceptable.
[5] Emergency use vehicles, such as ambulances and rescue vehicles, are unacceptable.

Catastrophes such as industrial explosions, airplane crashes, nuclear reactor breakdowns, or terrorist activities likewise occur with too little regularity to create a predictable pattern. Ideally, insurance rates allow for unpredicted losses. Still, a major catastrophe is likely to cause an underwriting loss for that year for most if not all affected insurers. However, failure to predict the unpredictable does not necessarily indicate inadequate underwriting.

Premium Volume

Part of evaluating an insurer's combined loss and expense ratio, both on an aggregate basis and by type of insurance, involves the extent to which the insurer's premium volume goals have been met. Premium volume and underwriting policy are directly related. Tightening underwriting standards typically causes an insurer's premium volume to decline. Conversely, loosening underwriting standards typically causes an insurer's premium volume to increase.

Premium volume is a component of the financial performance ratios commonly used by the insurance industry. In statutory accounting, the loss ratio is calculated by dividing incurred losses by earned premiums. The expense ratio divides underwriting expenses by earned premiums. The sum of those ratios is the financial basis combined ratio. The combined ratio as calculated by A.M. Best Co., which is also referred to as the trade basis combined ratio, uses the same loss ratio but divides underwriting expenses by net written premiums to determine the expense ratio. Underwriting expenses are divided by net written premiums because most expenses are associated with placing business on the books rather than maintaining it, thereby making the trade basis combined ratio more accurate than the financial basis combined ratio. However, analyzing on a trade basis has the following limitations:

- The extent to which the insurer's expenses are related to net written premiums (calculated at policy inception) rather than earned premiums (calculated over the policy life) varies by type of insurance. Up-front costs, such as commissions and acquisition expenses, also vary by type of insurance.

- Certain types of specialty insurance, such as boiler and machinery, have significant continuing expenses for inspections, and the timing of these expenses relates more closely to earned premiums. This is also true for workers' compensation insurance, but to a lesser extent. Consequently, using the trade ratio to compare insurers with different mixes of business can be misleading.

The combined ratio is considered the accepted measure of an insurer's underwriting performance. A combined ratio of less than 100 percent indicates profitable underwriting results, and a combined ratio of more than 100 percent indicates unprofitable underwriting results. Exhibit 4-5 illustrates how changes in premium volume can affect insurer underwriting results. The exhibit contrasts the results using both the financial and trade combined ratios. When measured on a *financial* basis, this insurer's underwriting results improved; when measured on a *trade* basis, results deteriorated. Although this is an extreme

EXHIBIT 4-5

Underwriting Results—Financial and Trade Bases

This exhibit shows a hypothetical example of an insurer experiencing a 25 percent drop in net written premiums as a result of a more restrictive underwriting policy. On a financial basis, the combined ratio improved from 102.0 to 96.0. On a trade basis, however, the insurer's combined ratio deteriorated from 99.9 to 102.2. Underwriting results should be analyzed on both bases to accurately determine the effect of changes in premium volume.

	Year 1	Year 2
Net written premiums	$10,000,000	$7,500,000
Earned premiums	9,500,000	9,000,000
Underwriting expenses	3,990,000	2,790,000
Incurred losses	5,700,000	5,850,000

Financial Basis

Loss ratio:

$$\frac{\text{Incurred losses}}{\text{Earned premiums}} \quad \frac{\$5,700,000}{\$9,500,000} = 60.0\% \qquad \frac{\$5,850,000}{\$9,000,000} = 65.0\%$$

Expense ratio:

$$\frac{\text{Underwriting expenses}}{\text{Earned premiums}} \quad \frac{\$3,990,000}{\$9,500,000} = 42.0\% \qquad \frac{\$2,790,000}{\$9,000,000} = 31.0\%$$

Financial basis combined ratio   102.0%   96.0%

Trade Basis

Loss ratio:

$$\frac{\text{Incurred losses}}{\text{Earned premiums}} \quad \frac{\$5,700,000}{\$9,500,000} = 60.0\% \qquad \frac{\$5,850,000}{\$9,000,000} = 65.0\%$$

Expense ratio:

$$\frac{\text{Underwriting expenses}}{\text{Net written premiums}} \quad \frac{\$3,990,000}{\$10,000,000} = 39.9\% \qquad \frac{\$2,790,000}{\$7,500,000} = 37.2\%$$

Trade basis combined ratio   99.9%   102.2%

example, it shows why both combined ratios should be analyzed for accurate evaluation of the effect of an insurer's change in underwriting policy.

Loss Development Delays

With certain types of insurance, particularly liability insurance, a considerable amount of time can elapse between when a loss is reported and when a claim is settled. This is known as a loss development delay or "long tail." Reserves are established as soon as the loss is reported, but significant inaccuracy exists in estimating ultimate loss costs that will be paid at some future date. The longer the time between the estimate and the ultimate claim settlement, the greater the inaccuracy is likely to be. That inaccuracy has two major components.

The first major component of inaccuracy as a result of loss development delay is changes in reserves for reported losses. With liability insurance, reserve amounts frequently change because of the time that elapses between loss notification and claim settlement. The loss ratio as an indicator of underwriting performance relies heavily on the accuracy of reserve estimates because the incurred losses used for loss ratios include both paid losses and outstanding loss reserves. The more time that elapses between loss notification and claim settlement, the less accurate the initial reserve estimate is.

The second major component of inaccuracy as a result of loss development delay is changes in reserves for incurred but not reported (IBNR) losses. If a liability insurance policy is written on an occurrence basis, the insurer provides coverage for property damage or bodily injury that occur during the policy period even if claims for such damage or injury are not submitted until after the policy has expired. Policies written on an occurrence basis can have an unlimited discovery period between the date an insured event occurs and the date of the discovery and subsequent claim. The accuracy of IBNR losses greatly affects the accuracy of loss data. Accuracy is less of a problem with claims-made forms. If a policy is written on a claims-made basis, the insurer provides coverage only for claims first made against the insured during the policy period. Theoretically, a claims-made policy would not cover losses that have not been reported by the end of the policy period.

In practice, however, claims-made policies often cover losses reported after the policy period because they provide for "extended reporting periods." Thus, IBNR losses can be a problem under either type of policy.

Non-Financial Measures

The second way to evaluate underwriting results is to use non-financial performance measures. These measures evaluate individual underwriters and underwriting departments on their actions rather than on their results. Underwriting should produce favorable financial results over the long term, barring uncontrollable variables, if underwriters do the right things and adhere strictly to underwriting guidelines. The following are non-financial measures used to evaluate underwriting results:

- Selection
- Product mix
- Pricing
- Accommodated risks
- Retention ratio
- Success ratio
- Service to producers

Some of these measures clearly apply only to commercial underwriting departments, but others can be used for both personal and commercial insurance. Some of these measures can be evaluated during an underwriting audit.

Selection

This measure requires well-defined selection rules in the underwriting guide. The selection rules should define highly desirable, average, and below-average types of insureds, and each underwriter, branch, or region should have a goal regarding the balance of the three types of insureds. During an underwriting audit or review, the insurance written by a particular under-writer, branch, or region can be segmented into the three types, and the percentages of the book of business written for each type can be evaluated.

Product Mix

This measure requires a statement in the underwriting guide about the desired product mix for new and renewal business. For example, if products liability losses are adversely affecting the entire book of business, the product mix standard might require a reduction in manufacturing classes and a concerted effort to increase writing insurance for contractor, service, and mercantile classes. The actual book of business can be compared to the desired book of business.

Pricing

Premiums being charged can be compared to pricing standards to measure premium adequacy. In commercial insurance, insurance rates are typically modified to reflect features specific to the account being underwritten. Pricing standards indicate the extent to which these modifications depart from standard pricing. By indicating the credits underwriters apply to indi-vidual accounts, an underwriting audit might reveal that profitability in a type of insurance is being sacrificed for growth.

Accommodated Risks

This measure requires a log in which all accommodated risks are entered along with the reasons for the accommodations. Evaluating the log as part of underwriting audits and reviews can reveal whether accommodations are made too frequently and can ensure that the producer has increased volume or has fulfilled some other promise in exchange for the accommodations.

Retention Ratio

The **retention ratio** is the percentage of business renewed. Most, if not all, of the underwriting monitoring would have been completed for existing policies. All else being equal, keeping those policies on the books offers more profit potential than acquiring new business, which involves acquisition costs. Too low a retention rate might indicate serious deficiencies, including poor service to producers, noncompetitive pricing, or unfavorable claim service. This measure requires careful monitoring of the renewal rate and any trends.

Retention ratio
The percentage of insurance policies renewed.

Success Ratio

Success ratio
The ratio of insurance policies written to those that have been quoted to applicants for insurance.

The **success ratio**, sometimes called the "hit ratio," is the ratio of business written to business quoted. This measure is typically used in commercial insurance. Data must be gathered for a large number of quotations to determine the average range for this ratio. Ratios that are either inordinately high or low might require investigation. A high success ratio might indicate any of the following:

- Competition is easing.
- Rates are inadequate or lower than other insurers' rates.
- Coverage is broader than other insurers'.
- Underwriting selection criteria are deteriorating.

A low success ratio might indicate any of the following:

- Competition is increasing.
- Rates are too high.
- Coverages or forms are too restrictive.
- Selection criteria are too strict.
- Service is poor.

Service to Producers

Producers usually measure insurers on the basis of their service. An insurer can also measure its service to producers by establishing a set of minimum acceptable standards for certain types of service. The actual performance of each underwriter, branch, or region being measured is compared with the targeted level of performance. An example of one such standard appears in Exhibit 4-6.

EXHIBIT 4-6

Example of "Service to Producers" Underwriting Standards

Category	Minimum Acceptable Standard
1. Quotations	3 working days
2. New policies	3 working days
3. Replies to correspondence	2 working days
4. Cancellations, endorsements, certificates	5 working days
5. Direct cancellation notices	Same-day service
6. Renewals	No later than 10 days before expiration

SUMMARY

The practice of underwriting insurance policies began when insurance emerged as a commercial enterprise. In modern practice, underwriters strive to develop a larger market share of profitable business. Adverse selection, a natural opponent of this objective, occurs when the applicant for insurance presents a higher-than-average probability of loss than is expected from a truly random sample of all applicants.

The underwriting process consists of a six-step decision-making process:

1. Evaluating loss exposures
2. Determining underwriting alternatives
3. Selecting an underwriting alternative
4. Determining the appropriate premium
5. Implementing the decision
6. Monitoring the loss exposures

This chapter discussed each of the steps in the process in a way that can be applied to any specific type of insurance or insurance product. Hazard identification and analysis are a crucial part of the line underwriter's job. Hazards can be categorized as moral, morale, physical, and legal.

An underwriter can make what appears to be a good underwriting decision but end up with poor results. The reverse is also true. Common problems with evaluating individual underwriting results are the span of time between the decision and the results, and factors that are outside the underwriter's control. Several underwriting performance measures are more subjective and do not rely on account profitability.

Insurers typically distinguish between the day-to-day tasks of line underwriters and the management-oriented functions of staff underwriters. Although this distinction is not universal, it does help to differentiate between underwriters who make individual risk decisions and those who establish general policy guidelines for the insurer. Establishing underwriting policy is a key objective of senior management. Effective implementation of underwriting policy is a criterion for the success of any insurer. An insurer's underwriting policy promotes the type of account and classes of business anticipated to produce a growing and profitable book of business. Although almost any restriction on acceptable business can be imposed, limitations apply to what an underwriting policy can contain and to the factors that affect that policy.

As in most businesses, financial ratios are used to indicate the success of the underwriting effort. Key ratios are the loss ratio, expense ratio, and combined ratio. A combined ratio of less than 100 percent indicates profitable underwriting results, and a combined ratio of more than 100 percent indicates unprofitable underwriting results. The combined ratio ignores investment income, an important component of an insurer's overall profitability. Various financial and non-financial methods of measuring underwriting results were also reviewed in this chapter.

The general process of underwriting covered in this chapter applies to both property and liability loss exposures. The next chapter discusses the specifics of underwriting property loss exposures.

Chapter 5

Direct Your Learning

Underwriting Property Insurance

After learning the content of this chapter, you should be able to:

- Given a case, evaluate property loss exposures using the COPE model.

- Explain how to underwrite property values.

- Given a case, analyze the loss exposures for the following causes of loss:

  - Fire
  - Lightning
  - Explosion
  - Windstorm
  - Hail
  - Vandalism and malicious mischief
  - Water damage
  - Flood
  - Earthquake
  - Collapse

- Describe the underwriting considerations when evaluating the loss exposures for the following causes of loss:

  - Riot and civil commotion
  - Sprinkler leakage
  - Sinkhole collapse and mine subsidence
  - Volcanic action
  - Terrorism
  - Weight of ice, snow, or sleet
  - Theft

- Given a case, analyze the loss exposures for each of the following types of insurance:

  - Business income
  - Commercial crime insurance
  - Marine insurance

- Describe the loss control function and its goals.

- Explain how loss control cooperates with other insurer functions.

- Describe the loss control services provided by insurers.

Develop Your Perspective

What are the main topics covered in the chapter?

In this chapter, a wide range of direct and indirect causes of loss for property are addressed from an underwriting perspective. Some causes of loss, such as fire, require extensive evaluation. This chapter also describes the loss control function and its goals.

Consider the underwriting evaluations for each cause of loss.

- What are the unique factors for each cause of loss?

- How can underwriters make accurate policy-selection decisions based on these factors?

- How does the loss control function cooperate with other insurer functions?

Why is it important to learn about these topics?

Causes of loss or loss exposures are the focus of an underwriting review. As part of that review, an underwriter gathers information to determine the extent of the potential losses for a new application or for an existing policy.

How can you use what you will learn?

Analyze direct and indirect causes of loss for property loss exposures.

- Compare the loss potential for two or more properties considered for purchase or lease. Include the loss exposures for each property as a factor in the purchase or lease decision.

- How can loss control assist underwriters in preventing or reducing losses arising from the direct and indirect causes of loss?

Chapter 5

Underwriting Property Insurance

Underwriting loss exposures related to the fire cause of loss has been a significant responsibility of property underwriters, and underwriting such loss exposures dominates the discussion in this chapter. This chapter also discusses underwriting other property loss exposures; the consequences of property loss; and underwriting crime, ocean marine, and inland marine loss exposures. Finally, the chapter examines the loss control function performed by many insurance organizations. Loss control is directly related to property insurance underwriting and performs a customer service function.

UNDERWRITING FIRE INSURANCE

Fire is generally the most significant cause of loss for most forms of property insurance involving buildings and personal property. Although most fire losses are partial losses and loss frequency is typically low for any given insured, fire can still produce a total loss.

Fire underwriting typically focuses on physical hazards, although moral and morale (or attitudinal) hazards are also important. Property underwriters analyze the following four areas, traditionally referred to with the acronym "COPE":

1. Construction
2. Occupancy
3. Protection
4. External loss exposures

Construction

The first area that property underwriters analyze is construction. The construction of the covered building, or the building that contains insured property, is a primary underwriting consideration. The building's construction characteristics relate directly to its ability to withstand damage by fire and other causes of loss and to protect its contents.

The insurance application and an inspection report provided by the producer or loss control representative identify a building's construction. Advisory organizations publish building construction information for buildings subject to specific rating. If an underwriter needs additional information, independent inspection companies can be hired to conduct a property survey.

Construction Classes

Insurance Services Office (ISO) divides building construction into six classes.[1] Construction classes reflect the construction materials' ability to resist fire damage. Ratings consider (1) the vertical load-bearing members that ultimately support the building's weight and (2) the materials used in the roof and floors, which spread the weight across the vertical load-bearing members. The six ISO construction classes, in descending order, are as follows:

Class 6—Fire-resistive construction

Class 5—Modified fire-resistive construction

Class 4—Masonry noncombustible construction

Class 3—Noncombustible construction

Class 2—Joisted masonry construction

Class 1—Frame construction

Fire-resistive construction
Construction that incorporates load-bearing members and that has a fire-resistance rating of at least two hours.

ISO Class 6 is fire-resistive construction. In a building of **fire-resistive construction**, the structure's load-bearing members can withstand fire damage for *at least two hours*. The construction materials are either (1) noncombustible with a fire-resistance rating of at least two hours or (2) protected by a noncombustible covering such as concrete, masonry, plaster, or gypsum that provides at least a two-hour fire-resistance rating. Fire-resistive ratings are assigned to construction material based on laboratory evaluations in test furnaces. Evaluations certify that materials can withstand fire damage under certain weight loads regardless of whether materials can be repaired or reused. The performance of such materials can differ significantly under actual fire conditions.

The load-bearing components of a fire-resistive building do not buckle or collapse as readily as those of other construction types. This is a higher standard than requiring that the structure not burn, because even though a structure does not burn, the fire's intense heat can still cause a building's load-bearing components to collapse. Fire-resistive construction is superior to other types of building construction, but it is not "fireproof."

Modified fire-resistive construction
Construction that has load-bearing walls and columns of masonry or reinforced concrete construction and that has a fire-resistance rating of one to two hours.

From an underwriting standpoint, fire resistive is the best type of construction to prevent damage from most causes of loss. In addition to resisting fire damage, the strength of a fire-resistive structure gives it superior resistance to causes of loss such as windstorm, earthquake, and flood.

ISO Class 5 is modified fire-resistive construction. A building of **modified fire-resistive construction** has bearing walls (walls supporting the weight of the upper floors and roof) and columns of masonry or reinforced concrete construction. It is similar to fire-resistive construction, except that the material's fire-resistance rating is *one to two hours*.

Masonry noncombustible construction
Masonry construction or construction that includes exterior walls of fire-resistive construction with a fire-resistance rating of not less than one hour.

ISO Class 4 is masonry noncombustible construction. In **masonry noncombustible construction**, the building's exterior walls are made of self-supporting masonry materials, and the floors and roof are made of metal or some other noncombustible or slow-burning material. The exterior walls are made of construction with a fire-resistive rating of not less than one hour.

A typical masonry noncombustible building has a masonry nonbearing wall surface, a concrete floor, a metal deck roof, and an unprotected metal frame. Low initial cost and low maintenance have made this type of construction extremely popular.

ISO Class 3 is noncombustible construction. A building of noncombustible construction has exterior walls, roof, and floor constructed of and supported by metal or other noncombustible materials such as gypsum. Although these buildings are noncombustible, they are not fire resistive. The buildings' unprotected steel structural supports twist and bend when subjected to the heat of a typical fire (see Exhibit 5-1). If this type of building is filled with combustible contents, structural failure is extremely likely in a serious fire.

EXHIBIT 5-1

Light Noncombustible Building After Fire

Photo by Kim Holston.

Even though these structures are constructed of noncombustible material and do not provide fuel for a fire, their susceptibility to damage makes them only marginally safer from a fire underwriting perspective than joisted masonry or frame construction (described next).

ISO Class 2 is joisted masonry construction. **Joisted masonry construction** has load-bearing exterior walls made of brick, adobe, concrete, gypsum, stone, tile, or similar materials, with floors and roofs of combustible materials. Joisted masonry construction is also called ordinary construction, ordinary masonry, brick, wood joisted, and brick joisted. Exterior walls can be fire-resistive construction with a fire-resistance rating of at least one hour or can be masonry construction. The walls are self-supporting, meaning that

Joisted masonry construction
Construction that has load-bearing exterior walls made of brick, adobe, concrete, gypsum, stone, tile, or similar materials; that has floors and roofs of combustible materials; and that has a fire-resistance rating of at least one hour.

they stand without support from the building's frame. Because the exterior walls are load bearing, many underwriters regard them as part of the building's frame. Interior columns and floors are of combustible material, usually wood.

Joisted masonry buildings are found in most major metropolitan areas, especially in northern states. The need for the exterior walls to support the structure's weight limits the height to which these structures can be built. Joisted masonry construction is rarely used for buildings higher than five stories and is typically used for buildings of three stories or fewer.

When a joisted masonry building suffers an intense fire, only a shell is left—the bare exterior walls. Walls can even fall or be pulled or pushed down by collapse of the roof or wooden support beams. The bricks in brick walls can be damaged beyond use by heat of sufficient intensity and duration. In the more frequent, less intense fires, the exterior bearing walls usually remain in usable, or nearly usable, condition; they continue to support the roof, and the walls and roof provide some protection for the interior.

Mill construction, also known as heavy timber construction, is a type of joisted masonry construction that uses heavy timbers for internal support of the floors and roof. In this construction type, no concealed areas exist under the roof and floors that might permit a fire to go undetected. The heavy wood floors serve as a firestop, slowing the spread of fire.

The size of the wood members used in mill construction gives these buildings structural strength. Fires that would consume the light joists used in typical joisted masonry might only char the heavy timber beams used in mill construction.

Frame construction
Construction that has load-bearing components made of wood or other combustible materials.

ISO Class 1 is frame construction. In **frame construction**, the building's load-bearing components are made of wood or other combustible materials. In addition to the direct damage caused by a fire, frame construction can suffer structural damage because the weight-bearing supports are combustible. Frame construction is used in many dwellings and small mercantile buildings. Buildings of mixed construction, such as wood frame with brick veneer, stone veneer, aluminum siding, or stucco, are classified as frame buildings.

Construction Materials

As previously mentioned, the construction of a building's weight-bearing members is a basic underwriting consideration for the fire cause of loss. The interior finishing materials used on walls, floors, and ceilings; the insulation; and the roofing also affect a structure's combustibility and underwriting desirability.

Interior finish includes paint, paneling, and other wall coverings, as well as floor and ceiling materials. Underwriters must consider several interior finish characteristics, including their ability to spread fire, the fuel provided for a fire, and the smoke and noxious gases emitted while burning. Each of these characteristics affects the structure's overall property loss potential and the occupants' safety.

Relatively noncombustible interior finishes include plaster, gypsum, and wallboard. Combustible interior finishes include wood or plywood, fiber ceiling tiles, and plastic wall coverings. Even fire-resistive buildings can have an interior finish that is highly combustible, such as an office with elaborate furnishings, draperies, and wall coverings. Certain paints, varnishes, wall-papers, and other surface coatings, when added to other combustible finishes, could contribute significantly to the building's fuel load. The **fuel load** (also called the **fire load**) indicates the expected maximum amount and type of combustible material in a given fire area, including material for structural elements and contents. Even the adhesives used in floor or ceiling tile can substantially affect a building's capacity to sustain or fuel a fire.

Interior finishing materials might be not only a property hazard but also a threat to life safety. A fire that consumes combustible interior finishes can generate highly toxic gases that circulate quickly throughout a building. For example, a 1980 fire that started in a first-floor restaurant of the MGM Grand Hotel in Las Vegas involved highly combustible finishing materials on the walls and ceilings. As they burned, these materials generated hot smoke and gases that seeped into stairwells and elevator shafts. These toxic gases were then dispersed throughout the building's twenty-six floors, killing eighty-four occupants, many on upper floors. These deaths occurred not only because the interior-finish fumes were toxic, but also because vertical openings were not properly protected.[2] Another example of the influence of interior finishes is the tragic Rhode Island nightclub fire in February 2003. In this case, pyrotechnics used as part of a musical act ignited soundproofing materials, starting a fire that engulfed the building in less than five minutes and caused almost 100 deaths.

Insulation is another construction material that can be problematic. Common fiberglass insulation is often installed with a paper backing. Insulation material can also include combustible substances such as finely chopped paper treated with fire-retardant chemicals. Combustible insulation is sometimes found in the interior walls of otherwise highly fire-resistive buildings, where it is used as a sound barrier.

Whether insulation is installed to conserve heat or to suppress sound, underwriters should try to determine its flame spread, fuel contribution, and smoke contribution characteristics. This information should be available from the insulation manufacturer. Because of rising energy costs, insulation has been added to many existing structures. Insulation can contain the heat of a fire within a building, concentrating it on structural members. Such an insulated building could, therefore, weaken and collapse more quickly than anticipated.

In addition to considering the construction materials used for interior finishes and insulation, underwriters should consider the construction materials used in roofing. A roof's exterior surface not only keeps out the

Fuel load, or fire load
The expected maximum amount of combustible material in a given area of a building, including both structural elements and contents.

weather but also provides a barrier against fires in adjacent or nearby buildings, as sparks and embers falling from fires outside the building can make contact with roofs.

Roof coverings vary in the fire resistance they provide. Asphalt shingles are probably the most common roof covering for residential buildings. Although they are somewhat combustible, they are excellent barriers to severe fire exposures when properly constructed and installed. Conversely, combustible materials such as wood shake shingles or tar paper afford almost no protection. Consequently, many municipalities prohibit using untreated wood shingles in congested sections of major metropolitan areas.[3]

Additional Construction Characteristics

Aside from analyzing a building's construction type and construction materials, underwriters must consider additional characteristics such as age, building height, fire divisions, building openings, and building codes.

The age of a building is the first additional construction characteristic that underwriters should consider. The following age factors should be noted:

- A different building code might have been in effect when the building was constructed. Consequently, the building might lack protective features and systems generally considered essential today.
- Complying with current building codes might increase the cost of making repairs after a loss.
- Heating, cooling, electrical, and fire protection systems might be obsolete.
- The building might have been intended for a different occupancy and might not be suitable for its current use.
- Conversion and remodeling might have created concealed spaces in which fire could burn undetected and spread rapidly.
- Alterations and repairs made over the years might have left unprotected openings in vertical and horizontal firestops.
- The building's condition might have deteriorated for numerous reasons, including normal wear and tear, hard use, or lack of maintenance.
- The value of an older building might be difficult to determine, especially if the builder used construction techniques and materials that are no longer available.

Although proper maintenance mitigates the effects of age and deterioration, all buildings eventually wear out. The degree of obsolescence or deterioration is directly related to the type of construction, the occupancy, the physical abuse of the building, and the quality of the owner's maintenance. A frame structure normally shows its age more quickly than a joisted masonry building. However, an office occupancy in a frame structure with good maintenance might be preferable to a fire-resistive building with minimal maintenance occupied by a foundry, for example.

Construction methods and materials have changed over time. For example, building materials used in the 1930s have long been abandoned. Forty years ago, electrical systems were designed primarily for lighting, whereas modern wiring systems are designed to handle space heating, air conditioning, computer systems, and heavy appliances.

A building that was designed for a particular commercial occupant fifty years ago might be inadequate for the business that occupies the building today. The weight of equipment and stock associated with a business might have increased since the building was designed and built. In addition to the increase in hazard that occurs because of the change in occupancy, the building's structural integrity has probably deteriorated over time.

Building height is the second additional construction characteristic that underwriters should consider. Buildings present unique problems when their height restricts the capability of the local fire service to fight fires from outside. The tallest extension ladders can reach 120 feet, but many municipal fire services are not capable of fighting a fire from the exterior of a building that exceeds 100 feet high (eight or nine floors). The National Fire Protection Association (NFPA) defines a high-rise building as one that is at least 75 feet tall.

In a high-rise building, the fire department has to fight the fire from inside—if possible. In one high-rise fire, the fire department could not approach the building because of flying glass caused by heat-shattered windows. Firefighters were forced to enter the building through a parking garage that provided access to the basement.

Controlling combustible contents in high-rise buildings is crucial. Such buildings should not contain occupancies that create a high fire hazard or a heavy fuel load. High-rise structures are commonly used as offices, apartments, and hotels, occupancies that present a low fire hazard. However, offices often store highly combustible paper files that create a high fire hazard.

High-rise structures sometimes have restaurants or bars on upper floors. Restaurants are a hazardous occupancy, and, when located on upper floors without adequate control or private protection, they constitute a significant fire hazard.

Property underwriters must realize that the fire department's first priority is the safety of a building's occupants. When lives are endangered, firefighters concentrate on human safety before fighting the fire.

When evaluating a high-rise structure, underwriters must consider the structure's fire-resistive characteristics and also the presence or absence of approved horizontal and vertical barriers designed to confine a fire to its area of origin.

A building's fire divisions are the third additional construction characteristic that underwriters should consider. While vertical integrity is the solution to many fire problems in high-rise structures, fire divisions are the analogous

Fire division

A section of a structure so well protected that fire cannot spread from that section to another, or vice versa.

Fire wall

A wall that resists the spread of fire by serving as a fire-resistive barrier.

Parapet

A vertical extension of a fire wall that extends above a roofline.

Fender wall

An extension of a fire wall through an outer wall.

solution for fires in buildings with large horizontal areas. A **fire division** is a section of a structure so well protected that fire cannot spread from that section to another. Many structures have a total horizontal area approaching one million square feet, making fire divisions critical.

A **fire wall** restricts the spread of fire by serving as a fire-resistive barrier. Interior walls might not be of sufficient fire resistance to qualify as a fire wall. Generally, fire walls must consist of at least eight inches of masonry material; however, fire wall adequacy also depends on the combustibility of building contents. A fire wall must also be free standing, which means that it must support its own weight without assistance from other building components. A load-bearing wall might not be a fire wall.

Fire walls are not effective if fire could easily spread over or around them. To prevent fire from spreading, fire walls must extend above a combustible roof and through exterior walls. Vertical extensions of a fire wall above the roofline are called **parapets**. The Factory Mutual Research Corporation (FMRC) recommends that parapets extend at least thirty inches above the roofline. Parapets can be higher or lower depending on local building codes.[4] Extensions of the fire wall through the outer walls are known as **fender walls**. They are common in frame construction that uses masonry interior fire walls to create fire divisions. In many frame apartment structures, fender walls also provide privacy to terraces and patios.

A definite firestop is a special class of fire wall that is of substantial construction. At the least, such a wall must have a minimum fire-resistance rating of four hours with no openings, even if protected.

For multiple-story buildings of fire-resistive construction, some underwriters recognize the vertical as well as horizontal firestops. Underwriters reason that a floor with a two-hour fire-resistance rating is effective in preventing the vertical spread of fire, just as fire walls are effective in preventing the horizontal spread of fire. However, because fire spreads more readily vertically than horizontally, few underwriters give the same weight to fire-resistive floors as they do to fire walls.

Building openings are the fourth additional construction characteristic that underwriters should consider. Openings that pierce firestops increase fire loss potential. Although the building's original construction might have been appropriate, electricians and heating and air conditioning contractors, for example, might have installed equipment that penetrates vertical and horizontal firestops. For example, a high-rise structure nearing completion in New York City had noncombustible structural members that were adequately protected and had at least a two-hour fire rating. Subcontractors subsequently diminished the protection of structural members by removing insulation from the structural steel members and resurfacing them with a protective coating. When a fire occurred, the steel members were weakened and required replacement. It cost several million dollars to replace major building supports in this structure.

Buildings contain many openings that, without additional protection, can violate the integrity of a fire division. These openings include doors between fire divisions, floor openings for stairs between floors, elevators, dumbwaiters, and conveyor belts. In most circumstances, fire doors can protect these openings. The most common causes of unprotected openings are oversight and poor loss control.

Openings in fire walls are sometimes needed if a building is to serve its intended purpose. If a fire wall is to perform its function, fire doors must protect those openings. Fire doors are classified based on their ability to resist fire. The classification scheme NFPA uses ranges from doors that withstand fire for three hours to those that withstand fire for one-third of an hour. Approved doors have a rating seal on the door's edge.

A fire door in a fire wall must be capable of withstanding the same fire as the wall itself. A one-hour fire door in a two-hour fire wall, for example, reduces the fire protection rating of the entire wall to one hour. A vertical opening such as an elevator or a stairwell is protected only when it is completely segregated into a separate fire division. A properly constructed elevator shaft or stairwell constitutes a building within a building.

A fire door cannot be effective if it is propped open. Each door must be automatically self-closing and unobstructed. Doors that must be left open to permit efficient industrial operations are fitted with fusible links that melt and release the door when the temperature reaches a predetermined level. This permits the doors to close automatically when exposed to the heat of a fire.

Building codes are the fifth additional construction characteristic that underwriters should consider. **Building codes** are local ordinances or state statutes that regulate the construction of buildings within a municipality, county, or state. Well-designed and properly enforced building codes can reduce insured losses, especially from such causes of loss as windstorm and earthquake.

Building codes
Local ordinances or state statutes that regulate the construction of buildings within a municipality, county, or state.

Until recently, underwriters usually had to rely on their own resources to evaluate the effectiveness of building-code enforcement. ISO has developed the Building Code Effectiveness Grading Schedule (BCEGS). The BCEGS program includes grades from 1 to 10, indicating the effectiveness of a community's building code. The schedule emphasizes mitigation of losses resulting from natural hazards, such as wind and earthquakes. A BCEGS grade of 1 indicates a municipality with exemplary commitment to building-code enforcement.[5]

Occupancy

Construction is the first area underwriters analyze in the COPE model. Occupancy is the second. Like construction, a building's occupancy affects property loss frequency and severity. The specific type of personal property, or contents, on insured premises clearly influences property loss potential. Most occupancies are subject to common hazards and special hazards, discussed next. Some occupancies, such as restaurants, have unique hazards, discussed at the end of this section.

Occupancy Categories

Underwriters have traditionally grouped occupancies into the following six categories to help analyze their hazards:

1. Habitational
2. Office
3. Institutional
4. Mercantile
5. Service
6. Manufacturing

The first occupancy category is the habitational occupancy. Habitational occupancies include apartments, hotels, motels, and nursing homes. Habitational occupancies are often in the control of someone other than the building owner, so detecting or controlling hazards can be difficult. Often, superior habitational occupancy results when the owner performs most of the building maintenance. Such maintenance demonstrates to the underwriter that the owner cares about the building's condition. Also, regular maintenance permits the owner regular access to occupant-controlled areas that might have deteriorated because of tenant neglect. Unfavorable conditions that are identified can then be corrected.

Habitational occupancies, especially those in the hospitality industry, are often affected by fluctuations in the economy. The owner's financial stability correlates directly with the business's vacancy rate. An account's vacancy rate can be evaluated by comparing it with the average vacancy rate of similar operations in the area.

The second occupancy category is the office occupancy. Office occupancy is a relatively low-hazard category. Materials found in offices are usually of limited combustibility and only slightly susceptible to damage. Buildings used primarily for office occupancies can have unusual features, such as restaurants or heliports. Likewise, office occupancies can exist in any type of structure and often share the building with other occupancies.

The third occupancy category is the institutional occupancy. Institutional occupancies include schools, churches, hospitals, and property owned by governmental entities. Governmental entities often operate habitational properties such as public housing and nursing homes. Institutional occupancies also include special-purpose facilities such as prisons and police and fire stations. Risk retention groups, municipal pools, and other alternative risk-transfer programs are commonly used to insure public entities. To avoid adverse selection, an underwriter might sometimes need to determine why institutional property is being submitted for a traditional insurance program.

The fourth occupancy category is the mercantile occupancy. Mercantile occupancies include businesses that buy and sell goods and merchandise, whether wholesale or retail. Department stores, clothing stores, hardware stores, specialty shops, and grocery stores are examples of mercantile occupancies. The combustibility of a mercantile operation's contents varies by type of stock sold. A sporting goods store might stock ammunition and camping-stove fuel. Hardware stores and home centers normally have large quantities of flammables and combustibles, such as paints, varnishes, solvents, lumber, curtains, and wallpaper. The stock of mercantile occupancies is usually of significant value and is susceptible to fire, smoke, and water damage. Clothing is especially subject to severe loss from smoke and water damage, and a hardware store's stock can rust from the water used in fighting a fire. Health authorities usually require food exposed to fire and smoke to be withdrawn from sale. Therefore, a small fire can produce a large loss in this occupancy category.

The fifth occupancy category is the service organization category. Service occupancies include businesses that perform an activity or a service for the customer rather than create or sell a product. This category includes dry cleaners and auto service stations. The hazards presented by a service occupancy are usually specific to the service being performed. Dry cleaners, for example, have several occupancy hazards. Lint accumulation presents a fire and an explosion hazard. Dry cleaners also have large boilers for the hot water used in cleaning, and irons and presses could serve as ignition sources. Many of the solvents used in dry cleaning are flammable and need to be handled and stored properly.

The sixth occupancy category is manufacturing operations. Manufacturers convert raw stock into finished products. The hazards of occupancies in this category vary widely by the product being manufactured. For example, a steel manufacturer has blast furnaces, rolling mills, and associated steel processing equipment, while a pasta manufacturer has an extensive drying process that creates a severe dust hazard.

Characteristics of Contents

Different types of occupancies present different types of underwriting concerns based on the characteristics of the contents at the insured location. The loss potential of a particular occupancy can be evaluated by examining the contents' ignition sources, combustibility, and damageability.

Ignition sources are the first characteristic of contents that underwriters should evaluate. Ignition sources provide the means for a fire to start. Underwriters must know the principal sources of ignition associated with the occupancy or the use of the covered building. Potential ignition sources include the following:

- *Friendly fires that escape containment.* Hostile fires can result from "friendly" open flames (such as in a fireplace) and heaters, smoking, lamps, furnaces, and ovens and space heaters, as well as from welding and cutting torches.

- *Friction that generates enough heat to ignite nearby combustible material.* Sources of friction include hot bearings, rubbing belts, grinding, shredding, picking, polishing, cutting, and drilling.
- *Electricity that produces sparks or heat that can ignite exposed combustibles.* Static electricity frequently causes sparks. Lighting fixtures, overloaded circuits, and worn wiring can release potentially damaging amounts of heat.
- *Certain chemical reactions, called exothermic reactions, that produce heat sufficient to cause ignition.*[6] Sources of exothermic reactions include substances such as magnesium or phosphorus, resulting in fires that are difficult to contain and extinguish.

Many industrial occupancies have obvious ignition sources as well as other, more subtle hazards.

Combustibility is a second characteristic of contents that underwriters should evaluate. The contents' combustibility determines how quickly the material ignites, the rate at which a fire spreads, and the intensity or amount of heat a fire generates. Gasoline, for example, ignites easily, spreads fire quickly, and burns with explosive intensity.

Materials that are highly combustible include the following:

- Light combustible materials such as thin plywood, shingles, shavings, paper, cotton, and other fibers
- Combustible dusts such as those produced when refinishing bowling alley lanes or refining flour
- Flammable liquids
- Combustible gases such as hydrogen
- Materials subject to spontaneous combustion
- Explosive materials, acids, and oxidizing agents[7]

The combustibility of a building's contents affects the underwriting desirability of the building. Regardless of the contents' combustibility, the insured's management practices in controlling its hazards can make a significant difference in the acceptability of the account.

Damageability is a third characteristic of contents that underwriters should evaluate. Damageability includes more than the ability to burn. Property that is not burned might still be damaged by smoke or by water used to extinguish the fire. The damageability of contents is a major underwriting consideration when determining the probable maximum fire loss to contents. Even a small and quickly extinguishable fire can cause a severe loss to highly damageable contents like expensive clothing, furniture, or electronic equipment.

Occupancy Hazards

The physical hazards that any occupancy presents can be classified into two categories: common hazards and special hazards. **Common hazards** exist in almost every occupancy. Underwriters generally recognize four broad (though not mutually exclusive) sources of common hazards:

1. Housekeeping practices
2. Heating equipment
3. Electrical equipment
4. Smoking

The first source of common hazards is housekeeping practices. Every occupancy generates waste and trash. Housekeeping practices hazards include uncollected litter, improper storage, and improper disposal. Uncollected litter can contribute significantly to the spread of fire. Paper, oily items, packing materials, and discarded smoking materials are common examples of this hazard. Many industrial operations use significant amounts of lubricant that produce oily waste and litter. Janitorial work frequently involves oily substances or is performed where oil and grease are present. An accumulation of greasy soot in vents and flues, particularly over cooking stoves, is a significant hazard.

Usually, wastes must be stored temporarily. Depending on the material and the nature of the storage, the waste's concentration and confinement can increase or decrease the hazard. When neatly stacked and enclosed, paper and cardboard, for example, resist burning better than the same material piled haphazardly and loosely. However, oily materials in a confined space are subject to spontaneous combustion. Good housekeeping also requires separating materials that react with one another. Trash and waste should be stored in noncombustible containers.

Incinerating waste on the insured premises requires special precautions. Incinerators are an ignition source. Mixtures of wastes present special problems, because some explode when burned or emit toxic gases. A properly designed and operating incinerator can control these hazards.

The second source of common hazards is heating equipment. Furnaces and other heating equipment present a hazard in that they are potential sources of ignition. The hazard exists primarily in the equipment's burners or heating elements; however, the equipment itself and the pipes, ducts, and flues leading from it also radiate heat. Some sources of heat present greater hazards than others. Wood-burning stoves and salamanders (portable heaters), for example, present a greater hazard than gas furnaces, because fuel cannot be controlled or withdrawn once added to the fire. Sparks from wood-burning stoves and portable heaters can also ignite nearby combustible material.

Common hazards
Hazards existing in almost every class of business occupancy, usually referring specifically to (1) housekeeping, (2) heating equipment, (3) electrical equipment, and (4) smoking.

The third source of common hazards is electrical equipment. The NFPA reports that most of the fires started by electrical motors and appliances are caused by careless use, improper installation, or poor maintenance. Management's interest in regular maintenance is a major factor in fire loss prevention.

The fourth source of common hazards is smoking. The fire hazard presented by smoking and lit cigarettes increases as the number of persons passing through the premises increases. This hazard is also affected by the organization's smoking policy. Health concerns unrelated to fire safety have led many organizations to prohibit indoor smoking, but smoking still remains a significant cause of fire losses.

To control fire caused by smoking and matches, smoking must be prohibited in certain areas, and cigarettes, cigars, and matches must be handled safely where smoking is permitted. Management's smoking policy and its enforcement are important in controlling this hazard. Smoking illegal substances presents additional problems; because these smokers are already breaking rules, they sometimes choose no-smoking areas where they are unlikely to be observed.

In addition to common hazards, occupancies have special hazards, special hazards of the class, and special hazards of the risk. Hazards that increase the likely frequency or severity of loss but that are typical for the type of occupancy are called **special hazards of the class**. Examples include cooking in a restaurant or using volatile chemicals in a manufacturing plant.

Special hazards of the class
Hazards that are typical for the class of loss exposures.

Almost every class of occupancy has a hazardous activity that can reasonably be expected based on the nature of the occupancy. Underwriters must be familiar with the operations and hazards that are typical of the classes they handle.

Special hazards of the risk
Hazards that are created by the activities of a particular business and that are not typical of other businesses with which it would be classed.

Some businesses engage in activities that are not typical of other businesses in their class. Those activities create **special hazards of the risk**. These hazards are neither contemplated by the underwriter nor considered in standard rates for that class. A maintenance garage for a large fleet of trucks or taxicabs, for example, might contain a small body shop with welding equipment. The garage creates special hazards of the class, but the auto body work, typically performed by an auto body shop, creates special hazards of the risk. Identifying special hazards of the risk usually requires a physical inspection of the insured's business.

Protection

After construction and occupancy, protection is the third area in the COPE model that underwriters analyze. The quantity and quality of fire protection available to individual properties vary widely. Fire protection is of two types:

1. Public or municipal protection provided by towns and cities
2. Private protection provided by the property owner or occupant

Although some exceptions exist, dwellings and small commercial buildings depend almost entirely on public protection, while large commercial buildings have private fire protection systems supplemented by public protection.

Public Protection

Public fire protection is defined as fire protection equipment and services made available through governmental authority to all properties within a defined area. The organization of public fire protection varies by community. Municipalities and sometimes counties often provide protection to all properties within their political boundaries. However, fire district boundaries are sometimes drawn where they make the most effective use of available equipment and personnel.

AAIS personal and commercial insurance fire rates recognize fire protection classifications, simply defined as follows:

- *Protected*—Building is located within 1,000 feet of a fire hydrant and is within five road miles of a responding fire department.
- *Partially Protected*—Building is located more than 1,000 feet from a fire hydrant and is within five road miles of a responding fire department.
- *Unprotected*—Building is located in an area that is classified as neither protected nor partially protected.[8]

ISO independently evaluates public fire protection and publishes a public protection classification (PPC) for each community. The PPC is an integral part of the ISO property insurance rating process. Most underwriters need only a basic understanding of the municipal grading system, but more extensive knowledge permits them to evaluate the relationship between private and public protection.

The PPC system rates the quality of a public fire service on a scale of 1 to 10. The scale measures the adequacy of the equipment available to the public fire service, the water supply, and response time available for property in a particular area. Class 1 represents the ideal; it is not reasonable to expect any community to achieve this rating. Classes 1 through 8 apply to properties in protected communities, while Classes 9 and 10 apply to unprotected communities. Properties that are located too far from a water supply adequate for fire suppression fall into Class 9. Properties that have no public fire protection service available fall into Class 10.

A single public protection class does not always apply to the property in an entire municipality or fire district. Geographic features sometimes prevent prompt fire service response to property in some areas, and water mains and hydrants in some areas might not extend to all properties that a given fire service protects. These considerations produce a higher public protection class number (indicating lower-quality public fire protection).

A given property might also have a public protection class inferior to the community as a whole, for two principal reasons. First, the property might

Public fire protection
Fire protection equipment and services made available through governmental authority to all properties within a defined area.

present a loss exposure to fires that are more challenging than the fire service is equipped to handle, such as flammable metals or large quantities of flammable liquids. Second, the fire service might lack adequate year-round access to the property, especially when the property owner maintains private access roads. The owners of some seasonal properties in cold climates make no arrangements for snow plowing because they are closed for the winter. Snow accumulation on the roads periodically makes such properties inaccessible to fire services. The PPC considers this and assigns a class of 9 or 10 for those properties.

Private Protection

Property insurance underwriting evaluates not only public fire protection systems but also private fire protection systems. Fire protection systems consist of prevention, detection, and suppression measures.

Prevention

Many measures can be taken to prevent fires from occurring or to minimize the damage that fires cause. Fires can be prevented by controlling heat sources and by separating fuel and heat. Fires can also be prevented by controlling arson. Various building design features, discussed at the beginning of the chapter under "Construction," can limit or slow the vertical or horizontal spread of fire or reduce the damageability of property exposed to fire.

Heat sources can sometimes be reduced or eliminated. Sometimes furnaces, forges, or kilns are larger or hotter than necessary, or the number of heating devices can be reduced. Sometimes hot water, for example, can be used instead of an open flame. When heat is a byproduct, various options, such as fluorescent lighting, can sometimes reduce heat sources. Cooling systems can dissipate heat energy. Electrical energy can be controlled with circuit breakers and adequate grounding.

Fuel and heat can often be separated by ensuring that flammable or combustible materials are kept away from fixed-location heat sources. For example, trash, paper, and flammable liquids should not be stored in the furnace room. Restaurant cooking stoves and their vent systems should be cleaned periodically to prevent the buildup of greasy deposits. Mobile heat sources, from equipment such as welding torches and portable heaters, present a special challenge because the hazards continually change. Such equipment is taken where it is needed and is not necessarily restricted to use in areas free of fuels or combustible materials.

Detection

Early fire detection is important because the size of a fire increases exponentially with time, and large fires are more difficult to suppress than small fires. Major detection systems include (1) a guard service with a clock system, (2) a private patrol service, (3) smoke and heat detectors, (4) an automatic local alarm, and (5) a central station alarm or remote station system. Sprinkler systems often have a local or central station alarm that is triggered by the flow of water within the system.

The effectiveness of a guard service depends on its guards' alertness. A clock system verifies that the guard makes regular rounds. Guards carry devices that time-mark their routes through the premises. The disadvantage of a basic clock system is that the watchperson's alertness cannot be determined until the device is reviewed. Many businesses have connected certain locations to a central station. If these locations are not checked by the watchperson, central-station personnel follow up.

Small merchants or businesses often employ private patrol services to check for break-ins. In many areas, business and industry associations provide private patrol services as a member benefit. A guard visits each business several times during the night to ensure that all doors and windows are secure and that fire has not broken out. Some private patrol services employ a clock system to verify that guards complete their assigned rounds on schedule. Although they provide some security, private patrols are unlikely to discover a fire on a timely basis.

The use of smoke detectors in private residences and businesses has increased significantly with the development of inexpensive, battery-powered smoke detectors. NFPA standards require that smoke detectors be wired directly to an AC power source in all newly constructed dwellings or buildings. NFPA 74 also recommends that residential smoke detectors be located outside each sleeping area, on each floor serving as living quarters, and in the basement. Most smoke detectors perform independently, sounding an alarm only at the location of the detected smoke. More advanced systems connect the smoke detectors so that all the alarms sound simultaneously. Often, these advanced systems also serve as burglar alarms by sounding a different alarm tone to indicate break-ins.

Heat detectors can be operated independently of suppression devices but are most frequently combined with devices like automatic sprinkler systems. Heat detectors are slow to activate, which makes them less desirable than smoke detectors. Heat detectors are used when other detection devices are not effective or are triggered too easily. Small storage rooms in which heat buildup would be rapid or kitchens in which some smoke is a usual byproduct might be better protected by heat detectors. Heat detectors activate when heat causes a physical or an electrical charge in a material or gas. They can also respond to a specific temperature or to a predetermined rate of increase in the ambient temperature.

To perform their intended function, smoke and heat detectors must be connected to an alarm, which can be local, central station, remote station, or proprietary. A **local fire alarm system**, triggered by smoke or heat, sounds an alarm inside or outside the building. The system relies on occupants or passersby to report the alarm to fire or police officials. Consequently, local alarms are not considered effective in reporting fires.

A **central station system** is a private service with personnel who monitor the systems of commercial establishments and, sometimes, residences. When an

Local fire alarm system
A detection system, triggered by smoke or heat, that sounds a gong, siren, or another audible alert inside or outside the building.

Central station system
A private detection service that monitors the systems of multiple businesses and/or residences and that calls appropriate authorities or dispatches its own personnel when an alarm is activated.

alarm is activated, the service either calls the appropriate authorities or dispatches its own personnel to investigate. Central station alarm systems eliminate the need for human intervention at the scene and offer a better solution to fire detection than local alarms. A central station alarm, with or without sprinklers, greatly increases the likelihood of a rapid response to a fire, which should greatly reduce both insured and uninsured losses. The disadvantage of this method is its relative cost.

Remote station systems and *proprietary alarms* are similar to central station systems, except that they do not signal a commercially operated central station. A remote alarm directly signals the local police and fire stations. A proprietary system directly signals a receiving station located on the protected premises, notifying on-site personnel.

Suppression

Fire detection devices can alert people to evacuate the property. But for property underwriting purposes, prompt fire detection does no good unless the fire that has been detected can then be suppressed. Public protection was discussed previously. Private fire suppression methods fall into four categories: (1) portable extinguishers, (2) standpipes and hoses, (3) automatic sprinkler systems, and (4) private fire brigades.

Portable fire extinguishers should be available in every business and residence. To be effective, extinguishers must be maintained regularly, and users must be trained to operate them. Most fire extinguishers are classed as "ABC," meaning they can be used on all types of fires. Class "D" extinguishers are designed for fires involving flammable metals. NFPA publishes standards that indicate the number and type of portable fire extinguishers that a property should have based on size and occupancy.

Standpipe and hose systems consist of water supply pipes located inside buildings and equipped with standard fire department connections at regular intervals. In a multistory structure, standpipes are commonly located in stairwells or fire towers with a hose connection at each floor landing. When the building covers a large horizontal area, standpipe hose connections are typically spaced at regular intervals throughout the floor. Standpipe systems usually have fire hoses attached so that both the fire service and the building's occupants can use them. A valve at the standpipe station controls water flow to the hoses. Even without attached hoses, standpipes are an invaluable aid to firefighters. By delivering water to the interior areas and upper floors of a building, they eliminate the need for firefighters to drag charged hoses across long distances to reach a fire. Standpipe systems can draw their water from the building water supply, but they do not always contain water. All standpipe systems have a fire department connection, sometimes called a "siamese connection," outside the building. This allows the fire service to pump additional water into wet standpipe systems for more effective fire suppression.

Automatic sprinkler systems are the most effective means of suppressing a fire. **Automatic sprinkler systems** consist of a series of interconnected valves and pipes with sprinkler heads. Commonly, each sprinkler head contains a heat-sensing element that responds individually to the heat generated by a fire. Contrary to what is depicted in some television shows and movies, only the sprinkler heads directly exposed to the fire's heat release water. The exception is a deluge system, discussed later, which is used only under special circumstances.

Automatic sprinkler systems respond more quickly than any other fire suppression system and deliver water where it is needed. Sprinkler systems always require their own water supply, but they also come equipped with an external fire department connection to supplement water and pressure.

Most automatic fire sprinkler systems are **wet pipe sprinkler systems**, meaning that the pipes always contain water under pressure. The water is released immediately when a sprinkler head opens. In areas in which the sprinkler lines are exposed to temperatures below freezing, a dry pipe system might be more appropriate. The pipes in **dry pipe sprinkler systems** contain compressed air or an inert gas that holds a valve in the water line shut. The opening of a sprinkler head allows water to flow through the previously dry piping to the sprinkler head. Dry pipe systems respond more slowly to fire than wet pipe systems because the gas must leave the system before water can flow through the sprinkler heads.

A dry pipe system is *not* advisable if water damage to sensitive property is a concern. When a fire can be expected to involve flammable liquids or live electrical equipment, extinguishants like dry powder and carbon dioxide are more appropriate and effective. Properly protected restaurants, for example, use dry chemical or CO_2 extinguishing systems, often called Ansul systems (Ansul is the leading manufacturer of such systems), to protect hoods over cooking equipment and ducts that disperse the heated air and combustion products. Water is not an appropriate extinguishing agent where heavy accumulations of grease are common.

Some property owners have gas extinguishing systems. The gas disrupts the chemical reaction in a fire, thereby eliminating the extensive damage to contents caused by water from sprinkler systems.

Pre-action sprinkler systems, used where property is highly susceptible to water damage from damaged sprinklers or piping, consist of a sprinkler system controlled by an automatic fire detection device, such as a smoke detector or heat detector. The sprinkler system valve remains closed until the smoke or heat detector opens it in response to fire conditions. Before the system discharges water, the detection component must sense a fire, and heat must activate a sprinkler head. **Deluge sprinkler systems** are similar to pre-action systems, except that sprinkler heads are always open. When a fire activates a detection device, water is simultaneously discharged from all sprinklers in the system, flooding or "deluging" the protected areas.

Automatic sprinkler systems
Fire sprinkler systems with a series of interconnected valves and pipes with sprinkler heads. Each sprinkler head usually contains a heat-sensing element that responds individually to the heat generated by a fire.

Wet pipe sprinkler systems
Automatic fire sprinkler systems with pipes that always contain water under pressure, which is released immediately when a sprinkler head opens.

Dry pipe sprinkler systems
Automatic fire sprinkler systems with pipes that contain compressed air or another inert gas that holds a valve in the water line shut until an open sprinkler head releases the gas and allows water to flow through the previously dry pipe to the sprinkler head.

Pre-action sprinkler systems
Automatic fire sprinkler systems with automatic valves controlled by smoke or heat detectors.

Deluge sprinkler systems
Automatic fire sprinkler systems with valves that remain open and that are controlled by an automatic fire detection device, such as a smoke or heat detector.

Both sprinkler and standpipe systems can be connected to an alarm that alerts a monitoring station to the flow of water through the pipes. A sprinkler alarm can be connected directly to the fire department. Both sprinkler and standpipe alarms can be connected to a central station that monitors them constantly and responds to any water flow. Sprinkler and standpipe alarms provide early notification of both fires and sprinkler leakage. Some alarms can still be connected only to a local alarm outside a building.

Private fire brigades are found only in the largest industrial complexes, such as petrochemical plants, and rural areas in which municipal fire protection is unavailable or considered inadequate. Underwriters should evaluate private fire departments in the same way that they evaluate public fire departments. They should gather information about the number and training of personnel as well as about the amount and type of equipment and its location within the industrial complex.

External Loss Exposures

External loss exposures
Loss exposures outside the area owned or controlled by the insured.

Construction, occupancy, and protection are the first three areas in the COPE model that underwriters analyze. **External loss exposures** are the last area. External loss exposures are outside the area owned or controlled by the insured. Single-occupancy loss exposures and multiple-occupancy loss exposures present different underwriting challenges.

Single-Occupancy Loss Exposures

A single-occupancy loss exposure exists when the property being underwritten consists of a single building, fire division, or group of buildings, all owned or controlled by the policyholder. The external loss exposures come from adjoining properties. One example is the loss exposure created by buildings situated close enough to permit a fire in that exposing building to spread to the insured (exposed) building. Another example is the loss exposure created by combustible materials such as brush, woodlands, or trash surrounding the open areas of the exposing building. External loss exposures are by definition outside the policyholder's control. Often, little can be done from a loss control standpoint to reduce external loss exposures.

Exposing Buildings

An exposing building is one that significantly increases the possibility of a fire in the insured building. A fire that erupts in an exposing building is an exposure fire. In addition to the intensity and duration of the exposure fire, other factors that influence the severity of an exposure fire in an exposing building include the following:

1. Type of construction of the exposing (adjacent) and exposed (insured) buildings
2. Height and width of the exposure fire

3. Openings in the exterior walls of the exposing and exposed buildings

4. Type of combustible contents in the exposure fire

5. Protection for openings in the walls of the exposed building

6. Interior finish of the exposing and exposed buildings

7. Distance between the exposing and exposed buildings

8. Shielding effects of noncombustible construction between the exposing and exposed buildings

9. Wind direction and velocity at the time of the fire

10. Public and private fire protection[9]

Fire walls, fire doors, special barriers, and parapets reduce the probability that an external fire will spread to the insured property. Clear space between buildings, good water supply, quick response from the fire department, and internal and external automatic sprinkler systems are additional methods of controlling external loss exposures. The methods by which the loss exposure between two buildings can be reduced include the following:

- Complete automatic sprinkler system protection
- Blank walls of noncombustible materials facing the exposure
- Barrier walls (self-supporting) between the insured building and the exposure
- Extension of exterior masonry walls to form parapets or fender walls
- Automatic outside water curtains for combustible walls
- Elimination of openings by filling them with construction equivalent to the wall
- Glass block panels in openings
- Wired glass in steel-sash windows (fixed or automatic closing) in openings
- Automatic or deluge sprinklers outside over openings
- Automatic (rolling steel) fire shutters on openings
- Automatic fire doors on door openings
- Automatic fire dampers on wall openings[10]

Adequate clear space enables firefighters to respond properly to a fire in an exposing building and reduces the likelihood that the heat from the fire will ignite the exposed building. Clear space should be free of materials that could provide fuel for a fire. An alley filled with trash, for example, would not qualify as adequate clear space.

Other Loss Exposures

Other external loss exposures can markedly increase the likelihood of a fire loss. Examples include loss exposures created by lumberyards, gasoline storage tanks, brush, or woodlands. An open area surrounding a structure and containing nothing but brush presents an external loss exposure, and major brush fires have swept through developed areas with catastrophic results.

Multiple-Occupancy Loss Exposures

In a multiple-occupancy building, persons other than the policyholder own or control portions of the fire division that contains the insured property. If the policyholder occupies part of a building that is divided from the rest of the building by an approved fire wall, that part is considered a single occupancy; the rest of the building is then treated as an exposing fire division. However, if the policyholder occupies part of a building with combustible walls separating the insured property from the other occupancies, a multiple-occupancy loss exposure exists. For example, shopping centers commonly have walls that can be moved to resize store areas to meet the needs of new occupants. Most office buildings occupied by more than one tenant are also multiple-occupancy buildings.

When evaluating a multiple-occupancy building, underwriters consider the occupancy class of the other occupants. In a typical commercial shopping center of brick construction, for example, a shoe store could be exposed by a restaurant or a paint store in adjacent portions of the same fire division.

Another factor to consider is the amount of protection available against fire originating in exposing occupancies. Even when no fire wall separates occupancies, a noncombustible wall provides some protection. However, the walls separating some occupancies could be no more than drywall partitions, and the entire fire division might have one continuous attic.

UNDERWRITING PROPERTY VALUES

The insurance buyer, with the insurance producer's help, requests a limit of insurance to provide adequate protection. Property underwriters confirm the adequacy of the policy limits. This section explains why it is important for underwriters to verify that property is properly insured to value.

Property insurance provides coverage to the extent of the insurable interest of insured parties. Property insurance policies invariably include a valuation provision specifying the method used to determine the insured property's value at the time of loss. The most common property valuation methods are replacement cost and actual cash value. Actual cash value is sometimes defined as replacement cost minus depreciation; factors other than depreciation are also often considered. Property is insured to value when the amount of insurance on that property approximates the policyholder's insurable interest in the property's insurable value.

An underinsured property owner—one who has not purchased insurance to value—will not be completely indemnified if the property is destroyed. This is the most obvious reason to purchase insurance to value. However, total losses are relatively uncommon, and lower limits of insurance have lower premiums. Therefore, insurance policies include coinsurance clauses and other insurance-to-value provisions to encourage purchasing insurance to value. The coinsurance clause provides this encouragement in the form of a penalty: An insured who does not purchase insurance to, say, 80 percent of the property's insurable value will not recover in full for a partial loss to that property. Ninety percent and 100 percent coinsurance provisions are also common. Comparable provisions in homeowners, dwelling, and businessowners policies penalize policyholders by providing actual cash value coverage rather than replacement cost coverage for property that is underinsured.

Insurable value, which is based on the valuation provision in the insurance policy, is different from *market value* or *book value.* The property's market value is based on the price it could command in a free market. For example, a building's market value depends heavily on its location and the value of the land on which it is situated. Book value, used for accounting and tax purposes, includes the acquisition cost of property and accounting depreciation, which generally have little bearing on the insurable value.

Insurance to value provides better policyholder protection against a total loss, and policyholders who are insured to value will not face a coinsurance penalty at the time of loss. The insurer also benefits when underwriters encourage insurance to value because insurance to value promotes the following:

- Higher limits of property insurance—These limits generate higher property insurance premiums that properly reflect the insurer's loss exposures.

- An adequately insured book of business—An underinsured book of business generates inadequate premiums that, in turn, can contribute to an underwriting loss.

- Competitive status for the insurer—An underwriting loss caused by underinsurance can indicate the need for higher property insurance rates, which, in turn, make the insurer less competitive.

Clearly, it is preferable to insure to value with rates that reflect the loss exposure than to underinsure property at inflated rates. Underwriters can confirm insurance to value on new business by using various appraisal tools, including tools that might be available from the insurer's loss control department. Various vendors offer building and contents valuation services for a fee.

Having adequate limits of insurance on new business does not necessarily ensure ongoing insurance to value. Underwriters must also consider the effects, if any, of inflation. At policy renewal, the underwriter should reassess the values exposed to loss and adjust limits accordingly.

UNDERWRITING PROPERTY CAUSES OF LOSS

Property insurance underwriters almost always evaluate the estimated probability and extent of damage by the fire cause of loss and the related causes of loss of lightning and explosion. ISO statistics show that the fire, lightning, wind, and hail causes of loss accounted for 55 percent of homeowners insurance incurred loss dollars in 2000.[11] Other important causes of loss that must be considered are vandalism and malicious mischief, water damage, collapse, flood, and earthquake.

Fire

Underwriters use the COPE model—construction, occupancy, protection, and exposure—primarily to analyze the fire cause of loss and to estimate the most severe fire loss that the policyholder is likely to sustain. The two most commonly used measures of loss severity are amount subject and probable maximum loss, discussed subsequently. Underwriters use the policy's coverage and limits, along with the amount subject and probable maximum loss, to determine the amount the insurer might be obligated to pay if a covered loss occurs.

Amount subject
The total value exposed to loss at any one location from any one event.

Amount subject represents a worst-case scenario—the total value exposed to loss from any one event. **Amount subject** measures the loss exposure to a single loss and varies by cause of loss. The insurer's amount subject can be different from the insured's amount subject. For example, an insured might have two locations one-half mile apart. A single fire probably would not affect both locations, but they both might be susceptible to total loss from the same tornado. If each location contains a single fire division, then the amount subject for fire insurance at each location would be the total value at risk at that location. The amount subject for a tornado, however, would be the sum of the values exposed to loss at both locations. If the policyholder insured each location with a different insurer or retained a substantial share of the property loss exposure, then the policyholder's and the insurer's amounts subject would not be the same. Likewise, if the insurer provided property insurance for more than one insured at a location, then the insurer would have an amount subject to fire loss greater than that of any single insured. This situation can result, for example, when an insurer covers both landlord and tenant, or when an insurer covers several stores within a shopping center's single fire division.

Probable maximum loss (PML)
An estimate of the largest likely loss.

After evaluating the amount subject, an underwriter uses experience and judgment to determine the largest likely loss, or **probable maximum loss (PML)**. For example, an underwriter might decide that a total loss to a high-rise fire-resistive structure is conceivable but unlikely. (The World Trade Center twin towers' collapse vividly illustrated that a total loss to a high-rise building is possible even when considered unlikely.) The underwriter would therefore set the PML at less than the full value of all insured property at that location. Determining the amount subject and probable maximum loss requires best guesses of an insurer's loss exposure. Underwriters following similar logic in amount subject and PML calculations might develop different values because judgment plays a crucial role in their determination. Probable maximum loss calculations are subjective estimates. Actual losses commonly exceed the PML that an underwriter has determined for a particular loss exposure.

Lightning

Insurance policies covering fixed-location property on land have almost always paired lightning with fire. Lightning frequently causes a fire, and even trained observers cannot always determine which cause of loss caused the damage. However, lightning can and does cause insured damage indepen-dently of fire. For example, lightning can strike an electricity transmission line and generate a power surge. The surge can cause extensive damage inside buildings serviced by the power line. Damage by high voltage to an insured's electrical system can destroy it, even if no fire ensues.

Even though lightning strikes cannot be prevented, various loss control measures can mitigate their effect. A property owner can limit surge damage by installing an external surge protector on power lines entering the building. Many types of electrical equipment, such as computers and electric motors, warrant interior surge protectors. Properly installed and maintained lightning rods can reduce the probability that a lightning strike will result in a fire. Underwriters should determine whether such devices are in place for proper-ties in areas prone to lightning strikes.

Explosion

Explosion, defined as any violent expansion of gases into the atmosphere, is another cause of loss closely related to fire. The most common types of explosion are the following:

- Combustion explosions (ignition of flammable clouds)
- Pressure explosions (rupture of confined spaces)

Combustion Explosions

The first type of explosion that concerns underwriters is a combustion explosion caused by fire that develops so rapidly that gases expand violently and explode. Combustion explosions occur when a flammable cloud of dust, vapor, mist, or gas encounters an ignition source.

Underwriters evaluate the techniques an applicant or a policyholder has in place to prevent combustion explosions. Preventing combustible clouds from forming is the surest protection against combustion explosions. Fire can occur only when the mixture of fuel and oxygen falls within its flammable range. Two effective techniques for preventing combustion explosions are to limit the amount of fuel in the atmosphere and to restrict the supply of oxygen that reaches the fuel.

Underwriters also look for techniques that minimize damage from the explosions that do occur. Venting minimizes explosion damage by relieving pressure on the building itself and by directing the force of the explosion away from property susceptible to damage. Isolating the potential source of an explosion by placing spaces or barriers between the source and the prop-erty that might be damaged is also effective.

Pressure Explosions

A second type of explosion that concerns underwriters is a pressure explo-sion, which occurs when a container bursts because it cannot contain internal pressure. Explosion of pressure vessels is the principal underwriting concern. Pressure vessels common to most occupancies include water heaters, tanks, boilers, and process equipment in manufacturing occupancies. Equipment breakdown insurance covers explosions of steam boilers and piping, while commercial property forms insure against explosions of other pressure vessels. Homeowners forms protect against both.

Pressure explosions occur in fired vessels when heat causes the contents of the vessels to expand beyond capacity. Fired vessels include water heaters, fired kettles, and hot water boilers. Unfired pressure vessels rely on mechanical means, such as compressors, to build and maintain internal pressure. Fire that reaches a pressure vessel can cause an explosion. Although fire is the cause of loss, underwriters should evaluate this loss potential as part of the explosion loss exposure.

Windstorm

Virtually all personal and commercial property insurance policies include windstorm among the covered causes of loss. Although many windstorms cause only local damage, others cause widespread damage and qualify as catastrophes. Hurricanes and tornadoes are the two most significant causes of windstorm loss.

Windstorm is a difficult cause of loss to underwrite. Short of identifying particular susceptible geographic areas and not writing property insurance or excluding windstorm coverage in those areas, it is difficult for underwriters to limit the consequences of any windstorm that might occur.

Windstorm coverage is generally available in most parts of the United States, giving most insurers a good geographic spread of risk. In most areas, adverse selection is not a problem, partly because property owners with little loss exposure to windstorm damage purchase windstorm coverage as part of a package of causes of loss. Additionally, reinsurance is frequently used to mitigate the effects of catastrophic windstorm losses.

Hurricanes

Most hurricane damage results from the effect of high wind on exposed property. Wind-driven rain can also penetrate buildings and cause significant damage. Most of that rain enters buildings through holes the wind creates in the roof or walls, and the resulting damage is therefore covered by the windstorm cause of loss. When a hurricane comes ashore, it drives a wall of high water called a storm surge before it. Storm surges threaten primarily coastal properties, but they can also impede drainage by raising the water level in rivers, streams, and bays. Finally, the heavy rains that a hurricane produces cause flooding alone or in combination with the storm surge.

Studies of hurricane damage provide insight into effective means of controlling wind losses. Several lessons for controlling wind damage were also learned from the buildings affected by Hurricane Andrew in 1992, one of the most damaging hurricanes to hit the continental U.S. and one that resulted in insured losses of more than $15 billion in the U.S.:

- Windstorm is a more serious consideration for personal rather than commercial insurance underwriters. One- and two-family dwellings sustained most of the damage in Hurricane Andrew, while fully engineered structures fared well overall.

- A building's survival in a windstorm depends on how well its outer walls and roof keep weather out.

- Buildings that adhere to sound codes avoid or sustain only minimal windstorm damage. In Hurricane Andrew, maximum sustained winds probably did not exceed 125 miles per hour,[12] only slightly higher than the design requirement of the South Florida Building Code, which applied to the entire affected area. Structures built to code should have weathered the storm with nominal damage but did not.

- Enforcing building codes is essential in coastal areas.

Underwriters can use the BCEGS to evaluate building codes.

Because losses from hurricanes often simultaneously affect many insured properties, underwriters must do more than evaluate individual submissions. Managing a book of business is essential. Insurers must be highly aware of their aggregate loss exposures from a single storm. Several insurers became insolvent and many more were financially weakened because of Hurricane Andrew. Exhibit 5-2 shows the growth in insured hurricane losses over a fifty-year period.

Staff underwriters use computer models to project the total windstorm loss exposure for an entire book of business. This projection allows underwriters to keep this loss exposure to a level that would not weaken the insurer financially. To manage its aggregate windstorm loss exposure, an insurer has to restrict the number of loss exposures it writes in a given geographic area. An insurer can elect to restrict its writings by establishing a target expressed as a desirable market share, policy count, or total insured value.

Tornadoes

Tornadoes are small but particularly violent windstorms. No part of the United States is immune to tornado damage, but the Great Plains of the Midwest and the Southeast are most prone to it. Exhibit 5-3 illustrates tornado-activity distribution across the nation. Tornadoes occur year-round but peak in the spring, and they are random and largely unpredictable. Tornado watches and tornado warnings alert people when a windstorm is imminent. Other than taking measures like lowering awnings and protecting patio furniture, people usually can do little to protect their property when a tornado strikes.

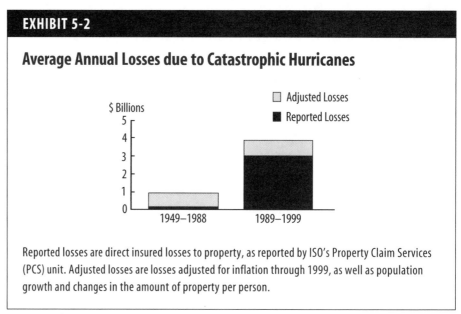

EXHIBIT 5-2

Average Annual Losses due to Catastrophic Hurricanes

Reported losses are direct insured losses to property, as reported by ISO's Property Claim Services (PCS) unit. Adjusted losses are losses adjusted for inflation through 1999, as well as population growth and changes in the amount of property per person.

Source: "A Half Century of Hurricane Experience," http://www.iso.com/studies_analyses/hurricane_experience/intro.html (accessed January 6, 2003).

Tornadoes owe their destructive power to their compact size, powerful winds, and the upward movement at the vortex wall. Their winds exceed any reasonable building standards. Tornadoes also subject property to rapid changes in wind direction and uplift forces. They can lift cars and heavy farm machinery from the ground and deposit the remains miles away. Tornadoes destroy any property squarely in their path. Buildings and property at the edge of a tornado's path could escape serious structural damage. Property close to the path can sustain minor to severe damage. As with hurricanes, underwriters must do more than evaluate individual submissions for the tornado cause of loss and need to manage this exposure on the basis of the overall book of business.

Hail

Destructive hail falls almost exclusively during violent thunderstorms. Hail-stones can be more than five inches in diameter and weigh more than one and one-half pounds. Damage to growing crops accounts for nearly 80 percent of all hail losses, but hail can also cause severe damage to auto and house windows, neon signs, and fragile structures such as greenhouses. Aluminum siding and roofing materials are particularly susceptible to hail damage.

Little can be done to prevent hail damage. However, underwriters need to be aware of the areas where hailstorms are relatively common. Property under-writers sometimes limit their writing of property coverage in areas that have historically had more than their share of hailstorms.

EXHIBIT 5-3

Total Number of Tornadoes by State—2000

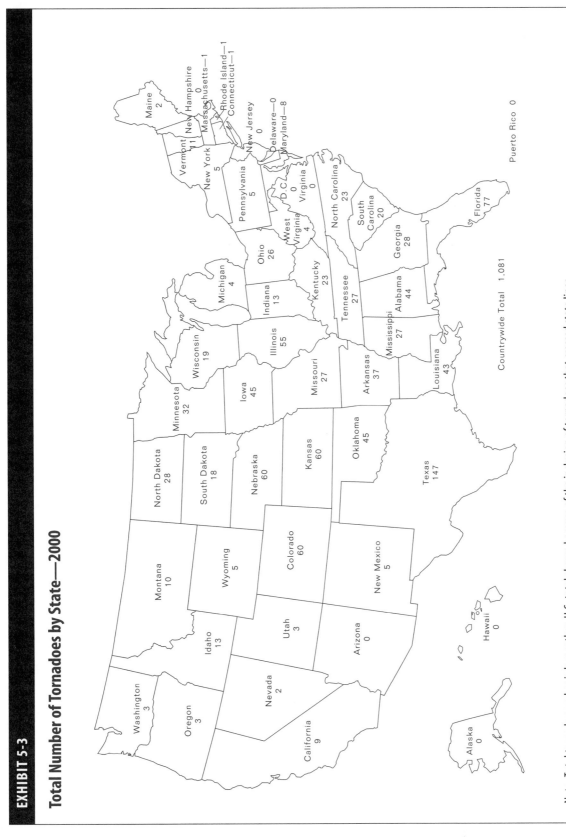

Note: Total tornado number is larger than U.S. total shown because of the inclusion of tornadoes that crossed state lines.

Source: U.S. Department of Commerce, Storm Prediction Center, National Weather Service.

Adapted with permission from *The Fact Book 2002: Property/Casualty Insurance Facts* (New York: Insurance Information Institute, 2002), p. 89.

Vandalism and Malicious Mischief

Vandalism can occur anywhere, but it is most common in urban areas. Because groups of children and young adults are more likely to commit vandalism than older adults, urban areas with many children are likely to have a high incidence of vandalism. Schools, churches, parks, playgrounds, youth centers, and other places where young people gather can be targets for vandalism; nursing homes and other geriatric institutions generally are not.

Vacant or unoccupied property also tends to attract vandals. Many property insurance policies address this cause of loss by limiting or excluding coverage on property that has been vacant for a specified period.

Despite the foregoing comments, vandalism has traditionally attracted little underwriting attention because it usually produces relatively small and infrequent losses. Loss frequency is more of an underwriting concern than severity, and an appropriately set deductible reduces the insurer's loss payments. Some observers have noted that terrorist attacks against property might be categorized as vandalism. Others have recognized that computer hacking and other cyber attacks might qualify as vandalism.

Water Damage

Many homeowners and commercial property coverage forms insure against certain types of water damage. Losses caused by accidental discharge, overflow, or leakage of water or steam from plumbing, heating, and cooling systems are the most commonly covered losses. Water damage caused by flood is usually excluded because of its catastrophic nature.

Poor maintenance causes most water-damage losses. Flat roofs are another source of water-damage losses, as water can soak through the roof covering. Damage occurs most often when water accumulates or "ponds" in the roof's low areas. In cold weather, packed snow and ice can block roof drains, preventing melted snow or ice from draining.

Although water damage occurs frequently, most claims are relatively minor. Exceptional cases occur when a leak persists over an extended time period because the leak is hidden or because the property is unoccupied, so nobody notices the leak. Water damage that is not repaired promptly can foster the growth of mold, especially in humid climates. Mold damage can require expensive remediation efforts. Mold is most likely to be a concern in buildings with a high level of human occupancy, such as apartment or hotel buildings, schools, hospitals, or offices.

Flood

Most private insurance policies covering buildings and other fixed-location real property exclude coverage for flood losses. However, other types of policies, especially those covering personal property, such as auto insurance policies and inland marine floaters of all types, typically do cover the flood cause of loss.

Floods typically occur in low-lying areas—or in areas that are low relative to the surrounding terrain—and they result when rain or snow falls faster than what the land can drain. Some locations flood annually, while others face no known flood losses. Many areas might flood no more frequently than once every one hundred years, but accurately predicting in which years those floods will occur is not possible.

Underwriters must recognize when covered property is in a location susceptible to flooding of any type. Six types of flood are common:

1. Riverine floods occur when rivers, streams, and other watercourses rise and overflow their banks. Floods can result from either heavy rainfall or snow melt upstream in their drainage basins.
2. Tidal floods arise from high tides, frequently driven by high winds offshore, and from tropical storms making landfall or passing closely offshore. They affect bays and the portions of rivers along the coast.
3. Wind floods occur wherever a strong wind holds back a large body of water from its normal drainage course and raises the water level. Back bays behind barrier islands are especially susceptible to wind floods. Water that cannot escape through normal channels can flow out of these bays across the barrier islands.
4. Rising water levels downstream can prevent drainage upstream, causing a backwater flood. Backwater floods can extend for a substantial distance upstream.
5. Ice jams sometimes develop as ice thaws and begins to move downstream. Ice jams block the flow of water, causing it to back up and to flood upstream areas. If the ice jam breaks suddenly, it can cause flooding downstream.
6. Accidental floods are caused by the failure of flood control systems. A dam might break, causing flooding downstream. Blocked floodgates and spillways cause upstream flooding.

The National Flood Insurance Program (NFIP) is managed by the Federal Insurance and Mitigation Administration (FIMA), part of the Federal Emergency Management Agency (FEMA). Through the NFIP, the federal government is the largest flood insurance underwriter in the United States.[13] Some commercial insurers provide flood coverage under commercial policies.

Information on flood causes of loss is widely available from FEMA, and protective measures can often be taken. Underwriting flood loss exposures successfully requires analyzing the known probability that a flood will occur at a certain location and then establishing a rate adequate to cover the anticipated loss exposure that the insurer assumes.

Earthquake

Many geographic regions have significant earthquake loss exposures. Underwriters must limit their total earthquake loss exposures within each such region to protect against a catastrophic loss from a single seismic event.

Earthquake underwriting considerations include three major factors:

1. Areas of earthquake activity
2. Soil conditions
3. Building design and construction

Areas of Earthquake Activity

The Pacific Coast from Alaska to California is the most seismically active area of the United States, and 90 percent of all earthquakes in the United States occur in California and western Nevada. The most severe earthquake ever recorded, however, occurred in 1811 along Missouri's New Madrid Fault.

The U.S. Geological Survey has assessed the chance of damaging seismic activity in various parts of the United States, as illustrated in Exhibit 5-4.

Soil Conditions

Buildings built on bedrock or supported on piling driven into bedrock are well protected from earthquake damage. Buildings built on consolidated soil of long standing (thousands of years), such as limestone and some clay, withstand earthquake damage better than buildings built on unconsolidated soil, such as sand, gravel, silt, and some clays. Buildings built on filled land, common in many large cities, are particularly susceptible to earthquake damage. Unconsolidated filled land (as well as certain other types of unconsolidated soils) is subject to liquefaction during an earthquake, becoming so unstable that it acts like a liquid.

Building Design and Construction

An earthquake causes horizontal stresses that weight-bearing columns and walls in most buildings are not designed to bear. Most buildings are designed to carry a vertical load, the weight of the structure and its contents. An earthquake-resistant building, on the other hand, has all of its structural members tied together securely so that the building moves horizontally as a single unit when subjected to earthquake forces. If not tied together, walls and columns can move from under the floors they were designed to support, causing the building to collapse.

Joisted masonry construction, which is rigid, is particularly susceptible to structural failure during earthquakes. A frame building, however, is more flexible and "gives" during earthquakes, often sustaining relatively minor damage, such as cracked plaster. Brick facing, stone veneer, and tile roofs often sustain earthquake damage. Tilt slab construction, which is sometimes

EXHIBIT 5-4

Seismic Potential for the Contiguous United States

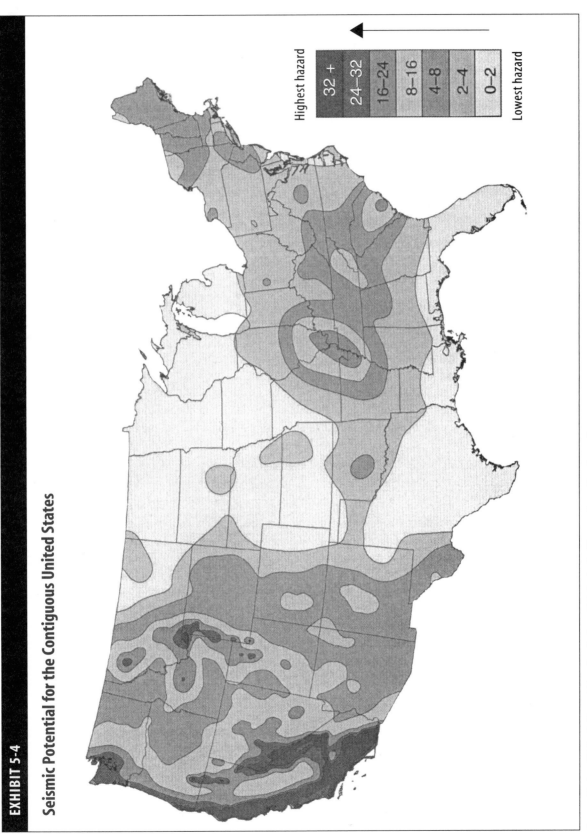

Highest hazard

32 +

24–32

16–24

8–16

4–8

2–4

0–2

Lowest hazard

Source: National Seismic Hazard Mapping Project, U.S. Geological Survey, http://geohazards.cr.usgs.gov.

found in light industrial buildings and warehouses, is also susceptible to earthquake damage. Fire-resistive construction survives most earthquakes with slight damage. When evaluating the earthquake exposure, underwriters must consider these three underwriting factors to determine which loss exposures are acceptable for coverage.

Collapse

Buildings collapse because of the weight of ice, snow, or sleet; defective design or construction; deterioration; and the weight of people, personal property, or water. Regular inspection and good maintenance should prevent such losses. The most common collapse problem involves rain water that accumulates on flat roofs when drains are blocked, but any unusual weight on a roof can cause it to collapse. Many roof structure designs do not contemplate the load of property or people, but that is not always apparent to the people who use a building.

Some buildings have collapsed from the cumulative effect of vibration. Very old structures were not designed with modern traffic in mind. For example, a nineteenth-century hotel in New York City collapsed without warning. Engineers identified subway and truck vibrations as the cause. Poor construction caused the collapse of a ceiling at the Port Authority Trans Hudson (PATH) Transportation Center in Jersey City, New Jersey. The plaster on the metal lath ceiling hung suspended from the reinforced concrete structure and collapsed as two PATH employees worked above it. The design had anticipated this load, but the contractor had cut corners, omitting every fourth suspender and spreading the rest out. Vibrations from passing PATH trains, combined with the weight of the maintenance workers and their equipment, caused the collapse.

Anticipating all potential causes of collapse is impossible. Underwriters can concentrate on the quality of a structure's design, construction, and maintenance. Novel or unusual designs are more prone to collapse than traditional ones. The ceiling of the PATH Transportation Center embodied a standard design widely used in building lobbies. Its collapse resulted in numerous inspections to make certain that poor workmanship did not affect similar ceilings elsewhere in the building. When a building's roof collapses because rain cannot run off it, poor maintenance or design is usually the cause. Other building parts are likely to be affected by similar maintenance or design defects.

Other Causes of Loss

Property insurance obviously covers many other causes of loss besides those previously discussed. Property underwriters must consider these causes of loss when the location or other loss exposure characteristics suggest they might be significant. For example:

- *Riot and civil commotion*, which includes any disruption of public order, are related covered by even the most basic property insurance. Historically, the loss exposures affected most either are located in urban areas or operate businesses that attract protesters with a political or moral agenda.

- *Sprinkler leakage* is a potential cause of loss for loss exposures with an automatic fire-extinguishing system. Underwriting concerns concentrate on (1) damageability of the contents and (2) the sprinkler system's physical condition, maintenance, and design. In almost all cases, the advantages of a sprinkler system as a fire-control device more than offset the possibility that the sprinkler system itself might be a source of property damage.

- *Sinkhole collapse* occurs where underground rivers and streams have carved channels out of solid limestone or dolomite bedrock. Sinkholes are common in Florida, and they also occur in other areas. Underwriters rarely analyze sinkholes as a specific cause of loss affecting the underwriting decision.

- *Mine subsidence*, a cause of loss similar to sinkhole collapse, can occur when a structure is built over the site of an abandoned mine shaft or tunnel. Underwriters need not consider this cause of loss unless property is in an area with mines; even then, this cause of loss is not usually evaluated unless losses have occurred in the area. These losses are relatively rare.

- *Volcanic action* suddenly became a significant cause of loss with the 1980 eruption of Mount St. Helens in Washington State. However, volcanic activity in the continental U.S. is so rare that the cause of loss usually requires no specific consideration.

- *Terrorism* suddenly became a significant cause of loss in the U.S. with the September 11, 2001, attacks. Although the federal government has provided a financial backstop for major terrorism losses, insurers remain exposed to terrorism losses of insureds that have not accepted a terrorism exclusion. Insurers face the challenge of pricing terrorism coverage despite a lack of credible historical data on loss frequency, loss severity, or the types of loss exposures most likely to experience a terrorism loss.

- *Weight of ice, snow, or sleet* is not generally a problem in the Sun Belt. However, cold snaps occasionally cause problems to roofs in the south that were not designed to handle snow or ice. Buildings in areas generally exposed to wintry weather can be susceptible to this cause of loss, especially if they involve large, flat spans of roof and inadequate drainage.

- *Theft* is a significant cause of loss covered in most homeowners policies and in commercial property policies written on a risk of direct physical loss ("all-risks") basis. Underwriting theft and related causes of loss are discussed later in the context of crime insurance.

UNDERWRITING BUSINESS INCOME AND EXTRA EXPENSE LOSS EXPOSURES

A category of insurable losses, sometimes referred to as *indirect, time element,* or *use and occupancy (U&O)* losses, occur as a consequence of the policyholder's inability to use its property following direct damage or loss to property. For example, a family often cannot live in their house, and a store often cannot operate its business, after the building is partially damaged or completely destroyed. The longer normal activity is interrupted—while rebuilding the structure and preparing it for use or occupancy, or while replacing production machinery—the greater the covered loss.

The homeowners policy offers "loss of use" coverage, which indemnifies the policyholder when his or her house is made uninhabitable by a covered cause of loss. Additional living expense coverage compensates the policyholder for extraordinary expenses incurred while the residence is being repaired. Fair rental value is the amount of rent that could have been fairly charged to a tenant for the premises had no loss occurred. Loss of use coverage also indemnifies the policyholder when a civil authority prohibits the policyholder from occupying the residence because of a covered cause of loss to other property. Dwelling policies contain similar coverages.

A common commercial counterpart to this coverage is found in the business income coverage forms. Under these coverage forms, the insurer pays the policyholder the actual loss sustained because of a necessary interruption of the policyholder's business operations arising from direct physical damage to property by a covered cause of loss. Both versions of the business income coverage form include coverage for extra expenses that helps to reduce the business income loss. One version adds extra expense coverage, which provides for the additional expenses incurred by the policyholder to minimize the interruption of operations even when the extra expenses do not reduce the loss of business income. Insureds who are more concerned with uninterrupted business operations than with loss of business income can purchase extra expense coverage separately. Various coverage options are available.

Businessowners policies usually include business income coverage on an actual loss sustained basis, often with fewer conditions or restrictions than separate business income or extra expense policy forms. Underwriters must recognize situations in which the business income loss exposure is more severe than contemplated by the simplified businessowners rate structure.

A covered loss of use, business income, or extra expense loss cannot occur without direct damage to property at the insured premises (not necessarily the insured's property) by a covered cause of loss. Analysis of the physical, moral, and morale (or attitudinal) hazards therefore begins with an analysis of the direct damage loss exposure. If business income or extra expense coverage is written separately, analysis of the COPE factors is required. With homeowners or dwelling insurance, or when the business income form is added to a direct damage policy, presumably this analysis is made. Additionally, the underwriter must consider both the probable maximum loss and factors affecting the interruption period.

Probable Maximum Business Income Loss

Determining the applicant's probable maximum business income loss is a complicated task involving the following two steps:

1. Evaluate the potential loss magnitude by projecting expected earnings for the coverage period. This evaluation is crucial in determining the amount of coverage necessary. However, any projection of future income is an estimate.

2. Select a coinsurance percentage that approximates the expected interruption period, should loss occur. The chosen coinsurance percentage is roughly related to the expected period of business interruption. For example, a business that anticipates a maximum period of interruption to be six months might select a 50 percent coinsurance clause. Businesses requiring more than a year to recover from a loss should consider a 125 percent coinsurance clause.

Requesting appropriate limits and selecting a coinsurance percentage are the insured's and producer's responsibility. However, commercial property underwriters should assist producers and applicants, when necessary, with determining appropriate limits and percentages and encouraging insurance to value.

Probable Period of Interruption

Underwriters must consider the time dimension when underwriting time element coverages. Any factor that lengthens the likely period of interruption increases the insured's potential loss amount. To evaluate the time dimension, the underwriter must consider the time required to rebuild the insured premises, the seasonality of the business, bottlenecks and computer nerve centers, long production processes, and disaster contingency plans.

The severity of a business income loss is not necessarily related to the underlying direct damage loss severity. A relatively minor fire destroying only 5 percent of the insured's building and personal property might result in a total business income loss up to the policy limit if, for example, the destroyed property included a custom-made piece of machinery, vital to the manufacturing process, that could not be replaced in less than one year.[14]

Rebuilding Time

The time period required to rebuild the insured's building or the building containing the insured's premises is a major factor in determining loss exposure. Specialized structures requiring long construction periods, lengthy delays in obtaining permits, severe climatic conditions inhibiting construction during certain times of the year, and congested urban locations are all factors that increase loss exposure. The absence of these characteristics makes a loss exposure more desirable to underwriters.

Seasonality

A seasonal business such as a toy store or ski resort with, say, 80 percent of its business concentrated in a three-month peak season, could suffer a severe business income loss from a relatively short shutdown at an inopportune time of year. Conversely, the time of year when a loss occurs has little effect on a nonseasonal business whose income stream is spread evenly across the year.

Bottlenecks and Computer Nerve Centers

The term "bottleneck" can apply to a machine, process, or building that is essential to the continued operation of an entire facility or manufacturing plant. For example, several products manufactured on different assembly lines might all flow through the same oven; if that oven is out of operation, no product can be completed. A flow chart of the production process often reveals one or more bottlenecks through which every product must pass.

A relatively minor direct damage loss involving a bottleneck can lead to a severe business income loss. If a vital process is duplicated on machines in separate fire divisions, the loss exposure is greatly reduced.

Although bottlenecks usually result from manufacturing processes, a congested area or an unusual building configuration can also create them.

Computer systems play a central role in many business operations. Relatively minor damage to a computer system can halt an entire operation. This is obviously a concern for manufacturing or processing plants operated by a central computer system. Many other businesses could be similarly affected, although the effect might not be as obvious. A large hotel, for example, might be virtually unable to operate when its computer system is down, because clerks cannot tell what rooms are occupied, and they cannot make reservations or produce bills.

Long Production Processes

If the insured's normal manufacturing or processing operation takes an unusually long time to complete, the underwriter must consider the time required to get stock in process back to the point at which it had been before the loss. For example, if a product must be aged or seasoned, destruction of the facility could lead to a lengthy interruption, because the aging or seasoning period would be added to the period necessary to restore the facility and its machinery to operating condition. Examples of such operations include wineries, leather processing, or cheese processing.

Disaster Contingency Plans

The existence of a current, sound disaster contingency plan is a positive underwriting factor. Proper planning before any loss occurs can reduce the probable length of interruption. A disaster contingency plan includes detailed written plans to restore the production process if part or all of the facility and equipment were destroyed. The disaster contingency plan should indicate what would be necessary if each part of the process were destroyed. The plan could also indicate whether continuation of the operation would be feasible following certain types of damage. If it were, extra expense insurance might be indicated, either instead of business income coverage alone or in a combined form.

UNDERWRITING CRIME INSURANCE

Crime is a significant cause of loss for both personal and commercial insureds. Most crime loss exposures for individuals and families are covered under homeowners policies and inland marine floaters. Theft coverage for personal property can be added by endorsement to a dwelling policy. The ISO homeowners policy does not define "theft," but it is generally understood to include burglary, robbery, and larceny.

The crime coverage needs of commercial insureds vary substantially, and coverage options are available to meet those varied needs. Commercial crime losses can arise from two broad areas: (1) crimes committed by employees and (2) crimes committed by others, which include burglary, robbery, or theft. The rest of this section is devoted to commercial crime loss exposures. However, many of the loss control measures and character issues are just as relevant for personal crime loss exposures.

Employee Dishonesty Loss Exposures

Employee dishonesty loss exposures have the following unique characteristics:

- Employees have ready access to money and other valuable property. They learn the company's routines and schedules and the habits of fellow employees. They can discover what controls employers have in place and how well the controls work.

- Losses can be hidden from discovery. Unlike burglary and robbery, which by definition are visible crimes, employee theft involves stealth and can often be concealed for months or years.

- Large losses are common. The thief's access to property continues until the crime is discovered. The length of time of access, in turn, contributes to the size of the loss.

- Employers are often reluctant to believe that employees might steal from them. That reluctance often leads to practices that create opportunities for theft, greatly increases exposures to loss, and creates a problem of adverse selection for the insurer.

- Employers might be reluctant to prosecute employees who steal. Many employers will not sign complaints or testify at criminal proceedings against their employees. They might want to avoid bad press; to accept the culprit's hard-luck story; or to quickly resolve the situation, especially when the employee promises restitution.

- Incidents of employee theft might be frequent, but they are usually hidden until large losses have accumulated. For example, an embezzler typically steals small sums of money over a long time period and is caught only when the sum is so large that the embezzler cannot continue to conceal it.

Many commercial insureds overlook the employee dishonesty loss exposure, and only a small percentage of mercantile establishments purchase employee dishonesty coverage. Employee dishonesty losses are significant, and they are estimated to cost businesses more than any other form of crime. Nonetheless, employee dishonesty insurance is profitable for insurers and available for most types of insureds.

Underwriting Employee Dishonesty Loss Exposures

Employee dishonesty insurance is often included in businessowners policies and commercial package policies without receiving much specific underwriting attention. However, underwriters should be satisfied that certain conditions, such as the following, exist before issuing a policy:

- No evidence of a moral hazard exists. (If it does, other coverages probably should not be written either.)
- Burglary and robbery loss control systems should be in place and maintained, because defenses against external crime also deter employee crime.
- As with other coverages, amounts of insurance should fall within the limits prescribed by the insurer's underwriting guidelines.
- The organization should be managed soundly. Management controls provide evidence of management's care and concern.

Controlling Employee Dishonesty Losses

Minimizing employee dishonesty losses requires strict adherence to management controls. Listed below are controls, applicable to almost all organizations, that improve underwriting acceptability:

- New hires are screened for prior criminal activity, and their references are checked.
- Seasoned employees are evaluated before they are promoted, especially for promotions or transfers into sensitive positions.
- A substance-abuse screening program is in place. Underwriters regard this as a positive sign because substance dependency creates potential for employee dishonesty.
- The rate and level of employee turnover is appropriate given the insured's business. Because employee turnover can increase the insured's loss exposure, underwriters normally evaluate this loss exposure by requesting a list of all employees, their positions, and their hire dates.

- Termination procedures are well defined. The computer passwords of employees who had worked in sensitive areas are revoked, and keys or access cards are returned upon termination.

- Management is sensitive to dramatic changes in employee behavior, such as sudden or drastic lifestyle changes, which might indicate employee dishonesty.

- Periodic audits are conducted to evaluate accounts receivable, cash accounts, inventories, and disbursements.

- Bank reconciliations are done to ensure that company and bank records agree.

- Employees monitor one another via a division of authority among employees.

- Annual vacations are required. This acts as a control because some embezzlement methods require a daily adjustment of records.

- Duties are rotated, a practice that helps to uncover irregularities or defalcations.

- Two-person or dual control systems are in place on some items, such as the vault, cash, and other items susceptible to theft.

Robbery, Burglary, and Theft Loss Exposures

Crime committed by others includes acts such as robbery, burglary, and theft. Definitions used in crime insurance policies often differ from those generally used, and underwriters must be aware of the crime coverage form definitions, whether they involve cause of loss (e.g., robbery, burglary, theft, disappearance) or personnel (e.g., watchperson, custodian, messenger).

Underwriting Robbery, Burglary, and Theft Loss Exposures

Underwriters analyzing robbery, burglary, and theft loss exposures consider the following five factors:

1. Susceptibility and marketability
2. Property location
3. Occupancy
4. Public protection
5. Coverage and price modifications

The first factor that underwriters consider when analyzing robbery, burglary, and theft loss exposures is an item's susceptibility to being stolen and its marketability. These characteristics are usually considered together, but an underwriter should be able to recognize them separately.

The size, weight, portability, visibility, and accessibility of property determine how susceptible it is to being stolen. The property's size or weight does not in itself reduce its susceptibility to being stolen. For example, a forty-ton steel truss bridge was stolen from a West Virginia creek in the late 1950s. However, large or bulky items generally have low susceptibility to being stolen. On the other hand, jewelry, clothing, small electrical appliances, precious metals, books, and hand tools are highly susceptible. The higher the property's value relative to its bulk and weight, the more susceptible it is to being stolen.

A combination of factors determines an item's marketability. Property that is widely used has more potential customers. Property that is difficult to trace is more marketable. The economy is often key, making a surprising variety of property highly marketable for some time.

The second factor that underwriters consider when analyzing robbery, burglary, and theft loss exposures is property location. Topography, neighborhood, climate, and the local crime rate can tell underwriters what kind of losses to expect. Seasonal occupancy, typical of a resort, for example, makes loss from an off-season burglary more likely. Crime occurs more often in some areas than in others, and underwriters should consider crime statistics. Urban areas have a higher crime rate than suburban and rural areas, but that gap seems to be narrowing.

Crime statistics often reflect the experience of entire cities or counties, which is of little value to underwriters. These statistics are not complete because many victims do not report crimes, especially in areas where they occur most often. Underwriters who want accurate data in a form they can use must develop their own data. Having reliable, objective data is especially important in underwriting to avoid unfair discrimination.

The third factor that underwriters consider when analyzing robbery, burglary, and theft loss exposures is occupancy. A reporter once asked Willie Sutton, a notorious bank robber of the 1940s and 1950s, why he chose to steal from banks when there were easier targets. His answer was, "Because that's where the money is." Some occupancies generally have a great deal of cash or other valuable property on hand. Those occupancies include banks, savings and loans, credit unions, check-cashing services, grocery stores, stadiums, arenas, churches, and buildings where charitable events are held.

Some businesses are conducted in obscure locations where criminal activity might not be readily detected or operate during hours when few people are around to deter criminals. Those businesses include public warehouses and twenty-four-hour convenience stores.

The fourth factor that underwriters consider when analyzing robbery, burglary, and theft loss exposures is public protection. Public protection reflects the quality of the local criminal justice system. How soon do police respond to alarms and crime reports? How often do prosecutors obtain convictions? Effective public protection means lower crime rates and fewer crime losses. To gauge the quality of public protection, the underwriter must know the area in which the insured's business operates.

The fifth factor that underwriters consider when analyzing robbery, burglary, and theft loss exposures is coverage and price modifications. Underwriters usually have some latitude in handling commercial crime insurance applications. Sometimes, applicants know what coverage they want and will turn to another insurer if the requested coverage is not provided. Often, however, the applicant simply requests the broadest coverage available at the lowest price. Insureds who request crime insurance are often willing to accept counteroffers made by an underwriter who is trying to write the account. Possible modifications include changing coverage, limits, pricing, and deductibles, and adding endorsements requiring protective safeguards.

Requests for policies providing broad coverage do not always match underwriting guidelines. Rather than reject the account, the underwriter might offer narrower coverage. For example, an underwriter might offer the applicable crime coverage form combined with a commercial property coverage form and the broad causes-of-loss form, rather than the special causes-of-loss form. Generally, however, transforming marginal accounts into acceptable accounts using coverage modification is difficult.

For most other types of insurance, the insured purchases a policy limit close to the value of the exposed property. With crime insurance, the policy limit more often reflects the probable loss amount. Total crime losses are rare; most insureds assume that only partial crime losses will occur. This assumption, the absence of a coinsurance requirement, and the desire to minimize premiums tend to reduce the policy limit and to increase problems associated with underinsurance.

For most property insurance, underwriters encourage insurance to value. With crime insurance, however, an underwriter is usually satisfied with policy limits much lower than the amount of the values insured. Because too much insurance can create a moral hazard, most underwriters do not want to provide crime insurance to full value even if the insured requests it.

Because crime insurance does not contain a coinsurance clause, the insured is not penalized for having inadequate limits. Partial losses can equal or exceed policy limits. Underinsurance can lead to underpricing, so underwriters must consider the amount subject when pricing crime coverage.

Because policy limits tend to be low relative to the amount at risk, the probable maximum loss per occurrence usually equals the amount subject. More than one covered crime loss can occur during the policy period, so underwriters who provide commercial crime coverage should recognize that total losses might exceed the policy limits.

Deductibles in crime insurance serve the same purposes as they do in other types of insurance. They eliminate small, more predictable losses, and they tend to make the insured more conscious of the benefits of loss control.

Policyholders knowledgeable about insurance recognize the value of retaining small, frequent losses that often can be readily contained through loss control techniques and financed with current cash flow. However, deductibles are not used as underwriting tools in crime insurance as often as they might be.

The deductible for crime insurance should at least equal the deductible amount that applies to other types of losses to the insured's business personal property.

A protective safeguards endorsement warrants that certain safeguards are in place. If the insured fails to protect the property as promised, the insurer is not contractually obligated to pay any resulting losses.

Some courts dismiss warranties in insurance policies. In crime insurance, however, courts are more likely to rule that breach of warranty negates coverage, because the insured's promise is clearly material to the underwriting decision. However, underwriters cannot assume that courts will require the insured's full warranty compliance. A good faith effort to comply is almost always sufficient. For example, the failure of a central station alarm service solely because of a power or telephone service outage does not breach the warranty. The situation is different, however, if the utility cuts off electrical service because the insured has failed to pay its bills. A warranty's intent is not to create a loophole through which an adjuster can deny liability. Rather, the warranty in a protective safeguards endorsement requires the insured to make a good faith effort to maintain the specified level of protection.

Warranties ensure that the loss exposure is appropriately rated. Insurers almost always require a warranty for any protective system that earns a rate credit. Underwriters might also regard a system as essential even when it does not qualify for a reduced rate. If the underwriter demands that protective systems be installed, the protective safeguard endorsement should be added to the crime policy to enforce the system's maintenance throughout the policy period.

Controlling Robbery, Burglary, and Theft Losses

A good prospect for crime coverage implements loss control measures and uses them diligently. Crime loss exposures respond well to loss control efforts. Private protection systems to prevent or reduce loss include the following:

- Safes and vaults
- Cages, special rooms, and limited-access areas
- Indoor and outdoor lighting
- Fences and walls
- Protection of openings on the premises (gates, doors, windows, and skylights)
- Guard services
- Alarm systems
- Electronic surveillance systems
- Inventory control and other management activities

Private protection systems generally serve two important functions: to prevent crime losses and to reduce losses that do occur.

Safes, vaults, fences, and so on rarely prevent access for a criminal who is strongly motivated. However, protection systems frustrate, confuse, and delay criminal activity, thereby reducing losses or causing a criminal to seek an easier target.

Although even the best protection systems do not eliminate loss, their value as a deterrent cannot be overemphasized. After moral hazard, private protection is the most important consideration in crime insurance underwriting.

Underwriting guidelines should indicate the protection level that a particular class or location requires. The two main categories of private protection devices are barriers to criminal access and detection devices. Barriers include devices that protect the premises, safes, and vaults. Detection devices are guards, alarms, and surveillance systems.

UNDERWRITING MARINE INSURANCE

Ocean marine is one of the oldest forms of insurance. Ocean marine underwriters have historically insured both oceangoing hulls and their cargoes. The "warehouse-to-warehouse" clause added land transportation coverage as well. Inland marine insurance, peculiar to the United States and Canada, grew out of a willingness of ocean marine underwriters to provide coverage for goods and equipment in transit within North America. Using the ocean marine tradition of broad insuring agreements, inland marine coverages grew rapidly and began competing with fire and casualty insurers. This conflict led to the development of the **Nationwide Marine Definition** in 1933, amended in 1953 and 1976, which defined the coverage areas within which marine coverage could be offered.

Nationwide Marine Definition
Definition of the kinds of loss exposures and coverages that can be classified under state insurance laws as marine and inland marine insurance.

Ocean Marine Insurance

Ocean marine insurance is divided into four major categories: (1) yachts, (2) commercial hulls, (3) protection and indemnity, and (4) cargo. Some differences exist between the underwriting considerations for yachts or other private vessels and those for commercial hulls and cargoes.

Yachts

The first category of ocean marine insurance is for yachts. Underwriting for all yachts (private vessels), whether they be twenty-foot sailboats or one-hundred-foot oceangoing powerboats, considers seaworthiness, navigable waters and season, and operator experience.

Seaworthiness is based on a vessel's age, construction, and maintenance. Typically, the older a vessel is, the lower its value and the greater its chance of being a constructive total loss should any damage occur. Most insurers limit the age of vessels they insure.

Construction quality varies by manufacturer, so the vessel's manufacturer is an important underwriting consideration. Fiberglass construction is a significant improvement over wooden construction. Modern fiberglass construction is lightweight and includes foam interlayers that significantly reduce the possibility of sinking. Fiberglass hulls also require less hull maintenance than wooden vessels.

All vessels, regardless of their construction, require regular maintenance. Underwriters can obtain information on a particular vessel through a marine survey that provides a comprehensive evaluation of the vessel's value and condition.

Navigation warranty
Part of a yacht insurance policy that restricts coverage to the navigational area for which the hull, the equipment, and the operator's experience are appropriate.

In addition to considering seaworthiness, underwriters consider the navigable waters and season in which yachts are operated. Underwriters use a navigation warranty as a major underwriting tool. The **navigation warranty** restricts coverage to the navigational area for which the yacht, the equipment, and the operator's experience are appropriate. The perils of the seas differ greatly by area and by season within the same area. Putting to sea during hurricane season in the Caribbean or during winter in Maine, for example, is not prudent. A navigation warranty suspends coverage when a vessel is used under conditions other than those agreed to with the underwriter.

Operator experience is the last underwriting consideration for yachts. Operator experience is an extremely important underwriting consideration. Many insurers give credit to operators who have completed Power Squadron or Coast Guard Auxiliary courses. Membership in an organized yacht club generally indicates the policyholder's dedication to his or her pastime and often implies sound experience and training. Many insurers use automobile motor vehicle records as an indicator of an operator's ability to operate equipment safely.

Commercial Hulls

The second category of ocean marine insurance is for commercial hulls. When evaluating commercial hulls, underwriters must consider some of the same basic types of information that they consider for yachts: seaworthiness, the navigable waters and season, and master and crew experience. However, the sources of information are different. Various registers of shipping provide a commercial vessel's physical characteristics. The "flag" or nation under which a ship is registered determines the ship's safety regulations and the frequency of inspections. An inspection determines the state of maintenance.

Protection and Indemnity

The third category of ocean marine insurance is for protection and indemnity. Protection and indemnity (P&I) provides liability coverage to a vessel owner for bodily injury, illness, death, and damage to the property of others arising out of the ownership, use, or operation of the vessel.

In underwriting, the hazards affecting hull loss potential also affect P&I loss potential. Inadequate training of a crew, for example, might keep a fire from being extinguished, allowing the fire to damage the hull and injure or kill crew members. Perhaps the two most important underwriting considerations are the owner's financial stability and the master's and crew's experience. A financially stable owner is more likely to have safe, well-maintained vessels, with a lower likelihood of both P&I and hull losses, than an owner who is financially weak. Likewise, an experienced master and crew will incur fewer losses than an inexperienced master and crew. Marine underwriters generally believe that an older, well-maintained vessel with a top-notch crew is a better risk than a new vessel with an inferior crew. Human error, not mechanical failure, is the cause of many accidents at sea. When evaluating the crew of a vessel or fleet, underwriters consider the nationality, experience, and training of crew members, officers, and captains.

Cargo

The fourth category of ocean marine insurance is for cargo. Many businesses have ocean marine loss exposures because they import components, raw materials, and finished goods from overseas. Many also export goods.

When underwriting cargo insurance, the policyholder's business reputation is important. The policyholder should have as a primary interest the safe arrival of the cargo at its destination. A policyholder who, for example, tries to save money by minimizing the amount of packing cannot be underwritten profitably.

Underwriters insure a wide variety of cargo. Cargo such as pig iron ingots has very low susceptibility to loss or damage, but cargo such as fine glassware and china can be damaged easily. Fishmeal or burlap cargoes can present extraordinary fire hazards. Auto parts and liquor cargoes are very attractive to thieves. Some chemicals become worthless if they are exposed to air, and certain electronic devices require expensive recalibration if they are even slightly damaged. Any bulk shipment or any shipment of raw materials presents its own unique problems. Some cargo has particular hazards, shown in Exhibit 5-5.

Through the "warehouse-to-warehouse" clause, ocean cargo insurance also includes land transit from the originating warehouse to the dock and from the dock at the port of destination to the consignee's warehouse, which usually involves thousands of miles. Therefore, not only the ports between which goods are shipped but also the land transportation used from warehouse to warehouse are major underwriting concerns. In some ports, ships must be unloaded by lighters, which are small, self-propelled vessels or barges. This increases the probability of cargo damage. Also, some ports are known to have high crime and damage rates.

Much of today's cargo is shipped in large, enclosed metal boxes known as containers, which are similar to semitrailers without the chassis. Containers can be "stuffed" at the original point of shipment and unloaded at their destination, thereby eliminating extra handling at the port. Containerization can reduce pilferage and weather-damage losses, provided the container is watertight and carries the merchandise from warehouse to warehouse. Because at least one-third of all containers are shipped on deck, however, the loss exposure to heavy weather and washing overboard is greatly increased. Shipment hijack and cargo breakage from shifting are additional loss exposures. Terrorism is another loss exposure; bombs or other devices concealed in a container can be difficult to detect.

Finally, cargo location on the ship is an important consideration. Deck cargo is subject to wind, water, and wave damage to a much greater extent than is cargo stowed below deck. Certain cargoes such as rough lumber are usually unaffected by shipment on deck.

EXHIBIT 5-5

Common Cargo Hazards

Auto parts	Pilferage and theft in certain areas of the world where new cars are not readily available
Automobiles	Marring, denting, and scratching
Canned goods	Rusting, denting, and theft
Chemicals in paper bags	Shortage and contamination from torn bags
Fine arts	Handling damage and theft
Fishmeal	Highly susceptible to heating damage and fire
Fresh fruit	Extremely sensitive to temperature change and difficult to keep from spoiling
Glass	Breakage and staining
Grain	Shortage and weevil damage
Household effects	Breakage, marring, chipping, scratching, shortage, and water damage
Liquids in bulk	Leakage, shortage, contamination
Lumber (cut)	Shortage, staining, and handling damage
Machinery	Rust and breakage of parts
Paper in rolls	Chafing, cutting, and water damage
Rags	Fire and shortage
Refrigerators and stoves	Marring, scratching, chipping, and denting
Scrap metal	Alleged shortage because of difference in scale weights at origin and destination
Steel products	Rusting, bending, and twisting
Television sets	Breakage of picture tubes
Textiles	Hook damage, theft, and water damage

Inland Marine Insurance

In terms of forms and rates, inland marine insurance is divided into filed and nonfiled classes.

- **Filed classes** are inland marine classes for which advisory organizations are required to file loss costs, rules, and forms. Filed classes have been selected for greater regulatory scrutiny than other inland marine classes because they tend to have many policyholders with reasonably homogeneous loss exposures. Most filed policies have relatively inflexible coverage and rates. Typical filed classes include the commercial articles coverage form, equipment dealers coverage form, physicians and surgeons equipment coverage form, sign coverage form, theatrical property coverage form, film coverage form, floor plan coverage form, jewelers block coverage form, mail coverage form, accounts receivable coverage form, and valuable papers and records coverage form. Two major categories of filed classes are jewelry and furs, which are also the two largest personal insurance classes.

- **Nonfiled classes** are developed and rated according to an individual insurer's underwriting practices. About one-half of all inland marine coverage is written on nonfiled forms. Nonfiled classes cover a vast array of loss exposures, from bridges and tunnels to power tools. Depending on insurer practice, an underwriter can freely modify any nonfiled forms, thereby providing a great deal of flexibility. Often, a manuscript policy must be designed to cover an unusual or a one-of-a-kind loss exposure.

Filed classes
Inland marine classes for which advisory organizations are required to file loss costs, rules, and forms.

Nonfiled classes
Inland marine classes rated according to the individual insurer's underwriting practices.

The following sections discuss some of the nonfiled coverages that generate the largest premium volume.

Contractors' Equipment

Contractors' equipment policies insure almost any type of mobile equipment that contractors use, including hand-held tools, mobile cranes, excavators, and bulldozers. This equipment is used in construction projects, not only by small contractors but also by businesses engaged in tunneling projects worth hundreds of millions of dollars. The typical coverage form provides direct physical damage coverage on a risk of direct physical loss ("all-risks") basis.

Key factors in underwriting this coverage are the equipment's use and scope of operations. Other factors include the following:

- The equipment's size and value
- The equipment's type, age, maintenance, supervision, operating characteristics, and protection
- The equipment operator's experience and accident record
- The policyholder's financial status
- The concentration of equipment at a single site
- Loss history
- Labor relations

Builders' Risk/Installation

Builders' risk coverage can be written on either commercial property or inland marine insurance forms. Many underwriters prefer nonfiled inland marine forms that permit rating and coverage flexibility. Those forms include transit coverage for building materials brought to a site. Coverage for flood and earthquake, subject to sublimits and high deductibles, is usually available as an optional coverage under an inland marine builders' risk policy.

Buildings under construction face the same loss exposures as completed buildings, but buildings under construction are often more vulnerable because protective safeguards are not yet in place. Underwriters should be aware of the following conditions that might increase the hazards for a building's fire loss:

- Water mains that might not be completed
- Fire hydrants that are operational but that might not be near the building
- Standpipes that might not be connected in high-rise buildings
- Sprinkler systems that might not be installed or activated
- Heat and smoke detectors that might not be installed
- Construction activities that introduce new heat sources, such as welding
- Salamanders (portable stoves) that are used for heat

Construction sites are susceptible to theft and vandalism losses unless security precautions are taken. Such precautions include installing fences, lighting, and alarm systems on trailers and storage sheds and employing security guards.

Buildings with large roof spans have an increased chance of collapsing before all of the needed supports are in place. Buildings are particularly susceptible to wind damage before exterior walls and roofs are in place.

Transportation

Goods shipped by truck, air, rail, and mail can be covered by inland marine insurance. The covered causes of loss are usually very broad, frequently risk of direct physical loss ("all-risks"), and they routinely include flood and earthquake. Transportation insurance can provide coverage for the following interests:

- The shipper, any party who hires another to transport cargo
- The carrier that actually transports (or carries) goods for another
- The consignee, the party designated for delivery

The terms of sale and common law determine which party bears the risk of loss to property in transit. The underwriter must consider who bears the risk of loss and therefore has an insurable interest, how susceptible the cargo is to damage, and what steps have been taken to protect against foreseeable losses. Deregulation of the trucking industry has made it common practice to place the risk of loss on the shipper or consignee. Terms of sale usually include a provision to transfer title to the goods and the risk of loss from the seller to the buyer at a defined point. The underwriter must be aware of the arrangements that cover insured shipments and their implications.

Instrumentalities of Transportation and Communication

The principal instrumentalities of transportation and communication are bridges; tunnels; pipelines; wharves, docks, and piers; radio and TV towers and stations; and dry docks and marine railways and cranes. Instrumentalities of transportation and communication are fixed-location structures and present many of the same loss exposures as any other type of real property. Additionally, because of their specialized nature, such structures are subject to some unique loss exposures.

Regarding these instrumentalities, the primary areas of concern for underwriters include the structure's construction and maintenance and any unique loss exposures and hazards that might exist. Bridges and tunnels, for example, might be exposed to trucks carrying gasoline or explosives, and they might be targets for terrorist activities. Television towers are susceptible to ice buildup in severe winter storms, increasing the likelihood of a collapse in high winds. Pipelines are susceptible to earthquake damage. Wharves, docks, and piers might be damaged by high waves as well as by ships colliding with them.

Bailee Coverages

Bailee coverage is provided in many inland marine policies, either as a section of coverage in a policy providing other coverage, such as the jewelers block, or as a separate policy. Bailee coverage is also provided as one coverage in other nonmarine forms, such as the garage coverage form or the building and personal property coverage form.

Bailee coverage is a hybrid coverage that combines concepts from both property and liability insurance. The cleaners and dyers customer's policy, for example, provides insurance coverage for damage to property in the bailee's custody; in this respect, it resembles property insurance. However, covered property is not owned by the bailee; in this sense, the coverage resembles liability insurance. However, coverage applies even when the bailee is not legally responsible for the loss.

When underwriting bailee coverages, the underwriter must evaluate many of the same factors affecting both property loss exposures and liability loss exposures. Coverage does not apply unless covered property is damaged by a named cause of loss, so normal property underwriting factors generally apply. However, relevant liability factors must also be considered, as well as any factors peculiar to the type of business involved. For example, if the bailed property includes jewelry or furs, the theft cause of loss and related loss control measures must be evaluated carefully.

LOSS CONTROL

The loss control function supports underwriters in determining which loss exposures to insure. Loss control representatives can provide information to underwriters that enables them to make better underwriting decisions. Principally, this information consists of field inspection reports on the premises and operations of new applicants and existing policyholders who would like to renew their policies. Inspection reports should provide a clear picture of the applicant's loss exposures and related hazards in terms that the underwriter will understand. Additionally, an insurer's loss control department can provide technical support to its underwriting department in many areas, such as fire hazards of new building materials, health hazards of materials or production processes, and new techniques or equipment for materials handling.

Loss control can also assist underwriters in modifying an applicant's loss exposures to meet eligibility limits. After an applicant has been accepted, loss control can be instrumental in helping the policyholder to remain within underwriting guidelines and thereby qualified for policy renewal. Sometimes, loss control can even be called on to "rehabilitate" a marginal account that underwriting has already accepted because of competitive considerations.

However, an insurer's loss control representatives not only serve as the underwriter's eyes and ears, but they also provide a valuable service for policyholders. The insurer's loss control services help the insured to prevent losses or reduce their effect. Because loss control representatives are often the only insurer employees that the insured meets, they also serve an important public relations and communications role. By contributing to improved underwriting decisions, helping policyholders control their losses, and maintaining the insurer's image, loss control representatives help to determine the insurer's success.

After describing the goals of insurer loss control activities, this section discusses the importance of cooperation between loss control and other insurer functions. Finally, it covers in greater detail the specific loss control services that insurers provide.

Many insurers employ individuals who specialize in loss control. The term **loss control** refers collectively to loss prevention and loss reduction.

- **Loss prevention** focuses on lowering the frequency of losses—in other words, preventing losses from occurring or from occurring as often.
- **Loss reduction** focuses on lowering the severity of the losses that do occur.

Many loss control measures serve a dual purpose by lowering both loss frequency and loss severity. Burglar alarms, for example, discourage burglars from attempting a crime (lowering loss frequency), and they detect burglaries that do occur (lowering loss severity).

Insurance personnel who perform loss control activities have varying titles, such as safety specialist or loss control engineer. This text collectively refers to

Loss control
A risk management technique to reduce loss frequency or loss severity.

Loss prevention
A loss control technique to lower the frequency of losses.

Loss reduction
A loss control technique to lower the severity of losses that occur.

loss control personnel as "loss control representatives." Loss control representatives are often members of an insurer's loss control department, which might be centralized in the home office or decentralized in field offices.

Goals of Insurer Loss Control Activities

Insurers conduct loss control activities to achieve several goals, which correspond to the overall goals of insurers.

Earn a Profit

Loss control activities can help insurers to reach their profit goals in several ways, as follows:

- *Improving underwriting decisions.* By inspecting the premises and operations of insurance applicants, loss control representatives can improve the information on which the underwriting department bases its decisions about which applicants to accept and how to price coverage. Better underwriting information enables the insurer to do a better job of selecting policyholders and pricing its coverage at a competitive level that produces an underwriting profit.

- *Improving premium volume.* Loss control personnel often recommend loss control measures that can change a marginal account to an acceptable account, thereby increasing the insurer's premium volume while meeting underwriting guidelines.

- *Encouraging policyholder loss control.* Loss control representatives can influence policyholders to exercise loss control activities by working with them to identify loss control opportunities and safety improvements.

- *Reducing insureds' losses.* Loss control representatives can continue to monitor policyholders and suggest appropriate loss control measures as the policyholders' loss exposures change. Consequently, loss control representatives can reduce losses that the insurer must pay, thereby helping to keep the insurer's book of business profitable.

- *Providing an additional revenue source.* Traditionally, insurers provided loss control services only to their policyholders and did not charge a fee in addition to the policy premium. Many insurers today also sell unbundled loss control services to firms that have chosen to retain, or self-insure, their losses. Some insurers also provide their policyholders with supplemental loss control services for a fee in addition to the policy premium. Several major insurers offer access to a variety of experts, such as nurses, ergonomic specialists, industrial hygiene specialists, engineers, attorneys, and chemists.

- *Reducing errors and omissions claims against the insurer.* Competent loss control service reduces the possibility of errors and omissions claims by policyholders or others alleging injury because of the insurer's negligence. The errors and omissions liability loss exposure also can influence an insurer's decision about what types or levels of loss control services to provide.

Meet Customer Needs

Some insurers offer loss control activities in response to insurance customers' needs, particularly commercial and industrial customers. This demand has resulted partly from the pressures of legislation such as the Occupational Safety and Health Act, the Consumer Products Safety Act, the Comprehensive Environmental Response Compensation and Liability Act, and the Americans with Disabilities Act. The threat of large liability judgments in certain areas has also contributed to the demand for loss control services.

By exercising sound loss control, organizations make their accounts more attractive to underwriters (especially during a hard market); lower their insurance premiums; reduce disruption to operations following accidents; remain socially responsible; fulfill occupational safety and health standards; comply with local, state, and federal laws; and improve their financial performance.

By satisfying customer needs for loss control services, insurers can attract new customers, retain satisfied customers, and gain a competitive advantage over insurers that do not provide these services.

Comply With Legal Requirements

Some states require insurers to provide a minimum level of loss control service to commercial policyholders. Insurers comply with these laws not only to meet the state's legal requirements, but also to minimize the possibility of errors and omissions claims by policyholders.

Fulfill Duty to Society

Insurers greatly benefit society by providing financial resources to help individuals and businesses recover from accidental losses. However, preventing accidents is even better. An occupational injury can cause pain, suffering, and loss of income for an individual and his or her family. A fire at a large factory can cause loss of business income, employee layoffs, and contingent business income losses for the firm's suppliers. The sum of all accidental losses has a profound adverse effect on society.

Insurers have an ethical obligation to use their expertise wisely. By assisting policyholders in preventing or reducing accidental losses, insurers pursue humanitarian goals and benefit society at large. This is true even when the insurer derives no direct financial benefit from its loss control services.

Cooperation Between Loss Control and Other Functions

An insurer's loss control efforts are most effective when they complement the activities of other insurer departments. The principal opportunities for loss control cooperation are with underwriting, marketing, premium auditing, and claims.

An insurer and its policyholders can also benefit from cooperative relationships between the loss control function and external organizations. These external organizations include independent agents or brokers and trade associations that engage in loss control activities.

Loss Control and Marketing

Loss control can be an important ally to the insurer's marketing staff in meeting its goals. By inspecting an applicant's premises and recommending ways of reducing hazards, loss control personnel can make the difference between the applicant's being rejected or accepted by the insurer's underwriting department. By making marginal accounts acceptable, loss control helps marketing to reach its sales goals. Loss control can also help marketing by proving to policyholders that it understands their business operations and associated hazards. The loss control representative can offer valuable advice on improving safety, advice that is particularly important for accounts that are eager for this type of help.

After applicants become policyholders, loss control can play a key role in retaining them as customers. In fact, a commercial policyholder might have more regular contact with the insurer's loss control representatives than with any other employee of the insurer. By providing professional and courteous service, loss control personnel can create customer goodwill.

Finally, through their direct contact with policyholders, loss control representatives can learn what insurance coverages or services policyholders need or want. By conveying this information to the appropriate marketing or sales personnel, loss control representatives can assist the marketing department in either meeting a policyholder's specific needs or developing product enhancements that will appeal to many policyholders. For example, a loss control survey might reveal that the policyholder has acquired new property that is not adequately covered under the existing policy. If conveyed to the appropriate marketing staff, this information might lead to the sale of additional coverage to that policyholder. If several insureds experience the same problem, that information could lead to a decision to revise the insurer's policy forms to provide better coverage for newly acquired property.

Loss Control and Premium Auditing

In one respect, the jobs of loss control representatives and premium auditors are similar, because both visit the policyholder's premises and have direct policyholder contact. Loss control representatives typically visit the policyholder at the beginning of the policy period, while premium auditors visit at the end. Because premium auditors often arrive after it is too late to correct recordkeeping deficiencies resulting from the policyholder's lack of knowledge or misunderstanding, loss control personnel can use the opportunity provided by the inspection to pave the way for the premium audit.

To take advantage of this opportunity, however, premium auditors must communicate their needs to the loss control representatives. If they are aware of those needs, loss control representatives can, for example, note the location of the accounting records and the name of the person to contact at audit time. They can also record the names, titles, and duties of executive officers. Their description of operations could be a starting point for the auditor's classification of loss exposures. Loss control representatives might even estimate the payroll by classification or at least the number of employees per department. They can report the existence of any new operations. If properly informed, they can also advise the policyholder about recordkeeping requirements and the need for certificates of insurance. Finally, they can offer the assistance of the insurer's premium auditors to deal with any complex questions about the audit. Problems can therefore be prevented before it is too late.

Loss Control and Claims

A partnership between loss control and claims can be just as valuable to an insurer as the partnership between loss control and underwriting, marketing, or premium auditing. The loss control department needs claim experience information to direct loss-control resources and efforts to crucial areas. The claim department relies on loss control for loss exposure data and background information that can support the loss adjusting process if a loss occurs. Claim and loss control personnel should discuss common concerns and review loss cases regularly.

The claim experience information that can be useful to loss control includes frequency and severity of losses by type of insurance, by cause of loss, by the kind of business the insured engages in, and by worker occupation. Regarding individual accidents, particularly in the workers' compensation area, loss control can also benefit from information about the type of accident, the body part injured, how the accident occurred, and perhaps other details from the adjuster's report. Loss control staff can use this information to (1) identify areas for research, (2) target loss exposures for additional attention, (3) identify characteristics associated with particular types of losses, and (4) develop alternatives to control losses.

Loss control personnel are usually well informed in engineering, mechanical, and technological areas with which claim personnel might be unfamiliar. Therefore, loss control specialists can assist claim personnel with solving technical problems that accompany claims. The loss control department can provide codes, standards, technical opinions, laboratory analyses, and other assistance to the claim department when investigating and settling claims. A loss control specialist can design product recall procedures to assist claim personnel and insureds in controlling specific product losses.

Loss Control and Producers

The traditional role of producers regarding loss control was to encourage the policyholder's loss control activities and to coordinate the efforts of the insurer's loss control personnel with the insured. Producers still perform this traditional role, which might be the only role played by many small to medium-sized agencies or brokerage firms. However, large producers have progressed well beyond this traditional role.

Many large agencies and brokerages maintain their own loss control departments, and some can furnish services on par with those offered by insurers. If a policyholder is receiving loss control services from both the insurer and its producer, the loss control entities of both organizations should strive to coordinate their efforts for the mutual benefit of all parties involved, particularly the policyholder.

Loss Control Services Provided by Insurers

The following insurer loss control services are discussed:

- Conducting physical surveys
- Performing risk analysis and improvement
- Developing safety management programs

An insurer with the necessary resources might provide services in all three categories for some of its policyholders.

Conducting Physical Surveys

The first loss control service is conducting physical surveys. This consists mainly of collecting underwriting information on a customer's loss exposures, including such details as building construction type(s), worker occupations, site diagrams, and fire protection systems. Less experienced loss control representatives are often assigned to this type of work.

On a typical survey, a loss control representative inspects the customer's premises on a walking tour and interviews the customer's management to discover details that might not be apparent from the tour. The loss control representative evaluates loss exposures and associated hazards relating to the following:

- Fire, windstorm, water damage, burglary, and other causes of property loss
- Legal liability arising out of premises, operations, products, completed operations, automobile, mobile equipment, environmental impairment, and other sources of liability
- Employee injuries relative to working conditions, machinery hazards, and employee safety practices

In addition to evaluating loss exposures and physical hazards, the loss control representative evaluates management's commitment to loss control and employee attitudes about safety-conscious behavior. So, the loss control representative might obtain insight into the possibility and extent of both moral and morale (or attitudinal) hazards.

At the tour's conclusion, the loss control representative meets with management to ask questions, discuss loss exposures and hazards, and share suggestions for controlling hazards identified during the survey. After leaving the customer's premises, the loss control representative organizes the information in a formal report. An example of portions of a loss control report is shown in Exhibit 5-6.

In connection with a physical survey, loss control representatives also make written recommendations that can help the customer eliminate or control loss exposures. Typically, recommendations are generated when a loss control representative identifies a loss exposure that falls below a satisfactory level. With mercantile loss exposures, for example, a common recommendation is to control slip-and-fall hazards by improving the maintenance program for aisles, steps, and stairwells.

If the customer has requested insurance on a building or buildings valued above a particular threshold, such as $500,000, the survey report might also include a property valuation. By determining the building's actual cash value, functional value, or full replacement cost, the appropriate limit of insurance can be determined.

Physical surveys benefit both the underwriter and the insured in the following ways:

- The survey report helps the underwriter gain a better understanding of the loss exposures being insured. Underwriters often provide an insurance quotation with the condition that various loss control recommendations in the survey report be implemented.
- The policyholder can gain a better understanding of its loss exposures and what steps could be taken to prevent or reduce losses, comply with applicable laws and regulations, and provide a better working environment for employees, all of which can increase employee morale and productivity.

If a property valuation is part of the survey, the policyholder can be more confident of an adequate recovery in the event of a total loss and less likely to incur a coinsurance penalty in the event of a partial loss.

Performing Risk Analysis and Improvement

The second loss control service is performing risk analysis and improvement. In addition to completing a physical survey and loss exposure and hazard evaluation, the insurer's loss control representative might analyze the customer's loss history (risk analysis) and submit written recommendations (improvements) to the business owner or manager about how to reduce hazards that have previously led to losses. Ordinarily, a loss control representative contacts the policyholder within sixty to ninety days to check the policyholder's progress in complying with the recommendations.

EXHIBIT 5-6

Short Form Loss Control Report

IIA Insurance Companies

429 Smithtown Rd., Anywhere, PA 22484

INSURED
Terry's Casual Wear

PERSON INTERVIEWED
Theresa Mason

MAILING ADDRESS
4814 Hwy. 17 South, N. Myrtle Beach, S.C.

SURVEY DATE
6/28/X3

LOSS CONTROL REPRESENTATIVE
John Henderson

LOCATION SURVEYED
SAME

POLICY NUMBER
CRO7234525

EXPLAIN OR MAKE RECOMMENDATIONS FOR ALL CIRCLE ○ ANSWERS

A. RISK OVERVIEW

OVERALL RISK	LOSS CONTROL	PREMISES CONDITION	HOUSEKEEPING	PRIOR LOSS	OPINION OF RISK
☐ Low	☑ Good	☑ Good	☑ Good	○ Yes	☑ Good
☑ Medium	☐ Fair	☐ Fair	☐ Fair	☑ No	☐ Fair
○ High	○ Poor	○ Poor	○ Poor		○ Poor

B. DESCRIPTION OF OPERATIONS

1. Description of business and/or operations:
   Retail clothing store

C. GENERAL DATA

1. Insured is: ☑ Owner ☐ Tenant ☐ Lessee
2. Insured is: ☑ Corporation ☐ Partnership ☐ Individual
3. Yrs. in business: 5   At this location 3
4. Business hours: 10 to 11
5. Estimated gross annual sales: $ 225,000
6. Neighborhood is: ☑ Commercial ☐ Rural ☐ Residential ☐ Industrial

7. Neighborhood is: ☑ Stable ○ Other
8. Does business appear successful? ☑ Yes ○ No
9. Management attitude satisfactory? ☐ Yes ○ No
10. Other occupants in building? ☐ Yes ◉ No
    If YES, describe:

Continued on next page.

BUILDING

1. Year built: 20X0
2. Building height (stories & ft./story): 1
3. Exterior wall construction: Frame Wood Cover: Wood shingle
4. Floor construction: Wood
5. Roof const.: Support: Wood Deck: Metal Cover: Metal
6. Area (include basement only if finished): sq. ft. 1,320
7. ☐ Fire Resistive ☐ Ordinary ☑ Frame
   ☐ Non-Combustible

8. Vertical openings:
   Stairways protected? ☐ Yes ○ No ☑ None
   Elevators protected? ☐ Yes ○ No ☑ None
   Elevators: # of passengers: _____ # of freight: _____
9. Int. finish: Walls: Wood Ceiling: S/R
10. Building condition satisfactory? ☑ Yes ○ No
11. Basement in building? ○ Yes ☑ No
    If YES, ☐ Full ☐ Partial _____%
    ○ Finished ☐ Unfinished

HAZARDS

1. Heating type: FA central loc elsewhere
   A. Fuel ☐ Gas ☑ Electric ☐ Wood/Coal ☐ LP Gas ☐ Oil
   B. Appears safely arranged? not seen ☐ Yes ○ No
2. Air conditioning? ☐ Yes ○ No
   Type: ☑ Central ☐ Package ☐ Portable ○ Other
3. Electrical type: ☐ Conduit ☑ Romex ☐ Fuses
   A. Overcurrent Protection: ☑ Cir. Brkrs.
   B. Appear safely arranged? ☑ Yes ○ No
4. Are the following satisfactory?
   A. Housekeeping ☑ Yes ○ No
   B. Maintenance ☑ Yes ○ No
   C. Trash Removal ☑ Yes ○ No
   D. Smoking Control ☑ Yes ○ No
   E. Flam./Combust. liquids ☐ Yes ○ No ☑ None noted
   F. Welding/hot work ☐ Yes ○ No ☑ None noted
   G. Other special hazards ☐ Yes ○ No ☑ None noted

FIRE PROTECTION

1. Risk within city limits? ☑ Yes ○ No
2. Fire department: ☐ None ☑ Paid ☐ Volunteer
3. Distance to fire dept.: 1/3 Miles
4. Number of hydrants and distance: 1 at 50'; 1 at 370'
5. Adequate fire extinguishers? ☑ Yes ○ No
   Size and type: 2A
6. Extinguishers properly tagged and serviced? ☑ Yes ○ No
7. Sprinkler system? ☑ Yes ☐ No
   A. Coverage: ○ Full ○ Partial _____%
   B. Alarm: ☐ Full ☐ Local ☐ Central Station
8. Fire detection/alarm system? ☑ Yes ☐ No
9. Watchman service? ☑ Yes ☐ No
10. Fire dept. name and class: N. Myrtle Beach

Operations

Your insured is a corporation that has been in business for five years. It has been in business at the present location since the shopping mall was constructed three years ago. The mall has numerous small shops and restaurants built up on a boardwalk over a small inlet, approximately 3,000 feet from the Atlantic Ocean. Insured leases this space for a clothing store, selling ladies' moderately priced casual wear and a few accessories, such as purses, belts, etc. Also, a small line of costume jewelry is in one case at the counter.

Building

The building is three years old, of wood frame construction, and found to be in good condition and well maintained. The building is on wood pylons, and a portion of the building is above the water (see diagram and photo).

Heating and Air Conditioning

Heat and air conditioning are ducted from elsewhere in the mall and are said to be water-controlled and thought to be electric; however, the unit was not located. The insured said she believes the units are near Hwy. 17, several hundred feet from the building.

Wiring

Wiring is Romex with breaker protection. This appears to be in good condition and is three years old.

Protection

Insured is located in North Myrtle Beach, and the North Myrtle Beach fire department will respond there. No unusual fire department obstructions were noted.

Portable extinguishers were posted all around the mall area, and these were properly tagged and serviced. Also, a Z100 Moose digital alarm system protects the shop. This has heat detectors as well as infrared motion detectors, and insured states she believes this is directly monitored by the fire department. The alarm system was installed by the owners of the mall, and apparently these are present in every location.

Much of the mall is sprinklered, and there is a PIV valve fifty feet outside the insured's location; however, this particular shop is not sprinklered.

Security guards are employed by the mall, and the insured said that they patrol this area twenty-four hours a day.

Liability

The shop was in good condition from a liability standpoint. Stock is neatly stored and arranged in a clutter-free manner. Floor covering, lighting, and egress are good, and there are marked exits. All parking is controlled by the mall.

Losses

Contact states no losses have occurred under these coverages. They did have one business interruption loss during Hurricane Hugo in 1989.

Comments

Because of premises and building conditions, as well as good controls and the nature of insured's operation, this risk rates "good" for all coverages surveyed.

Note

Initially, we visited insured on 6/20; however, the contact was not in. We phoned back on several occasions before she contacted us on 6/28 to obtain loss and other information.

Recommendations

None are deemed necessary at this time.

Continued on next page.

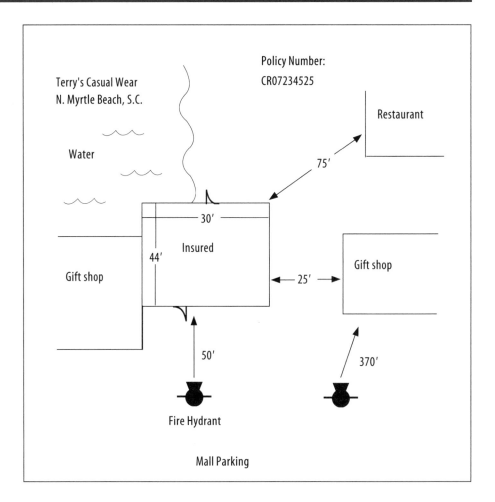

To support the risk analysis and improvement effort, the insurer's loss control representatives can provide training, informational, or counseling services. Some examples of these services are safety programs, technical loss-control information resources, fire protection systems testing and evaluation, and pre-construction counseling.

A safety program is a series of presentations on safety-related subjects to raise workers' awareness of loss exposures and appropriate safety behaviors. Typical subjects are fire safety, driver safety, and machine operation safety. The selection of subjects is based on an analysis of the policyholder's loss exposures or trends in loss experience. Priority is given to subjects that could significantly improve the policyholder's loss experience. Films, slide shows, and videotapes can be shown in conjunction with training programs or can be loaned to policyholders as requested.

Safety programs develop positive safety attitudes among all workers, improve workers' understanding of safety-related matters, and help workers accept responsibility for their role in the organization's safety program. To prepare the policyholder's managers for assuming a leadership role in loss control, the insurer might also conduct supervisory safety training sessions.

Many insurers also serve as a convenient source of technical loss control information. Information sought by the policyholder might relate to specific hazards and appropriate controls, the interpretation of standards, or particular safety management products or suppliers. By providing this information, the insurer helps the policyholder save time and effort in obtaining information needed to make informed loss control decisions. The insurer also builds a working relationship with the policyholder that can help to retain the policyholder's account.

Many insurer loss control departments enter into service contracts with their policyholders or other clients to provide periodic testing and maintenance for fire protection (and detection) systems, which must be tested regularly to ascertain their reliability during emergencies. The insurer's principal concerns are whether the system will respond in an emergency and whether the system is designed properly for the policyholder's current loss exposures.

When business owners expand existing facilities or build new structures, they often overlook the connection between construction features and insurance rates. Generally, rating credits can be given for noncombustible or fire-resistive construction, sprinkler systems, smoke detectors, burglar alarms, security hardware, and other features. A pre-construction review by the insurer of the drawings and specifications allows the policyholder to see how insurance rates and underwriting acceptability will be affected by the new construction. Any plan alterations the policyholder desires can then be made at minimal cost before construction begins.

Developing Safety Management Programs

The third loss control service is developing safety management programs. This service is usually coordinated by senior loss control staff members, often called loss control consultants, who have the advanced technical and communications skills needed for this type of service.

Developing safety management programs begins with a complete evaluation of the policyholder's operations, just as in risk analysis and improvement loss control services. After reviewing the policyholder's evaluation, loss control consultants assist the policyholder in establishing loss control goals, selecting appropriate loss control measures, organizing the resources necessary to implement the chosen loss control measures, and establishing procedures to monitor the program.

Because of several concerns, the policyholder is ordinarily responsible for implementing the program without direct assistance from the loss control consultant. These concerns include errors and omissions liability, lack of authority to exercise a management role in the policyholder's business, and the need for management to have program ownership. After being implemented, the program must be monitored to determine whether adjustments are needed. The consultant can provide a great deal of technical assistance in the monitoring phase of the program.

The consultation process normally requires frequent visits to the policyholder's premises to gather initial information, plan the review with management, and follow up to monitor the program.

Factors Affecting Service Levels

Every insurer must decide what levels of loss control service to provide to which policyholders. Several factors influence insurers' decisions.

Personal Insurance

An insurer that writes only personal insurance is unlikely to provide extensive loss control services. The relatively small premium for a typical personal auto or homeowners account does not justify the expense necessary to conduct on-site safety inspections.

During personal insurance underwriting, insurers sometimes request their agents or salespeople to photograph a house or an auto or to verify a car's vehicle identification number. Insurers might provide producers with checklists to ensure that certain items are either requested specifically of the applicant or identified during the producer's drive-by. An example of a checklist is shown in Exhibit 5-7. Producers can effectively implement loss control programs when provided with explicit instructions. When insuring exceptionally high-valued property—such as a mansion or a yacht—the insurer might use specifically trained loss control representatives to develop underwriting information or recommendations for reducing physical hazards.

Apart from on-site inspections, an insurer can promote loss control among its personal insurance policyholders by publishing educational bulletins or by offering rate discounts for home security systems, deadbolt locks, automobile anti-theft devices, driver education, or other loss control measures. An insurer might also support industry associations that disseminate information, conduct research, lobby legislators, or otherwise support loss control efforts to benefit society. Fire safety and highway safety are two major areas addressed by such associations.

Commercial Policyholder Size

The large premiums generated by commercial policyholders and the increased values at risk often make it economically feasible to provide such insureds with loss control services. The level of service rendered to a commercial policyholder can depend on the account's size. Typically, an insurer devotes more resources to accounts that generate a substantial premium.

Sometimes, policyholders might want a higher level of service than the insurer normally provides with its insurance. Policyholders who want supplemental services can purchase them for a fee in addition to the policy premium. Because the cost of these services is not built into the insurance premium charge, policyholders who do not want or need supplemental services are not required to subsidize the costs of them.

EXHIBIT 5-7

Personal Insurance Property Report

PERSONAL INSURANCE PROPERTY REPORT

DATE   November 1, 20XX
POLICY NUMBER   PCA 123 4579
NAME   Willis Bethea
MAILING   Providence Road
ADDRESS   Malvern, PA 19355
PROPERTY
LOCATION
(IF OTHER THAN ABOVE)

PHOTOS
☑ ATTACHED
PHOTOS _____
(IF MORE THAN ONE)
☐ NOT AVAILABLE

AMT. OF COVERAGE $ 194,000

OBSERVATIONS

1. Apprx. Year Built: ___1977___   OTHER:

2. Number of Stories: ☐ 1 ☑ 2 ☐ 3   ☐ _____

3. Occupancy:
   ☑ Single Family   ☐ Two Family   ☐ _____

4. Predominant Constr. Material:
   A. Dwg. ☑ Frame ☐ Brick   ☐ Solid   ☐ _____
                Veneer   or Stone   Brick
   B. Roof ☑ Comp. ☐ Tar &   ☐ Wood   ☐ _____
            Shingle   Gravel   Shingle
   C. Outbuildings ☐ None   ☑ Frame   ☐ _____
                    ☐ Masonry ☐ Metal

5. Condition:
   A. Dwg.   ☑ Good   ☐ _____
   B. Roof   ☑ Good   ☐ _____
   C. Outbuildings ☐ None   ☑ Good   ☐ _____

6. Neighborhood:
   A. Type ☑ Residential ☐ Commercial
            ☐ Rural   ☐ _____
   B. Status ☐ Improving ☑ Stable   ☐ _____

7. Protection:
   Approximate Distance in Feet to Nearest Hydrant   100 ft
   Approximate Distance in Miles to Nearest
   Responding Fire Department   1-1/2 mi

8. Liability Hazards:
   ☑ Outside Pool   ☑ Fenced   _____
   ☐ Horses   ☐ Unfenced
   ☐ Large Dogs   ☐ Business use

9. Hazards Noted: ☐ None
   ☐ Vacant or   ☐ Isolated or   ☐ Difficult Access
     Seasonal   Hidden   for Fire
     Property   ☐ Wood Stove   Department
   ☐ Dead Trees   ☐ Combustible   ☐ Open
     or Limbs   Brush or Debris   Foundation
   ☐ Adjacent   ☐ Flooding or
     Property   High Water   ☐ Other

VALUES

DIAGRAM—SHOW DIMENSIONS

Utility shed
Deck
Covered porch
Two-car garage

Estimated replacement cost using:
   ☑ Room count method
   ☐ Square foot method
   $ 210,000

CUSTOM HOME FEATURES:
_____
_____
_____
_____
_____

Date of Report ____9/1/20XX____
Agency: ___F.A. Smith, West Chester___
Inspector: ___Bill Smith___

REMARKS—RECOMMENDATIONS FOR IMPROVEMENT
_____
_____
_____
_____
_____

Types of Loss Exposures Insured

The loss control services an insurer provides depend to some degree on the types of loss exposures the insurer is willing to cover. An insurer that covers large and complex industrial firms needs skilled personnel and sophisticated equipment to meet the loss control requirements of such firms. It needs, for example, personnel and equipment to do the following:

- Test and evaluate the effects of noise levels on employees
- Appraise the hazards to employees of solvents, toxic metals, radioactive isotopes, and other substances
- Assist in the design of explosion suppression systems or fire-extinguishing systems for dangerous substances or easily damaged equipment
- Evaluate products liability loss exposures and prepare programs to minimize such loss exposures
- Deal with many other complex and specialized loss control problems

On the other hand, an insurer that deals primarily with habitational, mercantile, and small manufacturing loss exposures might be able to maintain a much less sophisticated loss control department.

SUMMARY

Property underwriting focuses on fire as a cause of loss. Most of the tools that property underwriters use to evaluate loss exposures are related to the fire cause of loss. Because fire is a predominant cause of loss, it is important that underwriters properly review that loss exposure to help achieve overall insurer profitability.

Property insurance underwriters use the "COPE" model to remind them of the four basic areas that should be analyzed for every application: construction, occupancy, protection, and external loss exposures.

Building construction is divided into six classifications: fire resistive, modified fire resistive, masonry noncombustible, noncombustible, joisted masonry, and frame.

Occupancy is described in terms of combustibility and damageability. Hazards fall into two categories: common hazards found in most commercial buildings and special hazards unique to the specific occupancy. Occupancy hazards and the degree of their control must be evaluated to determine to what extent they increase or decrease loss potential.

Protection can be classified as either public or private. Public protection consists of those services provided by a local government entity. ISO's public protection classes group property into one of ten categories based on the fire protection present. Private protection measures are provided by the property owner or tenant and range in sophistication from hand-held fire extinguishers to a fully equipped fire station at a manufacturing facility or an oil refinery. Private protection measures can be further categorized as prevention, detection, or suppression.

A consideration of external loss exposures broadens an underwriter's perspective to include areas and buildings adjacent to the loss exposure being evaluated. Availability of clear space, presence of surrounding brush, heights of exposing structures, and the occupancies of those structures are examples of underwriting concerns.

Although fire is the predominant cause of loss in property underwriting, other important causes of loss must be considered. These include lightning, explosion, windstorm, hail, vandalism and malicious mischief, water damage, flood, earthquake, collapse, and other causes of loss.

Underwriting business income includes measuring the largest loss of net income and estimating the probable period of interruption. The size of the net income loss is reflected in the selection of the coverage limits and the coinsurance percentage. The likely length of interruption is determined through sales projections and tempered by seasonal cycles and general economic conditions. Other considerations are the estimated rebuilding time, the time needed to return to the same level of production, and the presence of a disaster contingency plan that could reduce the period of interruption.

Crime insurance covers intentional losses caused by persons other than the policyholder to money and securities and to property other than money and securities through causes of loss such as employee dishonesty, burglary, robbery, and theft. Evaluating crime loss exposures other than employee dishonesty involves examining five factors: susceptibility to being stolen and marketability, property location, occupancy, public protection, and coverage and price modifications.

Ocean marine insurance is divided into four major categories: yachts, commercial hulls, protection and indemnity, and cargo. The underwriting criteria used to evaluate yachts include the vessel's seaworthiness, navigable waters and season, and operator experience. Commercial hull insurance underwriting involves the same concerns as yachts, but the values involved are more significant. Protection and indemnity (P&I) is liability insurance that provides coverage for claims arising out of a vessel's ownership and use. Also covered is liability for injuries to crew members. Ocean cargo insurance involves importing and exporting a wide variety of cargoes. Underwriting considerations focus on the susceptibility of the cargo to damage and how it is packed. Inland marine insurance is provided under numerous filed and unfiled coverage forms and classes. The ones discussed in this chapter represent the largest classes based on premium volume.

The chapter concludes with a discussion of the loss control function, which provides underwriters with important information needed to make sound underwriting decisions.

The discussion of the underwriting function is completed with the next chapter. Like this chapter on underwriting selected types of property insurance, the next chapter introduces liability underwriting basics for several important kinds of insurance.

The next chapter deals with underwriting liability insurance and describes the bases of legal liability and underwriting considerations for different types of liability insurance.

CHAPTER NOTES

1. Insurance Services Office, *Commercial Fire Rating Schedule* (New York: Insurance Services Office, 1983), pp. 3–4.

2. Glenn Puit, "MGM Grand Fire: The Deadliest Day," *Las Vegas Review-Journal,* Nov. 19, 2000, http://www.lvrj.com/lvrj_home/2000/Nov-19-Sun-2000/news/14818667.html (accessed January 6, 2003).

3. National Fire Protection Association, *Fire Protection Handbook,* 17th ed. (Quincy, Mass.: National Fire Protection Association, 1991), pp. 6–35—6–36.

4. *Fire Protection Handbook,* 17th ed., p. 6–23.

5. Insurance Services Office, *Mitigation online,* http://www.isomitigation.com/bcegs.html (accessed November 6, 2002).

6. *Fire Protection Handbook,* 17th ed., p. 1–44.

7. *Fire Protection Handbook,* 17th ed., p. 1–44.

8. American Association of Insurance Services Commercial Properties Manual— Pennsylvania, Rev 3.0, p. 4 (not dated). http://www.aaisdirect.com/aaistmep/4118896633 (accessed October 14, 2002).

9. *Fire Protection Handbook,* 17th ed., p. 6–8.

10. *Fire Protection Handbook,* 17th ed., p. 6–9.

11. Insurance Information Institute, *The Fact Book 2003* (New York: Insurance Information Institute, 2003), p. 66.

12. Gary G. Nichols and Sam Gerace, "A Survey of Hurricane Andrew" (Birmingham, Ala.: Southern Building Code Congress International, 1993).

13. For more information on these organizations and the NFIP, see http://www.fema.gov.

14. Robert B. Holtom, *Commercial Fire Underwriting* (Cincinnati: The National Underwriter Co., 1989), p. 140.

Chapter 6

Direct Your Learning

Underwriting Liability Insurance

After learning the content of this chapter, you should be able to:

■ Describe the three sources of legal liability.

■ Describe the loss exposures covered by and the underwriting considerations for commercial general liability insurance.

■ Describe the loss exposures covered by and the underwriting considerations for professional liability insurance.

■ Describe the loss exposures covered by and the underwriting considerations for personal liability insurance.

■ Explain how the regulatory environment affects personal auto insurance underwriting.

■ Describe the loss exposures covered by and the underwriting considerations for auto insurance.

■ Describe the loss exposures covered by and the underwriting considerations for workers' compensation insurance.

■ Describe the underwriting considerations for umbrella and excess liability insurance.

■ Explain why premium audits are conducted.

■ Describe the premium auditing process.

■ Explain why premium audits must be accurate.

Develop Your Perspective

What are the main topics covered in the chapter?

This chapter describes the factors considered in underwriting general liability, professional liability, personal liability, auto, workers' compensation, and umbrella and excess liability insurance. Also discussed are the legal bases for liability and the premium audit process.

Consider the legal basis for liability in the United States.

- How does this legal foundation create liability exposures in all of the various forms described in the chapter?

Why is it important to learn about these topics?

However unintentional or unexpected liability losses might be, some factors increase the chance that an organization or individual might injure or harm others and be the subject of a liability claim or lawsuit.

Analyze these factors and the role of underwriting.

- How does underwriting select and price policies to reflect the exposures presented?
- What does underwriting do to protect the financial stability of your insurance organization?
- What regulations restrict an underwriter's ability to select and price policies freely?

How can you use what you will learn?

Judge the general liability exposures for a local business.

- What property or activities increase its potential for loss?
- How could the business decrease its potential for being the subject of a liability claim or lawsuit?

Chapter 6

Underwriting Liability Insurance

This is the last of three chapters that describe property-liability insurance underwriting. Underwriting varies by type of insurance because each type of liability insurance covers different loss exposures. This chapter, therefore, focuses on key underwriting considerations for different types of liability insurance and concludes by discussing premium auditing.

SOURCES OF LEGAL LIABILITY

Underwriters who are responsible for reviewing applications for liability insurance must understand the legal concepts that underlie this insurance. This understanding assists underwriters in accurately determining the loss exposures of these applications. Liability policies cover damages that the insured becomes legally obligated to pay as the result of a covered loss. Legal liability is ordinarily based on torts, statutes, or contracts. This section briefly examines the concept and sources of legal liability.

Legal Liability

United States law is based on common law (decisions of courts), state and federal statutes (written laws enacted by legislative bodies), and contract law (civil law dealing with contracts). The legal system provides citizens with certain rights. These rights include freedom from bodily injury or damage to property caused by the negligent or intentional acts of others.

The law recognizes two classes of wrongful acts, with corresponding legal remedies:

1. Criminal acts—Crimes against others, which are also offenses against society. Persons found guilty of crimes are generally fined and/or jailed.
2. Civil acts—Civil wrongs violate the rights of individuals by tort or by breach of contract. Parties who commit civil wrongs are usually required to pay money damages to those who are wronged.

Liability is created when the law imposes a civil obligation on the wrongdoer to compensate the injured party for the financial consequences of the wrongful act. The party who is wronged and who files suit seeking relief is called the plaintiff. The party the plaintiff charges with committing the wrong is the defendant.

Liability insurance
Insurance that covers losses resulting from bodily injury to others or damage to the property of others for which the insured is legally liable and to which coverage applies.

Liability insurance covers losses resulting from bodily injury to others or damage to the property of others for which the insured is legally liable and to which coverage applies. Liability insurance covers the following three sources of legal liability:

1. Torts (tort liability)
2. Contracts (contractual liability)
3. Statutes that impose liability without regard to fault (statutory liability)

Torts

Tort
Wrongful act (other than a breach of contract) committed by one person against another for which a civil lawsuit in a court can provide a remedy.

The first source of legal liability is torts. A **tort** is a wrongful act (other than a breach of contract) committed by one person against another for which a civil lawsuit can provide a remedy. A person who has committed a tort might be held liable for damages.

Torts can be intentional or negligent. Liability insurance typically covers torts caused by negligence but might also cover certain torts caused intentionally. A tort can also be based on absolute liability or vicarious liability. Such torts might be covered by liability insurance. Each type of tort is discussed separately, but in practice the lines between the various types of torts are often imprecise.

Negligence

Negligence
Failure to act in a manner that is reasonably prudent or failure to exercise an appropriate degree of care under given circumstances.

Negligence is the failure to exercise the degree of care that a reasonably prudent person would exercise to avoid harming others. The following four elements are required to bring a civil suit for negligence:

1. Legal duty owed to the plaintiff to use due care.
2. Failure to conform to the standard of care required in the situation, which creates an unreasonable risk of harm. Courts measure conduct by the standard of the reasonable person, who is a figurative person exhibiting the standard of conduct that society expects.
3. Causal connection exists between the negligent act and the bodily injury or property damage.
4. Bodily injury or property damage.

Bodily injury or property damage caused by negligence often occurs when one person is on another person's premises. Traditionally, courts have recognized three classes of persons whose rights the law protects while they are on the premises of another party. Most courts hold that a person is liable for any injury or damage that is reasonably foreseeable.

The following list indicates the three levels of duty owed to others when they are on another's premises, with the highest degree of care owed to an invitee and the lowest, to a trespasser.

1. An **invitee** is a person who enters the premises for the owner's or the occupant's financial benefit. For example, a customer who comes into a store is an invitee.

2. A **licensee** is any other person who enters the premises with permission. For example, a social guest is a licensee.

3. A **trespasser** is anyone who enters the premises without permission. For example, a burglar is a trespasser.

Intentional Torts

In contrast to negligence, **intentional torts** generally involve a wrongful act or omission intended to cause harm. Intentional torts include the following:

- Assault and battery
- Unlawful detention (false imprisonment, false arrest)
- Defamation (libel, slander)
- Invasion of the right of privacy
- Copyright violations

Strict Liability

In various situations, tort liability can be imposed when the defendant acted neither negligently nor with intent to cause harm. This type of legal liability is commonly referred to as **strict liability** (or "absolute liability"). The term "strict liability" is also used to describe liability imposed by certain statutes, such as workers' compensation laws. Common examples of strict liability imposed under tort principals include the following:

- Abnormally dangerous instrumentalities
- Ultrahazardous activities
- Sale of dangerously defective products

Vicarious Liability

In some situations, the law holds one person liable for the torts of others. Relationships that can create such **vicarious liability** include the following:

- A principal-agent relationship
- An employer-employee relationship
- A parent-child relationship
- A contractual relationship
- A partnership

An agent is someone who acts for another person, called the principal. A principal might be liable for the torts of an agent acting within the agency's scope. Likewise, an employer might be liable for the acts of employees in the

Invitee
Person who enters a premises for the financial benefit of the owner or occupant.

Licensee
Person who enters a premises with the owner's or occupant's permission.

Trespasser
Person who enters a premises without the owner's or occupant's permission.

Intentional torts
Category of torts that involves a wrongful act or omission of a type intended to cause harm.

Strict liability
Liability imposed without regard to fault.

Vicarious liability
Liability arising when one party is held liable for the actions of another party.

course of their employment under the doctrine of *respondeat superior* ("let the master respond"). Generally, a parent is not liable for the torts of a minor child merely because of the family relationship, but the law recognizes exceptions. A child sometimes acts as the parent's agent or employee. Parents might also fail to exercise reasonable care in controlling a child for the safety of others.

Closely related to vicarious liability is the concept of negligent entrustment. For example, a boat owner might negligently entrust his boat to somebody who causes an accident because he or she lacks the skills needed to operate the boat. Claims of negligent entrustment are against the person who negligently entrusts property to another. Claims are based on negligence, not vicarious liability.

Damages

Damages are the remedy the law provides for torts. Damages are money the law entitles the plaintiff to recover for bodily injury, personal injury, or property damage. In addition to paying money as damages, a court can order the plaintiff to mitigate damages by protecting against further injury or damage.

Court-awarded money damages are usually categorized as compensatory or punitive:

- Compensatory damages compensate the injured party for the harm caused by the defendant's wrongful act.
- Punitive damages punish defendants whose conduct is willful, wanton, or grossly negligent.

Liability insurance always covers compensatory damages but adheres to applicable state and federal law on punitive damages. Liability insurance coverage for punitive damages varies by state law. Damages are discussed in greater detail in the claim chapters of this text.

Statutes

The second source of legal liability is statutes. Statutes can impose legal liability on certain persons regardless of whether they committed a tort or assumed contractual liability. Statutes can impose legal obligations on certain persons or organizations to compensate others if certain events occur. The workers' compensation system is an example of U.S. statutory liability. Workers' compensation statutes require every employer to pay prescribed benefits for occupational injury or illness of any employee (subject to exceptions in some states) arising out of and in the course of employment. These statutes require prompt compensation to injured employees without the need for lawsuits.

Contracts

The third source of legal liability is contracts. Legal liability based on con-tracts can arise out of either a breach of contract or an agreement to assume another party's liability. A breach of contract occurs when a party does not perform as promised in the contract. The injured party can sue for money damages or seek the remedy of specific performance, whereby the court orders the defendant to do what he or she contractually promised to do. Hold-harmless or indemnity agreements are contractual provisions whereby one party agrees to assume the liability of another party for damages in situations in which the first party would not otherwise be liable. For example, in a building lease, a tenant might agree to assume responsibility for all injuries occurring on the premises, including any caused by the landlord.

UNDERWRITING COMMERCIAL GENERAL LIABILITY

Commercial general liability insurance provides coverage for loss exposures in the following five liability categories:

1. Premises and operations liability
2. Personal and advertising injury liability
3. Premises medical payments liability
4. Contractual liability
5. Products and completed operations liability

For many years, the preceding list represented distinct "coverages" that might be purchased individually in separate forms or endorsements. Now, they are all available through the Insurance Services Office (ISO) Commercial General Liability Coverage Form (CGL).

This section discusses the loss exposures and the hazards an underwriter would consider when evaluating these loss exposures.

Premises and Operations Loss Exposures

The primary loss exposures facing most businesses are those for *either* their premises *or* their operations. General liability insurance covers the loss exposures of the insured's business premises and operations.

- **Premises liability loss exposures** arise from the policyholder's ownership or possession of real property.
- **Operations liability loss exposures** arise from a policyholder's business operations conducted away from its own premises and from uncompleted work. To distinguish operations loss exposures from **completed opera-tions loss exposures** (liability for damage or injuries arising from finished work), underwriters frequently refer to the former as *operations in progress* (injuries arising while work is being performed).

Premises liability loss exposures
Liability loss exposures that arise from the ownership or possession of real property (the premises).

Operations liability loss exposures
Liability loss exposures that arise from a policyholder's business activities conducted away from its own premises and from uncompleted work.

Completed operations loss exposures
Liability loss exposures that arise from an organization's finished work.

Liability underwriters tend to evaluate a business's loss exposures in terms of its "premises risks" or "operations risks." For example, underwriters consider a retail store a premises risk, and a building contractor, an operations risk. This does not assume that the loss exposures of the risk are exclusively premises or operations. Underwriters recognize that insureds whose loss exposures are primarily related to their premises also face incidental liability for the loss exposures of their operations in progress. Likewise, when the operations-in-progress loss exposures are primary, underwriters recognize the existence of incidental premises loss exposures.

Various factors increase premises liability loss exposures. Consider a retail store, for example—a typical premises risk. A long-established store with a good reputation and a steady business is more likely to attract customers than a new or declining store. A higher level of customer traffic suggests higher premises loss exposures.

Location can also contribute to customer traffic and, therefore, to the extent of loss exposures. Suppose an urban electronics store opens a new branch in a suburban indoor mall. A mall usually has several well-known, large stores that attract traffic to other, smaller stores in the mall. Mall customers are more likely to enter the premises of the mall electronics store than pedestrians are to enter a similar store on a typical city street. A greater concentration of mall customers is also likely during evenings or weekends. Even if total sales volume were average for the store's class of business, the mall electronics store would probably have a relatively greater concentration of customers at certain hours. A mall's setup and customer traffic make it less likely that customers would be able to exit the premises quickly in the event of a fire. In contrast, most weather-related loss exposures decrease for a store located in a mall, because indoor malls tend to eliminate premises hazards such as icy walkways or sidewalks.

Underwriters must also consider the legal status of persons likely to be on the premises. What is the policyholder's legal duty to these persons, and what standards of care are expected? The policyholder must demonstrate behavior that is consistent with the standard of care required. The underwriter can compare the policyholder's required degree of care with that of an average risk in the same classification. For example, a retail store with mostly adult customers might need to exercise reasonable care, but a toy store attracting many children might need to exercise additional care.

Because bodily injury claims tend to produce larger losses, bodily injury loss exposures are usually a primary underwriting concern. An underwriter cannot, however, ignore the potential for property damage losses. Property damage losses include claims not only for the value of the damaged property but also for the loss of its use.

When evaluating premises and operations loss exposures, underwriters need to consider physical hazards as well as the relation of any contractors or subcontractors to the policyholders that might affect loss exposures.

Physical Hazards

The physical hazards relating to premises and operations liability loss exposures fall into three categories:

1. *Common hazards* are physical hazards common to many premises, such as those that induce slips and falls. Common hazards frequently include uneven stairs, tears in carpets, inadequate lighting, congested aisles, poor housekeeping, and defective heating or electrical equipment. The underwriter tries to determine what hazards or conditions increase the likelihood of bodily injury or property damage for which the owner or lessor of the premises would be held liable.

2. *Special hazards of the class* are physical hazards, such as chemicals, dust, and explosives, that occur only in certain types of businesses.

3. *Special hazards of the risk* are physical hazards found in businesses that conduct operations that are not typical of the class to which they belong. Underwriters must identify any special hazards of the risk and decide whether they present unacceptable liability loss exposures. These hazards could evolve from an incidental operation, a gradual diversification of operations, or an assumption of operations not contemplated when the loss exposure was originally insured and rated. When special hazards of the risk exist, the business has loss exposures beyond those anticipated by the standard rates for the class.

To properly evaluate the physical hazards of premises loss exposures, underwriters consider the entire premises. When the primary loss exposures arise from the premises' interior, underwriters cannot overlook the exterior loss exposures. Injuries can be caused outside the premises by broken or icy sidewalks, parking lots in poor condition, falling signs, playground equipment, swimming pools, and other features of the premises. Forklift trucks or other mobile equipment could cause injury inside or outside the premises, depending on the equipment's type and use.

In addition to evaluating bodily injury loss exposures, an underwriter considers the physical hazards that can cause property damage losses. Torn or stained clothing and damage to vehicles in parking lots are the most common property damage losses. Additionally, pollution has become one of the most significant sources of severe losses, which should be considered when the insured requests limited pollution coverage under the general liability coverage form. For example, an apartment house could have an oil-fired heating system fed from an underground storage tank. The underground tank presents a serious leakage loss exposure that most underwriters would prefer be handled by environmental impairment liability specialists.

Generally, businesses with substantial premises loss exposures, such as apartment houses and office buildings, have minimal operations loss exposures. Businesses with small premises loss exposures, such as service businesses and contractors, have substantial operations loss exposures. An electrical contractor will usually have a place of business, but it is not likely to be a substantial loss exposure affecting risk selection. A store and shop where electrical fixtures are sold and repaired, on the other hand, would present premises loss exposures that an underwriter would have to assess separately. Typically, contractors have few premises loss exposures, but they have substantial operations loss exposures because of installation and repair work. An electrical contractor who has a sales and repair operation on the premises has both premises loss exposures and operations loss exposures.

The hazards related to operations loss exposures vary more than those related to premises loss exposures. Some service or contracting risks have heavy machinery or mobile equipment; some use flammables and blowtorches; some rent or lease equipment; and some blast, excavate, or erect. The builders of ranch-style residences and high-rise apartments do similar work, use similar tools, and create loss exposures at construction sites, but the similarity ends there. The high-rise building contractor uses steel girders, land-leveling equipment, and cranes, often in heavily populated areas.

Operations-type risks generally have a greater potential for property damage losses than do premises-type risks. The major sources of property damage losses are fire, collapse, water damage, and, in some cases, pollution. Using heavy equipment has the potential to cause serious property damage.

Contractors and Subcontractors

A policyholder could be held liable for the negligent acts of contractors or subcontractors hired to perform work. Generally, a property owner or con-tractor who hires an independent contractor is not liable under common law for the independent contractor's negligent acts. An independent contractor performs the work without specific direction about *how* to perform the work. In some cases, however, courts have held that an independent contractor is a de facto employee. This ruling eliminates the principal's or contractor's common-law immunity. Determining who is responsible for activities that cause injury or damage is a problem, particularly when contractors and subcontractors are individuals without employees. The injured party can easily claim that the property owner directed the work.

The law also holds the insured vicariously liable for duties that cannot be delegated to others. A principal has a duty to select competent independent contractors and to provide adequate supervision to protect the public from injury. Therefore, either a land owner (as a general contractor's employer) or a general contractor (as a subcontractor's employer) could be held liable to third persons for the negligent acts of contractors or subcontractors. Admit-tedly, the policyholder's liability for the acts of others is less significant than liability for its own acts. However, the potential loss exposure exists, and coverage is provided by commercial general liability insurance. When rating business operations other than a contractor, no special classification or rating rules exist for subcontractors, because the potential exposure is minimal. When the policyholder is a contractor, the underwriter must determine whether subcontractors carry adequate insurance. If they do, only a small charge is made to cover those loss exposures for which the policyholder might be held liable for the subcontractor's work.

When the identity of subcontractors is known, the insurer can require certificates of insurance from the subcontractors. The underwriter treats subcontractors who fail to provide evidence of insurance as though they are the insured's employees and charges the appropriate premium for their loss exposures. However, an insured usually does not know in advance which subcontractors it will hire during the policy term. This uncertainty places the underwriter at a disadvantage because the subcontractors cannot be evaluated before the policy is written. The underwriter must then rely on the policyholder's reputation in hiring competent subcontractors.

Personal and Advertising Injury Loss Exposures

Personal and advertising injury is automatically included as Coverage B in the ISO CGL coverage form, unless it is specifically excluded by attaching an endorsement to the policy. Because it is a part of the coverage form, underwriters do not usually evaluate this loss exposure closely unless the policyholder's operation is one for which personal injury or advertising injury losses might occur frequently. Based on this evaluation, the underwriter can decide to exclude both personal injury and advertising injury or to eliminate coverage for advertising injury only.

Personal injury loss exposures include the policyholder's legal liability arising out of libel; slander; false arrest; wrongful eviction; invasion of the right of private occupancy; and infringement of copyright, trade dress, or slogan. Underwriters would evaluate the personal injury loss exposure for department or other retail stores because of potential false arrest of suspected shoplifters. Likewise, hotels, motels, or apartment occupancies could present a personal injury loss exposure for wrongful eviction or invasion of privacy. Many insurers provide a listing of occupancies for which personal injury coverage should be evaluated within their underwriting guidelines.

The coverage provided under the CGL form for advertising liability is on an incidental basis only, and the form excludes personal injury and advertising injury committed by an insured whose business is advertising, broadcasting, publishing, or telecasting. This coverage is intended for businesses that purchase advertising to sell their own products or services, not for a company that is in the advertising business.

Premises Medical Payments Loss Exposures

Medical payments coverage is also automatically included as Coverage C in the CGL coverage form. Underwriters do not individually underwrite this loss exposure but do consider the medical payments loss exposure as part of the premises or operations loss exposures. Medical payments provides coverage for medical expenses of persons other than the insured who are injured on the policyholder's premises or because of the policyholder's operations. Medical payments coverage does not, however, require the policyholder to be legally liable to pay for them. Because of this, the limits for medical payments coverage are usually much lower than those for bodily injury or property damage, typically $5,000 or $10,000 per person. Medical payments coverage can be excluded by attaching an endorsement to the policy, but this is rarely done.

Contractual Liability Loss Exposures

With a few exceptions, commercial general liability policies cover any liability the insured assumes under a contract related to the business.

Hold-Harmless Agreements

Hold-harmless agreement
Contractual provision that obligates the indemnitor to assume the indemnitee's legal liability.

Indemnitor
Party in a hold-harmless agreement who assumes the other party's liability.

Indemnitee
Party in a hold-harmless agreement whose legal liability is assumed by the indemnitor.

A contractual provision under which one party assumes the liability of another is called a **hold-harmless agreement**. Under this agreement, one party, the **indemnitor**, agrees to *indemnify and hold harmless* the other party, the **indemnitee**. Like an insurance policy, a hold-harmless agreement is an indemnity contract. However, the indemnitor in a hold-harmless agreement is not in the business of assuming others' risk, and a hold-harmless agreement is rarely a separate contract. It is usually a clause in a contract that has a broader purpose.

The two parties to a hold-harmless agreement often presume that one party assumes the other party's entire liability. They rely on the indemnitor's liability insurance to protect both parties from liability losses. Certain types of hold-harmless agreements, however, fall outside the scope of liability insurance. Statutes in most states also limit using hold-harmless agreements in certain situations. Some courts have found that hold-harmless agreements are so vague that they are meaningless because extremely broad assumptions of liability might violate public policy. In these situations, the indemnitee has not transferred the loss exposure, despite the hold-harmless agreement.

An underwriter cannot know at policy inception what liability an insured will assume during the policy period. Therefore, when evaluating this loss exposure, an underwriter must usually rely on the insured's reputation and past practices.

Products and Completed Operations Loss Exposures

Any business that makes, sells, distributes, or even gives away products has loss exposures that can lead to products liability. Many service businesses, such as builders and repair shops, have loss exposures from the work they perform for others.

Sources of Products Liability

This section deals with the three sources of liability for product sale, manufacture, and distribution:

1. Breach of warranty
2. Negligence
3. Strict liability in tort

It is not uncommon for the plaintiff to assert all three causes of action in a products liability suit.

Breach of warranty is the first source of products liability. Breach of warranty is based on breach of contract. In every sale of merchandise, the seller implies warranties of merchantability and fitness for the product's intended use. The seller can also make an express warranty of fitness for a specific purpose. Because breach of warranty has limitations as an effective basis for products liability, the courts also recognize other grounds for products liability.

Breach of warranty
Source of liability based on laws that protect consumers who purchase products that do not perform as expected.

Negligence is the second source of products liability. Negligence applies to a broad range of persons who have no contractual relationship with the seller, and negligence is often difficult to prove. A plaintiff can rarely point to a specific act of negligence in a products liability suit.

Many products cannot be manufactured free of danger, and these products' hazards are not always obvious. The manufacturers of such products have a duty to warn potential consumers of any danger that is not public knowledge. Failure to give adequate warning is the most common charge of negligence in products liability suits.

Strict liability in tort is the third source of products liability. Strict liability in tort is the most common basis for products liability suits; it imposes liability on any person who produces an unreasonably dangerous product.

Products Loss Exposures

Underwriting generally focuses on the product itself. The underwriter is concerned about the product's potential to harm the public—that is, the product's loss frequency and severity.

Determining the inherent hazards of the product is, therefore, the first and most important step in underwriting a product. A product that is not inherently hazardous has a relatively minor loss exposure, and vice versa. Consider two products: a power lawn mower and a metal chair. The lawn mower is a much more hazardous product than the chair because the mower's inherent characteristics increase the likelihood of loss.

The applicant's business, the limits of liability, and the business's size and scope are important in underwriting both types of products. However, the quantity of underwriting information needed varies with the type of product.

In fact, most insurance applications have a section (or the insurer has a separate questionnaire) that requires specific information about products liability loss exposures.

In underwriting products liability loss exposures, underwriters ask the following questions:

- What are the product's inherent hazards?
- What representations or promises are made to the consumer in the sales material and advertising?
- Do technical manuals for complex products accurately reflect the safety precautions required in the product's assembly and repair?
- Does the product's packaging adequately protect the product so that it will operate properly when used?
- Are the instructions easy to read and understand?
- Does the product's warranty overstate the capability of the product?
- Are loss control efforts introduced into the product's design and production phases?
- Is a complaint-handling system in place to identify flaws and prevent injury and damage?
- Are quality-control checks incorporated into the product's manufacture?
- Are accurate records kept of products and components so that defective products can be identified and recalled?
- Have product lines changed to increase the inherent hazards?
- What is the applicant's position in the channel of distribution?
- Who is the product's ultimate consumer?

Plaintiffs increase their chances of winning a products liability lawsuit when they assert more than one ground for recovery, thereby increasing underwriting losses. The owner of a sport utility vehicle, for example, was injured when the vehicle overturned on a road. A court found that the propensity to overturn did not render the product unreasonably dangerous; it was a reasonable hazard for an off-road vehicle. Consequently, the plaintiff lost the strict liability in tort suit. The manufacturer's advertising, however, had portrayed the vehicle as a suitable family car. An appeals court ruled that this allowed a jury to infer that the manufacturer had breached an express warranty of fitness for a specific purpose. The court upheld the award against the manufacturer on those grounds.[1] This suit was decided based on the insured's advertising rather than on the product's inherent hazards.

Completed Operations Loss Exposures

Completed operations loss exposures include construction, service, repair, and maintenance activities. The characteristic that distinguishes completed operations loss exposures from products loss exposures is the insured's completed work that can cause injury or damage.

Generally, businesses that perform services have primarily operations loss exposures rather than premises loss exposures. Businesses with operations loss exposures are likely to have *completed* operations loss exposures. Underwriting focuses on the applicant's activities or operations that could cause a loss, particularly those performed off-premises. How work is performed is important to the underwriter in evaluating loss exposures of both operations in progress and completed operations. Quality of workmanship and equipment, supervision of employees, technical skill, reputation, and experience are all areas the underwriter considers when evaluating operations loss exposures. If an underwriter finds significant shortcomings in any of these areas, he or she might conclude that the operations loss exposures are significant. These same areas are important in evaluating completed operations loss exposures. For example, faulty workmanship is likely to cause a loss while the work is being performed and is also likely to cause a loss after the work has been completed.

Careless or faulty work could damage customers' premises and could even cause a fire. Careless or faulty work could also cause a loss after the work has been completed and the workers have left the premises. The injury or damage that results then falls within completed operations loss exposures. Careless or faulty work is likely to increase loss frequency to the same degree for both operations in progress and completed operations.

The completed operations loss exposures that the underwriter needs to consider vary by class of business. Consider, for example, the loss exposures faced by a contractor building high-rise apartments. While constructing a building, workers can cause extensive property damage from fire, collapse, or water, as well as bodily injury from falling objects, the operation of equipment, and the use of construction materials and tools. After the apartments are inhabited, fire or collapse could cause even more serious injuries and damage. If the cause of such a fire or collapse could be traced to the contractor's faulty workmanship, the insurer who underwrote the completed operations loss exposures would be responsible for the loss.

At the other extreme, a piano tuner could damage the customer's property while performing his or her work, but it is extremely unlikely that injury or damage resulting from this work would occur after the work has been completed. Logically, piano tuning is an operations classification in which completed operations loss exposures are included in the premises and operations insurance rate.

When evaluating an applicant for completed operations coverage, the underwriter must determine the likelihood and severity of potential losses by evaluating the applicant's business. Completed operations loss exposures for a given business can be considerably different from the completed operations loss exposures for other businesses in the same class.

UNDERWRITING PROFESSIONAL LIABILITY INSURANCE

Traditionally, professional liability insurance included only insurance covering liability arising out of providing professional services to others. Examples of such professional liability insurance include medical professional liability ("malpractice") insurance or errors and omissions insurance for accountants, attorneys, insurance agents and brokers, and other professionals. Today, the term "professional liability" is also used to encompass insurance that is not limited to professions but is purchased widely by all types of organizations. Three such types of insurance are directors and officers liability insurance, fiduciary liability insurance, and employment practices liability insurance.

Professional Liability Loss Exposures

Commercial general liability (CGL) policies explicitly exclude most professional liability loss exposures. Moreover, claims covered under professional liability policies do not necessarily involve liability for bodily injury, personal injury, or property damage that could be covered by CGL policies. The loss exposures covered by professional liability insurance include mistakes; errors or omissions in rendering professional service; or wrongful acts, depending on what professional liability coverage is involved. Professional liability underwriting naturally focuses on professional liability loss exposures rather than premises, operations, products, or completed operations loss exposures. Professional liability insurance is usually written by insurers who specialize in that type of insurance.

The many forms of professional liability insurance cover a broad range of loss exposures, each with unique underwriting considerations. This text does not examine specific professions or types of coverage. It does, however, highlight some common concerns of underwriters handling professional liability insurance.

Occurrence Versus Claims-Made Coverage

Underwriters must recognize the difference between occurrence and claims-made coverage and the problems associated with occurrence coverage. The first problem is that professional liability losses tend to be large and infrequent, and claims for these losses are often filed and settled many years after the occurrence on which the claim is based. The second problem is that it is often difficult to determine whether the professional liability insurance has been underwritten and priced properly until many years after the premium has been collected. To alleviate these problems, many professional liability policies provide claims-made coverage. Claims-made coverage covers liability claims that are made (submitted) during the policy period for covered events that occur on or after a retroactive date and before the end of the policy period. The retroactive date is the date on or after which bodily injury or property damage must occur to be covered. With such coverages, the insurer knows much sooner than with occurrence coverage what claims are made for any given year. Extended reporting periods, common in claims-made coverage, provide a useful coverage extension for the insured but delay the insurer's final results. Retroactive dates are also important underwriting considerations in claims-made policies, because an early retroactive date extends the period during which covered events must have occurred.

Settlement Conditions

Underwriters also need to consider the policy's settlement conditions. Most professional liability insurers insist on the right to settle out of court without the policyholder's consent. However, some professional liability policies contain a condition that requires the insured's consent. The difference is significant to the underwriter: The insurer's claim and defense costs could increase if the insurer cannot settle a claim without the insured's consent.

depends on policy

Defense Costs

The treatment of defense costs is another underwriting consideration. In some policies, defense costs are paid in addition to policy limits; in others, defense costs are included within policy limits. The insurer's possible maximum loss is greater when defense costs are payable in addition to policy limits.

— depends on policy

Deductibles and Self-Insured Retentions

Although deductibles are not commonly used with most types of liability insurance, large self-insured retentions (SIRs), typically $10,000 or more, are common with professional liability insurance. By requiring the insured to participate substantially in any loss, SIRs provide a strong incentive for the insured to prevent losses.

Other Factors

One factor that underwriters also need to consider is social and business trends that affect a particular type of professional liability insurance. For example, the accounting scandals of the past few years significantly increased the frequency and severity of directors and officers liability claims and led underwriters to evaluate this type of insurance much more closely than they had in the past. A second factor that underwriters should consider is the uncertain labor market of the past few years and its likely effect on employment practices liability claims for wrongful termination or other employment grievances. A third factor is declining profitability for certain types of professional liability insurance. Underwriters for insurers still providing medical professional liability insurance should closely evaluate new applicants whose insurance had been written by insurers that found such insurance unprofitable.

Medical professional liability is one of the largest classes of professional liability insurance. The physician's medical specialty is an important underwriting consideration. Those generally considered to be in the high-risk category are anesthesiologists, neurosurgeons, plastic surgeons, obstetrician-gynecologists, and cardiovascular surgeons. The general practitioner has fewer loss exposures, particularly if no surgery is performed.

Professional liability underwriters consider the following attributes of physicians: degrees and/or licenses held, membership in professional organizations, certification, recertification (continuing education), years in practice, type of clientele, associates (that is, fellow workers), and whether the doctor practices as an individual or as a member of a professional association. All of these attributes indicate something about the doctor's position within the medical community, which often plays a major role in defending suits. The physician's professional reputation is important in malpractice cases, and the insurer often seeks other physicians to speak on behalf of the insured's professional competence.

Specialty area is also an important underwriting consideration in lawyers' professional liability. A law firm that specializes in corporate practice involving many complex cases has many more loss exposures than a firm dealing exclusively in small probate and real estate work.

Evaluating the specialty area applies to other professionals as well, including insurance agents, real estate brokers, and accountants and auditors. Large accounting firms have experienced not only professional liability losses but also a loss of reputation as a result of their activities in certifying the financial records of publicly held companies. The loss exposure is greater for a firm auditing large public companies than for a firm auditing a number of small, privately held companies.

UNDERWRITING PERSONAL LIABILITY INSURANCE

Personal liability insurance is designed for individuals and their families. Generally, this insurance covers liability arising from the premises, operations, and products of an individual or a family. Personal liability insurance is part of every homeowners policy. It can also be purchased with a dwelling fire policy or alone. It covers liability that does not arise out of the applicant's business or profession or out of the use of most motor vehicles, airplanes, hovercraft, or large watercraft. Personal liability insurance applies to the premises where the applicant maintains a residence and to the non-business activities of the policyholder and household members.

Residence Premises Loss Exposures

All property owners, as well as tenants in control of property, are faced with the loss exposure of injury to people who come onto the property. This loss exposure can be increased by an attractive nuisance hazard. An

attractive nuisance is an alluring or unusual object or structure (usually man-made), such as a swimming pool or a treehouse, that might entice children onto the premises. These hazards are in addition to the common premises hazards of uneven or icy sidewalks, poorly maintained steps and porches, and poorly lighted hallways. Large sliding glass doors also present a hazard if they lack decals or some other way to call attention to the glass. These doors produce substantial losses when guests walk or run through them. A significant underwriting factor is the policyholder's attitude about maintaining the premises. The underwriter can evaluate premises hazards through photographs or personal inspections conducted by the producer or by independent inspection services.

Attractive nuisance
Potentially harmful object or structure so inviting or interesting to children that it would lure them onto someone's premises.

Residence liability losses are infrequent but can be severe. Therefore, loss experience can be extremely volatile in all except large books of business. Personal liability insurance is usually sold as an incidental part of a package that includes property insurance. Even when sold alone, personal liability insurance has a relatively low premium.

The expense factor of this low premium does not permit extensive investigation and inspection of the premises. Consequently, the underwriter faces highly unpredictable losses that must be underwritten based on little information. So, some insurers have developed supplementary forms to capture needed information. These forms might ask some of the following questions:

- Are large or potentially vicious dogs present?
- Does the applicant own or keep horses?
- Does the residence have objects or structures that might attract children, such as a swimming pool, hot tub, backyard gym, swings, slides, or climbing bars?
- Does an incidental office occupancy loss exposure exist?
- Is the residence under construction or being renovated?
- Does the applicant rent all or part of the dwelling to others?

Personal Activity Loss Exposures

Personal liability insurance extends coverage to all activities not specifically excluded and does not limit coverage to personal activities at the residence premises. Insured incidents might include injury or damage caused by an unlicensed recreational vehicle or property damage intentionally caused by children. Products and completed operations liability is not excluded, so coverage would apply, for example, if the insured furnishes food for a potluck dinner that makes guests sick.

Sports liability is one area of major underwriting concern. Injuries caused while golfing, hunting, fishing, and playing team sports are typical loss exposures. The underwriter usually cannot determine the applicant's activities. The producer is the only possible source of this information and might know whether the applicant has a particularly strong interest in an area that could present an atypical loss exposure.

Other Underwriting Factors

Some other relevant underwriting factors are not directly related to the premises or the applicant's activities, including occupation, claim history, and credit scores.

- The occupation of the applicant might indicate possible business loss exposures on the premises.

- Past losses might indicate future losses. Applications usually request information on all losses during the past several years. In addition, many underwriters participate in C.L.U.E.® (Comprehensive Loss Underwriting Exchange), "a claim history information exchange that enables insurers to access prior claim information in the underwriting and rating process. C.L.U.E. Personal Property reports contain up to five years of personal property claims matching the search criteria submitted by the inquiring insurer. Data provided in C.L.U.E. reports includes policy information such as name, date of birth and policy numbers, and claim information such as date of loss, type of loss and amounts paid.... More than 90 percent of insurers writing homeowners coverage provide claims data to the C.L.U.E. Personal Property Database."[2]

- Many insurers use credit scores to evaluate applicants. Insurance credit scores are based on complex formulas reflecting various factors in a person's credit history, such as payment history, late payments, and number of open accounts. Various studies have shown a statistical correlation between credit scores and insured losses. However, credit scores are highly controversial because no intuitive connection exists between a person's credit history and the probability of a homeowners loss. Various laws have been proposed to limit or prohibit the use of credit scores in personal insurance underwriting.

UNDERWRITING AUTO INSURANCE

Most people in the United States regard driving a car as a right. In some parts of the country, driving a car is a virtual precondition for employment. For these and other reasons, the public frowns on any institution or system that makes it more difficult for people to own or operate motor vehicles.

Motor vehicles provide essential transportation. They also cause the death and disability of thousands of people each year. When the head of a household is killed or disabled in an auto accident, dependents suffer serious economic loss. Insurance recovery might be the only thing that keeps the innocent victim from becoming dependent on the welfare system.

Exhibit 6-1 shows that the death rate from traffic accidents in the United States between 1996 and 2001 has declined slightly. However, economic losses from accidents increased from $115.6 billion in 1995 to $230.6 billion in 2000[3] because increases in the cost of automobile repair and medical treatment have outpaced improvements in highway safety.

Auto and highway design, operator licensing, traffic density, vehicle inspection, and traffic law enforcement all affect accident frequency and severity. The regulatory and legal environment have an even more direct effect on underwriting results.

EXHIBIT 6-1

Traffic Deaths, 1996–2001

Year	Deaths	Annual % change	Death rate per 100 million vehicle miles	Death rate per 100,000 motor vehicles
1996	42,065	+0.6%	1.7	20.86
1997	42,013	−0.1%	1.6	20.64
1998	41,501	−1.2%	1.6	19.95
1999	41,717	+0.5%	1.6	19.61
2000	41,945	+0.5%	1.5	19.33
2001	42,116	+0.4%	1.5	19.03

Source: U.S. Department of Transportation, National Highway Traffic Safety Administration.

Adapted with permission from *The Fact Book 2003* (New York: Insurance Information Institute, 2003), p. 99.

The Regulatory Environment

Auto underwriting must comply with many legislative and regulatory requirements that limit an underwriter's options. Underwriting discretion is especially limited in personal auto insurance.

To ensure that financial resources are available to compensate auto accident victims fairly, regulation has brought about the following:

- Financial responsibility laws
- Compulsory auto liability insurance laws
- Shared market mechanisms
- Mandatory uninsured motorists coverage
- No-fault auto laws
- Restrictions on cancellations and nonrenewals

This section discusses the characteristics of each of these.

Financial Responsibility Laws

Financial responsibility laws require a motor vehicle's owner or operator to show proof of financial responsibility in one of three instances:

1. After an auto accident that causes bodily injury or property damage greater than a specified dollar amount

2. After conviction for serious offenses, such as reckless driving, driving under the influence of alcohol, or leaving the scene of an accident

3. After failure to pay a final judgment arising from an auto accident

The requirement for filing proof of insurance affects underwriting. The insurer might have to file a form verifying that the owner or operator who had an accident and did not have insurance at the time now has coverage. Financial responsibility laws require that insurance remain in effect until a notice of termination is filed with the Department of Motor Vehicles. Financial responsibility laws also extend insurance coverage to all vehicles owned by the insured, whether or not all of the insured's cars are listed in the insurance policy.

Compulsory Auto Liability Insurance Laws

Compulsory auto liability insurance laws require the registered owners of all motor vehicles to have insurance with at least the minimum legal limits, which vary by state. A typical state minimum is 20/40/10, meaning the driver should have at least $20,000 per person bodily injury coverage, $40,000 per accident bodily injury coverage, and $10,000 property damage coverage.

Motorists must be able to produce evidence of current insurance when requested by law enforcement officers or other authorities. Consequently, the insurer must provide current documentation to all insured drivers. Compulsory insurance laws might also require insurers to notify the Department of Motor Vehicles when a policy has been cancelled and to provide continuous coverage until the cancellation notice has been effected properly.

Residual Market Mechanisms

A law requiring auto liability insurance does not guarantee that every driver can find a private insurer willing to provide the coverage. So, every state has developed a residual market mechanism to underwrite the insurance needs of drivers who cannot obtain liability insurance in the voluntary market. The four types of residual market mechanisms are:

1. Automobile insurance plans
2. Joint underwriting associations
3. Reinsurance facilities
4. State funds

The first type of residual market mechanism is the automobile insurance plan. An automobile insurance plan (AIP), also called an assigned risk plan, assigns drivers to insurers that are plan members. Each insurer is usually required to accept assignments based on its share of the voluntary market in the state. The AIP requires that applicants be rejected by the voluntary market before they can apply to the AIP. Policyholders in the plan should pay a higher rate than those in the voluntary market. Sometimes, however, plan rates for drivers with good records have been lower than those in the voluntary market.

This residual market mechanism does not guarantee that participating insurers will be assigned a cross-section of rejected drivers. Therefore, the underwriting experience of individual insurers varies partly based on the luck of the draw from the pool of rejected drivers. Underwriters have no control over the drivers they eventually must underwrite.

The second type of residual market mechanism is joint underwriting associations. Joint underwriting associations (JUAs) operate as insurers. They appoint servicing insurers to handle all insurer functions. State law usually requires all insurers that write auto coverage in that state to participate in a JUA. JUA profits and losses are evenly distributed among insurers based on their voluntary market share.

The third type of residual market mechanism is reinsurance facilities. States with reinsurance facilities require all voluntary insurers to be servicing insurers of the residual market. Under this arrangement, insurers accept all auto insurance applicants who have a valid driver's license. The insurers issue policies, collect premiums, and settle claims. However, if an applicant for auto insurance is considered a high-risk driver, the underwriter has the option of assigning the driver's premiums and losses to the reinsurance facility. The profits or losses on those policies are shared evenly among all insurers. One often-cited advantage of this mechanism is that drivers are not aware that they have been rejected and placed in the residual market.

The fourth type of residual market mechanism is state funds. Maryland operates a state fund as its residual market mechanism. Operating funds for the Maryland Automobile Insurance Fund (MAIF) are received from the insurance premiums written with MAIF. MAIF receives no state funding, and the State of Maryland is not responsible for any debts or obligations of the Fund.[4]

Mandatory Uninsured Motorists Coverage

Compulsory auto liability insurance has not been successful in keeping uninsured drivers off the roads. Some states require all drivers to have uninsured motorists coverage, which compensates the policyholder for medical expenses and loss of income (and, in some states, property damage) arising out of the use of an uninsured motor vehicle. This coverage is activated when the owner of an uninsured motor vehicle is at fault in an accident with the policyholder or when the policyholder is the victim of a hit-and-run driver.

No-Fault Auto Insurance Laws

Many states have no-fault auto insurance laws. The majority of these states require both first-party no-fault insurance and third-party auto liability insurance. Many no-fault laws restrict in some way an injured party's right to sue. Pennsylvania, New Jersey, and Kentucky offer programs that allow policyholders to waive their rights to sue, except in some limited circumstances, in return for a reduced premium. Underwriters must understand the applicable no-fault provisions and coverage requirements in the jurisdictions where they provide automobile insurance.

A typical no-fault law requires first-party medical coverage and loss of earnings coverage for auto accident victims in all cases. Many states also provide survivors' and funeral benefits as well as payment for replacement services required by the injured party.

Restrictions on Cancellations and Nonrenewals

In response to public pressure, most states have enacted laws that restrict the reasons for which insurers can cancel or nonrenew auto policies. In most states, the restrictions apply to both personal and commercial policies. In some states, requirements for personal auto policies are more restrictive. Some statutes specify the acceptable reasons to cancel or nonrenew. Others rely on the insurance department to establish the restrictions. Laws also specify the time period required for insurers to notify policyholders that their policy will be cancelled or will not be renewed. In most cases, this notice ranges from thirty to sixty days before the policy's cancellation date or expiration date.

Cancellation and nonrenewal restrictions have important underwriting implications: Once a policyholder has been insured, it can be difficult or impossible to cancel that policyholder's insurance. Underwriters must also make certain that they review pending renewals well before the policies' expiration date so that they can comply with the nonrenewal notification period imposed by law. Although legislators generally restrict cancellation and nonrenewal rights with the intention of improving insurance availability, these restrictions often make underwriters more selective.

Insurance Requirements for Commercial Autos

To protect the public against uninsured or underinsured commercial vehicles, the Motor Carrier Act of 1980 requires certain motor vehicles to meet financial responsibility requirements based on their operation and the type of commodity they carry. Some carriers are required by law to have liability limits as high as $1 million or even $5 million.

Motor carriers meeting the financial responsibility requirements through insurance must get their commercial auto insurance policy endorsed. The MCS-90 endorsement imposes additional responsibilities on the insurer. It amends the insurance policy to comply with the act and removes some of the defenses that the insurer would have without the endorsement. For example, with the endorsement, the insurer is responsible for injuries caused by insured-owned vehicles not identified on the policy or from trucking routes not described in the application. Additionally, the Motor Carrier Act requires insurers to give motor carriers thirty-five days' cancellation notice and the Department of Transportation thirty days' notice. Insurer payments for claims not normally covered by the insurance policy but required because of the MCS-90 can be recovered from the insured. Unfortunately for the insurer, it is unlikely that the insured will pay. Underwriters usually analyze a motor carrier's financial stability when evaluating an application.

Personal Auto Loss Exposures

The personal auto policy (PAP) covers the ownership and operation of vehicles by families and individuals. Insurers usually evaluate the loss exposures presented by an applicant by evaluating factors related to the driver. The underwriting guide reflects management's evaluation of these factors, most of which are also used to classify and rate the applicant. Various systems are used to evaluate the loss potential of personal auto applicants. Many insurers use credit scores, which were discussed previously in connection with personal liability insurance. Other major underwriting factors that are considered in most private passenger auto underwriting guides include the following:

- Age of operator
- Age and type of auto
- Auto use
- Driving record
- Territory
- Gender and marital status
- Occupation
- Personal characteristics
- Physical condition of driver
- Safety equipment

Age of Operator

The operator's age is important in determining the likelihood of losses. Rating plans in virtually all states consider age and charge considerably higher rates for young drivers. Whether the higher rate completely offsets the increased loss potential remains for the underwriter to judge.

Data compiled by the National Safety Council indicate that although only 5.2 percent of all drivers were under age twenty in 2001, they accounted for 13.4 percent of all accidents and 11.5 percent of fatal accidents. This disproportionate relationship of age, accident frequency, and accident severity does not change until operators reach age thirty-five.[5] Exhibit 6-2 presents complete accident frequency by age for 2001.

EXHIBIT 6-2

Motor Vehicle Accidents and Deaths by Age

Accidents by Age of Driver, 2001

Age group	Number of drivers	Percent of total	Drivers in fatal accidents	Percent of total	Drivers in all accidents	Percent of total
Under 20	9,956,000	5.2%	6,400	11.5%	2,850,000	13.4%
20-24	16,386,000	8.5	8,000	14.4	3,100,000	14.6
25-34	34,967,000	18.1	11,500	20.6	4,670,000	21.9
35-44	42,732,000	22.1	10,900	19.6	4,350,000	20.4
45-54	37,823,000	19.6	8,500	15.3	3,160,000	14.8
55-64	23,481,000	12.1	4,600	8.3	1,620,000	7.6
65-74	16,030,000	8.3	2,900	5.2	890,000	4.2
Over 74	11,925,000	6.2	2,900	5.2	660,000	3.1
Totals	**193,300,000**	**100.0%**	**55,700**	**100.0%**	**21,300,000**	**100.0%**

Note: Percent of total columns may not add because of rounding.
Source: National Safety Council.

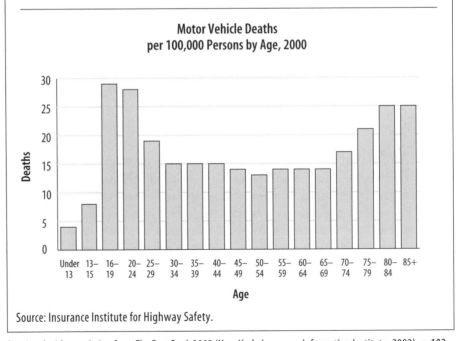

Motor Vehicle Deaths per 100,000 Persons by Age, 2000

Source: Insurance Institute for Highway Safety.

Reprinted with permission from *The Fact Book 2003* (New York: Insurance Information Institute, 2003), p. 102.

Age and Type of Auto

The age of an auto generally indicates its mechanical condition. Although some old autos are in outstanding mechanical condition, a correlation exists between age and mechanical condition.

The type of auto also affects underwriting acceptability. Sports cars and sport utility vehicles might be driven differently than station wagons and sedans, depending partly on geographic area. The physical damage premium should reflect the damageability and cost of auto repairs.

Auto Use

Other things being equal, the longer an auto is on the highway, the greater the probability of its being in an accident and incurring a loss. Long commuting distance or business use of an auto affects rates because those factors increase loss potential. Rates reflect the following classifications of auto use:

- Cars driven for pleasure use only
- Cars driven to work in a carpool in which drivers rotate driving responsibility
- Cars driven to work more than three miles but fewer than ten miles one way
- Cars driven to work more than ten miles one way
- Cars driven for business use

The classification for pleasure use only includes driving to work fewer than three miles one way. Underwriters must determine whether the driving mileage indicated is excessive in view of the rate that applies and should consider this when pricing the policy.

Driving Record

Underwriters evaluate a driver's prior accidents and prior moving violations. The driver's prior loss history might indicate poor driving habits, recklessness, or simply a lack of skill. Certain moving violations indicate a disregard for safety, while others indicate carelessness. The applicant or insured, index bureaus, and motor vehicle records are sources of underwriting information. Yet information on driving records is often incomplete.

Territory

Liability and physical damage losses vary by the driver's principal place of garaging and where the vehicle is used. For example, a driver might garage her car in a rural area but drive it every day through dense traffic to her job in a major city.

Theft and vandalism occur more frequently in congested urban areas, with on-street parking, than in less-populated areas where cars are generally parked in driveways or garages. Drivers are more likely to be involved in auto accidents in urban areas but more likely to be involved in *fatal* accidents in rural areas.

Other territorial considerations are unrelated to population density. Some areas of the country have severe winter weather, which causes slippery roads. Other areas have sandstorms that frequently cause other-than-collision losses to paint and windshields.

Gender and Marital Status

Underwriters have long recognized the correlation between gender, marital status, and loss experience. Age is a related factor. For example, young female drivers are generally considered to be better insureds than young male drivers. For many years, young female drivers paid the same premiums as adult drivers. However, recently, young women have paid more than adult drivers in most states, but still considerably less than young men.

Exhibit 6-3 illustrates that there are more male than female drivers in crashes, that female drivers have a higher crash rate per mile driven, and that male drivers are more likely to be involved in fatal accidents.

The marital status of younger drivers is both a rating and an underwriting factor. Married male drivers under age thirty usually pay less than their single counterparts because married persons in that age group generally tend to be more mature and responsible than single persons of the same age. Their marital status also suggests that they spend more time at home.

Some states regulate the use of gender and marital status for underwriting purposes. A few states prohibit price discrimination on the basis of gender or marital status; in these states, both men and women pay the same rates.

Occupation

The relationship between a person's occupation and driving habits is controversial. Some underwriting guides make distinctions on this basis; others do not. Certain occupations, such as traveling salespersons, require extensive driving and increase the probability of loss. Rates should reflect auto use.

Personal Characteristics

Underwriters often order consumer investigation reports to provide information on the personal characteristics of applicants and other drivers. This information is subjective and must be evaluated carefully.

As mentioned previously, many insurers use credit scores to evaluate the stability of insurance applicants. Studies have demonstrated a positive correlation between a poor insurance score using information in a credit report and higher insurance losses. Critics of insurers' use of credit scores suggest that the connection between the two factors is nonspecific and that the connection could mask factors that are prohibited for evaluation purposes, such as race.

EXHIBIT 6-3

Sex of Drivers Involved in Crashes, 1992–2001

| | Drivers in All Crashes | | | | Drivers in Fatal Crashes | | | |
| | Male | | Female | | Male | | Female | |
Year	Number	Rate*	Number	Rate*	Number	Rate**	Number	Rate**
1992	12,700,000	88	8,100,000	103	40,200	28	13,000	17
1993	12,900,000	87	8,200,000	101	40,400	27	13,500	17
1994	12,400,000	82	7,600,000	90	38,200	25	14,600	17
1995	10,600,000	69	7,000,000	80	37,500	24	13,000	15
1996	11,400,000	73	7,500,000	84	42,300	27	15,100	17
1997	14,300,000	90	9,600,000	103	43,600	27	16,100	17
1998	12,700,000	77	8,600,000	90	40,800	25	15,300	16
1999	10,600,000	63	7,400,000	74	30,400	18	11,800	12
2000	15,200,000	90	9,900,000	100	45,600	27	15,800	16
2001	12,700,000	74	8,600,000	82	40,800	24	14,900	14

* Number of drivers in all accidents per 10 million miles driven.

** Number of drivers in fatal accidents per 1 billion miles driven.

Source: National Safety Council.

Adapted with permission from *The Fact Book 2003* (New York: Insurance Information Institute, 2003), p. 103.

Physical Condition of Driver

Physical impairments might be a problem if allowances for the impairment have not been made. Auto modifications made to accommodate a driver with physical impairments and the driver's demonstrated driving mastery usually make the applicant acceptable.

Safety Equipment

Many new cars come equipped with advanced safety systems, and underwriters have begun to consider these safety features. For example, underwriters often allow rate discounts for antilock braking systems and side air bags. General Motors vehicles with the OnStar system, which combines global positioning system technology and wireless communication technology, have also earned rate credits from some insurers.

Commercial Auto Loss Exposures

In commercial auto underwriting, underwriters use the same factors to evaluate the loss exposures of insurance applicants as they do to determine appropriate rates. Factors relating both to the driver and the vehicle are considered.

Factors that underwriters consider for commercial vehicle drivers include their motor vehicle record, especially if it indicates any violations; accident history; and experience with operating commercial motor vehicles. The federal Commercial Motor Vehicle Safety Act (CMVSA) of 1986 requires drivers of large vehicles (trucks with a gross vehicle weight of 26,000 pounds or more, buses that can carry more than sixteen passengers, and vehicles that transport hazardous materials) to hold a commercial driver's license (CDL). The act requires that drivers pass both written and road tests. Drivers are forbidden from holding more than one CDL, which makes concealing a history of accidents and violations more difficult.

Private passenger vehicles owned or operated by a business would be covered under a commercial auto policy. The underwriting considerations, however, are similar to those of a personal auto loss exposure.

Underwriters also consider factors relating to the vehicle. Trucks, tractors, and trailers, as well as truckers hauling exclusively for one firm, are classified and rated using the following four factors:

1. Vehicle weight and type
2. Vehicle use
3. Radius of vehicle operation
4. Special industry classifications

Vehicle Weight and Type

The damage resulting from an auto accident is related to the size, weight, and speed of the vehicles involved. Commercial tractor-trailer rigs can weigh 80,000 pounds or more when loaded, and they often travel at or above the maximum posted speed, so these vehicles are more likely than others to cause severe damage when an accident occurs. Large trucks are also difficult to maneuver in heavy traffic or on small inner-city streets, a factor that increases loss potential.

Vehicle Use

How and to what extent commercial vehicles are used varies significantly. Some vehicles might be used almost continually to haul goods, while others might be used only to travel to and from job sites, remaining parked most of the time. The ISO *Commercial Lines Manual (CLM)* classifies trucks and tractor-trailers into service, retail, and commercial use. Each of these classifications is described in the *CLM* and is reflected in determining the primary classification to which the vehicle is assigned. The use classification reflects the extent to which the vehicle is driven.

- Service use applies to vehicles that are used principally to transport personnel or material to job sites. These vehicles are often driven to job sites at the start of a shift and remain there until the shift is over. Because they are used to the least extent, service vehicles receive the lowest rate.

- Retail use means that the vehicle is used primarily for deliveries to and pickups from households. Drivers frequently follow unfamiliar routes and operate on tight schedules. This use class receives the highest rate.

- Commercial use applies to any vehicle that does not fall into one of the preceding two classes.

The underwriter verifies that vehicles are properly classified to ensure that sufficient premium is charged for the loss exposure.

The *Commercial Lines Manual* also provides classifications for public use vehicles. Public use vehicles include taxis, public livery vehicles, van pools, and school and church buses, as well as charter and sightseeing buses. These classifications and rating factors reflect the unique characteristics of these loss exposures involving multiple passengers in a single vehicle.

Radius of Vehicle Operation

The distance traveled, as well as the nature of that travel, can affect accident frequency. Trucks operated over long distances might be more likely to have more severe accidents than those operated locally. There are several reasons for this. First, a driver who operates a truck over long distances might not be as familiar with the route and its hazards as are drivers who operate trucks locally. Second, long-distance trucking is more likely to be more strictly scheduled. If drivers are rushing to meet a delivery deadline, resulting fatigue and excessive speeds can increase accident frequency. Third, because long-haul trucks are large and usually travel at high speeds, they are typically involved in more severe accidents than trucks used within a city or town. While accidents involving long-haul trucks have a relatively high severity, this is partly offset by the frequency of accidents that occur with other vehicles as a result of congested city traffic and the stop-start nature of city driving.

Special Industry Classifications

Special industry classifications, or secondary classifications, consist of seven major industry classifications, each of which is further divided into subclassifications. The numerous classifications permit the capture of meaningful data by specialized use, even though most of the subclassifications within a classification have the same rate. The major classifications are as follows:

- *Truckers*—Vehicles used to transport the goods or materials of others; this does not include moving household goods, office furniture, or fixtures and supplies.

- *Food delivery*—Vehicles that wholesale food distributors and food manufacturers use to transport raw and finished products.

- *Specialized delivery*—Delivery vehicles such as armored cars or autos for delivering film, magazines or newspapers, mail and parcel post, and similar items.

- *Waste disposal*—Vehicles transporting waste material for disposal or resale.

- *Farmers*—Vehicles owned by farmers and used in farming operations.
- *Dump and transit mix trucks and trailers*—Vehicles that have no other appropriate classification and that have an incidental dumping operation.
- *Contractors*—All vehicles used by contractors, other than dump trucks.
- *Not otherwise specified*—Vehicles that cannot be classified in any other group.

From an underwriting perspective, trucks or tractor-trailers with special industry classifications can present additional concerns and require the underwriter to gather more information. For example, trucks with a food-delivery secondary classification might operate under tight timetables or might require specialized equipment, such as refrigerated units. Although the application of a special industry classification should result in a premium that reflects any increase in loss exposure, the underwriter needs to ensure that all necessary loss controls are in place. The loss control department can provide valuable assistance to the underwriter with this assessment.

Commercial Auto Loss Control

An insurer's loss control activities are important to achieving and maintaining the underwriting profitability of an account. Loss control representatives can assist the policyholder with making drivers and managers more safety conscious. Loss control can also aid the insured with developing vehicle inspection programs that address problems identified in loss control reports and with creating a positive approach to safety through safety programs.

Loss Control Reports

The loss control report can be an important source of information for the underwriter when monitoring existing commercial auto accounts. The report confirms and supplements information listed on the application, such as the type, scope, and efficiency of operations or the physical condition of vehicles.

The policyholder's accident record is an important guide in recommending improvements to the policyholder. For example, several backing losses may indicate a need for additional loss control systems. Better rear-view-mirror systems help, but they cannot always let the driver see well enough to avoid backing losses. Several proximity alarms are available that alert drivers to blind spots directly behind and to the sides of the vehicle.

Frequent theft or vandalism losses could indicate a need for better vehicle protection. The type and extent of protection would be determined at least partly by the vehicle's location when stolen or vandalized. Finally, the location of losses reported by the loss control representative can alert the underwriter to the fact that the radius of operations is greater than that originally indicated on the application.

Additionally, because of the higher physical damage deductibles usually written on commercial autos, many small accidents are not reported. This omission makes the loss frequency appear better than it is. The vehicle condition also deteriorates if damage from a small accident is not repaired. Consequently, the loss control report includes information on uninsured losses or accidents that are under the deductible amount.

Safety Programs

Policyholders with a fleet of autos should have a formal, written safety program. When monitoring an existing account, an underwriter can learn a good deal about a policyholder by examining the details and records of the safety program. Small commercial auto accounts should also have a plan, even if it is informal and not written.

The following are the essential elements of a good fleet safety program:

- Driver selection
- Driver training and motivation
- Equipment control
- Accident reporting and review
- Periodic evaluation of drivers and vehicles
- Program enforcement and reinforcement
- Management support of the program

Some policyholders also conduct periodic on-the-road evaluations of their drivers to see whether they obey laws and follow company procedures. This is a positive underwriting factor, but these evaluations must be followed up with corrective action. It does little good to discover which drivers are speeding if the policyholder does nothing about it. These evaluations and their results should be included in the safety-program records that the underwriter reviews.

Some independent firms specialize in road patrol (that is, on-the-road spot-checks of drivers). Companies may hire such firms to check their vehicles. In some cases, they authorize the road patrol firm to pull over the drivers, where laws and highway conditions permit, to check further into the driver's and the truck's conditions. Using a road patrol is a positive factor in the underwriter's evaluation, but only if the firm uses the resulting reports to take corrective action. Underwriters should request the reports filed on drivers and should ask what corrective action, if any, was taken.

UNDERWRITING WORKERS' COMPENSATION INSURANCE

Workers' compensation insurance protects employers against statutory liability losses, incurred under workers' compensation statutes. Benefits include death benefits, disability income, medical expense, and rehabilitation expense as required by applicable workers' compensation laws. Workers' compensation benefits are compulsory in all states except New Jersey, South Carolina, and Texas. Even in those states, most employers have workers' compensation insurance.

The workers' compensation and employers' liability policy also provides employers' liability coverage for employers whose employees are killed or injured or who acquire an occupational disease in the course of their employment. Employers' liability insurance covers employers for their legal liability to an employee for bodily injury arising out of and in the course of employment that is not covered under the workers' compensation law.

The standard workers' compensation and employers' liability policy provides complete coverage for employee bodily injury except for specified exclusions. The policy provides both blanket coverage for obligations imposed by the state workers' compensation law and broad coverage for other employers' liability. This broad coverage and the additional flexibility provided by endorsements spare policyholders the necessity of revising their insurance program when a new location is established or some other business change occurs.

Workers' compensation benefits vary by state. The same policy can be used for basic coverages in various states because the compensation laws of those states, not the policy provisions, control the conditions of coverage. Workers' compensation laws are specifically incorporated into the policy contract by policy reference. Therefore, an underwriter must read applicable statutes in order to interpret the policy. Workers' compensation insurance loss experience is closely related to changing economic, regulatory, and political environments, which often vary by state.

Underwriting Guidelines

The loss exposures covered by general liability and workers' compensation insurance are subject to many of the same hazards, and the same type of analysis is required to evaluate those hazards.

Each insurer's underwriting management, with the support of staff underwriters, evaluates individual classes of business and decides which to accept. Management communicates the insurer's preferences to line underwriters via underwriting guidelines and bulletins. A conservative insurer might want to avoid high-hazard classes of business such as steeplejacks or window washers. This same insurer might be willing to write some contractors but might want to avoid roofing and insulation contractors. Other insurers might target their marketing efforts to high-hazard classes. As with other types of insurance, there is no single right way to underwrite workers' compensation.

Some insurers use the experience rating modification as an index of the account's desirability within its class. A modification greater than 1.00 requires investigation. It might be the result of one large loss. The insured might also have implemented loss control procedures to prevent similar future losses. If an experience-rated policy does develop adverse results during the year, the experience rating mechanism ensures that the policyholder will be penalized in future policy periods. It does not matter who provides coverage because experience modifications are calculated by the applicable state's workers' compensation rating organization. This provides a financial incentive for effective loss control. Experience rating provides an accurate method to capture statistics about an applicant. Loss records indicate both past losses and future trends.

Underwriting Considerations

Line underwriters use the insurer's guidelines to evaluate individual accounts. The primary factors they consider are on-premises and off-premises hazards. Other factors also demand special attention, including management's attitude about safety, the number of temporary and seasonal workers, subcontractors the insured engages, and the potential for cumulative trauma disorders or occupational disease.

Since September 11, 2001, workers' compensation underwriters have placed more emphasis on the concentration hazard. The World Trade Center attack clearly demonstrated that an employer with a large number of employees at a single location faces the possibility that a single incident could result in many injuries or deaths. A catastrophic loss could arise from many causes, but the loss exposure could be greatest for employees working in prominent properties that might be terrorism targets.

On-Premises Hazards

On-premises hazards relating to housekeeping and maintenance are found in virtually all occupations, while special hazards of the class are peculiar to a particular operation or industry. Special hazards of the risk must also be considered where applicable.

Housekeeping

From an underwriting standpoint, housekeeping refers to the physical layout of the workplace, its cleanliness, and its operating efficiency. Housekeeping includes not only tidiness but also machinery arrangement, aisle placement and adequacy, stair cleanliness, and freight-elevator opening and stair marking.

Maintenance

Poorly maintained machinery presents an inherent danger. A good program of plant and machinery maintenance indicates a positive attitude toward work safety. The absence of such a program indicates carelessness or a lack of awareness, which can cause or increase injuries.

Other Hazards

Specific hazards might be present in a particular firm as a result of the type of machines, equipment, materials, and processes used in its operation. These specific hazards require controls such as machine guards, exhaust systems, and materials-handling devices designed to meet the requirements of the particular situation.

Most accidents occur as a result of either an unsafe act (88 percent) or an unsafe condition (10 percent).[6] An unsafe act or practice by an employee might be failing to use the proper personal protective equipment. Workers might, for example, fail to wear dust masks or air-supplied respirators in dust-laden atmospheres or fail to follow safe lifting procedures when moving heavy containers. The firm management can influence employee behavior. Its hiring policy, safety program, and enforcement of safety rules can increase or reduce injuries on the job. Premises inspections can indicate the extent to which the insured tolerates unsafe actions. Unfortunately, employees might act differently during an inspection than at other times. Losses can also occur when supervisors do not enforce safety rules continuously.

Unsafe conditions are generally easier to identify than unsafe acts. Offices usually present a minimum loss exposure to dangerous conditions involving machinery, chemicals, and similar hazards. Some potential exists for slips and falls and even for back strain from improperly lifting files, boxes of paper, and similar heavy objects.

The pace of business and the demands placed on workers increase the frequency of stress-related workers' compensation claims. Emerging technologies and increased use of computers have led to claims for cumulative trauma and claims related to radiation emitted by video display terminals (VDTs). Long periods of work with a VDT can also cause eye fatigue and other physical ailments.

In a factory, the manufacturing process and the type of materials used are important to underwriters. The loss history of the policyholder and others in the same industry provides information on the types of losses that might occur. In woodworking, for example, operating sharp cutting tools at high speeds can result in serious lacerations. Other processes present the potential for burns.

The rating structure considers the differences in relative hazards among occupational classes. A machine shop is more hazardous than an office, for example. The underwriter must determine to what extent the policyholder is typical of its class. The machine shop must be evaluated relative to some guidelines that indicate the conditions usually found in a typical machine shop. The presence of additional hazards not found in other machine shops or the heightening of typical hazards because of poor maintenance or house-keeping would indicate a less desirable exposure.

Off-Premises Hazards

Employees in some firms fulfill all their employment duties on the premises. Employees in other firms have a great deal of travel or off-premises work. The off-premises hazard has three elements: (1) the duration of travel, (2) the mode of transportation, and (3) the hazards at remote job sites. Contractors, for example, are subject to a constantly changing work environment as they move from one job site to another. The hazards faced by a residential building contractor vary significantly from those of a commercial building contractor.

Consider two accounting firms with identical payrolls. Accountants for Firm A do all their work on the firm's premises. In Firm B, which does a great deal of auditing for construction firms, accountants travel much of the time. This travel is done in private autos as well as in commercial and corporate aircraft. Traffic accidents or plane crashes could result in serious workers' compensation losses for Firm B, whereas the off-premises transportation hazard is not present for Firm A.

The use of corporate aircraft can result in a multiple-fatality workers' compensation loss in the event of a crash. The potential for multiple losses is also present when several employees share the same vehicle when traveling on business.

The same techniques for evaluating on-premises hazards can be used for off-premises hazards.

Management Attitude and Capability

In evaluating management of an insured firm, the underwriter considers the willingness and ability of management to minimize hazards and reduce losses.

If a firm does not have a safety program, or if the program exists only on paper with no management effort directed toward its implementation, managerial indifference can usually be assumed.

A firm that has insufficient financial resources might be unable or unwilling to implement a safety program. Some of the first areas cut back in an economic recession are worker training, maintenance, and safety.

Employee morale and claim consciousness often reflect management attitude toward workers' compensation and industrial safety, and the degree of managerial skill. If employee morale is low, grievances against management might motivate workers to file false or exaggerated claims for workers' compensation to escape an unpleasant work environment. A poorly managed firm is likely to have worse-than-average workers' compensation loss experience.

Temporary and Seasonal Workers

Many businesses employ temporary or seasonal workers who are generally not as well trained as permanent workers. Any lack of training increases the risk of injury.

A growing number of firms are using leased employees. Employers use vendors or professional employer organizations (PEOs) to provide employees, thereby reducing expenses related to maintaining a full-time workforce. For workers' compensation coverage, this practice raises the question of who employs these workers, the leasing company or the firm that hires them. This is an important consideration when attempting to segregate payrolls to calculate experience modifications and to collect other statistical data for a particular group of employees. Some state regulators and legislators have permitted master policies to be issued for all workers of a PEO. Other states have prohibited the use of master policies based on concerns that they allow individual employers to escape applicable experience modifications by using leased workers. The National Council on Compensation Insurance (NCCI) has developed several endorsements for use with workers' compensation policies covering leased workers. These endorsements clarify whether coverage applies to leased workers, non-leased workers, or both.[7]

Subcontractors

Most workers' compensation laws hold a contractor responsible for workers' compensation benefits to employees of its uninsured subcontractors. The standard workers' compensation policy automatically insures this loss exposure. Therefore, underwriters must ascertain whether a subcontractor loss exposure exists and, if it does, evaluate it and charge the appropriate rate. The policyholder must either prove that the loss exposure has been insured by the subcontractor or pay a rate based on the subcontractor's payroll as well as the insured's own payroll.

Cumulative Trauma Disorders

Cumulative trauma disorders, sometimes referred to as repetitive strain injuries (RSI), arise from a series of minor stresses over a period of time. These relatively minor injuries accumulate until they cause a disability or require medical treatment. Examples of cumulative trauma disorders include deafness as a result of a long-term exposure to high noise levels or kidney damage from years of jolting in the cab of a truck. Also, the increased use of computer keyboards has caused some office workers to lose feeling in their hands. This injury, called carpal tunnel syndrome, results from cumulative trauma. Most states now recognize cumulative trauma disorders as compensable injuries.

The major difficulty associated with determining compensability for these injuries is distinguishing between normal aging conditions, or conditions to which the general public is subject, and those that are truly job related. Determining financial responsibility is a related concern.

Occupational Disease

Workers' compensation laws provide benefits for some diseases in addition to injuries from accidents on the job. The definition varies by state, but an occupational disease is generally one resulting from causes the worker faces on the job and to which the general public is not exposed. Some of the occupational diseases covered by the various state workers' compensation laws are silicosis (from exposure to silica dust); asbestosis (caused by inhalation of asbestos fibers); radiation (including ionizing radiation); tuberculosis; pneumoconiosis (black lung); and heart or lung disease for certain groups, such as police or firefighters.

It is more difficult to predict the frequency and severity of occupational diseases than of work-related accidents. Exposure to unfavorable conditions at work does not always cause occupational disease. Accidents, on the other hand, are easy to identify.

In an industrial setting, hazard analysis includes monitoring the work environment for the presence of industrial poisons that can enter the body by ingestion, inhalation, or skin absorption. Analyzing the toxicity of the various chemical compounds used in a particular process provides a means of evaluating the related occupational disease hazards.

Occupational Safety and Health Act

The Occupational Safety and Health Act (the Act) of 1970 sets safety standards for employers and imposes penalties for violations of the standards. The Act also created the Occupational Safety and Health Administration (OSHA) to enforce those standards. The Department of Labor enforces the act. Safety inspectors may enter working premises at any reasonable time to inspect the premises, equipment, and environment. When a violation is detected, a citation describes its exact nature. The employer has fifteen working days after receiving written notice of the violation to notify the Department of Labor that either the citation or the penalty assessed will be contested. Any willful violation that results in an employee's death is punishable by a fine of up to $10,000 or imprisonment of up to six months. A second conviction imposes double penalties.

All employers subject to the act are required to keep occupational injury records for employees. Every employer must maintain a log of recordable cases of occupational injuries and illnesses and supplementary records of each case of occupational injury or illness. The Act defines a recordable case as one involving an occupational death; occupational illness; or occupational injury involving loss of consciousness, restriction of work or motion, transfer to another job, or medical treatment (other than first aid).

OSHA safety inspections and logs are a source of underwriting information. The log can be used to identify types of losses, loss frequency, and loss duration in terms of lost workdays. The log can also be used to verify other loss information submitted with the insurance application. However, OSHA records are no substitute for underwriting on-site inspections.

Experience in the red meat industry demonstrates that employers can control cumulative trauma disorders. Workers in this industry suffered so many injuries caused by repetitive movements that OSHA made it the target of a special campaign. New safety rules resulted, which employers adopted and enforced. Consequently, injury rates fell dramatically. Several years after making the red meat industry the target of its first special campaign, OSHA praised employers in this industry for the improved loss rates they had achieved.

Maritime Occupations

Maritime loss exposures are those related to occupations involving work on vessels while at sea or in close proximity to bodies of water, such as on docks, on piers, or in terminals. It is important for underwriters to understand the policyholder's operations before including any endorsement to the workers' compensation policy when maritime loss exposures are involved, because different coverage applies for different occupations.

Some employee injury claims come within federal rather than state jurisdictions. Federal laws entitle certain groups of workers to compensation for work-related injuries regardless of fault. The effect of these laws is similar to state workers' compensation laws. The difference is that the schedule of benefits and administrative procedures are established by federal laws. Consequently, applicable rates for insurance coverage differ under federal laws. The principal federal laws covering on-the-job injuries for maritime occupations are the United States Longshore and Harbor Workers' (USL&HW) Compensation Act and the Merchant Marine Act. The latter is more commonly known as the Jones Act and is intended to cover masters and crew members of vessels.

Some insurers avoid any workers' compensation loss exposures falling under federal jurisdiction because they require specialized underwriting expertise or because reinsurance agreements may contain restrictions for maritime loss exposures. Even an underwriter with many years of other underwriting experience would find it difficult to evaluate maritime loss exposures because of their complexity.

Maritime loss exposures can be overlooked when certain occupations or employees conduct occasional tasks that fall outside their regular duties, creating a "gray area" for coverage. These are employees who are not regular masters or crew members of vessels who usually clearly fall under the Jones Act or dockworkers who are covered under the USL&HW Act.

An example is a boat repair business that usually operates at an inland location. If an employee were injured at this workplace, benefits would be paid according to state workers' compensation laws. If, however, the employee boarded a vessel on water to make an emergency repair and was injured, a question could arise as to whether state or federal law would determine workers' compensation benefits. In many cases, benefits under the federal law are greater, so the injured employee would seek coverage under USL&HW. This same question can also arise with contractors. Painting, carpentry, electrical, and other trade contractors may routinely operate on land and never present a maritime loss exposure. If, however, an employee of a contractor were to be injured while involved in an operation on or near navigable waters, the question of state versus federal jurisdiction could arise.

Underwriters often discover this type of loss exposure only when a claim is presented. Underwriters must always be alert to the existence of potential maritime loss exposures. For proper coverage to be provided, the appropriate endorsements must be attached to the policy with the correct classification and the proper premiums charged for the additional loss exposure.

Underwriters can assess maritime loss exposures by reviewing certificates of insurance, the type of equipment owned, a list of jobs in progress, and previous loss experience. Some producers may request a USL&HW

endorsement on every workers' compensation application or as part of every request for insurance proposal, even when no obvious maritime loss exposure exists. In those situations, the underwriter must discuss the operations with the producer to determine whether a maritime exposure exists and then must determine what coverage can and should be provided.

An underwriter can discover USL&HW Act exposures in many typical construction and erection operations. Too often, the discovery results from a claim. They can be indicated in many ways, including persons to whom certificates of insurance are issued, the type of equipment owned, a list of jobs in progress, claims under other coverages, and so on. Some producers located near navigable waters attach a USL&HW Act coverage endorsement to every workers' compensation policy, just to be safe, even if such exposures are not contemplated when the policy is issued. In those situations, the underwriter must instruct the producer to indicate clearly when a maritime exposure is anticipated.

Residual Market—Workers' Compensation

When employers are unable to obtain workers' compensation coverage in the voluntary market, they seek to meet their statutory requirements in the residual market. Residual markets vary by state and include state funds, joint underwriting associations (JUAs), or assigned risk plans. Twenty states have either a monopolistic state fund or a competitive state fund.[8]

The Workers Compensation Insurance Plan (WCIP) is an assigned risk program that distributes applicants among all insurers in the state based on the percentage of their participation in the voluntary market. NCCI administers the Workers Compensation Insurance Plan on behalf of regulatory authorities in twenty states. NCCI also administers the National Workers Compensation Reinsurance Pool (NWCRP, or National Pool), which reinsures most of the business written in the state pools.[9]

UNDERWRITING UMBRELLA AND EXCESS LIABILITY INSURANCE

Many policyholders need high limits of liability coverage not offered in standard liability policies. Businesses and individuals often have significant assets that need protection from potentially catastrophic liability claims. Severe losses can result from multiple-passenger auto accidents, gasoline truck explosions, building collapses, hotel fires, and defective products.

Personal and Commercial Umbrella Liability Insurance

Umbrella liability insurance, both personal and commercial, is designed to cover large, low-frequency losses. It does not provide primary insurance in most cases, nor does it cover all losses. Most umbrella policies have a deductible or self-insured retention that the policyholder must pay. The retention for a commercial policy is usually $10,000, and the retention for a personal policy is usually $250.

Umbrella policies are not standardized. Policy language, as well as underwriting rules and guidelines, vary by insurer. Most umbrella policies are designed to serve three functions:

1. Provide excess liability limits above all specified underlying policies
2. Provide coverage when the aggregate limits of the underlying policies have been exhausted
3. Provide coverage for gaps in the underlying policies

An umbrella policy requires that liability insurance with agreed limits of liability be maintained on the underlying policies. If this is not done, the umbrella will respond as though the required underlying coverage exists.

Underwriting umbrella policies requires a careful analysis of the same loss exposures covered by the underlying policies, as well as additional loss exposures covered by the umbrella but not by underlying coverage. Umbrella policy underwriters must thoroughly know not only what coverage is provided by underlying policies but also how the applicant's underlying policies have been modified through endorsements.

Providing an umbrella policy above a private passenger auto policy can raise some additional concerns. State laws might require uninsured motorists coverage equal to the underlying policy's bodily injury liability limits unless rejected by the policyholder. The insurer might not be willing to provide such high limits on uninsured motorists coverage or to leave the decision to the policyholder. A similar problem exists in states that permit the stacking of policy limits. In those states, the courts have permitted the policyholder to combine the limits for each vehicle insured under the policy.

Excess Policies

Excess policies increase the limits of liability on one or more underlying policies but do not broaden coverage. Umbrella policies, in contrast, provide coverage in some situations when underlying coverage does not exist. Excess policies are frequently written on a layered basis, with several policies providing successively higher limits.

As with umbrella policies, loss frequency is not a problem with excess policies; rather, severity is the problem. Specific excess policies are seldom underwritten as underlying policies are. Insurers believe that if the primary policy is acceptable, then the excess policy is acceptable also. The excess insurer often relies on the primary insurer's underwriting judgment. However, the excess liability underwriter should also consider any catastrophe loss exposures, such as the potential for a major explosion that could cause many injuries and serious damage to adjacent property.

PREMIUM AUDITING

The premium audit function supports the underwriting function by providing additional information on loss exposures covered. As part of the premium auditing process, premium auditors can notify underwriters of new loss exposures or additional operations that are uncovered. The premium audit function also supports the insurer's profit goal by ensuring that appropriate premiums are charged for policies provided. This section of the chapter discusses the reasons for premium audits and the premium auditing process.

For many commercial insurance policies, the premium paid at the beginning of the policy period is a provisional premium based on an estimate of the extent of operations to be insured. At the end of the policy period, typically one year, the policyholder's records are examined, or audited, by a premium auditor to determine the audited premium. In conducting a **premium audit**, the premium auditor examines the insured's records to determine how extensive the insured's operations were. If they were more extensive than estimated, an additional premium is charged. If less extensive, the insured receives a partial refund.

> **Premium audit**
> Methodical examination of a policyholder's operations, records, and books of account to determine the actual exposure units and premium for insurance coverages already provided.

Premium auditing is performed for many of the coverages discussed in this chapter, including workers' compensation and general liability policies, which are rated on a per $100 of payroll premium base. General liability policies might also be rated on a dollar sales basis. Commercial auto policies for large fleets are rated based on the vehicles that are exposed to loss during the policy period. Although premium auditing most often involves liability insurance, some property insurance policies, such as those covering fluctuating inventory values, are also subject to premium audit. These premium bases are also called exposure units. An exposure unit is the fundamental measure that is used to calculate the policy premium.

Premium auditors help insurers obtain the information needed to calculate current premiums and to establish future rates. By safeguarding the accuracy of the information on which insurance rates are based, premium auditors help to make the insurance mechanism work as intended.

Reasons for Premium Audits

Insurers conduct premium audits for the following reasons:

- To determine correct premiums
- To meet regulatory requirements
- To collect ratemaking data
- To inhibit fraud
- To reinforce policyholders' confidence
- To obtain additional information

Determine Correct Premium

When a policy is written subject to audit, the actual premium can be calculated only after the end of the policy period when the exact exposure units or premium bases during the policy period are known. Usually, the rules and rates manual for the type of insurance involved strictly defines the procedure, specifies inclusions and exclusions in the premium base, and defines distinct rating classifications. Mastering these rules requires considerable effort and practice.

Policyholders have the accounting information or other data that are used to determine the premium base, but they rarely understand insurance manual rules well enough to present the information in the necessary form. A skilled premium auditor, employed by the insurer, usually assembles the information and determines the actual earned premium. Even if the insured can provide the necessary premium data, having a premium auditor inspect the original books of account makes the insurer more confident that the data are accurate.

Meet Regulatory Requirements

Although state rules vary, they often require premium audits of workers' compensation accounts. By requiring workers' compensation coverage, the state also assumes an obligation to ensure that such coverage is provided fairly and equitably. By ensuring that rating data are accurate and properly classified, premium audits help states to fulfill that obligation.

Collect Ratemaking Data

Class rates can be actuarially credible only if they are based on accurate data regarding incurred losses, earned premiums, and insured exposure units for each rating class. Claim reports provide the necessary information on claims for a given period. Premium volume and total insured loss exposures by class are based on the data from premium audits.

A detailed class-by-class breakdown of exposure units obtained by a premium audit is necessary for the insurer's statistical report to the advisory rating organizations (rating bureaus), as well as for billing purposes. When an advisory organization has credible statistics showing premium volume, loss experience, and total insured exposure units for each rating class, its actuaries can calculate appropriate loss costs that are used to establish rates. These data usually must be filed with state regulators to support rate increases or other rate filings.

Inhibit Fraud

Occasionally, business owners deliberately attempt to reduce their insurance premiums by presenting false or misleading information to the insurer. For example, underreporting payroll reduces premiums based on payroll.

Policyholders are far less likely to submit false or misleading information when they know the information might be checked and independently verified by a premium auditor. Uncovering fraud is not the primary purpose of premium auditing, but diligent premium auditors have often uncovered deceptive business practices. Therefore, even random premium audits help to safeguard the integrity of premium computation and collection.

Reinforce Policyholders' Confidence

Most policyholders want to deal fairly with insurers and to be dealt with fairly by insurers. Competent premium audits increase policyholders' confidence that they are receiving fair treatment. A premium computed from a meticulous audit has credibility when the policyholder knows the auditor obviously exercised due care in collecting and verifying the data. Observing the audit process counters the notion that premium adjustments are arbitrary and conveys the impression that all policyholders are, and in fact must be, treated according to uniform and equitable standards. A good premium auditor also explains the audit procedure to the policyholder so any premium adjustment does not surprise the policyholder.

The benefits of a competent audit extend beyond the premium audit itself. A policyholder with a favorable impression of the insurer is less likely to look for another insurer at renewal time or when the need for additional coverage arises. Having gained from the audit procedure a greater understanding of how the premium is determined, a policyholder might improve recordkeeping, especially when having properly segregated records reduces the premium charges. The policyholder might also be more receptive to loss control advice or other services the insurer can provide.

Obtain Additional Information

A premium audit might generate additional underwriting information about the policyholder, such as an incorrect classification or a new loss exposure that the underwriter had not previously identified. Such information can be extremely useful to the underwriter in determining whether to renew a policy. Premium audit information can also identify marketing opportunities and assist the claim department in adjusting certain types of losses. Finally, a premium audit is a source of feedback on the insurer's image and effectiveness.

Premium Auditing Process

To be sure that their information is accurate and complete, premium auditors follow a systematic process for each audit. At each stage of the audit, premium auditors make judgments about the particular case and decide how to proceed. Sometimes they need more information about the operations, more records, or an explanation of an apparent discrepancy. These judgments are necessary because premium auditors must be satisfied that the information they obtain is reasonable and reliable. The stages in the premium auditing process provide a framework for organizing the countless decisions auditors must make.

Planning

Because insurers cannot afford the expense of auditing every auditable policy every year, they must decide which policies to audit. In some cases, the insurer might determine that the audit is not worth the cost and elect (when permissible by regulators) to waive it. In doing so, the insurer considers the policy and its endorsements, prior audit reports, and the potential reliability of a voluntary report from the policyholder.

A voluntary report (also called a policyholder's report) is a form that the policyholder completes and returns to the insurer's premium audit department. The insurer includes instructions to assist the policyholder in capturing the exposure unit information required to adjust the premium for the expired policy period. An example of a policyholder's report is shown in Exhibit 6-4. Once the insurer receives the voluntary audit report, it might choose to accept it, to perform a two-year audit at the end of the next policy period, or to initiate an immediate field audit to confirm the voluntary audit report.

Field audits (also called *physical audits*) are personal examinations of the policyholder's books and records. Field auditors must judge how long each audit will take and must decide how to schedule audit appointments efficiently. For each audit, auditors must anticipate the classification and loss exposure questions that might be asked and must determine the premium base and any necessary allocations. They then must plan how to approach the audit, what records to use, where the records are located, whom to contact, and which questions to ask. Planning greatly improves the efficiency and quality of the premium audit.

The decision about whether to conduct a field audit is influenced by legal requirements, premium size, the insured's operations, prior audit experience, nature of the policy, cost of auditing, geographical factors, and staffing requirements. For example, a workers' compensation audit might be legally required. Advisory organization rules usually require audits of all policies involving a premium above a certain amount and might restrict audit waivers to no more than two in a row. Advisory organization rules also restrict classification changes, except under specific circumstances.

Reviewing Operations

Before they look at the books, skilled premium auditors determine the nature of the operations insured; observe the nature of the operation and compare it to similar businesses, looking for classifications that might not be shown on the policy; assess management quality and cooperation to determine how to proceed with the audit; and report any significant information to the underwriting department. Additionally, auditors note organizational changes and new loss exposures and are always alert to other clues about the nature and direction of the insured's business.

EXHIBIT 6-4

Policyholder's Voluntary Report

POLICYHOLDER'S REPORT

Your Insurance Policy was issued on an **estimate** of the premium bases listed below. We now need the **actual amounts** so we can figure the premium. Please fill in the amounts for the period of time shown in the section called **Reporting Period**. If you have any questions, **please contact your agent.** We will appreciate your response by the **due date**. Thank you.

NAME AND ADDRESS OF AGENT	NAME AND ADDRESS OF COMPANY
Elliott B. Arnold Agency P. O. Box 1224 AGENCY CODE Atlanta, GA 30301 3207	IIA Insurance Company P. O. Box 1000 Springton, PA 19809

NAME AND ADDRESS OF INSURED	POLICY NUMBER	KIND OF POLICY
John's Sporting Goods, Inc. 1972 Olympic St. Atlanta, GA 30301	WC 1234	Workers Compensation

	POLICY PERIOD MONTH-DAY-YEAR TO MONTH-DAY-YEAR	DATE
	6-6-X5 TO 6-6-X6	6-7-X6
	REPORTING PERIOD	DUE DATE
	6-6-X5 TO 6-6-X6	7-6-X6

CODE	DESCRIPTION/LOCATION	PREMIUM BASE	AMOUNT	RATE	PREMIUM
8017	Retail Stores N.O.C.	Remu-neration		3.73 per $100	

☐ COMPLETE   ☐ DO NOT COMPLETE THIS SECTION   EXECUTIVE OFFICERS/PARTNERS/ PROPRIETORS

TITLE	NAME	SPECIFIC DUTIES	EARNINGS
			DO NOT INCLUDE IN UPPER SECTION

Who keeps your records? __David Schneider__
NAME

Where are they kept? __178 Trimmings Ct.__
ADDRESS

Signature _David Schneider_   Title __Treasurer__

Phone Number __522-3054__   Date __7-1-X6__

RETURN TO   ☑ COMPANY   ☐ PRODUCER

The policyholder often does not communicate changes or new operations to the producer or the insurer. Even if such information is reported, it might be sketchy, faulty, or otherwise insufficient for underwriting purposes. A premium auditor should supply underwriting with details about ownership and operations that are sufficient for rating purposes. The auditor should also indicate the proper classifications for any new loss exposures. Other items of interest to the underwriting department include the experience of the new operation's management, the financing of the operation, the marketing of its product(s), the derivation of its income, and any information about unusual hazards.

Determining Employment Relationships

After analyzing the policyholder's operations, premium auditors must determine who the policyholder's employees are for types of insurance for which premiums are based on payroll. These determinations are not always simple. Employees' payroll might constitute the premium base for both workers' compensation and general liability policies, but the definition of "employee" is not necessarily the same for both coverages.

The premium basis of workers' compensation policies includes the payroll of every person considered an employee under workers' compensation laws. Therefore, the premium auditor must distinguish between employees and independent contractors. Moreover, applicable workers' compensation laws vary by state. Many policyholders do not realize that they must obtain certificates of insurance from their subcontractors; otherwise, premium auditors must include the subcontractors' payroll in the premium base.

Finding and Evaluating Books or Records

Premium auditors can examine all books or records of the policyholder related to insurance premiums. Auditors must decide, however, which records provide the necessary information most efficiently and reliably. They must evaluate the accounting system to determine record accuracy and to identify any alternative sources to confirm the data.

In addition to meeting accounting standards, insureds should set up their records to take full advantage of insurance rules and requirements. Producers can assist in this process. For example, insureds should separate their payroll records by classification and arrange their records so that auditors can easily identify previously unreported classifications. Payroll records should identify the bonus part of overtime pay, which cannot be included in the premium basis. The basis of premium includes other forms of remuneration, such as vacation pay, tool allowance, bonuses, commissions, sick pay, the value of board and lodging, and other money substitutes.

For large accounts, auditors frequently visit a prospective policyholder before the insurer accepts the account or shortly after acceptance. During this pre-audit survey, the premium auditor confirms the information on the application. Often, the auditor can also assist in setting up appropriate bookkeeping procedures.

Auditing the Books

The auditor's job involves not only counting the loss exposures but also classifying them correctly. Classifying an account properly can be a complex task. Rating manuals contain numerous rules and exceptions, and policyholders' operations change over time. Particularly when a policy does not generate premium sufficient to justify an on-site inspection or a loss control report, a premium audit can uncover any classification changes necessary to revise coverage. The premium auditor's expertise with classification questions can help underwriters to maintain the proper classifications of the insured's operations and to align the deposit premium with the loss exposures covered by the policy. Proper classifications are important because:

* If the classification is incorrect and the rate on the policy is too high, the policyholder is being overcharged and consequently might be placed at a competitive disadvantage when bidding for jobs or pricing products. Such a situation could have serious legal ramifications if the insurer has acted negligently.

* If the classification is incorrect and the rate on the policy is too low, an account is less likely to be profitable for the insurer. Premiums might decrease, but claims and expenses do not decrease when a policyholder is classified incorrectly.

When premium auditors examine the policyholder's accounting records, they must determine how much evidence suffices to ascertain the loss exposures and classifications with a reasonable degree of confidence. If evidence is not readily available, they must balance the time and expense of obtaining it against its potential effect on the audit.

Analyzing and Verifying Premium Data

Once premium auditors have obtained the data necessary for calculating the premium, they must decide whether the data are reasonable. Do they add up? Do they seem complete? Do they reflect every step of the policyholder's operations? Are they consistent with industry averages? For example, are the ratios of payroll to sales or labor to materials reasonable considering the nature of the operation? Can deviations from expected amounts be explained? Auditors should verify premium data in accounting records and reconcile any discrepancies. Premium auditors must use considerable judgment when analyzing and verifying premium data to ensure the validity of the audit findings.

Reporting the Findings

No premium audit is complete until the auditor summarizes the results in writing and transmits them to the billings and collection unit. Naturally, auditors should clearly summarize billing data so that the insurer can process the audit without delay. Additionally, premium auditors must show how they obtained the data; they must present the data in a manner that enables others to retrace their steps. The premium auditor should describe the policyholder's operations succinctly and explain any deviations from normal expectations. Premium auditors must also identify other significant information obtained during the audit and communicate it effectively to the appropriate people.

Importance of Accurate Premium Audits

The insurance mechanism relies on each insurer to measure and classify loss exposures correctly. Premium audit errors can distort the insurer's rating structure and cause significant problems for both the insured and the insurer.

Importance for the Insured

If audit errors occur, policyholders do not pay the proper premium for their insurance. Some policyholders pay more than their proportional share for the loss exposures covered; others pay less than their share.

Experience rating bases an insured's current premium on the insured's past experience (exposure units and losses). When data on those exposure units and losses are incorrect, the experience modification is incorrect, resulting in the insured's paying inaccurate future premiums.

Importance for the Insurer

Incorrect or incomplete premium audits affect the insurer in the following ways:

- *Customer retention.* If undetected premium-audit errors cause overcharging of some policyholders and undercharging of others, the overcharged policyholders might switch to another insurer to obtain coverage at a lower premium. The insurer loses premium volume while retaining the policyholders whose premium is not commensurate with their loss exposures.

- *Goodwill.* When policyholders are informed of errors in the premium audit, the insurer's image suffers. Policyholders could lose confidence in the insurer's competence and might consider switching to another insurer. Policyholders who continue their coverage with the insurer despite an incorrect audit might be unwilling to cooperate in a claim investigation or to implement loss prevention measures. Perhaps the biggest cost, however, is the marketing and underwriting effort expended to secure business that is subsequently lost because of premium audit mistakes.

- *Efficiency.* Unless premium audits are complete and correct, additional work is generated for both the premium audit department and the insurer's other departments. Redoing the audit taxes the resources of the premium audit department. Other departments might become involved in attempting to explain the error to the policyholder. Underwriters have to correct their records. The accounting department must make the appropriate adjusting entries and issue a corrected bill.

- *Collections.* Policyholders are not likely to pay premium bills they believe or suspect to be incorrect. Even when the problem is eventually resolved, the insurer's cash flow suffers as a result of any delay.

Importance for Insurance Rates

Premium audits affect the equity and accuracy of class rates in the following ways:

- *Consistency and accuracy of classification determinations.* If premium auditors in one area of a state consider a particular industrial class to be in classification X, while the premium auditors in another part of the state consider it to be in class Y, then the inconsistency distorts the resulting loss data from both classes and leads to inequitable rates for all policyholders in the state for those two classes. Equally important in the ratemaking procedure is accurately classifying claims. By notifying the claim department when additional classifications are assigned and by reviewing the classification of past claims at the time of an audit, premium auditors can assist the claim department in accurately classifying losses as well as loss exposures.
- *Measurement of the exposure unit base.* An audit error, not in classification but in determining the exposure units, also distorts the rate structure. Either underreporting or overreporting the exposure units affects the rate for that class.

SUMMARY

Underwriting liability insurance presents many challenges for underwriters. Legislation and court decisions require frequent changes to policy forms and underwriting guidelines. Such an environment requires underwriters to update their knowledge and skills continually to remain current with emerging issues. Underwriters must also understand the legal concepts that form the bases of liability insurance.

Commercial general liability provides coverage for bodily injury or property damage arising from loss exposures relating to premises owned or operated by the insured, as well as business operations conducted away from the premises. Commercial general liability insurance also provides coverage for negligent acts of contractors or subcontractors and for injuries caused by products manufactured or sold by the insured. Underwriters need to know the hazards related to the policyholder's premises, operations, and products. Personal liability insurance covers similar loss exposures; however, these loss exposures arise out of individual and family activities rather than business operations.

Professional liability insurance covers incidents that arise out of a policyholder's professional responsibilities. The standard of care required of a professional is greater than that of an ordinary individual. Because of the expertise required to write this coverage, only a small number of insurers are actively involved in providing it.

Effective personal auto underwriting requires an appreciation of the regulatory and legal environments that affect this type of insurance. The residual market and how its costs are shared have created a challenging environment for insurers in many states. Insurers are often granted little latitude in underwriting personal auto coverage. Several states do not permit insurers to reject applicants, and some states limit underwriting criteria to just a few factors.

Commercial auto underwriting is less controversial but is influenced by regulatory requirements on personal autos. In addition to considering drivers, underwriters consider the vehicle weight and use, radius of operation, and special industry classifications. Effective loss control programs can significantly affect the profitability of a commercial auto account.

Workers' compensation insurance covers employers for workplace injury to employees. Workers' compensation benefits are determined by law and include death, disability income, medical expenses, and rehabilitation costs. Underwriters must extensively investigate and evaluate hazards to ensure that a given account can be priced profitably. Many of the loss exposures are similar to those covered under general liability. The principal difference is that the policyholder's employees, rather than the general public, are exposed to potential injury. The Occupational Safety and Health Act has created a resource of statistics that an insurer can use to evaluate a class of business and that an underwriter can use to evaluate an individual applicant. Some employers present maritime-related occupations that fall under federal jurisdiction, unlike most workers' compensation exposures. Maritime loss exposures can exist where the underwriter would not expect, such as in certain construction or erection-type operations. Unfortunately, some of these loss exposures might not be discovered until a claim is presented to the insurer.

Umbrella and excess liability policies are available to provide higher coverage limits than those provided by the primary policies. Personal and commercial umbrella policies provide additional liability coverage over underlying policies as well as coverage when no primary coverage exists. Excess policies are usually found only in the commercial market and provide additional limits over underlying policies.

This chapter concludes by discussing the premium audit function. Premium auditors play an important role in commercial insurance because of the number and size of policies now written with a variable premium base.

Premium audits are used to determine correct policy premiums, to meet regulatory requirements, to collect ratemaking data, to inhibit fraud, and to reinforce policyholders' confidence in the insurer.

Because of their direct contact with policyholders, premium auditors also have an opportunity to refer specific observations to various insurer departments. Auditors can notify underwriters of incorrect classifications, inadequate exposure unit estimates, or previously unidentified loss exposures.

Information gathered during the premium audit process can provide new opportunities for the marketing department in developing new products.

Underwriters work closely with premium auditors in evaluating liability coverages. The premium audit department assists insurers by making certain that correct premiums are charged and by increasing customer satisfaction with and confidence in the insurer.

Underwriting is a behind-the-scenes activity from the insured's perspective. Claim adjusting, however, is the heart of the insurance product from the insured's perspective. The next chapter begins the discussion of the claim function.

CHAPTER NOTES

1. *Denny v. Ford Motor Co.*, 84 NY 2d, 1018 (1995).

2. http://www.choicepoint.com/industry/insurance/pc_ins_up2.html (accessed December 20, 2002).

3. National Highway Traffic Safety Administration, "The Economic Impact of Motor Vehicle Crashes, 2000," May 2002, http://www.nhtsa.dot.gov (accessed June 11, 2002).

4. Maryland Automobile Insurance Fund mission statement, February 25, 2000, https://www.maif.net/missstmt.htm (accessed December 20, 2002).

5. National Safety Council Web site, http://www.nsc.org/library/facts/yngdrive.htm (accessed June 11, 2000).

6. W. Heinrich, *Industrial Accident Prevention*, 4th ed. (New York: McGraw-Hill, 1959), p. 13.

7. National Council on Compensation Insurance, Guide to Employee Leasing, http://www.ncci.com/nccisearch/Industry/Employee/elhome.htm (accessed January 13, 2003).

8. Alliance of American Insurers, *Residual Markets: Workers Compensation, 2000 Experience* (Downers Grove, Ill.: Alliance of American Insurers, 2002), p. 1.

9. National Council on Compensation Insurance, "Residual Markets Overview," http://www.ncci.com/ncci/web/news/infostop/residual/OverviewWCIP.htm (accessed January 13, 2003).

Chapter 7

Direct Your Learning

Ratemaking

After learning the content of this chapter, you should be able to:

■ Describe the goals and ideal characteristics of ratemaking.

■ Explain how actuaries are involved in the ratemaking process.

■ Describe rate components and ratemaking terms.

■ Describe factors that affect ratemaking.

■ Given a case, calculate a rate.

■ Describe the following ratemaking methods:

    a.   Pure premium

    b.   Loss ratio

    c.   Judgment

■ Describe the steps in the ratemaking data development process.

■ Describe the policy-year, calendar-year, and accident-year data collection methods.

■ Explain why and how ratemaking data are adjusted.

■ Explain how to prepare rate filings.

■ Explain how ratemaking varies by type of insurance.

■ Explain why and how increased limits factors are used.

Develop Your Perspective

What are the main topics covered in the chapter?

This chapter describes the ratemaking goals of regulators and insurers and the processes applied in ratemaking. These processes include the methods of gathering statistics, adjustments for loss development factors and trending, and territorial and class relativities. Ratemaking methods and variations by type of insurance are illustrated.

Determine methods of ratemaking for a specific type of insurance with which you are familiar.

- How are statistics for this type of insurance gathered and applied?
- What adjustments are made to the statistics?
- What relativity factors are applied?
- What are the real-world factors that would complicate the ratemaking process for this type of insurance?

Why is it important to learn about these topics?

Ratemaking is the projection of past loss experience into rates that will, it is hoped, develop future premiums that will pay for losses and expenses and provide a margin for profit and contingencies. Actuaries use the processes described to develop the rates that are documented and submitted to the states in rate filings. By understanding the processes involved, you can appreciate the importance of the development of statistics, which are the basis of rate development and future premium income.

Consider how errors in statistics can affect rate development.

- How might the use of inaccurate statistics or the choice of inappropriate rating processes affect an insurer's premium revenue?

How can you use what you will learn?

Assess your own organization's ratemaking process.

- What statistics are used, and how are they gathered?
- Are the processes described in this chapter applied, or are other calculations required?

Chapter 7

Ratemaking

This chapter begins by describing **ratemaking** goals from the perspective of both regulators and insurers. Next, it briefly describes the persons or organizations that are responsible for ratemaking. Rate components and ratemaking terms are then introduced and factors that affect ratemaking are examined.

Next, the chapter studies three different ratemaking methods: the pure premium method, the loss ratio method, and the judgment method.

As sound ratemaking is based on data, the next major portion of the chapter discusses ratemaking data development. The chapter concludes by comparing ratemaking for different types of insurance.

This chapter focuses on how past loss statistics are used to develop future rates. No matter how complete and accurate these statistics might be, they can only tell what has happened in the past. Ratemakers cannot foretell the future, and they cannot guarantee that the future will resemble the past. They can only use their best judgment in interpreting developments and trends in order to anticipate what is most likely to occur in the future.

Ratemaking
The process insurers use to calculate insurance rates, which are a premium component.

RATEMAKING GOALS

Insurance ratemaking is challenging, because the amounts of fortuitous future losses and their associated expenses are unknown when rates are developed. In light of this uncertainty, insurers try to develop rates that meet their goals as well as regulatory goals.

As discussed in Chapter 2, the primary regulatory goals of ratemaking are that rates be adequate, not be excessive, and not be unfairly discriminatory. From the insurer's perspective, the primary goal of ratemaking is to develop a rate structure that enables the insurer to compete effectively while earning a reasonable profit on its operations. To accomplish this, the rates and pricing guidelines must result in premiums that adequately cover all losses and expenses and that leave a reasonable amount for profits and contingencies.

This ratemaking goal complements the underwriting goal, which is to develop and maintain a profitable book of business. To maintain its book of business, the insurer must have competitive rates. To be profitable, the insurer must have adequate rates. To enable an insurer to be competitive and profitable, rates should ideally have five characteristics. Rates should:

1. Be stable.
2. Be responsive.
3. Provide for contingencies.
4. Promote loss control.
5. Be simple.

Rates do not always have all of these characteristics. Also, some characteristics conflict with others, and compromises are often necessary.

Stable rates are highly desirable because changing rates is expensive. Additionally, sudden, large rate changes cause dissatisfaction among customers and sometimes lead to regulatory or legislative actions. However, rate stability could conflict with the responsiveness characteristic, which suggests that rates should change promptly in response to external factors that affect losses. Rate stability might also conflict with the characteristic that rates should provide for contingencies, such as unexpected variations in losses and expenses.

Ratemaking systems should address the fourth characteristic, promote loss control, by providing lower rates for policyholders who exercise sound loss control. For example, policyholders who install burglar alarm systems receive a reduction in their crime insurance rates. Lower fire insurance rates are charged to policyholders who install automatic sprinkler systems at their premises. On the other hand, policyholders who engage in activities that tend to result in more losses, such as persons who use their cars for business, generally pay higher rates.

Ratemaking systems should also be simple enough for producers and underwriters to apply and for policyholders to understand. Policyholders range from naive personal insurance customers to sophisticated corporate risk managers with advanced designations and degrees. The level of insurance expertise is generally much lower for personal insurance customers than for commercial insurance customers.

RATEMAKING RESPONSIBILITY

Actuary
A person who uses complex mathematical methods and technology to analyze loss and other data used in determining insurance rates.

Actuaries usually supervise ratemaking activities. An **actuary** is a person trained in applying mathematical techniques to insurer operations. Many large insurers employ one or more staff actuaries, whereas small insurers tend to rely on actuarial consultants. Insurers that employ staff actuaries may also retain actuarial consultants either because their staff actuaries lack expertise in specific areas or because the insurers believe that outside consultants can be more objective. Additionally, insurers might retain actuarial consultants to ease periodic workload peaks. Regulatory authorities and reinsurers sometimes require insurers to provide a consulting actuary's opinion verifying the accuracy and reasonableness of the staff actuaries' work.

Insurers having a large enough pool of loss data to be statistically credible calculate their own prospective loss costs to develop insurance rates. Prospective loss costs are one component of insurance rates and reflect the amount needed to pay future claims plus loss adjustment expenses. These insurers then add an amount for future expenses and for profit and contingencies to the developed loss costs.

Other insurers obtain actuarial services from advisory organizations. These advisory organizations, among other things, collect loss data and calculate prospective loss costs for various types of insurance. The prospective loss costs are then supplied to insurers.

When using prospective loss costs supplied by advisory organizations, each insurer must apply its own loss cost multiplier to determine its insurance rate. The loss cost multiplier reflects the amount needed to pay future expenses, such as acquisition expenses, overhead, and premium taxes. The loss cost multiplier also includes a factor for profit and contingencies. One insurer's rates might differ from another insurer's rates, even though both use the same prospective loss costs, because of variations in each insurer's loss cost multiplier.

The four principal advisory organizations are the following:

1. Insurance Services Office (ISO)
2. American Association of Insurance Services (AAIS)
3. National Council on Compensation Insurance (NCCI)
4. Surety Association of America (SAA)

A few other specialized advisory organizations exist. Advisory organizations maintain contact with regulatory authorities to facilitate approval of rate filings. For some types of insurance, and in some jurisdictions, rates are set by the state insurance department, rather than by advisory organizations. Advisory organizations also provide some services that are not actuarial, such as drafting insurance policies.

RATE COMPONENTS AND RATEMAKING TERMS

This section reviews the components of an insurance rate and discusses common ratemaking terms.

Rate Components

An insurance rate consists of the following three components:

1. An amount needed to pay future claims and loss adjustment expenses (prospective loss costs)
2. An amount needed to pay future expenses, such as acquisition expenses, overhead, and premium taxes (expense provision)
3. An amount for profit and contingencies (profit and contingencies factor)

The first component of an insurance rate is equivalent to the prospective loss costs supplied by advisory organizations or developed by insurers with large enough pools of loss data. The second and third components are equivalent to a loss cost multiplier. Once the insurance rate is calculated, it is multiplied by the appropriate number of exposure units to produce a premium.

The next section discusses common terms used in the ratemaking process. Because the most important and complex part of the ratemaking process is the projection of losses, a later section of this chapter discusses the methods used to estimate and project loss amounts.

Ratemaking Terms

Pure premium
The amount included in the rate per exposure unit required to pay losses.

The **pure premium** is the amount included in the rate per exposure unit required to pay losses.

Expense provision
The amount that is included in an insurance rate to cover the insurer's expenses and that might include loss adjustment expenses but that excludes investment expenses.

The **expense provision** is the amount added to the rate required to pay expenses. Such expenses include acquisition expenses; general expenses; premium taxes; and licenses and fees paid to government, regulatory, and advisory organizations.

Loss adjustment expenses
The expenses associated with adjusting claims.

Loss adjustment expenses are the expenses associated with adjusting claims and are examined in more detail in subsequent chapters. Some loss adjustment expenses, such as legal fees to defend a claim, are included in the pure premium instead. Consequently, these expenses are not also included in the expense provision.

Earned exposure unit
Exposure unit for which an insurer has provided a full year of coverage.

The **earned exposure unit** is the exposure unit for which the insurer has provided a full year of coverage.

Profit and contingencies
An amount included in the insurance rate to protect insurers against the possibility that actual claims or expenses will exceed projections.

Insurers add a loading for **profit and contingencies**. This loading protects the insurer against the possibility that actual losses and expenses will exceed the projected losses and expenses included in the insurance rate. If excessive losses or expenses are not incurred, the funds generated by the loading produce additional profit for the insurer.

Investment Income

A property-casualty insurer performs two distinct operations: insurance operations and investment operations. The insurance operations write policies, collect premiums, and pay losses. The investment operations use the funds generated by the insurance operations to buy bonds, stocks, and other investments to earn an investment profit. The return from these investments is called investment income.

Traditionally, property-casualty insurers did not consider their investment returns directly when calculating insurance rates. They may, however, have considered investment returns informally when determining allowances for profits and contingencies. Today, insurers commonly consider investment results explicitly in their rate calculations. Some states even require that investment income be considered explicitly. Sophisticated models are available that can be used to include investment returns in the insurance rate.

The investment return earned by an insurer depends largely on the types of insurance written, the loss reserves, and associated unearned premium reserves. Property losses are usually paid relatively quickly, while liability losses often are not paid until years after losses occur. Consequently, an insurer's loss reserves for liability insurance are usually much greater than its loss reserves for an equivalent amount of property insurance. Because the assets that offset loss reserves are invested to produce income for the insurer, investment returns are more likely to affect liability insurance rates than property insurance rates.

RATEMAKING FACTORS

Estimating future events and costs in the real world is subject to uncertainty. Areas of uncertainty that affect ratemaking include estimation of losses and delays in data collection and use.

Estimation of Losses

The key to developing insurance rates that are adequate to pay future claims is estimating the amount of losses for those claims. Past loss experience is generally used as a starting point to estimate future losses. Ratemaking is based on estimating losses from past coverage periods and then adjusting those losses for future conditions. For example, adjustments could be made to past loss experience for anticipated future inflation or for changes in benefits mandated by legislation.

However, past loss experience may not be completely known because not all covered losses are paid immediately. At any point in time, many losses have been incurred but not yet paid. The difference between the estimated loss amount that will be required to be paid and the actual loss amount paid to date is the loss reserves. This section explains how ultimate losses for past experience are estimated and why it is difficult to accurately estimate incurred losses for any given time period.

Insurance rates are based partly on incurred losses. Incurred losses include both paid losses and outstanding loss reserves. Loss reserves are estimates of future payments for losses that have already occurred, whether the losses are reported or not reported. Insurers are legally required to show loss reserves as liabilities on their balance sheets. Because loss reserves are estimates, they are somewhat imprecise. Nonetheless, rates are based partly on such estimates. So, if loss reserve estimates are too low, rates will probably be too low. If loss reserves are too high, rates will probably be too high.

To illustrate simply, assume that rates for auto liability insurance are calculated based on losses that occurred in the most recent three-year period. The insurer's past experience indicates that 25 percent of losses are paid in the year the accident occurs, 50 percent are paid in the second year, and 25 percent are paid

EXHIBIT 7-1

Paid Losses, Loss Reserves, and Incurred Losses for Hypothetical Auto Liability Insurance as of the End of Year 3

Year	(1) Paid Losses	(2) Loss Reserves	(3) Incurred Losses
1	$10,000,000	$ 0	$10,000,000
2	7,500,000	2,500,000	10,000,000
3	2,500,000	7,500,000	10,000,000
Total	$20,000,000	$10,000,000	$30,000,000

in the third year. Exhibit 7-1 shows the losses for each year in the three-year period, with Year 1 being the earliest year and Year 3, the most recent year.

The information in Exhibit 7-1 can be interpreted as follows:

- The *paid losses* in Column (1) are the amounts paid from January 1 of Year 1 up to and including December 31 of Year 3. The insurer has already paid this money to claimants.

- The *loss reserves* shown in Column (2) are the insurer's best estimates, as of December 31 of Year 3, of the amounts it will pay in the future for losses that occurred during each one-year period. Because all losses that occurred in Year 1 have been paid, no loss reserve exists for Year 1.

- Column (3), which is incurred losses for a given period, is the sum of Columns (1) and (2).

If the insurer in Exhibit 7-1 insured 100,000 cars each year during this three-year period, it provided 300,000 *car-years* of protection. A car-year represents the loss exposure of one car insured for one year. In this case, each car-year for which the insurer has provided coverage represents one earned exposure unit. If the 300,000 car-years are divided into the $30 million of incurred losses, the insurer needs a pure premium—the amount needed to pay losses—of $100 per car per year ($30,000,000/300,000 = $100) to pay its losses during this past three-year period. This example includes not only paid losses but also loss reserves.

If the pure premium indicated by this experience period were used to develop rates for a future year, any inadequacy in past loss reserves would also make future rates inadequate. In theory, an insurer could avoid this problem by waiting for all claims to be paid before using loss data to calculate rates. When all claims incurred during a given period have been paid, loss reserves for that period no longer exist. In practice, however, waiting would create problems. If the rate filing were delayed for several years to permit all claims to be settled, then factors like inflation, changes in traffic conditions, and so forth would have a greater chance of changing the loss exposure. The effects of these factors might be greater than the effects of errors in estimating loss reserves.

EXHIBIT 7-2

Payout Pattern for Automobile Liability Insurance Year 1 Losses

Year	(1) Paid Losses to Date	(2) Unpaid Losses Reported	(3) Unpaid Losses IBNR	(4) Estimated Losses for Year 1
12/31/X1	$ 5,051,145	$13,837,205	$9,592,239	$28,480,589
12/31/X2	10,780,845	12,906,866	4,187,646	27,875,357
12/31/X3	16,036,708	9,058,737	2,036,246	27,131,691
12/31/X4	19,667,531	6,782,231	79,247	26,529,009
12/31/X5	22,268,032	4,308,212	0	26,576,244
12/31/X6	24,714,163	3,136,059	0	27,850,222
12/31/X7	25,088,249	860,395	0	25,948,644

Exhibit 7-2 shows the payout pattern reported by one insurer for auto liability insurance. In Exhibit 7-2, Year 1 is the year in which the accidents occurred, Year 2 is the following year, and so forth.

Paid Losses

Column (1) of Exhibit 7-2 shows the actual amount the insurer paid to the end of the year for losses *arising from insured events that occurred during Year 1*—$5,051,145 in Year 1. In Year 2, the insurer paid an additional $5,729,700 for these insured events, bringing total loss payments to $10,780,845. By the end of Year 7, the insurer paid a total of $25,088,249 in losses for insured events that occurred in Year 1.

Reported But Not Paid Losses

Column (2) of Exhibit 7-2 shows the insurer's annual year-end *estimates* of the amounts it will pay for losses for insured events that occurred in Year 1 that have been reported but not yet paid. This amount decreases each year as claims are settled, becoming a relatively small amount of $860,395 at the end of Year 7.

Incurred But Not Reported (IBNR) Losses

Column (3) shows the insurer's *estimates* of future payments to pay losses for insured events that occurred in Year 1 but that have not yet been reported. These estimates are known as incurred but not reported (IBNR) losses. The insurer assumed that all auto insurance losses incurred in Year 1 had been reported by the end of Year 5, so the IBNR figure is zero for Year 5 and later.

The amounts in Columns (2) and (3) are *estimates* of future payments. The amounts in Column (2) are usually based on estimates by claim department personnel of the amounts to be paid on individual claims. The amounts in Column (3) are usually calculated by actuaries based on historical data. The amounts ultimately paid seldom, if ever, equal the estimates, and the differences are sometimes substantial.

Incurred Loss Estimate

Column (4) of Exhibit 7-2 shows the insurer's estimate of the losses incurred during Year 1 as of December 31 of each year. Incurred losses include both paid and unpaid losses. The unpaid losses include both reported and IBNR losses. Therefore, Column (4) is the sum of the amounts in Columns (1), (2), and (3).

Column (4) shows that the insurer estimated that at the end of Year 1, it would pay a total of $28,480,589 to settle all of the auto liability losses for Year 1. By the end of Year 7, the insurer had reduced that estimate to $25,948,644. With only $860,395 of outstanding losses at the end of Year 7, the estimate in the last line of the exhibit is a more accurate estimate of the loss amounts ultimately payable for Year 1 than the estimate made at the end of Year 1.

If the insurer in Exhibit 7-2 had used its estimated incurred losses at the end of Year 1 for ratemaking purposes, the resulting rates would have been too high by approximately 10 percent:

$$\frac{\$28,480,589 - \$25,948,644}{\$25,948,644} = 9.8\%.$$

On the other hand, rates based on underestimated losses could lead to inadequate rates, underwriting losses, and possibly even insolvency.

Actuaries have methods for correcting consistent errors in estimating future losses. Loss development methods are described later in this chapter.

Delay in Data Collection and Use

As mentioned, responsiveness is a desirable ratemaking characteristic. Because conditions are constantly changing, any delay between when data are collected and when they are used tends to reduce rate accuracy. A delay inevitably occurs between when losses are incurred and when those losses are reflected in rates charged to customers. The delay can span several years. During this period, economic or other factors can increase or decrease the rates the insurer should charge if the premium is to reflect the expected losses.

The delay in reflecting loss experience in rates stems from several sources, including the following:

- Delays by policyholders in reporting losses to insurers
- Time required to analyze data and prepare a rate filing
- Delays in obtaining state approval of filed rates
- Time required to implement new rates
- Time period during which rates are in effect, usually a full year

When a rate is in effect for a full year, the last policy issued under that rate could be issued 365 days (one year) after the effective date of the rate filing, and the policy's coverage under that rate continues until policy expiration, yet another year later. This delay is illustrated in Exhibit 7-3.

EXHIBIT 7-3

Delay Caused When Rates Are in Effect One Full Year

1/1/X1 ---------------------------------- 12/31/X1 ---------------------------- 12/31/X2

| Beginning of Policy Year First Policies Issued | Last Policies Issued for This Policy Year | Policies Issued 12/31/X1 Expire |

Exhibit 7-4 shows a reasonably typical schedule for developing, approving, and implementing new rates for auto insurance. Exhibit 7-4 assumes that the insurer is basing its new rates on its loss experience for a prior three-year period, called the **experience period**. Data from the experience period are collected and analyzed in the ratemaking process.

Experience period
The period for which all pertinent statistics are collected and analyzed in the ratemaking process.

EXHIBIT 7-4

Chronology of a Rate Filing

1/1, Year 1	Start of experience period, first loss incurred
12/31, Year 1	
12/31, Year 2	
12/31, Year 3	End of experience period
3/31, Year 4	Start of data collection and analysis
7/1, Year 4	Rates filed with regulators
9/1, Year 4	Approval of rates received
1/1, Year 5	New rates initially used
12/31, Year 5	Rates no longer used
12/31, Year 6	Last loss incurred under this rate filing

---

The experience period in Exhibit 7-4 begins on January 1 of Year 1. Data are collected for the three-year period beginning on that date and ending on December 31 of Year 3.

In Exhibit 7-4, the analysis phase of the ratemaking process begins only three months after the end of the experience period. Some insurers wait longer to start the ratemaking process in order to permit loss data to mature. Many losses incurred during the experience period would not yet have been reported to the insurer.

Exhibit 7-4 assumes that the new rates will become effective on January 1 of Year 5, one year after the end of the experience period. They will remain in effect until December 31 of Year 5, two years after the end of the experience period. However, the policies issued on December 31 of Year 5 will remain in force until December 31 of Year 6. Consequently, the last loss under these rates will be incurred three years after the end of the experience period and six years after the beginning of the experience period, when the first losses occurred on which the rate calculation was based.

Some insurers shorten this process slightly by filing new rates every six months or issuing six-month policies. Others follow a longer cycle.

Other Factors

Both loss severity and loss frequency affect an insurer's loss experience during any given period. Economic inflation or deflation during the inevitable delay previously discussed also affects the average cost of a loss (severity). Finally, legislative or regulatory changes such as modification in rules governing claim settlement can affect the number of losses (frequency). Rates calculated without regard to these factors could prove to be grossly inadequate or grossly excessive.

These factors are difficult to quantify, but they clearly affect losses. Some factors that affect the size and frequency of losses cannot be identified or measured directly, but their aggregate effect on losses can be determined with reasonable accuracy by trending, an actuarial technique discussed later in the chapter.

Insurance rates are also based on the insurer's projected expenses. Like losses, expenses can change over time, and any projected changes must be considered in the ratemaking process. Rather than using past expenses, it is sometimes more relevant to use judgment or budgeted expenses, especially when conditions change dramatically. Ratemakers are also challenged to allocate general administrative expenses properly among different types of insurance.

RATEMAKING METHODS

Insurers commonly use the following three ratemaking methods:

1. Pure premium method
2. Loss ratio method
3. Judgment method

These three methods are compared in Exhibit 7-5.

EXHIBIT 7-5

Ratemaking Methods

Method	Data Required	Uses
Pure premium method	• Incurred losses • Earned exposure units • Expense provision • Profit and contingencies factor	To develop rates from past experience (Cannot be used without past experience)
Loss ratio method	Actual loss ratio, calculated from: • Incurred losses • Earned premiums Expected loss ratio, calculated from: • 100% − expense provision	To modify existing rates (Cannot be used without existing rates; cannot be used to determine rates for a new type of insurance)
Judgment method	Rates based on experience and judgment	To develop rates when data are limited (Requires skilled judgment)

Pure Premium Ratemaking Method

The first ratemaking method is the **pure premium method**, which involves the following four steps:

1. Calculate the pure premium.
2. Estimate the expenses per exposure unit.
3. Determine the profit and contingencies factor.
4. Add the pure premium and the expense provision and divide by one minus the profit and contingencies factor.

Pure premium method
A method for calculating insurance rates using estimates of future losses and expenses, including a profit and contingencies factor.

Step 1 in the pure premium method is to calculate the pure premium. The *pure premium* (the amount needed to pay losses or prospective loss costs) is calculated by dividing the dollar amount of incurred losses by the number of earned exposure units. For example:

$$\text{Incurred losses} = \$4 \text{ million}$$

$$\text{Earned car-years} = 100{,}000$$

$$\text{Pure premium} = \frac{\text{Incurred losses}}{\text{Earned car-years}}$$

$$\text{Pure premium} = \frac{\$4{,}000{,}000}{100{,}000} = \$40.$$

Step 2 in the pure premium method is to calculate expenses per exposure unit based on the insurer's past expenses, except investment expenses, and possibly loss adjustment expenses. If loss adjustment expenses are included in the pure premium, then they are excluded from the expenses. Investment expenses are not directly reflected in rate calculations. If expenses are $1.7 million, then expenses per exposure unit are:

$$\frac{\$1,700,000}{100,000} = \$17.$$

Step 3 in the pure premium method is to determine the profit and contingencies factor. In this example, a factor of 5 percent is used.

Step 4 in the pure premium method is to add the pure premium and the expense provision per exposure unit and divide by one minus the profit and contingencies factor.

For example, if the pure premium is $40, the expenses per exposure unit are $17, and the profit and contingencies factor is 5 percent, the formula would be:

$$\text{Rate per exposure unit} = \frac{\text{Pure premium} + \text{Expenses per exposure unit}}{1 - \text{Profit and contingencies factor}}$$

$$= \frac{\$40 + \$17}{1 - 0.05}$$

$$= \frac{\$57}{0.95}$$

$$= \$60.$$

The rate per exposure unit of $60 is equal to the pure premium of $40 (the amount required to pay losses or loss costs) plus an additional $17 (the amount required to pay expenses) and $3 (for profit and contingencies).

Some insurers separate their expenses into two components: fixed expenses and variable expenses. Fixed expenses are stated as a dollar amount per exposure unit. Variable expenses are stated as a percentage of the rate. For example, the insurer in the preceding example might decide that its cost for issuing a policy and collecting the premium is $2.50 per car-year, regardless of premium size, rating class, or rating territory. Its other underwriting expenses vary by premium size, and the total of such expenses equals 12 percent. The formula to calculate the rate per exposure unit in this case would be:

$$\text{Rate per exposure unit} = \frac{\text{Pure premium} + \text{Fixed expenses per exposure unit}}{1 - \text{Variable expense percentage} - \text{Profit and contingencies factor}}$$

$$= \frac{\$40 + \$2.50}{1 - 0.12 - 0.05}$$

$$= \frac{\$42.50}{0.83}$$

$$= \$51 \, (\text{rounded}).$$

The new rate per exposure unit of $51 is equal to the pure premium of $40 (the amount required to pay losses or loss costs), fixed expenses of $2.50, variable expenses of $6 (rounded), and $2.50 (rounded) for profit and contingencies.

The pure premium method can be used to develop rates based on past experience. An insurer that needs to modify its current rates could apply the pure premium method, or it could use the loss ratio method.

Loss Ratio Ratemaking Method

The second ratemaking method is the **loss ratio method**. This method adjusts an existing insurance rate either upward or downward to reflect changing conditions. In its simplest form, the loss ratio method uses two loss ratios—the actual loss ratio and the expected loss ratio of the insurer during the selected experience period:

Loss ratio method
A method for determining insurance rates based on a comparison of actual and expected loss ratios.

1. Actual loss ratio $= \dfrac{\text{Incurred losses}}{\text{Earned premiums}}$

2. Expected loss ratio $= 100\% - $ Expense provision.

In this method, profit and contingencies are included in the expense provision because the method modifies a current insurance rate.

The expected loss ratio plus the expense provision always add up to 100 percent.

The following is the loss ratio ratemaking equation in its simplest form:

$$\text{Rate change} = \frac{\text{Actual loss ratio} - \text{Expected loss ratio}}{\text{Expected loss ratio}} .$$

If the rate change percentage is negative, it indicates a rate reduction. If positive, it indicates a rate increase. For example, if the actual loss ratio equals 54 percent and the expected loss ratio equals 60 percent, then the rate change is a decrease of 10 percent, as shown below:

$$\frac{\text{Actual loss ratio} - \text{Expected loss ratio}}{\text{Expected loss ratio}} = \frac{(0.54 - 0.60)}{0.60}$$

$$= \frac{-0.06}{0.60}$$

$$\text{Rate change} = -0.10 = -10\%.$$

In this case, the insurer's actual loss ratio was better than the targeted loss ratio. Based only on this information, it appears that the insurer could lower its rates and still make the desired profit on business subject to these rates. Lower rates would probably also attract additional business that, in turn, would produce greater profits.

The loss ratio ratemaking method cannot be used to calculate rates for a new type of insurance, because neither an actual loss ratio for the calculation nor an old rate to adjust is available. For a new type of insurance, either the pure premium method or the judgment method must be used.

Judgment Ratemaking Method

Judgment ratemaking method
A method for determining insurance rates that relies heavily on the experience and knowledge of an actuary or an underwriter who makes little or no use of loss experience data.

The third ratemaking method is the **judgment ratemaking method**. This method is the oldest ratemaking method and is still used for some types of insurance. With this method, underwriters determine rates primarily on the basis of their experience and judgment. Although the judgment ratemaking method might use limited or no loss experience data, an experienced underwriter generally has a sense of what rates have produced desired results in the past. The judgment ratemaking method is still used for ocean marine insurance, some inland marine classes, and aviation insurance and when limited data are available, such as with terrorism coverage.

RATEMAKING DATA DEVELOPMENT

This section describes the steps in ratemaking data development. The insurer's staff might perform these steps, or an advisory organization might perform some or all of them. The major steps in the ratemaking data development process are:

- Collect data
- Adjust data
- Determine territorial and class relativities
- Prepare rate filings and submit rate filings to regulatory authorities as required

Collect Data

Three ratemaking data collection methods are discussed in this section:

1. Policy-year data collection method
2. Calendar-year data collection method
3. Accident-year data collection method

To obtain and maintain usable data, each insurer must code data when transactions occur. Some coding is prescribed by advisory organizations, but many insurers collect more data than advisory organizations require. Information about specific policies is collected most conveniently when policies, endorsements, and invoices are issued. Claim data are collected when claims are reported, reserves are established or changed, checks or drafts are issued, or claims are closed.

Before collecting ratemaking data, the insurer must determine the kinds of data to collect.

- For the pure premium ratemaking method, actuaries need incurred losses, earned exposure units, the expense provision amount, and a profit and contingencies factor.

- For the loss ratio method, actuaries need incurred losses, earned premiums, and the expense provision amount (including a profit and contingencies factor).

If rates are to vary by rating class and territory, data must be collected for each class and territory.

Ideally, the incurred losses, earned premiums, and earned exposure units should be based on the same group of policies. However, this is not always practical, so approximation techniques are used. For example, as will be explained, sometimes it is most practical to compare premiums during one twelve-month period with losses for a slightly different twelve-month period, even if these two periods do not involve exactly the same policies.

The three ratemaking data collection methods are summarized in Exhibit 7-6.

Policy-Year Data Collection Method

The first ratemaking data collection method is the **policy-year method**. This method involves analyzing earned premiums, exposure units, and incurred losses associated with a particular group of policies that were issued during a specific twelve-month period—for example, all policies first issued from 1/1/X1 to 12/31/X1. For year-long policies, the coverage period for this group of policies spans two years because policies issued on 12/31/X1 expire one year later, on 12/31/X2. All premiums for a policy are linked directly to that policy, including the original premium; additional premiums; and return premiums resulting from premium audits, retrospective rating plans, policy changes, and similar transactions. Exposure units, incurred losses, and allocated loss adjustment expenses are also linked to the policies that cover them.

Policy-year method
A method of collecting ratemaking data that analyzes all policies issued in a given twelve-month period and that links all losses, premiums, and exposure units to the policy to which they are related.

The policy-year method is the only ratemaking data collection method that exactly matches losses, premiums, and exposure units to a specific group of insureds.

Two major disadvantages apply to the policy-year ratemaking data collection method:

1. It takes longer to gather data for this method than for the calendar-year and accident-year methods.

2. It involves some additional expense to gather data that are used only for ratemaking. The data used in the other two methods are gathered in part as a byproduct of the insurer's accounting operations. Although this additional expense was once considered a major disadvantage of the policy-year method, automated recordkeeping has made the extra cost of compiling policy-year statistics much less significant.

Delays in concluding data collection can be overcome partly by estimating the ultimate values of data for which final values are not yet available. However, potential errors in estimating such values reduce the "apples-to-apples" advantage of the policy-year method.

Calendar-Year Data Collection Method

Calendar-year method
A method of collecting ratemaking data that estimates both earned premiums and incurred losses by formulas from accounting records.

The second ratemaking data collection method is the **calendar-year method**. This method involves analyzing data that are used for accounting purposes. An insurer's transactional accounting records show the insurer's written premiums and unearned premium reserves for a given calendar year. They do not, however, show information more directly relevant for ratemaking—earned premiums, incurred losses, or exposure units. This information must be approximated using accounting data.

Earned premiums must be calculated as follows from written premiums and unearned premium reserves:

Earned premiums = Written premiums for the year
+ (Unearned premiums at the beginning of the year
− Unearned premiums at the end of the year).

This formula provides a reasonably accurate estimate of the actual earned premiums. Computed this way, the earned premiums might not reflect additional premiums or refunds resulting from premium audits or retrospective rating plans on the insured's previous policies, but the discrepancies should be relatively small for most insurers.

Under the calendar-year ratemaking data collection method, incurred losses must also be estimated by formula:

Incurred losses = Losses paid during the year
+ (Loss reserves at the end of the year
− Loss reserves at the beginning of the year).

That formula sometimes results in inaccuracies because the estimated incurred losses for a given year might be distorted by changes in reserves for losses that occurred in previous years.

Such inaccuracies can be substantial with liability insurance or other types of insurance commonly involving delays between the date of loss occurrence and the date when resulting losses are paid. However, large inaccuracies are unlikely for insurance such as inland marine and auto physical damage, for which most losses are paid relatively quickly. For such insurance, calendar-year statistics might be sufficiently accurate.

Calendar-year data reflect how insurers must report their income on their financial statements. These data are available quickly, and compiling them involves little additional expense. However, insurer accounting records usually do not contain exposure unit data. Consequently, calendar-year data

EXHIBIT 7-6

Ratemaking Data Collection Methods Compared

Ratemaking Data Collection Method	Data Analyzed	Advantages	Disadvantages
Policy-year	For policies issued during a one-year period. (Note: coverage period for such policies might span two calendar years): • Earned premiums, including • Initial premiums • Additional premiums • Return premiums • Exposure units, including any adjustments • Incurred losses that arise under those policies, including allocated loss adjustment expenses	Apples-to-apples exact matching of losses, premiums, and exposure units to a specific group of insured entities	• Longer delays in gathering statistics than in other rate-making methods • Additional expense in gathering data that are used only for ratemaking
Calendar-year	Data used for accounting purposes. For a given calendar year, earned premiums calculated from: • Written premiums • Unearned premium reserves as: Unearned premiums at the start of the year, plus written premiums during the year minus unearned premiums at the end of the year • Losses are calculated as: Losses paid during the year (regardless of when losses occur) plus changes in reserves (for all years' losses—current and prior—where changes in reserves = Total reserves year-end minus total reserves at the beginning of the year)	• Statistics available immediately • Little expense involved in compiling data	• Accounting records do not contain exposure unit data. • Least accurate of the three ratemaking methods.
Accident-year	• For a given calendar year, earned premiums calculated the same way as calendar-year method • Losses for all accidents that occur during the period	• Can be more accurate than the calendar-year method, because it uses incurred losses during a specific year • Faster than the policy-year method, because policy year need not be completed	• Neither earned premiums nor incurred losses are tied directly to a specific group of policyholders. • Accident-year data are slightly more expensive to compile than calendar-year data.

cannot be used alone in the pure premium ratemaking method unless exposure unit information is also collected separately. The calendar-year method is the least accurate ratemaking data collection method.

Accident-Year Data Collection Method

The third ratemaking data collection method is the accident-year method. The only difference between the calendar-year method and the accident-year method is how incurred losses are calculated. The calendar-year method calculates incurred losses using transactional accounting records. The **accident-year method** calculates incurred losses for a given period using all losses and claims arising from insured events that occur during the period. The claims can be either open or closed, but if they arose from an insured event that occurred during the specified period, they are included in incurred losses for that period.

Earned premiums for the accident-year ratemaking data collection method are calculated in the same way they are calculated for the calendar-year method. Incurred losses consist only of losses arising from insured events that occur during the period; they are not affected by changes in reserves for events that occurred in previous periods. Therefore, the accident-year method eliminates the largest source of error inherent in the calendar-year method.

The accident-year ratemaking data collection method achieves much of the accuracy of the policy-year method while preserving most of the economy and speed of the calendar-year method. The accident-year method might be more accurate than the calendar-year method, because it uses incurred losses during a specific year. It is faster than the policy-year method because it does not wait for the policy year to be completed to collect data.

Neither earned premiums nor incurred losses are based as directly on a specific group of policies under the accident-year method as they are with the policy-year method. Accident-year data are slightly more expensive to compile than calendar-year data, because they require separate tabulation of loss data.

Illustration

Exhibit 7-7 illustrates five claims, indicating how each would be classified under the three ratemaking data collection methods. All policies in Exhibit 7-7 are one-year policies. Each claim is assigned to only one year under both the policy-year and accident-year methods, although the year might not be the same for both methods.

In the calendar-year method, loss payments for a single claim could be made over several successive calendar years. Consequently, the calendar-year method is unsuitable for collecting ratemaking data for liability and workers' compensation insurance, because the delay in loss payment can be long and the loss reserves can be large relative to earned premiums. For those types of insurance, either the policy-year or accident-year method should be used. For

Accident-year method
A method of collecting ratemaking statistics that uses incurred losses for an accident year, which consist of all losses related to claims arising from accidents that occur during the year, and that estimates earned premiums by formulas from accounting records.

EXHIBIT 7-7

Policy-Year, Accident-Year, and Calendar-Year Hypothetical Data

(1) Claim Number	(2) Date of Occurrence	(3) Policy Effective Date	(4) Date Claim Reported	(5) Original Loss Reserve	(6) Change in Reserve	(7) Date of Reserve Change	(8) Amount Paid to Close	(9) Date Paid	(10) Policy Year	(11) Accident Year	(12) Calendar Year	(13) Calendar- Year Reserve
1	7-1-00	1-1-00	2-1-01	$100,000	—	—	$100,000	6-3-02	2000	2000	2001	
2	11-1-01	12-15-00	1-1-02	200,000	—	—	200,000	9-1-03	2000	2001	2002	
3	10-3-00	2-4-00	12-20-00	100,000	+$200,000	3-1-02	300,000	4-6-03	2000	2000	2000	$100,000
											2002	200,000
4	9-13-00	2-2-00	3-14-01	50,000	+100,000	4-4-02	300,000	5-3-03	2000	2000	2001	50,000
											2002	100,000
											2003	150,000
5	12-1-01	12-15-00	1-10-02	100,000	−50,000	3-1-03	150,000	2-1-04	2000	2001	2002	100,000
											2003	−50,000
All policies are for one-year terms.											2004	100,000

Notice how each claim is charged differently under the policy year, accident year, and calendar year:
- Policy years (Column 10) reflect the year in which the policy was effective.
- Accident years (Column 11) reflect the year in which the loss occurred.
- Calendar years (Column 12) reflect the year in which the loss was paid or reserves were changed.

fire, inland marine, and auto physical damage insurance, losses are paid relatively quickly, and loss reserves tend to be small relative to earned premiums. So, the calendar-year method might be satisfactory for ratemaking data collection, although it is still not as accurate as the other two.

Adjust Data

After data have been collected, they must be adjusted. Adjustment is necessary because the raw premium, loss, and exposure data reflect conditions from present and past periods, whereas the rates being developed will be used in the future. The possibility that past premiums in the raw data might have been written at several rate levels further complicates matters.

Actuaries must adjust premium and loss data to develop future premiums and losses. Actuaries use the following two ways of adjusting premium and loss data:

1. Apply loss development factors
2. Apply trending

EXHIBIT 7-8

Reported Losses (000s omitted)

| Accident Year | Months of Development | | | | Final |
	12	24	36	48	60
1	$10,000	$11,000	$12,000	$11,500	$11,000
2	9,000	10,500	11,000	10,750	
3	10,500	12,000	12,000		
4	9,750	11,000			
5	10,250				

- Each line shows successive estimates of reported losses for a different year.
- Year 1 is the oldest year, and Year 5 is the most recent year.
- Column (2) shows the insurer's estimate of its reported losses after twelve months of development.
- Column (3) shows the insurer's revised estimate at twenty-four months of development.
- Column (6) shows the actual losses reported at sixty months of development. The incurred losses are assumed to be known accurately at that point.

Only Year 1 has matured to sixty months. The other years are too immature, with Year 5 having developed only to twelve months.

Percentage Development

| Accident Year | Months of Development | | | |
	12–24	24–36	36–48	48–60
1	1.100	1.091	0.958	0.957
2	1.167	1.048	0.977	
3	1.143	1.000		
4	1.128			
5	—			
Average	1.135	1.046	0.968	0.957

One-year loss development factor = 0.957.
Two-year loss development factor = $0.968 \times 0.957 = 0.926$.
Three-year loss development factor = $1.046 \times 0.968 \times 0.957 = 0.969$.
Four-year loss development factor = $1.135 \times 1.046 \times 0.968 \times 0.957 = 1.100$.

The figures in this lower part of the exhibit are calculated from the data in the top of the exhibit. They show the ratio of reported losses from one period to the prior period.

- For Year 1, the reported losses increased 10 percent from twelve months of development to twenty-four months of development.
- An additional 9.1 percentage-point increase occurred from twenty-four months to thirty-six months.
- After thirty-six months, the estimate decreased each period in this case.
- The bottom line, labeled "Average," shows the arithmetic average of the numbers above it in that table. That is, it shows the average change during the period for all years for which data are available. For this example, these factors will be used directly to calculate the loss development factors. In practice, an actuary might modify the averages to reflect changing circumstances. For example, the claim department might have changed its reserving methods so that the past data are not a good indication of current reserve accuracy. Such adjustments are based largely on judgment.

Apply Loss Development Factors

The first way ratemaking data are adjusted is to apply loss development factors. Because insurers cannot wait for loss data to mature before revising rates, actuaries evaluate several years of loss data to determine trends in how these data have developed. Data analysis produces loss development factors. Immature data are then multiplied by a loss development factor to produce a sound estimate of the data that will result when losses have fully matured.

Calculating loss development factors is explained in the right column of Exhibit 7-8. Readers should study this information carefully to learn how loss

EXHIBIT 7-9

Developed Losses

Accident Year	(1) Reported Losses	(2) Loss Development Factors	(3) Developed Losses
1	$11,000,000	1.000	$11,000,000
2	10,750,000	0.957	10,287,750
3	12,000,000	0.926	11,112,000
4	11,000,000	0.969	10,659,000
5	10,250,000	1.100	11,275,000
Total	$55,000,000		$54,333,750

- Reported losses (Column 1) and loss development factors (Column 2) are taken from Exhibit 7-8.
- Column (3) = Column (1) × Column (2).

development factors are determined. Loss development factors are usually calculated by using a table of successive estimates of reported losses, as shown in the top left corner of Exhibit 7-8. Because of the shape of the loss development tables, they are often called loss triangles.

The resulting loss development factors required to bring immature losses to their ultimate value are shown in the lower left corner of Exhibit 7-8. These factors are then applied in Exhibit 7-9.

Exhibit 7-9 shows the developed losses for the five-year period shown in Exhibit 7-8. Developed losses represent a sound estimate of how the losses for each year will mature.

In Exhibit 7-9, no adjustment is made to the losses from Year 1, which are assumed to be fully mature. The losses for Year 2 are twelve months from maturity, so the one-year loss development factor (0.957, from the bottom of Exhibit 7-8) is applied. Losses for Year 5 are four years from maturity, so the four-year development factor is applied. The losses from the other two years are adjusted similarly.

In Exhibit 7-9, the developed losses are less than the reported losses both in total and for some individual years, which would not always be the case. Developed losses could be either more or less than reported losses. If loss reserves have been consistently underestimated in the past, developed losses will be higher than reported losses. If loss reserves have been consistently overestimated in the past, developed losses will be lower than reported losses.

The loss development factors calculated in Exhibit 7-8 and used in Exhibit 7-9 are for the dollar amount of losses. Development factors can be derived similarly for the number of claims.

Exhibit 7-10 shows the developed amount of losses, the developed number of claims, and the average claim severity for each year.

EXHIBIT 7-10

Developed Losses and Developed Claims

(1) Accident Year	(2) Developed Losses	(3) Developed Number of Claims	(4) Average Claim Severity
1	$11,000,000	9,167	$1,200
2	10,287,750	7,913	1,300
3	11,112,000	7,880	1,410
4	10,659,000	6,995	1,524
5	11,275,000	6,860	1,644
Total	$54,333,750	38,815	$1,400

- The developed number of claims in Column (3) would be derived through the use of loss triangles similar to those in Exhibit 7-8, using number of claims instead of loss amounts. The process is not illustrated in this chapter.

- The total in Column (4), $1,400, is a weighted average of the amount of claims, using the number of claims as weights. Alternatively, it can be calculated by dividing the total amount of losses ($54,333,750) by the total number of claims (38,815).

Apply Trending

The second way ratemaking data are adjusted is to apply trending. Loss development is an attempt to correct errors in reporting past losses and to estimate the ultimate settlement value of losses during a previous period. For ratemaking purposes, an estimate of losses for a future period is needed. The purpose of *trending* is to adjust the developed losses from the experience period to reflect conditions that are expected in a future period. Making the adjustment is commonly done by projecting past trends into the future.

Exhibit 7-10 shows that claim severity (average claim amount) was trending upward during the experience period. In Year 1, the average claim was $1,200. The average claim increased every successive year, and by Year 5 the average claim was $1,644.

At the same time, the developed number of claims was trending downward. Exposure unit data, introduced in Column (3) of Exhibit 7-11, show that the number of earned car-years decreased every year. Therefore, the decrease in the number of claims probably resulted from a decline in earned exposure units over the five years. It did not result from a decrease in claim frequency. Column (4) of Exhibit 7-11 indicates that claim frequency increased.

These trends can be projected into the future using two trending methods:

1. Linear trending
2. Exponential trending

EXHIBIT 7-11

Calculation of Claim Frequency

(1) Year	(2) Developed Number of Claims	(3) Earned Car-Years	(4) Claim Frequency
1	9,167	458,350	2.00
2	7,913	386,000	2.05
3	7,880	380,676	2.07
4	6,995	333,095	2.10
5	6,860	325,118	2.11
Total	38,815	1,883,239	2.06

- Column (4) represents claims per 100 earned car-years (4) = (2) ÷ [(3) ÷ 100].
- The total in Column (4), 2.06, is the average frequency.

The actual claim frequency, measured in claims per 100 earned car-years, actually rose slightly, from 2.00 to 2.11.

Linear trending assumes that the data being trended will increase or decrease by a fixed amount each year. For example, claim frequency will increase by 0.0275 claims per unit each year, and claim severity will increase by $111 each year. That is, in Year 6 claim frequency is projected to be 2.14 claims per 100 earned car-years and claim severity is projected to average $1,755 per claim.

Exponential trending assumes that data being projected will increase or decrease by a fixed percentage each year, as compared with the previous year. For example, claim frequency will increase 1.3 percent each year, and claim severity will increase 8.2 percent each year. That is, in Year 6 claim frequency is projected to be 2.14 claims per 100 earned car-years and claim severity is projected to average $1,779 per claim.

When losses are increasing, exponential trending has a compounding effect that usually results in higher projected future losses than linear trending. Therefore, when used in rate calculations, exponential trending results in higher premium rates in virtually all cases, all other things being equal. The differences can be substantial.

If a graph of the data shows that data are increasing or decreasing in a straight line, linear trending is recommended. If the rate of change appears to be accelerating or decelerating, exponential trending is appropriate.

Some support exists for using exponential trending for claim severity because inflation, which is an exponential factor, has a major effect on severity. However, generally little basis exists for using exponential trending for claim frequency.

Linear trending
A method of loss trending that assumes a fixed amount of increase or decrease for each time period and whose amount is in either dollars or number of claims.

Exponential trending
A method of loss trending that assumes a fixed percentage increase or decrease for each time period.

Determine Territorial and Class Relativities

After collecting and adjusting data, the next step in ratemaking data development is to determine territorial relativities. These relativities reflect the extent to which various geographic territories in a state deserve rates that are higher or lower than the statewide average rate, which is calculated as a benchmark.

Territorial relativities can be determined by comparing the estimated incurred loss ratio for each territory to the statewide average loss ratio. The earned premiums used in the loss ratio are based on the statewide average rate currently used, not on the territorial rate. This comparison produces factors that are applied to the statewide average rate to reflect experience in each geographic territory. In a congested territory, for example, auto insurance rates might be 8.6 percent higher than the statewide average rate, while in a rural territory, rates might be 20.2 percent lower.

If a given territory has a small number of claims, raw data regarding territorial loss experience are likely to vary widely over time. To reduce variability and keep rates relatively stable, a credibility factor might be used. The credibility factor limits the difference between the statewide average rate and the territorial rate.

Class relativities are used to develop rates for each rating class. Class relativities are determined similarly to territorial relativities. Once class relativities have been determined, the insurer can prepare a rate table showing rates for each territory and each rating class.

Prepare Rate Filings

After data have been collected and adjusted, and after territorial and class relativities have been determined, rate filings must be prepared. A rate filing is a document prepared for and submitted to state regulatory authorities. The form for and the amount of information required in a filing vary by state. Generally, the filing must include at least the following seven items:

1. Schedule of the proposed new rates
2. Statement about the percentage change, either an increase or a decrease, in the statewide average rate
3. Explanation of why the same percentage change does not apply to the rates for all territories and rating classes, if applicable
4. Data to support the proposed rate changes, including territorial and class relativities
5. Calculation showing how investment income is reflected in the rates, if applicable
6. Expense provision data
7. Explanatory material to enable state insurance regulators to understand and evaluate the filing

Depending on state law, formal approval of the filing by regulators might not be required. In some states, approval must be obtained before the rates are used. In other states, formal approval is not required by law, but many insurers prefer to obtain approval before use to avoid the possibility of having to withdraw the rates if regulators decide that rates do not meet statutory requirements.

The actuarial department, either with or without assistance from the legal department, frequently negotiates with regulators about rate filings. Actuaries are best qualified to answer any technical questions that the regulators might raise. However, some insurers prefer to delegate most of the contact with regulators to the legal department and to involve actuaries only as needed.

RATEMAKING IN DIFFERENT TYPES OF INSURANCE

Ratemaking can vary widely by type of insurance. These variations can result from the characteristics of loss exposures, regulatory requirements, political considerations, and other factors.

Some types of insurance use all three ratemaking methods to some degree. In workers' compensation, for example, the loss ratio ratemaking method is used to determine the statewide average rate increase or decrease, while the pure premium ratemaking method is used to determine class relativities. Of course, judgment is also used in trending and developing credibility factors.

Experience Period

Although an experience period of one to three years is common for auto insurance and other types of liability insurance, a five-year experience period is used almost universally for fire insurance because it is required by law in many states. The experience for each of the five years is usually not given equal weight. The experience for the most recent years is given greater weight to promote rate responsiveness.

The experience period for other property causes of loss, such as wind, is even longer—frequently twenty years or more. The purpose of that long experience period is to avoid the large swings in rates that would otherwise result when a major hurricane, a series of major tornadoes, or another natural catastrophe strikes an area.

Three factors can be considered in determining the appropriate experience period: (1) legal requirements, if any, (2) the variability of losses over time, and (3) the credibility of the resulting ratemaking data. Of course, factors (2) and (3) are related to some degree.

Loss Development Factors

The need for loss development factors varies by type of insurance. Applying loss development factors is essential for most types of liability insurance because of the long delay in loss settlement and the resulting large accumulation of loss reserves. An error in estimating the loss reserves could result in a substantial rate error, because the incurred losses used in ratemaking might include a substantial proportion of reserves for open claims.

However, losses for fire, inland marine, and auto physical damage insurance are settled much more quickly. The loss reserves for those types of insurance, therefore, tend to be a relatively small part of incurred losses. Also, open claims for those types of insurance can usually be estimated more accurately than for liability claims. Consequently, loss development factors are frequently not used in ratemaking for fire, inland marine, and auto physical damage insurance.

Trending

Trending practices also vary by type of insurance. For liability insurance, trending claim frequency and claim severity is common. For fire insurance, loss claim frequency is low and generally stable, so trending is restricted to claim severity. However, the average claim is not used to measure claim severity because the average fire insurance claim is likely to be distorted by infrequent, large claims. Consequently, a composite index, composed partly of a construction cost index and partly of the consumer price index, is used for trending.

In fire insurance, trending both losses and premiums is necessary. Losses are trended partly to reflect any effects of inflation on claim costs. However, inflation can also increase property values, and people tend to increase the amount of insurance to reflect the increased values. This increases insurer premium revenue. If the amounts of insurance kept pace perfectly with inflation, it would be unnecessary to trend losses for inflation. However, increases in amounts insured tend to lag somewhat behind inflation. Consequently, insurers trend both losses and premiums and offset the growth in premiums against the growth in losses. Premiums are also trended in other types of insurance for which the exposure units are affected by inflation. Examples include workers' compensation and some general liability insurance.

A special trending problem exists in workers' compensation insurance. Because the benefits for that insurance are established by statute, they can change suddenly and unexpectedly when the legislature is in session. A law amendment factor is used to adjust rates and losses to reflect statutory benefit changes. Actuaries can estimate with reasonable accuracy the effects of a statutory benefit change on the losses insurers will incur under their policies. Unlike other trending, rate increases resulting from statutory benefit changes might apply to outstanding policies as well as renewals.

For boiler and machinery insurance, trending is applied to loss control expenses because loss control expenses exceed the amount paid to settle losses. Trending is desirable for these expenses, because they constitute such a large portion of the rate.

Large Loss Limitations

Unusual rate fluctuations could result from occasional large losses, whether from large individual losses or from an accumulation of smaller losses from a single event, such as a hurricane. In liability insurance, these fluctuations are controlled by using only basic limits losses in calculating incurred losses. Basic limits losses are losses capped at some predetermined dollar amount, such as $25,000.

A similar practice is followed in workers' compensation insurance ratemaking. Individual claims are limited to a specified amount for ratemaking purposes. Another limitation applies to multiple claims arising from a single event. Both limitations vary over time and by state.

Loss limitations also apply in ratemaking for property insurance. When a large single loss occurs in fire insurance, only part of it is included in rate-making calculations in the state in which it occurred. The balance is spread over the rates of all the states. The amount included in the state depends on the total fire insurance premium volume in that state, so it varies substantially by state.

Most losses from catastrophe events, such as hurricanes, are excluded from ratemaking data and replaced by a flat catastrophe charge in the rates. The amount of the catastrophe charge is determined by data collected over a long time period to smooth the fluctuations that would otherwise result from such catastrophes.

Commercial insurers must also quote a separate charge applicable to the terrorism loss exposure. Because past loss experience with terrorism losses in the United States has been extremely limited, terrorism ratemaking presents a special challenge.

Credibility

Credibility is a measure of the predictive ability of data. In ratemaking, the credibility of past loss data is important in projecting future losses. Credibility assumptions vary by type of insurance. In auto insurance, statewide loss data are assumed to be fully credible. That assumption might be inappropriate for some small insurers who base their rates solely on their own loss data. Even the loss data for some large territories and rating classes might not be fully credible. For territories and classes with loss data that are not fully credible, rates are calculated as a weighted average of the indicated rate for the territory or class and the statewide average rate for all classes and territories combined. The credibility factor is used as the weight in the weighted average.

For fire insurance, due to the low average claim frequency, even the statewide loss data might not be fully credible. In that case, a three-part weighted average is used, combining the state loss data for the rating class, regional loss data of the rating class, and state loss data for a major group encompassing several rating classes. Again, credibility factors are used as weights.

Pure premiums for workers' compensation insurance are composed of three separate charges: a pure premium for medical costs, a pure premium for nonserious injuries, and a pure premium for serious injuries. A separate credibility table exists for each of these categories.

When data are less than fully credible, the rate change indicated by such data should be moderated by a credibility factor, a number between 0 and 1.

Increased Limits Factors

Liability insurance rates are first developed for basic coverage limits. Basic coverage limits for auto liability insurance in a particular state might be $25,000 for any one accident or loss. Data used in developing insurance rates for basic coverage limits include only losses associated with that amount of coverage.

Actuaries use various ratemaking techniques for coverage amounts in excess of basic coverage limits. The most common approach to establish rates for coverage limits in excess of basic coverage limits is to develop increased limits factors. Increased limits factors are a function of insurance rates for basic coverage limits. For example, the additional charge to increase auto liability limits to $300,000 for any one accident or loss might be expressed as 90 percent of the basic coverage limits rate, producing an increased limits factor of 1.90.

Charges to increase commercial liability insurance limits can, and frequently do, exceed 100 percent of the charge for basic coverage limits. Several reasons exist for large increased limits factors in general liability and workers' compensation insurance. First, commercial insurance customers often purchase liability limits that are much higher than basic coverage limits. Second, while loss severity does not increase uniformly with increased coverage limits, it could more than double the average loss severity experienced under basic limits policies. Third, increased limits losses are, by definition, large liability losses that typically take more time to settle. Therefore, expected loss development until ultimate claim settlements are concluded is more difficult to estimate accurately. Fourth, higher limits can also require a portion of the coverage to be reinsured, requiring the primary insurer to include a provision for reinsurance transaction expenses in its ratemaking calculations. Finally, because large losses occur less frequently than small losses, the variability of losses in higher coverage layers is greater than for basic coverage limits, resulting in lower data credibility and justifying an additional contingency loading.[1]

SUMMARY

The role of regulators is to protect the insurance customer. Therefore, regulators are more concerned that rates be adequate, not excessive, and not unfairly discriminatory among various classes of insureds.

Ratemaking is an important component of the overall insurance mechanism. From the insurer's perspective, rates should enable the insurer to be competitive and earn a reasonable profit. Insurers are also concerned about the stability, responsiveness, and simplicity of the rates used. Rates should also provide for unanticipated contingencies, such as errors in estimating losses and expenses.

Actuaries usually supervise the ratemaking process. The two most prominent actuarial functions involve ratemaking and verifying loss reserves.

Three ratemaking methods are used. The pure premium method involves calculating a pure premium, the amount needed to pay losses, and then adding an expense provision and applying a profit and contingencies factor. The loss ratio method determines a new rate by modifying an old rate, using a comparison of actual and expected loss ratios. The judgment method is used when little or no loss experience data are available for ratemaking and relies heavily on the knowledge and experience of an actuary or underwriter.

Ratemaking requires collecting a large amount of data. These data include incurred losses, earned premiums, number of claims incurred, and earned exposure units. Such data are best accumulated gradually as policies and endorsements are issued and claims are reported and paid. Insurers should determine what data will be collected and in what form.

The policy-year data collection method can be the most accurate. It is also the most expensive method and involves a longer collection delay than other methods. A policy year consists of all policies issued during a year, and the earned premiums include all premiums earned by those policies. These premiums include all related additional premiums under endorsements, premium audits, and retrospective rating adjustments. The incurred losses consist of all of the losses covered under those policies. Incurred losses are tied directly to the premiums that were intended to pay for them.

The calendar-year data collection method is less accurate than the other methods. However, calendar-year data are available quickly and with little additional expense because the data come from the insurer's accounting records. This method is inaccurate because incurred losses must be estimated from paid losses and reserves. Such estimates might be grossly inaccurate because of changes in reserves for outstanding losses.

The accident-year data collection method is a compromise between the other two methods. It preserves most of the accuracy advantages of the policy-year method while achieving much of the speed and economy of the calendar-year method. The incurred losses for the accident-year method include all claims arising from insured events that occurred during the year, whether closed or open. The earned premiums are the same as for the calendar-year method.

Insurance ratemaking would be simple if all insured persons and all loss exposures were identical and unchanging. The complexities of real-world ratemaking arise from variations in policyholders and loss exposures as well as from time-related changes in the insurance environment.

Once data have been collected, they must be adjusted before rates can be calculated. First, losses must be developed, a process intended to recognize patterns in the accuracy of estimating loss reserves. Next, trending is applied to project the previous losses for use in future periods.

Territorial and class relativities must also be determined so that rates for various classes and territories can be calculated. Credibility procedures might be applied at several stages of the ratemaking process to minimize the adverse effects of random fluctuations in losses.

The ratemaking process and methods described in this chapter are applicable to all types of property-casualty insurance, although ratemaking application might differ by type of insurance.

The next chapter provides an overview of the claim function and introduces the claim adjusting process. This is the first of three chapters on the claim topic.

CHAPTER NOTE

1. For additional information on ratemaking for increased limits of liability coverage see: Jeffery T. Lange, "The Interpretation of Liability Increased Limits Statistics," *Proceedings of the Casualty Actuarial Society*, vol. LVI (1969), pp. 163–173; and Glenn G. Meyers, "The Competitive Market Equilibrium Risk Load Formula for Increased Limits Ratemaking," *Proceedings of the Casualty Actuarial Society*, vol. LXXVIII (1991), pp. 163–185.

Chapter 8

Direct Your Learning

The Claim Function

After learning the content of this chapter, you should be able to:

- Describe the goals of the claim function.
- Describe the users of claim information.
- Explain how and with whom claim personnel interact.
- Explain how the claim function can be organized.
- Describe claim function management and settlement authority.
- Describe the claim adjusting process.
- Describe the types of claim reports.
- Explain why loss reserving is an important claim activity and how it operates.
- Explain how performance of the claim function is measured.
- Explain how claim activities are regulated.

Develop Your Perspective

What are the main topics covered in the chapter?

Claim adjusting handles the demands for claim payments. In that role, the claim department fulfills the insurer's promises to policyholders and helps the insurer achieve its profit objectives. The structure of the department and processes used can vary.

Speculate regarding the outcome if a claim department failed to fulfill its role for an insurer.

- How would an insurer's reputation and profitability change?

Why is it important to learn about these topics?

By understanding the goals and functions of claim adjusting, you can appreciate the crucial role it fills within an insurer. Adjusters are on the front line with customers and claimants. Adjusters represent the insurer in ensuring that claim payments are fair.

Judge the success of a claim function in fulfilling its goals.

- What activities are required to be successful?

How can you use what you will learn?

Compare an insurer's claim function with that described in the chapter:

- Are the claim adjusters' goals the same?
- What is the management structure and settlement authority?
- Is the claim adjusting process similar?
- How might processes be improved?

Chapter 8

The Claim Function

Individuals and businesses purchase insurance to protect themselves from the financial consequences of loss and to alleviate the worry associated with the possibility of loss. Once a loss occurs, the insurer is expected to fulfill its responsibility to the policyholder and to pay covered claims. **Claim adjusting** is the process of determining coverage, legal liability, and damages, and settling the claim.

This chapter lays the foundation for the study of claim adjusting by discussing goals of claim adjusting and the environment in which it is performed. The chapter also provides an overview of the claim adjusting process, focusing on aspects common to most types of claims. Issues particular to specific types of insurance are discussed in subsequent chapters.

Claim adjusting
The insurer function that handles demands for claim payments.

CLAIM ENVIRONMENT

The claim function exists to fulfill the insurer's promises to its policyholders. Because the claim function controls more than half of what insurers spend, its proper and efficient performance is important to an insurer's profitability. The loss payments, expenses, and other information generated by the claim department are essential to marketing, underwriting, and pricing insurance products. Claim personnel are among the most visible of insurer employees to policyholders and the public. Claim adjusters must be able to interact well with a variety of people. Managing, organizing, and delegating settlement authority effectively within claim departments contribute to their success.

Goals of the Claim Function

When establishing goals for the claim function, senior management should recognize the effect the claim function has on both the insurance customer and the insurer itself. This section discusses the following two primary goals of the claim function:

1. Complying with the contractual promise
2. Supporting the insurer's profit goal

Complying With the Contractual Promise

The first goal of the claim function is to satisfy the insurer's obligations to the policyholder as set forth in the insurance policy. Following a loss, the promise of the insuring agreement to "pay," defend, or indemnify in the event of a covered loss is fulfilled.

The insurer fulfills this promise by providing fair, prompt, and equitable service to the policyholder, either (1) directly, when the loss involves a first-party claim made by the policyholder against the insurer or (2) indirectly, by adjusting a third-party loss made by someone against the policyholder to whom the policyholder might be liable.

From the insurer's perspective, claims are expected, and adjusters must deal with them routinely. For the individuals involved, the loss occurrence and its consequences are not at all routine and can be overwhelming. Adjusters, therefore, routinely deal with policyholders and claimants in stressful situations. Insurance is marketed not only as a financial mechanism to restore policyholders to a pre-loss state but also as a way to ensure peace of mind. An adjuster should handle a claim in a way that promotes peace of mind for the policyholder who has suffered a loss. Were it not for insurance, administered through the claim adjusting process, recovery would be slow, inefficient, and difficult.

Supporting the Insurer's Profit Goal

The second goal of the claim function is supporting the insurer's profit goal. Most of the discussion about the insurer's profit goal focuses on the marketing and underwriting departments—key contributors to an insurer's success. However, it would be shortsighted not to recognize the claim function's role in helping insurers achieve an underwriting profit. This is accomplished primarily through controlling expenses.

Policyholders are entitled to a fair claim settlement. However, by overcompensating a policyholder or claimant, the insurer unnecessarily raises the cost of insurance for all of its policyholders. Overpaid claims can lower profits and result in higher policy premiums.

Conversely, underpaid claims can result in angry policyholders, litigation, or regulatory oversight. Policyholders and claimants are likely to accept the insurer's settlement offer if they believe they are being treated fairly. If a claim adjuster treats a policyholder or claimant unfairly, the insurer might find itself in a lawsuit. Claims that are mishandled and that eventually lead to litigation erode goodwill and generate increased insurer expenses.

An insurer's success is based to a great extent on its reputation for providing the service promised. A reputation for resisting meritorious claims can invalidate the effectiveness of insurer advertisements or its goodwill earned over the years.

Claim Information Users

The claim function provides valuable information to other insurer departments. The three primary departments that receive claim information are marketing, underwriting, and actuarial.

Marketing

The marketing department needs information about customer satisfaction, timeliness of settlements, and other variables that assist in marketing the insurance product. The marketing department recognizes that the other services the insurer performs for the policyholder are forgotten quickly if the insurer fails to perform well after a loss occurrence.

Many insurers that market commercial policies have developed "niche" products to address the needs of specific types of policyholders. The intent of these insurers is to become the recognized expert in certain business classes, providing a product and service that cannot easily be equaled elsewhere. The claim adjusting process can be a source of new coverage ideas and product innovations for niche marketers.

Producers must also have policyholder loss information to prepare renewal policies properly. Many commercial policies are subject to rating plans that affect the policy premium, based partly on the policyholder's loss experience. In personal insurance, personal auto policies might be surcharged when property damage claims are paid during the policy year.

Claim personnel must inform producers of court rulings that affect the insurer's loss exposures or pricing, such as interpretations of policy exclusions or application of limits.

Underwriting

Individual underwriters are interested in claim information for the specific accounts they have underwritten. A post-loss evaluation could reveal characteristics of the loss exposure that an underwriter should have detected when the application was originally reviewed. Even if obvious clues were not initially overlooked, reviewing the claim file can uncover operations and activities that the underwriter would have investigated more thoroughly had they been apparent on the application. In some instances, material aspects of the insured loss exposures have changed since the policy was first underwritten. These changes could prompt policy cancellation or nonrenewal. Underwriters also understand that losses occur on even the best accounts. A minor loss can create an opportunity for the underwriter to take corrective action, through the loss control department, that could prevent a subsequent major loss from occurring.

A number of similar claims might alert underwriting management to a problem for a particular type or class of policyholder. These claims might be the result of new processes or technologies being used by the class of policyholders as a whole. For example, some roofing contractors might have tried to speed the process of replacing composite roofs by moving the tar smelter to the roof of the structure being repaired. This practice might have caused a number of fire losses. An adverse court ruling could also cause the loss experience of a class of business to deteriorate or could increase the number of claims presented.

Actuarial

Actuaries need accurate information not only on losses that have been paid but also on losses that have occurred and are reserved for payment. Such information helps actuaries establish reserves for IBNR losses and project the development of open claims for which the reserves might change substantially over time before the claim is finally settled.

Claim Department Contacts

Other than the producer, the claim department is the contact within the insurer that is most visible to the public. Therefore, the claim department must interact effectively with outside contacts, such as the public, plaintiffs' attorneys, defense attorneys, regulators, and claim organizations and associations.

The Public

Although many insurers have a public relations department for advertising, the insurer's public image is determined largely by the claim department's behavior. When Consumers Union surveyed 34,000 readers of its publication *Consumer Reports*, those surveyed reported that "promptness in claim handling was the single most significant factor in deciding how much they liked a company's service." For the most part, survey respondents had been paid promptly for claims, with 70 percent saying they received their claim payment within fourteen days.[1] Delay in receiving claim payment is the primary claim-related complaint; it causes many claimants and policyholders to seek attorney representation.

The advent of technological improvements has allowed many insurers to improve the quality and speed of their claim service. Starting with the growth of cell phones and the Internet and progressing to improvements in wireless technologies, claim departments have found new ways to streamline the claim process and to improve customer satisfaction. Technology facilitates communications between field personnel and regional or local claim offices. Wireless technology can also eliminate many of the problems related to conventional communications systems in the event of catastrophe losses. Hurricanes, floods, or earthquakes can wreak havoc on the infrastructure required for phone or fax services. Wireless communication can alleviate some of these problems.[2]

Claim adjusters often deal with policyholders and claimants whose knowledge of insurance is unsophisticated. Adjusters must recognize that adjusting requires a high degree of integrity, involving more than just honesty.

Claimants' Attorneys

For some types of claims and in certain areas of the United States, claimants are more likely to hire attorneys, often leading to costly litigation. Although attorney representation can result in a higher payment by the insurer, representation does not necessarily result in higher settlements to claimants, because claimants must pay expenses and attorney fees from settlements. Attorney representation also does not guarantee a faster settlement.

Litigation of third-party claims has become one of the most visible and expensive problems facing liability insurers. Most insurers realize that litigation prevention must be an active part of the claim function.

Defense Attorneys

The duty to defend under liability policies is as important as, or more important than, the duty to indemnify. Many insurers spend as much money on fees for outside defense attorneys as they do on claim department staff salaries and independent adjusting fees combined. Managing defense expenses is an essential component of managing the overall claim function.

Insurers typically hire an attorney from the jurisdiction in which the claim is submitted. Most attorneys limit their practice to one or two counties within a state, affording them a familiarity with the local legal system. Attorneys from a particular jurisdiction are more likely to identify with the community and with potential juries. However, rising legal costs have made the use of in-house counsel for claim defense more attractive for many insurers, regardless of the advantages inherent in using local attorneys. Many insurers have created in-house law offices in major metropolitan areas to defend claims.

The ideal situation for the insurer is to avoid litigation altogether by promptly investigating and resolving claims. A litigated claim might indicate that some aspect of the claim adjusting process failed to operate properly. Perhaps the claim department was understaffed, or the individual adjuster did not recognize a legitimate claim or offered an unrealistic settlement amount. Alternatively, the adjuster might not have explained the merits of the insurer's case well enough for the claimant to recognize a valid settlement offer. Of course, even if the insurer presents a valid case, the claimant might still be convinced that the claim is worth more and seek an attorney.

State Regulators

State insurance regulators monitor insurers' activities in the claim settlement process. Regulators exercise controls by licensing adjusters, investigating consumer complaints, and performing market conduct investigations. Enforcement is usually handled through the Unfair Claims Settlement Practices Act or similar legislation.

Licensing

Not all states currently license adjusters, and no standard procedure or uniform regulation exists for those that do. Some states require licensure only for independent adjusters, who work for many insurers, or for public adjusters, who represent policyholders in first-party claims against insurers. Other states require staff adjusters to be licensed. Exhibit 8-1 shows a list of states that require licensing of independent adjusters.

Most states with licensing laws also require that adjusters or their employers post a bond or show evidence of a fidelity bond. Many states with licensing laws also require the applicant to pass a written examination, which might be given for one or more types of insurance. Some states also license vehicle-damage or property appraisers. A licensed attorney who is acting as an adjuster might be exempt from licensing requirements. Temporary permits or licenses are frequently granted to out-of-state adjusters that insurers use to adjust claims for major catastrophes.

EXHIBIT 8-1

Licensing of Independent Insurance Adjusters

States Requiring Adjuster Licenses

• Alabama	• Kentucky	• Oklahoma
• Alaska	• Maine	• Oregon
• Arizona	• Michigan	• Rhode Island
• Arkansas	• Minnesota	• South Carolina
• California	• Mississippi	• Texas
• Colorado	Montana	• Utah
• Connecticut	• Nevada	• Vermont
• Delaware	• New Hampshire	• Washington
• Florida	• New Mexico	• West Virginia
• Georgia	• New York	• Wyoming
• Hawaii	• North Carolina	• Puerto Rico (Terr.)
• Idaho		

• States that require more than the payment of a license fee.

© A.M. Best Company. Used with permission, *Best's Directory of Recommended Insurance Attorneys and Adjusters*, Volume II, 1998 Edition, p. 1068.

Consumer Complaints

Claim departments must also handle customer complaints made to state insurance departments. Most states have a specific time limit within which inquiries by the department must be answered or acted on. Failure to respond can result in expensive fines and even in the loss of the adjuster's—or his or her employer's—license. Nevertheless, the relationship between state insurance departments and adjusters is usually positive.

Market Conduct Investigations

Insurance regulators periodically perform market conduct investigations either as part of their normal audit of insurer activities or in response to specific complaints. The typical market conduct audit includes more than just claim practices; it audits all departments that interact directly with policyholders and claimants.

Organization of the Claim Function

No ideal organizational structure exists for the claim function. What is best is generally what works. What works reflects the insurer's overall organization, its size, its growth, and its willingness to use outside providers of claim services.

The claim function is either centralized or decentralized, and it can be further organized by type of insurance or class of business.

Centralized Versus Decentralized

Insurers can operate successfully with either a centralized or a decentralized claim operation. A centralized claim operation consists of either one home office at which all claims are handled or a home office with a few regional offices. Centralized operations can be more efficient than decentralized operations in terms of cost of office rental, supervisory overhead, information systems support, and support staff. This organizational approach works well when less supervision is required or when claims do not require personal inspection.

The advantages and disadvantages of decentralized operations are the reverse of those for centralized operations. Decentralization can be more costly and difficult to supervise, but it is preferable for claims that must be adjusted in person. Because many claim tasks, such as property inspections and witness interviews, cannot be done as well from a remote location, claims can never be centralized as effectively as can underwriting or processing support functions.

The type of insurance, the volume of business, the geographic location, and the density of loss exposures can determine how an insurer structures its claim operations, where it locates its field offices, and whether it uses inside adjusting procedures or a large number of field staff or independent field adjusters. An insurer that writes a substantial amount of workers' compensation insurance, for example, might locate a workers' compensation claim office in an area where its policyholders have many employees or where required by state law, or it might contract with a local independent adjusting firm in that area to handle claims.

By Type of Insurance or Class of Business

Some insurers organize the claim function by type of insurance or class of business—a property claim department handles first-party claims, a casualty claim department handles third-party claims, a marine department handles marine claims, and so forth. Other insurers organize by commercial and personal insurance. Responsibility for those types of insurance is usually subdivided into geographic regions. Some large personal insurers maintain a number of local claim offices, often several in a single metropolitan area. Some local offices might conduct one activity, such as appraising automobile physical damage claims. These small claim offices report to the nearest regional service center. Many insurers also permit their producers to handle minor claims directly with their policyholders.

Claim Function Management and Settlement Authority

The management structure and settlement authority of the claim function vary by insurer. Usually, the vice president of claims is a key member of the insurer's management team. Reporting directly to the vice president are one or more assistant vice presidents, who are responsible for individual insurance coverages. Reporting to each of those persons might be one or more claim managers. The level of settlement authority required to settle or deny a claim usually follows the chain of command within the insurer. The settlement authority granted to individuals varies by their experience, training, and education.

Below the senior level, claim adjusting personnel are organized by responsibility and authority into claim managers, examiners, supervisors, and adjusters. A diagram of a typical insurer claim department structure is shown in Exhibit 8-2.

Claim Managers

The person below the top executive level usually has the title of claim manager. Regardless of whether this individual works out of the insurer's home office, a regional office, or a branch office, the claim manager is usually the senior person in the claim department, involved in individual claim file decisions and loss management. The claim manager is often in charge of both claim files and the general administration and supervision of the claim department.

Examiners

Many insurers employ examiners at regional or home offices. Although an examiner's job description and title might vary by insurer, the examiner is primarily a claim analyst who assesses coverage, liability, and damage factors of claims; extends settlement authority to adjusters; and recommends settlement amounts or other authorization to a superior. The examiner might also be responsible for certain internal claim processes, such as preparing data input, reporting claims to a reinsurer, establishing a file reserve, or referring a claim file to counsel if a coverage or liability issue arises. Examiners are technical experts who do not usually supervise office staff.

EXHIBIT 8-2

Insurer's Claim Department Structure

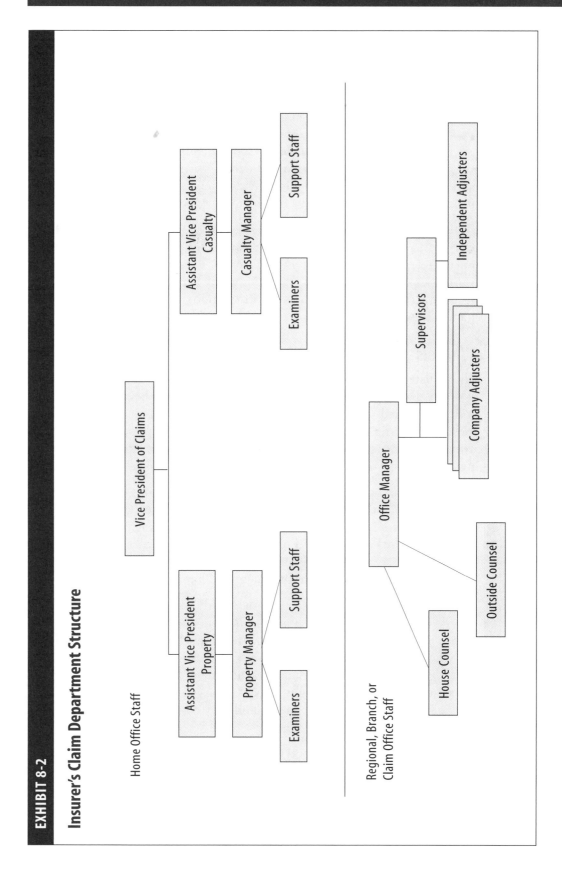

Home Office Staff

Vice President of Claims

Assistant Vice President Property

Assistant Vice President Casualty

Property Manager

Casualty Manager

Support Staff

Examiners

Support Staff

Examiners

Regional, Branch, or Claim Office Staff

Office Manager

Supervisors

House Counsel

Outside Counsel

Company Adjusters

Independent Adjusters

Supervisors

Most claim managers structure their departments into various units or subsections, either by type of coverage or by geographic location. Each unit is under a supervisor's direction. The claim supervisor is usually responsible for the unit's daily activities. The supervisor might serve in two capacities, both as a supervisor of claim personnel and as a supervisor of the claim files, giving guidance to assigned adjusters, appraisers, and other representatives on the routine investigation, evaluation, and disposition of the files. Usually, the supervisor also has authority over defense attorneys, independent adjusters, appraisers, and other outside service personnel with whom the insurer contracts.

The supervisor might have certain levels of settlement or denial authority and might be responsible for supervising any claim files that go into litigation and are referred to outside attorneys. Many insurers maintain a list of approved outside attorneys in the localities where their losses are most likely to occur, and they often provide specific instructions and state the authority granted to those attorneys.

Adjusters

Adjuster, or claim representative
A person responsible for investigating, evaluating, and settling insurance claims.

The **adjuster** is responsible for investigating, evaluating, and negotiating the coverage, liability, and damages related to a claim. Whether the adjuster's position is called "claim adjuster," "claim representative," or some other title, the adjuster is the insurer's direct contact with the policyholder, claimant, witness, or attorney; the liaison to the producer or broker; and the one, to a great extent, on whose shoulders the insurer's reputation rests.

An adjuster can be an employee of the insurer, an employee of an insurer-owned adjustment bureau or subsidiary firm, or an independent adjuster retained either on a contract basis or on an individual assignment basis. Staff adjusters usually have some authority to act and issue checks on behalf of the insurer without prior clearance once coverage has been confirmed, whereas an independent adjuster's authority might be limited.

Adjusters are usually employed either as "field" adjusters who operate outside the claim office or as "inside" adjusters who adjust claims from within the claim office. Field adjusters spend much of their time visiting the scene of a loss; interviewing witnesses; investigating damages; and meeting with policyholders, claimants, attorneys, and other persons involved in the claim. They might inspect damaged property themselves or work closely with damage appraisers, and they might attend trials and hearings on claims assigned to them.

Inside claim adjusting is appropriate for claims whose expenses are known or for claims that need little investigation. Examples of claims handled by inside adjusters are personal auto comprehensive claims for losses such as stolen hubcaps, broken windshields, and towing or workers' compensation claims involving only medical expenses. Inside adjusters might also be responsible for claims in litigation in which outside investigation is no longer necessary. The level of responsibility and the duties of inside adjusters vary from one insurer to another.

Independent Adjusters

Independent adjusters provide claim adjusting services to a variety of insurers and self-insureds. Independent adjusting firms derive revenue by charging insurers a fee for claim settlement services. These firms might be owned by insurance brokers, insurance groups, or their own shareholders.

National adjusting firms serve not only insurers but also large self-insured corporations and government agencies. They might also offer related services, such as medical cost containment programs, health and vocational rehabilitation services, property and vehicle damage appraisals, loss data processing, educational information, and so on.

Many large insurer groups and brokerage firms own their own independent adjusting firms. These firms provide countercyclical revenue so that even during periods of heavy losses, fee income from adjusting services is available to partially offset losses. Whenever possible, the insurer-owner uses its own facilities. Additionally, most independent adjusters actively solicit nonrelated insurer accounts. Many independent adjusters operate in a specific geographic region. These adjusters cite their familiarity with the producers, policyholders, claimants, and legal environment as a reason to employ them when claims occur in their region.

Independent adjusters enable an insurer to have comprehensive coverage of a geographic area without the expense of leasing office space, hiring staff adjusters, and incurring other expenses associated with operating a claim office. Most insurers use independent adjusters because claims can occur in places where the insurer does not have staff available. Many insurers keep full-time staff at minimal levels, so they must hire temporary employees or independent adjusters during periods of peak activity. Sometimes, insurers hire independent adjusters to handle claims outside the expertise of the insurer's adjusters, such as for pollution or asbestos claims. Access to specialized claim-handling expertise might be the deciding factor that wins the policyholder's account for the insurer.

In some "fronting" arrangements between businesses with high self-insured retentions (SIRs) and the insurer, the insured might be instrumental in selecting the independent adjusting firm that will handle claims on the insurer's behalf. Many of these firms operate autonomously, even maintaining trust accounts funded by the insured for payment of claims within the SIR and providing loss reports to the insurer and policyholders.

Insurers might also hire independent adjusters when they have been unable to hire permanent personnel or when they need to supplement staff during vacations. For catastrophic losses such as those caused by hurricanes or earthquakes, independent adjusting firms can supply claim adjusters to support the increase in claims.

Independent adjusters
Adjusters who handle claims on a case-by-case basis for a fee and who are not employees of insurers.

An insurer that routinely employs an independent adjusting firm usually provides instructions about where to report and how much authority the adjuster has to act on behalf of the insurer. Many insurers supply settlement checks to their approved independent adjusters and expect them to operate within the scope of their authority.

Public Adjusters

Public adjusters
Adjusters who represent policyholders to negotiate a settlement with the insurer in exchange for a fee or a percentage of the settlement.

Many states license **public adjusters**, who represent policyholders in property claims against insurers. These adjusters assist their clients in preparing the verification of loss, negotiating values with the insurer's adjuster, and preparing the settlement documents, such as the proof of loss forms. Public adjusters are generally paid a percentage, such as 10 percent, of the settlement the policyholder receives from the insurer, giving them an incentive to seek the highest possible settlement for their clients.

Many individuals and small businesses, without the time to deal with all of the documentation and negotiation required in a large fire or other property loss, find the services of a public adjuster convenient. When the insurer is acting responsibly and in good faith, using a public adjuster should not make a significant difference in the amount of the claim settlement. Any increase might be offset immediately by the public adjuster's fee.

Producers

Most independent-agency insurers permit their producers to handle minor claims within specific settlement authority or to assign independent adjusters. Extending settlement authority to producers expedites claim service. Producers like having the opportunity to remind their clients of the value of their services and to reevaluate policyholders' coverage. Additionally, many large commercial insurance producers employ claim personnel who assist policyholders with filing claims under policies serviced by the producer.

Most large personal insurers have completely separated their marketing and claim functions. Producers for these insurers obtain claim information from the policyholder and forward it to the regional service center for assignment to a local claim office. Some producers give the policyholder the telephone number of the insurer's claim service and a brief explanation of how the claim will be handled.

Other Claim Adjusting Personnel

Insurers rely on other experts to handle a specialized type or a particular aspect of a claim. Among these are specialist adjusters, origin and cause experts, material damage appraisers, reconstruction experts, private investigators, accountants, health and rehabilitation experts, medical cost containment consultants, professional engineers, and other support personnel.

Specialist Adjusters

Both independent and staff adjusters tend to specialize in specific areas of claims. Those who have completed certain educational requirements and have a certain amount of experience might be granted a special title, such as "general adjuster." An adjuster who handles a single type of coverage might use that specialty in his or her title—for example, "property adjuster" or "marine adjuster."

One type of specialist adjuster is a catastrophe adjuster, who travels to the location of disasters and remains there until all claims have been settled. Catastrophe adjusters are trained to handle natural disasters (such as floods, hurricanes, tornadoes, hail losses, earthquakes, and volcanic eruptions), man-made disasters, or multiple liability losses.

Some insurers and independent adjusting firms maintain pollution liability teams that are prepared to go anywhere a major loss has occurred. These teams mitigate damages as well as adjust claims. Their quick action helps to improve policyholders' perception of the insurer and to reduce the likelihood of class action suits.

Another type of specialty adjuster is the marine surveyor, or "average" adjuster, who exclusively handles loss to freight, cargo, vessels (including everything from small watercraft and yachts to oceangoing ships), and, occasionally, aircraft. ("Average" is a marine insurance term for loss.)

Origin and Cause Experts

Origin and cause experts attempt to determine where and how a fire began. These experts are often consulted for fires that have a suspicious origin or when the possibility of subrogation exists.

Material Damage Appraisers

Many adjusters are also trained as property or vehicle damage appraisers. The appraiser inspects the damage and, if it is repairable, estimates the repair cost. The appraiser then obtains an agreed repair price with a repair facility, contractor, body shop, or other organization that the policyholder or claimant has selected to make the repairs.

If an item is not repairable or is missing because of theft or other loss, the appraiser assists the adjuster in determining the value or replacement cost of the item and in disposing of salvage. Many insurers use wholesale replacement organizations that can obtain items commonly involved in losses at a lower price than can the policyholder. Insurers also use automobile salvage "pools" to sell to the highest bidder vehicles deemed to be a "total loss." Other companies assist adjusters in disposing of other salvage, such as merchandise from a commercial fire loss.

Reconstruction Experts

Some experts specialize in reconstructing the events of automobile accidents. They explain how an auto accident occurred and testify about the rate of speed at which the vehicles were traveling, the point of impact between the vehicles, and, in some cases, what the various drivers were able to see before the accident.

Private Investigators

Many insurers also employ the services of private investigators to conduct background and activity checks on claimants, for surveillance of claimants who are allegedly injured, to check financial records, to serve process, and for similar activities. Forensic engineers and highly trained arson investigators are also employed by insurers to investigate unusual or questionable losses. Many of these investigators operate as independent contractors. Most insurers also have their own special investigations unit (SIU).

Accountants

Accountants might be required to examine the books of a policyholder in first-party claims for loss of use and claims for damaged inventory. Accountants might also be used in liability claims to verify the financial losses submitted by claimants.

Health and Rehabilitation Experts

Liability insurers rely on a variety of medical specialists to assist with claim and medical management. Medical consultants and rehabilitation nurses also help to arrange independent medical examinations (IMEs) and to obtain second opinions before agreeing to a treatment or surgical process suggested by the attending physician.

Many states' workers' compensation laws now mandate a variety of vocational rehabilitation services, such as employment consultation and job retraining for disabled workers. Large workers' compensation insurers might operate their own rehabilitation firms as subsidiaries, and some independent adjusting firms have health and rehabilitation divisions that provide such services.

Medical Cost Containment Consultants

The insurer's health experts also review medical reports and audit bills from physicians and other medical providers. In a process called utilization review, the nurse or medical technician examines the physician's report to ascertain the diagnosis and determines whether the treatment being provided is reasonable and necessary for that diagnosis. Because most claims are for a specific injury or illness, the insurer does not want to pay for unreasonable charges or for services that are unrelated to the claim.

Professional Engineers

Many slip-and-fall cases involve steps, stairways, or sidewalks. Products liability cases often allege improper design. Professional engineers can help the insurer determine whether any Occupational Safety and Health Administration (OSHA) requirement or a building code was violated.

Support Personnel

In addition to the experts already described, claim departments might employ a variety of support personnel for technical and clerical functions. Large personal insurers might employ auto damage appraisers who inspect damaged vehicles locally and who either provide an agreed price for their repair or an assessment of value for a total loss. The insurer might also have other staff technicians who assist in certain aspects of loss, including special fraud investigators, coverage analysts, research librarians (especially for legal issues), and even laboratory and engineering assistants.

Unbundled Claim Services

Large commercial businesses commonly have both the necessary expertise and the desire to retain, rather than insure, losses. Although many of these businesses might have the financial resources and sophistication to manage claims without an insurer's services, they might not have or want to maintain the necessary in-house talent to handle their own claims.

Many insurers unbundle their services, permitting these businesses to purchase loss control, data processing, or claim adjusting services separate from insurance coverage. Independent adjusters or third-party administrators also offer their services directly to businesses choosing to self-insure their loss exposures. The unbundling of insurer services offers an opportunity for the claim department to generate revenue for the insurer without the exposure to underwriting risk.

CLAIM ADJUSTING PROCESS

The claim adjusting process is not uniform; the procedure each insurer follows in settling a claim may vary. Although settling similar types of claims requires taking similar steps, so many challenges arise in settling claims that insurers have developed extensive guidelines for claim adjusters to follow.

The way in which property and liability claims are handled differs significantly. This difference is reflected throughout the claim function in terms of how personnel specialize, which internal forms are used, and which procedures are followed. Although the distinction between property and liability underwriting has gradually diminished since the introduction of package policies, it remains to some extent in most claim operations. Policyholder claims can usually be categorized as either property (first-party) or liability (third-party). This section deals with some of the common elements of both types of claims.

Virtually all claims are legitimate requests of the insurer to fulfill its obligations. In evaluating a claim, the adjuster must consider whether the claim should be paid and whether any defenses to the claim exist. These determinations are similar to the screening process that underwriters use in reviewing applicants. The claim adjusting process involves the following four steps:

1. Determine whether the loss is covered by the applicable policy.
2. Determine the cause of loss and legal liability, if necessary.
3. Determine the amount of damages or extent of loss.
4. Settle the claim.

An adjuster investigates, evaluates, and answers each of these elements in the course of handling either a property or liability claim.

Determine Coverage

The first step in the claim adjusting process is to determine whether the loss is covered by the applicable policy. Paying a loss that is not covered by a policy is one example of mishandling a claim. It is probably the second-worst coverage mistake a claim adjuster can make. Denying coverage when it does exist is the most serious coverage mistake. It can result in bad-faith suits as well as enormous verdicts for extra-contractual damages. Making an accurate coverage decision is fundamental to good claim adjusting.

Claim departments typically have experienced personnel, each of whom works on claims resulting from only one, or few, types of coverages. Claim adjusters must have detailed knowledge of the policies with which they work. Every line and clause in a policy can affect the outcome of a claim. Good coverage analysis requires a methodical review of the specific policy for a given loss. Ultimately, coverage depends on (1) whether the loss or type of damage is covered by the insuring agreement and (2) whether any policy exclusion or condition eliminates or restricts coverage.

Insuring Agreement

Insuring agreements usually include brief statements such as this one from the Commercial General Liability coverage form, Coverage A:

> We will pay those sums that the insured becomes legally obligated to pay as damages because of "bodily injury" or "property damage" to which this insurance applies.[3]

Another example is this statement, from the Building and Personal Property Coverage Form:

> We will pay for direct physical loss of or damage to Covered Property at the premises described in the Declarations caused by or resulting from any Covered Cause of Loss.[4]

Although brief, such statements raise numerous questions. Defined terms, such as "bodily injury," "property damage," and "insured," implicitly exclude from coverage anything that is not within their definitions. For example, "property damage" is generally not considered to extend to fines, purely financial loss, or the diminution in value of property unrelated to physical damage. The "insured" in an auto policy does not include every person who might be driving an auto owned by the named insured (for example, a thief is not covered). The distinction between actual damage and loss of use is important in property insurance because different provisions might apply for each. Finally, insuring agreements typically reference other policy elements that must be fully understood before the insuring agreement itself can be understood.

Exclusions

All policy forms contain exclusions, and some coverage forms include extensive exclusionary language. Claim adjusters must carefully read and understand every policy exclusion applicable to a given loss. In most cases, the evidentiary burden of proof of the exclusion's applicability lies with the insurer. Coverage is usually excluded for one of the following reasons:

- Coverage is provided elsewhere.
- Most policyholders do not need the coverage.
- Occurrences are within the policyholder's control.
- Causes of loss are uninsurable.

Policies generally exclude coverage that is provided elsewhere. For example, auto and workers' compensation losses are excluded from general liability policies because they are covered by other policies.

Some exclusions exist because most policyholders do not need the coverage and do not want to pay additional premiums for unneeded coverage. For example, insureds whose property is located on flat and stable terrain have no need for volcanic eruption or earthquake coverage. Policyholders with these types of loss exposures must cover them with endorsements or separate policies and must pay the necessary additional premium for such coverage.

Some exclusions ensure that the policyholder does not have control over the loss occurrence. For example, general liability policies exclude claims arising out of intentional wrongdoing by the policyholder and (with some exceptions) out of the policyholder's failure to perform contractual obligations.

Other exclusions relate to causes of loss that are uninsurable because of the difficulty in spreading the loss exposures. For example, losses caused by war and nuclear accident would simultaneously affect many policyholders; therefore, insurance does not cover such causes of loss.

Conditions

The policyholder's duties after a loss are the most important policy conditions that claim adjusters handle. The exact wording of those duties varies by policy, but certain conditions are common to most policies. For example, the policyholder must promptly notify the insurer of any loss or suit and must cooperate in investigating, settling, and defending any claim. These and other policyholder duties are conditions precedent to the insurer's obligation to pay the claim. Insurers are cautious about rigidly enforcing compliance with some conditions in order to maintain customer goodwill and because most courts will not allow it.

Response to Coverage Issues

When a coverage issue arises, the claim adjuster must protect the insurer's interests and resolve the issue quickly. If no coverage applies, the adjuster must immediately inform the policyholder in writing, referring to specific policy provisions.

Reservation of rights letter
A letter providing notice to the insured that the insurer is investigating a claim that is issued to inform the insured that a coverage problem might exist, and that protects the insurer so it can deny coverage if necessary.

If coverage is uncertain, the adjuster must continue to handle the claim under a **reservation of rights letter** or **nonwaiver agreement** while resolving the coverage issue. Reservation of rights letters and nonwaiver agreements serve the same purpose. They allow the claim adjuster to continue to handle the claim without voiding the insurer's right to disclaim coverage later. Otherwise, the insurer's continued handling of the claim could be legally construed as a waiver of its right to deny coverage. The only difference is that the reservation of rights letter is issued unilaterally by the insurer, and the nonwaiver agreement contains the signature and consent of the policyholder.

Nonwaiver agreement
An agreement that is signed by the policyholder and that indicates that the insurer may investigate a claim while reserving the right to deny coverage if necessary.

Reservation of rights letters and nonwaiver agreements allow the claim adjuster to have the time necessary to resolve the coverage issue. This resolution might require additional investigation or the opinion of an attorney experienced in insurance coverage.

The policyholder should be advised immediately once a coverage decision has been made. Disgruntled policyholders frequently sue their insurers. The potential damages in such cases, including compensation for the policyholder's emotional distress and punitive damages, could be considerable. Consequently, most claim departments restrict authority to issue coverage denials to the claim manager, supervisory personnel, or home office.

Declaratory judgment
A ruling by a court to determine whether an insurance policy provides coverage.

Filing a declaratory judgment action is an alternative to unilaterally resolving a coverage issue. A **declaratory judgment** action is a lawsuit that asks the court to declare the rights of parties rather than to award monetary damages. Courts have acknowledged that the resolution of insurance policy coverage is a suitable issue for a declaratory judgment action. The drawbacks are that a declaratory judgment is expensive and in some jurisdictions the declaratory judgment action might not move through the court system any faster than the underlying suit that is the subject of the claim. Consequently, the declaratory judgment action might not be decided until the underlying action has been decided.

Determine Legal Liability

The second step in the claim adjusting process is determining whether the policyholder is legally liable. Legal liability is an important concept in third-party claims. The insuring agreements of the personal auto policy and the commercial general liability policy refer, respectively, to damages "for which any 'insured' becomes legally responsible" and "that the insured becomes legally obligated to pay." The phrases "legally responsible" and "legally obligated" are synonymous with the phrase "legally liable." **Legal liability**—the state of being legally liable for harm to another party—is a coverage requirement under a liability insurance policy. The insurer will not pay damages on the insured's behalf unless the insured is legally liable to pay them. Policyholders buy liability insurance to protect themselves against the financial consequences of legal liability.

Legal liability
The legal responsibility of a person or an organization for bodily injury or property damage suffered by another person or organization.

Sources of Legal Liability

Other than from criminal acts, which are almost invariably not covered by insurance, legal liability arises from three sources:

1. Torts
2. Contracts
3. Statutes

Torts

The first source of legal liability is torts, which encompass all noncontractual civil wrongs. Many criminal acts, such as assault and battery and fraud, are also torts. Claim adjusters must have a command of tort law because most torts are covered by insurance and because their possibility is the reason most policyholders have insurance policies. Torts are categorized by the behavior of the wrongdoer (called a tortfeasor)—that is, whether the tortfeasor has acted intentionally or negligently or, in some circumstances, regardless of how the tortfeasor has acted.

Contracts

The second source of legal liability is contracts. A legal liability to do something or to refrain from doing something can arise out of having made an agreement to that effect. The law enforces agreements as long as the other party (or parties) incurs a reciprocal obligation and the agreement is not for an unlawful purpose. Contracts are common in both business and personal life. Generally, contractual obligations are not insurable. However, exceptions to this general rule are common and important enough that claim adjusters need a sound working knowledge of contract law. In particular, contracts are frequently used to transfer statutory and common-law duties from one party to another.

Statutes

The third source of legal liability is statutes. An individual or a business might be required to do something or to refrain from doing something because a legislative body has enacted a law to that effect. For example, paying taxes and filing tax returns are legal requirements, as is refraining from polluting the land, air, and water. Many statutes are codifications of preexisting common law (judge or court-made law), and in such cases the statute pre-empts the common law. Violating a statute is also a tort.

Determine Amount of Damages

The third step in the claim adjusting process is to determine the amount of damages. Both first-party and third-party insurance policies indemnify policyholders or claimants for damages. Claim adjusters spend a great portion of their time investigating and evaluating damages. Insurance policies generally cover property damage, bodily injury, or both.

Property Damage

In first-party coverages, the term "property damage" means the direct physical destruction of or damage to property. Valuation for such damage is usually specified in the policy as either replacement cost or actual cash value. Replacement cost is the cost at the time of loss to replace what has been damaged. Actual cash value is usually replacement cost minus depreciation. Arguments about depreciation are common. Courts have held that any relevant factor can be considered in determining depreciation, including cost to replace, cost when purchased, expected life span, technological or style obsolescence, market value, and identifiable physical wear and tear.

As an alternative to paying money to settle a property claim, the insurer can choose to repair or replace property. These options can be exercised with personal property losses and with claims that are suspicious.

Loss of use, which can be a result of property damage or destruction, is an element of damage but is not necessarily covered under first-party coverages. Generally, homeowners policies have some coverage for loss of use. Many commercial property policies must have such coverage added by endorsement. In both cases, loss of use is usually not covered by property insurance unless the loss results from a covered type of property damage or destruction. In other words, loss of use is not covered when property simply ceases to function without having been damaged or destroyed. The measure of damages for loss of use is specified in the policy.

Property damage in liability claims also includes direct physical damage to the property and loss of its use. When property has been totally destroyed, claimants are not entitled to replacement cost unless the property had not depreciated at all. For partially damaged property that can be repaired, the cost of repair is an accepted measure of damages. That cost is the least amount of money required to return the claimant to his or her original condition. Loss of use can sometimes be measured by the cost of replacement services. However, all claimants in all liability claims are required to mitigate their damages. Claimants cannot allow loss of use damages to accumulate beyond the value of damaged property. Claimants must also expeditiously replace destroyed property.

Bodily Injury Damages

Bodily injury damages are covered by liability insurance and can fall into at least the following categories:

- Expenses for medical treatment
- Loss of earnings
- Pain and suffering
- Permanency
- Loss of consortium
- Future damages
- Punitive damages
- Survival and wrongful death
- Extra-contractual damages

Punitive damages, discussed below, and extra-contractual damages can arise in property damage cases as well, but they are more often related to bodily injuries.

Bodily injury damages with amounts that can be determined readily, such as for medical expenses and loss of earnings, are often called **special damages**. In addition to recovering special damages, claimants can recover **general damages**, whose monetary value is subjective and cannot easily be documented and which compensate for intangibles such as pain and suffering and scarring or disfigurement. Special damages and general damages together are called compensatory damages because they are designed to compensate the claimant for actual loss.

Punitive Damages

In those rare cases in which the defendant's conduct has been especially outrageous or willful, the jury or court can award punitive damages. As the term suggests, these damages are levied against the defendant as punishment and to deter others from engaging in similar behavior. Many states use the law or policy language to prohibit insuring such damages. Other states do not prohibit insuring punitive damages, so some policies do cover them. The U.S. Supreme Court has also upheld paying punitive damages with insurance.

Extra-Contractual Damages

The terms of insurance policies describe the circumstances under which and the amounts that the insurer must pay. However, in certain situations, insurers might be liable to their policyholders for amounts that are not covered by the policy or that exceed policy limits. Such situations can occur when the insurer has behaved improperly toward its policyholder. If the insurer denies a claim that should be covered, or knowingly makes a settlement offer in an amount well below the claim value, the insurer might ultimately be found to have acted in "bad faith." **Extra-contractual damages**

Special damages
Compensatory damages awarded for specific out-of-pocket expenses, such as doctor and hospital bills.

General damages
Compensatory damages awarded for losses, such as pain and suffering, whose monetary value cannot be documented easily.

Extra-contractual damages
Monetary awards that are against an insurer for its negligence to its insured and that are considered extra-contractual because they are beyond the insurance contract between insurer and insured.

are usually awarded in bad-faith cases because of an excessive verdict or because of the wrongful treatment of a policyholder, such as with a violation of the Unfair Claims Settlement Practices Act.

Settle the Claim

The fourth step in the claim adjusting process is to settle the claim. Every claim must be settled, and most means of settlement require some negotiation by the adjuster, unless the claim simply involves payment of a fixed amount.

Negotiation at many levels is a necessary part of settling a claim. Aspects of coverage might need to be evaluated and agreed on by the policyholder and the insurer. Other insurers might be involved when more than one policy covers a loss or when more than one party is responsible for damages. All of the damages must be assessed before settlement can be reached. Disputes over the damages might involve not only the adjuster and the policyholder or claimant but also repair facility operators, public adjusters, and individuals providing care or treatment for the injured person.

Additionally, the adjuster must become familiar with the producing agent, the third-party claimant or adverse party (if one exists), any witnesses, physicians, other experts who might be used, and the attorneys representing any parties involved in the claim. The adjuster's success in settling a claim depends on his or her familiarity and ability to negotiate with the persons involved. The relationships that the adjuster establishes determine whether the claim will be settled with ease or with difficulty.

A key to negotiating settlements in which all parties consider themselves to be winners is having complete and accurate information. Unless the adjuster has adequately investigated and evaluated all factors, the negotiating position will be weak and ineffectual and could result in litigation. When the adjuster wants to pay $5,000 but the claimant is demanding $50,000, the adjuster must have a strong justification for the settlement amount proposed. Both parties might need to reevaluate their positions. Adjusting requires personal control, salesmanship skills, a friendly disposition, and tolerance for frustration.

Information must often be shared. Some adjusters might believe that they should not discuss or share information that supports their position with a claimant or an opposing attorney, but unless they do, negotiations suffer.

Some insurers routinely use some form of advance payments for both first- and third-party claims. For major property losses, the insurer often gives the policyholder an advance for additional living expenses and even reconstruction costs and supplies before claim settlement. For liability losses involving both property damage and bodily injury, the insurer settles the property portion of the claim without waiting for the bodily injury settlement (in accordance with the Unfair Claims Settlement Practices Model Act).

Settling a claim could mean denying the entire claim or part of it. Claim denial can be difficult unless the adjuster has researched the claim thoroughly. To be successful and to avoid litigation, claim denial must be based on accurate information about coverage, liability, and damages. When a loss is not covered, the adjuster must be prepared to explain to the policyholder why that is so. Denial of coverage must be made as soon as practical after all facts are known.

Denying payment to a third party on the basis that the policyholder is not legally liable must be handled in a way that prevents or minimizes ill will. The adjuster must be certain that no liability exists and must be able to identify applicable policy provisions.

Claim Settlement Documents

Once the adjuster has received settlement authority from senior claim department personnel and the parties have agreed on a claim's value, the concluding documents are executed. Property claims are sometimes settled using a sworn statement in a proof of loss form. The policyholder submits this form as a sworn submission of the claim and as an offer to settle. The insurer can either accept or reject this offer. In questionable first-party claims or those with disputed facts, the policyholder might be provided with blank proof of loss forms to use in submitting a claim. If the claim is known to be fraudulent, the insurer might deny coverage based on the insured's act of submitting the "sworn" proof. Although some insurers treat the proof of loss form as a settlement document, others waive the formal filing of the form entirely, simply issuing a check for the agreed-on amount.

To close a third-party claim, a release is obtained from the claimant. A release is a legally binding document providing that, in exchange for the specific sums to be paid to the claimant, the claimant releases the policyholder from all claims arising out of that particular claim. The most commonly used release is the general release. The general release is appropriate in almost all situations except those for which a specific type of release is more suitable. An example of a general release is shown in Exhibit 8-3.

Attorneys have also drafted releases other than general releases for certain situations. In many cases, the language of the releases varies to conform with individual state law.

Claim Reports

The adjuster's reports are vital to the claim function and serve as an important part of the evaluation process, updating information about each claim so that proper action can be taken. Adjuster file notes are the basis of the more formal types of reports discussed next. With widespread use of computer networks, insurers and adjusters can now prepare and transmit many reports entirely by computer. Reports can be categorized as follows:

- Preliminary
- Status
- Summarized
- Closing

EXHIBIT 8-3

Release in Full of All Claims and Rights (General Release)

For and in consideration of the sum of _____

_____ ($ _____), receipt of

which is acknowledged, I release and forever discharge _____

_____, their

principals, agents, representatives, and insurance carriers from any and all rights, claims,
demands, and damages of any kind, known or unknown, existing or arising in the future,
resulting from or related to personal injuries, death, or property damage, arising from an
accident that occurred on or about the _____ day of _____,
20____, at or near_____.

This release shall not destroy or otherwise affect the rights of persons on whose behalf
this payment is made, or persons who may claim to be damaged by reason of the
accident other than the undersigned or any other persons.

I understand that this is a compromise settlement of all my claims of every nature and
kind whatsoever arising out of the accident referred to above, but is not an admission of
liability. I understand that this is all the money or consideration I will receive from the
above described parties as a result of this accident. I have read this release and understand it.

Signed this _____ day of _____, 20____, at _____ .

_____   _____
WITNESS

_____   _____
WITNESS

Preliminary Reports

The ACORD form is used by many producers to report the occurrence of a
claim to an insurer. A copy of the ACORD Property Loss Notice is shown in
Exhibit 8-4. Once the insurer has assigned the claim to an adjuster, many
insurers require a first report to be filed within a certain number of days after
the loss has been reported. These reports usually identify the names and
quantity of claimants and provide some initial evaluation of whether any
coverage issues need to be explored, along with preliminary information on
the aspects of liability involved in the claim. Above all, the report should
guide the examiner in establishing the initial reserve for the claim.

Status Reports

After the preliminary investigation has been completed, the insurer requires
periodic reports on the status of the claim. These reports are sent every thirty
days or over longer intervals if the claim is slow in developing, as is the case
with many injury losses. One important purpose of status reports is to facilitate

EXHIBIT 8-4

ACORD Property Loss Notice

ACORD™ **PROPERTY LOSS NOTICE**		DATE (MM/DD/YY) 8-24-XX

PRODUCER	PHONE (A/C, No, Ext):	MISCELLANEOUS INFO (Site & location code)	DATE OF LOSS AND TIME 7/29/XX	x AM PM	PREVIOUSLY REPORTED YES x NO

PROCTOR AGENCY
127 MAIN STREET
PLAINFIELD, OH

POLICY TYPE	COMPANY AND POLICY NUMBER		
PROP/ HOME	CO: IIA INSURANCE COMPANY		EFF:
	POL: HO 1894370		EXP:
FLOOD	CO:		EFF:
	POL:		EXP:
WIND	CO:		EFF:
	POL:		EXP:

CODE: 39542 SUB CODE:
AGENCY CUSTOMER ID:

INSURED		CONTACT	CONTACT INSURED	
NAME AND ADDRESS	SOC SEC #:	NAME AND ADDRESS		WHERE TO CONTACT

LEONARD HILLMAN
156 SIXTH AVENUE
PLAINFIELD, OH

JULIA HILLMAN

WHEN TO CONTACT

RESIDENCE PHONE (A/C, No)	BUSINESS PHONE (A/C, No, Ext)	RESIDENCE PHONE (A/C, No)	BUSINESS PHONE (A/C, No, Ext)
215-555-8181	215-555-5000		

LOSS

LOCATION OF LOSS		POLICE OR FIRE DEPT TO WHICH REPORTED

KIND OF LOSS	FIRE	LIGHTNING	FLOOD	OTHER (explain)	PROBABLE AMOUNT ENTIRE LOSS
	THEFT x	HAIL x	WIND		$3,000

DESCRIPTION OF LOSS & DAMAGE (Use reverse side, if necessary)

WIND AND HAIL DAMAGED ROOF   Sample

POLICY INFORMATION

MORTGAGEE   PLAINFIELD FEDERAL SAVINGS AND LOAN ASSOCIATION

☐ NO MORTGAGEE

HOMEOWNER POLICIES SECTION 1 ONLY (Complete for coverages A, B, C, D & additional coverages. For Homeowners Section II Liability Losses, use ACORD 3.)

A. DWELLING	B. OTHER STRUCT	C. PERSONAL PROP	D. LOSS OF USE	DEDUCTIBLES	DESCRIBE ADDITIONAL COVERAGES PROVIDED
$200,000	$20,000	$100,000	$40,000	$500	None

☐ COVERAGE A. EXCLUDES WIND
SUBJECT TO FORMS (Insert form numbers and edition dates, special deductibles)

FIRE, ALLIED LINES & MULTI-PERIL POLICIES (Complete only those items involved in loss)

ITEM	SUBJECT OF INS		AMOUNT	% COINS	DEDUCTIBLE	COVERAGE AND/OR DESCRIPTION OF PROPERTY INSURED
	BLDG	CNTS				
	BLDG	CNTS				
	BLDG	CNTS				

SUBJECT TO FORMS (insert form numbers and edition dates, special deductibles)   HO-290 REPLACEMENT COST COVERAGE

FLOOD POLICY	BUILDING:		DEDUCTIBLE:		ZONE	PRE FIRM POST FIRM	DIFF IN ELEV	FORM TYPE	GENERAL DWELLING	CONDO
	CONTENTS:		DEDUCTIBLE:							

WIND POLICY	BUILDING	DEDUCTIBLE	CONTENTS	ZONE	FORM TYPE	GENERAL DWELLING	CONDO			

REMARKS/OTHER INSURANCE (List companies, policy numbers, coverages & policy amounts)
ROOF LEAKING AFTER STORM. WATER DAMAGE TO CEILING IN ADDITION TO ROOF DAMAGE.

CAT #	FICO #	ADJUSTER ASSIGNED		ADJUSTER #	DATE ASSIGNED

REPORTED BY	REPORTED TO	SIGNATURE OF PRODUCER OR INSURED
LEONARD HILLMAN	ANN ADAMS	*Ann Adams*

ACORD 1 (1/96)   NOTE: IMPORTANT STATE INFORMATION ON REVERSE SIDE   © ACORD CORPORATION 1988 the constant reevaluation of the reserves being maintained on the claim. As factors involved in the claim change, the reserves might need to be increased or decreased. Sample status reports are shown in Exhibits 8-5 and 8-6.

Summarized Reports

The adjuster's next report is a detailed report on the claim investigation. Such a report is often called the "full formal" because it contains standard paragraph captions about coverage, liability, damages, and other loss factors. This report also outlines the key information already obtained and the information that needs to be investigated. Each topic might be given a separate heading in the report.

Closing Reports

The adjuster's final report usually outlines the basis of settlement or other conclusion of the claim. It also contains the documents necessary to close the claim, such as a copy of the settlement check, the release or proof of loss document, dismissal of any litigation, and final billings for any other services performed in the settlement, such as the defense attorney's or independent adjuster's fees.

Loss Reserving

Reserving losses for claims is a crucial adjusting task. The reserve represents the amount of money that the insurer anticipates will be needed to pay a particular claim. The reserve includes both the amounts owed to the policyholder or claimant(s) and, with some insurers, the funds required to cover the insurer's expenses. Estimating ultimate losses is a key adjusting skill acquired with experience and training. Failure to reserve properly, by either underestimating or overestimating the final cost of claims, can distort the insurer's financial statements. Underreserving is one of the major causes of insurer insolvency and bankruptcy.

The amount insurers pay for claims is a key element in calculating future rates. Actuaries base future rates not only on the amount of money the claim department has paid on both open and closed claims, but also on the amount reserved on open claims and reserved for incurred but not reported losses and reopened claims. Accuracy in reserving eventually translates into rates that accurately reflect loss potential. Claim departments must reserve claims consistently. Claim department management must communicate to the actuarial department any change in reserving practices so that any abnormalities that develop in loss reserve data can be recognized.

Improper reserving can (but should not) affect the outcome of individual claims. Overreserving claims can create a tendency to overpay claims or to settle too quickly without adequate negotiation. Underreserving claims, on the other hand, can cause the insurer to take too firm a position, a stance that can lead to litigation.

EXHIBIT 8-5

Six-Month Supervisor's Reserve Adequacy Review—Property

Supervisor	Policy No.	Insured	Loss Cause	Suit
Jones	CPP 6106442100	Westwide Mfg.	Fire	☐ Yes ☑ No

Claim Rep	Amount of Coverage	Loss Date	Date Reported	Age (mos.)	LAE to date
Harrison	500,000	4/5/0X	10/9/0X	6	NA

ALL LOSSES	Y	N	N/A	A/N*	BUILDING ONLY	Y	N	N/A	A/N*
Scope—loss items defined in file content	☑	☐	☐	☐	ACV/RCV Calculated	☑	☐	☐	☐
					Ownership Established	☑	☐	☐	☐
Cause/Origin—clearly noted in file	☑	☐	☐	☐	Coinsurance Noted	☑	☐	☐	☐
					Mortgage Noted	☐	☐	☐	☐
Limiting Clauses Identified	☐	☐	☑	☐	R/C Holdback Applied	☑	☐	☐	☐
Deductible Identified	☑	☐	☐	☐	Statement Taken	☐	☐	☐	☐
					CONTENTS				
					Police Report Obtained	☑	☐	☐	☐
					Property Verification of Items Involved	☑	☐	☐	☐

1. Are there any unresolved COVERAGE questions? ☐ Yes ☑ No
   a. If yes, are all proper steps being taken to resolve them? ☑ Yes ☐ No
   b. Needed actions:
   (1) <u>Report underinsurance to underwriting</u>
   (2) _____
   (3) _____

2. INVESTIGATION completed? ☐ Yes ☑ No
   a. Specific investigation needed:
   (1) <u>Check for other property lines</u>
   (2) _____
   (3) _____

3. DAMAGES/EXPOSURE
   a. Is file properly documented to reflect the company's exposure? ☑ Yes ☐ No
   b. If no, does file contain a plan to document damages/exposure? ☐ Yes ☐ No
   c. If ALE/BI is involved, are steps being taken to control expense? ☐ Yes ☐ No

4. REPORTING
   a. Are activity log notes clearly stated in file? ☑ Yes ☐ No
   b. Does the file contain a 90-Day Status Report? ☑ Yes ☐ No
   c. If defense attorney is involved, does the file contain an Initial Claim Analysis? ☐ Yes ☑ No

5. Does the file contain a PLAN FOR RESOLUTION? ☑ Yes ☐ No
   Additional steps needed to resolve:
   (1) <u>Arrange for salvage to be sold</u>
   (2) _____
   (3) _____
   (4) _____
   (5) _____

6. RESERVE ANALYSIS
   a. Have all reserve changes been posted in file? ☑ Yes ☐ No
   b. In view of your analysis of liability and damages, is the reserve adequate? ☑ Yes ☐ No

   Reserve: $ <u>300,000</u>   REVISED RESERVE: $_____

Signature: _____   Date: <u>10/9/0X</u>

*A/N: Action Needed

EXHIBIT 8-6

Six-Month Supervisor's Reserve Adequacy Review—Casualty

Policy #: _____ WC _____   Claim Rep: _____ Harrison _____

Date of Loss: _____ 1238607 _____   Super: _____ Jones _____

Age (Months): _____ 6 _____   SUIT?   ☐ Yes   ☑ No

LAE to date: $ _____ NA _____   Policy Limits Remaining: $ 200,000 _____

1. Are there any unresolved COVERAGE questions?   ☐ Yes   ☑ No
   a. If yes, are all proper steps being taken to resolve them?   ☐ Yes   ☐ No
   b. Needed actions:
      (1) _____
      (2) _____
      (3) _____

2. INVESTIGATION completed?   ☐ Yes   ☑ No
   a. Specific investigation needed:
      (1) Index claimant to review past claim
      (2) Consider peer review of chiropractic bills
      (3) _____
      (4) _____
   b. LIABILITY Analysis:
      Undisputed
      _____

   c. Is legal advice needed to assist in evaluating liability?   ☐ Yes   ☑ No

3. DAMAGES and INJURIES
   a. Are medicals and specials in the file?   ☑ Yes   ☐ No
   b. If not, have we obtained the information by phone?   ☐ Yes   ☐ No
   c. Has the claimant returned to work?   ☑ Yes   ☐ No
   d. DIAGNOSIS:
      (1) Cervical strain
      (2) _____ (3) _____
      PROGNOSIS: Full recovery

                                        SPECIALS: $ 3,750 _____

4. REPORTING
   a. Does the file contain 90-day report(s)?   ☐ Yes   ☐ No
   b. Does the file contain an Initial Claim Analysis?   ☐ Yes   ☐ No   ☐ N/A
   c. Does the file contain reports of depositions?   ☐ Yes   ☐ No   ☐ N/A

5. Does the file contain a PLAN FOR RESOLUTION?   ☐ Yes   ☐ No
   Additional steps needed to resolve:
   a. _____
   b. _____
   c. _____
   d. _____

6. RESERVE ANALYSIS
   a. Have all reserve changes been posted in file?   ☑ Yes   ☐ No
   b. In view of your analysis of liability and damages, is the
      reserve adequate?   ☑ Yes   ☐ No

   Reserve: $ _____   REVISED RESERVE: $ _____

   Signature: _____   Date: _____

Loss Adjustment Expenses

In addition to paying the policyholder's loss, the insurer is responsible for paying the expenses associated with the claim. The NAIC Annual Statement requires that insurer claim expenses be apportioned between defense and adjusting expenses. Claim costs that can be specifically identified with the settlement of a particular claim are **defense and cost containment expenses** (comparable to what was formerly called allocated loss adjustment expenses). Specific costs that can be assigned to a claim include fees such as those paid to an auto appraiser to inspect a vehicle damaged in an accident, to a photographer to take photos of the scene, and to a private investigator to do a background check on the claimant. Additionally, all the costs related to the policyholder's defense if the claim goes into litigation—including the attorney's fees and the fees for court reporters, copy services, process servers, and the appeal bond—can be allocated to the individual claim. The cost of engaging experts and any fixed amounts for medical cost containment expenses are also included in this expense category.[5]

Defense and cost containment expenses
Costs of adjusting a claim that can be assigned to a specific claim.

Expenses related to the claim function's overall operation are called **adjusting and other expenses incurred** (comparable to what was previously called unallocated loss adjustment expenses). These expenses include charges for the insurer's overhead expenses and adjustment expenses not included under defense and cost containment expenses.

Adjusting and other expenses incurred
Costs of adjusting a claim that relate to the overall operation of an insurer's claim function.

Properly allocating expenses between these categories is important because of state reporting requirements. Insurers frequently evaluate their expenses to compare the efficiency of their claim operations with those of other insurers.

IBNR

Claim departments are involved in establishing case reserves. Case reserves are the ultimate loss expectations for each individual claim. Insurers also establish bulk (or aggregate) reserves. Bulk reserves are developed to estimate (1) the growth in reported case reserves, (2) the losses that are assumed to have happened but that have not yet been reported, and (3) the additional cost of claims that are reopened after having been settled and closed. Collectively, these bulk reserve components are called "IBNR." "Pure" IBNR reserves are just those for claims not yet reported; the total IBNR reserve also includes an amount for case reserve deficiencies (reopened claims and growth in reported case reserves).

IBNR losses are highly relevant to the insurer's profit expectation but are only slightly relevant to an individual adjuster. The connection between the two is that case reserves are often used as a basis to calculate IBNR.

The claim department usually assists in establishing bulk reserves. Many insurers use a committee composed of underwriting, actuarial, accounting, claim, and senior management personnel to review recommendations for bulk reserves. Although a significant part of this procedure is an actuarial function, claim department management can provide valuable information on the validity of the individual case reserves (on which the IBNR estimates are based), changes in the methodology used to determine case reserves, catastrophic or large losses that could distort results, and changes in the legal climate and benefit levels that might affect the ultimate cost of claims.

Case Reserves

No system of bulk reserving can be accurate unless the underlying reserves on individual claims are reasonably accurate. Ensuring reserve accuracy often falls on the individual adjuster, supervisor, or claim examiner who is responsible for setting the initial reserve or on a special committee established to evaluate reserves.

The three standard methods of establishing case reserves are the:

1. Judgment method
2. Average value method
3. Tabular method

The effectiveness of these methods depends on how they are used and on recognizing their inherent weaknesses.

Judgment Method

Judgment method
A case reserving method in which the amount that will eventually be paid to settle the claim is estimated by a claim adjuster or another claim specialist.

One method of establishing case reserves is the **judgment method**. With this method, an adjuster or another person within the claim department estimates the amount that will eventually be paid to settle the claim, and a reserve is set up in that amount. Because this reserve is established based on one person's judgment, that person's estimating accuracy is crucial. Accuracy is influenced by the person's experience.

Management can establish guidelines to assist in the process, and some insurers use expert systems to help with establishing case reserves. Depending on the nature of the claim, the adjuster needs to know medical treatment costs, average repair or reconstruction time, local pricing factors, local plaintiff attorneys, treating physicians, local contractors, and other information that influences the claim's final cost. The subjective nature of the judgment method makes evaluating the adequacy of case reserves difficult, except in the aggregate.

Average Value Method

Average value method
A case reserving method that establishes a predetermined dollar amount of reserve for each claim as it is reported.

A second method of establishing case reserves is the **average value method**, which establishes a predetermined dollar amount of reserve for each claim as it is reported. This method is suitable for claims that occur regularly, such as automobile physical damage claims. This average value can apply to all claims within a type of insurance, such as physical damage for private passenger automobile, or it might vary by loss exposure within the type of insurance. For insurance with relatively small variations in loss size and relatively short delays in loss settlement, the average value reserve might not be changed during the life of the claim. For other types of insurance, an average value reserve might be established when a claim is first reported and then adjusted later, either upward or downward, as more complete information becomes available. The claim department can readily establish a reserve amount that can be used for all claims with small amounts and short settlement times, recognizing that the reserve amount will be high or low in specific claims but will even out overall. Incorrectly estimating the average claim amount can cause problems. A low reserve could influence the insurer to ignore a potentially serious claim. Mishandled claims or claims that go to litigation usually settle for more than the average value.

For liability insurance, the average value method is likely to produce inadequate loss reserves, especially for liability insurance claims that usually do not settle readily, such as medical malpractice. For such insurance, using an average reserve is appropriate when the claim is initially reported. The average amount can be modified once the claim can be reviewed in depth.

Tabular Method

A third method of establishing case reserves is the **tabular method**, which is similar to the average value method of reserving. Instead of using a selected average amount, the tabular method provides an "average" amount for all claims that have similar characteristics in terms of the claimant's age, health, and marital status. This method is used primarily for workers' compensation claims.

Tabular method
A case reserving method that establishes an "average" amount of all claims that have similar characteristics in terms of the claimant's age, health, and marital status.

The tabular method can be used for claims that involve a series of fixed or determinable payments to the claimant over a prolonged period of time. For example, some disability insurance claims require payment of a fixed sum over many years, provided the claimant remains alive and continues to be disabled. Payments are terminated if the claimant dies or recovers from the disability.

Calculations for the present value of future payments require assumptions about interest rates and the length of the disability. A mortality table can be used to estimate the probability of death and a morbidity table, to estimate the probability of recovery. For widow or widower benefits under workers' compensation, the claim can be terminated if the claimant remarries. A remarriage table, showing the probability of remarriage at various ages and periods of widowhood, is used to estimate the value of such claims.

The mortality, morbidity, and remarriage rates assumed in calculating tabular reserves are not realized exactly in most cases, as most claimants live longer or die sooner than indicated in the mortality table. However, if an insurer has a large number of such claims, the average mortality, morbidity, and remarriage rate of all claims combined should approximate the tabular rates fairly closely.

Reserving Work Sheets and Software

Insurers employ various reserve work sheets that require the claim adjuster to consider all claim factors. For a workers' compensation or bodily injury claim, the work sheet considers not only the known or anticipated medical costs but also the length and cost of disability, the injury's degree of permanency, and other special damage factors that influence the claim. Sophisticated computer programs are available to help claim adjusters consider all relevant factors in setting reserves.

For liability claims, the adjuster must also consider general damage factors, such as pain and suffering, that a jury considers in determining a claim award. Reserving work sheets also require careful evaluation of liability. Comparative negligence factors must be applied if applicable. If joint tortfeasors contribute or if the potential for subrogation exists, those cost-reducing factors must also be considered.

Property claims can also be systematically evaluated to include not only the direct damages that can be quickly appraised, but also the indirect damages, such as business income, extra expense, loss of use costs, and potential recoveries for salvage and subrogation, that develop only after considerable time has passed.

Reserving Problems

Reserving becomes a problem when reserves are inadequate or redundant. During an investigation, claims are reevaluated and reserves are updated to reflect newly discovered facts.

Stair-stepping
Incremental increases in claim reserves by the claim representative without any significant change in the facts of the claim.

Adjusters are often criticized for "stair-stepping" reserves, a practice that results when the claim is initially reserved inadequately and the reserves must be updated continually. **Stair-stepping** (or "reserve creep") often occurs in workers' compensation or other types of claims in which periodic payments are made. The adjuster, instead of establishing a sufficient reserve based on the realistic value of the claim, sets only enough reserve to cover costs for the immediate future. Then, when payments meet or exceed the established reserve, the figure is increased for another round of payments. The problem with stair-stepping is that the true value of the claim does not become evident to senior claim management until perhaps years after the initial reserve was set, meaning that cost-control procedures that might have helped to reduce the overall loss exposure were never considered. Furthermore, stair-stepping can mislead the insurer into delaying a report to a reinsurer or, in a serious liability claim, notifying the policyholder of a potential excess loss situation.

Few initial reserves on claims that are open for more than a few weeks remain accurate over the long run unless the loss is reserved for policy limits. Therefore, most claim reserves must be reevaluated as additional information about the loss is received. This reevaluation can occur often enough that the claim appears to be stair-stepped. However, reevaluation is quite different from stair-stepping, and the evaluation should more accurately represent both positive and negative loss factors.

Litigation

When a lawsuit arises for a liability claim, the insurer must decide whether to defend it. If the lawsuit is the first notice of the claim and liability is probable, the adjuster handling the claim might request an extension from the plaintiff's attorney while investigating and then try to settle the claim without incurring defense costs.

If the facts are already known and the policyholder's liability is clearly established or probable, the adjuster should try to settle the claim before incurring legal costs. The attorney might have filed the lawsuit only to protect against a statute of limitations or to get the insurer's attention if settlement negotiations had reached an impasse.

If, however, the plaintiff is seeking a settlement greater than the insurer believes is justified, the adjuster might decide to allow discovery to proceed to learn whether the plaintiff has any proof that the damages are as severe as alleged.

When the investigation shows that the claim is not covered because of either a lack of liability or damages, the insurer might decide to defend the lawsuit.

Insurers often speak of "nuisance settlements" of a claim or lawsuit for which either little liability or no proof of damages exists. To save the cost of defending such a suit, the insurer might pay or contribute a minimal amount to a settlement to resolve the lawsuit.

Even though insurers can reduce litigation expenses through insurance settlements, their litigation expenses are still significant. Many insurers spend as much money on outside defense attorneys as they do for their entire claim department because defending policyholders is one of the key promises of liability insurance. Consequently, it is essential to policyholders and to the insurer that claim personnel handle litigation well. When litigation cannot be avoided, claim adjusters must carefully select and direct defense counsel and must actively participate in litigation strategy to ensure proper policyholder defense and to control litigation expenses carefully.

A new or an unproved attorney who charges a minimum rate might be considered for routine claims for which the amount of damages is specific (as in property damage) or for which the action involves only subrogation collection. However, the insurer must select a seasoned, highly skilled defense attorney when allegations against the policyholder are severe, liability is questionable, and the damages are so severe that a jury might award compensatory damages that exceed the policyholder's policy limits.

Claim adjusters might need the assistance of various experts in addition to attorneys. For complex claims involving traffic accidents, building or construction sites, products, mechanical processes, and other loss exposures that could require expert testimony, the adjuster must have a pool of resources to use for witnesses. Someone with the most credentials might not be the best technical expert if that person cannot clearly explain to a jury in lay terms what happened. The adjuster must select specialists who not only are experts but also are impartial and well spoken.

Alternatives to Litigation

Alternative dispute
resolution (ADR)
Methods used to settle claims
that avoid litigation.

Because of the enormous expense of litigation and the delays that exist in many court systems, claim representatives should explore litigation alternatives. Adjusters use various approaches called **alternative dispute resolution (ADR)** as alternatives to litigation. ADR includes negotiation, mediation, arbitration, appraisals, mini-trials or summary jury trials, and pretrial settlement conferences. The insurance industry and the courts encourage using ADR, which is discussed in the next chapter.

Subrogation and Other Recoveries

Subrogation is the legal process through which an insurer assumes the right to pursue a legal action against a party who might be liable to the policyholder. Subrogation is one of the most effective post-loss control processes. Most subrogation occurs in workers' compensation, property insurance, and automobile physical damage claims.

An auto physical damage insurer frequently seeks to recover collision damages it paid to an auto owner from the liability insurer of the driver who struck the insured auto and was responsible for the accident. Insurers that have signed the Nationwide Inter-Company Arbitration Agreement sponsored by Arbitration Forums, Inc., can use arbitration panels of local claim adjusters to resolve disputes among themselves about liability issues related to claims under subrogation. This agreement also permits insurers to pursue deductible recovery on the insured's behalf. The panel's decision is binding and generally cannot be appealed. Insurers can also subscribe to several other types of intercompany and special arbitration agreements. Disputed uninsured motorists claims are often settled using arbitrators affiliated with the American Arbitration Association.

Claim Performance Measurement

Claim performance measures are internal standards by which claim departments and individual adjusters can be gauged. An insurer's claim function should be evaluated using two types of measures: (1) financial measures and (2) non-financial measures.

Financial Measures

The insurer's loss ratio is one of the most commonly used measures of evaluating the insurer's financial well-being. An increasing loss ratio could indicate that the insurer is improperly performing the claim function.

Increasing losses could also mean that underwriting failed to select above-average loss exposures or that the actuarial department failed to price the insurer's products correctly.

When the insurer's expense ratio increases, the claim function, along with other functions, is pressured to reduce expenses. Claim personnel could quickly reduce claim adjusting expenses in the short term by offering policy-holders and claimants the settlement demanded rather than the settlement deserved. However, to reduce adjusting expenses in the long term, inflated settlement demands should be resisted, researched, negotiated, and, if necessary, litigated.

Claim personnel can also reduce adjusting expenses by following claim procedures. The long-term consequences of not following acceptable claim procedures is an increase in the total cost of claims.

Another financial measure of claim performance is the accuracy with which claims are reserved. If the insurer must constantly transfer large sums on its financial balance sheet from surplus to reserves because of past underreserving, the claim department might be performing one of its primary responsibilities poorly.

Non-Financial Measures

Non-financial measures used to evaluate the claim function include the following:

- Turnover of claims
- Average cost of settlement
- Number and percentage of litigated files
- Litigation win/lose ratios
- Ratio of allocated to unallocated costs
- Average caseload per adjuster
- Staff turnover
- Customer satisfaction

The performance of individual adjusters can be measured using the following:

- File turnover
- Ratio of litigated to settled claims
- Average settlement costs compared to other adjusters with similar claims

The adjuster's position, level of experience and education, and degree of supervision must be considered when measuring performance. An adjuster with few settled but many litigated claims should be monitored carefully, as should an adjuster with a pattern of overpaying claims.

Unfair Claims Settlement Practices Legislation

The Unfair Claims Settlement Practices Model Act was developed by the National Association of Insurance Commissioners (NAIC) to establish standards to handle claims properly. Insurer activities prohibited by the Unfair Claims Settlement Practices Model Act are listed in Exhibit 8-7.

Under the provisions of the model act, if the insurance commissioner has reasonable cause to believe that an insurer is conducting business in violation of the act, he or she can issue a statement of charges to the insurer and can set a hearing date. If the hearing determines that the insurer has violated the act, the insurance commissioner issues a cease-and-desist order and can impose a fine.

The fine cannot exceed $1,000 for each violation and $100,000 altogether unless the violation was committed flagrantly and in conscious disregard of the act. In such cases, the penalty cannot exceed $25,000 for each violation or $250,000 in the aggregate.

The insurance commissioner can suspend or revoke the insurer's license if the insurer knew or reasonably should have known that the activity violated the act.

Additional penalties exist for violation of cease-and-desist orders.[6] Some states adopted the model act but not the specific penalty provisions. Other states have altered the model act or have deleted sections of it.

The Unfair Property/Casualty Claims Settlement Practices Model Regulation is a companion to the Unfair Claims Settlement Practices Model Act. As with the model act, individual state legislatures must choose to adopt the model law or some version of it and to enact it into law.

The regulation defines procedures and practices that constitute unfair claim practices in the following specific areas:

- File and record documentation
- Misrepresentation of policy provisions
- Failure to acknowledge pertinent communications
- Standards for prompt, fair, and equitable settlements applicable to all insurers
- Standards for prompt, fair, and equitable settlements applicable to automobile insurance
- Standards for prompt, fair, and equitable settlements applicable to fire and extended coverage-type policies with replacement cost coverage

Forty-five jurisdictions have adopted either the Unfair Claims Practices Model Act or similar legislation. Twenty-one states have adopted the Unfair Property/Casualty Claims Settlement Practices Model Regulation or similar regulations. Insurance regulators in states that have not adopted the model regulations must decide case by case what is considered an "unfair" practice.

EXHIBIT 8-7

Unfair Claims Settlement Practices

Committing or performing with such frequency as to indicate a general business practice any of the following:

A. Knowingly misrepresenting to claimants and insureds relevant facts or policy provisions relating to coverage at issue;

B. Failing to acknowledge with reasonable promptness pertinent communications with respect to claims arising under its policies;

C. Failing to adopt and implement reasonable standards for the prompt investigation and settlement of claims arising under its policies;

D. Not attempting in good faith to effectuate prompt, fair and equitable settlement of claims submitted in which liability has become reasonably clear;

E. Compelling insureds or beneficiaries to institute suits to recover amounts due under its policies by offering substantially less than the amounts ultimately recovered in suits brought by them;

F. Refusing to pay claims without conducting a reasonable investigation;

G. Failing to affirm or deny coverage of claims within a reasonable time after having completed its investigation related to such claim or claims;

H. Attempting to settle or settling claims for less than the amount that a reasonable person would believe the insured or beneficiary was entitled by reference to written or printed advertising material accompanying or made part of an application;

I. Attempting to settle or settling claims on the basis of an application that was materially altered without notice to, or knowledge or consent of, the insured;

J. Making claims payments to an insured or beneficiary without indicating the coverage under which each payment is being made;

K. Unreasonably delaying the investigation or payment of claims by requiring both a formal proof of loss form and subsequent verification that would result in duplication of information and verification appearing in the formal proof of loss form;

L. Failing in the case of claims denials or offers of compromise settlement to promptly provide a reasonable and accurate explanation of the basis for such actions;

M. Failing to provide forms necessary to present claims within fifteen (15) calendar days of a request with reasonable explanations regarding their use;

N. Failing to adopt and implement reasonable standards to assure that the repairs of a repairer owned by or required to be used by the insurer are performed in a workman-like manner.

Source: *NAIC Model Laws, Regulations, and Guidelines* (Kansas City, Mo.: NAIC, 1991), Tab: Unfair Trade Practices, p. 900-2-3.

All state insurance codes contain various rules and regulations that govern the practice of claim adjusting. Many states make insurers, their adjusters, and independent adjusters subject to the state's consumer-oriented Deceptive Trade Practices Act. These laws often leave the issue of what constitutes an unfair trade practice to juries, which can award triple damages.

States interpret their laws and regulations differently. For example, one state might require an adjuster to advise an unrepresented claimant of the statute of limitations, but another state might construe volunteering such information as the unauthorized practice of law. In another example, one state might require a vehicle damage appraiser to provide the insured with a list of shops that agree to repair a damaged vehicle for the appraised amount, but another state might view recommending any repair facility as a violation of law.

Insurers have rewritten the provisions of the model act, incorporated those provisions into their procedures, and added specific standards for adjusters to follow when the regulations provide none. Consequently, even adjusters who are not familiar with the act itself are following procedures that comply with the act. Enforcement of the Unfair Claims Settlement Practices Act is limited in most states. In only a minority of states can individuals exert a right of action based on the act in first-party claims. Even fewer states permit a right of action in third-party claims. In the remainder of states, enforcing the act is the full responsibility of the state insurance department.

SUMMARY

The insurer fulfills its contractual promise to the policyholder through the claim settlement process. Adjusters screen requests for payment to distinguish valid from invalid claims. Claims that fall within the bounds of coverage are assessed to determine their value and are then paid.

Most policyholders have little or no contact with their insurer except when the initial policy is written or when the premium is due. When a claim does occur, the adjuster is responsible for the reputation of the insurer. Fair and professional treatment of policyholders and claimants can do much to improve the image of the insurance industry, even on an individual, claim-by-claim basis.

Some insurers may think that any claim that goes to trial is a failure, even before the verdict has been determined. When a claim does go to trial, the adjuster must manage the defense counsel and communicate to plaintiff's counsel the insurer's settlement philosophy. Internally, adjusters must provide information to several departments, including the marketing, underwriting, and actuarial departments.

The structure of an insurer's claim organization is typically described in terms of its geographic or physical organization and its management/settlement authority. Claim offices are usually located close to policyholders so that service can be provided easily. Often, when claims occur outside the insurer's normal geographic scope, independent adjusters are employed to serve the policyholder. The management structure of a claim department is usually similar to that of any other insurer functional area. A distinguishing feature of a claim organization is that higher levels of settlement authority are assigned to individuals based on their responsible use of the claim authority already granted. Experience, knowledge, and the confidence of management are all factors considered in extending settlement authority.

In addition to handling claims outside the normal scope of operations, independent adjusters provide expertise for complex or unusual claims. Many insurers employ independent adjusters as a normal part of their business rather than expanding their own staffs.

The claim adjusting process can be described in terms of investigation, evaluation, negotiation, and settlement of coverage, liability, and damage issues. The steps in this process may vary between property and liability claims. Specific claim-handling differences and the unique characteristics of individual types of insurance are the subjects of subsequent chapters. The differences for adjusting property losses are discussed in the next chapter.

CHAPTER NOTES

1. "A Guide to Auto Insurance," *Consumer Reports*, October 1995, p. 642.

2. "Loss/Risk Management Insight: On the Scene Claims," *Best's Review*, December 2000, http://www.ambest.com (accessed November 19, 2002).

3. Commercial General Liability Coverage Form, CG 00 01 10 01, Insurance Services Office, 2000, p. 1.

4. Building and Personal Property Coverage Form, CP 00 10 04 02, Insurance Services Office, 2001, p. 1.

5. National Association of Insurance Commissioners, *Accounting Practices and Procedures Manual*, 2002 (Kansas City, Mo.: NAIC), pp. 55-3–55-5.

6. National Association of Insurance Commissioners, *NAIC Model Laws, Regulations, and Guidelines* (Kansas City, Mo.: NAIC, 1991), Tab: Unfair Trade Practices, p. 900.

Appendix

Claim Organizations and Associations

Although claim personnel represent one of the largest segments of people employed by the property-casualty insurance business, no single national organization or association exists for people who work in claims. However, several organizations are important to claim personnel. The National Association of Independent Insurance Adjusters (NAIIA) is open to independent adjusters who meet certain standards. The NAIIA distributes adjusting standards; maintains communications with insurers; encourages ethical practices; and conducts national, regional, and state meetings. The NAIIA publishes the *Blue Book of Adjusters*, which lists its members throughout the country and maintains educational resources available to any interested party.

The Property Loss Research Bureau (PLRB) and the Liability Insurance Research Bureau (LIRB) are dedicated primarily to education and research. They exist to provide expert research and analysis of claims and legal issues important to member companies. They also conduct an annual education conference that is open to anyone in the insurance business.

Property Claim Services, a division of the Insurance Services Office, provides catastrophe management and educational services to the industry. Its educational services include seminars, reference manuals, videos, and conferences.

The Loss Executives Association, consisting of claim experts in the property field, conducts seminars for its members. The Conference of Casualty Insurance Companies provides arbitration and educational services to its members. Through its many local offices, Arbitration Forums, Inc., administers various intercompany arbitration agreements, such as the Nationwide Intercompany Agreement and the Fire and Allied Lines Subrogation Arbitration Agreement.

The National Insurance Crime Bureau (NICB) was formed from the National Auto Theft Bureau (NATB) and the Insurance Crime Prevention Institute (ICPI). The NICB fights all forms of insurance fraud and crime, including automobile theft, medical fraud, and staged losses. It offers presentations on crime detection for claim representatives.

Local claim associations exist in most metropolitan areas. These groups are valuable sources of contacts within the local claim community and of information about local matters, such as defense law firms, public adjusters, plaintiff attorneys, and service providers. Most of the meetings these groups hold have both a social and an educational purpose. In fact, most meetings are organized around an educational presentation. Many state claim associations are also active and sponsor worthwhile educational programs.

Chapter 9

Direct Your Learning

Property Claim Adjusting

After learning the content of this chapter, you should be able to:

■ Explain how the questions that an adjuster must ask about property claims and their answers are important aspects of the adjusting process.

■ Describe insurable interests in property.

■ Describe what property is insured by property insurance and where and when it is insured.

■ Describe the causes of loss covered by property insurance.

■ Explain how the amount of loss is determined under property policies.

■ Describe the insured's duties after a loss.

■ Describe the challenges of adjusting the following types of property claims:

- Residential dwelling claims
- Residential personal property claims
- Commercial structure claims
- Business income claims
- Merchandise claims
- Transportation and bailment claims
- Crime claims
- Catastrophe claims

Develop Your Perspective

What are the main topics covered in the chapter?

This chapter describes how property claims are adjusted. Adjusting property claims is distinctly different from that of liability claims. Property claim adjusters focus on detailed insurance policy provisions. These general provisions and those of selected property policies are included.

Examine the detailed level of policy examination required in property claim adjusting.

- What facets of this process would create challenges for a claim adjuster?

Why is it important to learn about these topics?

Property claim adjusting requires attention to policy content and application of that content to a specific claim situation. Insight into this process provides an opportunity to review the skills required for this function.

Evaluate the knowledge and skills required to perform property claim adjusting and the adjusters' role in representing the company and safeguarding its profitability.

- Placing yourself in the role of an insurance executive, what level of expertise would you hope to build in your property claim adjusting staff?

How can you use what you will learn?

Investigate an insurer's property claim adjusting department:

- What type of policy losses does it adjust?
- How do the adjusters acquire their expertise?

Chapter 9

Property Claim Adjusting

The next two chapters each address a specific type of claim. This chapter discusses claims for property losses (claims for property damage under first-party insurance policies), and the next chapter discusses liability claims (primarily bodily injury claims under third-party insurance policies). This division is a natural one because claim adjusters are generally either property or liability specialists. Although claims for property damage can be made under third-party policies and injury claims made under first-party policies, claim personnel work mostly in either property damage, first-party claims or in bodily injury, third-party claims.

Property and liability claim specialists operate in different environments. Property claim adjusters are primarily concerned with applying detailed insurance policy provisions to specific situations. Liability claim adjusters are primarily concerned with how the legal system, which operates independently of insurance policy provisions, evaluates third-party claims and compensates claimants. Property claim adjusters evaluate and settle primarily objective, quantifiable losses. Liability claim adjusters evaluate and settle claims that are primarily subjective. "Pain and suffering," for example, one of the major elements of damages in bodily injury liability claims, is highly subjective.

PROPERTY CLAIM ADJUSTING PROCESS

The first part of this chapter discusses the general questions that adjusters must answer as part of the property claim adjusting process. These questions include the following:

- Who has an insurable interest in, and who is insured with respect to, damaged property?
- What property is insured under a policy, where is it insured, and during what time period?
- Against what causes of loss does the insurance protect?
- What is the dollar amount of the loss?
- What are the insured's duties after a loss?
- What procedures must the adjuster follow to settle the claim?

The answers to these questions are determined by applying the insurance policy provisions to specific situations. Answering these questions provides a framework for property adjusters to use for all kinds of property damage claims. An adjuster can answer most of these questions by consulting the policy and applying policy language to the given situation. An exception is determining the amount of loss. Insurance policies indicate how property will be valued in general terms. Adjusters, however, determine the dollar amount of damaged property covered by the policy at the time of the loss, not at the time the policy was issued.

The second part of the chapter deals with issues peculiar to specific types of claims.

Who Has an Insurable Interest? Who Is Insured?

The first set of questions an adjuster must answer about a property claim is, Who has an insurable interest and who is insured? Property insurance protects people or organizations from loss of the value of their interest in property. Accordingly, an insurable interest in property is a prerequisite to asserting a claim under an insurance policy.

An underwriter requires a prospective policyholder to have an insurable interest in property before issuing an insurance policy. This underwriting requirement is supported by language in the policy that limits all claim payments to the extent of the insured's insurable interest.

Interests in Property

Generally, anyone who would be financially harmed by the destruction of property has an insurable interest in that property. The simplest and most obvious example of an interest in property is ownership. A sole owner has complete interest in the property. However, numerous other interests, less than complete and sole, can exist, often simultaneously.

Joint ownership
A form of ownership in which two or more owners have an indivisible interest in property.

Tenancy by entireties
A form of joint tenancy ownership in which the co-owners are husband and wife, and when one spouse dies, property passes to the surviving spouse.

Ownership in common
A form of ownership in which two or more owners each have an identifiable fractional interest in property.

More than one person can own property simultaneously. Under **joint ownership**, two or more owners each have a complete, indivisible interest in the property. If one joint owner dies, ownership need not be transferred, because the other owner already has a complete interest in the property. Joint ownership between husband and wife is known as **tenancy by entireties**. **Ownership in common** involves two or more owners, each with an identifiable fractional financial interest in the property. Ownership in common is typical among partners.

A person or an organization can also have an interest in property that is not an ownership interest. Lessees of property have an interest in the use of the property for the life of the lease. Custodians of property, such as bailees, warehouse employees, and carriers, have an interest in the property to the extent of their fees and for their legal liability for the property's safe return to its owner. Finally, security interests can exist in almost any property. The secured party is generally a creditor of the property owner. A security interest is usually not evident by inspecting property. The secured party usually does not have possession of the property, and the property is not marked physically to show the interest. Security interests are created by contractual agreement or by law.

Policy Requirements for an Insurable Interest

Rather than listing the existence of an insurable interest as a precondition to coverage, insurance policies simply limit payment on any claim to the extent of the insured's interest. For example, the HO-3 policy states the following under Conditions Item A:

> …we will not be liable in any one loss: 1. To an insured for more than the amount of the insured's interest at the time of loss; …[1]

Under Loss Payment, Paragraph 4.d., the Business and Personal Property Coverage Form states:

> We will not pay you more than your financial interest in the Covered Property.[2]

Limiting claim payments to the extent of an insured's insurable interest and requiring all interests existing in the property to be specified are essential claim adjusting practices. Allowing the insured to collect more than its insurable interest in the insured property would provide a great incentive for the insured to deliberately destroy the property. Even when a policy has been properly underwritten, an insured's interest can change (for example, through divorce, marriage, or additional mortgages), creating opportunities for false claims if the insured's recovery is not limited to his or her actual insurable interest.

Identifying all insurable interests in the property enables the adjuster to treat every party fairly without compromising the insurer's rights. It also helps the adjuster identify other coverage on the same property. Whenever there are multiple insurable interests in property, each party might have its own insurance protecting its own interest. Another party's property or liability insurance might reduce the claim payments of the investigating insurer. Policies contain provisions to uphold the indemnification concept, such as the other insurance and subrogation clauses.

Coverage by Other Insurance

Parties with different interests who commonly have separate insurance policies are landlords and tenants, bailors and bailees, and mortgagors and mortgagees.

Landlords and Tenants

The relationship between a landlord and a tenant is determined by the lease agreement. The lease should specify precisely what property is subject to the lease; what rights of use or access, if any, the tenant has to the landlord's other property; the rights in the leased property that the landlord retains; the rights of the tenant to make improvements to the leased property; and the rights of the landlord to any improvements to the leased property at lease expiration. The lease should also specify whether the landlord and tenant waive rights of recovery against each other and whether the tenant is obligated to provide insurance for the landlord. An adjuster cannot determine the interests of either a landlord or a tenant in property without first reviewing the lease.

Although the lease determines the respective rights regarding the leased property, it does not determine coverage under an insurance policy. The landlord or the tenant might be named as an insured under the other's policy, or coverage might exist for the property of others in the insured's possession. Neither the landlord nor the tenant has any rights under the insurance coverage of the other unless indicated in the other's insurance policy.

Adjusters handling claims that potentially involve a landlord and a tenant must conduct a two-part analysis. First, what are the parties' respective interests in the property under the lease? Second, what rights does each party have under the applicable insurance policy in question? To recover under an insurance policy, a party must have both the right to do so under the policy *and* an insurable interest in some property covered by the policy.

Bailors and Bailees

The bailor-bailee relationship involves issues similar to the landlord-tenant relationship. The respective interests of the bailor-bailee in the property are determined by contract or, in the absence of a contract, by the law. Rights under an insurance policy are determined solely by the policy. Because of their legal liabilities and because of industry custom, bailees such as warehouse employees, carriers, and repairers typically have some sort of coverage for the property of others while it is in their possession.

Adjusters handling claims for owners of property damaged while in a bailee's possession usually rely on the bailee's insurer to handle the claim. Should the bailee's insurer deny liability, the owner's insurer must handle the claim. Subrogation claims against the bailee might be waived or otherwise affected by the agreement between the owner and the bailee.

Mortgagors and Mortgagees

The most common situation in which different interests are protected by common coverage is with owners and mortgagees. Mortgage agreements usually require the owner to name the mortgagee on the owner's insurance policy. Insurance policies grant rights to mortgagees that are separate and distinct from the owner's rights, so adjusters might have to protect a mortgagee even when the owner's coverage under the property is void.

In most cases, the mortgagee's interest is protected when claim settlement proceeds are used to repair the property. The adjuster should include the mortgagee's name on any claim settlement checks. Failure to do so might make the insurer separately liable to the mortgagee.

Identification of Insureds

Adjusters must carefully distinguish among a variety of people with rights and duties under a policy. A policy might identify a "first named insured," "named insureds," spouse of a "named insured," "insureds," and people whose property might be covered under a policy.

Generally, only the "first named insured," "named insured," or spouse of the "named insured" is entitled to make a claim. These specified individuals are likewise responsible for paying premiums and performing the insured's duties in the event of loss. In the event of the named insured's death, an adjuster can settle claims with the named insured's legal representative, either the executor or the estate administrator. These legal representatives are included in most policies' definition of "insured." Loss payees are parties, such as owners of leased office equipment, who do not have any rights greater than or independent of the policyholder, but the loss payee's name must be included on any claim settlement check.

Adjusters must deal with the right parties to avoid paying the claim to the wrong person and to avoid making any legal notices the insurer has given ineffective. Adjusters can determine which parties to deal with because the policy declarations identify the named insureds. The policy also indicates who can make claims and who must perform the insured's duties in the event of loss.

For cases in which the insurer can deny coverage to the first named insured or to the named insured's spouse, the adjuster must carefully check the policy for the rights the other insureds might have. If the policy language is unclear about such rights, the adjuster should consult legal counsel.

What Property Is Insured? Where Is It Insured? When Is It Insured?

The second set of questions an adjuster must answer about a property claim is, What property is insured? Where is it insured? and When is it insured? Policy provisions about what property is covered, where it is covered, and when it is covered are straightforward and usually do not cause disagreement between the insured and the adjuster. As part of determining what property is covered, adjusters must understand the difference between real and personal property. The two types of property might be valued differently (actual cash value versus replacement cost), might have different limits of coverage, and might have different coinsurance requirements. Real property is land and everything attached to it, such as buildings. Personal property is everything not considered real property.

Real Property

Buildings are real property and are easy to describe and identify. Most policies state the described buildings and structures at a given location. Other policies provide blanket coverage but still require a schedule of locations to identify the buildings to be insured.

Personal Property

Other than in inland marine policies, most personal property is covered under policies that are written for a fixed location (and that might be primarily concerned with coverage for a building at that location). Generally, the insured's personal property at the insured location is covered; the insured's personal property away from the insured location might be covered, depending on the policy; and personal property not owned by the policyholder is covered only at the insured location and while in the insured's care, custody, and control, often subject to a sublimit.

Fixtures are personal property that have become attached to and part of real property. In the event of a loss, the adjuster must determine whether a given "fixture" is real or personal property. Adjusters can determine whether fixtures are real property by asking the following three questions:

1. How permanently attached to the real property is the fixture? (For example, a furnace is a fixture, but a window air conditioner is not.)

2. Is the fixture well adapted to the real property? (For example, draperies that have been selected to match the interior decor of a particular room are real property, but non-custom window treatments are not.)

3. What was the intent of the owner? (For example, the owner would expect that shelves bolted to the wall would be removed when a tenant moved, but that built-in shelves would not be removed.)

Certain policy provisions specify whether a fixture is real or personal property. For example, the Business and Personal Property (BPP) coverage form allows fixtures to be classed as either "building" or "business personal property." The ISO Homeowners Special Form (HO-3) Loss Settlement provision requires that carpets, awnings, appliances, and outdoor antennae be valued as personal property, regardless of whether they might actually be fixtures.

Property Not Covered

Adjusters should check the exact policy before denying any claim. Insureds are entitled to a plausible and verifiable explanation from the adjuster of why their claims have been denied. For example, the adjuster might explain that the property is the sort that is usually covered elsewhere (for example, motor vehicles) or through specialty types of insurance (for example, valuable papers or livestock). Nevertheless, all claim denials should be in writing. Failure to provide a reasonable explanation for a claim denial with references to the policy and the facts of the claim violates of the Unfair Claims Settlement Practices Act.

Additional Coverages

Following a loss, insureds might ask the adjuster about whether, and to what extent, their expenses are covered by the policies' additional coverages. Adjusters should reach agreement about an expense before it is incurred. The adjuster's authorization of an expense under the additional coverages is contractually binding on the insurer, even if the expense in question is not covered.

Policy Period

In addition to the type of property and its location, adjusters must also verify that the loss occurred during the policy period. All property policy conditions state that coverage applies only during the policy period stated on the declarations page.

Against What Causes of Loss Does the Insurance Protect?

The third question an adjuster must answer about a property claim is, Against what causes of loss does the insurance protect? Most property insurance policies provide coverage only for direct physical loss. Adjusters must, therefore, recognize indirect or nonphysical types of losses.

The most important type of indirect loss is loss of use of property. Coverage for loss of use is provided as part of the package of coverages in the typical homeowners policy. In contrast, some commercial property policies do not automatically provide loss of use coverage. Unless the insured purchases such coverage, loss of use of property is not covered by these policies.

Even when loss of use is covered, direct physical loss to property is required to trigger such coverage and to measure its duration. For example, coverage for loss of business income applies only when the loss is caused by a direct loss to covered property resulting from a covered cause of loss or when civil authorities close the business because of a hazardous situation nearby. Such coverage begins after a brief waiting period after the covered property suffers direct loss and usually ends when the same property should be repaired or replaced.

Nonphysical losses include loss of value to property not caused by physical damage or destruction, such as obsolescence, loss of market, investment loss, and financial fraud. Loss of market is an important problem for claim adjusters. Insureds who operate seasonal businesses and who suffer losses at the busiest time of year frequently expect compensation for the diminished value of inventory that has gone unsold because of their losses. Assuming such inventory has not suffered physical loss, its diminished value is not covered.

Cause of Loss and Exclusions

Determining whether a loss has resulted from a covered cause of loss is usually a straightforward task for an adjuster. Causes of loss such as fire and windstorm, for example, lead to characteristic damage and are easy to verify. However, adjusters might encounter problems verifying certain causes of loss, particularly when exclusions apply. This section first deals with the following causes of loss that are difficult to verify:

- Water damage
- Collapse
- Theft
- Vandalism

This section then deals with the following troublesome exclusions:

- Gradual causes of loss
- Ordinance or law
- Faulty design, construction, or material
- Intentional acts of the insured

Water Damage

Property insurance policies that provide coverage for water damage generally limit such coverage to sudden and accidental overflow, breakage, or bursting of plumbing. In a given case, the exact wording of the coverage is crucial, because any type of water damage not within the defined cause of loss is not covered.

The most significant types of water damage that are usually not covered are gradual seepage and floods. Alone, these two types of water damage are easy to identify. Claim adjusters face difficulties, however, when these types of water damage are combined with covered losses. For example, a burst pipe might cause damage to property that has already suffered damage from gradual seepage. Except under certain policies covering against "direct physical loss" except as excluded (previously called "all-risks"), which might cover seepage, the adjuster must separate property damaged by seepage from other property and must determine how much of the damage to the former was caused by the seepage and by the burst pipe, respectively.

Water damage claims have increased in homeowners insurance because of changes in the design of homes. Many houses now have laundry rooms and water heaters located on the second floor, increasing the potential for greater damage as the result of a water claim. Newer homes also often have multiple bathrooms and many appliances such as dishwashers, icemakers, and water-softening equipment that also increase the likelihood of water damage claims.[3] Adjusters must carefully consider the cause of such losses and the applicable policies to determine coverage accurately.

Hurricanes frequently cause damage through a combination of wind, wind-driven water, and flooding. The typical property policy covers the damage caused by wind and wind-driven water (under specific circumstances), but not that caused by flooding. The adjuster must separate damages by cause of loss even if the owner has purchased flood coverage through the National Flood Insurance Program (NFIP).

Collapse

Collapse is a type of loss rather than a cause of loss. Recent Insurance Services Office policy forms treat collapse as an additional coverage. The effect of this treatment is to limit the coverage for collapse. Collapse is covered only when it results from the causes of loss specified in the additional coverage. Adjusters must be careful when handling claims involving two specific causes of collapse: hidden problems and defective construction.

Decay and insect and vermin damage are covered causes of collapse only if they are *hidden*. Conspicuous decay or insect or vermin damage should be repaired by the insured before further loss occurs. To determine whether the insured should have known of the damage that caused the collapse, claim adjusters must reconstruct how a structure looked before its collapse.

Defective construction is a covered cause of collapse only if the collapse occurs during construction. Policyholders have presented numerous claims to insurers for loss caused by defective construction. Property insurance policies are not intended to serve in place of a surety bond that protects the building's owner from the builder's mistakes.

Theft

Coverage for theft varies widely among property policies, from none to extensive. An adjuster handling a claim for loss caused by theft must be careful to review the relevant policy provisions thoroughly.

Assuming the policyholder has theft coverage for the type and location of property concerned, the adjuster's most difficult task is verifying the loss. Both the loss itself and its amount must be verified. Theft claims are the easiest for a dishonest insured to fabricate because little or no evidence remains. Even in legitimate cases of theft, often no evidence exists that a thief acted, that the property involved ever existed, or of the values and quantities of property involved. The insured's statements about the nature, quantity, and value of property allegedly stolen are admissible evidence in court. This admissibility means that an adjuster cannot deny a claim simply because the insured fails to provide receipts.

Adjusters can (and should) require policyholders with theft claims to report such claims to the police, and most insurance policies require the policyholder to do so. A policyholder's failure to file a police report will likely arouse the adjuster's suspicions. This is because people who falsify theft claims might be reluctant to involve the police because of the possibility of criminal sanctions for false reporting. On legitimate claims, the police occasionally recover stolen property, which mitigates the insurer's payment.

Disproving questionable theft claims is difficult. Adjusters must judge theft claims by how reasonable they are. Do the type and amount of property in question seem appropriate to the policyholder's standard of living? Does the policyholder claim unusual duplicates, such as two stereo systems or two sets of silver? Does the policyholder have documentation that is common, such as inventory records in a business or instruction manuals for consumer electronics? Ultimately, if the adjuster compels the policyholder to comply meticulously with every duty following loss and the adjuster's suspicions remain unproved, the claim is likely to be paid.

Vandalism

Vandalism is the intentional or malicious destruction of property. Accidental or negligent property destruction is not vandalism. Adjusters investigating unexplained damage to property cannot pay for such damage under the coverage for vandalism unless evidence of intentional or malicious wrongdoing exists. For example, landlords might report a tenant's abuse of property as vandalism. Unless evidence of maliciousness beyond mere carelessness is apparent, such abuse would not be considered vandalism.

Vandalism is likely whenever damage appears to have been caused by the actions of a person, rather than forces of nature, and the circumstances do not appear to be accidental. Examples include windows broken by rocks, spray-painted graffiti, and other deliberate defacement of property.

Gradual Causes of Loss

Gradual causes of loss include wear and tear, rust, decay, deterioration, latent defect, and rot. Losses from these excluded causes of loss present the same problems as those caused by water seepage.

Property that has suffered loss from any of these excluded causes of loss might suffer a subsequent loss that is covered. In such a situation, the adjuster must separate property that suffered the gradual damage from that which did not. Gradual damage to property might be included in a claim for subsequent covered loss, but the claim for such property is limited to the extent its value has been further diminished by the covered cause of loss. The gradual cause of loss might have already diminished the property's value to nearly nothing.

Ordinance or Law

Local ordinances or laws might require the demolition of a damaged structure. The cost of demolition might be more than the cost to rebuild the structure. Additionally, local ordinances or laws might require construction plans, methods, or materials that are different from, and more expensive than, those originally used in the damaged structure. Generally, property policies do not cover these additional costs unless a special endorsement has been added to the policy.

An adjuster handling a claim with such additional costs should ask contractors to prepare estimates as though the building were to be rebuilt as it
was, even though such rebuilding is not legal. Alternatively, complete
estimates can be prepared, as long as the added costs not covered are
identified and segregated.

Faulty Design, Construction, or Materials

As noted previously, property insurance policies are not designed to be surety
bonds for construction work. Losses caused by faulty design, construction, or
materials are generally excluded from coverage. The additional coverage for
collapse actually "gives back" coverage for faulty construction in limited
circumstances, such as when the collapse occurs during construction, remodeling, or renovation. For example, if faulty construction caused a fire, the
adjuster must segregate damage caused by the poor workmanship from that
caused by the fire and might initiate subrogation.

Intentional Acts of the Insured

The most obvious type of loss that should be, and invariably is, excluded
from coverage is loss caused intentionally by the insured. Fires are the most
common type of intentionally caused loss. Intentionally set fires are arson,
whether committed by the insured or not. Arson can also be committed for
revenge, in the commission of a crime, or by vandals. In those cases, innocent property owners are entitled to insurance coverage. Nevertheless, in the
insurance context, "arson" usually refers to a fire intentionally set by the
insured. When arson by the insured is suspected, most insurers involve their
special investigative units (SIUs) or outside legal counsel. The factors shown
in Exhibit 9-1 are indicators of arson.

To prove arson, an adjuster must prove (1) an incendiary fire (one that has
been set intentionally), (2) a motive on the insured's part, and (3) opportunity on the insured's part. An origin and cause expert, usually a scientist or
an engineer with expertise in identifying the cause of fires, can be used to
determine the cause of the fire.

With arson, the insured's motive is usually financial, and it might be shown by
demonstrating that the insured is better off financially with the insurance
proceeds and a vacant lot than with an intact building. Examining the
policyholder's books and records might reveal such information. Irrational
motives, such as anger toward a spouse or business partner, might also be the
cause of an arson. Opportunity to set the fire can be proved by demonstrating
that the insured was in the vicinity of the building soon before the fire started.

Once the investigation concludes that the insured committed arson, the
insurer need only deny the claim for breach of the policy conditions against
misrepresentation and because losses caused by intentional acts are excluded.

EXHIBIT 9-1

Indicators of Arson

General Indicators of Arson-for-Profit or Fire-Related Fraud

- Building or contents were up for sale at the time of the loss.
- Suspiciously coincidental absence of family pet at time of fire.
- Insured had a loss at the same site in the preceding year. The initial loss, though small, may have been a failed attempt to liquidate contents.
- Building or business was recently purchased.
- Commercial losses include old or nonsaleable inventory or illegal chemicals or materials.
- Insured or insured's business is experiencing financial difficulties, e.g., bankruptcy, foreclosure.
- Fire site is claimed by multiple mortgagees or chattel mortgagees.

Indicators at the Fire Scene

- Building is in deteriorating condition and/or lacks proper maintenance.
- Fire scene investigation suggests that property/contents were heavily over-insured.
- Fire scene investigation reveals absence of remains of noncombustible items of scheduled property or items covered by floaters, e.g., coin or gun collections or jewelry.
- Fire scene investigation reveals absence of expensive items used to justify an increase over normal 50 percent contents coverage, e.g., antiques, piano, or expensive stereo/video equipment.
- Fire scene investigation reveals absence of items of sentimental value, e.g., family Bible, family photos, trophies.
- Fire scene investigation reveals absence or remains of items normally found in a home or business. The following is a sample listing of such items, most of which will be identifiable at fire scenes except in total burns. Kitchen: major appliances, minor appliances, normal food supply in refrigerator and cabinets. Living room: television/stereo equipment, record/tape collections, organ or piano, furniture (springs will remain). Bedrooms: guns, jewelry, clothing, and toys. Basement/garage: tools, lawn mower, bicycles, sporting equipment, such as golf clubs (especially note whether putter is missing from otherwise complete set). Business/office: office equipment and furniture, normal inventory, business records (which are normally housed in metal filing cabinets and should survive most fires).

Indicators Associated With the Loss Incident

- Fire occurs at night, especially after 11 PM.
- Commercial fire occurs on holiday, weekend, or when business is closed.
- Fire department reports fire cause is incendiary, suspicious, or unknown.
- Fire alarm or sprinkler system failed to work at the time of the loss.

Adapted with permission of the National Insurance Crime Bureau.

Some insurers take steps to have the insured prosecuted by the criminal authorities, should the evidence be strong enough.

The policyholder could sue the insurer for the claim payment. To prevail in a civil suit, the insurer need have only the preponderance of the evidence in its favor. To prevail in a criminal suit, the state must prove its case beyond a reasonable doubt. The criminal standard of proof is more difficult. So, even if the policyholder is acquitted of criminal arson or if the authorities have declined to prosecute, the arson defense can still be used successfully by the insurer in a civil suit.

What Is the Dollar Amount of Loss?

The fourth question that an adjuster must answer about a property claim is, What is the dollar amount of loss? Insurance policies do not specify how adjusters should determine the amount of loss. Policies usually value property at "replacement cost" or "actual cash value" without further guiding the adjuster as to how "replacement cost" can be determined or what "actual cash value" might mean (for example, does it differ from "cash value" or "value"?). For property adjusters, this is the step in the claim adjusting process that determines damages.

Replacement Cost

Replacement cost is the cost to replace property with identical property or with property of like kind and quality at the time of the loss. Replacement cost settlement provisions spare adjusters the difficulties of determining actual cash value and convincing the policyholder to agree with that value.

Replacement cost
The cost to repair or replace property using new materials of like kind and quality with no deduction for depreciation.

Determining replacement cost is easier than determining actual cash value, yet several possibilities exist for disagreement with the policyholder. The adjuster and the insured must identify the property precisely. For personal property, the manufacturer's name, product description, and exact model or style numbers must be determined. For real property, the exact measurements and descriptions and an exact specification of the type and quality of materials, are necessary.

Once the property has been fully identified and described, the adjuster must determine the cost to replace it *at the time of loss*. The amount the insured originally paid for the property (generally less than the replacement cost or cost to replace) is irrelevant. The cost at the time of loss should be the amount at which the policyholder can buy the item of personal property.

If the exact type of property damaged or destroyed is no longer available, the adjuster can make settlement based on property of like kind and quality. Specific models and styles of goods are frequently discontinued. However, similar items are usually available, often from the same manufacturer. Settlement on the basis of such goods is rarely a problem with the policyholder, as long as the goods are of similar quality.

Adjusters obtain specific replacement cost information from catalogs, furniture retailers, and department stores. However, for specific losses, adjusters should consult the retailer from which the policyholder bought the property. Business personal property is normally replaced through the insured's usual suppliers and, therefore, might be available at wholesale prices. Many replacement service vendors specifically service the insurance industry and can provide insurers the best price on many products. Insurers have the option of replacing property rather than paying money to settle claims.

Determining replacement cost for building damage requires construction estimates. Proper estimates are based on the following factors:

- *Specifications.* Specifications state precisely what must be done, including whether to repair or replace the property, the exact type of materials, and the quantity of materials in exact dimensions or count.

- *Materials.* The total quantity of materials is determined based on the specifications. Material prices are based on prevailing material costs for projects similar to what is required by the policyholder's loss. Bulk discounts cannot be considered unless such quantities are needed.

- *Labor.* The hours of labor required for a particular job depend on the amount and type of material to be installed and the working conditions. Skilled estimators can calculate labor amounts fairly accurately. Additionally, published "standard" work rates are generally regarded as fair. For example, such rates might indicate that wallpaper can be hung at 200 square feet per hour.

- *Overhead.* Overhead represents the contractor's fixed costs of doing business or fixed specific costs attributable to the job. Examples include office space, telephones, insurance, permits, and job site offices. Generally, overhead is calculated as a percent of the cost of the job, usually 10 to 15 percent, depending on a contractor's circumstances. Costs that are specific to the job, such as permits, might simply be added in.

- *Profit.* Contractors are in business to earn a profit. The amount computed for overhead is *not* profit. Overhead represents very real costs for the contractor. Once overhead costs have been added to the job, profit is calculated as a percentage of total costs.

Most adjusters ask or hire contractors to provide estimates. Policyholders, or public adjusters working for them, likewise engage contractors to provide estimates. Unless all contractors involved provide estimates with detailed specifications, material, and labor, resolving disparities is difficult. Even when all parties have done detailed work, there is room for differences: Does property need to be replaced, repaired, or simply cleaned? Have measurements been rounded? What allowance is each contractor making for waste of materials or for difficult working conditions? What labor rate (dollars per hour) and rate of work does each contractor assume? Estimates might appear to be precise but probably include a great deal of judgment. Adjusters must be prepared to negotiate estimates in good faith and should be careful to use only contractors who provide legitimate estimates and good workmanship.

Computer software is available to help adjusters or contractors prepare estimates. The adjuster or contractor specifies the work to be done, the measurements, and the quantities, and the computer calculates the total cost of materials and the total hours and cost of labor and determines the total estimate. Computerized estimating programs are quick and provide well-formatted output. The computer cannot, however, spot unusual circumstances. Computerized estimating programs are a useful tool for those who already understand estimating, but they cannot teach estimating to a novice.

Whenever losses are settled on a replacement cost basis, determining the insured's compliance with insurance to value requirements must also be done on a replacement cost basis. This task can be tedious if the loss is small relative to the total value of insured property. The adjuster must estimate the value of a great deal of property not affected by the loss. Fortunately, there are shortcuts. With business personal property, the insured's accounting records will usually show what items the business purchased, when they were purchased, and for how much. The services of an accountant might be needed to extract this information from the accounting records. An estimation guide, which uses factors such as square footage and construction quality to determine how much it would cost to rebuild a building, offers a shortcut for determining a building's value.

Insurance policies generally do not permit replacement cost settlements until the property has been repaired or replaced. Such policy provisions exist to prevent unjust enrichment of the insured and to discourage intentional losses. Nevertheless, the insured might need funds to pay a contractor or merchant before repair or replacement is complete. The adjuster will either (1) release to the insured an actual cash value settlement, with the balance paid upon complete repair or replacement or (2) parcel out a replacement cost settlement as repair or replacement is gradually accomplished. Either of these approaches should be satisfactory to the policyholder.

Actual Cash Value

Actual cash value (ACV) is usually defined as replacement cost minus depreciation. Claim adjusters applying this formula must have a sophisticated understanding of depreciation. Although the formula is generally appropriate, claim adjusters must realize when it is not.

Depreciation represents loss of value. It is not limited to physical wear and tear, although physical wear and tear is obviously an important consideration in determining the depreciation of certain property, such as carpeting. When physical wear and tear is the chief cause of depreciation, adjusters usually apply straight-line depreciation, by which a fixed percentage of the property's value is deducted for every year of the property's useful life that the owner has enjoyed.

Aside from physical wear and tear, obsolescence is the main cause of depreciation. Obsolescence is caused by changes in technology and fashion and can have much more sudden and dramatic effects on the value of property

Actual cash value (ACV)
The replacement cost of property minus depreciation.

Depreciation
The physical wear and tear or technological or economic obsolescence of property.

than physical wear and tear. Clothing in last year's styles, even if untouched by wear and tear, has lost significant value. Property for which technology advances rapidly, such as electronics and computers, also loses value quickly.

Age alone, absent wear and tear or obsolescence, should not cause too much depreciation. For example, the frame carpentry (wall studs, floor joists, and so forth) of a 100-year-old house might be in as good a condition as when it was installed. While some obsolescence might occur in such frame carpentry, obsolescence can be difficult to identify in residential construction. Although the copper pipes used today are superior to the lead pipes found in older homes, frame carpentry techniques have changed little in 100 years. Furthermore, certain features of older construction are considered desirable.

Adjusters frequently rely on published guides to determine depreciation. Individual insurers have created such guides based on their experience. Trade groups have published guides for items such as clothing and household furnishings. However, adjusters should consider the characteristics of the property in question when evaluating actual cash value. For every loss that will result in an actual cash value settlement, the adjuster must determine depreciation for the property that has suffered loss.

For losses in which significant depreciation caused by obsolescence has occurred, guidebooks are likely to become obsolete sooner than the property in question. Guidebooks are primarily useful as a starting point for discussing depreciation caused by wear and tear. In many situations, the published rate of depreciation is perfectly appropriate; in others, it might not be.

Other Definitions of Actual Cash Value

As long as depreciation is understood to represent loss of value of any type, the "replacement cost minus depreciation" definition of "actual cash value" is usually appropriate. However, it is not appropriate in all circumstances.

Application of the "replacement cost minus depreciation" definition requires an ascertainable figure for replacement cost. Sometimes, no such figure exists. For example, antiques cannot be produced and sold new. Old buildings might feature construction methods that are no longer used. Finally, many adjusters mistakenly infer that the "replacement cost minus depreciation" definition allows only for deductions from the replacement cost. Certain property, such as some collectibles, is known to appreciate in value.

Some courts have defined actual cash value to mean fair market value. The fair market value of an item reflects both the "replacement cost minus depreciation" approach and the possibility that an item is irreplaceable. The market valuation of antiques and objects of art is generally regarded as fair. Additionally, a well-functioning market considers obsolescence and any other factor that affects value. A well-functioning market for a type of property is key to determining market valuation. Unfortunately, no substantial secondary market exists for many common items of property, such as used clothing, which most people regard as valueless. This situation is evolving with the advent of online outlets that deal in used items. Adjusters should not apply market valuation unless a well-functioning secondary market exists.

Other courts have avoided definitions based strictly on a formula of actual cash value. These courts have required adjusters to consider all pertinent factors, including physical wear and tear, obsolescence, market value, and any other relevant factors. This approach is known as the **broad evidence rule**.

Deductibles

Applying a deductible is a simple matter when a loss is otherwise fully covered. The deductible amount is subtracted from the amount of the loss, and the insured is paid the remainder. However, applying deductibles to a loss that is not fully covered is more difficult.

When a coinsurance penalty reduces the recoverable amount of loss, the insured benefits by having the deductible applied first, as shown in the following example:

$$\text{Loss} = \$10,000$$

$$\text{Actual Amount of Coverage} = \$60,000$$

$$\text{Required Amount of Coverage} = \$80,000$$

Deductible Applied First

$$\$10,000 \text{ loss} - \$100 \text{ deductible} = \$9,900$$

$$\frac{\$60,000}{\$80,000} \times \$9,900 = \$7,425$$

Coinsurance Applied First

$$\frac{\$60,000}{\$80,000} \times \$10,000 \text{ loss} = \$7,500$$

$$\$7,500 - \$100 \text{ deductible} = \$7,400.$$

Adjusters should use the first approach unless the policy explicitly states otherwise. The commercial building and personal property (BPP) form is an example of a policy that states otherwise. A loss might also not be fully covered because of the application of a sublimit. Applying sublimits is discussed subsequently.

Stated Values and Agreed Amounts

Some property policies are written on a scheduled basis, such as personal articles floaters and homeowners policy endorsements designed for scheduled property. Individual property items might be listed separately with a value assigned for each, or the property might be listed by class, such as cameras, furs, or jewelry. Some coverages provided on personal articles floaters are on

Broad evidence rule
Rule that requires adjusters to consider all relevant factors when determining the actual cash value of property.

Stated amount
A method of valuing property often described in an insurance policy as the least of (1) the actual cash value, (2) the cost to repair or replace, or (3) the applicable amount of insurance for the property.

a stated amount basis. The **stated amount** is typically determined by appraising the policyholder's property or by reviewing a sales receipt for the property in question. In the event of a loss, the insured is entitled to no more than the *least* amount of (1) the property's actual cash value, (2) the cost to repair or replace, or (3) the applicable amount of insurance.

Many policyholders believe that they are entitled to the stated amount regardless of the policy's valuation provision. However, the stated value is designed as a maximum amount the insurer will pay.

Agreed amount
A method of valuing property in which the insurer and the insured agree on the property's value at the time the policy is written and that states the amount in the policy declarations as the amount the insurer will pay in the event of a total loss to the property.

Fine arts and valuable papers are usually insured on an **agreed amount** basis. In the event of a loss, the insurer agrees to restore the property to its condition before the loss or to pay the agreed amount. The distinction between these properties and those covered on a stated amount basis is that the more valuable property is typically impossible to replace.

In dealing with agreed value losses, adjusters should be alert for possible fraud. Underwriters recognize the increased chance of moral and morale hazards and scrutinize applicants accordingly.

Repair or Replace Option

Claims are generally settled with money. Occasionally, adjusters prefer to settle claims by repairing or replacing the property as the policy allows. Adjusters might prefer not to repair or replace property because doing so opens up a new area for potential disagreement with the insured. The policyholder might expect the insurer to guarantee the repairs or certify the quality of a replacement item.

Adjusters choose the repair or replace option whenever it is significantly less expensive to do so. It might be less expensive to perform repairs or provide a replacement item when the insurer has discount purchasing arrangements through local contractors and retailers. Insurers frequently replace jewelry through wholesale channels. Repairing or replacing the property enables insurers to eliminate the financial incentive some insureds have to file unfounded claims. Insurers can also settle the claim with money based on the insurer's cost to replace the item.

Appraisal Clause

The appraisal clause found in every property insurance policy is used solely to settle disputes over the value of the property or the amount of loss.

Adjusters who work for years in property claims might never participate in an appraisal, but this does not mean that the clause is unimportant. The appraisal clause prompts the insured and the adjuster to do formally what the appraisal procedure requires. The adjuster provides the insured with estimates from contractors and other supporting documentation. The insured provides similar information to the adjuster. The adjuster and the insured, or the contractors working for them, negotiate their differences and almost always reach an agreement. The possibility of an appraisal procedure in which an impartial umpire settles the dispute gives both sides an incentive to negotiate in good faith.

What Are the Insured's Duties After a Loss?

The fifth question an adjuster must ask about a property claim is, What are the insured's duties after a loss? Every property insurance policy indicates duties the insured must perform after a loss. These duties are policy conditions. An insured is not entitled to loss payment unless these duties have been performed. The insured's performance of duties following a loss helps the adjuster to verify the extent and the dollar amount of the loss and to protect against fraudulent or exaggerated claims. Adjusters can waive certain duties if the circumstances warrant, but they are likely to hold the policyholder to strict performance when unusual circumstances surround the claim or when the claim seems suspicious. Requiring the insured to perform its duties protects the adjuster from a critical review in a subsequent claim audit. Additionally, making the policyholder follow legitimate claim settlement procedures might uncover fraudulent claims or policyholder misrepresentations.

Provide Prompt Notice

Obviously, nothing can be done with a claim until the policyholder notifies the insurer of the loss. The policyholder need not provide notice in any special form or in any special wording. The policyholder does not even have to give written notice; a telephone call suffices.

Although policies do not require the policyholder to give notice in any particular form, they do require that the notice be "prompt." An adjuster cannot properly investigate and evaluate a loss after too much time has passed. The prompt notice requirement rarely becomes an issue between insureds and insurers. Insureds are usually eager to report claims, and adjusters generally do not penalize the insured for delayed notice if a proper investigation is still possible. Courts generally require that the insurer suffer some prejudice to its rights before it can consider denying coverage. Nevertheless, lack of prompt notice (as well as breach of other policy conditions) is an issue, for example, when the insured repairs or replaces property before ever notifying the insurer of the loss.

In case of loss by theft, the insured is required to notify the police. In most states, it is a felony to submit false reports to the police, so the policyholder's duty to report thefts and other criminal violations discourages fraudulent claims. The BPP requires the insured to notify the police if a law is broken, which includes the occurrence of a possible theft. The common-sense interpretation of the BPP limits this duty to violations of *criminal* law only.

Homeowners policies provide coverage for lost or stolen credit cards. The insured must, however, notify the credit card or funds transfer card company.

Thereafter, the insured is not liable for improper and unauthorized charges. Should the insured fail to notify the credit card company, the insurer is not liable for any charges incurred after a reasonable time during which notice could have been given. An insured's lack of timely notice to a credit card company is rarely an issue between the insured and the insurer because most credit card agreements limit the cardholder's liability for unauthorized use to some small amount, such as $50.

Protect Property

The insured is required to protect the property from further loss by making emergency repairs (such as covering a damaged roof with a tarpaulin) and by implementing emergency safeguards. Such measures are a reimbursable part of the loss (subject to policy limits) as long as they are "reasonable" and "necessary." The insured usually seeks pre-approval of such measures from the adjuster. Adjusters are happy to approve these requests because they limit the loss. Nevertheless, the insured is obligated to take "reasonable" and "necessary" measures regardless of whether the adjuster's approval has been obtained. Failure to do so might void coverage for any additional loss that results.

Assist With the Loss Adjustment Process

Insureds have several duties that help expedite and conclude the claim settlement process. They must inventory all damaged property and, under certain policies, all undamaged property as well. The inventory must include quantities, values, and amounts of loss and might be required as part of, or independently of, the proof of loss. Without such an inventory, the adjuster would have difficulty organizing and analyzing the loss to personal property and would have to deal with continual additions to the claim for personal property.

The insured must show the damaged property to the adjuster. The purpose of this requirement is to preclude claims based on photographic or verbal evidence and to discourage exaggerated or fraudulent claims.

The insured must also allow books and other records to be inspected. The adjuster might personally inspect the insured's books or might hire an accountant to do so. The evidence in a policyholder's books and records is often essential to verify the existence and value of property. For example, property is often destroyed in all-consuming fires or as a result of theft.

Some insurance policies require the policyholder to cooperate. For example, the BPP lists among the insured's duties in the event of loss the duty to "cooperate with us in the investigation or settlement of the claim." The absence of such a duty in other policies means that the insured has no general duty of cooperation, although the lack of such a duty does not usually create any problems for the adjuster. The specifically listed duties—and, in particular, the duty to submit a proof of loss—are sufficient for the adjuster to obtain whatever is necessary from the policyholder.

Provide Proof of Loss

The proof of loss is a powerful adjustment tool, yet it is often not used, or is misused, by adjusters. A **proof of loss** is a written, signed, and sworn-to statement by the insured about the loss. It is the policyholder's official version of the loss and, because it is signed and sworn to, all statements it contains are material and, if false, are grounds to void the coverage. The formality of the proof of loss impresses policyholders with the importance of the statements made within it.

In a proof of loss, the insured is typically required to specify the time, place, and cause of loss; the interests in the property; any other insurance on the property; and detailed estimates, inventories, bills, and other documentation that prove the loss. The proof of loss should contain all of the information necessary for the adjuster to settle the claim, including an exact dollar figure for the loss.

Once a proof of loss has been submitted, the adjuster must respond promptly. Many states have laws specifying the number of days following receipt of a proof of loss that an adjuster has to either accept or reject the proof of loss or to tell the policyholder specifically what is further required. An adjuster who rejects a proof of loss should do so in writing and should state specific reasons for the rejection. The rejection letter should explain that the claim cannot be settled without a proper proof of loss and should ask the policyholder to submit a new proof if possible and still timely.

Many insurers routinely waive the proof of loss. On uncomplicated claims, doing so expedites settlement. The danger to insurers of routinely waiving proofs of loss on simple, straightforward losses is that adjusters might not spot nonroutine cases soon enough to implement the proof of loss requirement, waiving valuable rights.

Some adjusters require the insured to complete a proof of loss only at the claim's conclusion. At that point, the adjuster has presumably already agreed with the insured about the amount of settlement. However, to be most effective, the proof of loss should be required early in the adjustment process. On the other hand, a proof of loss that is completed after settlement is still a sworn statement of material fact and therefore could be the basis of a fraud defense.

Submit to Examination Under Oath

An **examination under oath** is a statement given by a person who has sworn to tell the truth before a court officer. Insurers rarely require an examination under oath, but when they do, they usually suspect policyholder fraud.

The examination under oath is a policy condition that the insured must fulfill, if required by the insurer. The insurer might require an examination even though the claim is not being litigated. The insured might have counsel present, but such counsel cannot interrupt, object, or ask questions. Although adjusters can conduct examinations under oath themselves, they are

Proof of loss
A written, signed, and sworn-to statement by the insured about a loss.

Examination under oath
A statement given by a person who has sworn to tell the truth before an officer of the court.

almost invariably conducted by an attorney working for the insurer and helping the insurer prepare its fraud case.

An examination under oath is usually conducted after the insured completes and submits a proof of loss. The proof of loss commits the insured to a certain story, and the examination under oath allows the insurer to clarify that story.

Public Adjusters

Sometimes a policyholder can engage a public adjuster to assist with a claim. In such cases, the public adjuster handles all of the insured's duties following loss (except that the insured must still sign and swear to any proof of loss and must appear for an examination under oath). The policyholder is free to engage a public adjuster, just as the policyholder is free to engage an attorney. The insurer's adjusters are required to handle claims with whomever policyholders designate to represent them.

What Procedures Must Be Followed To Settle the Claim?

The sixth question an adjuster must ask about a property claim is, What procedures must be followed to settle the claim? This determination is the final step in the claim adjusting process. Regardless of how a claim is investigated, it involves doing the following three things:

1. Determining the cause of the loss
2. Determining the amount of the loss
3. Documenting the cause and amount of the loss

Adjusters do one of the following or some combination thereof when they receive a new claim:

*   Accept the policyholder's word and settle the claim accordingly.
*   Employ experts to investigate the claim or refer it to an SIU.
*   Personally investigate the claim.

The smaller, simpler, and more straightforward a claim is, the likelier an adjuster is to settle it based on the policyholder's word. The larger, more complicated, or more questionable a claim is, the likelier an adjuster is to hire experts or involve an SIU.

Experts might be consulted to determine the cause of loss. Such experts include origin and cause scientists, accident reconstruction engineers, and private investigators. Other experts help to determine the value of a loss. These experts include contractors, accountants, and appraisers. Expert services are expensive but are essential when litigation is foreseeable, either following a claim denial or pursuant to subrogation.

The following sections explain how an adjuster personally investigates a claim.

Determining the Cause of Loss

An adjuster who personally investigates the cause of a loss inspects the damaged property, takes the policyholder's statement, or does both.

By personally inspecting the damaged property, the adjuster determines how the property has been damaged and identifies the property for purposes of verifying coverage. The effects of causes of loss such as fire, smoke, lightning, windstorm, hail, explosions, and vandalism are usually obvious, and a brief inspection can verify coverage.

The adjuster takes the policyholder's statement. Such a statement is informal compared to the proof of loss or examination under oath, but it is recorded. In some states, taking the policyholder's statement might preclude a subsequent proof of loss or examination under oath. When the policyholder's statement can be taken, the adjuster asks about the cause of loss, any other interests in or liens on the property, other insurance, steps taken to mitigate loss, documentation of the extent of loss, and any subrogation possibilities.

Determining the Amount of Loss

An adjuster who personally determines the amount of a loss must take careful, detailed inventories of personal property to specify the exact quantities and types of property and must prepare estimates for losses to buildings.

Most adjusters leave the item-by-item preparation of a personal property inventory to the insured. The adjuster spot-checks the physical property or double-checks against the policyholder's books and records. The adjuster must check the physical property sufficiently to determine appropriate depreciation.

An adjuster who prepares estimates must have extensive knowledge of construction practices, material prices, and labor allowances. Such adjusters usually have their own library of materials catalogs, manufacturers' price lists, and construction trade association guides.

An adjuster also develops a methodology for taking thorough specifications at a loss site. For example, an adjuster might take all outside measurements first, then go inside to take room measurements, and, finally, determine all mechanical and electrical specifications. Completed estimates are usually organized by trade, such as demolition, frame carpentry, finish carpentry, drywall, painting and decorating, plumbing, and electrical, or by room.

Documenting the Cause and Amount of Loss

When adjusters investigate and gather the information necessary to determine the amount of settlement checks, they should simultaneously create files that enable others to understand the claim, including the cause and amount of loss. All pertinent information should be in the file. Insurers need complete and accurate claim files to justify settlement payments, to audit claim procedures and claim-handling quality, and to transfer cases among adjusters. State insurance regulators and reinsurers are also interested in complete and accurate claim files.

Sometimes an adjuster's actions can cause the insurer to relinquish its rights unintentionally. The following section emphasizes the importance of documentation in preventing the relinquishment of the insurer's rights.

Avoiding Waiver and Estoppel

Waiver is the voluntary and intentional relinquishment of a right, and it can be expressed explicitly or implied by conduct. **Estoppel** is also a relinquishment of a right but results when someone's words or behavior cause another to rely, to his or her detriment, on those words or behavior. Estoppel bars the first party from asserting any rights inconsistent with his or her words or behavior. Estoppel can result from a waiver but can also be based on thoughtless, unintentional action on which the other party relies.

An adjuster's words and actions can cause waiver and estoppel of the insurer's rights. Although insurance policies require the insurer's written approval before they can be altered or amended, courts invariably deem adjusters to be agents of insurers with the power (if not the authority) to waive contractual conditions. Therefore, an adjuster's words and behavior can undo policy requirements. The most significant way in which adjusters can cause waiver and estoppel is by continuing to adjust a claim *after* a coverage problem has been discovered. A court can consider such behavior a waiver, or the policyholder might rely on such behavior, leading to estoppel.

Adjusters avoid the problems of waiver and estoppel with nonwaiver agreements or with reservation of rights letters. Exhibits 9-2 and 9-3 show a general nonwaiver agreement and a reservation of rights letter, respectively. In each of these documents, the insurer clearly indicates that nothing it does (through the adjuster) in handling the claim is intended as a waiver of any of the insurer's rights.

The general nonwaiver agreement is used whenever little is known about the loss and the adjuster wants to investigate without compromising the insurer's rights. The reservation of rights letter accomplishes the same objectives as the general nonwaiver agreement and also tells the policyholder about any specific problems, such as property or causes of loss that appear not to be covered or the policyholder's failure to perform any duties after a loss or to comply with other policy conditions. A reservation of rights letter has the same content as a nonwaiver agreement. It is sent (usually by certified mail) to the policyholder as a letter, usually when the policyholder refuses to sign a nonwaiver. Assuming that proof of receipt by the policyholder can be shown, a reservation of rights letter is as effective as a nonwaiver agreement. Once a determination has been made that the loss is covered, the reservation of rights letter is rescinded.

Once either a nonwaiver agreement or a reservation of rights letter has been issued, the adjuster must promptly resolve the coverage issue and must inform the policyholder. Should the adjuster fail to resolve the coverage issue and

Waiver
The voluntary and intentional relinquishment of a known right by an insurer that results in estoppel.

Estoppel
The principle that prevents the insurer from asserting a right that it has already waived.

EXHIBIT 9-2

Nonwaiver Agreement

Policy of insurance number _____HO 302 7648_____ was issued to ___Michael Doe___
by ___IIA Insurance Company___ to cover the period from___7-1-X7___ to ___7-1-X6___.
Coverage under this policy of insurance has been requested for an occurrence that took
place on _____12-21-X6_____ at _____Malvern, PA_____ . A dispute has arisen
about whether there is insurance coverage under the policy to protect___Michael Doe___
for any liability that is a result of the reported occurrence. The reason for the question of
coverage is _whether water damage was caused by repeated seepage._

Nevertheless, ___Leonard Phillips___ _____requests_____ that the
IIA Insurance Company investigate, negotiate, settle, deny, or defend any
claim or suit arising out of such accident or occurrence as it deems necessary.
IIA Insurance Company agrees to proceed with such handling of this case
only on condition that such action taken will not waive any right the Insurer may have to
deny any obligation under the policy contract, or be considered an admission of any
liability on the part of the company. It is further agreed that such action will not waive
any rights of the insured.

There may be other reasons for which coverage does not apply. We do not waive our right
to deny coverage for any other valid reason that may arise.

Nothing in this agreement precludes ___Leonard Phillips___ from retaining personal
counsel for his or her own protection.

Either party to this agreement may at any time terminate the agreement upon notice in
writing and proceed under his or her own unrestricted rights.

Signed this _____4th_____ day of _____May_____, 20_X7_ .

Jane Wilson	_Michael Doe_
Witness	Insured
	Additional Insured
Mary Harris	IIA Insurance Company
Witness	Insurance Company

BY: _____**John Davis**_____
For the Company

EXHIBIT 9-3

Reservation of Rights Letter

_____5/8_____ , 20 _X2___

TO: RE: Insured: Ruth Andrews

Claimant:

Date of Loss:

Policy Number:

We have received notice of an occurrence that took place at __Malvern, PA__ on
___4-1-X2_____. As a result of this occurrence, coverage has been requested under
policy number __BOP 5612112___, which was issued to
_____Ruth's Country Kitchen_____ by _____IIA Insurance Company_____.
There is a question whether coverage under the policy applies to this occurrence.

The nature of the coverage question is as follows:___whether it was lightning_____
___that caused the air-conditioning unit to fail_____.

_____IIA Insurance Company_____ will continue to handle this claim even
though a coverage question exists. However, no act of any company representative while
investigating, negotiating settlement of the claim, or defending a lawsuit shall be
construed as waiving any Company rights. The Company reserves the right, under the
policy, to deny coverage to you or anyone else claiming coverage under the policy.

There may be other reasons for which coverage does not apply. We do not waive our right
to deny coverage for any other valid reason that may arise.

You may wish to discuss this matter with your own attorney. In any event, we would
be pleased to answer any questions you might have concerning our position as
outlined in this letter.

Very truly yours,

_____IIA Insurance Company_____
Insurance Company

BY_____*John Davis*_____
For the Company

proceed to settle the claim, the claim payment constitutes a waiver and the insurer is estopped from raising the coverage issues again.

Determining Salvage Value and Subrogation Rights

Claim adjusters can minimize the insurer's losses by salvage and subrogation activities. Whenever an insurer pays the insured the full value of personal property that has suffered a loss, the insurer is entitled to take ownership of the property and can subsequently resell it. Any amount realized in the sale reduces the cost of the claim. Taking the salvage value of property that has been "totaled" is the insurer's option. The policyholder cannot require the insurer to pay full value for damaged property and then take over the salvage. Claim adjusters do not reduce the amount of a loss settlement because of the value of "expected" salvage. Instead, if salvage value is apparent, insurers usually pay full value to the insured and handle the salvage themselves.

Ordinarily, adjusters do not directly market salvage. They either sell or consign the property to professional salvage companies. The markets for salvaged property are specialized, variable, and irregular. Even insurers that frequently sell property salvageable from their losses find that they cannot compete in salvage markets. Salvage companies typically sell property on consignment for expenses incurred plus a percentage commission.

Salvors can provide more services to insurers than just selling damaged goods. They are expert in protecting and inventorying property. In certain situations when insureds want to sell the damaged property, a salvor can advise the insurer about the percentage of value remaining in the property. In those situations, the insurer settles the claim for the value of the property less its remaining salvage value. Insureds accept such settlements when they are confident that their efforts can realize more value from a "fire sale" than could the efforts of anyone else.

An insurer might have subrogation rights when a party other than the policyholder is responsible for causing the loss. When an insurer pays an insured for a loss under a policy, the insurer is substituted (subrogated) for the insured and obtains the insured's rights against any responsible party. Handling a claim involving potential subrogation is no different for an adjuster than handling any other claim, except that the adjuster must be especially thorough in establishing and documenting the cause of loss and might put the responsible party on notice of the liability claim.

If the responsible party has liability insurance and the two insurers cannot agree on a settlement amount, a subrogation claim is likely to be handled through the nationwide arbitration system operated by Arbitration Forums, Inc. Although this agreement applies only to claims between signatory parties and amounts of $100,000 or less, the agreement keeps many claims out of court. Settlements under this agreement are fair and are far less expensive than court settlements. Naturally, the claim adjusters for the two involved insurers can negotiate a settlement before arbitration.

When an insurer obtains an amount through subrogation efforts, it must first pay the attorney fees and other expenses of subrogation and then reimburse the insured for any deductible or any other amount of loss not covered. The insurer receives what is left.

ADJUSTING SPECIFIC TYPES OF PROPERTY CLAIMS

The rest of this chapter examines the challenges of adjusting losses for damage to particular types of property. Specific types of property loss claims raise specific issues. What is important in adjusting claims for residential structures may be unimportant when settling claims for common carriers, and vice versa.

Residential Dwelling Claims

Probably no job in the property-casualty insurance industry is more important or more rewarding than adjusting losses to people's homes. Protecting people from the financial and emotional devastation that can follow the destruction of a home is perhaps the insurance industry's most important task.

Adjusters handling losses to homes have two goals: (1) to address the policyholder's concerns and (2) to enforce policy provisions and protect the insurer's rights. Generally, little conflict exists between these goals, provided the loss is not suspicious and the adjuster and policyholder continually communicate and cooperate.

Of all the reported structure fires in the U.S., 56 percent involved dwelling property, as indicated in Exhibit 9-4. This percentage does not include fires in other residential structures such as apartment buildings, hotels or motels, college dormitories, or boarding houses. While dwelling forms cover many other causes of loss, fire is one of the major causes of loss for this type of insurance.

Insured's Concerns

Fortunately, most insureds who suffer a loss to their home have never experienced such a loss before. However, as a result, the emotional trauma of seeing their home damaged is compounded by uncertainty and anxiety about their insurance and the loss adjustment process. Many policyholders fear that an inadvertent error on their part might somehow void their coverage.

Following a serious loss to a home, an adjuster's three priorities should be:

1. Ensuring the physical safety of the policyholder's family
2. Ensuring the safety and security of the damaged home and its contents to prevent further damage
3. Explaining the coverage and adjustment procedure to the policyholder

EXHIBIT 9-4

Structure Fires by Type of Use, 2000[1]

Property	Estimated Number of Fires	Percent Change From 1999	Property Loss[2] ($ millions)	Percent Change From 1999
Public assembly	15,000	−6.3%	$ 365	−11.4%
Educational	7,000	−17.7	108	52.1
Institutional	7,000	−12.5	20	−13.0
Residential (total)	379,500	−0.9	5,674	11.4
One- and two-family dwellings[3]	283,500	0.4	4,639	12.5
Apartments	84,500	−4.5	886	5.2
Other[4]	11,500	−4.2	149	17.3
Stores and offices	23,500	−17.5	587	−10.9
Industry, utility, defense[5]	15,000	−14.3	778	−43.4
Storage in structures	33,000	−8.3	694	3.4
Special structures	25,500	0.0	275	47.1
Total	**505,500**	**−3.3%**	**$8,501**	**0.1%**

1. Estimates based on data reported by fire departments responding to the 2000 National Fire Experience Survey. May not include reports from all fire departments.

2. Includes direct property loss to contents, structures, vehicles, machinery, vegetation, or any other property involved in a fire. Does not include indirect losses, such as business income or temporary shelter costs.

3. Includes manufactured homes.

4. Includes hotels and motels, college dormitories, boarding houses, etc.

5. Does not include incidents handled only by private brigades or fixed suppression systems.

Source: National Fire Protection Association

Reprinted with permission from *The Fact Book 2002* (New York: Insurance Information Institute, 2002), p. 93.

Should doubts about coverage exist, the adjuster can issue a reservation of rights letter and can begin to address these priorities immediately.

Sometimes policyholders escape from their burning home with nothing but the clothes on their backs, which might be pajamas. An adjuster who deals with the insured at such a time can provide reassurance that the coverage extends to living expenses and replacement of personal property and can issue an advance on the settlement amount on the spot.

The insurance policy requires the insured to protect the property from further loss, yet the policyholder might be unsure about what that means. The adjuster should advise the policyholder of what is necessary and should recognize that such advice is equivalent to authorization of any attendant expense. Following a serious loss, the policyholder must usually turn off all utilities, drain all plumbing, secure or board up windows and doors to keep out vandals and trespassers, and secure tarpaulins or plastic sheets over any roof or wall openings to keep out the elements. Policyholders can do this work themselves or can hire contractors.

Once the insured's family and property are secure, the adjuster should thoroughly explain the coverage and the adjustment procedure and should answer any questions. This communication should take place at the first contact with the policyholder after the loss. For example, the adjuster should immediately communicate the existence of coverage for living expenses and emphasize the importance of the insured's good faith compliance with policy conditions. The adjuster should address policyholder questions. The policyholder should know what he or she should do the next day, the next week, and the next month.

Additional Living Expense

In the time immediately following a loss to a residence, policyholders appreciate additional living expense coverage because it helps to normalize their condition by paying for increased living expense after a loss.

The adjuster explains the scope of additional living expense and emphasizes to policyholders that they must obtain and keep receipts. Furthermore, although it is best to have receipts for everything, the policyholder must understand that compensation is only for *additional* living expense. Most policyholders can quickly grasp that normal living expenses for which they would be responsible even without the loss are not compensable. The adjuster explains that coverage is limited to the policyholder's normal standard of living. Policyholders should be encouraged to check with the adjuster before making a doubtful expenditure.

The insured's residence must be uninhabitable (because of a covered loss) before additional living expense coverage is available. Fortunately, most losses are small. With large (total) losses, the inhabitability of a residence is obvious. With other losses, whether a home is inhabitable might be harder to judge. Adjusters can best answer this question by asking themselves whether they would expect their own family to live in a place damaged as badly as the insured's home. The stench of smoke might make a home uninhabitable, at least until it can be ventilated or fumigated. The loss of just a refrigerator or a stove probably does not make a home uninhabitable, but loss of an entire kitchen or a sole bathroom probably would. Loss of a furnace (during a cold season) or a water heater would likewise probably make a home uninhabitable.

Contractors

Damage to the policyholder's home is adjusted based on estimates. The insurance policy obligates the insured to provide proof of damages. Contractors engaged by the insured should prepare detailed estimates that clearly show specifications, material costs, hours, and costs of labor, and additional expenses such as overhead, permits, and demolition and debris removal. Estimates that show only grand-total costs or trade-by-trade total costs are not suitable for claim settlements because it is impossible to see how such estimates differ from other estimates and to negotiate those differences.

Most adjusters prefer to negotiate differences in estimates directly with contractors because these individuals routinely handle construction issues. Estimates are likely to differ regarding specification of the work to be done, quality of materials, or hours of labor. Once the quality and hours have been specified, the costs of materials and labor can be determined.

Some insurers allow adjusters to recommend contractors to policyholders. Such recommendation helps policyholders who might otherwise not know honest, competent contractors who are interested in insurance repair work. However, making such recommendations creates some real dangers for the insurer. The policyholder might interpret the adjuster's recommendation as a guarantee that the contractor's estimate will be accepted or that its work will be good. Furthermore, some insurers fear that allowing adjusters to make recommendations might lead to the adjusters' receiving kickbacks and gratuities from contractors.

Some contractors treat estimating for insurance repairs differently from other estimating. They regard the work as more difficult or more complicated because it requires removing damaged sections and rebuilding. If all damaged property can be removed, estimating insurance repairs is identical to estimating new construction. Occasionally, if damage restricts or prevents access to property that needs repair, additional repair time and expense might be justified. Sometimes smoke, fire, and water damage might be hidden, which might also justify additional time and expense.

Restoration and Cleaning Services

Initially, many losses, especially losses caused by smoke and water damage, look far worse than they actually are. Although many types of water damage are not covered, water damage resulting from fire-fighting activity is covered (under the fire cause of loss) and is often a significant problem. Both smoke and water can cause increasingly worse damage to property the longer they remain untreated. Furthermore, smoke and water cause little or no damage to certain types of property if they are quickly removed. Professional cleaning and restoration services are available for such removal.

Although the adjuster can take an "arm's-length" approach to the policyholder's selection of a contractor, the adjuster must quickly become involved in hiring a professional cleaning and restoration service. Adjusters and insurers typically have contacts with such services, so they can quickly be used at the scene of a loss. The adjuster agrees on a price with the service providers and obtains the policyholder's authorization for those providers to begin work immediately. Rapid work by such services can save a great deal of property, minimize additional living expense, and reduce repair costs. Sometimes, cleaning alone is sufficient when early observations might have indicated that repainting would be necessary, or repainting alone is sufficient when it was thought replacement would be necessary.

Residential Personal Property Claims

Claims for loss to residential personal property present adjusters with some difficult challenges. Frequently, proof that the property existed and that it was lost is scarce. Evaluation is difficult to do with any confidence or accuracy. Finally, the dollar amount of such claims is frequently small, so the adjuster must constantly be aware of the adjustment costs relative to the value of the damaged property.

Inventory

Damaged personal property is usually available for the adjuster's inspection unless fire or theft caused the loss. Unfortunately, fire and theft are two of the most common causes of loss affecting personal property. Even when personal property is burned beyond recognition or is stolen, the insured must prepare an inventory.

Most homeowners do not have written records of their personal property. Few people can even provide an accurate account of all the clothes they own. Often they cannot remember where or when various items were bought. Despite the often minimal evidence of personal property, adjusters cannot refuse to settle such claims. Most people own a collection of personal property that is consistent with their income and lifestyle. An adjuster does not deny a claim for a reasonable inventory of personal property just because the policyholder could not provide documentation. Large purchases can often be documented by bank statements or credit card bills. Personal photographs might show the policyholder's home and furnishings in the background. In most instances, the adjuster can jog the policyholder's memory by going through a checklist of types of property. Included in such a checklist might be major furniture in each room; clothes (by category) for each person in the household; drapes; rugs; towels and linens; kitchen appliances and utensils; food and liquor; pots and pans; dishes; televisions; radios; stereo equipment; tapes and compact discs; telephones; power tools and hand tools; gardening equipment; office supplies and books; home computers; toys; framed pictures and art objects; sports equipment; bicycles; firearms; and jewelry.

Depreciation

Homeowners generally can produce no better evidence of their property's depreciation than of its existence. Sometimes they can remember where they made major purchases, and those stores might have exact records to provide evidence of purchase dates.

In the absence of specific evidence of the age or condition of property, certain assumptions can be made. Clothes wear out and are subject to fashion obsolescence at a predictable rate. Carpets become threadbare after a certain number of years. Kitchen appliances have a limited lifespan; kitchen utensils and pots and pans last longer. Major furniture can last a long time if it is not subject to abuse and is of classic styling. Policyholders and adjusters can usually agree on reasonable assumptions.

Depreciating items of property by groups, such as clothing, kitchen utensils, books, and children's toys, is undesirable, but might be necessary when the property cannot be inspected. Whenever the property is available for inspection, an item-by-item determination of depreciation should be possible.

Sublimits

The adjuster should explain the rationale of sublimits: some property is especially vulnerable to theft (for example, cash, jewelry, and firearms), and large coverage limits for such property would greatly increase the exposure to loss and the insurance premium. Other property (boats, valuable papers, and business property) is often covered by specialized policies. The adjuster could recommend that in the future the policyholder consider increasing coverage limits for that property.

Applying special sublimits is usually straightforward. A typical homeowners policy has numerous sublimits for specific types of property, such as cash, precious stones and jewelry, and firearms. Adjusters should first apply the deductible to any amount of the loss that is not covered because it exceeds a sublimit. For example, an insured with a $100 sublimit for cash and a $100 deductible who has lost $500 cash would recover only $100, and the deductible should not apply any further. The $400 loss in excess of the sublimit is more than sufficient to absorb the deductible. Although insurance policies do not explicitly require this approach, it is regarded among adjusters as a good and proper practice.

Scheduled Property

When the policyholder has special coverage for individual items of property, the adjuster often has more loss settlement flexibility than with ordinary personal property.

Individual property usually gets scheduled coverage because it is valuable, and the policyholder wants the broader causes of loss or risks of direct physical loss typically associated with scheduled items. Scheduled coverage usually identifies the property precisely. Consequently, the adjuster can contact merchants and appraisers who specialize in such property to determine whether it can be repaired, whether it can be replaced through a secondary market, how much its value has decreased because of a loss, and whether the insurer can buy at discount. Jewelry, camera equipment, and firearms are the types of property for which the insurer is likely to exercise its "repair or replace" option, because the insurer might be able to buy an exact replacement for less than the policyholder originally paid. The high value of these items also makes repair far more feasible than for lower-value property.

Commercial Structure Claims

Adjusting claims for losses to commercial structures is usually limited to highly skilled and experienced adjusters because the value of commercial structures can easily reach millions of dollars. Additionally, experienced adjusters are needed to deal with complex issues such as alternative methods of property repair and the value of depreciated property. Rarely can an adjuster handle losses to commercial structures without expert assistance. Investigating arson and considering the loss of use coverage for commercial structures is also more complex than for residential dwellings.

Architects and Contractors

Adjusters with substantial experience and expertise in estimating residential losses are not necessarily able to estimate losses for commercial structures. Construction principles, methods, materials, and available contractors are different for commercial structures. The adjuster usually must employ an architect to develop building specifications. The architect's fee is a legitimate element of the loss when architectural services are necessary.

Architectural plans dating from the building's construction are often still available. Those plans can provide valuable information about a building's details if a serious loss has occurred. They can also serve as the basis of reconstruction of the destroyed building. Even with such plans, the adjuster might have to hire another architect to identify changes in building codes or to design alternatives to obsolete construction features and building techniques. An architect can develop precise cost estimates or can hire professional estimators to do so.

Local contractors might not be adequate for reconstructing certain commercial structures. They might lack sufficient expertise, equipment, or staff for a large or complicated structure. The insured or his or her architect might have to solicit bids from contractors throughout the region or the country. The adjuster cannot necessarily settle the claim based on the lowest bid for the work. The low bidder might be lowest because the contractor's lack of experience caused a faulty estimate. The adjuster should choose the lowest bidder who is both responsible and capable. The architect can help the adjuster identify which bidders meet those criteria.

The adjuster must remember that the insurer's duty is to settle the claim with the policyholder, not to engage a contractor to perform the actual reconstruction. Soliciting bids from contractors is done to help the adjuster evaluate the loss. Only the insured should enter into contracts for the construction work.

Property's Actual Cash Value

The value of commercial structures is more variable than that of residences. Additionally, commercial structures are more likely than residences to significantly depreciate because of factors other than wear and tear.

The principle of supply and demand determines the value of a commercial structure. A portion of a structure's value depends on the profit a business derives from its use, or demand. The remainder of the structure's value depends on the cost of rebuilding that structure or of obtaining an alternative location, or supply. When demand is strong and supply is low, the value of commercial structures rises significantly. Alternatively, when demand is weak and supplies are high, values decline.

The demand for commercial structures fluctuates with the overall economy and with business conditions in particular industries. The more specialized a building is, the more the demand for its use parallels economic conditions in a particular industry. For example, the value of an auto assembly plant corresponds more to the demand for autos than to the value of other commercial structures.

The supply of commercial structures is characterized by frequent shortages and oversupplies. This phenomenon is caused by the amount of time required to build commercial structures. In times of shortage, buildings are planned that might not be completed until an oversupply of similar buildings exists.

An adjuster evaluating the actual cash value at the time of loss of a commercial structure must consider market conditions. The market might be such that the replacement cost of a structure has appreciated significantly since the structure was built. If so, the insured should be compensated appropriately. Alternatively, the value of a structure might have depreciated significantly.

Although commercial structures experience wear and tear, other significant causes of depreciation exist. Commercial structures are more susceptible than residences to economic and technological obsolescence. For example, an old warehouse might still be useful but less desirable than a new warehouse because its floor space is divided by pillars, its lighting is inadequate, its access roads and parking lots are in poor condition, its loading dock is not well designed, and its heating and ventilation are obsolete. Though still in use, the older, obsolete structure has far less value per square foot than a new structure. This difference is usually easy to document through commercial realtors. Realtors can quote the likely rental values of an old property and a new property. The difference in rental rates is a good gauge of depreciation.

The extent of depreciation a policyholder has taken in its financial records is irrelevant. Because financial depreciation reduces taxes, policyholders take it as fast as the tax laws allow. Therefore, most buildings have less actual depreciation than the amount recorded in the policyholder's financial records.

Problems With Mortgagee

The variability of the value is more of a problem for commercial structures than for residential dwellings. Commercial mortgage agreements usually make the mortgage amount completely due and payable upon the destruction of the structure. During depressed markets for commercial properties, mortgagees might see an insurance claim as their most likely chance of being paid the remaining mortgage. Therefore, the mortgagee might resist the owner's desire to rebuild the structure and want to be paid in full.

The adjuster cannot resolve this problem because it is between the structure's owner and the mortgagee. The adjuster must put the names of both the owner and the mortgagee on the claim settlement check and keep both parties advised of the settlement. Beyond these actions, the adjuster has no obligation to either party.

Contamination and Pollution Cleanup

Serious losses at commercial structures, especially at manufacturing and storage sites, might result in contamination and pollution. Adjusters should be concerned about such losses for three reasons.

First, the adjuster's own health and safety might be at risk from exposure to pollutants at the loss site. Firefighters might be obligated to notify the Environmental Protection Agency (EPA) or state environmental agencies of contaminated loss sites. When such agencies are involved, the adjuster should avoid the site until notified that entry is safe.

Second, the coverage for pollution cleanup is extremely limited in most policies. The adjuster must be familiar with these limitations and communicate them to the insured. Nevertheless, pollution caused by a covered cause of loss is often covered.

Third, the adjuster should have contacts with specialized technical services that can help the policyholder to decontaminate a site. The adjuster should not recommend such a service unless its cost is covered or unless the insured provides clear acknowledgment (preferably in writing) of being responsible for such costs. Although these technical services are expensive, they can often devise solutions that might be more practical, less expensive, and faster than EPA solutions.

Arson Investigation

As for a residential dwelling, the adjuster must prove three things to establish arson with a commercial structure: (1) incendiary fire, (2) motive, and (3) opportunity. As with suspected residential arsons, the incendiary fire can be proved by an origin and cause expert, and the insured's opportunity, investigated by an SIU. The only difference with commercial structures is that they have a higher rate of incendiary fires not caused by arson.

The main focus in cases of suspected arson to commercial structures is on the policyholder's motive. Such motive is almost always economic. Economic motive might exist even for a structure used regularly, provided the policyholder would be better off financially with the insurance settlement and vacant real estate. Usually in cases of suspected arson, the insured structure is owned by a failing business in need of cash. Such need can be established by having an accountant examine the policyholder's financial records. Indeed, considering the seriousness of the matter and the amount of money at stake, an adjuster should not consider asserting an arson defense without a solid accounting report that establishes motive.

Business Income Claims

Adjusters regard business income claims as highly complex. Proper settlement of these cases requires detailed analysis of and considerable speculation about extensive financial records. Nevertheless, adjusters can organize and simplify their task by concentrating on three issues and reminding themselves that the ultimate effect of a business income settlement is to put policyholders in essentially the same financial position they would have been in without their losses. The three issues are:

1. Identifying the best loss settlement approach
2. Determining business income loss
3. Determining the period of restoration

Identifying the Best Loss Settlement Approach

Business income claims can be settled prospectively or retrospectively. **Prospective settlements** are those made before the property has been repaired. **Retrospective settlements** are those made after the property has been repaired and the policyholder has resumed operations.

Prospective settlements
Settlements made before property has been repaired.

Retrospective settlements
Settlements made after property has been repaired and the policyholder has resumed operations.

Prospective settlements are desirable when the insured does not intend to repair the property or intends to make significant alterations. The policyholder can request a prospective settlement and is not required to wait until the property is repaired and operations resume to conclude the settlement. Provided the policyholder and the adjuster agree on all relevant loss data, settlement can be made immediately.

Nevertheless, retrospective settlements are probably more common. Once the property has been repaired and the policyholder has resumed operations, the amount of time taken to make repairs and the expenses incurred during the interruption are known. Furthermore, during the interruption of business, the policyholder is probably so preoccupied with reopening that the business income loss settlement becomes a secondary concern. Unfortunately, disagreeing about what the period of restoration *should* have been is more likely with retrospective settlements. Insurance covers only the time in which repairs *should* be made, not necessarily the amount of time taken to complete the repairs.

Determining Business Income Loss

Current ISO forms define "business income" as essentially net profit (or loss) plus continuing normal operating expenses. Business income is most easily understood when placed within the framework of business accounting.

A business determines its profit (or loss) by subtracting its expenses from its revenue. Revenue consists mainly of sales. Expenses consist of the cost to acquire the goods the business sells plus all other costs. For retailers, the cost of goods is called "cost of goods sold" and represents the cost to the retailers of acquiring goods from their suppliers. For manufacturers, the cost of goods is their own manufacturing cost.

Excerpts from the Business Income Report/Work Sheet for a manufacturer are shown in Exhibit 9-5. A business that completes this work sheet can determine the likely amount of its business income. This amount can be understood as either (1) revenue minus cost of goods sold minus operating expenses that discontinue or as (2) net profit (or loss) plus operating expenses that continue. These two amounts should be equivalent. Typically, both claim adjusters and policyholders find it easier to approach a loss settlement with the former definition: revenue minus cost of goods and discontinued expenses.

The adjuster cannot directly use the Business Income Report/Work Sheet to settle a claim. This work sheet lists projected amounts, and the claim should be settled based on actual loss data. Using the actual loss principle might seem to conflict with the prospective approach to settlement. For a prospective settlement, the adjuster and the insured make new projections of what the insured loss of business income is likely to be for the expected period of restoration. Any actual experience that has developed since the policyholder completed the work sheet should be used to make the best projection of the actual loss of business income.

Determining the Period of Restoration

The "period of restoration" is the time starting seventy-two hours after the loss and ending when the repairs should be complete. This period is so defined to compel the insured to make repairs and resume operations with due diligence and to allow for settlement when the insured neither makes repairs nor resumes operations.

The time in which repairs should be made can be determined by consulting with the contractors hired to do the work. Adjusters must remember that any such estimate from a contractor, even if made in good faith, is still an estimate. Contractors cannot control weather, interruptions in the availability of supplies or of subcontractors, or subcontractor behavior.

Many adjusters and insureds prefer to settle business income claims only after the repairs have been completed. However, at that point, the adjuster and insured might disagree over whether the insured used due diligence to

EXHIBIT 9-5

Business Income Report/Work Sheet

Business Income Report/Work Sheet
Financial Analysis
(000 omitted)

Income and Expenses	12 Month Period Ending 12/31/X4		Estimated for 12 Month Period Beginning 4/1/X5	
	Manufacturing	Non-Manufacturing	Manufacturing	Non-Manufacturing
A. Gross Sales	$ 10,050	$ _____	$ 10,350	$ _____
B. Deduct: Finished Stock Inventory (at sales value) at Beginning ...	– 500	XXXXXX	– 550	XXXXXX
....	9,550	XXXXXX	9,800	XXXXXX
C. Add: Finished Stock Inventory (at sales value) at End	+ 533	XXXXXX	+ 480	XXXXXX
D. Gross Sales Value of Production	$ 10,083	XXXXXX	$ 10,280	XXXXXX
E. Deduct:				
Prepaid Freight—Outgoing	– 0	– _____	– 0	– _____
Returns & Allowances	– 20	– _____	– 21	– _____
Discounts	– 30	– _____	– 32	– _____
Bad Debts	– 25	– _____	– 27	– _____
Collection Expenses	– 0	– _____	– 0	– _____
F. Net Sales		$ _____		$ _____
Net Sales Value of Production	$ 10,008		$ 10,200	
G. Add: Other Earnings from your business operations (not investment income or rents from other properties):				
Commissions or Rents	+ 0	+ _____	+ 0	+ _____
Cash Discounts Received	+ 0	+ _____	+ 0	+ _____
Other	+ 10	+ _____	+ 15	+ _____
H. Total Revenues	$ 10,018	$ _____	$ 10,215	$ _____

Copyright, ISO Commercial Risk Services, Inc., 1994   **CP 15 15 06 95** ☐

Continued on next page.

Income and Expenses	12 Month Period Ending 12/31/X4		Estimated for 12 Month Period Beginning 4/1/X5	
	Manufacturing	Non-Manufacturing	Manufacturing	Non-Manufacturing
Total Revenues (Line **H.** from previous page)	$ 10,018	$ _____	$ 10,215	$ _____
I. Deduct:				
Cost of goods sold (see next page for instructions)	– 5,725	– _____	– 5,900	– _____
Cost of services purchased from outsiders (not your employees) to resell, that do not continue under contract	– 0	– _____	– 0	– _____
Power, heat and refrigeration expenses that do not continue under contract (if **CP 15 11** is attached)	– N/A	XXXXXX	– N/A	XXXXXX
All ordinary payroll expenses or the amount of payroll expense excluded (if **CP 15 10** is attached)	– N/A	– _____	– N/A	– _____
Special deductions for mining properties (see next page for instructions)	– N/A	– _____	– N/A	– _____
J.1. Business Income exposure for 12 months	$ 4,293	_____	4,315	_____
J.2. Combined (firms engaged in manufacturing & non-manufacturing operations)	$ _____		$ _____	

The figures in **J.1.** or **J.2.** represent 100% of your actual and estimated Business Income exposure for 12 months.

K. Additional Expenses:

1. Extra Expenses—form **CP 00 30** only (expenses incurred to avoid or minimize & to continue operations) .... $ _____ $ _____

2. Extended Business Income and Extended Period of Indemnity—form **CP 00 30** or **CP 00 30** (loss of Business Income following resumption of operations, up to 30 days or the no. of days selected under Extended Period of Indemnity option) .... + _____   + _____

3. Combined (all amounts in **K.1.** and **K.2.**)... $ _____

complete the work. Generally, adjusters do not penalize policyholders for delays caused by factors beyond their control. Adjusters also do not penalize the policyholder for any delays caused by the settlement of the property damage claim. Delays in settling the underlying claim could be caused by the policyholder, the adjuster, or both.

Extra Expense

Claims for extra expense can be settled only retrospectively. For extra expenses to be covered, they must be incurred to avoid or minimize the suspension of business. For example, a retailer might lease a temporary selling location to maintain sales. The policyholder could profit if the adjuster paid extra expense based on projections. Also, the adjuster cannot adequately monitor whether the insured used the payment appropriately or simply pocketed it.

Extra expense might also be incurred to repair damaged property and is covered *to the extent it reduces the business income claim*. The adjuster can authorize expedited construction methods or relatively expensive contractors if the business income loss is thereby reduced.

Use of Accountants

Probably no type of claim requires as much use of accounting assistance as business income claims. Most adjusters are not trained to analyze the hundreds of entries that record individual transactions of an ongoing business. Adjusters cannot review historic data and determine the policyholder's "normal" operating expenses.

Therefore, some accounting firms specialize in claim work. These firms already understand the policy coverages and can explain them to the policyholder's accountant. Adjusters find that business income claims run smoothly when one of these accounting firms is hired to work with the policyholder's accountant.

Merchandise Claims

Merchandise that the policyholder holds for sale is a special type of business personal property. Its valuation raises unique issues; it offers the best opportunities for salvage and use of salvor services, and its claims must be settled in special ways.

Merchandise Valuation

The replacement cost of merchandise is the policyholder's cost to replace that merchandise. The policyholder usually has ongoing relations with its suppliers and can provide accurate information about their prices. If the policyholder regularly obtains discounts from its suppliers, the effective cost to the policyholder is less than what appears on supplier invoices. Replacement cost of a manufacturer's finished goods is the costs of manufacture.

Actual cash value standards can be difficult to apply to merchandise. Often, the goods have not depreciated, and actual cash value is equivalent to replacement cost. Depreciation caused by ordinary wear and tear is uncommon, but many goods suffer "shop wear." They are picked over and handled by so many people that they are no longer presentable as first-quality goods.

Merchandise is also subject to significant depreciation caused by obsolescence. An adjuster can identify situations of obsolescence even if he or she is unfamiliar with the product. If, before the loss, the policyholder was offering the product to the public at a discounted price or had stopped offering it altogether, the product has likely suffered obsolescence. In fact, good accounting practice requires that the inventory value of merchandise be reduced whenever its listed retail price is reduced. The adjuster can note such an accounting approach by the policyholder and can cite it as justification for settling claims at the reduced inventory figure. Fashion changes, technological changes, and seasonal selling patterns can all cause an inventory to become obsolete. Insurance is not designed to reimburse for such loss of value.

Salvage

Other than vehicles, merchandise is the only significant source of salvage for the insurance industry. As previously explained, adjusters and insurers rarely try to sell salvaged merchandise themselves; they employ professional salvage firms.

Salvage proceeds from the sale of damaged merchandise can be significant. Some merchants refuse to deal in damaged goods, no matter how superficial the damage. These merchants refuse to consider a loss settlement based on a percentage of the goods' value because in those merchants' markets, the goods are "worthless." Adjusters find it easiest to settle with such merchants for 100 percent of the goods' value and to take the merchandise for salvage.

Professional salvage firms can act quickly to protect goods from further damage, inventory and separate goods, and give advice to adjusters about the likely amount of residual value in damaged goods.

Reporting Form Losses

Inventories of merchandise are often insured under reporting form policies that require the policyholder to submit regular reports of value. Adjusters who handle claims for such merchandise must know what to do when the policyholder underreports its values or fails to report the values promptly. The following rules are based on ISO's value reporting form.

Following a loss to merchandise insured under a value reporting form, the adjuster must determine the value of the policyholder's inventory as of the date of the last report. The adjuster is not concerned with the inventory's value on the date of loss unless the inventory is totaled. Inventory analysis for a past date might require an accountant's assistance. If the policyholder underreported its inventory's value, the policyholder cannot recover the full loss amount. The policyholder can recover only the percentage of the loss that is equal to the percentage of inventory value it reported.

If the policyholder fails to submit a report when due, then the loss adjustment is based on the last report submitted. The adjuster does not pay more than the amount last reported. This rule might penalize the policyholder. However, should the policyholder fail to submit even the first required report, the adjuster does not pay more than 75 percent of what would otherwise have been paid. Applying this latter rule always penalizes the policyholder.

Importance of Negotiation

Adjusters sometimes settle merchandise losses based on a percentage of its value. Under these settlements, the merchant keeps the merchandise and is reimbursed for its decreased value. The adjuster is not required to pay full value for the merchandise or to dispose of salvage. Adjusters should try to negotiate such settlements with policyholders because they are mutually beneficial.

For example, suppose that following a merchandise loss, the adjuster believes that salvage of the damaged merchandise would yield about 35 percent of its insured value. It is not unusual for the policyholder in such a situation to assume it could sell the merchandise for a much higher percentage of value, perhaps 55 percent. This assumption might be true because the policyholder is a merchant in the business and is already organized to sell such merchandise. On one hand, the adjuster could total the merchandise and sell it as salvage for a net loss of 65 percent. Alternatively, the adjuster could try to negotiate settlement with the policyholder for some percentage less than 65 percent. The policyholder might be willing to take as little as 45 percent, because the policyholder believes it can still realize 55 percent by selling the merchandise itself. Any settlement figure between 45 percent and 65 percent is therefore fair *to both parties*.

This situation is common in merchandise losses. Each party must assess the situation accurately to negotiate effectively. The adjuster can get advice from a salvor or can negotiate based on personal experience with similar losses. Sound negotiating by the adjuster does not necessarily disadvantage the policyholder. A policyholder, knowledgeable of the value of the merchandise, can refuse unfavorable settlement proposals. The policyholder can invoke the appraisal clause or can challenge the adjuster to total the merchandise and try to realize the salvage value that the adjuster claims still exists.

Transportation and Bailment Claims

Property is frequently in the possession of someone other than its owner. Losses to such property create complicated legal and insurance policy coverage issues. Adjusters might have to handle claims for either the property owner or the party in possession of the property. An adjuster must carefully review the coverage, the law, and the contracts between the parties in these situations.

The most common circumstances in which property is in the possession of someone other than its owner are transportation and bailment situations. Carriers such as trucking companies, railroads, and air freight companies are in the business of transporting other people's property. Bailments include situations in which owners entrust their property to bailees such as cleaners, repairers, and warehousers. Bailment relationships are contractual, and the applicable contracts can affect both legal liability and insurance coverage.

Insurance Coverages

Adjusters handling transportation and bailment claims must orient themselves to the applicable insurance policy. Insurance policies exist for both the owner and for the other party involved. Policies written for motor truck carriers, bailees, warehouse workers, and so on might provide certain coverage for other parties. So, adjusters might find themselves settling a claim for one party under a policy that names some other party as the insured. For example, an adjuster might settle losses under a dry cleaner's policy for the dry cleaner's customers rather than for the named insured—the dry cleaner.

Owner's policies typically provide limited coverage for property away from the insured location. Unfortunately, an owner's coverage is often inadequate. An adjuster handling an owner's claim should check for off-premises coverage. If such coverage is inadequate, the adjuster should quickly settle for the available coverage and place the carrier's or bailee's insurer on notice of the claim. Owner's policies typically have "no benefit to bailee" clauses. These clauses clearly indicate that the owner's coverage does not extend to the carrier or bailee and that the owner's insurer retains its right of subrogation. However, as discussed later, subrogation rights might be affected by agreement between the parties. An owner with predictable off-premises loss exposures should obtain special coverage under floater policies or shipper policies.

Policies for carriers and bailees typically protect the interests of both the owner and the carrier/bailee. An adjuster handling claims under a carrier/bailee policy must usually settle two claims arising out of the same property loss: the owner's and the carrier/bailee's. The carrier/bailee has an interest in the property to the extent of its earned fees. Additionally, the carrier/bailee might be legally liable to the owner for the property's return (the extent of a carrier/bailee's legal liability is discussed subsequently). A carrier/bailee's insurance policy that extends to liability for the owner's property requires the adjuster working for the carrier/bailee's insurer to settle the owner's claim. Most policies of this sort allow the adjuster to deal directly with the owner and also allow the insurer to defend the carrier/bailee against the owner's claim rather than to pay it. Some carrier/bailee policies protect the owner regardless of the carrier/bailee's legal liability. Such policies are purchased to maintain customer goodwill. Owners expect to be reimbursed for damage to their property without hairsplitting over legal liability. This quasi-first-party coverage allows the adjuster to deal immediately with the owner before conducting an investigation of legal liability.

Legal Liability

Even in the absence of agreement between the parties, the law specifies the carrier/bailee's extent of legal liability to the owner. Because the relationship between the owner and the carrier/bailee is contractual, the terms of the contract between the parties also affect legal liability between them.

In the absence of an agreement to the contrary, the law makes common carriers liable for damage to an owner's goods. The only exceptions to this liability are for acts of God, war, negligence of the shipper, exercise of public authority, and inherent vice of the goods. Carriers usually limit the dollar amount of their liability in their **bill of lading**, which is a receipt for the goods and a contract for transportation. A **released bill of lading** limits the carrier's liability to a specified dollar amount. Owners and shippers with large loss exposures must pay high insurance rates for the carrier's increased liability. Adjusters handling losses in shipment *must* review the applicable bill of lading.

Other bailees are generally liable to the owner only for their negligence. Should a loss occur without any negligence on the bailee's part, the owner must bear the loss. Therefore, owners with significant off-premises loss exposures must obtain special coverage. A bailee's coverage might not apply. As with a transportation contract, a bailment contract can modify the parties' respective legal rights. A bailment contract might limit the dollar amount of a bailee's liability or might make the bailee strictly liable. An adjuster handling an owner's claim against a bailee for legal liability must read and understand the bailment contract. To the extent that the bailee's liability is limited, so too is any coverage for the owner that is based on liability. Furthermore, the subrogation rights of the owner's insurer might be limited. Most property insurance policies allow the insured to waive subrogation before a loss occurs. An adjuster who has paid a claim under an owner's insurance might find that the insured/owner has waived the bailee's liability beyond a certain dollar amount. Such a waiver likewise limits the insurer's subrogation rights.

Bill of lading
A document that serves as a receipt for property being shipped and that may also contain the contract of carriage between the shipper and the carrier.

Released bill of lading
A bill of lading that limits the carrier's liability for cargo loss in return for charging a lower freight rate than would be charged for carrying the cargo subject to full valuation.

Crime Claims

Property losses caused by crime present a significant challenge to adjusters. The property in question is usually gone, along with the best evidence of the property's value. Adjusters handling such claims usually have a higher level of doubt and uncertainty than with other property claims.

On crime losses, the adjuster's most important duties are to verify the exact cause of loss, to verify the property's existence and value, and to investigate any fraud possibilities.

Verify Exact Cause

Because crime insurance is expensive, policy forms covering crime losses are narrowly focused. The policyholder should have just the form or forms needed for that insured's significant loss exposures. For example, under the ISO Crime Coverage Form, Insurance Agreement 3 provides broad coverage (theft, disappearance, or destruction) for only one category of property (money and securities), but Insuring Agreement 4 provides coverage for a broad category of property ("any tangible property other than money or securities") but only for two causes of loss (robbery of a custodian and safe burglary only).[4]

Once the adjuster has carefully determined the policyholder's coverage, he or she determines the exact cause of loss. The coverage forms provide crime definitions that indicate whether a particular loss is covered. For example, burglary, by definition, requires signs of forcible entry or exit. This requirement might not exist under a particular state's definition of burglary in its criminal code. Nevertheless, for coverage to apply to a loss, the cause must satisfy the policy definition.

The adjuster interviews and obtains statements from every party knowledgeable about the alleged crime. Although taking statements is not standard practice for ordinary property losses, it is for crime losses. A robbery victim should be asked to furnish a complete account of the incident. The person who discovered a burglary should be interviewed in depth. The scene of a reported burglary must be inspected. Most policies require the policyholder to report such crimes to the police, and the adjuster should obtain whatever report or investigation results the police prepare. Unfortunately, police in many high-crime areas spend little time and effort tracking down burglars and might not ever investigate the crime.

An essential aspect of an adjuster's investigation into a crime loss is to determine whether the theft was an inside job. "Theft" by the policyholder is not theft at all; it is fraud. Theft by employees is covered only under employee dishonesty (fidelity). For a burglary, the policy requirement of evidence of forcible entry or exit benefits the adjuster. In the absence of such evidence, the adjuster can deny the claim without necessarily accusing the insured or the insured's employees of fraud. For employee theft, the policyholder is usually suspicious of employee involvement and might have an idea about who is involved. Adjusters should not repeat unproved, slanderous accusations but should take statements from all suspects and then decide whether sufficient evidence exists to alert the police to likely suspects or whether to deny the claim.

Verify the Property's Existence and Value

An adjuster can find it difficult, but not impossible, to verify the existence and value of stolen property. Businesses should have inventory records indicating property quantity and value. Although inventory records are not perfect, they are usually fairly accurate. Many crime policies preclude using inventory records to prove the occurrence of a crime because inventory "shrinkage" is a widespread phenomenon usually caused by unrecorded sales, discarding of damaged merchandise, and employee pilferage. However, inventory records can be used as evidence of the stolen property's quantity and value.

If the adjuster is suspicious about the loss, then he or she can check with the policyholder's suppliers. These suppliers should have complete records on the types, quantities, and values of goods shipped to the policyholder. The adjuster can also check with suppliers to determine whether the policyholder has submitted false inventory data to the adjuster claiming receipt and presence of goods that never existed.

Investigate Fraud Possibilities

Adjusters tend to be suspicious of all crime losses. Nevertheless, legitimate crime losses are the norm, so unless the adjuster can develop evidence to the contrary, insured crime losses must be settled. The policyholder has a motive for fraud whenever its inventory is obsolete or not selling well. The adjuster should learn as much as possible about the policyholder's general business condition through credit reports, financial statements, and tax records. If those reports show deterioration in the policyholder's financial condition, the adjuster could consider the possibility that the claim is fraudulent.

Employees are often the best sources of evidence of policyholder fraud. Employees might witness the removal of property that is subsequently reported stolen or might be aware of irregularities in the policyholder's bookkeeping. An adjuster investigating a suspicious loss could contact employees at their homes, where they might feel more comfortable discussing questionable business practices.

Catastrophe Claims

Hurricanes, floods, tornadoes, earthquakes, and fires or explosions causing widespread damage affect entire communities. The insurance industry's role in helping communities recover from catastrophes represents the industry at its finest. Property adjusters respond to catastrophes, and their response includes pre-loss and post-loss planning.

Pre-Loss Planning

Claim departments would be overwhelmed by catastrophes if they did not plan for them. They must respond to catastrophes by having a sufficient number of adjusters in potential disaster areas while maintaining acceptable service throughout the rest of the country.

Certain areas of the United States, such as the Gulf and Atlantic coasts during hurricane season, are most likely to "host" disaster recovery teams. Claim offices in these areas should prepare kits that include forms, maps, telephone directories, temporary licenses, tape measures, clipboards, calculators, and anything else a visiting adjuster needs to operate on the road.

Although state insurance regulators vary as to how strictly they enforce licensing requirements following a catastrophe, every adjuster who is likely to be called into an area should be licensed.

The insurer's administrative departments must be prepared to rent office space; to have telephones, copy machines, desks, and other equipment installed; and to procure temporary living quarters and rented cars on short notice.

Local agents or the underwriting department must establish a system by which adjusters can confirm coverage simply and reliably.

Post-Loss Planning

Adjusters on "storm duty" must work long hours and be separated from their families and normal lives for long periods. Additionally, catastrophes cause the adjuster to modify normal claim adjusting procedures. Adjusters often pay claims with less documentation than usual. They might also reimburse the insured for the insured's own labor in cleaning up the property, a circumstance that is especially common following catastrophes. Claims that would normally require an in-person inspection might be handled by telephone.

Local agents should be familiar with the insurer's claim practices so they can advise policyholders on how to begin loss recovery. The agents should advise policyholders of what documentation they must maintain and what actions they should take immediately after a loss.

Contractors' services might be at a premium after a catastrophe. However, contractors from around the country flock to the disaster area to help mitigate the shortage. Policyholders should be advised to be very careful about to whom they release money. Unscrupulous persons might take advantage of people who are shocked, confused, and suddenly holding cash.

SUMMARY

Several questions must be answered about every property claim, and those questions form a framework for property claim adjusters to use for all kinds of property damage claims.

The first questions ask who has an insurable interest in the property and who is insured. The next questions ask what property is insured and at what location. Adjusters also need to know what causes of loss are provided under the insurance policy, the dollar amount of the loss, the insured's duties after a loss, and the procedures to be followed to settle the claim.

Although losses from fire and windstorm are fairly clear-cut, problems can arise from losses caused by water damage, collapse, theft, vandalism, gradual causes, ordinance or law, faulty construction, and intentional acts of the policyholder. Indirect losses are financial losses resulting from loss of income or extra expenses to remain in operation.

After determining that coverage is in order for the policyholder, the property, and the cause of loss, the adjuster must answer the question, What is the dollar amount of loss? Policies usually value property at replacement cost or actual cash value without specifying how the adjuster is to determine those amounts. Determining replacement cost is usually easier than determining actual cash value.

Every property insurance policy specifies duties the insured must perform after a loss. These duties include notifying the insurer of the loss, protecting the property from further loss, assisting the insurer with the loss adjustment process, providing proof of loss if required, and submitting to examination under oath if requested. Some policyholders hire public adjusters to handle the contractual duties imposed after a loss.

Loss adjustment procedures include determining the cause of loss, determining the amount of loss, and documenting the cause and amount of loss. Salvage and subrogation activities offer the adjuster an opportunity to minimize the insurer's losses.

Losses to commercial structures can easily reach millions of dollars. In those cases, adjusters often confer with architects and contractors to determine the value of a commercial structure and the extent of loss. Problems can arise with mortgagees. Serious losses at commercial structures can result in contamination and pollution. Suspected arson is also a concern.

Business income claims can be highly complex, and settlement often requires a detailed analysis of financial records by an accountant.

Merchandise that the policyholder holds for sale is a special type of business personal property. The valuation of merchandise for sale raises unique issues: it offers the best opportunities for salvage and the use of salvor services, and claims for it must be settled in special ways.

Transportation and bailment losses can create complicated legal and coverage issues. Adjusters might have to handle claims for either the owner or the party in possession of the property. A claim adjuster must carefully review the coverage, the law, and the contracts between the parties in these situations.

Property losses caused by crime are among the greatest challenges adjusters face. When handling crime losses, the adjuster's most important duties are to verify the exact cause of loss, to verify the property's existence and value, and to investigate any fraud possibilities.

Catastrophes—hurricanes, floods, tornadoes, earthquakes, fires, or explosions—can cause widespread damage that affects entire communities. The adjuster's response to these losses should include pre-loss and post-loss planning. The next chapter ends the discussion of the claim function by discussing how the claim adjusting process applies to liability claims.

CHAPTER NOTES

1. Homeowners 3—Special Form, HO 00 03 10 00, Insurance Services Office, Inc., 1999, p. 13.
2. Business and Personal Property Coverage Form, CP 00 10 04 02, Insurance Services Office, Inc., 2001, p. 10.
3. Barbara Bowers, "Shelter From the Storm," *Best's Review*, November 2002, p. 58.
4. Commercial Crime Coverage Form, CR 00 21 03 00, Insurance Services Office, Inc., 1998, p. 1.

Chapter 10

Direct Your Learning

Liability Claim Adjusting

After learning the content of this chapter, you should be able to:

■ Describe the steps in the liability claim adjusting process.

■ Explain how and why adjusters use negotiation and other settlement techniques in adjusting liability claims.

■ Describe the litigation process.

■ Describe the challenges of adjusting each of the following types of claims:

- Auto bodily injury liability claims

- Auto property damage claims

- Premises liability claims

- Operations liability claims

- Products liability claims

- Workers' compensation claims

- Professional liability claims

Develop Your Perspective

What are the main topics covered in the chapter?

Once coverage has been established, resolving liability claims depends on the law of liability and damages. The issues and challenges in handling specific types of liability are covered.

Examine the role of the law in settling liability claims.

- What skills must liability claim adjusters possess to perform their role effectively?

Why is it important to learn about these topics?

Liability claim adjusting requires distinctly different skills from those required for property claim adjusting. By understanding the differences, you can appreciate why insurance companies typically divide these functional responsibilities.

Contrast the skills required for property and liability claim adjusting.

- What diverse skills are required?
- How might an insurance organization develop a claim department that supports the skills required and the tasks to be accomplished?

How can you use what you will learn?

Consider the structure of the claim adjusting department in your own organization.

- What training, management, and support are provided?
- How might the structure be changed to facilitate the duties adjusters must perform?

Chapter 10

Liability Claim Adjusting

Liability claim adjusting differs so significantly from property claim adjusting that most insurer claim operations are organized separately into either property or liability coverage units. For personal insurers, liability claim adjusting might consist primarily of adjusting third-party auto, homeowners, or personal umbrella liability claims. Insurers servicing commercial customers might have the same claim department personnel adjust auto liability and general liability claims, while workers' compensation and auto physical damage claims are organized into separate units within the claim department. (Although workers' compensation is not a traditional liability-based coverage, workers' compensation claim adjusting is discussed in this chapter.)

Claim personnel usually specialize in adjusting property or liability insurance claims. Once coverage has been established, resolving liability claims depends more on determining legal liability and damages than on an insurance policy's terms. Legal liability and damages exist apart from insurance policy terms. Liability insurance policies protect the policyholder against the financial consequences of legal liability. Therefore, liability claim adjusters spend most of their time and effort investigating and evaluating the legal aspects of liability and damages and relatively less time than property claim adjusters enforcing and evaluating insurance policy terms.

In liability claims, the insured is not the person with the claim. The party with a liability claim *against* the insured is the claimant. This party is also referred to as the third party. The insurer has no contract with, and the liability adjuster has no contractual obligations to, the claimant. Although most insurers consider it to be both ethical and in their own best interests to deal with claimants promptly and responsively, the adjuster has more leeway in dealing with a third-party claimant than with the insured. Most insurance department regulations and market conduct studies, for example, are more solicitous of the interests of first-party insureds than of third-party claimants. Additionally, third-party claimants are more frequently represented by an attorney than are first-party insureds.

Liability claims include both property damage and bodily injury liability. Although liability claims for property damage exist, they represent a relatively minor percentage of the total dollars paid on all liability claims. The predominantly injury-oriented nature of liability claims distinguishes their settlement from property damage claim settlement. The evaluation of bodily injuries by both claimants and adjusters is more subjective and uncertain than the evaluation of property damage, and, therefore, negotiation plays a greater role in settling bodily injury claims than it does in settling property damage claims.

This chapter begins by describing the core functions that adjusters perform in all liability claims. Coverage for the claim in question must be determined. The adjuster must investigate and evaluate both legal liability and damages. Finally, the adjuster must settle the claim, either through negotiation or through the courts. The second half of this chapter describes issues that are important in settling specific types of claims, including auto liability and property damage, premises, operations, products, workers' compensation, and professional liability claims.

LIABILITY CLAIM ADJUSTING PROCESS

The four steps in adjusting a liability claim, which are not necessarily completed sequentially, are as follows:

1. Determining coverage
2. Determining legal liability
3. Determining damages
4. Negotiating and settling the claim

Rarely are coverage, legal liability, and damages determined quickly and easily. Making these determinations requires investigation and documentation, which consume most of an adjuster's time. This section explains how liability adjusters complete the steps in the claim adjusting process.

Determining Coverage

The first step in the liability claim adjusting process is determining coverage. The essential coverage clause of most liability insurance policies is simple. For example, Coverage A of the Commercial General Liability (CGL) form states, "We will pay those sums that the insured becomes legally obligated to pay as damages, because of 'bodily injury' or 'property damages' to which this insurance applies."[1] Therefore, any type of bodily injury or property damage for which the insured is allegedly liable is covered, unless it is specifically excluded. When determining coverage, adjusters are primarily concerned with the possible application of exclusions. Nevertheless, the essential coverage clause raises important issues. Under Coverage A of the CGL, the claim must be for "bodily injury" or "property damage." Under most auto liability coverages, the claim must also arise out of the use of certain autos by certain individuals. Therefore, a claim that is not for "bodily injury" or "property damage" or that does not arise out of the use of certain autos is not within the essential coverage provisions.

This section describes how claim adjusters determine whether a claim is covered by addressing the major issues that adjusters face.

Claimant's Allegations

When a liability claim is first presented to an adjuster, the facts might be unknown or disputed. Without knowing the facts, how can an adjuster determine coverage?

The claimant's allegations determine coverage, even if those allegations are disputed and even if they are eventually proved untrue. Liability policies protect the insured against legal claims and the cost to defend them, regardless of whether the claims are valid or groundless. Protection against false, unproved, and unprovable claims is a crucial part of the protection provided by liability insurance policies. An adjuster determining coverage must first consider the claimant's allegations at face value even if those allegations might not be covered or if coverage might be doubtful.

Coverage Problems

Adjusters face difficulty whenever coverage for a claimant's allegations is doubtful. This difficulty occurs when some aspects of a claim are covered and others are not, and when coverage for the entire claim is questionable. Clear communication with the insured and prompt action by the adjuster are essential to protect both the insured's and the insurer's interests. Whenever coverage is doubtful or not applicable to part of a claim, the adjuster must explain clearly, in writing, why this is so and what both the adjuster and the policyholder must do.

If part of a claim is clearly not covered, the adjuster must explain to the insured why not, with reference to specific policy provisions. The adjuster must explain that the insurer will continue handling the claim but that the insured might have to contribute to an eventual settlement or judgment. The adjuster should invite the insured to engage a private attorney in the claim. Usually, in these situations, the insured neither involves a private attorney nor contributes to a settlement. This is so because part of the claim *is* covered, and the insurer must continue to defend the claim and must pay any applicable settlement unless part of the claim is clearly not covered. Because most liability claims are settled without clearly specifying the basis of liability or the elements of damages, the insurer usually pays the entire settlement.

When coverage for the entire claim is doubtful, the adjuster must explain to the insured why, in writing, and must explain what the adjuster will do. The adjuster usually investigates further. Pending this investigation, the adjuster reserves the insurer's right to deny coverage should the facts so indicate. After issuing a letter advising the insured of a coverage problem and reserving the insurer's rights, the adjuster must promptly investigate and make a coverage determination. If coverage is found to apply, the insured is informed. If coverage does not apply, a prompt letter of denial is forwarded to the insured.

Insurers can resolve coverage questions through declaratory judgment actions in court. These actions result in a court declaration of the rights of parties. Many jurisdictions allow courts to declare rights of parties whenever a controversy arises in the investigation of a claim. Unfortunately, declaratory judgment actions have drawbacks. They are likely to generate thousands or tens of thousands of dollars of legal expense; therefore, they are not feasible for small and moderately sized claims. Furthermore, in many jurisdictions, declaratory judgment actions do not move through the courts any faster than other cases. A declaratory judgment that takes years does not serve its purpose. The insurer has to pay to defend the policyholder throughout that time and might have had to settle the claim in the meantime. Filing a declaratory action, if unsuccessful, also complicates the defense of the underlying action.

Whenever coverage does not apply to a claim, the insured should receive a written explanation, and a copy should go to the producer. If a lawsuit has been filed, the insured must be told exactly how much time he or she has to file a response with the court. Additionally, an adjuster should direct the insured to engage a private attorney.

Bodily Injury and Property Damage

As noted, liability insurance policies usually apply only to claims for bodily injury or property damage. The most likely exception is the personal injury coverage of the CGL, which extends to damages that are not limited to bodily injury and property damage. Attorneys use the term "personal injury" to refer to "bodily injury" claims as defined in insurance policies. In insurance, "personal injury" refers to specific policy coverage for defamation, false arrest, advertising injury, and malicious prosecution.

Generally, insureds submit claims only for bodily injury or property damage. However, not all insureds have a clear idea of what their insurance covers and submit any claim in the hope that it might be covered. Therefore, adjusters occasionally encounter claims for damages other than bodily injury or property damage.

Money damages are an appropriate remedy for both bodily injury and property damage and are normally included in the relief sought in a lawsuit. Lawsuits that seek only injunctions, and not money damages, are generally not for bodily injury or property damage. An adjuster must be careful not to deny coverage too hastily in a lawsuit seeking injunctive relief. A number of such suits concern ongoing bodily injuries and seek an injunction to stop further injury. This is true especially for claims of interference with use of property. Because loss of use of property is included within the definition of "property damage," a lawsuit based on such alleged damage might be covered.

Lawsuits alleging breach of contract resulting only in financial harm or lawsuits alleging financial fraud are more clearly not covered, because they do not concern claims for bodily injury or property damage. Likewise, regulatory fines or minor criminal fines are not property damage and are not covered.

Claims for emotional injury only, without physical bodily injury, present more difficult coverage issues. Generally, if the court cases of the applicable jurisdiction allow a tort claim based on emotional injury only, then an emotional injury would constitute bodily injury for coverage purposes. Increasingly, more jurisdictions accept emotional injury as bodily injury.

Intentional Acts

Because insurance is designed to cover accidental events, liability insurance policies generally exclude coverage for the insured's intentional acts. This is an important exclusion for adjusters because claimants often allege that the insured acted intentionally. Unfortunately, applying this exclusion is difficult, because adjusters must uncover the answers to two questions: (1) Did the insured intend the result of his or her action or merely intend to commit the action without contemplating the injurious outcome? and (2) Can intentional acts be excluded when the claimant also alleges negligence or strict liability on the insured's part? An additional question can be, Is the insured liable for the intentional acts of an agent or a servant, if the insured is vicariously liable?

Adjusters cannot rely on the intentional act exclusion unless they are familiar with the law in their state regarding its meaning. For example, in some states, an assault might not be excluded as an intentional act unless the insured intended the resulting harm. This standard makes the exclusion much harder to apply than in states that consider an intentional assault covered as long as the insured intended to commit the assault. States that require an indication that the policyholder intended the harm do not require that the insured intended the precise harm that occurred. Furthermore, the intent to cause harm might be inferred from the commission of the assault. Unfortunately, an insurer cannot deny coverage, hoping that a court infers intent.

The distinction between intending the act and intending the harm has been at the center of numerous suits by insureds seeking coverage under their homeowners liability insurance for acts of sexual molestation. Many of these cases involve victims who are small children. The insureds in these cases have alleged that they were insane or severely emotionally disturbed or that they did not believe they were causing harm. Some courts have accepted those arguments and awarded coverage. Other courts have rejected the insured's arguments and have ruled that the intent to harm exists, as a matter of law, regardless of what the insured says about his or her mental state. Consequently, most homeowners policies now have a specific exclusion for sexual molestation.

Applying the intentional act exclusion is difficult when the claimant also alleges negligence or strict liability on the insured's part. Based on the claimant's allegations, part of the claim is covered and part is not. In such situations, the insurer must defend the insured. If the opportunity arises, the adjuster might also have to settle the claim completely. Upon settlement, no distinction is made between which parts of the settlement are for which allegations. The case is settled as a whole, and coverage issues cannot be resolved in a settlement. The same problem exists even when a case is litigated to a verdict. In a few states, courts require juries to identify damages awarded count by count. Otherwise, the verdict is expressed as a single sum of money and does not resolve any coverage issues. Sometimes the insurer can prove through a lawsuit's discovery process that the policyholder must have intended the behavior, and this evidence could be the basis for denying coverage. However, an insurer taking this approach is acting contrary to the insured's best interests and must do so through a separate attorney. The attorney hired by the insurer to defend the insured cannot simultaneously work for the insurer to prove that the insured acted intentionally.

Contractual Obligations

Generally, liability insurance does not guarantee that insureds will perform their contractual agreements. However, adjusters cannot deny coverage for all claims based on breach of contract. Contractual obligations are frequently involved in covered claims.

The consequences of a breach of contract might be covered even if the breach itself is not. For example, a contractor might be hired to erect a wall. Should the contractor do the work negligently and the wall collapse on a person, the cost of rebuilding the wall (the contract's subject) would not be covered, but bodily injury to the person would be. Adjusters frequently encounter this type of claim.

Certain contractual obligations might be directly insured by liability policies. For example, the CGL excepts from its contractual exclusion (therefore provides coverage for) contractual liability assumed in a lease and contractual liability assumed for another's torts for bodily injury or property damage. Both of these contractual obligations affect coverage.

As with claims involving alleged intentional acts, claims of contractual breach might be combined with claims of negligence or strict liability. Such claims generally involve products or professional liability. The breach of contract aspect of these claims is usually incidental. Adjusters handling such claims often realize that they will not differentiate between the intentional act and the contractual breach so that they do not inform the insured that part of the claim should technically not be covered. Failure to so advise the insured is equivalent to granting coverage for the entire claim, which is probably what the adjuster intends.

Property Under the Insured's Control

Insureds often submit claims for property damage to another's property that has been damaged while in the insured's care, custody, or control or while the insured was working on it. Such property damage is clearly excluded from coverage by the typical liability insurance policy.

Insureds are usually not aware of what is or is not covered. Adjusters can identify care, custody, or control situations with minimal investigation. The adjuster can then usually direct the insured to the first-party coverage that deals with these situations.

Property damage to the insured's product itself, to the insured's work itself, or to property that the insured has sold or given away is likewise excluded from typical liability policies. However, claims for consequential bodily injury and damage to another's property are usually covered. Adjusters frequently encounter these situations and must carefully distinguish between bodily injury and property claims that are covered and those that are not.

Determining Legal Liability

The second step in the liability claim adjusting process is determining legal liability. This section describes the procedures an adjuster follows to determine legal liability. Proper investigation is essential in determining legal liability. The ability to conduct a complete and proper investigation is one of the core skills of claim adjusting. The adjuster's investigation is guided by the facts that must be established to determine legal liability. These facts are dictated by the legal principles applicable to the situation. Many legal principles are relevant to claim adjusting, including tort liability, criminal liability, contractual liability, statutory liability, and vicarious liability. This section describes these principles as they apply to claim adjusting and describes the defenses that can be asserted against liability claims.

Investigation

A claim's initial report usually states nothing more than, "Insured involved in auto accident at 10th and Washington," or "Claimant fell at insured's store." The adjuster must gather the additional facts.

The adjuster organizes the investigation according to what information is needed and what is most important. For example, regarding the loss reports previously cited, the adjuster would want to know the potential claimants' names, addresses, and telephone numbers and whether any of them were injured. On learning these facts, the adjuster would want to know each claimant's account of the accident. When a claimant's account of an accident is committed to a statement, he or she cannot easily change it later.

An adjuster should also obtain the insured's account of the accident. The insured is required to cooperate and usually is eager to do so. The claimant might exaggerate, embellish, or falsify his or her account if not questioned promptly. In addition to preserving evidence, prompt contact reassures the claimant about the insurer's responsiveness and greatly reduces the chance that the claimant will hire an attorney.

Taking statements from witnesses is standard practice with liability claims. A good statement has a proper introduction of both the witness and the adjuster and systematically covers all relevant facts. An adjuster should even cover areas with which the witness is likely to be unfamiliar. Having a witness respond "I don't know" prevents that witness from later inventing evidence on the same point. As long as a witness is available to testify, a statement given out of court cannot be used as evidence, except for impeachment.

Most statements are recorded on audiotape, which is convenient for the adjuster and preserves the witness's words. Tapes are easy and inexpensive to reproduce should the witness want a copy.

Adjusters also collect evidence in other forms, such as police reports, photographs and diagrams of accident scenes, and products or objects involved in claims. Evidence should be collected promptly to preserve the accident scene before changes occur. For example, skid marks wear away quickly. Such evidence is useful for checking the credibility of witness statements and to provide direct evidence of what happened. A police report should never substitute for the adjuster's own investigation unless all parties agree about the facts of the accident.

Obtaining all of the relevant evidence is the most important aspect of any investigation. Once all evidence has been gathered, the adjuster must evaluate its credibility and must decide what most likely happened. Adjusters should be constantly evaluating the credibility of evidence as it is received.

Adjusters quickly learn that in many cases, the "truth" is never known for sure. All that is available is evidence, and one piece of evidence can contradict another. The best the adjuster can do is to evaluate the relative credibility of the evidence. Although the evidence credibility might not be the same in every case, it decides the outcome of claims.

For witnesses to be completely credible, they must have had an opportunity to observe the facts, must remember those facts accurately, must have the ability to communicate those facts, and must have no motive to distort the facts. Most witnesses are deficient in at least one of these areas. They might have had a good opportunity to observe but might have a poor memory. They might have a good memory but be so inarticulate that the adjuster must lead them through their entire statement, introducing the possibility of distortion. An adjuster must also remember that a witness might be biased but honest or might be articulate but have been unable to really see what happened.

Tort Liability

A tort is a civil wrong not arising out of breach of contract. Some torts, such as assault, can also be crimes, and others, such as professional malpractice, can also be breach of contract. Generally, though, the law provides a remedy for torts because the wrongdoer (called a tortfeasor) has behaved in a manner that falls below acceptable legal standards and has caused bodily injury to another or damaged another's property.

Negligence is the usual basis of tort liability. Adjusters and attorneys use the term "negligence" to refer both to negligent behavior and to a cause of action in negligence. A cause of action in negligence requires a legal duty owed to the claimant, a breach of that duty that causes harm, a causal connection between the breach and the harm, and actual bodily injury or damage on the claimant's part.

When a person has failed to behave carefully and prudently, that person has likely breached a duty of care. Negligent behavior is common. An adjuster investigating a claim involving potentially negligent behavior usually proceeds by investigating what the insured could have done differently to prevent the accident. If the insured could have reasonably avoided the accident, the insured is probably negligent. Violations of certain laws, such as traffic laws, are deemed negligence per se. These laws are designed to fix the standard of care for all people subject to the law. Anyone who drives must observe the traffic laws, and failure to do so is negligence.

It is not enough for the bodily injury of a person to be "caused by" another for compensation to result; **proximate** (or legal) **cause** must also exist. This legal concept requires that an unbroken chain of events must link the "cause" and the injurious "event." Although "proximate" means close, a proximate cause is not necessarily physically close or close in time to its outcome. The proximate cause requirement protects a wrongdoer from responsibility for remote, unforeseeable consequences. Proximate cause is most likely questioned when the injurious outcome is also caused by intervening negligence. The intervening negligence could eliminate proximate cause between the original negligence and the injurious outcome.

Proximate cause
An event that sets in motion an uninterrupted chain of events contributing to a loss.

Damages are an essential part of an action in negligence. Unless negligent behavior causes bodily injury or property damage to another party, the wrongdoer escapes any legal consequences.

Tort liability can also be based on behavior other than negligence. Intentional torts include assault, battery, false arrest, false imprisonment, conversion (theft), defamation, trespass, and fraud. Although many of these torts are crimes and all involve intentional conduct, an adjuster cannot assume they are excluded. Indeed, personal injury coverage includes many of these torts. Convicting the policyholder of a crime is generally conclusive evidence that a tort was committed.

Torts can also be based on strict liability (or "absolute liability"), which is liability that exists regardless of whether the insured was negligent. The term strict liability is often used in regard to products liability claims and is imposed because some defense, such as improper use of the product, might be available. Absolute liability is generally imposed for activities such as operating aircraft, storing explosives, or having wild animals on premises, even if they have been tamed—such as in a zoo or circus. For such hazardous activities, the possibility of a loss is almost inevitable, and persons who engage in these activities are held liable for damages regardless of fault.

An adjuster investigating tort liability must know all of the elements of the tort(s) in question so that tort liability can be recognized. Claimants are unlikely to say, "I have an action in negligence against your insured." Instead, they say, "I fell and was injured at your insured's store."

Criminal Liability

Criminals are legally liable in civil courts to their victims. As noted, criminal acts are generally intentional, but that does not automatically mean they are excluded by insurance.

Anyone, including a convicted criminal, who seeks insurance coverage for a victim's claim is required by the insurance policy to cooperate with the insurer. Adjusters frequently find that convicted criminals are not cooperative even though they have a duty to be so. Those accused of crimes are often unable to cooperate with the adjuster if doing so jeopardizes their Fifth Amendment rights.

A convicted criminal's lack of cooperation might have little practical significance. A conviction is conclusive evidence that the crime was committed. Therefore, the criminal's cooperation would not help to defend the claim. An adjuster handling a claim filed against a convicted criminal must often concede liability, but not necessarily coverage.

In the case of an accused, the adjuster can usually wait until the criminal proceedings have concluded before demanding the insured's cooperation. Criminal cases generally proceed much faster than civil cases, so the insurer is usually not prejudiced by the adjuster's waiting.

Contractual Liability

A party who breaches a contract is legally liable to the other party to the contract. If such breach causes bodily injury or property damage, the breaching party's liability insurance might cover the claim. As noted, certain contractual obligations might be covered by liability insurance.

In cases of alleged breach of contract, the adjuster must thoroughly review the entire applicable policy. The adjuster must investigate the insured's behavior to determine whether it constitutes a breach of contract. Finally, the adjuster must investigate all potential contractual defenses. Did the claimant breach the contract first, thereby excusing further performance by the policyholder? Did a precondition for the insured's contractual obligations not occur or fail to be met? Did the insured and the claimant substitute a new contract for a previous one?

In cases of contractual hold-harmless agreements and assumptions of liability, the adjuster must scrutinize the contract to determine whether it applies to the situation in question. Courts interpret such contracts narrowly, and an adjuster should do so as well. For example, in many hold-harmless agreements, the insured agrees to hold another harmless for claims that arise out of the insured's conduct. Should the situation in question involve negligence on the part of others, especially the party seeking protection under the agreement, the agreement might not apply. Courts might also invalidate contracts that are against public policy, that attempt to transfer liability for a nondelegable duty, or that contain ambiguous language.

Statutory Liability

Except for workers' compensation, insurance is generally not designed to cover a policyholder's statutory obligations. (Workers' compensation laws create an obligation for employers even when negligence is not an issue.) Nevertheless, should a statute violation cause bodily injury or property damage, the policyholder's liability coverage might apply. For example, violating a traffic law and injuring someone is covered by auto liability insurance.

Not all statutory violations that cause bodily injury or property damage are covered by liability insurance. For example, intentionally dumping pollutants is excluded. An adjuster handling a case involving an alleged statute violation must determine what the statute requires, what the policyholder did, and whether any insurance policy exclusion applies.

Vicarious Liability

Frequently, adjusters must investigate the possibility of vicarious liability, which is liability imposed on a party because of that party's relationship to a wrongdoer. For example, employers might be liable for the acts of their employees, and principals might be responsible for the acts of their agents. Most claims against commercial policyholders involve vicarious liability because corporations are legal entities that act through their employees.

For adjusters, the most important issue regarding vicarious liability is the scope of employment or agency. An employer is liable for the acts of its employees only while they are acting within the scope of their employment. For example, if an employee goes home and assaults a neighbor, the employer is not liable. Unfortunately for adjusters, the scope of employment is not always clear cut. For example, employees often make brief deviations from their employer's business to attend to personal matters. Whether such deviations occurred and when they ended are difficult to determine. An adjuster handling such situations must thoroughly investigate such deviations. Another difficult situation for determining scope of employment arises when an employee attempts to conduct the employer's business by prohibited means, such as driving at illegally high speeds from one appointment to another. Usually, the law deems these situations to be within the scope of employment. The adjuster handling such situations often faces difficulty because the employer might overstate the extent to which it made its rules and prohibitions known to the employee.

Defenses to Liability Claims

Adjusters are interested in possible defenses to any claim they handle. As they investigate liability, adjusters also investigate possible defenses. The most useful defenses are absence of negligence, comparative or contributory negligence, assumption of risk, and statute of limitations.

Absence of Negligence

Absence of negligence is not so much a defense as it is a failure to prove the claimant's case. Nevertheless, adjusters should consider absence of negligence as a possible defense. Many accidents occur through no one's fault. Claimants often assert claims believing that the mere occurrence of the accident entitles them to compensation. For example, a claimant who twists an ankle while walking through undeveloped land might expect compensation from the landowner. Yet it is not because of the owner's negligence that the surface of the undeveloped property is uneven. Nature does not provide smoothly paved walkways, and anyone walking through natural terrain cannot expect such. Another unfortunately common example is auto accidents involving child pedestrians who dart into traffic. In many of those situations, it would have been impossible for the driver to have seen or anticipated the child's behavior or to have stopped the car in time. Defending these cases requires careful preparation, however, because any hint of negligence on the driver's part might render the driver liable. Children involved in these cases are frequently younger than seven years old and are therefore legally incapable of negligence.

Comparative or Contributory Negligence

Comparative or contributory negligence exists whenever a claimant's own fault contributes to causing his or her bodily injury. Such negligence is common. Under comparative negligence laws, the claimant's recovery is reduced in proportion to the claimant's share of fault. In other words, if a claimant's negligence is a 25 percent cause of the accident, the claimant's recovery is reduced by 25 percent. Under some comparative negligence laws, claimant fault in excess of 50 percent completely bars the claimant from recovery. However, in "pure" comparative negligence states, a claimant can be 99 percent at fault and still recover 1 percent of the damages. In the few states that recognize contributory negligence, any fault on the claimant's part completely bars the claimant from recovery.

Assumption of Risk

The assumption of risk defense applies whenever a claimant knows of a risk and voluntarily assumes it anyway. For the defense to be valid, the claimant's behavior must be both knowing and voluntary. Assumption of risk is frequently confused with comparative negligence. For example, participating in sports such as downhill skiing includes a risk of injury, but it is not negligent to participate. Knowing that risk, many people choose to participate anyway.

Statute of Limitations

Each state has statutory time limitations on the right to file lawsuits. The amount of time varies by state and by the type of legal claim; time limits can range from two to fifteen years, depending on the circumstances. Failure to file a lawsuit within the allotted time waives any obligation on the tortfeasor's part so that an expired statute of limitations can serve as an absolute defense.

Determining Damages

The third step in the liability claim adjusting process is determining damages. Adjusters must determine and document damages before settling a claim. Doing so usually takes more time than determining liability. Determining liability often takes a few days, whereas determining damages can take weeks, months, or longer. Adjusters usually rely on outside experts for damage information, such as doctors for bodily injury; appraisers, contractors, or repairers for property damage; and accountants or economists for financial factors.

Damages in bodily injury liability claims are usually proved with medical reports and bills, hospital records, and employer information. The adjuster must assemble this documentation throughout the time in which the claimant continues to receive treatment. So, settling a bodily injury claim often does not occur until treatment has concluded or until a clear prognosis and course of future treatment are known. Damages in property damage claims are proved with repair estimates or with actual bills for repair and rental. Most of this section concerns damages in bodily injury claims because those claims account for the majority of liability claim dollars spent. The rest of this section describes property damage liability claims and how they differ from first-party property damage claims.

Bodily Injury Claims

To investigate and document claims properly, adjusters must understand every element of damages for which the law provides compensation. The claimant has the burden of proving the damages. Nevertheless, the adjuster must investigate the nature and value of damage.

Damages can be classified as either special damages or general damages. Special damages are established for losses that can be quantified, such as loss of earnings. General damages are for intangible losses, such as pain and suffering. These damages are highly subjective, but they are the largest and most important element of damages in bodily injury claims. Adjusters, claimants' attorneys, and claimants often do not agree about how to evaluate general damages. Nevertheless, those involved are regularly required to negotiate and settle claims involving general damages.

Assuming legal liability is unquestioned and damages are not affected by policy limits, general damages are usually considered to be several times as great as special damages. Some adjusters consider only medical expense (often referred to as "medical specials") in determining a multiple for general damages and then add in the unmultiplied amount of lost earnings. Other adjusters multiply all specials.

The multiple-of-specials approach to general damages is often criticized as inappropriate in most cases. It has no logical basis nor any "official" recognition in case law. Nevertheless, it is widely practiced by both claimants' attorneys and adjusters.

Expenses for Medical Treatment

Medical expenses include expenses for emergency care, physicians' services, hospital care, nursing and rehabilitation treatment, medications, medical devices and equipment, and even transportation to receive medical care. Medical expenses must be related to the bodily injury, necessary to heal the bodily injury, and reasonable in amount. Although unrelated medical expenses should not be compensable, they are often submitted for payment. Many claimants have preexisting medical conditions for which they were already or should have been receiving treatment. Bills for these treatments are often included with bills for accident-related treatment. Preexisting problems and unrelated problems that develop after an accident are not the liability insurer's responsibility unless the bodily injury exacerbates a preexisting condition.

Medical treatment must be necessary to be compensated. Medical treatment is usually controlled by the claimant and the claimant's physician. Insurer arguments against the prescribed treatment are fruitless after the fact. Second-guessing the treating physician is not easy, but, with a solid case, an insurer can avoid payment for unnecessary treatment.

Finally, medical treatment must be reasonable in amount and cost. Although insurers do not have any statutory, regulatory, or contractual controls over physicians and hospitals, they are neither required to reimburse a course of treatment nor to pay bills that they can show are excessive.

Because adjusters lack the experience and expertise necessary to evaluate the necessity and frequency of medical treatment, insurers have begun to employ utilization review services. These services represent a recognized specialty within the medical field. By assessing medical treatment and bills, they can advise when a course of treatment is unnecessary, unrelated to the specific injury, or redundant with other treatment.

Adjusters might also audit medical bills by using a specialized computer program or by hiring a vendor that provides this service. These audits check bills submitted for duplicate charges, treatment code errors, reasonable and customary charges, inaccuracies, and other factors that might lead to incorrect billing.

In many states, the defendant must pay the medical expense, even if it has been covered by another source of insurance, such as health insurance. This is known as the **collateral source rule**. The rationale of this rule is that defendants should not benefit from the prudence of injured parties in insuring themselves. This rule also extends to other collateral coverage, such as disability insurance for lost earnings. Recently, some states have modified or abolished the collateral source rule, allowing a defendant to deduct recovery for expenses covered by other insurance.

Collateral source rule
A tort law that prevents the tortfeasor (defendant) from deducting from the amount owed to the victim (plaintiff) any goods, services, or money the victim received from other "collateral" sources (e.g., insurance benefits) as a result of the tort.

Loss of Earnings

Any amount that a claimant would have earned during a disability period is recoverable. Lost wages are established by verifying the extent and period of disability and the claimant's earnings. The extent and period of disability are medical issues that must be determined by a physician familiar with the physical demands of the claimant's job. A physician who expresses an opinion about disability without knowing the demands of the claimant's job cannot be reliable, unless the claimant's condition disables the claimant from any work at all. The adjuster must usually rely on a physician's written report to evaluate a claimant's disability. Should the adjuster doubt the alleged disability, the claimant can be examined by a physician of the adjuster's choosing. An independent medical exam can always be obtained when a claim is in litigation. If not, the claimant need not consent. Those who refuse to consent should raise the adjuster's suspicions.

Earnings are verified easily for a claimant who receives a salary or who works regular hours for wages. The claimant's employer or the claimant's tax returns can verify earnings. Earnings of self-employed claimants and claimants who own their own businesses are more difficult to verify. Tax returns can be helpful, but business conditions for such claimants change yearly. The issue in every case is what the claimant would have earned during the disability period, not what was earned just before disability. It might be necessary to contact the claimant's customers and clients or to hire an accountant to review the claimant's books. The lost time of a claimant who is a businessowner is especially difficult to verify because the business can often carry on temporarily without the owner.

Pain and Suffering

Pain and suffering is an intangible factor in every bodily injury case and is usually the largest component of damages. It includes inconvenience, anxiety, and other types of distress. The amount awarded in a suit, or agreed on in a claim settlement, depends on the medical expense amount, the disability's length, the severity and nature of the bodily injury, the locale where the lawsuit is tried, the attorneys' respective skill at creating sympathy and favorable impressions, the sympathies created by the parties, and many other factors. The question a claim adjuster faces in evaluating pain and suffering is, What would a jury award? Proper evaluation requires a good deal of experience, but even experienced claim adjusters are well aware of how inaccurate they could be in a given case. Claimants' attorneys are also under the same pressure, and this mutual pressure causes many settlements. In clear or fairly clear liability cases when policy limits are not an issue, settlements for pain and suffering usually constitute the largest component of damages and might be for amounts several times the medical expense, loss of earnings, or both.

Pain and suffering
Intangible injuries, including inconvenience and anxiety as well as pain and suffering associated with a physical injury.

Permanency/Disfigurement

In addition to having chronic pain, claimants sometimes suffer scarring or loss of bodily function that might not cause pain but that reduces the quality of life. Permanent bodily injuries and scars are evaluated similarly to pain and suffering—unscientifically. For example, burns or other scars on the face would be considered differently if they were on the claimant's back or another less visible area. On the other hand, damages for permanent bodily injuries that reduce earning capacity can be determined more accurately.

Loss of Consortium

Loss of consortium is an element of damages that generally belongs only to the injured party's spouse. Some states permit payment to other family members such as a parent or grandparent. Other states limit consortium payments to the spouse. Consortium traditionally consists of sex, society, and services. Sex means the loss of sexual relations because of the bodily injury. Society means the loss of enjoyable companionship because of the bodily injury. Services means the loss of useful services that the injured party formerly performed for the spouse, such as housekeeping, home repairs, or child care. This element of damages is also difficult to evaluate, and sometimes it is estimated as a percentage of the underlying injury damages. Plaintiff attorneys do not usually emphasize this aspect of a lawsuit with a jury because of the common attitude that spouses take each other "for better or for worse." Nevertheless, this element of damages and a spouse who inspires sympathy can increase the amount of damages awarded.

Future Damages

Any of the previous elements of damages that can be expected to continue into the future should be included in a settlement or jury verdict. With serious bodily injury, future damages—such as future medical expenses, future lost earnings and future pain and suffering—can exceed the damages incurred. Because of inflation, future damages can be larger, in their face amount, than present damages. However, any future damages that can be specified in amount should be adjusted to their present value. This procedure recognizes that a dollar received in the future is worth less than a dollar received today.

Survival and Wrongful Death

Survival actions
Legal causes of action that existed for the deceased before his or her death.

The term "survival and wrongful death" refers to both the action and the damages. **Survival actions** are legal causes of action that existed for the deceased before his or her death. In other words, had the deceased lived, he or she could have pursued these actions as in any other lawsuit. The claims for the medical expense, lost earnings, and pain and suffering up to the time of death are elements of a survival action and are evaluated similarly to other lawsuits. However, actions that precede a death lose some value upon death because the claimant cannot testify on his or her own behalf.

Wrongful death action
Legal causes of action that exist for the survivor of the deceased.

A wrongful death action is different. In concept, a **wrongful death action** belongs to the deceased's survivors. This action is designed to compensate survivors for the loss of the deceased and arises only upon death. Evaluating wrongful death actions is complicated. Only certain people are entitled to recover under a wrongful death action. If none of these people exist, the wrongful death action is worth very little. Most deaths involve eligible beneficiaries because most states allow spouses, parents, or children to recover, and most people have one or more such relatives. Even if eligible beneficiaries exist, their recovery might be limited to the benefits they would have received from the deceased. For parents and adult children claiming for one another, the amount of the financial benefit from the deceased might be small. Many states allow recovery for loss of companionship, but this element of damages is usually moderate, except for spouses. Financial dependence allows for the largest recoveries. Minor children are presumed to be financially dependent on their parents, and spouses are presumed to depend financially on each other. Some states provide for a loss-to-the-estate measure of damages to the eligible beneficiaries. Under this measure, the deceased's future cost of maintenance is subtracted from future earnings to determine a net contributions figure, or an estimate of the deceased's estate. Under loss-to-the-estate measures of damages, the future damages should be discounted to their present values.

Property Damage Claims

In some respects, determining damages in third-party property damage liability cases is easier than in first-party property damage claims. The adjuster need not worry about deductibles, special sublimits, coinsurance, or damages caused by both covered and noncovered causes.

However, in third-party claims, the law allows a deduction for depreciation from replacement cost. Determining depreciation can be as complex as it is in first-party claims. The adjuster must consider physical wear and tear; obsolescence because of fashion, seasonal, and technological changes; market value; and any other relevant factors. However, as in first-party claims, depreciation can be negligible, and a replacement cost settlement can be appropriate in many cases.

One important difference between first-party and third-party property damage claims is that the property owner's own negligence is irrelevant in first-party claims, but it can be a major factor in settling third-party claims. In contributory negligence states, the owner's fault in causing the loss is a complete bar to recovery. In comparative negligence states, the owner's fault reduces the recovery by a proportionate percentage or might even completely bar recovery.

A property damage claimant is in a relatively weaker bargaining position with the adjuster than a bodily injury claimant because of the smaller or more definite value of property damage claims and the expense of litigating them. Some restrictions on adjusters address this situation. For example, adjusters do not want to incur unnecessary legal expense. If liability and value are clear, most adjusters prefer to pay the claim and close their file rather than litigate. Claim managers strongly discourage having a property damage claim go to lawsuit, and such a lawsuit would be scrutinized to see whether the adjuster had neglected to make legitimate settlement efforts. Furthermore, the Unfair Claims Settlement Practices Act, a version of which is in effect in most states, requires adjusters to attempt settlement when liability is reasonably clear and forbids stalling on one claim settlement to influence another's settlement. This latter rule is especially applicable to auto accident cases in which the property damage claim might be ready for settlement while the bodily injury claim is still a long way from being settled.

Many property damage liability claims first appear as subrogation claims from other insurers. The adjuster for the liability insurer should respond to the claim as an adjuster would respond to a claimant. Should the adjusters for the respective insurers be unable to negotiate a settlement, the claim can be resolved by intercompany arbitration. The Property Subrogation Arbitration Agreement covers most first-party subrogation claims. The Nationwide Inter-Company Arbitration Agreement covers auto physical damage claim subrogation. The arbitrators in these claims decide issues of both liability and damages, and their decision cannot be appealed. The vast majority of U.S. insurers subscribe to these agreements.

Negotiating and Settling Claims

The fourth step in the liability claim adjusting process is negotiating and settling claims. Everything an adjuster does on a claim should be directed toward settlement. The vast majority of liability claims are settled without going to lawsuit. The vast majority of claims that do go to lawsuit are settled before trial. Settling liability claims is the most valuable service liability claim adjusters perform for insureds, claimants, insurers, and society. The courts would be overwhelmed if even a small percentage of claims that are settled were tried. It is also in the insurers' best interests for adjusters to settle liability claims. Insurers would pay more in legal fees and verdict amounts than they would pay in settlements if they were to try all the claims that they could settle. Therefore, negotiating to settle claims is a key responsibility of claim adjusters. Negotiation involves discussing all issues and arriving at a mutually satisfactory disposition of the claim.

Duty to Settle

Liability insurance policies usually give insurers the right to settle claims, but they do not impose a duty to settle because insurers might want to litigate a claim. The insurer must have the right to litigate to protect itself against frivolous, fraudulent, or unfounded claims. The threat that a claim might be litigated helps keep many dubious claims from ever being asserted.

Adjusters tend to believe that settling claims is expedient and in insureds' and claimants' best interests. However, a legal obligation to settle arises when the value of a liability claim approaches or clearly exceeds the insured's policy limit.

Insureds buy liability insurance for peace of mind. Almost nothing disturbs that peace of mind as much as being party to a lawsuit and enduring a trial. Even if they are ultimately successful, most people are unsettled by the experience of a trial. A settlement shields the insured from this experience. Indeed, a settlement protects the insured from even being sued. Insureds generally want claims to be handled without troubling or involving them too much. Because settling is also in the insurer's best interests, it seems to be the best option for all concerned.

When the value of a claim approaches or exceeds the insured's policy limit, making settlement becomes a legal obligation and is no longer just good judgment. The insurer, rather than the insured, controls the defense and claim settlement. If a verdict exceeds the insured's policy limit, however, the insured has to pay the excess. This situation creates a potential conflict. Absent a duty to settle the claim and once the claim's value approaches or exceeds the policy limit, the insurer would have little to lose by going to trial because the insurer might face the payment of a relatively low award. However, the insured would end up paying damages exceeding the policy limit.

To prevent insurers from exploiting this situation, courts require them to make reasonable efforts to settle within policy limits and to accept settlement offers within policy limits whenever the value of the claim exceeds policy limits. An insurer that rejects a settlement offer within policy limits does so at its own risk. Although courts have not made insurers absolutely liable for excess verdicts following the rejection of a settlement, convincing a court that the excess verdict was unforeseeable after it has been rendered is difficult. If a court thinks that an insurer unreasonably rejected settlement, it would probably hold the insurer responsible for the damages exceeding policy limits. This is one type of **bad-faith claim** against the insurer.

Pressures to Negotiate

Both sides to a claim are pressured to negotiate by the possibility of an undesirable outcome at trial. This pressure is probably felt more strongly by insurers than by claimants, except when claimants face a serious risk of a defense verdict.

Even claimants who face little chance of losing at trial overwhelmingly prefer to settle than to litigate. Indeed, the typical liability claimant probably underestimates his or her claim for settlement; claimants typically settle for less than they could reasonably expect from a trial. This outcome probably occurs because claimants are far less able than insurers to risk an adverse result and because claimants' attorneys make much more money for their time by settling claims than by trying them.

For most liability claimants, a claim might be a once-in-a-lifetime event, and their bodily injuries might create trauma for them. Claimants make an enormous emotional investment in their claims and can be devastated by an adverse result at trial. An adverse result could simply be a verdict amount much less than anticipated and not even a complete loss. In contrast, for insurers, each claim is another piece of business to be handled expeditiously. With such differing emotional investments, claimants and insurers approach settlement differently.

Plaintiff and defense attorneys face similar professional pressures. It is almost always in their clients' best interests to settle. Yet to develop their professional skills and to gain credibility, they need trial experience. Trying cases, however, is enormously stressful. Juries are unpredictable, clients can be unforgiving, and professional reputations can be made or destroyed by a single case.

Adjusters are also highly motivated to limit and control legal expenses. Both claim department management and corporate management monitor legal expenses closely. Adjusters are reprimanded for allowing claims to go to trial unnecessarily and for failing to pursue settlement throughout the course of litigation.

Bad-faith claim
A claim that implies or involves actual or constructive fraud, a design to mislead or deceive another, or a neglect or refusal to fulfill some good-faith duty or some contractual good-faith obligation.

Negotiation Strategies

In a typical claim settlement, negotiations begin with a demand by the claimant's attorney for a specific sum of money. The opening demand is usually a high evaluation of the claim. The adjuster sometimes makes the opening settlement offer to "adjust" the attorney's expectations. Usually, however, the adjuster responds to the attorney's demand with a settlement offer that is a lower evaluation of the claim. The attorney and the adjuster discuss the strengths of their cases and the weaknesses of the other side's case and exchange further counterdemands and counteroffers. If they believe they can settle, they continue to negotiate until they agree on a specific settlement amount. With an unrepresented claimant, the adjuster is much more likely to make the first settlement offer. Claimants are often unfamiliar or uncomfortable with the negotiation process. Typically, adjusters must establish trust and try to make realistic initial offers with unrepresented claimants. Thereafter, if the claimant and the adjuster believe they can agree on a settlement, they continue to discuss the claim until they reach settlement.

Neither adjusters nor attorneys consider willingness to negotiate a weakness. Both sides know that the vast majority of claims settle. Anyone who avoids or refuses negotiations might appear inexperienced or disorganized. Good negotiators can take strong positions and encourage the other side to continue the process.

Properly preparing for and intelligently evaluating a claim are essential prerequisites to good negotiating. Proper preparation consists of the adjuster's investigation and documentation of liability and damages. The final step in proper preparation is the adjuster's review of the file to ensure that he or she can discuss all aspects of the claim. Simultaneously, the adjuster must evaluate the claim intelligently. The adjuster determines both a good first offer and a probable range of settlements. Every adjuster can settle claims without consultation only up to a specified dollar limit. Beyond that limit, the adjuster must obtain settlement authority from higher-level claim personnel. Requests for settlement authority are usually presented in writing and summarize the facts, the liability details, the bodily injury, and the special damages.

Adjusters want to communicate several messages with their first offer and throughout the negotiation process. They want to communicate an intelligent evaluation of the claim; nothing discredits an adjuster faster than being obviously unaware of a claim's value. Adjusters also want to communicate their confidence in their position and willingness to litigate the claim. In this respect, both the adjuster and the insurer should have experience litigating claims. The adjuster must also be sure that a credible defense attorney is involved should the claim already be in lawsuit. Finally, communicating some flexibility in one's position is important. Undervaluing a claim and being inflexible risk stalling negotiations and incurring needless litigation expense. However, overly generous offers and concessions might make an opponent too optimistic and inflexible.

Most adjusters and attorneys negotiate cooperatively and constructively. Such a negotiation style is safe and effective. Nevertheless, this is not the only style of negotiation. Some parties negotiate in a hostile, competitive, and belligerent manner, which can also be effective but much riskier.

Settlement Techniques

Most claims are settled using a general release, in which the claimant releases the insured of all liability for the claim and the insurer agrees to pay the claimant the agreed settlement amount. Specialized releases address particular situations, such as those involving joint tortfeasors and minors.

For claims by married individuals, the claimant's spouse should also be a party to the release to dispose of his or her consortium claim. For claims in which a lawsuit has been filed, the settlement must include the lawsuit's dismissal by the claimant. The claimant's attorney files a simple notice in the court records stating that the claim has been settled.

Liability claims are usually settled with a lump-sum payment. Sometimes, the settlement requires both a lump-sum payment at the time of settlement and a series of payments into the future. These are called **structured settlements**. Although structured settlements are usually made on high-value claims, such settlements have no minimum-size claim. Structured settlements are especially useful when the claimant is likely to experience regular damages into the future, such as loss of income, or when the adjuster suspects that the claimant might be unable to effectively manage a lump-sum payment.

Structured settlement
An agreement in settlement of a lawsuit involving specific payments made over a period of time.

Structured settlements are attractive to insurers because they enable them to offer more dollars in the total settlement at a lower present cost than with a lump-sum payment. Insurers can fund their future obligations with annuities purchased from other insurers, usually life insurance companies. The present cost of an annuity is less than what the annuity will pay in the future.

Many insurers also use **advance payments** to discourage claimants from hiring attorneys. Advance payments are made as the claimant incurs medical or other expenses. Payments are paid without receiving a release in return, but the claimant must sign a receipt acknowledging payments and that the advance payments count toward final settlement.

Advance payment
A payment made to a claimant following a loss to cover the immediate expenses resulting from that loss.

Some insurers practice **walk-away settlements**, in which the insurer pays the claimant a lump-sum settlement and takes no release. These settlements are most appropriate for small claims. Insurers that advocate this practice say it promotes excellent public relations, enhances assertive claim handling, and encourages claimants to refrain from bringing suit. In claims in which the claimant does sue, the insurer is entitled to credit for what it has paid.

Walk-away settlement
A settlement that involves lump-sum payments made by insurers to settle claims and that does not require a release from the claimant.

Litigation

All liability claim adjusters should be familiar with litigation. Ultimately, courts determine both liability and damages for any claim that is not settled. Claimants might have to go to court to obtain compensation. Insurers and adjusters must understand how courts operate and how courts balance the rights and interests of plaintiffs and defendants.

Defending lawsuits is a significant part of the protection policyholders buy through liability insurance policies. Insurers have both the right and the duty to defend the policyholder. Adjusters must understand and properly handle this right and duty.

Civil procedure
Rules by which courts conduct civil trials. Civil trials concern the judicial resolution of claims by one individual or group against another.

Lawsuit procedures are governed by **civil procedure**, that part of the law that establishes rules for litigation in civil cases. Adjusters must understand civil procedure to contribute to case strategy and to control defense attorney conduct.

Because attorney fees are a major expense for liability insurers, adjusters implement a variety of controls designed to minimize legal expense. Therefore, adjusters must simultaneously ensure the insured's proper defense, develop strategy, direct litigation, and manage legal expenses. Properly handling litigation is one of the most challenging tasks in claim adjusting and one of the most important of any insurance activities.

Role of Courts in Resolving Claims

Although the majority of claims are settled before suit is filed and the majority of suits are settled before trial, the courts play an essential role in settling claims. Courts provide an incentive to negotiate. A policyholder could not be held legally liable without a court determination. Insurers would not need to protect policyholders without the threat of legal liability.

Nevertheless, courts are not fast, inexpensive, or predictable. Claimants who might otherwise rely on courts to determine their rights against policyholders have an incentive to negotiate. Claimants who do rely on courts find that they wait many years, spend considerable money on legal expenses, and often end up with a result no better than they could have achieved in settlement.

The adverse psychological effects of litigation tend to mount as time progresses, a circumstance that increases incentives to settle. Just before the trial, the pace of depositions and motions usually increases. These pretrial activities place great stress on the parties and their attorneys and indicate what trial will be like. Following pretrial activities, many parties conclude that they prefer a settlement for a definite amount, with relief from the aggravation and stress of litigation, to the difficulty and uncertain outcome of a trial.

The values that attorneys and adjusters place on claims are derived from actual results of claims litigated to conclusion. Claims that are litigated to conclusion therefore have important effects on all other claims. Although only a small percentage of claims are decided by court verdicts, those verdicts influence the price of all claims.

Duty to Defend

In addition to paying amounts for which the insured is legally liable (up to policy limits), insurers are also obligated to defend their insureds against lawsuits. This obligation is a valuable aspect of liability insurance. Many times, the insurer's duty to defend is more important to the insured than the duty to indemnify.

Many claims take a long time and a great deal of effort to settle. Other claims cannot be settled at all and are concluded by a trial and verdict. In both of these cases, legal expenses can be extraordinary. Thousands and then tens of thousands of dollars in legal expenses can quickly accumulate on ordinary claims, such as auto liability and premises liability claims. Complex claims can result in legal expenses well into six figures.

Claims can be difficult to settle because of unreasonableness on the part of plaintiffs or defendants. Plaintiffs can make settlement demands so unreasonably high that the defendant's insurer is not even tempted to settle. Likewise, insurers can make settlement offers far below what the plaintiff is likely to be awarded in a trial or fail to evaluate a claim realistically. (Usually, once a claim is in lawsuit, the insurer's defense attorney realistically evaluates the claim, even if the claim adjuster has failed to do so.) Another type of lawsuit that is difficult to settle involves claims of multiple codefendants, all of whom insist they have no liability and refuse to settle. Complete mutual refusal by a group of codefendants to make a settlement offer can ruin negotiations, even in claims involving clearly innocent and severely injured plaintiffs. The better practice, in such claims, is for the defendants to cooperate to settle the plaintiff's claim and then to arbitrate or to negotiate their respective shares of the settlement. Unfortunately, this rational approach is often difficult to adopt because of the number of claim adjusters and attorneys involved.

The insurer's duty to defend is especially important in frivolous, fraudulent, or meritless claims. Absent the insurer's duty to defend, plaintiffs would be in a strong position to coerce settlements from defendants who lack the resources or the ability to resist lawsuits. For liability insurance claims, plaintiffs face an opponent with tremendous resources and experience in defending lawsuits: the insurer. When insurers defend frivolous lawsuits to a verdict, they spend far more on defense than on claim indemnification. When insurers settle frivolous lawsuits, they usually do so because settling saves an equal or a greater amount of legal expenses.

The insurer's duty to defend is also its right. The insurer can select the defense attorney, and the insured is then obligated to cooperate with that chosen attorney. As long as it is solely liable for the claim, the insurer can dictate defense strategy. The insurer can unilaterally decide to settle or to continue a claim's defense. Although the defense attorney is professionally obligated to serve the insured's interests above all, the insurer pays the defense attorney and therefore dictates all defense decisions. As long as the insured is not financially exposed to the claim, the defense attorney takes direction from the insurer. Taking direction from the insurer in this situation does not compromise the insured's interests, as long as the defense attorney is not involved in matters in which the insured and insurer might be adverse, such as a coverage issue. Defense attorneys hired to defend the insured should never be used to advise the insurer on coverage issues in the same case.

The insurer's right and duty to defend suits is complicated for claims in which coverage is doubtful or in which part of the claim is clearly not covered. Generally, an insurer must defend an *entire* claim whenever a plaintiff's allegations for *any part* of the claim are covered. Coverage applies according to the plaintiff's allegations, not according to the claim's merits. Otherwise, insureds would be without coverage when they need it most—when faced with unfounded claims. However, plaintiffs often assert claims that are clearly not covered (such as intentional wrongdoing) in the same lawsuit as claims that are covered (such as ordinary negligence) or assert claims that might not be covered at all (such as a claim in which it is doubtful whether the bodily injury or property damage occurred during the policy period). In these claims, the insurer must defend the entire lawsuit, but the insured has a right to involve an attorney of the insured's choosing at the insured's expense. When two defense attorneys are involved, the insurer's attorney has the right to control the case as long as the insurer's money is at stake. The insurer's attorney attempts to involve and obtain the approval of the insured's private attorney in all major decisions. Should the insurer's attorney ever disagree with the insured's private attorney, the insurer is likely to be financially responsible for any consequences.

Civil Procedure

Court cases proceed according to rules of civil procedure. Although details vary by state and county, the basic framework of civil procedure is the same throughout the U.S. The five stages of a lawsuit are pleadings, discovery, motions, trial, and appeal.

Pleadings

Pleadings
Formal written statements of the facts and claims of each party to a lawsuit.

Summons
A legal document issued by the clerk of the court requiring the sheriff or another officer to notify the person named that an action has commenced against him or her and that he or she must answer the complaint.

Complaint
A document listing what the defendant has done to harm the plaintiff and the amount of money the plaintiff wants to recover.

Answer
A document that responds to the plaintiff's allegations and that can include defenses to the complaint.

The first stage of a lawsuit is pleadings. The **pleadings** are papers filed with the court clerk in which each side gives its account. A lawsuit is initiated with either a **summons**, a simple notice to the defendant that a lawsuit has been filed, or a **complaint**, a listing of allegations in which the plaintiff establishes his or her case. The extent of detail required in a complaint varies by jurisdiction, but all jurisdictions require that a complaint notify the defendant of the nature of the case. Within a specified time, usually twenty or thirty days, the defendant must file an **answer** in response to each of the plaintiff's allegations. As part of the answer, the defendant can also raise affirmative defenses.

The defendant can join additional defendants by filing a cross-complaint against other parties who might ultimately be found responsible for the cause of action being brought against the defendant. Additional defendants must file an answer to the cross-complaint.

The initial pleadings that join a party to a lawsuit, whether a summons, complaint, or cross-complaint, are served on the party (usually personally) by a court officer, such as a sheriff or sheriff deputies. In federal courts, U.S. marshals perform this task. Thereafter, court rules usually allow papers to be served by private parties or by mail.

Discovery

The second stage of a lawsuit is discovery. Once all parties have filed their pleadings, the issues are clear and discovery can begin. **Discovery** is the formal process by which each party obtains the evidence and information known to the other parties. Discovery can be by written **interrogatories**, a series of questions the other party must answer in writing; by **deposition**, a series of oral questions and answers that are recorded by a court reporter; by requests for documents, whenever documentary evidence is at issue; or by requests for admission, written statements that the receiving party must either accept or dispute. Because depositions are the most expensive and time-consuming form of discovery, most attorneys prefer to use the other forms of discovery first to narrow the issues. Nevertheless, depositions are usually essential to preparing a case. Discovery might also include a right of inspection, whenever the physical makeup of an object or a place is important, or a right of independent medical examination, whenever a party's health and physical condition are at issue. Once all discovery is complete, each side should thoroughly know the opposing side's case and what evidence the opposing side will use at trial.

Discovery
A pretrial exchange of all relevant information between the plaintiff and defendant.

Interrogatories
Specific written questions or requests raised by one party to a lawsuit that the opposing party must answer in writing.

Deposition
A recorded and transcribed testimony of a witness obtained through oral questions or written interrogatories that is used to prepare for a lawsuit.

Motions

The third stage of a lawsuit is making motions. Motions can be made at any point from suit initiation to appeal. A **motion** is a formal request to the court for a decision or ruling. A motion can be narrow and specific, such as a request for the court to allow or disallow a specific item of discovery, or comprehensive, such as a request for the court to terminate the lawsuit in favor of the moving party. An example of the latter is a **motion for summary judgment**, in which the moving party asks the court to decide the case in its favor, usually after only pleadings or discovery has been completed and before trial. A motion for summary judgment is essentially an argument that no real issues exist and that, as a matter of law, the moving party is entitled to judgment.

Motion
A formal request for the court to take a particular action.

Motion for summary judgment
A pretrial request to enter a judgment when no material facts are disputed.

Trial

The fourth stage in a lawsuit is the trial. Barring summary judgment or settlement, a case goes to trial. At trial, each side presents its evidence and has an opportunity to cross-examine and counter the other side's evidence. Either a judge or a jury decides which party's case is more persuasive and renders a verdict accordingly. When a jury decides a case, the judge explains to the jury the relevant law and explains what factual issues the jury must resolve.

Appeal

The fifth stage in a lawsuit is the appeal. Following a verdict, the losing party can file an appeal. An appeal is a request to a higher court to overturn the trial decision. On appeal, the case is *not* heard again in its entirety. Only alleged errors of law, not issues of fact, can be argued on appeal. Examples of errors of law are that inadmissible evidence was admitted or that the trial judge misstated the law to the jury. Occasionally, on appeal a party asks the higher court to change the law or to announce new law. Courts have the inherent power to change, add to, or interpret the law. Consequently, common law evolves. Because appeals can succeed only in cases of legal error, most trial verdicts are not appealed. The trial marks the end of most claims.

Legal Expense Control

Defending liability lawsuits is tremendously expensive. Consequently, insurers are extremely sensitive to legal expenses and have adopted a number of strategies to control them. Adjusters are responsible for implementing and enforcing those strategies.

Most claim departments use only certain preapproved law firms to defend liability lawsuits. Those law firms usually specialize in insurance defense work and are familiar with insurers and their needs. In exchange for a volume of business, such law firms usually work at a lower hourly rate than other attorneys and law firms with comparable skills and experience.

Claim departments usually require monthly or quarterly bills on active cases. These bills must be broken down by tenth of an hour or quarter-hour segments and must show exactly which attorney did what work in the time billed. Adjusters or specialized legal auditing firms can check these detailed bills against the actual file and the attorney's original time sheets to verify charges.

Many claim departments require law firms to submit budgets for each case or to quote a fixed price for the entire case. Sometimes fixed prices can be established for predictable work, such as completing pleadings or conducting a deposition. Many claim departments require adjusters to preapprove all depositions or motions. Adjusters must have a sophisticated understanding of trial evidence and strategy to exert such controls in a way that does not jeopardize the defense.

Ultimately, the best control of legal expenses is complete avoidance of the legal process. Adjusters should settle cases that can be settled before they go to lawsuit or before discovery and trial have caused enormous expenses to accumulate.

Alternative Dispute Resolution

For various reasons, potential litigants are often unable to resolve their disputes without third-party assistance. Traditionally, courts were used in this role to resolve disputes. The rising costs of allowing courts to resolve disputes and the enormous backlog of cases in the court system have caused potential litigants to search for alternative ways of resolving disputes.

Alternative dispute resolution (ADR) refers to any number of forums for settling claims outside the traditional court system. The most common ADR forums are negotiation, mediation, arbitration, appraisals, mini-trials, and pretrial settlement conferences. The courts have recently annexed some of these forums as a way of relieving the backlog of cases in the court system.

Negotiation is the primary ADR forum for resolving claims outside litigation. Litigation is sometimes the sign of a poorly functioning negotiation process. Because of improper training or supervision, adjusters might make inadequate offers to claimants. Claimants' attorneys might file frivolous lawsuits in the hope of receiving a settlement because of the sheer "nuisance value" of the claim. Claim supervisors and managers should monitor the negotiation process to ensure that it is working properly. If the parties in dispute have acted in good faith, they should have fully explored the possibilities of resolution by direct negotiation before starting a lawsuit.

When direct negotiations fail, the parties can use mediation as an ADR forum. **Mediation** can be considered negotiation with a referee, called a mediator. In mediation, the parties in dispute present their case to the mediator, whose role is to facilitate an amicable resolution. The mediator listens to each side present its case, identifies the weaknesses in the arguments or in the evidence presented, proposes alternative solutions, and helps improve the relationship between the parties. The mediator does not normally decide the case for the parties but instead assists them in reaching a mutually agreeable settlement. The fact that both sides must agree with the ultimate outcome makes mediation an attractive choice. The downside to mediation is that disputes sometimes remain unresolved. After investing time and money in mediation, the opposing parties must then consider some other ADR forum or litigation.

Mediation
A negotiation process in which a neutral outside party helps participants examine the issues and develop a mutually agreeable settlement.

Another ADR forum is arbitration. In **arbitration**, the parties present their cases to a disinterested third party (the arbitrator) who acts as a judge (and often is an active or a retired judge) in weighing the facts presented and making a decision based on the evidence. Arbitration's advantage is that a decision is made. Whether the participants must accept this decision depends on the type of arbitration agreement into which the parties entered. In binding arbitration, the participants are required to accept the arbitrator's decision. In nonbinding arbitration, neither party is required to accept the arbitrator's decision. However, the arbitrator's decision provides the "winner" with leverage in future negotiations. Arbitration Forums, Inc., is one well-known national organization that insurers use to resolve intercompany disputes. Its most popular forum is the Nationwide Inter-Company Arbitration Agreement, which is used to resolve automobile subrogation claims.

Arbitration
A process in which the parties in a dispute agree to submit their controversy to a private body that will make a decision that can be final and binding.

An **appraisal** is a unique ADR forum. (It should not be confused with the damage estimates of an automobile or a property damage appraiser.) An appraisal, in this context, is a method of resolving disputes between insurers and their insureds. The appraisal process and its scope are specifically described in the insurance policy. Exhibit 10-1 shows the appraisal provision from the ISO

Appraisal
A method of resolving disputes between insurers and insureds over the amount owed on a covered loss.

HO-3 policy. The appraisal provision resolves disputes over the *amount owed* on a covered loss, but it does not determine whether coverage exists.

EXHIBIT 10-1

Appraisal Provision From ISO HO-3 Policy

Appraisal. If you and we fail to agree on the amount of loss, either may demand an appraisal of the loss. In this event, each party will choose a competent appraiser within 20 days after receiving a written request from the other. The two appraisers will choose an umpire. If they cannot agree upon an umpire within 15 days, you or we may request that the choice be made by a judge of a court of record in the state where the "residence premises" is located. The appraisers will separately set the amount of loss. If the appraisers submit a written report of an agreement to us, the amount agreed upon will be the amount of loss. If they fail to agree, they will submit their differences to the umpire. A decision agreed to by any two will set the amount of loss.

Each party will:

a.   Pay its own appraiser; and

b.   Bear the other expenses of the appraisal and umpire equally.

Source: Homeowners 3—Special Form (HO 00 03 10 00), Copyright 1999, Insurance Services Office, Inc.

Mini-trial, or **summary jury trial**
An abbreviated version of a case that allows parties to present evidence and arguments to a panel that acts as a jury and that has no authority to make a binding decision but that can pose questions and offer an opinion on the outcome of a trial based on the evidence.

Pretrial settlement conference
Meeting of the judge and the parties' lawyers in a judge's conference chamber two or three weeks before the trial to narrow the issues to be tried, to stipulate the issues and evidence to be presented at trial, and to help settle the case.

A **mini-trial** or **summary jury trial** is an ADR forum that closely resembles the traditional legal system in that representatives (usually attorneys) present an abbreviated version of their case to a panel that acts as a jury. The jury's decision can be binding or nonbinding. The rules of evidence and procedure law normally coincide with those of traditional courts. Critics argue that little cost saving is achieved. The main advantage is that the litigants do not have to wait months or years to have their cases heard.

A **pretrial settlement conference** is also an ADR forum that almost all states now require. The conferences are sanctioned by the court and are normally conducted by the judge who is presiding over the case. Lawsuits have already been filed for these cases. The purpose of the pretrial settlement conference is to force litigants to make one last effort to resolve the claim in lieu of going to trial. The judge's role is similar to that of a mediator, but sometimes the judge subtly expresses to the litigants his or her opinion of their positions.

ADJUSTING SPECIFIC TYPES OF LIABILITY CLAIMS

The adjuster's general duties to investigate; to determine coverage, liability, and damages; and to settle claims exist in all liability claims. The challenges in performing these duties vary by claim. General principles of liability and damages apply somewhat differently to different situations.

The remainder of this chapter describes the challenges that exist in various types of liability claims. This section first addresses auto bodily injury and auto physical damage claims. Auto physical damage claims are not traditional liability-based claims but are part of the auto policy, which is a liability coverage form. It then discusses claims arising out of premises, operations, and products, the situations typically covered by general liability insurance. This section concludes by addressing the specialized areas of workers' compensation claims, professional liability claims, and environmental and toxic tort claims.

Auto Bodily Injury Liability Claims

Auto accidents generate the most common type of liability claim. Nevertheless, auto accidents can cause some of the worst bodily injuries and the most expensive claims. New adjusters begin in auto claims because, fortunately, a majority of relatively minor claims exist and because the liability principles are well known.

Although auto claims are a traditional training ground for liability adjusters, auto claims can be complicated regarding coverage determination; accident reconstruction; and coordination with no-fault, workers' compensation, and uninsured motorists claims.

Coverage Determination

Coverage determination is simple only when the accident involves the named insured as the driver and a vehicle specifically listed on the policy. Situations in which the named insured, or some other insured, has coverage while driving a vehicle not listed on the policy or when someone other than the named insured is using a covered vehicle are more complicated.

Usually, when an insured is driving another's vehicle, that other vehicle's coverage covers any loss. However, the other vehicle's coverage sometimes does not apply or is inadequate. In the event of the insolvency of the vehicle's insurer or the exclusion of coverage for any reason, the driver's insurer must take over the claim. Adjusters who "inherit" cases under these circumstances often find claim investigation and management inadequate or completely absent.

Inadequate policy limits are more common than the inapplicability of the vehicle's coverage. The adjuster working for the driver's insurer can adopt different strategies, depending on the circumstances. If the underlying coverage is far less than the claim's value, the adjuster for the driver's insurer should become heavily involved in the claim or should ensure its handling. If the underlying coverage is adequate to pay the claim, the adjuster for the driver's insurer is likely to take a less active role.

Accident Reconstruction

The facts of most auto accidents are not difficult to ascertain. The points of impact on each vehicle indicate at what angle and from what direction the two vehicles came into contact. The extent of damage to the vehicles provides some indication of the vehicles' speeds. The parties to an auto accident usually differ more over how culpable they think each party is than over what happened. Fortunately for adjusters, clear right-of-way rules apply when two vehicles converge on the roads. Also, whenever the parties disagree about what happened, adjusters or accident reconstruction experts might be able to determine the facts. Accident reconstruction experts are most helpful in determining vehicle speed and what a driver should have been able to see at the time of an accident.

Vehicle speed is determined by examining skid marks and vehicle damage. Skid marks are reliable indicators of speed because once the brakes are locked, vehicles stop according to their weight, the road grade, the road surface, and speed. All of these factors except speed are known or can be precisely measured after an accident. When, instead of coming to a complete stop, a vehicle collides with another vehicle, an accident reconstruction expert can determine that the vehicle was traveling no slower than a certain speed based on the skid marks. This information can be sufficient to disprove a party's statements or to establish liability. The point at which skid marks begin can establish when and where the driver first reacted to a hazard, an essential piece of evidence when driver inattention is an issue.

Accident reconstruction experts can also determine what a driver should have been able to see just before impact. The exact time of day and weather conditions at the time of the accident can usually be established. The driver's lines of sight can be determined according to vehicle type and driver height. The effects on visibility of curves or hills in the road are also considered. All of this information can be combined to determine whether a driver reacted promptly to a hazard or was slow and inattentive. That determination is essential in claims in which the driver alleges a sudden and unavoidable hazard or in which the claimant's comparative negligence is at issue. Comparative negligence is frequently an important issue in auto accident claims. Often, the insured can be primarily at fault, but the claimant is also substantially negligent for failing to respond to a hazard.

Coordination With Auto No-Fault and Workers' Compensation

An adjuster handling auto liability claims must frequently deal with other insurers that provide auto no-fault or workers' compensation benefits to an injured claimant. Another insurer can provide the adjuster with detailed medical information. The adjuster can stay abreast of the claimant's bodily injury to ensure that the liability claim reserves for the claim are adequate. The other insurer can provide medical information because it has a subrogation claim for the medical expense amount. In jurisdictions in which subrogation is possible, the other insurer is obligated to submit medical information to other insurers involved with the claim to support its claim.

However, difficulties can arise between the adjuster and the other insurer whenever subrogation rights do not exist or comparative negligence is an important issue. In the absence of subrogation rights, the other insurer should not release any medical information about the claimant to the adjuster without authorization. Eventually, the claimant must release medical information to the adjuster, but the claimant is likely to want control over any such release. As a professional courtesy, another adjuster might be willing to comment on the adequacy of the liability claim reserves, but the other adjuster might be accused of invading the claimant's privacy should any medical information be revealed.

Uninsured Motorists Coverage

Policyholders purchase uninsured motorists (UM) coverage to protect themselves against motorists who do not have liability insurance. Under this coverage, the policyholder is treated similarly to claimants, while uninsured motorists are often unavailable and uncooperative parties who are treated like insureds. Denying a claim under uninsured motorists coverage might have immediate legal ramifications for the insurer that would not be present if the claimant were a third party.

Attorney representation in an uninsured motorists claim is almost inevitable in many parts of the country. Once policyholders realize that opposing drivers are uninsured, they assume that legal representation is essential. Unfortunately, dealing with the policyholder as a claimant leaves the adjuster with no favorable witness because the uninsured driver is usually unavailable or uncooperative. A person who drives without insurance or causes hit-and-run accidents is usually not a credible witness, even if available and cooperative. Therefore, uninsured motorists claims are extremely difficult to defend with respect to liability or on the basis of comparative negligence.

The adjuster has limited powers to defend uninsured motorists claims. In the event of any disagreement over the settlement amount, the policyholder can require arbitration. Arbitration is less expensive and less time consuming than litigation. Furthermore, arbitrators are usually attorneys who are aware that the claim involves the policyholder versus the insurer. Arbitrators tend to give the policyholder the benefit of every doubt. Unfortunately, fraud and exaggeration can be at least as common in uninsured motorists claims as they are in third-party liability claims.

In many states, purchasing uninsured motorists coverage is required in order to meet state financial responsibility laws. The adjuster must be aware that some exclusions and other policy provisions might contradict state statutes. Courts have ruled that whenever policy language and state statutes conflict, the statute prevails. For example, in some states requiring uninsured motorists coverage for every vehicle, courts hold that policyholders can stack liability limits. Therefore, if a policyholder has three cars with $100,000 uninsured motorists coverage on each, he or she would be entitled to $300,000 coverage despite the fact that this was not permitted by the auto policy. Adjusters must be familiar with any state statutes that might affect the coverage of the claims they are handling.

Uninsured motorists (UM) coverage rarely applies to claims in which the responsible motorist has some liability insurance coverage, but in which that coverage is inadequate.

Underinsured Motorists Coverage

Because states' minimum liability-limit requirements have not kept pace with rising medical costs, insurers have offered underinsured motorists (UIM) coverage to help counter that problem. The ISO Underinsured Motorists Coverage endorsement PP 03 11 defines an "underinsured motor vehicle" as "a land motor vehicle or trailer of any type to which a bodily injury liability bond or policy applies at the time of the accident but its limit for bodily injury liability is less than the limit of liability for this coverage."

The following illustrates an underinsured motorist:

• Allen, a policyholder for Company A, has a Personal Auto Policy (PAP) with a $100,000 UIM limit. He is involved in an accident with Bob, a policyholder with Company B.

• Bob, who is responsible for the accident, has a $25,000 bodily injury limit on his PAP.

• Bob's motor vehicle would be considered "underinsured" regarding Allen's UIM coverage.

Using the same illustration, the following explains how UIM coverage applies in most states:

• Allen suffers bodily injury with $200,000 in damages.

• Allen collects $25,000, the bodily injury limit, from Bob's policy.

• The ISO UIM endorsement limits coverage by the following provision: "...the limit of liability shall be reduced by all sums paid because of the 'bodily injury' by or on behalf of persons or organization who may be legally responsible...." So, Allen is entitled to $75,000 from his own UIM coverage (Allen's $100,000 UIM limit *minus* Bob's $25,000 bodily injury limit).

The purpose of the UIM coverage is to guarantee the policyholder a specific limit of coverage (in this example, $100,000). In this illustration, Allen would be uncompensated for his damages over $100,000. Consequently, courts in some states have construed the policy wording differently to provide additional coverage above the liability limit collected from the responsible party's insurance policy. Such courts might award a total of $125,000 in compensation for Allen's injuries (Allen's $100,000 UIM limit *plus* Bob's $25,000 bodily injury limit).

Auto Property Damage Claims

In addition to bodily injury, auto accidents can also result in the insured becoming legally liable for damage to property such as buildings, appurtenant structures, landscaping, contents of over-the-road shipments, or other vehicles. These third-party losses are covered under auto property damage liability. Because the property that is damaged in auto accidents is most frequently other vehicles, the claims for such damage are handled similarly to first-party property damage losses. First-party property damage losses are covered under the physical damage section of the auto policy. Such losses might involve damage resulting from collision, fire, flood, or theft of the vehicle. Damaged autos are usually first inspected by an appraiser who writes a damage estimate that is forwarded to the adjuster assigned to the claim. These auto damage appraisers have expert knowledge of auto body repair methods and costs. Once the appraisal is received, the adjuster confirms coverage and pays the loss. As part of this process, the adjuster should explain the claim process to the insured and remain in contact with the insured to resolve any problems. The insurer will pursue subrogation, if appropriate and, if successful, will promptly reimburse any deductible paid by the insured.

Handling third-party property damage liability claims correctly is an essential part of good relations with both insureds and third-party claimants. Calculating constructive total losses accurately and obtaining agreement on repair prices are key tasks in properly adjusting these claims. Also, the adjuster can assert comparative negligence to mitigate full responsibility for property damage arising out of an accident involving the insured.

As with first-party claimants, an adjuster should provide prompt service to third-party claimants. If the third-party claimant is injured, courteous and professional service in handling the property damage can hasten the settlement of any bodily injury claim that might be asserted. If the claimant is not injured, the law might require the adjuster to negotiate any property damage liability claim with the aggrieved party. An adjuster is permitted to make good-faith comparative negligence arguments but should be willing to negotiate an equitable settlement.

Constructive Total Losses

When the cost to repair a vehicle plus its remaining salvage value equals or exceeds the vehicle's pre-loss value, the vehicle is a **constructive total loss**. It does not make sense financially to repair a constructive total loss, even if it is possible to make satisfactory repairs. By paying the vehicle's pre-loss value and taking the salvage, the insurer pays less overall. For example, assume a car worth $3,500 before the loss suffers $3,000 of damage and retains $1,000 of salvage value. Rather than pay $3,000 for repairs, the insurer should pay $3,500 for the title to the car and obtain $1,000 in the salvage market, for a net loss of $2,500. Insurers are in a better position to dispose of salvage efficiently than is the average person.

Constructive total loss
A loss that occurs when the cost to repair damaged property plus its remaining salvage value equals or exceeds the property's pre-loss value.

Neither insureds nor claimants, however, are required to "sell" their cars to insurers, as the preceding example might imply. Should the insured want to keep the car, the adjuster is entitled to take account of the salvage value. For example, using the values in the preceding paragraph, the vehicle's actual cash value before loss ($3,500) minus the vehicle's ACV following loss ($1,000) equals the amount of the loss ($2,500) paid to the claimant or insured.

Agreed Repair Prices

If a vehicle can be repaired, the adjuster should obtain an agreed repair price from the body shop selected by the insured or claimant. This agreement demonstrates that the adjuster's evaluation of the loss is legitimate and prevents disputes between the insurer and the claimant or between the owner and the body shop. Although the adjuster should try to agree on a repair price, the choice of a body shop should be left to the claimant. Many states have enacted "anti-steering" laws that restrict an insurer from directing a claimant to a particular repair shop.

Premises Liability Claims

Businesses that regularly have members of the public on their premises, such as retail stores, restaurants, banks, and hotels, probably experience more premises liability claims than any other type of liability claim. Premises liability claims are usually relatively minor fall-down claims, but nevertheless, they are important to the claimant and the policyholder. Responsively handling such claims can reduce their cost to the insurer and can preserve goodwill toward the policyholder.

Adjusters handling premises liability claims must establish good rapport with the claimant, both to establish the cause of the accident and to determine comparative negligence. Witnesses and employees of the policyholder can often help the adjuster in these efforts.

Determining the Cause of the Accident

Legal liability in premises liability claims is determined by negligence theories. Typically, the claimant asserts that the policyholder failed to maintain the premises in a reasonably safe condition. Under the law of negligence, the policyholder should be judged by how a reasonably prudent person would behave under the same circumstances.

The standard of care for property owners is traditionally qualified by the claimant's status on the premises. An owner owes only a slight level of care toward a trespasser, primarily a duty not to inflict intentional injury. An intermediate level of care is owed to licensees, a group that includes social guests, letter carriers, and solicitors. A property owner owes a high level of care to business invitees, those who are on the premises at the owner's invitation to do business with the owner. This group of claimants includes customers of the business. Some jurisdictions have eliminated this level of care classification, requiring instead that a reasonable level of care is the duty owed to all.

On learning that a customer has had an accident on the premises, most policyholders are genuinely solicitous of the injured person, out of both human decency and a sense of self-protection. Most policyholders want to preserve their customers' goodwill and forestall possible legal actions against them. Injuries to pride and dignity are as common as bodily injuries, and policyholders find that injured customers respond well to genuine concern. Some policyholders in these circumstances insist that the customer be seen by a physician and promise to pay whatever medical expense is incurred. Policyholders who take this approach should have medical payments coverage. Medical payments coverage is usually obtained for exactly this situation: taking care of a customer regardless of fault. Policyholders who do not have medical payments coverage probably violate their liability insurance policy conditions by making promises of payment, yet such promises do not usually cause trouble with insurers. If doing so settles the claim, adjusters are usually willing to pay for minor medical expenses, regardless of fault, under liability coverage.

Maintaining rapport with claimants in premises liability claims is important. A claim from a dissatisfied claimant who seeks legal representation usually costs the insurer much more to settle than a claim from a satisfied claimant. So, most adjusters handling premises liability claims do not push liability issues if a claim can be settled for medical expenses only.

When premises liability claims cannot be settled quickly and easily, liability issues are important. For business invitees, the insured owes a high level of care. So, almost any factor in the environment of the insured premises contributing to the accident could indicate negligence on the policyholder's part. The floor might be uneven, slightly defective, or too slippery. The lighting might be insufficient or the environment, too distracting. The policyholder might have failed to warn the public of a hazard or to barricade the hazard. The policyholder might have failed to conduct sufficient premises inspections to be aware of a new hazard. Sometimes (but rarely), claimants fall down on smooth, even, dry, clear, well-lighted, and unobstructed surfaces. However, the claimant can usually blame some other aspect of the premises for the accident.

Adjusters investigating premises liability claims should solicit statements from the claimant and all witnesses who can testify about either the accident or the condition of the accident scene. If the scene is substantially the same as when the accident occurred, the adjuster should take photos. The adjuster should also determine the policyholder's cleaning, maintenance, and inspection practices and should obtain copies of any logs or other records of such. If the policyholder uses an independent contractor for cleaning or maintenance work, the adjuster should determine the scope of that contractor's duties, obtain copies of the contracts, and determine what role in the accident the contractor might have played.

Determining Comparative Negligence

Regarding liability for their accident, claimants in premises liability claims are often in a difficult position. Unless their accidents were caused by a hidden hazard, claimants usually provide one of the following three reasons for the accident: (1) they had no idea what caused their accident, (2) they knew of the causes but failed to observe and avoid them, or (3) they were aware of and observed the causes before the accidents but encountered them anyway. Regarding liability, these three reasons amount to (1) no negligence on the policyholder's part, (2) comparative negligence on the claimant's part, or (3) assumption of the risk by the claimant. A common example of the first situation is a fall down smooth, even, well-lighted stairs. Most policyholders that have the public on their premises maintain their stairways well, and the policyholder's defense is that the fall on the stairs is the claimant's own fault. An example of the second situation is a claimant who falls on an obvious hazard, such as debris on the floor. The defense of claims of this sort is weaker whenever something in the environment, such as a sales display, was a conspicuous distraction or whenever the policyholder should have known of the hazard and eliminated it before the accident. An example of the third situation is a claimant who voluntarily walks across an obvious hazard, such as a torn-up or an icy sidewalk. The defense of this third situation is weakened if the claimant had no choice. The assumption of risk defense cannot be applied unless the claimant acted voluntarily.

Operations Liability Claims

Regarding liability theories and defenses that apply, claims arising out of a policyholder's operations are similar to premises claims. The key difference is that operations liability claims usually focus on an unsafe act rather than an unsafe condition. Additionally, the policyholder in operations liability claims is typically a contractor rather than an establishment open to the public.

Bases of Liability

A policyholder's operations are alleged to be responsible for an accident whenever the accident results from an unsafe or improper act by the policyholder or the policyholder's employees, whenever the policyholder fails to provide proper supervision of another party for whom it is responsible, or whenever the policyholder has contractually assumed liability.

Construction sites and construction operations are inherently dangerous. Unsafe acts and conditions are common. Consequently, many contractors and construction companies pay high premiums for workers' compensation and general liability insurance. Such companies often devote great effort to promoting safety, to controlling costs, to avoiding unfortunate injuries, and to complying with OSHA standards. Consequently, the policyholder's workers might not be forthcoming, honest, and complete in response to the adjuster's inquiries; the policyholder's supervisors might be defensive or brusque. Therefore, following an accident, the adjuster must realize that determining liability will be particularly challenging.

When investigating operations liability claims, the adjuster should begin by investigating exactly how the claimant's accident occurred. Exactly where did the accident occur? What workers were in the vicinity? Who employs and supervises these workers? Exactly what were these workers doing at the time of the accident? What equipment were they operating? What did each of them see? Even in the face of evasion and reluctance from witnesses, an adjuster can usually establish what happened through a thorough and methodical investigation.

A contractor might be responsible for its own employees as well as for the supervision of others. Under many construction contracts, a general contractor has duties to ensure workplace safety, and individual contractors might be responsible for their own subcontractors. The duty to supervise might be an explicit contractual obligation, a custom of the trade that is implied in the contract, or a requirement under general tort principles. When faced with a case of potential improper supervision, an adjuster usually assumes that the primarily responsible party is the workers' employer. Nevertheless, the adjuster should thoroughly investigate what supervisory steps the policyholder actually took. Did the policyholder communicate with its subcontractors about safety? Did the policyholder conduct inspections, give warnings, or otherwise enforce safe practices?

Contractual Assumptions of Liability

In addition to their direct responsibility for their workers and their duty to supervise others, contractor-insureds are often liable for the property damage and bodily injury caused by others because they have assumed contractual liability. Liability assumed by contract is different from liability for failure to supervise. When a contractor assumes liability for another, it is responsible for that other party's liabilities. In contrast, liability for failure to supervise is based on the contractor's own failure, not the failure to supervise or liabilities of another.

The legal interpretation of contractual liability can be complex. Generally, courts recognize contractual assumptions of liability as valid but interpret them narrowly. An adjuster examining an assumption of liability clause must determine whether it requires defense and indemnity or just indemnity. Does the assumption of liability extend to all liabilities of the indemnified party or just to liabilities that arise out of the indemnifying party's behavior? Does the assumption of liability extend to the project site's owner or to the indemnified party's subcontractors? If the adjuster has any doubts about interpreting the assumption of liability clause, he or she should seek the advice of claim supervisors, claim managers, or legal counsel.

Insurance coverage for contractual assumptions of liability varies. So, adjusters handling contractual liability claims must check policy wording carefully. Again, if coverage is unclear or doubtful, adjusters should seek opinions from their superiors or staff advisers and should issue a reservation of rights letter to the policyholder until the matter is resolved.

When an adjuster handles an assumed liability claim, the adjuster must investigate with the indemnified party and its employees as though they were the insured. If the indemnified party has been sued, the adjuster might consider providing its defense, even if the contract does not strictly require it. If the adjuster's insurer must indemnify the party in question, providing its defense as well might be preferable. Whether to do so is a question of the insurer's policy that can also depend on the strength of the claim and the willingness of the party in question to relinquish control of its defense.

Preservation of the Accident Scene

For a claim involving operations, the adjuster should immediately try to preserve the accident scene through photos, diagrams, and detailed measurements. Construction sites change rapidly, and witnesses' memories can become confused and vague.

In addition to preserving the precise scene of an accident, photos can provide many important incidental details. Photos can show the exact stage of the project at the time of the accident, including the exact stage of each subcontractor's work. Photos can show which contractors were on the scene on the day of the accident. Photos can also show the presence or absence of safety measures and precautions. On large or well-organized projects, the owner, architect, or general contractor might have daily records of progress, including photos.

Products Liability Claims

Any party that manufactures or sells a product that harms another can be liable for that harm. An adjuster handling products liability claims must investigate all possible bases of liability and all applicable defenses.

Bases of Liability

Other than traditional negligence theories, products liability can be based on breach of warranty or strict liability in tort.

Warranty
A promise, either written or implied, such as a promise by a seller to a buyer that a product is fit for a particular purpose.

A **warranty** is any contractual promise about the product that accompanies the sale. The warranty that guarantees performance or durability is one type of warranty. An alleged breach of warranty can be based on an express warranty (described in the next section) or on an implied legal warranty. Many written sales contracts explicitly disclaim any warranties, express or implied, unless included in the written contract.

Express warranty
An explicit statement about a product that often accompanies the sale of a product.

An **express warranty** is any explicit statement about the product that accompanies the sale. For example, a statement that reads, "These hedge clippers can easily cut through branches up to one-quarter-inch thick" could be the basis of liability if the hedge clippers failed to so perform and caused bodily injury or property damage. Express warranties can allow a claimant to assert a products liability claim that might not be sustainable on negligence or strict liability grounds. In the absence of an express warranty, the principal advantage to claimants of a products liability claim based on a warranty is that the statute of limitations is usually longer than for such a claim based on a tort.

Strict liability in tort differs from negligence, yet the claim investigations for both are similar. Under strict liability, the nature of the product is the issue, not the defendant's behavior. Specifically, the issue is whether the product is defective in a way that makes it unreasonably dangerous, not whether the defendant was negligent.

Product and Manufacturer Identification

The product in question must be carefully identified for subsequent identification of the manufacturer. Many retailers sell products that are manufactured elsewhere but that carry their store label. Many products have component parts from sources other than the assembling manufacturer.

Unless the manufacturer can be identified, the retailer is responsible to the claimant. A retailer can usually verify whether it sold a particular type of product at a particular time. The retailer can usually also identify the source from which it bought its merchandise.

Defending products liability claims is significantly different for manufacturers than for wholesalers or retailers. If a wholesaler or retailer resells a product in the same condition in which it left the manufacturer, the manufacturer is responsible for indemnifying the wholesaler or retailer from any products liability claims. An adjuster handling a wholesaler or retailer products liability claim can usually withdraw from the claim once the manufacturer's insurer is involved. Nevertheless, because the wholesaler or retailer is liable as far as the public is concerned, an adjuster for a wholesaler or retailer should be prepared to handle the claim should the manufacturer go out of business or be unidentifiable, insolvent, uninsured, or unwilling for any reason to handle the claim. Usually, however, manufacturers want to defend their products and their retailers for business reasons.

Use of Experts

Once a product has been identified, the issue of liability depends on whether the product could have been made safer and still perform its intended function. Some products are inherently dangerous. For example, power tools cannot perform their intended function without simultaneously being capable of severe bodily injury.

Determining liability in products claims often involves redesigning the product after an accident. The feasibility of redesign can be determined only through expert opinion. Both the plaintiff and the defendant must hire an engineer or another expert who can provide an opinion. Adjusting products liability claims is, therefore, expensive. Most manufacturers consider the expense of having an engineer or expert worthwhile because manufacturers face potentially millions of claims from product users. Because the policyholder has often been in business for years, the policyholder can probably provide the adjuster with the names of engineers and experts. However, adjusters must consider any financial stake such people might have in their relations with the policyholder and whether they are defending their own designs.

Review of Warnings and Instructions

Often, in products liability claims, the product itself cannot realistically be redesigned, so the plaintiff alleges that the warnings and instructions that accompanied the product were inadequate and that the product was defective.

When faced with such an allegation, the adjuster must review all information accompanying the product. The adjuster should determine whether the warnings and instructions provided, if followed, would have prevented the claimant's accident. If not, the adjuster should try to determine what additional warning would have been necessary to prevent the claimant's accident. The adjuster should also investigate whether the claimant read the instructions. If the claimant asserts that he or she did, the adjuster should ask the claimant to repeat whatever he or she remembers. Should it appear that the claimant never read the instructions, or forgot everything that he or she read, the claimant will have a difficult case to prove. Any alleged shortcomings in the manufacturer's instructions cannot be a cause of the claimant's accident if the claimant never read or cannot remember them.

Improper Use

Claimants are often injured while using products in ways that are not intended or foreseeable. For example, claimants can suffer bodily injuries by using a lawn mower to trim hedges or by using prescription drugs for conditions other than those for which they were prescribed.

Adjusters who suspect improper use should obtain detailed statements from the claimants. If the claimant is not available for a statement, the adjuster might be able to obtain an account of what happened from the claimant's emergency-room records or from an initial report by the claimant to a state or federal consumer products regulatory agency.

Workers' Compensation Claims

The workers' compensation system operates differently from the liability system. The majority of work-related bodily injury claims are compensated regardless of fault and usually without judicial intervention. These claims are covered under Part One of the Workers Compensation and Employers Liability Insurance policy. Part One of this policy theoretically provides the exclusive remedy for bodily injury claims caused or aggravated by conditions of employment. A small percentage of bodily injury claims fall under Part Two of the Workers Compensation and Employers Liability Insurance policy, which is the Employers Liability coverage part. Employers' liability is a liability-based third-party coverage under which the employee must prove negligence. It is an exception to the exclusive remedy approach used for workers' compensation coverage. Employers' liability coverage applies to employees who are excluded from workers' compensation laws by employment exemptions, such as agricultural workers, or to employees who have rejected compensation benefits under elective statutes in certain states. Employers' liability also provides coverage for care and loss of services to a spouse and to family members of an injured employee who suffer bodily injury as a consequence of the employee's bodily injury. Two additional types of claims would not be covered under workers' compensation coverage but would be covered under employers' liability coverage:

1. Third-party-over claims—for example, when an employee of the insured sues a third party, such as a machine manufacturer, for a work-related bodily injury, and the third party then sues that employee's employer.

2. Dual capacity claims—for example, when an injured employee sues his or her employer in a capacity other than as employer, such as in a products liability suit.

The claim adjusting process used for employers' liability is similar to the process used for other third-party claims. Because these claims are uncommon, this discussion focuses on handling workers' compensation claims rather than on employers' liability claims. Although the compensability of work-related bodily injuries is usually straightforward, adjusters handling workers' compensation claims must investigate them diligently. Additionally, the medical aspects of workers' compensation claims can be extraordinarily complex and expensive.

Investigating Compensation Cases

Workers' compensation claims that involve only medical expenses, such as a single visit to the emergency room, are usually processed with no investigation. The policyholder's word is accepted as proof that the accident occurred on the job and that the injury is work related.

Should an accident involve lost time from work, the adjuster is likely to conduct an investigation. Statements are obtained from the claimant, the employer, and any witnesses. The purpose of these statements is to establish that the bodily injury is work related, that the bodily injury was not preexisting, what the likely period of disability will be, and whether relations between the employee and employer are such that the claimant might have staged the claim or might be inclined to exaggerate the disability. The adjuster must document the employee's earnings so that the employee's disability compensation can be calculated properly.

The adjuster's investigation of the accident can be an important part of the employer's loss control program. Many policyholders are concerned about their workers' compensation costs. Additionally, these policyholders want to reduce workplace injuries for humanitarian reasons, to forestall any OSHA or state labor department investigation, and to maintain productivity in their business. Many insurers are active in loss control and depend on their adjusters' investigations for guidance about where to devote their efforts.

Controlling Medical Expenses

Workers' compensation medical expenses are potentially unlimited. The law requires the employer (or its insurer) to pay all necessary and reasonable medical expenses related to the bodily injury sustained on the job. Consequently, workers' compensation policies have no policy limits. A small percentage of workers' compensation claims account for an enormous percentage of the medical expenses paid by workers' compensation insurers.

Workers' compensation adjusters have limited tools with which to challenge medical expenses. The employee-patient is not required to co-pay any portion of the expenses, as is common with health insurance expenses. Workers' compensation insurers often do not have the bargaining power that health insurers have with medical providers. Furthermore, many states do not have fee schedules or other controls over medical expenses. Consequently, workers' compensation medical expenses have risen faster in the past decade than healthcare expenses in general.

To control medical expenses, some workers' compensation insurers have entered into agreements with **preferred provider organizations (PPOs)**, through which the insurer receives a discount on the usual medical expenses in exchange for a volume of referrals. This type of agreement is feasible only in states that allow the employer or insurer to select the treating physician.

As with liability claims for other types of bodily injury, insurers also control workers' compensation medical expenses by conducting medical bill audits. Most workers' compensation insurers conduct bill audits to identify charges that are excessive, fabricated, or redundant. Specialized bill auditing firms can perform this service for workers' compensation insurers. Bill audits usually result in more than enough savings to justify the expense of the audit.

Utilization review services, discussed previously, are another valuable tool to control medical expenses by determining whether medical treatment is necessary. However, before an insurer can deny reimbursement for medical treatment, the insurer must be certain that experts from the utilization review service are willing and able to testify on its behalf. Because workers' compensation laws are designed to protect workers regardless of fault, insurers should not deny claims without strong grounds for doing so.

Workers' compensation claims can also include claims for psychological conditions, which are very expensive. The causes of psychological conditions are complex and can include a combination of work-related and nonwork-related factors. Furthermore, the recovery from and cure of psychological conditions are often difficult to verify. So, claims for psychological conditions are expensive to investigate and difficult to terminate.

Claims for work-related stress disability can involve a complex interaction of employer-employee difficulties, preexisting personality disorders, and difficulties outside the workplace. Adjusters are generally not competent to evaluate these claims. However, experts in the fields of psychology and psychiatry specialize in defense evaluations of psychological conditions.

The most sophisticated form of medical expense control is **medical management**. Medical management controls medical expenses on the small percentage of claims that involve high medical expenses. Those claims usually involve permanent bodily injuries that require tens of thousands of dollars of medical expenses annually for the remainder of the claimant's life. Medical management ensures that the claimant receives care in appropriate facilities with appropriate specialists. Rehabilitation facilities can specialize in certain bodily injuries, such as brain trauma, quadriplegia, burns, or blindness. Medical management can enable an injured claimant to live independently rather than in an institution. By specializing in the care of serious permanent bodily injuries, medical management specialists can both ensure optimum treatment for claimants and medical expense control for insurers.

Controlling Disability Expenses

Controlling disability expenses is probably the foremost challenge for workers' compensation adjusters. Claims in which the claimant loses no time from work and claims in which the claimant returns to work promptly are relatively simple and straightforward. Claims in which disability extends over a long or an excessive period are the biggest challenges and expense for workers' compensation insurers.

Workers' compensation insurers generally do not have the legal power simply to stop claim payments if they believe the disability has ended. Once a claim has been initially accepted as compensable, the insurer can end disability payments only by agreement with the claimant or by order of the compensation commission. If the claimant does not agree, cases before the compensation commission can take months to resolve. Compensation commissions generally decide in the claimant's favor and usually resolve doubtful cases against the insurer. Should the commission find in the insurer's favor and allow disability payments to stop, the claimant is not required to reimburse past payments. So, in jurisdictions in which compensation claims take months to resolve, the claimant is assured of compensation for those months, no matter the outcome.

Some claimants in difficult disability cases are antagonistic toward the employer or about their work. The adjuster can do little about such antagonism. However, such behavior usually becomes obvious during the adjuster's investigation and signals that the case could be difficult.

Adjusters can control disability expenses by insisting that the treating physician explain why the claimant cannot perform his or her job responsibilities. Many treating physicians certify disability without any real understanding of the physical demands of the claimant's job responsibilities. For almost any physical impairment, some jobs, or aspects of jobs, can be performed by someone with that impairment. Therefore, physicians cannot simply assume that certain impairments prevent employees from performing their jobs.

An adjuster can also work with the employer to modify the employee's job by removing its most physically demanding parts. Claimants who return to limited-duty work are usually on the road to recovery. Adjusters handling disability claims can encourage claimants to think in terms of returning to work by constantly asking them what aspects of their work they are still incapable of performing. Adjusters can then suggest job modifications to the employer.

Professional Liability Claims

Liability claims for professional malpractice are generally handled by specialized insurers and adjusters. These claims require a specialized determination of liability and a complex determination of damages. Because of the importance of these claims to the policyholder's professional reputation, the policyholder is usually involved in his or her own defense, and these claims are likely to be litigated to verdict rather than settled.

Professional liability claims can be asserted against people who provide professional services, such as physicians, engineers, architects, attorneys, accountants, or insurance agents.

Determining Standard of Care

Professionals are not necessarily at fault for negative outcomes. Physicians cannot guarantee a complete cure for every patient. Attorneys cannot win every case. Accountants cannot guarantee the financial health of a business or an investment.

Professionals are required to exercise the standard of care accepted in their profession. In other words, professionals should perform their services competently. Malpractice claims are usually proved by experts who testify that the defendant should have behaved or decided differently, given the facts and circumstances when the professional services were rendered. An adjuster investigating a malpractice claim should constantly ask what could have and should have been done differently at every point.

Physicians are part of a nationwide profession with professional journals and modern communications readily available. However, no physician is held to the standard of the leading expert in the field. If appropriate care of a patient requires leading-edge expertise, the average physician should not be judged as negligent for failing to provide such expertise.

Many physicians are found at fault for failing to obtain a patient's informed consent. Physicians are required to explain their care to their patients; they should explain the treatment options and risks associated with each. Should a physician fail to explain the risks of treatment, he or she might be liable to the patient, even if the adverse outcome is an unavoidable risk. Physicians must exercise judgment in how much they tell patients, because exhaustive explanations would confuse most patients. Nevertheless, a physician who fails to fully inform a patient of the risks of treatment could be responsible for any negative outcome. Proving that the physician obtained informed consent is difficult because many physicians do not document their discussions with their patients. After a negative outcome, patients often claim not to have understood the risks they faced, and the physician cannot prove otherwise.

Determining Damages

Damages in medical malpractice claims are similar to those in other bodily injury cases, except that the physician is not liable for the underlying condition that initially caused treatment. Determining damages requires expert testimony about how much the patient's condition would have improved or progressed with proper treatment. Often these determinations are only matters of probability.

For alleged attorney malpractice, the underlying legal matter from which the malpractice claim arose must be relitigated or reconsidered in the professional liability claim. The damages in the malpractice claim depend on how much better the result obtained in the underlying legal matter should have been.

Determining damages in other types of malpractice claims is similar. Expert testimony is used to establish what the claimant's condition would have been had proper professional services been rendered.

Defending Malpractice Claims

Generally, malpractice claims are litigated by only the most sophisticated plaintiff and defense attorneys. The policyholder is also likely to be heavily involved in the claim's defense.

As malpractice suits became more common, the insurers that handled them resisted easy settlement. Often, the policyholder had to consent in writing to any settlement. Absent such consent, the verdict had to be litigated. As the strength of the defense became obvious, only the most talented plaintiff attorneys accepted these cases. To match the skills of the plaintiff attorney, insurers increasingly relied on specialized defense attorneys. Currently, a general practice attorney rarely handles a malpractice case.

Many professional malpractice insurance policies require the policyholder's consent to settlement. The policyholder is more personally concerned about the outcome of the professional malpractice claim than about the outcome of other claims because the policyholder's professional reputation is at stake. Some policies require the policyholder who rejects a proposed settlement to be responsible for any verdict in excess of the proposed settlement.

An adjuster involved in a professional malpractice claim must investigate the possibility of defenses. In medical malpractice claims, for example, the patient could be responsible for failing to divulge all relevant information to the physician, for failing to follow the prescribed course of treatment, or for failing to report complications.

SUMMARY

This chapter describes how liability claims are adjusted. Once coverage has been determined in a liability claim, the insurance policy plays a much smaller role than in the settlement of a property claim. Liability claim adjusters are primarily concerned with the laws of liability and damages, which exist apart from the insurance policy.

The basic law of negligence applies to most liability claims that adjusters handle, but adjusters must also consider strict liability for products and specific statutory liability for certain auto accidents.

Damages in bodily injury claims include medical specials, loss of earnings, and general damages. Determining and evaluating general damages are essential skills for liability claim adjusters because general damages are often the main element of the claim. Because general damages are subjective, much room for negotiation exists in liability claims. Most successful liability claim adjusters are excellent negotiators who enjoy the challenge.

Should negotiations prove unsuccessful, liability claim adjusters must know how to guide claims through the court system. Doing so requires knowledge of court procedures and the ability to deal with and manage attorneys.

Specific types of liability claims present their own unique challenges, and this chapter concludes with a review of these challenges. Experienced liability claim adjusters are familiar with the difficulties that can arise for various types of claims. Determining coverage for auto bodily injury claims can be complicated and might require accident reconstruction experts and coordination with auto no-fault, workers' compensation, and/or uninsured motorists claims. When adjusting premises liability claims, the adjuster must first determine the cause of accidents according to negligence theories to establish whether the policyholder is liable for injuries arising from the accident. Adjusting operations liability claims is similar to adjusting premises liability claims; however, operations liability claims generally focus on an unsafe act rather than on an unsafe condition within the premises. For products liability claims, the adjuster must investigate all possible bases of liability and applicable defenses before settling the claim.

Workers' compensation claims are compensated regardless of fault and are, therefore, an exception to the liability system. Workers' compensation adjusters must still investigate all claims thoroughly to accurately determine not only compensation amounts but also all medical expenses for the worker's on-the-job bodily injury. Professional liability claims are usually handled by adjusters who specialize in this type of claim. Professional liability claim adjusting requires a focused determination of liability, and determining damages is complex in most cases.

This chapter concludes the discussion of the claim function. The next chapter covers reinsurance and includes a discussion of the reinsurance market and types of reinsurers, as well as reinsurance program administration.

CHAPTER NOTE

1. Commercial General Liability Coverage Form, CG 00 01 10 01, Insurance Services Office, 2000, p. 1.

Chapter 11

Direct Your Learning

Reinsurance

After learning the content of this chapter, you should be able to:

■ Explain how reinsurance operates and how it benefits policyholders.

■ Describe reinsurance marketing systems and the functions of reinsurance.

■ Describe the categories and types of reinsurance.

■ Given a case, determine how the primary insurer and the reinsurer would share the amount of insurance, the premium, and covered losses under quota share and surplus share treaties.

■ Given a case, determine how the primary insurer and the reinsurer would share losses under per risk excess of loss, per policy excess of loss, per occurrence excess of loss, and aggregate excess of loss treaties.

■ Evaluate the effectiveness of per risk excess of loss, per policy excess of loss, per occurrence excess of loss, and aggregate excess of loss treaties in providing stabilization of loss experience, large-line capacity, catastrophe protection, and surplus relief.

■ Explain why a primary insurer would use facultative reinsurance instead of treaty reinsurance.

■ Explain how finite risk reinsurance operates.

■ Describe the factors that should be considered in developing a reinsurance program.

■ Given a case, evaluate the reinsurance needs of an insurer and recommend a reinsurance program to meet those needs.

■ Explain how reinsurance retentions and limits are set.

■ Describe the information that the reinsurer and the primary insurer usually request from one another when negotiating reinsurance agreements.

■ Explain how reinsurance intermediaries operate and how they are compensated.

■ Describe the role of the primary insurer and the reinsurer in reinsurance program administration.

■ Explain how reinsurance is regulated.

Develop Your Perspective

What are the main topics covered in the chapter?

This chapter discusses the primary functions of reinsurance, which include stabilizing loss experience, improving large-line capacity, providing catastrophe protection, and providing surplus relief. Other functions include providing underwriting guidance and facilitating withdrawal from a territory or type of business. The process of obtaining, administering, and regulating reinsurance is also described in this chapter.

Compare the profiles of insurers in the chapter to your own organization.

- Based on these examples, what reinsurance limits, retentions, and types of reinsurance might fit the needs of your organization?

Why is it important to learn about these topics?

In underwriting a reinsurance treaty, a reinsurer considers the primary insurer's management, financial strength, and other existing reinsurance agreements. A reinsurance agreement is individually tailored and priced.

Consider the factors involved in tailoring a reinsurance agreement.

- How would a reinsurer view the characteristics of your organization in developing a reinsurance agreement?

How can you use what you will learn?

Investigate your organization's reinsurance needs.

- How might your organization's current goals change its reinsurance requirements?

Chapter 11

Reinsurance

Insurers, like other types of organizations, have numerous property and liability loss exposures. Some of an insurer's loss exposures—for example, exposure to fire damage loss to the company's office building—are common not only to insurers but also to other types of organizations.

An insurer can use essentially the same risk management techniques to manage its underwriting risk as it uses to manage its other risks.

- An insurer can *avoid* underwriting risk to some extent by not operating in a certain state or by not selling a particular type of insurance.
- An insurer can *control* underwriting risk by following sound underwriting guidelines, by charging adequate rates, and by providing loss control and claim services to policyholders.
- An insurer can *finance* some of its underwriting risk by transferring the potential financial consequences of certain loss exposures it insures to another insurer.

This chapter focuses entirely on the last technique—risk financing through transfer of loss exposures to other insurers. This transfer is known as reinsurance. This chapter also examines several interrelated topics, including basic terms and concepts; reinsurance marketing systems; reinsurance functions; types of reinsurance; and reinsurance program development, negotiation, program administration, and regulation.

BASIC TERMS AND CONCEPTS

Reinsurance can be thought of as "insurance on insurance," because it refers to insurance through which one insurer transfers to another insurer (called the reinsurer) some or all of the potential financial consequences (liability) of certain loss exposures it cedes to the reinsurer. The potential financial consequences are the payable amounts of insurance that cover the loss exposures ceded to the reinsurer. The loss exposures ceded could relate to a single subject of insurance (such as a building), a single policy, or a group of policies. An insurer that transfers the liability for the loss exposures it cedes to a reinsurer is variously referred to as the reinsured, the ceding company, the cedent, the direct insurer, or the primary insurer. Although all of these terms are acceptable, this chapter uses the term **primary insurer** to denote the party to a

Reinsurance
Insurance through which one insurer transfers to another insurer (called the reinsurer) some or all of the potential financial consequences (liability) of certain loss exposures it cedes to the reinsurer.

Primary insurer
An insurer that transfers the liability for the loss exposures it cedes to a reinsurer.

Reinsurer
An insurer that accepts the liability for loss exposures ceded by another insurer.

Ceding commission
A fee paid to a primary insurer by a reinsurer to compensate the primary insurer for acquisition costs such as state premium taxes, agents' commissions, and other operating costs.

Reinsurance limit
The maximum amount that the reinsurer will pay for a claim and that is commonly stated in the reinsurance agreement.

Retrocession
A contractual agreement in which one reinsurer transfers part of the liability for its loss exposures assumed under reinsurance agreements to other reinsurers.

Cut-through endorsement
An endorsement that provides that, in the event of the insolvency of the primary insurer, the reinsurer directly assumes the obligations of the primary insurer.

reinsurance agreement that cedes loss exposures to a reinsurer. The **reinsurer** is the party to the reinsurance agreement that accepts the loss exposures ceded by the primary insurer.

The consideration paid by the primary insurer to the reinsurer is called the reinsurance premium. Depending on the type of reinsurance agreement, the reinsurer might pay the primary insurer a **ceding commission** to compensate the primary insurer for the expenses of acquiring the underlying (or original) policy. Sometimes the ceding commission is used to share part of the profit the reinsurer has earned on profitable transferred loss exposures.

The primary insurer usually retains some of the liability for loss exposures it cedes to the reinsurer. The primary insurer's retention can be expressed as a dollar amount, a percentage of the original amount of insurance, or both. A **reinsurance limit**—the maximum amount that the reinsurer pays for a claim—is also commonly specified in the reinsurance agreement. The primary insurer retains all liability above the reinsurance limit unless it has another reinsurance agreement for the liability that exceeds the reinsurance limits.

Reinsurers, like primary insurers, can transfer to other reinsurers some of the liability they have accepted in reinsurance agreements. A **retrocession** is the agreement under which one reinsurer, called the retrocedent, transfers some or all of the liability it has assumed or will assume for certain loss exposures to another reinsurer, called the retrocessionaire. Retrocession is very similar to reinsurance except for the parties involved in the agreement. As illustrated in Exhibit 11-1, reinsurance and retrocession enable worldwide insurance risk transfer.

With reinsurance, insurers can better meet the needs of the public and handle their own risk portfolios more efficiently. Reinsurance helped to enable the U.S. insurance industry to withstand about $20 billion of insured losses from Hurricane Andrew in 1992 and an estimated $40 billion of insured losses from the terrorist attacks of September 11, 2001.

Policyholders benefit from reinsurance (see the adjacent text box for a summary of the benefits), but they are not a legal party to reinsurance agreements. The primary insurer is solely responsible for indemnifying its policyholders for all covered losses regardless of reinsurance covering the same losses. Whether the primary insurer receives timely or appropriate reimbursement from the reinsurer for the loss exposures it has reinsured is a legal matter between the primary insurer and the reinsurer. So, if the primary insurer becomes insolvent or fails to meet its obligation to pay a claim, the policyholder cannot collect directly from the reinsurer. However, the following two exceptions to this general rule can apply:

- First, the reinsurer might authorize the primary insurer to attach a so-called cut-through endorsement to the policies of certain insureds. A **cut-through endorsement**—also called an assumption certificate or an assumption of liability endorsement—modifies the underlying policy so that the primary insurer's obligation under the underlying policy becomes the

EXHIBIT 11-1

Worldwide Insurance Risk Transfer

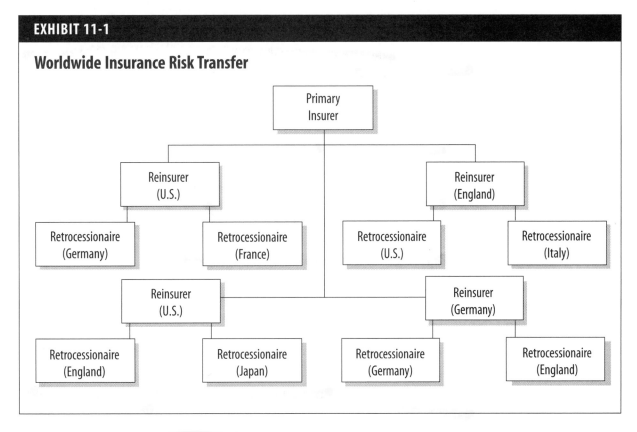

reinsurer's direct obligation in the event of the primary insurer's insolvency. This endorsement is usually attached to a property insurance policy when a mortgagee is concerned with the financial rating of the insurer providing insurance coverage on the financed property. Also, risk managers of large commercial policyholders often request cut-through endorsements.

- Second, the organization might file a claim directly with the reinsurer when the organization purchases reinsurance for its captive insurer or for a pool of which the organization is a member.

Reinsurance Benefits to Policyholders

Even though an insurer's policyholders are not parties to the insurer's reinsurance agreements, reinsurance nevertheless provides several benefits to policyholders:

- Reinsurance enables policyholders to obtain all of their insurance from one insurer, thereby avoiding coverage gaps and possible problems collecting payments for covered losses that might exist when buying insurance from several insurers.

- Reinsurance helps to stabilize and improve the primary insurer's loss results, thereby effectively increasing the likelihood that the insurer remains solvent and is able to pay policyholders' claims for covered losses.

- Reinsurance allows small insurers to compete effectively against large ones, thereby increasing the coverage options available to policyholders.

REINSURANCE MARKETING SYSTEMS

In the U.S., any licensed insurer can market reinsurance unless prohibited by statute or charter. Few such prohibitions exist, and many primary insurers sell some reinsurance. Even relatively small insurers can participate in various reinsurance pools and syndicates. Reinsurance marketing systems include the following:

- *Professional reinsurers.* Professional reinsurers serve the reinsurance needs of primary insurers. Professional reinsurers can work with primary insurers directly or indirectly through reinsurance intermediaries.

- *Reinsurance departments of primary insurers.* Primary insurers that also provide reinsurance usually conduct reinsurance operations through separate departments (or as separate insurers in the group).

- *Reinsurance pools, syndicates, and associations.* Reinsurance pools, syndicates, and associations are groups of unrelated (i.e., not under common ownership) insurers that band together to underwrite or share reinsured loss exposures jointly. Some pools write reinsurance only for member insurers of the pool. Others write coverage only for nonmember insurers, and still others write coverage for both members and nonmembers.

Nonadmitted alien reinsurer
A reinsurer that is not licensed to do business in the U.S. but operates there.

If permitted, primary insurers in the U.S. can cede loss exposures to nonadmitted alien reinsurers. **A nonadmitted alien reinsurer** is a reinsurer that is not licensed to do business in the U.S., but operates there. Transactions with nonadmitted alien reinsurers account for a sizable portion of the reinsurance business in the U.S. Insurers based in the U.S. also sell much reinsurance abroad, but not nearly as much as they buy abroad.

Reinsurance intermediary
The party between a primary insurer and the reinsurer who assists in completing the reinsurance agreement.

Reinsurance can be placed directly with a reinsurer or through an intermediary. **A reinsurance intermediary**, also known as a reinsurance broker, provides various services to primary insurers and reinsurers, including coverage and premium negotiation, claim adjusting, accounting, and underwriting advice. As compensation for its services, a reinsurance intermediary receives a commission, called a brokerage fee, from the reinsurer. Some reinsurers use their own personnel to sell reinsurance and do not ordinarily accept loss exposures from reinsurance intermediaries. Such reinsurers are known as direct writer reinsurers.

REINSURANCE FUNCTIONS

It might seem unusual for an insurer to go to the trouble and expense of selling a policy and then paying a reinsurer to accept some or all of the liability for certain loss exposures. However, reinsurance can alleviate several practical business constraints, such as the need to insure large loss exposures, to protect policyholders' surplus from adverse loss experience, or to finance growth.

Different types of reinsurance are available. Each effectively performs one or more functions. So, the reinsurance that an insurer obtains depends mainly on what constraints or problems the insurer must address in order to reach its goals. Before analyzing the types of reinsurance, it helps to consider the six functions that reinsurance serves. The first four functions are primary functions. The last two functions are additional functions that reinsurance can provide.

1. Stabilize loss experience
2. Improve large-line capacity
3. Provide catastrophe protection
4. Provide surplus relief
5. Provide underwriting guidance
6. Facilitate withdrawal from a territory or type of business

Stabilize Loss Experience

The first primary function of reinsurance is to stabilize loss experience. Smoothing the peaks and valleys of the loss experience curve is an important function because an insurer must have a reasonably steady flow of profits to attract and retain capital and to increase its capital and surplus to support growth. Insurance losses sometimes fluctuate widely because of demographic, economic, social, and natural forces, as well as because of chance. Stabilizing loss experience is closely related to providing catastrophe protection, discussed later.

To illustrate how reinsurance could stabilize an insurer's loss experience over a ten-year period, assume that an insurer purchases reinsurance that places a $20 million ceiling on the total amount of all losses the insurer will pay each calendar year for a particular type of insurance. Exhibit 11-2 shows how such reinsurance might work. Alternatively, an insurer might purchase reinsurance that limits its maximum loss payment to $25,000 per claim; however, this approach would not protect a primary insurer from an accumulation of losses as does the first example.

Improve Large-Line Capacity

The second primary function of reinsurance is to improve large-line capacity. **Large-line capacity** is an insurer's ability to provide a large amount of insurance under a single policy, such as $100 million of property coverage for a commercial office building. Few insurers are willing and able to provide such high limits alone because that exposes them to potentially devastating underwriting results. Moreover, most state insurance regulations prohibit an insurer from retaining a single loss exposure, net of reinsurance, that exceeds 10 percent of its policyholders' surplus. (Policyholders' surplus is an insurer's net worth, equal to the insurer's assets minus its liabilities.)

Large-line capacity
A primary insurer's ability to provide a large amount of insurance under a single policy.

Reinsurance can help insurers improve their large-line capacity. For example, a primary insurer might insure a commercial building worth $100 million, retain

EXHIBIT 11-2

Stabilization of Loss Experience

Hypothetical Loss Experience of an Insurer for a Type of Insurance

Time Period (Year)	Losses (000)	Amount Reinsured (000)	Stabilized Loss Level (000)
1	$ 10,000	$ —	$10,000
2	22,500	2,500	20,000
3	13,000	—	13,000
4	8,000	—	8,000
5	41,000	21,000	20,000
6	37,000	17,000	20,000
7	16,500	—	16,500
8	9,250	—	9,250
9	6,000	—	6,000
10	10,750	—	10,750
Total	$174,000		
Average Annual Losses = $17,400			

The total losses are $174,000,000, or an average of $17,400,000 each time period. If a reinsurance agreement were in place to cap losses to $20,000,000, the primary insurer's experience would be limited to the amounts shown in the stabilized loss level column. The broken line that fluctuates dramatically in the graph below represents actual losses, the dotted line represents stabilized losses, and the horizontal line represents average losses.

Graph of Hypothetical Loss Data

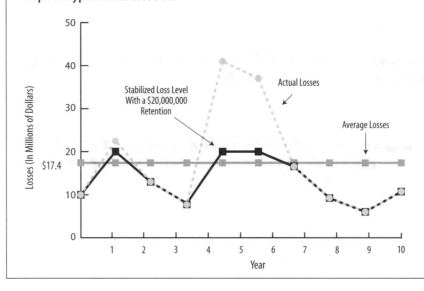

$10 million of the liability, and transfer the rest of the liability, or $90 million, to a reinsurer. With this reinsurance agreement, an insurer can provide the full amount of insurance requested on this large loss exposure while keeping its retention to an acceptable level.

Provide Catastrophe Protection

The third primary function of reinsurance is to provide catastrophe protection. Insurers are subject to catastrophe losses from natural as well as man-made disasters. Without reinsurance, an insurer can suffer serious financial harm or even insolvency when a large number of its insured loss exposures are concentrated in an area that experiences a catastrophe. The appropriate type of reinsurance, when arranged properly to meet the insurer's needs, can help an insurer minimize the effect of catastrophic losses.

To protect itself against catastrophic losses, an insurer might, for example, purchase reinsurance that provides up to $50 million of coverage per hurricane when the total amount of loss from a single hurricane exceeds a certain amount that the insurer can safely retain. Reinsurance that limits the net amount a primary insurer must pay for all claims resulting from a single occurrence can also help to stabilize the insurer's loss experience over time.

Provide Surplus Relief

The fourth primary function of reinsurance is to provide surplus relief. **Surplus relief** is a flow of funds into a primary insurer's policyholders' surplus when policyholders' surplus has been reduced by the insurer's rapid growth in written premiums. Generally, insurance regulators consider an insurer to be overextended when its net written premiums (gross written premiums, direct and reinsurance assumed, less reinsurance ceded), exceed its policyholders' surplus (its net worth) by a ratio of more than three to one. For reasons to be discussed, rapid growth of an insurer's written premiums can cause a "surplus drain" that results in an unacceptable premium-to-surplus ratio. Reinsurance that provides surplus relief can help a growing insurer to keep its premium-to-surplus ratio at a level that permits further growth.

Surplus drain results from accounting rules that specify when revenues and expenses must be recognized in an insurer's financial statements. According to these rules, insurers must recognize expenses immediately but cannot treat ✳ the associated revenues as fully earned on the same date. For example, when an insurer issues an insurance policy, it must immediately recognize the full amount of the agency commission as an expense. However, the insurer cannot recognize the associated policy premium as revenue until it is actually earned, pro rata, over the policy period. The difference in amount resulting from this mismatching of expenses and revenues must be supported by, and therefore reduces, the insurer's policyholders' surplus. So, these accounting rules can reduce the underwriting capacity of newly formed or fast-growing insurers whose premium revenue does not increase as quickly as their policy acquisition expenses.

Surplus relief
A flow of funds into an insurer's policyholders' surplus when policyholders' surplus has been reduced by the insurer's rapid growth in written premiums.

To illustrate the application of these accounting rules, assume that an insurer has written a policy covering a commercial building for an annual premium of $20,000 and has incurred acquisition expenses of 25 percent of the premium, or $5,000. On the insurer's balance sheet, this transaction increases the insurer's liabilities by $20,000 (because the $20,000 policy premium must be put into the unearned premium reserve), while the insurer's assets increase by only $15,000 because the acquisition expenses have already been recognized. The $5,000 difference between assets and liabilities results in a $5,000 decrease in policyholders' surplus, thereby reducing the insurer's underwriting capacity. If, however, the insurer has a type of reinsurance in which the reinsurer pays the primary insurer ceding commissions, the insurer can obtain some surplus relief. The ceding commission paid by the reinsurer is immediately recognized as revenue to the primary insurer, thereby offsetting the effect of the immediately charged policy acquisition expenses by the amount of the ceding commission.

Provide Underwriting Guidance

One additional function of reinsurance is to provide underwriting guidance. Reinsurers deal with many insurers in the domestic and global markets. Consequently, reinsurers accumulate a great deal of information about coverages, rating, underwriting, and claim adjusting. This information can help primary insurers, particularly small insurers or large insurers planning to expand the types of insurance they offer. For example, a medium-sized insurer might reinsure 95 percent of its umbrella liability insurance over a period of years and rely heavily on the reinsurer's expertise in underwriting and pricing that insurance.

Providing underwriting expertise can be a very important service to property-casualty insurers. Reinsurers must be careful when offering advisory services so that they do not reveal or use proprietary information obtained through confidential relationships with other insurers.

Facilitate Withdrawal From a Territory or Type of Business

A second additional function of reinsurance is to facilitate withdrawal from a territory or type of business. An insurer might sometimes make a business decision to stop insurance operations in a particular territory or to stop writing a particular type of business. An insurer uses several approaches to implement this decision. The insurer can simply stop writing new business and renewing existing policies and wait for all existing policies to expire. Or, the insurer can (to the extent permitted by applicable cancellation laws) cancel all policies in effect and return the unearned premiums to its policyholders. Either of these two approaches can be unwieldy, expensive, and likely to create ill will among policyholders, producers, and state insurance regulators. Either approach also leaves uncertainty about the insurer's outstanding claims, which must be settled, and about new claims, which might continue to be filed even after the insurer ceases operations.

Another approach is for the primary insurer to transfer the liability for all outstanding policies to a reinsurer. By purchasing reinsurance, the insurer can avoid creating ill will resulting from policy cancellation while transferring its obligations for existing and new claims to the reinsurer. An arrangement by which an insurer cedes the loss exposures for an entire type of insurance, all of the policies sold in a particular territory, or book of business to a reinsurer in order to withdraw from that business is known as **portfolio reinsurance**.

REINSURANCE TYPES

No single reinsurance agreement performs all the reinsurance functions. Instead, reinsurers have developed various types of reinsurance, each being effective in helping insurers meet one or more goals. A primary insurer often combines several reinsurance agreements to meet its particular needs. Each reinsurance agreement is tailored to the specific needs of the primary insurer and the reinsurer.

Reinsurance transactions are of two types. The first type of transaction uses one agreement for a group of loss exposures and is called treaty reinsurance. The second type of transaction uses one agreement for each loss exposure and is called facultative reinsurance.

- In **treaty reinsurance**, the primary insurer agrees in advance to cede certain types of loss exposures according to the terms and conditions of the reinsurance agreement, called a treaty. Treaty reinsurance is characterized as being "obligatory," because the primary insurer must cede, and the reinsurer must assume, the loss exposures falling within the treaty. Treaty reinsurance premiums and claims are settled periodically (for example, quarterly), and most treaties are automatically renewed annually until canceled by either party.

- In **facultative reinsurance**, the primary insurer negotiates a separate reinsurance agreement for each loss exposure it wants to reinsure. Similarly, the reinsurer is under no obligation to accept any particular loss exposure offered: it can decline the loss exposure or make a counteroffer to the primary insurer. So, facultative reinsurance is often characterized as being "non-obligatory," because the primary insurer is free to decide which loss exposures it wants to reinsure and the reinsurer is free to accept or reject each loss exposure.

The two types of treaty and facultative reinsurance are pro rata and excess of loss reinsurance. These types of reinsurance reflect how amounts of insurance, premiums, and losses are to be divided between the primary insurer and the reinsurer.

- In **pro rata reinsurance** (or proportional reinsurance), the amount of insurance, the premium, and the losses are divided between the primary insurer and the reinsurer in the same agreed proportion. For example, if the reinsurer accepts 75 percent of the amount of insurance under a given policy, the reinsurer receives 75 percent of the premium and must pay 75 percent of each covered loss under the policy. Pro rata treaties have a

Portfolio reinsurance
Reinsurance that transfers to the reinsurer liability for an entire type of insurance, territory, or book of business after the primary insurer has issued the policies.

Treaty reinsurance
An agreement in which the primary insurer agrees to cede certain types of loss exposures, and the reinsurer agrees to accept the loss exposures that fall within the treaty.

Facultative reinsurance
An agreement that is negotiated separately for each loss exposure the primary insurer wants to reinsure and that gives the reinsurer the right to accept or reject each loss exposure.

Pro rata reinsurance
An agreement in which the amount of insurance, premium, and losses are divided between the primary insurer and the reinsurer in the same agreed portions (proportional reinsurance).

reinsurance limit that applies to each loss exposure that is subject to the treaty. Loss exposures requiring higher amounts of insurance can be reinsured, but the excess liability is retained by the primary insurer unless otherwise reinsured.

Excess of loss reinsurance
An agreement that requires a reinsurer to pay that portion of a loss that exceeds the primary insurer's retention up to the reinsurance limit (nonproportional reinsurance).

- In **excess of loss reinsurance** (or nonproportional reinsurance), the primary insurer and the reinsurer do not share each loss proportionately as in pro rata reinsurance. Instead, the excess of loss reinsurer is involved only if a loss exceeds the primary insurer's retention, which is also called the reinsurer's attachment point. The reinsurer pays only the amount exceeding the retention, subject to the reinsurance limit.

As shown in Exhibit 11-3, both facultative reinsurance and treaty reinsurance can be written on either a pro rata or an excess of loss basis. Finite risk reinsurance, as illustrated in the exhibit, is a nontraditional type of reinsurance that is also discussed later.

EXHIBIT 11-3

Types of Reinsurance

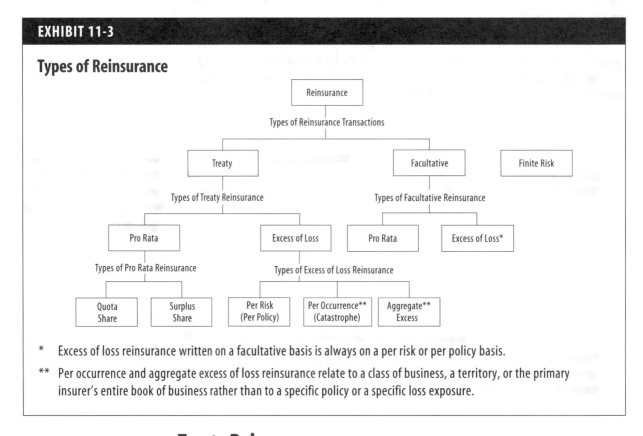

*   Excess of loss reinsurance written on a facultative basis is always on a per risk or per policy basis.

**   Per occurrence and aggregate excess of loss reinsurance relate to a class of business, a territory, or the primary insurer's entire book of business rather than to a specific policy or a specific loss exposure.

Treaty Reinsurance

The first type of reinsurance transaction is treaty reinsurance. Most insurers depend heavily on treaty reinsurance because it provides distinct advantages over facultative reinsurance. The reinsurer is obligated to accept all loss exposures that are subject to the treaty's terms. Consequently, the primary insurer can underwrite, accept, and reinsure such loss exposures without prior consultation with the reinsurer on each pending application. Also, because prior negotiation is not required, the handling expense for each policy included in the reinsurance agreement is less under treaty reinsurance than under facultative reinsurance. Whether an insurer chooses to use a pro rata or an excess of loss treaty is determined by the kind of loss exposures to be reinsured, the primary insurer's financial needs, and other factors.

Pro Rata Treaties

Pro rata reinsurance is often chosen by thinly financed or newly incorporated insurers because it is effective in providing surplus relief. Its effectiveness results from the practice of paying ceding commissions under pro rata treaties. Pro rata treaties can be used to reinsure either property or liability loss exposures, but property pro rata treaties are much more common.

The two types of pro rata treaties are *quota share treaties* and *surplus share treaties* (sometimes simply called "surplus treaties"). The principal difference between them is how each one indicates the primary insurer's retention.

Quota Share Treaties

Under a **quota share treaty**, the primary insurer cedes a fixed, predetermined percentage of the amount of insurance for every policy within the class or classes of business subject to the treaty. Even policies with the lowest amounts of insurance are ceded.

Quota share treaty
A pro rata reinsurance agreement under which the primary insurer cedes a fixed, predetermined percentage of every loss exposure it insures within a class or classes.

The primary insurer's retention is stated as a percentage of the amount of insurance so that the dollar amount of its retention varies by amount of insurance. The reinsurer assumes the liability for the amount of insurance minus the primary insurer's retention, up to the limit of the reinsurance treaty. The percentage of premium that the reinsurer receives (minus the ceding commission) and the percentage of each loss the reinsurer must pay is the same as the percentage of the liability for the amount of insurance it assumes. An example of a quota share treaty is shown in Exhibit 11-4.

Quota share treaties have the advantage for primary insurers of being simple to administer because the reinsurer receives the agreed percentage of all covered premiums. The principal disadvantage of a quota share treaty for the primary insurer is that the reinsurer receives a large share of the premium for presumably profitable business. Because of this disadvantage, quota share treaties are used by small insurers that have limited reinsurance options and by insurers that need surplus relief.

The effectiveness of quota share treaties in fulfilling the four primary functions of reinsurance is as follows:

- Quota share treaties are the most effective means of providing surplus relief because the primary insurer receives a ceding commission on every policy covered by the reinsurance agreement.

- Quota share treaties are not effective in stabilizing loss experience because they do not affect the primary insurer's loss ratio.

EXHIBIT 11-4

Quota Share Treaty Example

Assume that Insurance Company has purchased from Reinsurance Company a quota share treaty with a $250,000 limit and a retention of 25 percent and a cession of 75 percent. Insurance Company has written three policies. Policy A insures Building A for $10,000 for a premium of $100, with one loss of $8,000. Policy B insures Building B for $100,000 for a premium of $1,000, with one loss of $10,000. Policy C insures Building C for $150,000 for a premium of $1,500, with one loss of $60,000. The table and graph below show how the amounts of insurance, premiums, and losses under these policies would be split between the primary insurer and the reinsurer. In each case, the primary insurer retains 25 percent of the amount of insurance and the premium and pays 25 percent of the losses. However, the dollar amount of its retention increases as the amount of insurance increases.

Division of Amount of Insurance, Premiums, and Losses Under Quota Share Treaty

	Primary Insurer (25% Retained)	Reinsurer (75% Assumed)	Total
Policy A			
Amount of Insurance	$2,500	$7,500	$10,000
Premium	25	75	100
Loss	2,000	6,000	8,000
Policy B			
Amount of Insurance	$25,000	$75,000	$100,000
Premium	250	750	1,000
Loss	2,500	7,500	10,000
Policy C			
Amount of Insurance	$37,500	$112,500	$150,000
Premium	375	1,125	1,500
Loss	15,000	45,000	60,000

Total Reinsurance Losses = $58,500

Total losses are less than the $250,000 treaty limit, so loss payments are not affected by policy limits.

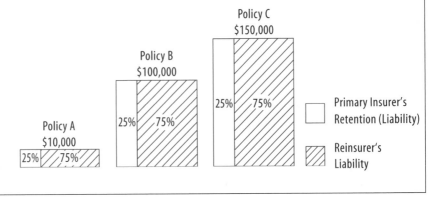

- Quota share treaties can be reasonably effective in improving the primary insurer's large-line capacity, depending on the retention percentage specified by the treaty. However, quota share treaties are not as effective in that regard as surplus share and per risk excess of loss treaties, which are discussed subsequently.

- Although quota share treaties can lessen the effect of a catastrophe, they do not provide adequate protection for catastrophes because they place no cap on the aggregate loss. Reinsurers sometimes include a per occurrence limit in quota share treaties, which further limits the usefulness of these treaties for protecting the primary insurer from an accumulation of losses that is typical following catastrophic events.

Exhibit 11-5 indicates the effectiveness of quota share treaties and compares their effectiveness at performing the four primary reinsurance functions with that of other types of treaties.

EXHIBIT 11-5

Functions of Specific Types of Treaty Reinsurance

Type of Reinsurance	Stabilize Loss Experience	Improve Large-Line Capacity	Provide Catastrophe Protection	Provide Surplus Relief	Main Purpose
Pro rata quota share	No	Yes	No	Yes	To provide surplus relief
Pro rata surplus share	No	Yes	No	Yes	To provide large-line capacity while providing some surplus relief
Excess of loss per risk or per policy	Yes	Yes	Yes, to some extent, but not purchased for purpose	No	To provide large-line capacity while stabilizing loss experience
Excess of loss per occurrence	Yes, to the extent losses fluctuate because of an accumulation of losses from a single occurrence	No	Yes	No	To protect against catastrophic losses from one event
Aggregate excess of loss	Yes	Yes, but not purchased for this purpose	Yes	No	To stabilize loss experience

Surplus Share Treaties

Surplus share treaty
A pro rata reinsurance agreement in which the reinsurer assumes pro rata responsibility for only that portion of a loss exposure's liability that exceeds a stipulated dollar amount.

Under a **surplus share treaty**, only those underlying policies whose amounts of insurance exceed a stipulated dollar amount are covered by the treaty. When the amount of insurance for the underlying policy exceeds this stipulated dollar amount, or *line*, the reinsurer assumes the "surplus liability," which is the difference between the underlying policy's amount of insurance and the primary insurer's line. This surplus liability is what the primary insurer cedes to the reinsurer.

The primary insurer and the reinsurer share premium and losses proportionally. The primary insurer's share of the premium and losses is that proportion that the line bears to the underlying policy's amount of insurance. The reinsurer's share of the premium and losses is that proportion that the amount of ceded liability bears to the underlying policy's amount of insurance. The following is an illustration:

Underlying policy's amount of insurance	$125,000
Primary insurer's line	$ 25,000
Surplus liability or ceded amount of liability	$100,000

Primary Insurer's Proportional Share of Premiums and Losses

Primary insurer's line	$ 25,000
Underlying policy's amount of insurance	$125,000

Reinsurer's Proportional Share of Premiums and Losses

Surplus liability or ceded amount of liability	$100,000
Underlying policy's amount of insurance	$125,000

For the preceding illustration, the primary insurer would receive 20 percent of the underlying policy's premium and would pay 20 percent of any losses covered by the underlying policy, subject to the limits of the underlying policy. Likewise, the reinsurer would receive 80 percent of the underlying policy's premium and would pay 80 percent of all losses covered by the underlying policy, subject to the limits of the underlying policy.

Surplus share treaties usually permit the primary insurer to adjust the amount of its line based on the quality of the loss exposure. Primary insurer underwriters use *line authorization guides* (insurer-developed manuals) for assistance with selecting an appropriate line for each loss exposure. The line authorization guide usually specifies minimum and maximum lines for each loss exposure based on objective hazard characteristics such as the loss exposure's construction type, fire protection, and occupancy. In surplus share treaties, the primary insurer fully retains every loss exposure whose amount of insurance is less than the applicable line. The primary insurer must cede every loss exposure whose amount of insurance exceeds the applicable line, and the reinsurer must accept that loss exposure.

The capacity of a surplus share treaty is often expressed in terms of the number of lines. For example, an insurer with a $50,000 line and a five-line surplus share treaty can provide a combined underwriting capacity of $300,000, or the sum of $50,000 from the primary insurer and $250,000 from the reinsurer. Exhibit 11-6 illustrates how the amounts of insurance, premiums, and losses can be shared under a surplus share treaty.

To obtain large-line underwriting capacity in excess of an existing surplus share treaty, a primary insurer can purchase surplus share treaties in layers. For example, if a primary insurer has a five-line surplus share treaty with a $50,000 retention and obtains a second-layer five-line surplus share treaty, the primary insurer's total capacity per policy becomes eleven times its retention, or $550,000. Like quota share treaties, surplus share treaties are renewable annually until canceled by either party.

Surplus share treaties provide a more logical approach to purchasing reinsurance than do quota share treaties, because no loss exposure whose amounts of insurance fall below the primary insurer's minimum line is ceded. Accordingly, a principal advantage to the primary insurer of surplus share treaties over quota share treaties is that primary insurers do not cede loss exposures that they can afford to retain.

A disadvantage of surplus share treaties compared to quota share treaties is the primary insurer's increased administrative expense. Because not all loss exposures are ceded and retention amounts can vary by type of loss exposure, the primary insurer must maintain a record of the loss exposures that are ceded.

The effectiveness of surplus share treaties in fulfilling the four primary reinsurance functions is as follows:

- The main purpose of surplus share treaties is to provide large-line capacity. Surplus share treaties are superior to quota share treaties in providing large-line capacity because under a surplus share treaty, the primary insurer can obtain multiple lines of reinsurance coverage up to the treaty limit. In contrast, under a quota share treaty, the primary insurer's total dollar liability increases in direct proportion to that of its reinsurers, limiting the primary insurer's large-line capacity.

- Because surplus share treaties normally provide ceding commissions to the primary insurer, they can also provide surplus relief. However, they are less effective than quota share treaties in providing surplus relief because under surplus share treaties, no loss exposures are ceded for policies with amounts of insurance less than the minimum retention.

- Like quota share treaties, surplus share treaties are not effective in stabilizing loss experience or providing catastrophe protection.

EXHIBIT 11-6

Surplus Share Treaty Example

Assume that Insurance Company has purchased from Reinsurance Company a surplus share treaty with a retention of $25,000 and a reinsurance limit of $250,000. This would be referred to as a "ten-line surplus share treaty," because the primary insurer's reinsurance coverage would be up to ten times its retention amount. The table and graph in this exhibit show how this treaty would apply to the same three policies used in the quota share treaty exhibit. For Policy A, the reinsurer assumes no liability because the amount of insurance is less than the $25,000 retention. For Policy B, the proportion in which premiums and losses are shared is determined by the retention divided by the amount of insurance. The same applies to Policy C. Under a quota share treaty, the percentage retention remains constant, and the dollar amount of retention increases as the amount of insurance increases. Under a surplus share treaty for amounts of insurance above the retention, the dollar amount of retention remains constant while the percentage retention decreases as the amount of insurance increases.

Division of Amount of Insurance, Premiums, and Losses Under Surplus Share Treaty With $25,000 Retention and $250,000 Reinsurance Limit

	Primary Insurer (% Retained)	Reinsurer (% Assumed)	Total
Policy A			
Amount of Insurance	$10,000 (100%)	$0 (0%)	$ 10,000
Premium	100	0	100
Loss	8,000	0	8,000
Policy B			
Amount of Insurance	$25,000 (25%)	$ 75,000 (75%)	$100,000
Premium	250	750	1,000
Loss	2,500	7,500	10,000
Policy C			
Amount of Insurance	$25,000 (17%)	$125,000 (83%)	$150,000
Premium	250	1,250	1,500
Loss	10,000	50,000	60,000

Policy A
No participation
by the reinsurer

Policy B
$100,000
25% / 75%

Policy C
$150,000
17% / 83%

Primary Insurer's Retention (Liability)

Reinsurer's Liability

Bordereau

A **bordereau** (for which the plural is "bordereaux") is a document that shows details of all individual loss exposures ceded under pro rata treaty reinsurance agreements. Previously, primary insurers submitted monthly or quarterly bordereaux to their reinsurers, as required by a clause in their treaties. Few reinsurers today require a bordereau clause in the reinsurance agreement. Nevertheless, primary insurers continue to keep such details in their cession registers, which can be audited by their reinsurers according to an "inspection of records" clause in the treaty.

Bordereau
A document showing details of all individual loss exposures ceded under pro rata treaty reinsurance agreements.

Excess of Loss Treaties

Excess of loss treaties (commonly called excess treaties) differ from pro rata treaties in that the primary insurer and the reinsurer do not share the amounts of insurance, premiums, and losses in the same proportion. In fact, *no insurance amount is shared under excess of loss treaties*, only losses and premiums. The reinsurance premium is usually stated as a percentage of the primary insurer's premium revenue for the covered types of business, but the percentage is subject to negotiation and varies by type of business and by insurer.

The reinsurer is responsible only for losses that exceed the retention or for loss exposures that are subject to the excess of loss treaty. Although coverage provided by a pro rata treaty is typically concurrent (identical) with the coverage provided by the primary insurer's policy, the coverage provided by an excess of loss treaty is not necessarily the same as that of the primary insurer's policy.

The capacity of an excess of loss treaty is expressed in terms of the retention and the reinsurance limit, such as the following:

$800,000 xs $100,000 for each and every loss

The reinsurer indemnifies the primary insurer up to $800,000 in excess of the first $100,000 of loss. The primary insurer is responsible not only for its $100,000 retention but also for any amount of the loss above the combined $900,000 capacity—the sum of the retention plus the reinsurance limit—unless the primary insurer has or can obtain another reinsurance agreement.

Three of the most frequently used excess of loss treaties are the per risk or per policy excess of loss treaty, the per occurrence excess of loss treaty, and the aggregate excess of loss treaty. They differ substantially in operation, as explained in the next section.

Per risk excess of loss treaty
A reinsurance agreement applied to property insurance policies under which a retention and a limit of coverage apply separately to each loss exposure insured by the primary insurer.

Per Risk or Per Policy Excess of Loss Treaties

In a **per risk excess of loss treaty**, the retention and the reinsurance limit apply separately to each loss exposure ceded by the primary insurer. (A single loss exposure might be one building or all buildings insured under a single policy.) In contrast, the retention and the limit in a **per policy excess of loss treaty** apply separately to all of the loss exposures under each *policy* ceded by

Per policy excess of loss treaty
A reinsurance agreement applied to liability insurance policies under which a retention and a limit of coverage apply separately to each policy issued by the primary insurer.

the primary insurer. Per risk excess of loss treaties are common in property reinsurance, and per policy excess of loss treaties are common in liability reinsurance. In both types of treaties, the retention is stated as a dollar amount of loss, and the reinsurer is liable—unless the primary insurer has agreed to a percentage participation in losses exceeding its retention—for all losses to any one loss exposure in excess of the retention and up to the agreed reinsurance limit.

When entering into a per risk or per policy treaty, most insurers set their retentions high enough so that they transfer to the reinsurer only the liability for the less-frequent, large claims. However, some insurers set their retentions low enough so that reinsurance claims occur frequently. Treaties with such low retentions are frequently called **working covers** (or working excess layers). Working covers help primary insurers to stabilize their loss experience. A small or an inexperienced insurer might choose a working cover to minimize its liability until it gains confidence in the types of business written.

Working cover
A per risk or per policy excess of loss treaty with such low retentions that the reinsurer expects moderate to heavy loss activity.

The retention under a per risk or per policy excess of loss treaty *applies separately to each subject of insurance*. For example, if Insurance Company insured Company A's building at 1110 Main Street and Company B's building next door at 1112 Main Street and both buildings burned, then the retention under a per risk excess of loss treaty would apply separately to each building. If Insurance Company issued automobile liability policies to each of the preceding firms and an auto accident occurred covered by both policies, the retention under a per policy excess of loss treaty would apply separately to each policy. As the next two sections explain, the retention applies differently for the other types of excess of loss treaties.

Unlike pro rata treaty reinsurers, excess of loss treaty reinsurers do not participate in all losses with primary insurers, but rather only in those that exceed the primary insurer's retention, and then only in the loss amount that exceeds the retention. This difference is emphasized here because it is a frequent source of confusion. Exhibit 11-7 shows how a primary insurer and a reinsurer divide responsibility for losses under a per risk excess of loss treaty.

From the primary insurer's viewpoint, the principal advantage of per risk or per policy excess of loss treaties compared to pro rata treaties is that less premium is shared with the reinsurer. Consequently, the primary insurer earns income on the investment of these premium savings. Administration expenses are also lower because fewer reinsurance claims are processed. Also, monitoring loss exposures reinsured, as is required under a surplus share treaty, might not be necessary because the excess of loss treaty is concerned only with losses.

EXHIBIT 11-7

Per Risk Excess of Loss Treaty Example

Assume Insurance Company has purchased from Reinsurance Company a per risk excess of loss treaty with a $25,000 retention. The table and graph below show how losses will be split. Policy A and Policy B have losses below the retention amount, so the reinsurer is not involved. Policy A (see Exhibit 11-6) has a limit of only $10,000, so even a total loss will not come under this treaty. No mention is made here of amounts of insurance or premium amounts because they are not relevant to the division of losses under an excess of loss treaty.

Division of Losses Under Per Risk Excess of Loss Treaty With $25,000 Retention

	Loss Amount	Insurance Company	Reinsurance Company
Policy A Loss	$ 8,000	$ 8,000	$ 0
Policy B Loss	10,000	10,000	0
Policy C Loss	60,000	25,000	35,000

Policy C
$60,000 Loss

$35,000

$25,000

Policy A
$8,000 Loss

Policy B
$10,000 Loss

Primary Insurer's Retention

Reinsurer's Share of the Loss

The effectiveness of per risk and per policy excess of loss treaties in fulfilling the four primary reinsurance functions is as follows:

- Per risk or per policy excess of loss treaties are effective in stabilizing the primary insurer's loss experience because they lessen the effect of large losses, which contribute disproportionately to loss experience fluctuations. The reinsurer's loss experience is not the same as that of the primary insurer in any given year. However, over the long run, each primary insurer should expect to pay its own losses plus the reinsurer's operating expenses and profit—that is, the primary insurer relinquishes part of its profits in the good years to transfer its losses to the reinsurer in the bad years, thereby stabilizing its loss experience over time.

- Per risk or per policy excess of loss treaties are effective in providing large-line capacity because they absorb the large losses that limit the primary insurer's ability to insure large loss exposures. These treaties are much more effective in this regard than quota share treaties and more effective than surplus share treaties, particularly if the reinsurance premium expense is considered.

- Per risk excess of loss treaties provide catastrophe protection because they pay the amount in excess of the primary insurer's retention on each individual loss. However, they are far less effective in this regard than per occurrence excess of loss treaties, because a catastrophic loss can affect a large percentage of the insurers' policies written in a geographic area.

- Excess of loss treaties are generally not as effective as pro rata treaties in providing surplus relief because ceding commissions are normally not paid by the reinsurer to the primary insurer.

Per Occurrence Excess of Loss Treaties

Per occurrence excess of loss treaty

A reinsurance agreement that indemnifies the primary insurer when the losses for an occurrence exceed the primary insurer's retention.

Under a **per occurrence excess of loss treaty**, the reinsurer agrees to indemnify the primary insurer for losses in excess of the primary insurer's retention, subject to a reinsurance limit, when two or more losses (or policies, or specifically scheduled subjects of insurance) are involved in one accident, occurrence, or event. Per occurrence excess of loss treaties can be used for either property or liability loss exposures.

Property insurers are prone to large accumulations of losses arising from a single event, such as a hurricane or an earthquake, that can damage many insured properties simultaneously. Most of the individual covered losses are relatively small, but the accumulated covered losses can be staggering. A **catastrophe excess of loss treaty**—another name for a per occurrence excess of loss treaty when applied to property coverages—helps insurers manage such large accumulated covered losses.

Catastrophe excess of loss treaty

A reinsurance agreement that helps the primary insurer manage a large accumulation of losses from a single event, such as a hurricane or an earthquake.

Per occurrence excess of loss treaties play an important role in liability insurance, too, especially when the primary insurer needs large-line capacity for a single type of liability insurance or simultaneous coverage for multiple types of liability insurance. For example, an insurer writing workers' compensation insurance might consider per occurrence excess of loss reinsurance protection for that type of insurance. Or, it might combine multiple types of liability insurance—for example, workers' compensation, auto liability, and commercial general liability—subject to a single per occurrence excess of loss treaty. When the per occurrence retention is set higher than the limit of any single liability policy, the reinsurance coverage is sometimes known as a *clash cover* because it requires losses under two or more policies to exceed the per occurrence retention.

Like the retention under per risk and per policy excess of loss treaties, the retention under a per occurrence excess of loss treaty is stated as a dollar amount of loss. The difference is that all of the net losses—total losses less deductions for all other per risk or per policy reinsurance agreements at lower layers of the reinsurance program—arising from a single occurrence are totaled to determine when the retention for the per occurrence excess of loss treaty has been satisfied. Accordingly, the primary insurer and the reinsurer must carefully evaluate the reinsurance agreement's definition of occurrence, which can be quite detailed. For example, a treaty might contain a definition of occurrence that contains separate clauses applicable to several different sets of covered causes of loss. The clause defining occurrence regarding windstorm might read as follows:

> As regards windstorm, hail, tornado, hurricane, cyclone, including ensuing collapse and water damage, the term "occurrence" is defined as all individual losses sustained by the Company [that is, the primary insurer] occurring during any period of 72 consecutive hours arising out of and directly occasioned by the same event. However, the event need not be limited to one state or province or states or provinces contiguous thereto.

The definition of occurrence is important because it controls the application of the retention and the reinsurance limit. The retention applies separately, but only once, to each occurrence, as does the reinsurance limit. According to the definition of occurrence quoted previously, if a hurricane traveled up the East Coast and caused wind damage over three days, then all of the damage would result from a single occurrence. Consequently, the primary insurer would be required to absorb only one retention, and the reinsurer's liability would not exceed the treaty's limits. (The definition quoted is illustrative. Different reinsurers, or even the same reinsurers for different treaties, might use different definitions.)

Per occurrence excess of loss treaties are usually written for an annual period and cannot be canceled by either party.

The effectiveness of per occurrence excess of loss treaties in fulfilling the four primary reinsurance functions is as follows:

- Per occurrence excess of loss treaties are effective in stabilizing loss experience to the extent that such fluctuations result from an accumulation of losses from a single occurrence.

- Per occurrence excess of loss treaties might enhance large-line capacity, depending on the circumstances, but are not purchased to fulfill that function.

- Per occurrence excess of loss treaties protect against an accumulation of losses resulting from a single event and are therefore the most effective type of reinsurance treaty for catastrophe protection.

- Per occurrence excess of loss treaties do not provide surplus relief, because the reinsurer usually does not pay a ceding commission.

Aggregate Excess of Loss Treaties

Under an **aggregate excess of loss treaty**, the reinsurer agrees to indemnify the primary insurer when the primary insurer's aggregate losses for a certain period, usually one year, exceed the retention for the type of underlying insurance the treaty covers. The retention can be stated in dollars, as a loss ratio, or as a combination of the two. When the retention and reinsurance limit are stated

Aggregate excess of loss treaty
A reinsurance agreement under which the reinsurer begins to pay when all of the primary insurer's losses for some stated period of time exceed the retention stated in the treaty.

in dollars, the aggregate excess treaty is usually called an *aggregate excess of loss treaty*. When the retention and reinsurance limit are stated as loss ratios, the aggregate excess treaty is usually called a *stop-loss treaty*.

The primary insurer can negotiate the size of its retention, but the reinsurer usually does not agree to a retention so low that it would guarantee the primary insurer a profit. Moreover, the reinsurer normally includes a participation requirement in the reinsurance agreement to discourage the primary insurer from relaxing its underwriting or loss adjusting standards once its retention has been reached. Sometimes, the reinsurer requires that the primary insurer maintain other treaties as a condition of providing the aggregate excess of loss treaty.

Aggregate excess of loss treaties are less common than the other forms of excess treaties. However, they have been used with some frequency for crop-hail insurance and for small insurers providing other types of insurance.

The effectiveness of aggregate excess of loss treaties in fulfilling the four primary reinsurance functions is as follows:

- Aggregate excess of loss treaties are the most effective of all types of reinsurance for stabilizing the primary insurer's loss experience because these treaties eliminate fluctuations in aggregate loss amounts.

- Aggregate excess of loss treaties can enhance large-line capacity by providing greater aggregate limits on an insurer basis, but they are not purchased for that function.

- Aggregate excess of loss treaties provide catastrophe protection because the caps they put on losses incurred in one year could also limit the insurer's liability for an accumulation of losses from a single event.

- Aggregate excess of loss treaties do not provide surplus relief because they do not usually provide ceding commissions to the primary insurer.

Facultative Reinsurance

The second type of reinsurance transaction is facultative reinsurance. Facultative reinsurance is obtained on an individual loss exposure basis, allowing the primary insurer to choose the loss exposures it wants to cede. Likewise, the reinsurer is under no obligation to assume the loss exposures offered by the primary insurer and therefore can decline the offer or make a counteroffer. If the reinsurer decides to assume the loss exposures offered by the primary insurer, the reinsurer formalizes the reinsurance agreement by issuing a facultative certificate of reinsurance to the primary insurer.

Underwriting facultative reinsurance is substantially different from underwriting treaty reinsurance. In underwriting a treaty, the principal focus is on the primary insurer's management, the types of insurance to be reinsured, and the primary insurer's loss experience for the types of insurance to be covered under the treaty. The reinsurer, however, does not underwrite individual loss exposures under the treaty. With facultative reinsurance, the reinsurer underwrites each loss exposure individually as it is submitted for consideration.

Facultative reinsurance has several potential disadvantages. When a primary insurer cedes loss exposures facultatively, it incurs the administrative expense of handling the loss exposures separately. The primary insurer bears the uncertainty that reinsurance might not be available under the terms and at the rates it wants. Because the reinsurer individually underwrites the loss exposures, the primary insurer must furnish prospective reinsurers with detailed information about the loss exposures it wants to cede—essentially the same information that a prudent primary insurer requires when considering an application from its own applicant. The primary insurer discloses additional competitive information (for example, insurance rates) to potential reinsurers. The reinsurance rate could be set higher than was the insurance rate on the underlying policy if, for example, the reinsurance market is hard.

Despite these likely disadvantages to primary insurers, they can find facultative reinsurance useful in the following four situations:

- First, an insurer might not have any treaty covering a particular type of insurance because it rarely writes that type of insurance. When an insurer wants to write that type of insurance as an accommodation in order to attract or retain key policyholders, facultative reinsurance can make that possible. Additionally, facultative reinsurance enables primary insurers, particularly small or new ones, to provide coverage on large loss exposures that would otherwise exceed their individual underwriting capacity.

- Second, treaties have exclusions. A treaty might exclude coverage for "target loss exposures" or loss exposures related to certain hazardous operations. "Target loss exposures" refers to high-value properties such as large art museums, major bridges, and nuclear generating facilities that require concurrently purchasing insurance from several insurers. A primary insurer can use facultative reinsurance to cede those loss exposures excluded under its applicable treaties.

- Third, treaties have upper limits. Like the size of the primary insurer's retention, the reinsurance limit can affect the reinsurer's loss experience and is a major determinant of reinsurance cost. A primary insurer can cede facultatively the portion of a loss exposure that exceeds the reinsurance treaty's limit.

- Fourth, a primary insurer can use facultative reinsurance to protect its treaties from adverse loss experience. Continuing an existing treaty on favorable terms, or perhaps on any terms, depends on the quality of the loss exposures ceded under the treaty. A favorable reinsurance treaty can facilitate the primary insurer's operations and profitability. Some treaties include a profit-sharing commission that bases reinsurance rates or ceding commissions directly on losses incurred during the current or most recent policy periods. So, an insurer can use facultative reinsurance for loss exposures that might adversely affect its treaty reinsurance. Because each facultative submission is an independent transaction and is underwritten separately, a loss under one facultative agreement has little or no effect on the terms or rates for subsequent transactions.

Facultative reinsurance can be effective in providing large-line capacity to the primary insurer. It helps the insurer stabilize its loss experience by limiting the effect of a single large loss. Also, the facultative reinsurer can provide expert advice about loss exposures, price, policy terms, and conditions. Because facultative reinsurance must be negotiated separately for each loss exposure, it is not likely to provide significant surplus relief unless a very large number of facultative agreements are negotiated. This same characteristic prevents facultative reinsurance from effectively providing catastrophe protection.

Types of Facultative Reinsurance

Like treaty reinsurance, facultative reinsurance agreements can be pro rata or excess of loss. **Pro rata facultative reinsurance** functions similarly to a surplus share treaty except, of course, that each facultative agreement relates to a single loss exposure. **Excess of loss facultative reinsurance** also operates just like a per risk or per policy excess of loss treaty—that is, the reinsurer is involved only if the loss exceeds the primary insurer's retention and pays only the amount of loss in excess of the retention, subject to the reinsurance limit.

Although pro rata facultative reinsurance is the traditional approach to reinsuring property loss exposures, excess of loss facultative agreements are used with hazardous, complex, and high-value properties. Excess of loss reinsurance has also been the traditional form of facultative reinsurance for liability and workers' compensation loss exposures.

The pricing for excess of loss facultative reinsurance for property loss exposures depends on numerous factors, including the facultative underwriter's judgment, statistics from the reinsurer's experience with similar loss exposures, guides such as Lloyd's first loss scale, and prevailing market conditions. For liability loss exposures, the per policy excess of loss reinsurance premium is usually based on the increased limits factors used by the primary insurer. However, the reinsurance premium might be higher or lower than the primary insurer's increased limits premium, depending on the facultative reinsurer's judgment about the adequacy of that premium for the particular loss exposure.

Facultative Obligatory Treaty Reinsurance

Some reinsurance agreements are hybrid and have both treaty and facultative reinsurance elements. Reinsurers sometimes enter into what is known as facultative obligatory treaties or automatic facultative treaties. In a facultative obligatory treaty, the primary insurer can opt to retain or cede a certain loss exposure (a facultative element), but the reinsurer is bound to accept all loss exposures ceded according to the treaty agreement (an obligatory treaty element). So, a high degree of trust must exist between the parties in a facultative obligatory treaty. Otherwise, the primary insurer could cede only poor loss exposures, disadvantaging the reinsurer.

Facultative obligatory treaty reinsurance provides several advantages to the primary insurer. The insurer can select the loss exposures it wants to cede, and

Pro rata facultative reinsurance
A reinsurance agreement for individual loss exposures in which the reinsurer shares a pro rata portion of the losses and premiums of the ceding insurer.

Excess of loss facultative reinsurance
A reinsurance agreement for individual loss exposures in which the primary insurer pays all losses up to its agreed retention and the reinsurer pays losses in excess of the retention up to the reinsurance limit.

the reinsurance for those loss exposures is guaranteed. Therefore, the primary insurer has an immediate capacity to provide insurance for large loss exposures—ten to twenty times the primary insurer's retention—when, for example, the primary insurer has used all the capacity available under its other treaties. Primary insurers usually place a facultative obligatory treaty as a layer above treaty agreements consisting of quota share and surplus share treaties.

Finite Risk Reinsurance

An additional type of reinsurance is known as **finite risk reinsurance**. Broadly speaking, finite risk reinsurance is a nontraditional reinsurance agreement for a limited (or "finite") amount of risk and on which anticipated investment income is expressly acknowledged as an underwriting component. Because this type of reinsurance is sometimes purchased to improve the primary insurer's balance sheet, it is often referred to as financial reinsurance.

Finite risk reinsurance can be arranged to protect an insurer against a combination of a traditionally insurable loss exposure (for example, building loss caused by explosion) and a traditionally noninsurable loss exposure (for example, possibility of loss due to economic variables such as product demand and market competition). Finite risk reinsurance can effectively handle extremely large and unusual loss exposures, such as catastrophic losses resulting from an oil-rig explosion or an earthquake.

Finite risk reinsurance agreements usually transfer very little underwriting risk; some of them might transfer no underwriting risk at all. Finite risk reinsurance agreements usually transfer investment risk, timing risk, or both. Underwriting risk is the possibility that the losses actually paid over the coverage period will be greater than expected. Investment risk is the possibility that an investment portfolio will yield a lower return than expected. Timing risk is the possibility that losses will be paid more quickly than expected.

A finite risk reinsurance agreement typically has a multi-year term—three to five years, for example—so it spreads risk as well as losses over several years, subject to an aggregate limit for the agreement's entire term. With finite risk reinsurance, the primary insurer can rely on long-term protection, and the reinsurer can rely on a continual flow of premiums. Finite risk reinsurance provides the primary insurer with a predictable reinsurance cost over the coverage period. Consequently, both the insurer and the reinsurer tend to be flexible in negotiating finite risk reinsurance pricing and terms.

Finite risk reinsurance premiums can be a substantial percentage—70 percent, for example—of the reinsurance limit. This relationship between premium and reinsurance limit reduces the reinsurer's potential underwriting loss to a level that is much lower than the potential underwriting loss typically associated with traditional types of reinsurance.

Generally, finite risk reinsurance is designed to cover high-severity losses. The finite reinsurer commonly shares profits with the primary insurer when it has favorable loss experience or has generated income by investing the prepaid

Finite risk reinsurance
A nontraditional reinsurance agreement for a limited amount of risk.

Not more than 2 (pt.)
More investment question
not underwriting

premium. This profit-sharing income can compensate the primary insurer for the higher-than-usual premium for finite risk reinsurance. The finite risk reinsurer does not assess any additional premium even if its losses exceed the premium.

REINSURANCE PROGRAM DEVELOPMENT

A well-planned and well-executed reinsurance program is valuable to a primary insurer. It can help to stabilize loss experience, provide large-line capacity, provide catastrophe protection, and provide surplus relief. In a catastrophe, a good reinsurance program can mean the difference between survival and failure. An optimal reinsurance program requires careful planning by the primary insurer, possibly with assistance from reinsurers, reinsurance intermediaries, and consultants.

Many kinds of reinsurance exist, and, with rare exceptions, any primary insurer can find a combination of reinsurance agreements that meets its needs. Developing such a reinsurance program requires carefully analyzing the primary insurer's needs, retentions, reinsurance limits, and reinsurance costs, including those beyond the reinsurance premium.

Determining Reinsurance Needs

The reinsurance needs of a primary insurer depend on several factors that must be considered in designing a comprehensive reinsurance program. The six most important factors are the following:

1. Stability of loss frequency and severity
2. Loss exposures subject to catastrophes
3. Number of exposure units
4. Available financial resources
5. Stability and liquidity of investment portfolio
6. Growth plans

Stability of Loss Frequency and Loss Severity

The first factor used to determine reinsurance needs is stability of loss frequency and loss severity. Stability of loss frequency and loss severity are important characteristics of the types of insurance written by a primary insurer that help to determine the insurer's reinsurance needs.

Reinsurance is much more effective at reducing loss severity variations than at reducing loss frequency variations. For large individual losses, both surplus share and per risk excess of loss treaties are especially effective. The choice between them should be based on cost and the need for surplus relief. Facultative reinsurance also effectively controls large losses from exceptionally hazardous or unusually large loss exposures. However, the delays and heavy administrative burden associated with facultative reinsurance limit its use to relatively unusual situations.

Although none of the common forms of reinsurance deals directly with loss frequency variations, several forms of reinsurance can reduce their financial effect. Perhaps the best form of reinsurance for reducing the financial effect of loss frequency (especially if reinsurance costs are ignored) is an aggregate excess of loss treaty. An aggregate excess of loss treaty caps the primary insurer's loss ratio (subject to percentage participations and treaty limits), whether caused by frequency (an accumulation of losses) or severity (catastrophe losses).

Loss Exposures Subject to Catastrophes

The second factor used to determine reinsurance needs is loss exposures subject to catastrophes. Several types of insurance (such as homeowners and commercial property) are especially susceptible to catastrophic causes of loss such as windstorm, earthquake, and hail. Other types of insurance (such as crime and equipment breakdown) have less serious catastrophe loss exposures.

In designing a catastrophe reinsurance program, a primary insurer must carefully analyze the geographic distribution of its loss exposures. Such an analysis should consider the number of exposures that could be damaged in a single occurrence and the maximum aggregate amount of damage from such an occurrence. Extensive data are available to assist with such an analysis. Data on the occurrence and intensity of hurricanes, tornadoes, and earthquakes are available from various government agencies. Insurance loss data are available from industry organizations. Such data are also essential in setting retentions and reinsurance limits under catastrophe excess of loss treaties.

Number of Loss Exposures Insured

The third factor used to determine reinsurance needs is the number of loss exposures insured. According to the law of large numbers, an insurer with a large number of loss exposures should have a more stable loss ratio than one with a small number, all else being equal. The increased stability resulting from large numbers reduces the need for reinsurance. Of course, the number of loss exposure units needed to provide stability differs by type of insurance. A type of insurance that has frequent, small losses can achieve stability with a smaller number of loss exposures than one that has infrequent, large losses.

For example, an insurer that specializes in physical damage coverage for private passenger automobiles could achieve reasonable stability with a relatively small number of loss exposures. Some catastrophe reinsurance might be needed unless the loss exposures are widely distributed across the country. In contrast, it is doubtful that any attainable number of loss exposures would provide acceptable stability without reinsurance for an insurer that specializes in property insurance on large industrial facilities. Such an insurer would likely need a relatively complex reinsurance program, involving both treaty and facultative agreements, regardless of the number of exposure units.

Available Financial Resources

The fourth factor used to determine reinsurance needs is available financial resources. The financial resources available to the primary insurer affect its reinsurance needs in two ways: through its need for stability and through its need for surplus relief. An insurer with a weak surplus position needs a highly stable net loss ratio to avoid serious financial difficulties and possible insolvency. A weak surplus position can also require the use of pro rata reinsurance to provide surplus relief.

An insurer with a strong surplus position can afford to have a more volatile loss experience because it has the financial strength to absorb some unanticipated losses. However, the absolute size of the insurer's surplus is not the only consideration. The quality of the surplus, as indicated by the invested assets that support it, must also be considered.

Stability and Liquidity of Investment Portfolio

The fifth factor used to determine reinsurance needs is the stability and liquidity of a primary insurer's investment portfolio. If an insurer plans to rely on its surplus to absorb unanticipated losses, that surplus must be invested in assets that are (1) readily marketable and (2) immune from wide market price fluctuations. Otherwise, the surplus might be insufficient to pay losses in a timely manner.

An insurer that holds large amounts of common stock in its investment portfolio needs to be more heavily reinsured than an insurer that holds short-term bonds, all other things being equal, because the common stock might be marketable only at a substantial loss in an unfavorable market. A portfolio of long-term bonds might also sustain substantial market losses. Many insurers have a considerable investment in the stock of subsidiaries or other related insurers. Such stock is often not traded publicly and therefore is not readily sold to pay losses. An insurer that invests a large part of its assets in a wholly owned subsidiary needs to have a substantial reinsurance program, because the subsidiary's stock might not be marketable when unusual losses occur.

Growth Plans

The sixth factor used to determine reinsurance needs is an insurer's growth plans. Generally, an insurer that plans to grow rapidly needs to be reinsured more heavily than one that plans to grow slowly, because of the following:

*   A rapidly growing insurer's new business constitutes a large part of its premium volume. The loss ratio on new business is likely to be higher and less predictable than the loss ratio on business that has been seasoned through renewal underwriting.

- A rapidly growing insurer is more likely to need surplus relief than an insurer that is growing slowly. An insurer might earn a reputation for being unreliable if it has to discontinue writing new business because it has already written too much.

A primary insurer might reduce its long-term profits by entering into a reinsurance agreement because it has potentially ceded away profitable loss exposures. Sacrificing these profits is a short-term strategy that enables the primary insurer to continue to grow and possibly to earn greater future profits.

Example 1—Large Multi-Line Stock Insurer

The first example is a stock insurer with annual direct written premiums of $1 billion and policyholders' surplus of $500 million. The insurer has averaged 10 percent annual growth over the past decade and expects to continue to grow at about the same rate.

The insurer's ratio has exceeded 100 each year for the last decade, averaging 102 for the current period. It has reported an operating profit each year for the last decade, but the profit has been small in some years. A high-grade portfolio of bonds and other fixed-income securities accounts for about 95 percent of its invested assets. The remaining five percent consists of carefully selected preferred and common stocks.

The insurer writes commercial automobile insurance, commercial general liability, commercial multi-peril, and commercial fire and allied lines insurance. It insures small to medium-sized commercial and industrial loss exposures. A survey of its outstanding policies showed that about 95 percent of its liability policies had occurrence limits of $10 million or less, and about 95 percent of its property policies provided coverage of $15 million or less. Management has decided to set its treaty limits to cover those amounts and to depend on facultative reinsurance for the policies with higher limits.

The insurer does not need surplus relief, so no pro rata reinsurance is purchased. Per risk or per policy excess of loss treaties are purchased for both property and liability loss exposures. Management has decided that the insurer can afford to assume individual losses up to 0.5 percent of direct written premiums, or 1.0 percent of policyholders' surplus. Consequently, the retentions under the treaties are set at $5 million per loss. Treaty limits are $5 million for liability and $10 million for property losses. Therefore, the primary insurer's retention and the treaty limits fully cover about 95 percent of all policies issued.

The properties insured by the primary insurer are spread widely across the country, but several areas have high concentrations of values subject to catastrophe losses. The worst of those is a metropolitan area on the Gulf Coast, where management estimates that a direct hit by a major hurricane could cause up to $50 million in losses. A catastrophe treaty with a limit of $50 million and a retention of $5 million is purchased.

Example 2—Small Multi-Line Mutual Insurer

The second example is a small mutual insurer whose business is confined to a single state. The insurer has annual direct written premiums of $20 million and policyholders' surplus of $5 million. It writes homeowners insurance and property insurance for small commercial loss exposures. It is headquartered in a city on the south Atlantic coast, and about half of its business is in or near the coastal region. Virtually all of its policies provide windstorm coverage; many also provide earthquake coverage. Minor quakes occur in or near its headquarters city several times each year. The most recent damaging quakes occurred in the nineteenth century.

An analysis of the geographic distribution of its business indicates that a major hurricane could cause losses of as much as $10 million to the properties currently insured. An earthquake could cause losses of as much as $5 million. Its investment portfolio consists primarily of U.S. government bonds, with some bonds issued by its home state and local governments within that state. The insurer has experienced moderate growth in the past and expects to continue to grow at about five percent each year. Although it has shown an operating profit in most years of the last decade and for the decade as a whole, its loss ratio fluctuated substantially over the past decade even though no major catastrophes occurred during that period.

With a premium-to-surplus ratio of 4 to 1, this insurer needs surplus relief if it is to continue to grow. Consequently, a quota share treaty is needed. Management has decided to cede 25 percent of its loss exposures under a quota share treaty, and the reinsurer has agreed to pay a 25 percent ceding commission. That transaction reduces its net written premiums to $15 million, and the ceding commission increases its policyholders' surplus to $6.25 million, giving it a premium-to-surplus ratio of less than 3 to 1. That ratio is acceptable to the regulatory authorities in the insurer's home state.

Management has decided that an aggregate excess of loss treaty offers the best solution for stabilizing the insurer's loss experience. A reinsurer has offered to provide such a treaty with the retention of an 80 percent loss ratio. The reinsurer pays 95 percent of losses in excess of the retention along with its proportional share of loss adjustment expenses. However, the reinsurer is willing to provide that aggregate excess of loss treaty only if the primary insurer purchases a per occurrence excess of loss treaty with a limit of at least $8 million and a retention of $500,000 or less. The per occurrence excess of loss treaty applies only to the primary insurer's net losses after deducting amounts recoverable under the quota share treaty. The aggregate excess of loss treaty applies only to the primary insurer's net losses after deducting recoveries under both the quota share treaty and the per occurrence excess of loss treaty. The per occurrence excess of loss treaty applies only to property losses. The other two treaties apply to liability losses under the homeowners policies also.

Setting Retentions

Primary insurers, reinsurance intermediaries, and reinsurers often apply models in setting retentions, but the usefulness of these models usually depends on the predictive value and accuracy of the underlying data.

Nonetheless, setting retentions is still more a matter of judgment than an exact science. However, some general considerations apply.

The method of setting retentions varies by type of treaty as well as by other factors. The purpose for buying a pro rata treaty differ from the purposes for buying an excess of loss treaty, so the factors considered in setting the retention also differ.

The principal purpose for choosing a pro rata treaty instead of an excess of loss treaty is to obtain surplus relief. Consequently, the amount of surplus relief needed is an important factor in setting the retention. The amount of surplus relief received is a function of the percentage of premium ceded and the ceding commission percentage received.

The principal purposes of excess of loss treaties are to stabilize loss experience and to provide large-line capacity. Providing large-line capacity is a function of the treaty limit rather than the retention. Therefore, the principal consideration in setting the retention of an excess of loss treaty is the size of loss that the primary insurer can absorb without undue effect on the policyholders' surplus or the loss ratio for the type of insurance included in the treaty. The size of the loss is, in turn, a function of the premium volume and the primary insurer's policyholders' surplus.

Most states have a statutory provision that sets an upper limit on an insurer's retention under its reinsurance treaties. That provision usually states that an insurer cannot retain an amount on any one loss exposure in excess of 10 percent of the insurer's policyholders' surplus. So, if an insurer has policyholders' surplus of $10 million, its legal maximum net retention for any one loss exposure would be $1 million. Very few insurers retain their legal maximum.

One of the principal purposes of excess of loss reinsurance is to stabilize loss experience. It seems logical, therefore, that the primary insurer should retain that part of its aggregate losses that is reasonably stable and predictable and should reinsure that part that is not. However, that simple statement raises two complex questions. First, what is meant by "reasonably stable and predictable"? Second, given criteria for "reasonably stable and predictable," how does one determine what portion of aggregate losses meets those criteria?

Insurers' management have different criteria for what is reasonably stable and predictable. However, a general rule applies. Losses can be said to be reasonably stable and predictable if the maximum probable variation is not likely to affect the insurer's loss ratio or policyholders' surplus to an extent unacceptable to management.

For example, one insurer's management might conclude that it could accept a maximum variation of three percentage points in the loss ratio and a change of nine percent in policyholders' surplus due to chance variation in losses during the year. Another insurer with less policyholders' surplus or less venturesome management might decide that it could risk only two percentage points of the loss ratio and four percent of policyholders' surplus. All other things being equal, the second insurer would probably set a lower retention. Of course, setting retentions requires balancing the desirability of stability against the undesirability of high reinsurance costs. Lowering the retention increases stability, but it also increases reinsurance costs.

Based on the foregoing considerations, various quantitative methods have been used to set the retention level under a per risk or per policy excess of loss treaty. These methods, which are not described in detail here because they are beyond the scope of this text, assume that the primary insurer should retain losses within the size category in which sufficient frequency exists for reasonable predictability.

Setting the retention for a catastrophe treaty (per occurrence excess of loss treaty) is a two-step process. The first step is for management to decide how much policyholders' surplus and how many percentage points of loss ratio the insurer can risk on one year's catastrophes. These numbers must then be translated into dollars.

The second step is to estimate the maximum number of catastrophes that might reasonably be expected to occur in one year. That number depends on the types of insurance concerned, the territory in which the primary insurer operates, and the concentration of insured loss exposures within the territory. For jurisdictions that have windstorm pools, the effects of such pools must be considered when setting windstorm retentions. The retention per catastrophe is found by dividing the number of dollars from the first step by the number of catastrophes from the second step.

Retention setting is easier under an aggregate excess of loss treaty than under any other kind of reinsurance. The primary insurer sets its retention at the lowest loss ratio (1) for which the reinsurance premium is affordable and (2) that is acceptable to the reinsurer. Those two considerations almost inevitably result in a retention loss ratio somewhat higher than the primary insurer's break-even loss ratio.

Most of this discussion of retention setting has ignored the cost of reinsurance and the reinsurer's role in setting retentions. However, those considerations cannot be overlooked in actual practice. Most insurers purchasing excess of loss treaties accept retentions higher than they would prefer, either to reduce reinsurance costs or to satisfy the reinsurer's requirement.

Under surplus share treaties, the reinsurer's position might be reversed—that is, the reinsurer might sometimes insist on a lower retention than the primary insurer prefers. Under a surplus share treaty, no reinsurance is provided on loss exposures for which the amount of insurance is less than the retention. Consequently, a very high retention means that the reinsurer is excluded from participating in a large part of the primary insurer's business. If the business below the retention is the most desirable part of the primary insurer's portfolio, the reinsurer might insist on a lower retention to enable it to participate in that business.

If the primary insurer carries several treaties that might cover the same loss exposures, the retention under each treaty should be set by considering the relationships among the treaties. For example, an insurer's reinsurance program might have a quota share treaty, a per risk excess of loss treaty, and a catastrophe treaty. The retention under the catastrophe treaty should be higher if that treaty is written for the benefit of both the primary insurer and quota share reinsurer than if written only for the benefit of the primary insurer.

To illustrate the difference, assume that the retention under the quota share treaty is 25 percent and the retention under the catastrophe treaty is $1 million. Assume further that a catastrophe causes losses totaling $3 million for loss exposures reinsured by the catastrophe treaty. If the catastrophe treaty is written for the primary insurer's benefit only, the treaty would not pay any of the losses. The primary insurer's portion of the losses would be 25 percent, or $750,000, which is less than the catastrophe retention.

If the catastrophe treaty is written for the benefit of the primary insurer and the quota share reinsurer, the catastrophe reinsurer would pay $2 million, assuming that the treaty limit is at least that high. The quota share reinsurer would then pay 75 percent of the remaining $1 million, leaving the primary insurer with a net retention of only $250,000.

A similar analysis could be done for the per risk excess of loss treaty and the quota share treaty or, for that matter, for all three treaties. This is another reason why an insurer's reinsurance program should be carefully integrated and not merely a collection of treaties.

Setting Reinsurance Limits

Setting reinsurance limits for pro rata and per risk or per policy excess of loss treaties is only slightly less subjective than setting retentions. Limits for these treaties, combined with the primary insurer's retention, should be sufficient to cover a substantial majority of the loss exposures insured by the primary insurer. Exactly how large a majority will be covered depends on cost, because reinsurance costs increase as the reinsurance limit increases and the retention remains constant. This increased cost for a higher reinsurance limit must be weighed against the premium, administrative expense, and inconvenience of facultative reinsurance for those loss exposures not fully covered by treaties.

Setting limits for catastrophe treaties is even more subjective. The goal is to set a limit just adequate to cover the largest catastrophe that might reasonably be expected. The difficulty is determining the potential loss amount for the largest catastrophe likely to occur. The primary insurer's past loss experience is not a satisfactory guide. Catastrophe losses are notoriously variable, and the largest catastrophe the insurer sustained in the past might not be the largest that is likely to occur in the future. Additionally, circumstances change. For example, the insurer might now be writing more business in a catastrophe-prone area than it wrote in the past.

By carefully analyzing catastrophe data and the insurer's concentration of loss exposures, an insurer can reasonably estimate the largest amount of aggregate losses it is likely to sustain in a single hurricane, earthquake, flood, or other natural disaster. Although such analyses are time consuming and expensive, they are necessary to ensure that the primary insurer has adequate catastrophe reinsurance limits. Some reinsurers and reinsurance intermediaries have computer models to assist in these analyses. Because reinsurers and reinsurance intermediaries have already collected necessary historical data, the primary insurer need provide only its own data on the distribution of insured loss exposures.

The limit for an aggregate excess of loss treaty should be set at an amount adequate to cover the highest loss ratio the primary insurer might reasonably expect to sustain, provided the reinsurance premium for such a limit is acceptable to the primary insurer's management. Unfortunately, no reliable method of accurately estimating loss ratio variations exists. However, three factors should be considered in this regard. The first factor is the type of insurance written. A property insurer can expect a greater loss ratio variation than a liability insurer can because of catastrophe loss exposures covered by property insurance. Having a catastrophe treaty (in addition to the stop-loss treaty) lessens the variation caused by catastrophes.

The second factor is the insurer's size. All other things being equal, a small insurer (measured by premium volume) can expect more loss ratio variation than a large one. The small insurer would, therefore, need a higher treaty limit relative to its premium volume.

The third and perhaps most important factor is the geographic distribution of the insurer's loss exposures. An insurer with loss exposures concentrated in one territory is much more vulnerable to loss ratio variations than an insurer with a nationwide spread of loss exposures. Again, this is primarily because of variations caused by catastrophes.

In setting the limit for any kind of reinsurance, the interaction among all applicable treaties must be considered. For example, the limit for an aggregate excess of loss treaty can be lower if the insurer carries adequate catastrophe reinsurance. Also, the limit of a catastrophe treaty can be lower if it applies only to the primary insurer's retention after recoveries from pro rata reinsurance, rather than to the direct losses.

Determining Reinsurance Cost

The cost of reinsurance might not be easy to determine because the cost is not simply the premium paid to the reinsurer. Other costs must be considered.

Reinsurance transfers some loss reserves and unearned premium reserves from the primary insurer to the reinsurer. Because the assets offsetting these reserves are invested, this transfer results in some loss of investment income to the primary insurer. The loss of investment income is likely to be greater under a pro rata treaty than under an excess of loss treaty because the reinsurance premium for a pro rata treaty is usually greater. However, some investment income is lost in either case, and the lost income is an additional cost of the reinsurance.

The cost to the primary insurer of administering the reinsurance program must also be considered. Facultative reinsurance is especially expensive to administer because each reinsurance agreement must be negotiated individually. Pro rata treaties, especially surplus share, are generally more expensive to administer than excess of loss treaties because of the more detailed recordkeeping and the greater frequency of reinsurance claims. In any case, the cost of administering the program must be considered in evaluating reinsurance costs.

REINSURANCE NEGOTIATIONS

Reinsurance negotiations to secure the particular types of reinsurance that the primary insurer wants can be conducted in several ways, depending on the nature of the primary insurer's and the reinsurer's operations, the kind of reinsurance concerned, and other factors. This section discusses in general terms some of the major factors involved in negotiating reinsurance agreements.

Information Needed

The primary insurer's first step in reinsurance negotiations is compiling the necessary information. Depending on the kind of reinsurance, the required information might be voluminous, and compilation might require a substantial effort. Favorable reinsurance terms and rates might depend on the thoroughness of the data the primary insurer provides.

The information required in reinsurance negotiations varies by reinsurance agreement. In treaty negotiations, the reinsurer is interested primarily in information about the primary insurer's management and underwriting operations. Little attention is given to individual loss exposures insured; instead, the reinsurer is concerned about product mix and geographic spread. In facultative negotiations, the reinsurer is interested primarily in the details of the individual loss exposure and only secondarily in the primary insurer's management and underwriting operations. Of course, if the subject of negotiation is a facultative obligatory treaty, then the information needed would be essentially the same as for any other treaty. However, the reinsurer might underwrite the primary insurer's loss exposures even more carefully because of the greater opportunity for adverse selection under a facultative obligatory treaty.

The reinsurer's principal considerations in underwriting a treaty are the following:

- The primary insurer's management characteristics
- The primary insurer's financial strength
- The primary insurer's underwriting policies and underwriting results
- The existence and terms of other reinsurance
- The primary insurer's loss experience

The integrity of the primary insurer's management is a major consideration. Opportunities exist for fraud in administering a reinsurance treaty, and fraud has occurred. The reinsurer is interested in more than just honesty. It is also interested in management's demonstrated capability and stability and the underwriting staff's experience and capabilities. Reinsurance treaties are intended to be long-term agreements. Consequently, the reinsurer is concerned with the possibility of a change in management, a change in management goals, or both.

A reinsurer is also concerned about the primary insurer's financial strength. The insolvency of a primary insurer normally does not increase the reinsurer's liability, but it does complicate treaty administration, and it could involve the loss of part of the reinsurer's premiums. The reinsurer's role might become especially complicated if many cut-through endorsements are outstanding, because the reinsurer might be required to adjust losses under such endorsements directly with the original insured.

Perhaps the most important considerations in reinsurance negotiations are the primary insurer's underwriting policies and underwriting results. Factors to consider in assessing an underwriting policy are shown in Exhibit 11-8.

EXHIBIT 11-8

Factors to Consider in Assessing the Primary Insurer's Underwriting Policy

1. What classes of business is the primary insurer writing?

2. Is it writing primarily personal, small mercantile, industrial, or other types of insurance?

3. What is its geographic area of operation?

4. Are the primary insurer's underwriting guidelines (e.g., acceptable, prohibitive, and submit-for-approval lists) satisfactory?

5. Are its gross line limits and net line limits for surplus share treaties in keeping with its financial strength?

6. Are the primary insurer's loss control and loss adjustment practices adequate for the classes of business written?

7. Have the primary insurer's underwriting results been satisfactory in the types of insurance covered by the proposed reinsurance treaty?

8. Does the primary insurer anticipate any substantial changes in its management, marketing, or underwriting practices?

9. Are the primary insurer's rates adequate for the loss exposures covered under the treaty?

The existence and terms of other reinsurance are also important. In property insurance, for example, pro rata reinsurers are interested in the terms of any catastrophe treaty and other excess of loss reinsurance. Is that reinsurance written only for the primary insurer's interest, or does it also protect the pro rata reinsurer's interest?

Also, the reinsurer is concerned about the primary insurer's loss experience over the most recent several years. Loss ratio is especially important in connection with a pro rata treaty because it is used for underwriting selection, rating, and setting commission terms. The reinsurer is concerned about not only the level of the loss ratio but also its stability or volatility over time.

The discussion to this point has concentrated on the information the reinsurer is likely to require from the primary insurer. However, in most reinsurance negotiations, the primary insurer is also interested in obtaining information about the reinsurer. The information the primary insurer needs, while less detailed, is approximately the same as that which any customer needs in purchasing insurance. Is the reinsurer financially sound and well managed? Are its claim practices satisfactory? Can it offer the services that the primary insurer needs? Are its rates competitive? Is it licensed in the primary insurer's state of domicile, or can it make other arrangements so that the primary insurer can take credit for the reinsurance in calculating its unearned premiums and loss reserves?

Reinsurance Intermediaries

The first step in negotiating any agreement is for the parties to get together. The primary insurer and reinsurer may get together directly or work through a reinsurance intermediary.

The function of a reinsurance intermediary is essentially the same as that of any other intermediary: to bring together two potential contracting parties and to assist them in agreeing on contract terms. The reinsurance intermediary, in this case, is compensated for those efforts through a commission paid by the reinsurer. The commission might be small compared with the commission rates paid to primary insurance brokers—frequently as low as one percent of the reinsurance premium. However, the premiums are often large, so the dollar amount of commission can also be large.

When reinsurance is handled by a reinsurance intermediary, premium payments usually pass through the reinsurance intermediary from the primary insurer to the reinsurer. Also, loss payments and premium refunds pass through the reinsurance intermediary from the reinsurer to the primary insurer. The reinsurance intermediary might be able to earn substantial investment income on these funds in its custody, adding significantly to its income.

Should a primary insurer use a reinsurance intermediary to negotiate its reinsurance program even though many large reinsurers are willing to deal directly? No single answer applies to all cases. The answer depends on an insurer's own needs and circumstances.

If the primary insurer is well staffed with people who are thoroughly familiar with reinsurance and who are capable of designing its reinsurance program and of negotiating its reinsurance agreements, it might not need a reinsurance intermediary. Consequently, the primary insurer might be able to negotiate a slightly lower reinsurance cost because of the absence of a brokerage commission.

However, many insurers, especially small and medium-sized ones, do not have the personnel needed to manage their reinsurance effectively. They must rely on an outside person for advice. That person could be a consultant or an employee of a reinsurer, but frequently that person is a reinsurance intermediary.

A reinsurance intermediary handles the reinsurance needs of several primary insurers. Experience with a variety of issues enables reinsurance intermediaries to develop expertise in handling reinsurance problems. This expertise, when coupled with knowledge about available reinsurance markets and access to them, can make a reinsurance intermediary a valuable ally in reinsurance program negotiations.

Reinsurance intermediaries offer one other advantage. Some reinsurers might not be staffed to deal directly with potential reinsurance buyers. This is particularly likely for small professional reinsurers and primary insurers with limited reinsurance operations. Also, some very large reinsurers deal only through reinsurance intermediaries. A reinsurance intermediary might provide the only practical means of access to such reinsurers, either through a pool managed by the intermediary or through individual negotiation.

Most of the reinsurance premiums controlled by intermediaries are for treaty reinsurance. Many intermediaries prefer not to handle facultative reinsurance agreements because of the extensive amount of effort and paperwork involved in handling individual agreements.

Whether the reinsurance intermediary is acting as the primary insurer's representative or the reinsurer's is not always clear. The question is important because it could determine, among other things, whether a reinsurance agreement is void because of misrepresentation or concealment.

For example, the primary insurer might make full disclosure to the reinsurance intermediary, but the reinsurance intermediary might fail to transmit a material fact to the reinsurer. If the reinsurance intermediary is the primary insurer's agent, the treaty might be voidable at the reinsurer's option for concealment. If the reinsurance intermediary is the reinsurer's agent, the treaty would not be voidable because it would be assumed that the reinsurer has the same knowledge as the reinsurance intermediary. Consequently, no concealment would have occurred.

In most cases, the courts have held that a reinsurance intermediary is the primary insurer's agent. However, a reinsurance intermediary could become the reinsurer's agent either by specific contractual agreement or by the reinsurer's actions that lead the primary insurer to believe that the intermediary is the reinsurer's agent.

Reinsurance Commissions

Reinsurance transactions can involve two kinds of commissions: (1) the ceding commission that the reinsurer pays to the primary insurer and (2) the brokerage commission that the reinsurer pays to the reinsurance intermediary. The ceding commission reimburses the primary insurer for the expenses it incurred in selling and servicing the loss exposures ceded to the reinsurer. Such commissions are common under pro rata treaties but not under excess of loss treaties. The ceding commission amount is negotiable and usually depends on (1) the primary insurer's actual expenses (including acquisition costs along with administrative, information system, and accounting costs); (2) the reinsurer's estimate of the premium volume and loss experience expected under the treaty; and (3) the competitive state of the reinsurance market at the time the treaty is negotiated. Treaties frequently adjust the ceding commission retrospectively if the actual loss ratio under the treaty varies substantially from the expected loss ratio.

Brokerage commissions vary, but a typical commission might be one percent to two percent of the premium on pro rata treaties and five percent to ten percent on excess of loss treaties. The higher commission on excess of loss treaties reflects the fact that they produce lower premiums while requiring substantially the same amount of effort on the reinsurance intermediary's part. Therefore, a higher commission is needed to provide the same dollar remuneration. Some reinsurance intermediaries negotiate a fee for their services to the primary insurer instead of a commission.

REINSURANCE PROGRAM ADMINISTRATION

Reinsurance program administration is a joint effort by the primary insurer and the reinsurer. Each has specified duties, obligations, and rights under the reinsurance agreement.

Primary Insurer's Role

After the reinsurance agreement has been negotiated and has become effective, the heaviest burden of administration falls on the primary insurer. The primary insurer is obligated to conduct its underwriting and loss adjusting as contemplated by both parties when they negotiated the reinsurance or to notify the reinsurer of any substantial changes.

The primary insurer is free to exercise its best judgment in underwriting individual loss exposures or in adjusting individual claims, and the reinsurer is bound by the primary insurer's actions in such matters. In words common to reinsurance, the reinsurer "follows the fortunes" of the primary insurer.

A treaty might require the primary insurer to notify the reinsurer promptly upon receiving notice of a large claim, and the reinsurer might reserve the right to participate in investigating or defending such claims. These rights are exercised only in unusual circumstances.

The primary insurer should design its information systems to capture and process the data required to fulfill its administrative duties. If the reinsurance program is simple, including only quota share and excess of loss treaties covering all policies issued by the primary insurer with the same retentions and limits, data requirements can be simple. In such cases, the primary insurer needs to collect only direct premium data to calculate the reinsurance premiums payable to the reinsurer. Data for individual losses are needed to apply retention and reinsurance limits. Such data are needed for other accounting purposes in any case, so little additional burden arises for reinsurance administration.

For catastrophe excess of loss treaties, the primary insurer must code losses so that those arising from catastrophes can be identified. Similarly, for a clash cover, occurrences must be identified so that all losses arising from a single occurrence can be readily identified. A clash cover is an excess of loss reinsurance agreement that protects the primary insurer against an accumulation of losses.

A surplus share treaty might have slightly more complex data requirements. The primary insurer must have sufficient data to determine the portion, if any, of each of its loss exposures ceded to each surplus share reinsurer. Such information is essential to calculate both reinsurance premiums payable and reinsurance losses recoverable.

Extensive use of facultative reinsurance might require a more elaborate approach to fulfilling data needs. Each facultative reinsurance agreement is negotiated separately, so the retention, the limits, the premium, and even the reinsurer might be different for each agreement. Even the nature of the coverage (excess of loss or pro rata) might differ. The information system should be able to capture those differences.

Some of the primary insurer's underwriting practices might also require expanding the data requirements. If the primary insurer covers loss exposures that are excluded from one or more of its treaties, the policies covering such loss exposures should be coded to avoid paying reinsurance premiums for them and submitting reinsurance claims for them.

If the primary insurer elects not to cede an otherwise eligible loss exposure under a treaty (to protect its treaty or for other reasons), special coding is necessary to avoid errors in calculating reinsurance premiums or losses.

Special coding is also needed if the primary insurer elects a retention or reinsurance limit different from the standard retentions and limits provided by its treaties.

A properly designed data collection and information system greatly simplifies the reinsurance administrative process. It also simplifies the process of compiling data to negotiate renewal or replacement treaties.

The primary insurer is required to report premiums and losses, and perhaps other data, to the reinsurer by bordereaux or by such other means as the treaty might specify. The reinsurance agreement might also require the primary insurer to make its books and records available to the reinsurer at reasonable times and places so that the reinsurer can verify the reported data.

Exhibit 11-9 shows a section of a bordereau one primary insurer uses to report required information to its reinsurer. Exhibit 11-10 shows one form of current account statement one primary insurer uses to report reinsurance premiums and losses to a reinsurer that does not require a detailed bordereau.

Historically, bordereaux were required by virtually all reinsurers. That requirement is much less common today. Many reinsurers are willing to accept a current account statement such as that in Exhibit 11-10. Reinsurers rely on their contractual right to audit the primary insurer's books to guard against incorrect information.

EXHIBIT 11-9

Illustrative Bordereau—July 20X1

Insured	Policy	Effective Date	Expiration Date	Gross Premiums Ceded	Ceding Comm.	Net Premiums Ceded	Losses Paid	Loss Expenses Paid	Losses Outstanding	Balance Due to Reins.
Boat Manufacturer	CPP99406	07/03/X1	07/03/X2	$17,953	$ 4,488	$13,465	$ 825	$ 75	0	$12,565
Book Store	CPP88431	09/07/X0	09/07/X1	0	0	0	7,593	487	0	−8,080
Restaurant	CPP89976	11/13/X0	11/13/X1	0	0	0	12,576	793	$8,541	−13,369
Delivery Service	CPP97865	07/01/X1	07/01/X2	24,581	7,374	17,207	0	0	0	17,207
Total				$42,534	$11,862	$30,672	$20,994	$1,355	$8,541	$ 8,323

Summary

Gross Premiums Ceded	$42,534
Less Ceding Commissions	−11,862
Net Premiums Ceded	30,672
Less Loss and Loss Adjustment Expenses Paid	−22,349
Balance Due to Reinsurer	$ 8,323

EXHIBIT 11-10

Illustrative Reinsurance Current Account

Annual Statement Line	Gross Premiums Ceded	Ceding Comm.	Net Premiums Ceded	Losses Paid	Loss Expenses Paid	Losses Outstanding
01-Fire	$ 40,560	$10,140	$ 30,420	$ 20,321	$ 2,503	$ 45,654
02-Extended Coverage	13,471	3,347	10,124	4,783	3,977	26,894
05-C.M.P.	180,478	45,140	135,338	97,728	10,539	140,000
09-Inland Marine	53,547	13,436	40,111	21,649	2,374	27,652
Total	$288,056	$72,063	$215,993	$144,481	$19,393	$240,200

Summary

Gross Premiums Ceded	$288,056
Less Ceding Commission	−72,063
Net Premiums Ceded	215,993
Less Loss and Loss Adjustment Expenses Paid	−163,874
Amount Due to Reinsurer	$ 52,119

Reinsurer's Role

Under a smoothly functioning treaty, the reinsurer's duties, other than collecting premiums and paying claims, are minimal. Many reinsurers prefer to write excess of loss treaties with very high retentions so that claims are rarely submitted.

Yet the reinsurer performs additional duties. Although it ordinarily does not become involved in underwriting individual loss exposures or adjusting individual losses, the reinsurer can audit the primary insurer's underwriting and claim practices to ensure they are being implemented as anticipated. Large, individual losses can be examined partly to verify that proper claim adjusting and reserving practices are followed and partly to extract whatever underwriting implications they provide. The primary insurer can also consult the reinsurer about individual underwriting or claim problems.

Frequently, reinsurers become involved in litigation initiated by insureds and claimants against the primary insurer. This litigation seeks to obligate the reinsurer to share in punitive damage judgments or bad-faith judgments against the primary insurer arising out of the primary insurer's handling of claims covered under the reinsurance agreement. In most cases, courts have held that the reinsurer is not liable for such judgments because those judgments did not arise from the reinsurance agreement but from the primary insurer's errors or unfair practices. Coverage for those "extra-contractual obligations" is frequently provided under liability excess of loss treaties.

Claim Adjusting

Claim adjusting under the primary insurer's policies with its policyholders is typically left to the primary insurer. Reinsurance agreements usually permit the reinsurer to participate in adjusting direct claims that might result in reinsurance claims, but that right is exercised infrequently.

The claim adjusting procedure between the primary insurer and the reinsurer can vary by agreement and by type of treaty. Under a pro rata treaty, the primary insurer might be required to file a monthly statement or bordereau showing premiums due to the reinsurer and claim payments due from the reinsurer. If the premiums exceed the losses, the primary insurer remits the difference. If the losses exceed the premiums, the reinsurer remits the difference. Exceptionally large individual losses might be paid individually before the end of the reporting period as a convenience to the primary insurer.

Losses under a working cover or per occurrence excess of loss treaty might be handled by statement or bordereau as similarly outlined previously for pro rata treaties, because a substantial number of losses are expected under a working excess treaty. For excess of loss treaties with high retentions, losses are reported individually as they occur. The agreement usually requires the primary insurer to report all losses that are expected to exceed the retention or that involve a particular type of claim, such as a death or a brain or spinal injury, that is likely to be significant.

Claims for per occurrence excess of loss treaties are initiated only after the accumulated losses exceed the retention. At that point, the primary insurer begins presenting claims to the reinsurer as soon as it has paid them. Reinsurers often advance funds to primary insurers following a catastrophe instead of making the primary insurer pay the claims first. Some treaties are written with a "cash call" provision that contractually obligates the reinsurer to advance funds under specific circumstances.

Aggregate excess of loss treaties, when triggered, usually provide for an initial loss payment within a short time period, perhaps sixty days, after year-end. If the primary insurer's loss ratio has not been finalized at that time, a subsequent adjustment might be made. Although usually not contractually required, most reinsurers make initial payments before year-end if it becomes clear that the primary insurer's loss ratio will exceed its retention.

Effect of Competition

Reinsurance is a very competitive business, both domestically and internationally, which results partly from the relative ease of market entry. For example, a new reinsurer in the intermediary market does not need to invest large sums in building a marketing force.

In the U.S., an insurer's charter to write primary business usually also permits the primary insurer to write reinsurance for the same types of insurance. Therefore, little or no additional funding is required to capitalize a reinsurer.

Finally, a new reinsurer using reinsurance intermediaries needs only a minimal staff. Policyholder services are provided by the primary insurer, and the reinsurer need not become involved in these services except in unusual circumstances. Even staff in the reinsurer's claim department can be minimal because the primary insurer handles claim adjusting in most cases.

Primary insurers move in and out of the reinsurance business as market conditions change. Those market changes tend to destabilize reinsurance pricing and cause fluctuations in reinsurance availability.

When reinsurance is profitable, new reinsurers can be formed, and primary insurers enter the market to sell reinsurance. Those new reinsurers must offer some incentive to prospective customers, usually in the form of lower prices or higher ceding commissions. Established reinsurers must meet their new competitor's prices, leading to lower profits or possibly to underwriting losses and the resulting withdrawal of marginal reinsurers.

Effect of Inflation

Economic inflation causes the cost of claims to rise. With pro rata reinsurance, the effect of inflation is the same for the primary insurer and reinsurer except to the extent that some claims might exceed the treaty limit. Excess of loss reinsurers are affected by inflation in two ways. First, claims that would not have exceeded the primary insurer's retention now do. Second, increases in losses are borne exclusively by the reinsurer, limited only by the reinsurance limit.

Inflation affects excess of loss reinsurers to a substantially greater degree than pro rata reinsurers. The effects are felt at both ends of the treaty: the retention and the reinsurance limit. The excess of loss reinsurer covers the top part of the claims in excess of the retention, and, because those claims increase in severity with inflation, the increase is at the top. If a fixed retention is used rather than a variable one, the inflationary increase in losses above the retention does not affect the primary insurer's net loss.

If a fixed retention is used, the excess of loss reinsurer also suffers at the lower end of the loss distribution. The inflationary increase in the small losses pushes more of them over the primary insurer's retention, so the reinsurer must pay part of them.

REINSURANCE REGULATION

Reinsurance is subject to limited regulation. A principal purpose of insurance regulation is to protect insurance customers from unfair practices and insurer's insolvency. That protection was deemed necessary because of the unequal knowledge and bargaining power of insurers and insurance customers. Because the reinsurance business is conducted between two insurers, the knowledge and bargaining power of the parties is deemed to be relatively equal, so the protective shield of regulation is not considered necessary. Some also feared that rigid regulation of U.S. reinsurers would limit their ability to compete with alien reinsurers, both here and abroad.

Another factor that reduced the need to regulate reinsurance is the nature of the market and market participants. Traditionally, reinsurers were few in number and were well-financed, with a long history of ethical and sound business dealings. The market situation has changed drastically in recent years. Many new participants, both reinsurers and reinsurance intermediaries, have entered the market. Some of them have been found to lack ethical standards, financial strength, or both. The world of reinsurance has been shaken by several scandals in the U.S., the United Kingdom, Panama, Bermuda, and other places. Those scandals have brought about increased pressure for stricter reinsurance regulation. The New York regulation dealing with reinsurance intermediaries, shown in Exhibit 11-11, arose from one of the scandals—the insolvency of a reinsurance intermediary with large losses to both reinsurers and primary insurers.

EXHIBIT 11-11

New York Regulation 98

(1) Reinsurance intermediaries act in a fiduciary capacity for all funds received in their professional capacity and must not mingle them with other funds without the consent of the insurers and reinsurers they represent;

(2) Reinsurance intermediaries shall have written authorization from the insurers and reinsurers they represent, spelling out the extent and limitations of their authority;

(3) The written authority above must be made available to primary insurers or reinsurers with which the intermediary deals;

(4) No licensed intermediary shall procure reinsurance from an unlicensed reinsurer unless the reinsurer has appointed an agent for the service of process in New York;

(5) The intermediary must make full written disclosure of

    (a) any control over the broker by a reinsurer,

    (b) any control of a reinsurer by the intermediary,

    (c) any retrocessions of the subject business placed by the intermediary, and

    (d) commissions earned or to be earned on the business;

(6) Records of all transactions must be retained for at least ten years after the expiration of all reinsurance contracts.

Source: N.Y. Comp. Codes, Rules and Regulations Title 11 § 32.3 (a) (I), (filed 1982).

Current Reinsurer Regulation

Reinsurers domiciled in the U.S. and alien reinsurers licensed in the U.S. are subject to the same solvency state regulations as primary insurers. Reinsurers are required to file financial statements with state regulatory authorities and to adhere to state insurance regulations regarding reserves, investments, and minimum capital and surplus requirements. They must also undergo periodic examination by the appropriate state authorities. The solvency tests for reinsurers are the same as those applied to primary insurers. However, those requirements are not applied to *unlicensed* alien reinsurers because they are not within the jurisdiction of state (or federal) regulatory authorities. Much concern has arisen recently about possible insolvencies of some unlicensed alien reinsurers, but U.S. regulatory agencies can do little to prevent such insolvencies. Primary insurers and reinsurance intermediaries must rely on their own efforts to detect impending insolvencies of unlicensed alien reinsurers.

Reinsurance rates are not directly regulated in the U.S. The regulation of primary insurer rates could indirectly affect reinsurance rates, however. To the extent that reinsurers receive a reinsurance premium based on the premiums of primary insurers, reinsurers are affected by state insurance rate regulation. The adequacy of the reinsurer's premiums is directly affected by the adequacy of the primary insurer's premiums. Establishing the primary insurer's rates might place an effective ceiling on the amount the primary insurer can pay for reinsurance.

Reinsurance agreements are regulated to only a slightly greater degree than is reinsurance pricing. Such regulation is aimed at the primary insurer rather than the reinsurer because many reinsurers are not within the jurisdiction of state insurance regulators. State insurance regulators do not regulate reinsurance agreements as they do the policy forms used by primary insurers. Most states do, however, want reinsurance agreements to include a few specific clauses. Enforcing the requirement for reinsurers to include those clauses is indirect: the primary insurer is penalized when the clauses are not included.

Primary insurers are usually eager to take credit against their unearned premiums and loss reserves for premiums paid to and losses recoverable from reinsurers. The availability of those credits, referred to as credit for reinsurance, reduces the drain on the primary insurer's surplus from writing new business. Regulators motivate primary insurers to require some desirable clauses in their reinsurance agreements by withholding permission to take reserve credit for the reinsurance transaction unless the reinsurance agreements contain the specified clauses. Those clauses are not mandatory; a primary insurer that is willing to forgo the credit for the reinsurance transaction can enter into a reinsurance agreement that does not include them.

Insolvency clause
A clause that is required in reinsurance agreements indicating that the primary insurer's bankruptcy does not affect the reinsurer's liability for losses under the reinsurance agreement.

The required **insolvency clause** provides that the primary insurer's insolvency does not affect the reinsurer's liability for losses under the reinsurance agreement. The reinsurer pays the receiver or liquidator of the insolvent primary insurer for its creditors' benefit.

Intermediary clause
A clause that is required in reinsurance agreements indicating that the reinsurance intermediary is the reinsurer's agent for collecting reinsurance premiums and paying reinsurance claims.

More recently, some states have required an **intermediary clause** in reinsurance agreements. This clause provides that the reinsurance intermediary is the reinsurer's agent for collecting reinsurance premiums and paying reinsurance claims. So, the reinsurer assumes the credit risk that the reinsurance intermediary will be unable or unwilling to pay all of the premiums collected under its reinsurance agreements. The reinsurer also assumes the risk that the reinsurance intermediary will not transmit to the primary insurer all claim payments made by the reinsurer. This clause is beneficial to primary insurers because courts have held in most cases that the reinsurance intermediary is the primary insurer's agent. Consequently, in the absence of this clause, the risk of the reinsurance intermediary's insolvency would fall most often on the primary insurer and not on the reinsurer.

Insurance regulatory authorities can influence the selection of reinsurers by primary insurers. The value of most pro rata reinsurance agreements lies in the favorable accounting treatment afforded a reinsurance transaction. If state insurance regulators do not approve a reinsurer, they can deny the primary insurer any benefit of such a reinsurance agreement with the unapproved reinsurer. Some states permit the primary insurer to take the reserve credits only if the reinsurer is licensed in the state. Others permit the reserve credit if the reinsurer is licensed in any state. Finally, some states permit the reserve credit even if the reinsurer is not licensed anywhere in the U.S., provided the primary insurer obtains the state insurance department's permission before entering into the agreement. Reserve credit for reinsurance can also be permitted if reinsurance loss reserves are secured by a letter of credit or a trust fund.

SUMMARY

Insurers purchase reinsurance to finance some of their underwriting risk by transferring some or all of the potential financial consequences of certain loss exposures they cede to reinsurers. Through a transaction called retrocession, reinsurers in turn finance some of the risk they have assumed from primary insurers to other reinsurers, called retrocessionaires. Reinsurance and retrocession enable worldwide risk financing.

A policyholder is not a party to a reinsurance agreement between the primary insurer and its reinsurer unless a cut-through endorsement is attached to the primary insurer's policy with the policyholder.

The following entities provide reinsurance: professional reinsurers; reinsurance departments of primary insurers; and reinsurance pools, syndicates, and associations. Reinsurance can be placed directly with a reinsurer or through a reinsurance intermediary.

Reinsurance serves the following functions benefiting primary insurers: stabilize loss experience, improve large-line capacity, provide catastrophe protection, provide surplus relief, provide underwriting guidance, and facilitate withdrawal from a territory or type of business.

Reinsurance transaction are of two types: treaty reinsurance or facultative reinsurance. Treaty reinsurance is reinsurance for certain types of loss exposures under a prearranged reinsurance agreement called a treaty. In facultative reinsurance, the primary insurer negotiates a separate reinsurance agreement for each loss exposure it wants to reinsure.

Treaty and facultative reinsurance agreements are of two types: pro rata reinsurance or excess of loss reinsurance. Under pro rata reinsurance, the amount of insurance, the premium, and the losses are divided between the primary insurer and the reinsurer in the same agreed proportion. Under excess of loss reinsurance, the reinsurer is involved only if a loss exceeds the primary insurer's retention, and the reinsurer pays only the amount in excess of the retention, subject to the reinsurance limit.

The major types of pro rata reinsurance treaties are quota share and surplus share. The major types of excess of loss treaties are per risk or per policy excess of loss, per occurrence excess of loss, and aggregate excess of loss. The chapter illustrates the operation of each of these types of treaties. Each type of treaty is designed to accomplish one or more, but not all, of the functions of reinsurance.

Because facultative reinsurance is obtained on an individual loss exposure basis, it entails more expense for both the primary insurer and the reinsurer. Despite this drawback, facultative reinsurance enables a primary insurer to insure a type of loss exposure that is not covered by its treaties or provide an amount of insurance that exceeds its capacity. It also enables a primary insurer to "protect its treaties" by separately reinsuring a loss exposure that might otherwise have an adverse effect on the primary insurer's treaties.

The reinsurance program of a well-managed insurer plays a key role in meeting specific insurer goals. In designing a reinsurance program, insurers or their reinsurance intermediaries compare existing reinsurance agreements with their ever-changing needs. To be effective, reinsurance programs must be flexible enough to meet known and anticipated needs. Designing a reinsurance program involves determining reinsurance needs, setting retentions, setting limits, and determining reinsurance cost.

Reinsurance negotiations secure the reinsurance program that the primary insurer desires. Factors involved in reinsurance negotiations include compilation of information, use of a reinsurance intermediary, and reinsurance commissions.

After the reinsurance program is in place, it must be administered. The level of administration varies by the type of reinsurance. The cost of administering the reinsurance program is an additional consideration in selecting the components of a program.

Reinsurance is regulated less than primary insurance. The premise state regulators use is that in reinsurance, both parties to the agreement are knowledgeable about their rights and obligations. Insurance regulators have recognized that the insurance customer could suffer if reinsurance agreements are not met. In response, several proposals have been initiated to increase the level of regulatory supervision of reinsurers.

The discussion of insurer financial statements begins in the next chapter, which is the first of three chapters covering various aspects of insurer financial management.

Chapter 12

Direct Your Learning

Insurer Financial Statements

After learning the content of this chapter, you should be able to:

■ Identify who uses insurer financial statements.

■ Describe the elements of an insurer's balance sheet and income statement.

■ Describe the elements of an insurer's completed NAIC Annual Statement and the information those elements contain.

■ Explain how statutory accounting principles (SAP) and generally accepted accounting principles (GAAP) differ.

Develop Your Perspective

What are the main topics covered in the chapter?

This chapter explains how financial statements are used by insurers and how these statements differ from those used in other types of businesses. Also discussed are statutory accounting principles (SAP) and how SAP differs from generally accepted accounting principles (GAAP).

Compare financial statements of an insurer and of a noninsurance operation.

- How do these financial statements differ?

- Which elements are unique to the insurer, and how can this information be used to evaluate the insurer?

Why is it important to learn about these topics?

Insurer financial statements are an important source of information about the insurer, and several parties have an interest in this information.

Consider the parties who would use insurer financial statements.

- Why are these parties interested in this financial information?

- How does each of these parties use this information to evaluate the insurer?

How can you use what you will learn?

Review the Annual Statement of a property-casualty insurer.

- What information is available on the balance sheet of this statement?

- What additional information is provided within the supporting documents and schedules within the statement?

Chapter 12

Insurer Financial Statements

This chapter discusses what financial statements insurers use, who uses these statements, and how they differ from those of other types of businesses. Like all businesses, insurers prepare and publish financial statements to report the financial results the company has experienced and to depict its financial well-being. Many parties with a stake in an insurer's financial status review such statements with keen interest:

- Corporate managers use financial information in planning, monitoring company performance, and allocating resources.

- Investors seek financial information on companies in which they have invested. These investors expect a satisfactory return on their investments and will move their investments to other companies or industries if expected returns do not materialize.

- Regulators are primarily concerned with insurer solvency and depend on insurer financial statements to make decisions about financial requirements, surplus levels, and reserve amounts for individual insurers.

- Policyholders, producers, and risk managers are interested in the financial stability of the insurers with which they do business.

Two key financial statements that all businesses create are the balance sheet and the income statement. However, for an insurer, the same elements of each of these statements are different from those that appear on the statements of most businesses. The next section of this chapter provides an overview of these two financial statements, highlighting the elements that are unique to insurers. This is followed by a discussion of statutory accounting principles (SAP) and their effect on insurers, the Annual Statement and its supplements, and the balance sheet and income statements as presented within the Annual Statement.

This chapter concludes by analyzing the differences between SAP and generally accepted accounting principles (GAAP). These differences arise from the requirements of state insurance regulators who prescribe the rules, contents, and format for insurer financial statements.

WHO USES INSURER FINANCIAL STATEMENTS?

Insurer management, investors, regulators, policyholders, and others are all interested in insurers' financial condition and performance. The specific needs of these parties determine the type and format of the financial information provided by insurers.

Management

Insurer management establishes the insurer's goals, plans operations that will fulfill those goals, obtains and allocates the needed resources, monitors performance, and adapts as necessary.

Two primary goals of insurer management are to earn a profit and to maximize the value of the firm. Financial statements indicate how well management has accomplished these goals. These statements also provide feedback about the performance of particular classes of business and types of policies as well as serve as a source of detailed reports to support operations. For an insurer whose shares are publicly traded, these goals would likely be recognized as maximizing share value. Because profit and share value are determined by financial results, the importance of financial statements to management is obvious. However, in addition to serving as "report cards" for overall corporate performance, financial statements enable management to make numerous operational decisions.

Class of Business and Product Performance

Financial reports enable management to answer such questions as, How is a particular class of business or product performing? Are revenues being realized as expected? Are products priced competitively? Are too many resources devoted to unpromising classes of business?

If answers to such questions are unsatisfactory, management can take corrective action. Depending on financial results, management might expand or withdraw from a class of business, a product line, or a geographic area; might re-price certain products and services; and/or might prepare for a regulatory exam of financial performance.

Detailed Reports

Senior management needs financial reports that show progress against overall plans. These reports should reveal whether operational plans are unfolding as expected. Middle management regularly monitors financial performance relating to sales goals and expense budgets. Financial information can also be used to evaluate the performance of divisions, units, offices, and even individual employees.

The hierarchy of financial reports ranges from detailed reports on operating unit performance to summary financial statements for the entire enterprise. Management must prepare the financial reports required by regulators and tax authorities. However, these reports are likely to be too summarized and too infrequent to serve management's needs adequately.

Investors

Investors are those who own an insurer's shares of stock. They are interested in a good return on their investment and have many investment options. Investors make judgments on the value of investment opportunities based on information contained in the insurer's quarterly and annual financial reports. If an insurer's stock or the entire industry's stocks do not look promising, investors can easily move their money elsewhere.

From the investor's point of view, it is not enough for management to earn some profit. Management must produce enough profit to yield a satisfactory return to investors. These returns must be competitive with stocks and other financial investments of similar liquidity and riskiness. The returns of competing investments are publicized widely in the financial media. If insurers do not offer competitive returns, investors will move their capital elsewhere.

Rating Services

Several prominent rating services evaluate insurer financial reports to assess financial strength on behalf of potential policyholders and investors. (Note that because insurers are not usually funded by issuing bonds or other types of debt, not all rating services evaluate bonds from insurers.)

These rating services evaluate the information contained in insurer financial statements regarding the insurer's ability to grow, remain solvent, pay claims, and reward investors. In essence, these rating services review financial data to glean meaning from it.

Controlling Owners

Most investors are passive, with no interest in running the companies in which they invest. However, some actively participate in stockholder meetings and try to influence or even oust existing management. Investors with the largest ownership interest can exert the greatest control.

Some investors buy enough stock to control the company. Any takeover of a controlling interest requires careful analysis of the target company by the buyer. Such analysis extends to all aspects of the target company but particularly to its financial statements.

Regulators

State insurance departments are responsible for enforcing insurance laws in their states. One purpose of insurance regulation is to monitor insurer solvency—that is, to ensure that insurers can fulfill their promises to their policyholders. To protect policyholders against insurer insolvency, insurance laws and regulations impose financial requirements on insurers. These requirements include the following:

- Insurers must have minimum capital to begin operations and sufficient capital to continue operations.
- The amount of premiums an insurer can write is constrained by its capital.
- Premiums are considered earned over the period for which insurance protection is provided rather than when revenue is received.
- Reserves for incurred losses should be set at adequate levels to pay claims when due.

Adherence to these requirements is determined using information from an insurer's financial statements.

The NAIC Annual Statement

The primary financial statement that insurers prepare is the National Association of Insurance Commissioners (NAIC) Annual Statement, required by every state. The **NAIC Annual Statement** is a lengthy document that includes a balance sheet, an income statement, a cash flow statement, an account of changes to surplus, and numerous supporting schedules.

NAIC Annual Statement
The primary financial statement prepared by insurers and required by every state insurance department.

Statutory accounting principles (SAP)
The accounting principles and practices that are prescribed or permitted by an insurer's domiciliary state and that insurers must follow.

The rules created by the NAIC for completing the Annual Statement are known as **statutory accounting principles (SAP)**. The important features of the Annual Statement and SAP are described later in this chapter.

Other Financial Filings

In addition to providing financial reports to the state insurance department, insurers must provide them to other authorities, including the Securities and Exchange Commission (SEC) and the Internal Revenue Service (IRS).

Insurers whose stock is publicly traded must register and file reports with the SEC. After its initial registrations, any company registered with the SEC must file the 10-K and 10-Q financial statements with the SEC. The Form 10-K is an annual financial statement that companies must file within ninety days of the end of the reporting company's fiscal year. The Form 10-Q financial statement is filed quarterly and includes unaudited financial statements. This financial statement must be filed for each of the first three quarters of the reporting company's fiscal year. These financial statements, and other SEC filings, are available online at www.sec.gov/edgar.

Insurers must also file a federal income tax return. They are permitted to base their federal income tax on SAP, subject to adjustments. As is explained subsequently, insurers must immediately recognize expenses incurred to acquire insurance business even though premium revenue is earned ratably over the policy period. This moves expenses forward in time and thereby reduces net income and taxable income. In addition, insurers are permitted to recognize losses as they are incurred and reserved, which might be well before losses are paid. Although insurers must discount reserves to present value for tax purposes according to IRS rules, recognizing losses as incurred, rather than as paid, is a form of accrual accounting that moves expenses forward in time relative to cash flow, reducing net income and taxable income.

Policyholders, Producers, and Risk Managers

The majority of policyholders, even those who are sophisticated business people, are not skilled enough to judge the financial status of insurers. One key reason for insurance regulation is to protect such individuals from the potential consequences of insurer insolvency.

Property-casualty insurance might seem to be a relatively short-term transaction, but it involves longer-term relationships than some policyholders might recognize. While policy terms are generally just one year, claim settlements, especially with certain types of liability insurance, may not be made for years after a policy has expired. For policyholders who remain with one insurer for many years, this effect of long-tail claims may be compounded. Therefore, an insurer's financial strength is especially significant for policyholders who establish long-term relationships with one insurer.

Producers, both agents and brokers, are very concerned about the financial strength of the insurers with which they work. They might be professionally liable for errors and omissions if they knew or should have known about the financial difficulties of an insurer and placed a client's business with that insurer anyway. Producers follow the industry trade press closely and develop their own sources of information.

Often, risk managers must be more informed about insurer financial strength than other insurance customers. Sophisticated risk management programs for large loss exposures often include high-level retentions that involve insurers only after losses have reached a significant amount. Many of these losses would also be covered under reinsurance agreements because of their size. Concerns about the financial condition of insurers are complicated further by large losses that may be slow to develop over time. Because of higher attachment points, reinsurers are often more vulnerable to price inadequacy than are primary insurers, which could lead to financial difficulties. As part of administering an insurance program, the risk manager is required not only to monitor losses and attachment points but also to consider the potential effect of the financial strength of all insurers involved on the viability of the overall insurance program.

FUNDAMENTALS OF INSURER FINANCIAL STATEMENTS

The Annual Statement that insurers file with state insurance departments is a daunting-looking document. More than 100 pages long, it is packed with in-depth data covering numerous years and types of insurance. Yet it is summarized in financial statements that are supported by exhibits and supplements. The two key statements are the balance sheet and the income statement.

Insurers are like other businesses in that the balance sheet and income statement are the main financial statements they create. However, insurers are quite different from other businesses regarding the elements within these statements.

The Balance Sheet

For every organization, including insurers, a balance sheet is a listing, in dollars, of everything the organization owns and everything it owes to others, as of a specified date. What the organization owns are its assets, and what it owes to others are its liabilities.

A balance sheet also indicates the difference between an organization's assets and its liabilities. This difference is the organization's net worth. Net worth is positive if the organization owns more than it owes and negative if the reverse is true. Because net worth is defined as the difference between assets and liabilities (that is, Net worth = Assets − Liabilities), the balance sheet will always balance, even if net worth must be a negative number for a balance to exist. An organization with negative net worth has liabilities that exceed assets and is probably insolvent.

Conventionally, a balance sheet lists assets in a column on the left side and liabilities in a column on the right side. Net worth is usually listed after liabilities on the right. See Exhibit 12-1 for the general form of a balance sheet.

EXHIBIT 12-1	
General Form of a Balance Sheet	
Assets	Liabilities
	Net Worth

From a finance perspective, a balance sheet can be thought of as showing the sources and uses of an organization's funds. The liabilities and net worth of an organization indicate the source of its funding—it obtains funds from those to whom it owes money and from money initially provided by its owners or retained from earnings. An organization uses funds by investing in its assets. A for-profit business hopes to succeed by achieving a higher return on its assets than it must pay for its liabilities.

As indicated in Exhibit 12-2, an insurer balance sheet follows the same general form as for other organizations but has a few significant differences.

EXHIBIT 12-2

General Form of an Insurer Balance Sheet

Assets	Liabilities
	Surplus as Regards Policyholders

Designating an insurer's net worth as "surplus as regards policyholders" (or **"policyholders' surplus"** in more common industry usage) is more than just a labeling difference. All of the insurer's net worth is available to satisfy policyholder's claims before any owner is entitled to anything.

The other principal difference between an insurer's balance sheet and another organization's balance sheet is that different elements constitute the insurer's assets and liabilities.

Policyholders' surplus
The balance sheet item representing an insurer's net worth under statutory accounting.

Insurer Assets

Business assets typically include buildings, equipment, and inventory. However, most assets owned by insurers are intangible financial assets.

By far, the largest class of assets owned by property-casualty insurers is bonds. Bonds are debt obligations of the issuing organizations that typically pay to their owner (the bondholder) regular interest payments—annually or semiannually, for example—plus a repayment of the bond's face amount at its maturity date (typically ten to thirty years after the bond is issued). Bonds are attractive investments for insurers because, compared to other investments, they pay fairly predictable, periodic, secure income. It is very important for insurers to generate income from their investments to provide cash flow for payment of future losses.

Other financial investments that make up sizeable portions of insurer assets are stocks, cash, and cash equivalents (for example, money market funds and instruments). Insurers have certain important groups of receivables. A receivable is an asset because it represents money owed to the organization. For most insurers, the most important receivable is **"premium balances"** owed by agents. These balances arise from the delay between premium payment by policyholders to their agents and transmittal of these premiums by the agents to the insurer. For some insurers, funds due from reinsurers ("reinsurance recoverables") or from affiliated companies can be significant.

Premium balances
An insurer receivable consisting of premium amounts due from producers.

Insurers also own buildings; equipment, especially computer equipment; and office furnishings. However, these assets are relatively minor compared to the insurer's intangible financial assets.

Insurer Liabilities

Insurer liabilities are even more distinctive from the liabilities of other organizations than are their assets. The two principal liabilities are reserves for losses and for unearned premiums, both of which arise from the insurer's operations and both of which are unique to insurers.

Loss reserves
An insurer liability representing the insurer's obligation to pay claims that have occurred but have not yet been paid.

Insurer **loss reserves** are liabilities that recognize the insurer's obligation to pay claims that have occurred but have not yet been paid. The liabilities for loss reserves are included in the "Losses" element of the insurer's balance sheet. See Exhibit 12-3. Insurers also reserve amounts for the expenses they have incurred but not yet paid to settle such claims, a liability called **"loss adjustment expense reserve."** The liabilities for these expense reserves are included in the "Loss Adjustment Expenses" element of the insurer's balance sheet.

Loss adjustment expense reserve
An insurer liability representing the expense amounts it has incurred to settle claims that have not yet been paid.

Loss reserves arise because there is inevitably a delay between the occurrence of a covered loss and its settlement. Delays occur in reporting, investigating, and negotiating claims. For certain types of claims, such as auto physical damage, this delay might be only a few days or weeks. For other types of claims, such as litigated medical malpractice claims, the delay can span many years because of the legal process. Generally, first-party and property loss claims take less time to settle than third-party liability claims.

Loss reserves must be estimated, and estimates can be inaccurate. Reserve inaccuracies directly affect policyholders' surplus because the balance sheet must always balance. If reserves are too low, policyholders' surplus will be overstated (and understated when reserves are too high). Once inadequate reserves are properly recognized, policyholders' surplus will be reduced (or increased if reserves were originally set too high). This is a critical issue for insurers because policyholders' surplus is vital to insurer financial strength and ongoing viability.

Unearned premium reserve
An insurer liability representing the amount of premiums received from policyholders that are not yet earned.

The insurer's other principal liability is the **unearned premium reserve**. This liability represents the amount of premiums received from policyholders but not yet earned. Policyholders pay premiums before the period for which they are covered and sometimes pay the entire premium before the policy period begins. Although insurers receive cash for the premium at the start of the policy period, they earn premium proportionately as the policy period transpires. For example, on an annual policy, the insurer earns 1/365th of the annual premium as each day of the policy period passes. At the end of the policy period, all premiums received will be earned. But, in the meantime, insurers must recognize as a liability the unearned premium amounts they have received from policyholders.

Exhibit 12-3 indicates an outline of the main elements of an insurer balance sheet. Anyone who is familiar with these elements will readily be oriented to more complex, detailed statements, such as those contained in the Annual Statement.

EXHIBIT 12-3

Principal Elements of an Insurer Balance Sheet

Assets	Liabilities
Bonds	Losses
Stocks	Loss Adjustment Expenses
Cash	Unearned Premiums
Premium Balances	**Surplus and Other Funds**
Reinsurance Recoverables	Surplus as Regards Policyholders

The Income Statement

While a balance sheet is a snapshot of an organization's assets and liabilities as of a specific date, an income statement portrays financial results over a time period, usually a year or a quarter. An income statement also shows gains or losses from non-operating activities, such as the purchase or sale of assets.

An income statement is structured to calculate an organization's profitability. Generally, an organization is profitable when its revenues exceed its expenses. An organization earns revenue by selling its products or services; expenses are the costs incurred in producing that revenue. The general form of an income statement is shown in Exhibit 12-4.

EXHIBIT 12-4

General Form of an Income Statement

Revenues

− Expenses

Net Income

Conventionally, revenues are listed at the top of an income statement and expenses are listed below revenues. The "bottom line" of an income statement is net income, the difference between revenues and expenses, or profit.

The general form of an insurer's income statement is similar. The revenues from an insurer's underwriting operations are the premiums received from policyholders, and the expenses for an insurer are payments for losses covered by the insurer's policies plus the insurer's operating expenses. See Exhibit 12-5. Additionally, insurers earn income from investments. The precise terms for the elements of an insurer's income statement are explained next.

EXHIBIT 12-5

General Form of an Insurer Income Statement

Premiums
− Losses
− Operating Expenses
_____
Net Income From Operations

Earned Premiums

Insurers count premiums as revenue once they are earned, not when they are written or received. Therefore, "earned premiums" is the correct term for insurer revenues. Earned premiums in a given year can be calculated as:

> Unearned premiums at the beginning of the year
>
> + Net written premiums during the year
>
> − Unearned premiums at the end of the year
>
> = Earned premiums during the year.

The first two elements of this formula represent the premiums available to be earned during the year, while the third element represents premiums yet to be earned at year's end.

Incurred Losses and Loss Adjustment Expense

Insurers count the amount of their incurred losses as expenses against their income. Incurred losses are not the same as paid losses. For Annual Statement purposes, incurred losses in a given year are:

> Losses paid during the year
>
> + Loss reserves at the end of the year
>
> − Loss reserves at the beginning of the year.

The last two elements of this formula represent changes in reserves. If reserves increase during the year, incurred losses for the year are greater than paid losses. If reserves decrease during the year, incurred losses for the year are less than paid losses.

In calculating net income, loss adjustment expenses are also recognized as they are incurred. Therefore, loss adjustment expenses are calculated as expenses paid plus the change in loss adjustment expense reserves during the year.

Other Underwriting Expenses

Other underwriting expenses
An insurer expense item representing expenses arising from its underwriting activities, including sales commissions paid to producers, salaries and benefits for insurer staff, and other operating expenses.

Insurers also incur significant expenses from underwriting activities. These expenses are grouped as **"other underwriting expenses"** and include sales commissions to agents, salaries and benefits for the insurer's staff, advertising, rent, and other operating expenses.

Investment Earnings

The results from an insurer's underwriting operations alone would give an incomplete picture of the insurer's financial performance. Insurers earn income from invested assets. Investment income arises out of the fundamentals of insurance transactions. Policyholders pay their premiums before insurers pay losses. Between these periods of time, insurers hold funds that are available for investment.

While most solvent businesses have some funds available for investment, insurers invest on an altogether different scale. Indeed, investment earnings have been essential to insurer profitability and survival for years. For some time periods, insurers lose money on underwriting operations almost every year—yet they can remain in business because of investment results.

Investment earnings include investment income and net realized capital gains. Investment income comes principally from interest payments on bonds and dividend payments from stocks. Capital gains result when an asset, such as shares of stock, is sold for more than its purchase price. The gain is realized upon the sale. (Unrealized capital gains on investments result when an asset increases in value but is not sold. These gains are not included in an insurer's income statement.) "Net" realized capital gains refers to the net of capital gains over capital losses (also a possibility).

Exhibit 12-6 presents the important elements of an insurer's income statement.

EXHIBIT 12-6

Principal Elements of an Insurer Income Statement

Earned Premium
– Losses Incurred
– Loss Adjustment Expense Incurred
– Other Underwriting Expenses
Net Underwriting Gain (or Loss)
+ Investment Income
+ Net Realized Capital Gains (or Losses)
Net Income (Before Dividends or Taxes)

STATUTORY ACCOUNTING AND THE ANNUAL STATEMENT

The complete set of financial statements produced by an insurer is contained in the Annual Statement that must be filed with state insurance departments. The Annual Statement is based on statutory accounting principles (SAP) that form a complete system of accounting for insurers.

Statutory Accounting

Statutory accounting principles are "the principles and practices prescribed or permitted by an insurer's domiciliary state."[1] State insurance laws, regulations, and regulatory practices govern the accounting methods insurers must follow.

State Law Prevails

The NAIC has done significant work to standardize SAP. However, the NAIC cannot preempt state laws and regulations. To the extent that a conflict exists between SAP as promulgated by the NAIC and individual state laws or regulations, the state's rules will prevail for any insurer domiciled in that state. However, the NAIC requires every insurer that follows accounting practices and procedures that differ from the NAIC's rules to file a disclosure statement revealing: (1) a description of the practice and how it differs from NAIC rules and (2) the effect of such practice on net income and surplus. Such disclosure enables regulators in other states in which a particular insurer does business to see immediately how the insurer has varied from NAIC rules.

Annual Statement and Supplements

Insurers must file an Annual Statement with the insurance department of the state in which they are domiciled and, either directly or through filing with the NAIC, in every state in which they do business. Annual Statements are available to the public.

Every state insurance department requires insurers to file supplements with the Annual Statement. These supplements (1) contain elaboration, documentation, and details of matters not contained in the NAIC Annual Statement; (2) are primarily financial in nature; and (3) are of special interest to the particular state insurance regulator.

General Organization of the Annual Statement

Exhibit 12-7 shows the general organization of the significant elements of the Annual Statement as of 2002. This exhibit also indicates the physical organization of the Annual Statement except that the Schedules are not arranged strictly in alphabetical order in the Annual Statement. Note that the NAIC regularly revises the Annual Statement but that the elements listed have been stable features for many years.

The "Title Page and Jurat" identifies by legal name and NAIC company code number the company for which the Annual Statement is being filed and lists both a contact for purposes of the Annual Statement and the directors of the company. This initial page of the Annual Statement must be authenticated and signed by the company's president, secretary, and treasurer.

EXHIBIT 12-7

General Organization of the Annual Statement

Title Page and Jurat

Assets

Liabilities, Surplus and Other Funds

Underwriting and Investment Exhibit

> Statement of Income
>
> > Underwriting Income
> >
> > Investment Income
> >
> > Other Income
>
> Capital and Surplus Account

Cash Flow

> Cash from Operations
>
> Cash from Investments
>
> Cash from Financing and Miscellaneous Sources
>
> Reconciliation of Cash and Short-Term Investments

Underwriting and Investment Exhibit

> Part 1—Premiums Earned
>
> Part 1A—Recapitulation of All Premiums
>
> Part 1B—Premiums Written
>
> Part 2—Losses Paid and Incurred
>
> Part 2A—Unpaid Losses and Loss Adjustment Expenses
>
> Part 3—Expenses

General Interrogatories

Five-Year Historical Data

Schedules

> A—Real Estate
>
> B—Mortgage Loans
>
> BA—Other Long-Term Invested Assets
>
> D—Bonds and Stocks
>
> DA—Short-Term Investments
>
> DB—Derivative Investments
>
> E—Cash and Special Deposits
>
> F—Reinsurance
>
> P—Analysis of Losses and Loss Expenses

The next two pages of the Annual Statement—the "Assets" and "Liabilities, Surplus and Other Funds"—constitute a balance sheet and are the core of the Annual Statement. The "Statement of Income" is embedded within the "Underwriting and Investment Exhibit." The contrast between the Annual Statement's balance sheet and income statement is unmistakable. The balance sheet is elaborated over two pages, while the income statement occupies barely half a page, reflecting the greater importance the NAIC places on the balance sheet, which indicates solvency.

The "Capital and Surplus Account" shows all "Gains and (Losses) in Surplus." These gains and losses come from the "Net income" line of the "Statement of Income," net unrealized capital gains, and changes in surplus and capital accounts. The bottom line of this account carries over to the total "Surplus as regards policyholders" on the balance sheet.

The "Cash Flow" account is a conventional cash flow statement, similar to those of other businesses, showing sources and uses of cash from operations, investments, and financing activities. As indicated in Exhibit 12-8, sources of cash under the "Cash from Operations" section include premiums collected and investment income. Cash is used to pay losses, loss adjustment and underwriting expenses, and dividends to policyholders. Under "Cash from Investments," proceeds from the sale, maturity, or repayment of bonds, stocks, and other investment holdings are the sources of cash. The cost of investment acquisitions is the chief investment use of cash and is subtracted to determine a "Net cash from investments" figure. The final category in the Cash Flow account is "Cash from Financing and Miscellaneous Sources," in which any cash provided from surplus notes, borrowed funds, and other sources is shown. Payment of dividends to stockholders, transfers to affiliates, and repayment of outstanding loans are the chief uses of cash from financial and miscellaneous sources. In the "Reconciliation of Cash and Short-Term Investments" section of the Cash Flow account, the net change in cash and in short-term investments for the current year is calculated.

The various parts of the "Underwriting and Investment Exhibit" supply elaboration and detail for items that appear in the income statement or balance sheet.

The "General Interrogatories" explore matters that are not necessarily revealed in the financial statements, such as changes in the corporate charter or bylaws; dealings with affiliated entities, foreign owners, directors, officers, or shareholders of the company; control of capital stock by others; dealings with trade associations; unusual exposures and reinsurance arrangements; and receipt of promissory notes and letters of credit in lieu of premiums.

The "Five-Year Historical Data" section discloses five-year trends in the major balance sheet and income statement items, percentage allocations of the various invested assets to total invested assets, key operating ratios, and one-year and two-year reserve development factors for each of the five years.

EXHIBIT 12-8

Cash Flow

	1 Current Year	2 Prior Year
Cash from Operations		
1. Premiums collected net of reinsurance		
2. Loss and loss adjustment expenses paid (net of salvage and subrogation)		
3. Underwriting expenses paid		
4. Other underwriting income (expenses)		
5. Cash from underwriting (Line 1 minus Line 2 minus Line 3 plus Line 4)		
6. Net investment income		
7. Other income (expenses):		
7.1 Agents' balances charged off		
7.2 Net funds held under reinsurance treaties		
7.3 Net amount withheld or retained for account of others		
7.4 Aggregate write-ins for miscellaneous items		
7.5 Total other income (Lines 7.1 thru 7.4)		
8. Dividends to policyholders on direct business, less $ . . . . dividends on reinsurance assumed or ceded (net)		
9. Federal and foreign income taxes (paid) recovered		
10. Net cash from operations (Line 5 plus Line 6 plus Line 7.5 minus Line 8 plus Line 9)		
Cash from Investments		
11. Proceeds from investments sold, matured or repaid:		
11.1 Bonds		
11.2 Stocks		
11.3 Mortgage loans		
11.4 Real estate		
11.5 Other invested assets		
11.6 Net gains or (losses) on cash and short-term investments		
11.7 Miscellaneous proceeds		
11.8 Total investment proceeds (Line 11.1 to 11.7)		
12. Cost of investments acquired (long-term only):		
12.1 Bonds		
12.2 Stocks		
12.3 Mortgage loans		
12.4 Real estate		
12.5 Other invested assets		
12.6 Miscellaneous applications		
12.7 Total investments acquired (Lines 12.1 to 12.6)		
13. Net cash from investments (Line 11.8 minus Line 12.7)		
Cash from Financing and Miscellaneous Sources:		
14. Cash provided:		
14.1 Surplus notes, capital and surplus paid in		
14.2 Capital notes $ less amounts repaid $		
14.3 Net transfers from affiliates		
14.4 Borrowed funds received		
14.5 Other cash provided		
14.6 Total (Lines 14.1 to 14.5)		
15. Cash applied:		
15.1 Dividends to stockholders paid		
15.2 Net transfers to affiliates		
15.3 Borrowed funds repaid		
15.4 Other applications		
15.5 Total (Lines 15.1 to 15.4)		
16. Net cash from financing and miscellaneous sources (Line 14.6 minus Line 15.5)		
RECONCILIATION OF CASH AND SHORT-TERM INVESTMENTS		
17. Net change in cash and short-term investments (Line 10, plus Line 13, plus Line 16)		
18. Cash and short-term investments:		
18.1 Beginning of year		
18.2 End of year (Line 17 plus Line 18.1)		
Details of Write-Ins:		
7.401		
7.402		
7.403		
7.498 Summary of remaining write-ins for Line 7.4 from overflow page		
7.499 Totals (Lines 7.401 thru 7.403 + 7.498) (Line 7.4 above)		

Source: St Ives Burrups, "2002 Annual Statement Changes" (Marlton, N.J.: St Ives Burrups Insurance Division), 2002.

Like the parts of the "Underwriting and Investment Exhibit," the various Schedules provide the detail for items that appear in the income statement or balance sheet. Schedule DB requires disclosure of investments in derivatives, such as puts, calls, caps, options, and swaps. "Derivatives" are so called because they are contractual investments whose value is derived from the value of some other financial instrument. Indeed, the Annual Statement calls them "Replicated (Synthetic) Assets." Derivatives can be used conservatively to hedge exposures from other financial instruments or speculatively as gambles on the future. The particular use of derivatives is of great interest to the NAIC.

Balance Sheet

Exhibit 12-9 shows the consolidated balance sheet for the entire property-casualty insurance industry for 2001.[2] The elements explained in Exhibit 12-3 are highlighted in Exhibit 12-9 and constitute the major elements for insurers. The elements in Exhibit 12-9 that do not appear in Exhibit 12-3 are relatively minor and are rarely critical to an insurer's financial strength.

Key items on the balance sheet come from various supporting documents. For example, "Mortgage loans on real estate" comes from Schedule B, "Real estate" comes from Schedule A, "Cash" comes from Schedule E, "Other invested assets" comes from Schedule DA, and "Reinsurance recoverables on loss and loss adjustment expense payments" comes from Schedule F. Among the liabilities on the balance sheet, "Losses" and "Loss adjustment expenses" are the respective allocations for loss reserves and loss adjustment expense reserves that come from Part 3A of the Underwriting and Expense Exhibit, "Unearned premiums" comes from Part 2A of the Underwriting and Expense Exhibit, and "Surplus as regards policyholders" comes from the Capital and Surplus Account (on the next page of the Annual Statement).

Schedule D

Schedule D elaborates on the key invested assets: bonds, preferred stock, and common stock. Schedule D includes a "Summary By Country" that indicates investments in bonds, preferred stock, and common stock that originate from the U.S., Canada, or elsewhere.

Schedule D has the following six parts:

- Part 1 provides specific information for all bonds owned as of December 31 of the report year. Each bond the company holds must be listed.
- Part 2 provides detailed information for each preferred stock and each common stock the company holds as of December 31 of the report year.
- Part 3 lists all bonds and stocks acquired during the report year.
- Part 4 lists all bonds and stocks sold, redeemed, or otherwise disposed of during the report year.
- Part 5 lists all bonds and stocks both acquired and fully disposed of during the report year.
- Part 6 lists shares of subsidiary, controlled, and affiliated companies.

EXHIBIT 12-9

Consolidated Industry Totals

(000 omitted)

ASSETS	2001	2000	1999	1998	1997
1. Bonds	532,043,034	505,118,701	515,456,135	519,814,328	512,692,350
2. Stocks:					
2.1 Preferred stocks (Schedule D, Part 2, Section 1)	10,959,851	10,644,888	10,321,140	11,982,453	12,858,711
2.2 Common stocks (Schedule D, Part 2, Section 2)	164,632,096	183,372,676	196,965,534	188,136,429	172,960,473
3. Mortgage loans on real estate (Schedule B):					
3.1 First liens	1,964,603	1,551,180	1,841,438	1,916,210	2,173,872
3.2 Other than first liens	67,522	83,249	79,659	37,821	56,101
4. Real estate (Schedule A):					
4.1 Properties occupied by the company (less $ .... encumbrances)	8,170,306	8,549,017	8,345,483	7,867,695	7,653,553
4.2 Properties held for the production of income (less $ .... encumbrances)	1,015,808	—	—	—	—
4.3 Properties held for sale (less $ .... encumbrances)	340,580	996,267	1,064,443	1,003,587	1,433,528
5. Cash ($ ...... Schedule E, Part 1) and short-term investments ($ ...... Schedule DA, Part 2)	44,330,008	41,866,117	32,284,992	46,298,485	39,481,190
6. Other invested assets (Schedule BA)	32,961,768	31,192,148	28,987,471	16,625,485	13,977,176
7. Receivable for securities	1,946,035	2,916,920	1,679,946	1,151,303	1,138,786
8. Aggregate write-ins for invested assets	2,353,166	3,039,085	2,034,428	1,946,778	1,636,179
9. Subtotals, cash and invested assets (Lines 1 to 8)	800,784,777	789,330,250	799,060,669	796,780,574	766,061,919
10. Agents' balances or uncollected premiums:					
10.1 Premiums and agents' balances in course of collection)	34,386,260	18,878,549	19,128,299	19,175,376	18,172,221
10.2 Premiums, agents' balances and installments booked but deferred and not yet due					
(including $ .... earned but unbilled premiums)	49,730,969	41,447,106	39,514,262	37,212,608	36,521,840
10.3 Accrued retrospective premiums	3,754,329	3,740,763	4,097,990	4,336,407	4,698,566
11. Funds held by or deposited with reinsured companies	7,961,361	7,007,369	6,290,410	4,835,877	4,699,625
12. Bills receivable, taken for premiums	605,543	470,107	489,578	545,236	532,364
13. Amounts billed and receivable under deductible and service-only plans	1,538,338	—	—	—	—
14. Reinsurance recoverables on loss and loss adjustment expense payments (Schedule F					
Part 3, Cols. 7 and 8)	20,012,885	16,630,130	15,171,512	12,037,471	10,949,802
15. Federal and foreign income tax recoverable and interest thereon					
(including $ .... net deferred tax asset)	15,554,070	2,054,485	2,452,542	2,010,351	1,168,859
16. Guaranty funds receivable or on deposit	461,895	163,000	190,090	164,204	172,476
17. Electronic data processing equipment and software	1,970,483	2,205,764	2,536,986	2,576,035	2,294,113
18. Interest, dividends and real estate income due and accrued	8,063,995	8,234,821	8,526,646	8,654,465	8,606,425
19. Net adjustments in assets and liabilities due to foreign exchange rates	38,280	—	—	—	—
20. Receivable from parent, subsidiaries and affiliates	12,197,878	7,812,858	8,411,729	8,934,195	5,912,671
21. Equities and deposits in pools and associations	1,623,333	1,745,404	1,939,653	2,138,511	2,084,302
22. Amounts receivable relating to uninsured accident and health plans	99,939	110,273	91,393	67,039	30,535
23. Other assets non-admitted (Exhibit 1)	225	11,837	1,704	2,658	13,190
24. Aggregate write-ins for other than invested assets	13,880,210	12,167,133	10,405,454	9,295,578	8,137,149
25. TOTALS (Lines 9 through 24)	972,664,771	912,009,850	918,308,916	908,766,582	870,056,057
DETAILS OF WRITE-INS					
0801.					
0802.					
0803.					
0898. Summary of remaining write-ins for Line 8 from overflow page					
0899. TOTALS (Lines 0801 thru 0803 plus 0898) (Line 8 above)					
2401. Future investment income on loss reserves	113,008	183,472	198,457	214,574	217,658
2402. Other write-ins for assets other than invested assets	13,767,202	11,983,661	10,206,997	9,081,004	7,919,491
2403.					
2498. Summary of remaining write-ins for Line 24 from overflow page					
2499. TOTALS (Lines 2401 thru 2403 + 2498) (Line 24 above)	13,880,210	12,167,133	10,405,454	9,295,578	8,137,149

Continued on next page.

(000 omitted)

LIABILITIES, SURPLUS AND OTHER FUNDS	2001	2000	1999	1998	1997
1. Losses (Part 3A, Line 34, Column 8)	308,806,289	293,396,728	297,889,656	301,265,514	299,559,963
2. Reinsurance payable on paid loss and loss adjustment expenses (Schedule F, Part 1, Column 6)	6,828,458	4,999,835	4,491,304	3,642,966	3,829,726
3. Loss adjustment expenses (Part 3A, Column 9, Line 34)	62,959,264	63,101,517	64,129,233	63,930,124	63,791,019
4. Commissions payable, contingent commissions and other similar charges	3,291,331	2,162,655	2,566,665	2,532,717	2,593,662
5. Other expenses (excluding taxes, licenses and fees)	13,908,854	10,527,636	9,996,627	9,151,668	8,392,155
6. Taxes, licenses and fees (excluding federal and foreign income taxes)	4,594,222	2,879,815	2,786,429	2,711,741	2,705,606
7. Federal and foreign income taxes (including $............on realized capital gains (losses)) (including $............net deferrred tax liability)	13,645,966	2,727,892	3,007,364	2,613,438	2,824,457
8. Borrowed money $............and interest thereon $............	2,946,098	3,079,669	2,647,624	1,732,414	763,970
9. Unearned premiums (Part 2A, Line 37, Column 5) (after deducting unearned premiums for ceded reinsurance of $............and including warranty reserves of $......)	136,482,481	124,931,077	120,637,627	116,668,393	112,802,446
10. Dividends declared and unpaid:					
10.1 Stockholders	161,905	2,559,813	120,984	337,624	381,729
10.2 Policyholders	1,445,750	1,923,857	1,810,527	1,924,993	2,509,361
11. Ceded reinsurance premiums payable (net of ceding commissions)	19,520,104	—	—	—	—
12. Funds held by company under reinsurance treaties (Sch. F, Pt. 3, Col. 19)	24,436,428	14,862,218	11,310,881	9,961,253	9,236,843
13. Amounts withheld or retained by company for account of others	5,084,355	4,472,365	5,032,047	5,603,686	6,236,319
14. Remittances and items not allocated	1,710,202	1,412,243	1,491,466	1,659,522	—
15. Provision for reinsurance (Schedule F, Part 7)	5,471,002	5,198,852	4,683,668	3,870,995	3,719,706
— Excess of statutory reserves over statement reserves (Schedule P Interrogatories)	—	724,549	1,055,253	1,317,751	1,466,460
16. Net adjustments in assets and liabilities due to foreign exchange rates	668,654	648,853	606,716	720,990	665,298
17. Drafts outstanding	4,487,192	5,459,493	4,872,218	4,791,107	5,260,010
18. Payable to parent, subsidiaries and affiliates	8,451,982	5,409,002	6,817,030	8,006,155	4,321,515
19. Payable for securities	4,776,612	3,062,467	2,606,970	2,352,728	2,697,514
20. Liability for amounts held under uninsured accident and health plans	1,378	5,588	4,670	9,519	11,716
21. Capital notes $............ and interest theron $............	38,303	38,289	1,007	1,006	—
22. Aggregate write-ins for liabilities	33,286,971	41,064,822	35,394,778	30,633,076	27,807,582
23. Total liabilities (Lines 1 through 22)	663,003,801	594,649,233	583,960,742	575,439,379	561,577,058
24. Aggregate write-ins for special surplus funds	28,595,569	35,158,791	37,436,588	33,429,398	28,367,472
25. Common capital stock	3,059,016	7,023,632	7,108,587	6,964,431	6,218,317
26. Preferred capital stock	1,752,502	1,811,195	1,805,818	1,507,867	1,505,934
27. Aggregate write-ins for other than special surplus funds	361,405	507,295	494,536	459,101	467,196
28. Surplus notes	6,648,832	5,647,941	5,245,278	5,349,067	5,155,383
29. Gross paid in and contributed surplus	87,046,776	116,006,252	118,058,638	112,431,163	103,725,613
30. Unassigned funds (surplus)	163,120,002	152,164,618	165,217,529	173,639,787	163,463,974
31. Loss treasury stock, at cost:					
31.1..... shares common (value included in Line 25 $..........)	960,611	941,958	1,002,359	416,795	391,284
31.2..... shares preferred (value included in Line 26 $.........)	17,936	17,149	16,441	36,817	33,606
32. Surplus as regards policyholders (Lines 24 to 30, less 31) (Page 4, Line 36)	289,605,554	317,360,616	334,348,173	333,327,202	308,478,999
33. TOTALS (Page 2, Line 25, Column 3)	952,609,355	912,009,850	918,308,916	908,766,582	870,056,057
DETAILS OF WRITE-INS					
2201. Misc. conditional reserves	11,501,981	10,003,698	8,212,782	6,791,168	5,491,739
2203. Loss portfolio transfers	2,234,133	900,724	-1,615,136	-701,448	-538,652
2204. Discount on loss reserves	-678,880	-781,264	-286,684	-281,844	-264,160
2205. Other write-ins for liabilities	20,229,737	30,941,664	29,083,817	24,825,200	23,118,655
2298. Summary of remaining write-ins for Line 20 from overflow page					
2299. TOTALS (Lines 2201 thru 2205 plus 2298) (Page 22 above)	33,286,971	41,064,822	35,394,778	30,633,076	27,807,582
2401.					
2402.					
2403.					
2498. Summary of remaining write-ins for Line 24 from overflow page					
2499. TOTALS (Lines 2401 thru 2403 plus Line 2498) (Line 24 above)					
2701. Guaranty fund	255,455	253,847	250,788	257,207	257,605
2702. Other write-ins for other than special surplus funds	105,950	253,448	243,748	201,894	209,590
2703.					
2798. Summary of remaining write-ins for Line 27 from overflow page					
2799. TOTALS (Lines 2701 thru 2703 plus Line 2798) (Line 27 above)	361,405	507,295	494,536	459,101	467,196

Source: *Best's Aggregates & Averages, Property/Casualty*, 2002 Edition (Oldwick, N.J.: A.M. Best Company).

Values for purposes of Schedule D and the entire Annual Statement are determined by the NAIC's Securities Valuation Office (SVO).

Part 1A of Schedule D is especially important to the NAIC. It lists bond holdings by quality and maturity distribution. Quality ratings are determined by the NAIC. Exhibit 12-10 shows the heading information of Schedule D, Part 1A. The information shown in this heading and the quality classifications of "Class 1" through "Class 6" are shown for each of the following types of bonds:

- U.S. Governments
- Other Governments
- State, Territories, and Possessions Guaranteed
- Political Subdivisions of States, Territories, and Possessions Guaranteed
- Special Revenue and Special Assessment Obligations, Non-Guaranteed
- Public Utilities
- Industrial and Miscellaneous
- Credit Tenant Loans
- Parent, Subsidiary, and Affiliated

Schedule F

Reinsurance relationships critically affect the financial strength of insurers. Schedule F provides expanded information on an insurer's reinsurance arrangements and has the following seven parts:

- Part 1 provides details about assumed reinsurance—that is, reinsurance that the reporting insurer provides to other insurers.
- Part 2 provides details about portfolio reinsurance ceded or assumed.
- Part 3 provides details about ceded reinsurance, especially information about **reinsurance recoverables**. Reinsurance recoverables that prove to be worthless or uncollectible create a critical financial vulnerability for insurers. Except for certain provisions for unsecured reinsurance from unauthorized reinsurers and for overdue reinsurance, reinsurance recoverables are assumed to be assets that can be valued at face amount.
- Part 4 provides details of the aging of reinsurance recoverables.
- Part 5 provides details of **unauthorized reinsurance**, in particular the extent to which the reporting insurer has adequate security, such as letters of credit or funds held by the reporting insurer, for reinsurance recoverables due from unauthorized reinsurers.
- Part 6 provides details on reinsurance recoverables more than ninety days overdue, which requires special treatment.
- Part 7 determines a liability that must appear on the reporting insurer's balance sheet. The liability item "Provision for reinsurance" on page 3 of the Annual Statement is the balance sheet acknowledgment of late and unauthorized reinsurance.

Reinsurance recoverables
Amounts for losses and loss adjustment expenses owed to an insurer under reinsurance agreements covering paid losses.

Unauthorized reinsurance
Reinsurance agreements with reinsurers that are not licensed or otherwise authorized to do business in a primary insurer's state of domicile.

EXHIBIT 12-10

Schedule D, Part 1A

SCHEDULE D — PART 1A — SECTION 1

Quality and Maturity Distribution of All Bonds Owned December 31, At Book/Adjusted Carrying Values By Major Types of Issues and NAIC Designations

Quality Rating per the NAIC Designation	1 Year or Less	2 Over 1 Year Through 5 Years	3 Over 5 Years Through 10 Years	4 Over 10 Years Through 20 Years	5 Over 20 Years	6 Total Current Year	7 Col. 6 as a % of Line 10.7	8 Total from Col. 6 Prior Year	9 % from Col. 7 Prior Year	10 Total Publicly Traded	11 Total Privately Placed (a)
1. U.S. Governments, Schedules D & DA (Group 1)											
1.1 Class 1											
1.2 Class 2											
1.3 Class 3											
1.4 Class 4											
1.5 Class 5											
1.6 Class 6											
1.7 Totals											

Source: St Ives Burrups, "2002 Annual Statement Changes" (Marlton, N.J.: St Ives Burrups Insurance Division), 2002.

Income Statement

The income statement of the Annual Statement, shown in Exhibit 12-11, is brief. It contains a few elements in addition to what was shown in Exhibit 12-5, the elements of which are indicated in Exhibit 12-11.

Under "Underwriting Income," every important element comes from one of the parts of the Underwriting and Expense Exhibit. Premiums earned come from Part 1, which follows the formula for earned premiums [written premiums + unearned premiums end of prior year – unearned premiums end of current year] for each type of insurance. Losses incurred come from Part 2, which follows the formula for incurred losses [paid losses + loss reserves end of current year – loss reserves end of prior year] for each type of insurance. Loss expenses incurred and other underwriting expenses come from Part 3.

"Investment Income" comprises investment income from interest, dividends, and real estate, as reported in the Exhibit of Net Investment Income, and net realized capital gains, as reported in the Exhibit of Capital Gains/Losses.

Under "Other Income," the reporting insurer lists gains or losses from charge-offs of agents' balances, finance charges, and any other miscellaneous income. Also under this section, dividends to policyholders and taxes are deducted to arrive at net income. This net income flows to the Capital and Surplus Account.

Schedule P

Schedule P occupies more than fifty pages of the Annual Statement. It is titled "Analysis of Losses and Loss Expenses," but it accomplishes much more. It enables the NAIC and any other users to analyze on a year-by-year basis the reporting insurer's premiums earned versus losses incurred and other expenses and to determine how promptly the reporting insurer recognizes its loss reserve development.

The Annual Statement's income statement is problematic because it counts incurred losses as loss payments plus net changes to loss reserves. The problem with this formula is that changes to reserves can be caused by changes in the estimated amount of money that eventually will be paid for claims that arose in prior years. Any reserve change counts in this formula. The current year's net income can seem better or worse than it actually is depending on whether prior years' reserves are decreasing or increasing. One particular advantage of Schedule P is that it compares a given year's earned premiums with incurred losses for just the losses that occurred during that year.

The crucial purpose of Schedule P is to provide information to analyze loss reserve and incurred loss development. For a given year's losses, incurred losses consist of loss payments plus reserves for losses not yet paid. Hypothetically, loss reserves for a given year's losses should be set at their ultimate value as of January 1 of the following year because there will not be any more losses for the year just ended. Unfortunately, case reserves for known claims are rarely adequate by year's end. So, actuaries must estimate the amount

EXHIBIT 12-11

Annual Statement

	1 Current Year	2 Prior Year
UNDERWRITING AND INVESTMENT EXHIBIT **STATEMENT OF INCOME** **UNDERWRITING INCOME**		
1. Premiums earned (Part 1, Column 4, Item 34).		
DEDUCTIONS		
2. Losses incurred (Part 2, Column 7, Item 34).		
3. Loss expenses incurred (Part 3, Column 1, Item 25)		
4. Other underwriting expenses incurred (Part 3, Column 2, Item 25).		
5. Aggregate write-ins for underwriting deductions		
6. Total underwriting deductions (Items 2 through 5)		
7. Net income of protected cells		
8. Net underwriting gain or (loss) (Item 1 minus 6 plus line 7).		
INVESTMENT INCOME		
9. Net investment income earned (Exhibit of Net Investment Income, line 17).		
10. Net realized capital gains or (losses) (Exhibit of Capital Gains/Losses).		
11. Net investment gain or (loss) (Items 9 + 10)		
OTHER INCOME		
12. Net gain or (loss) from agents' or premium balances charged off		
(amount recovered $. . . . . amount charged off $. . . . .)		
13. Finance and service charges not included in premiums.		
14. Aggregate write-ins for miscellaneous income		
15. Total other income (Items 12 through 14)		
16. Net income before dividends to policyholders and before federal and foreign income taxes (Items 8 + 11 + 15)		
17. Dividends to policyholders		
18. Net income, after dividends to policyholders but before federal and foreign income taxes (Items 16 minus 17).		
19. Federal and foreign income taxes incurred		
20. Net income (Item 18 minus 19) (to Item 22)		
CAPITAL AND SURPLUS ACCOUNT		
21. Surplus as regards policyholders, December 31 prior year (Page 4, Column 2, Item 38)		
GAINS AND (LOSSES) IN SURPLUS		
22. Net income (from Item 20)		
23. Net unrealized capital gains or losses		
24. Change in net unrealized foreign exchange capital gains (losses).		
25. Change in net deferred income tax		
26. Change in non-admitted assets (Exhibit 1, Item 5, Col. 3)		
27. Change in provision for reinsurance (Page 3, Item 16, Column 2 minus 1).		
28. Change in surplus notes		
29. Surplus (contributed to) withdrawn from protected cells.		
30. Cumulative effect of changes in accounting principles		
31. Capital changes:		
31.1 Paid in		
31.2 Transferred from surplus (Stock Dividend)		
31.3 Transferred to surplus		
32. Surplus adjustments:		
32.1 Paid in		
32.2 Transferred to capital (Stock Dividend)		
32.3 Transferred from capital.		
33. Net remittances from or (to) Home Office		
34. Dividends to stockholders.		
35. Change in treasury stock (Page 3, Item 34.1 and 34.2, Column 2 minus 1).		
36. Aggregate write-ins for gains and losses in surplus.		
37 Change in surplus as regards policyholders for the year (Items 22 through 36).		
38. Surplus as regards policyholders, December 31 current year (Items 21 plus 37) (Page 3, Item 35)		
DETAILS OF WRITE-INS		
0501.		
0502.		
0503.		
0598. Summary of remaining write-ins for Item 5 from overflow page		
0599. TOTALS (Items 0501 thru 0503 plus 0598) (Item 5, above)		
1401.		
1402.		
1403.		
1498. Summary of remaining write-ins for Item 14 from overflow page		
1499. TOTALS (Items 1401 thru 1403 plus 1498) (Item 14, above)		
3601.		
3602.		
3603.		
3698. Summary of remaining write-ins for Item 36 from overflow page		
3699. TOTALS (Lines 3601 thru 3603 plus 3698) (Item 36, above)		

Source: St Ives Burrups, "2002 Annual Statement Changes" (Marlton, N.J.: St Ives Burrups Insurance Division), 2002.

needed to make reserves complete at year's end and determine year-end total reserves accordingly. Estimating total reserves requires great skill and judgment and is subject to error.

An insurer's balance sheet need show only a solitary liability entry for "Losses" and another for "Loss adjustment expenses" (see Exhibit 12-3). These aggregate liabilities consist of different elements, which are described differently by different sources, such as the NAIC and the Casualty Actuarial Society.

The NAIC's codified principle concerning loss reserves, Statement of Statutory Accounting Principles, No. 55, Unpaid Claims, Losses and Loss Adjustment Expenses, states, in part:

> The following are types of future costs…which shall be considered in determining the liabilities for unpaid losses and loss adjustment expenses:
>
> a. Reported Losses: Expected payments for losses relating to insured events that have occurred and have been reported to, but not paid by, the reporting entity as of the statement date;
>
> b. Incurred But Not Reported Losses (IBNR): Expected payments for losses relating to insured events that have occurred but have not been reported to the reporting entity as of the statement date. As a practical matter, IBNR may include losses that have been reported to the reporting entity but have not yet been entered into the claims system or bulk provisions. Bulk provisions are reserves included with other IBNR reserves to reflect deficiencies in known case reserves.

Schedule P of the Annual Statement parallels this classification of future costs (see Exhibit 12-12). The Part 1–Summary of Schedule P labels loss reserves as "Losses Unpaid," consisting of "Case Basis" and "Bulk + IBNR" categories.

The Casualty Actuarial Society has adopted a slightly different definition of loss reserves:

> A loss reserve is a provision for its related liability. A total loss reserve is composed of five elements, although the five elements may not necessarily be individually quantified:
>
> 1. case reserve
> 2. provision for future development on known claims
> 3. reopened claims reserve
> 4. provision for claims incurred but not reported
> 5. provision for claims in transit (incurred and reported but not recorded) [3]

The first element is parallel to the NAIC's "Case Basis" reserves, and the other four elements together are parallel to the NAIC's "Bulk + IBNR."

Schedule P enables the NAIC or any other user to look backward and see how well the reporting insurer estimated its reserves year by year over the past decade. The NAIC computes one-year and two-year loss reserve development factors. Excessive and chronic reserve development (positive or negative) indicates that the reporting insurer has not adequately estimated its losses and has been misstating (under or over) its surplus. This is a serious problem because loss reserves are the element of the balance sheet whose value is both large and most uncertain.

EXHIBIT 12-12

Schedule P, Part 1, of the Annual Statement

SCHEDULE P — ANALYSIS OF LOSSES AND LOSS EXPENSES
SCHEDULE P — PART 1 — SUMMARY

($000 omitted)

Years in Which Premiums Were Earned and Losses Were Incurred	Premiums Earned			Loss and Loss Expense Payments						10	11	12
	1 Direct and Assumed	2 Ceded	3 Net (1 – 2)	Loss Payments		Defense and Cost Containment Payments		Adjusting and Other Payments		Salvage and Subrogation Received	Total Net Paid (4 - 5 + 6 - 7 + 8 –9)	Number of Claims Reported– Direct and Assumed
				4 Direct and Assumed	5 Ceded	6 Direct and Assumed	7 Ceded	8 Direct and Assumed	9 Ceded			
1. Prior	X X X X	X X X X	X X X X									X X X X
2. 1993												X X X X
3. 1994												X X X X
4. 1995												X X X X
5. 1996												X X X X
6. 1997												X X X X
7. 1998												X X X X
8. 1999												X X X X
9. 2000												X X X X
10. 2001												X X X X
11. 2002												X X X X
12. Totals	X X X X	X X X X	X X X X									X X X X

	Losses Unpaid				Defense and Cost Containment Unpaid				Adjusting and Other Unpaid		23	24	25
	Case Basis		Bulk + IBNR		Case Basis		Bulk + IBNR				Salvage and Subrogation Anticipated	Total Net Losses and Expenses Unpaid	Number of Claims Outstanding– Direct and Assumed
	13 Direct and Assumed	14 Ceded	15 Direct and Assumed	16 Ceded	17 Direct and Assumed	18 Ceded	19 Direct and Assumed	20 Ceded	21 Direct and Assumed	22 Ceded			
1.													X X X X
2.													X X X X
3.													X X X X
4.													X X X X
5.													X X X X
6.													X X X X
7.													X X X X
8.													X X X X
9.													X X X X
10.													X X X X
11.													X X X X
12.													X X X X

	Total Losses and Loss Expenses Incurred			Loss and Loss Expense Percentage (Incurred/Premiums Earned)			Nontabular Discount		34	Net Balance Sheet Reserves After Discount	
	26 Direct and Assumed	27 Ceded	28 Net	29 Direct and Assumed	30 Ceded	31 Net	32 Loss	33 Loss Expense	Inter-Company Pooling Participation Percentage	35 Losses Unpaid	36 Loss Expenses Unpaid
1.	X X X X	X X X X	X X X X	X X X X	X X X X	X X X X			X X X X		
2.											
3.											
4.											
5.											
6.											
7.											
8.											
9.											
10.											
11.											
12.	X X X X	X X X X	X X X X	X X X X	X X X X	X X X X			X X X X		

Note: Parts 2 and 4 are gross of all discounting, including tabular discounting. Part 1 is gross of only non-tabular discounting, which is reported in Columns 32 and 33 of Part 1. The tabular discount, if any, is reported in the Notes to Financial Statements, which will reconcile Part 1 with Parts 2 and 4.

Source: St Ives Burrups, "2002 Annual Statement Changes" (Marlton, N.J.: St Ives Burrups Insurance Division), 2002.

Part 1 allows a direct comparison of earned premiums and losses incurred (payments plus reserves) for that same year for each of the past ten years. These amounts are reported as of the date of the Annual Statement. The experience for the earliest years should be more accurate and is not likely to have changed significantly from the previous Annual Statement.

Part 1 of Schedule P divides loss and loss expense payments into "Loss Payments," "Defense and Cost Containment Payments," and "Adjusting and Other Payments" and further divides each of these into "Direct and Assumed" and "Ceded." "Salvage and Subrogation Received" are netted out of direct and assumed loss payments. Reserves for losses are labeled "Losses Unpaid" and are divided into "Case Basis" and "Bulk + IBNR," and each of these is separated into "Direct and Assumed" and "Ceded." Reserves for loss adjustment expenses are labeled "Defense and Cost Containment Unpaid" and "Adjusting and Other Unpaid."

The Summary reports for Parts 2, 3, and 4 of Schedule P are shown in Exhibit 12-13. Parts 2, 3, and 4 of Schedule P are loss development triangles. These show how losses for a given year, both paid amounts and estimated amounts as yet unpaid, have developed from year to year. A given row in a loss development triangle can be read left to right as showing how much was reported for that year when it ended (the first cell), how much was reported for that same year at the end of the next year (the next cell to the right), and so on up to the current report year. Losses that mature quickly should show little development beyond the next two years or so. In contrast, losses for certain types of insurance, such as medical malpractice, continue to develop for many years. Part 2 shows development of incurred losses (payments plus reserves). Part 3 shows development for paid losses. Part 4 shows development for bulk and IBNR reserves. Note that year-to-year development can be negative (although rarely so for paid losses).

Schedule P is as long as it is because a Part 1, Part 2, Part 3, and Part 4 is shown for each of the following types of insurance:

- Homeowners/Farmowners
- Private Passenger Auto Liability/Medical
- Commercial Auto/Truck Liability/Medical
- Workers' Compensation
- Commercial Multiple Peril
- Medical Malpractice – Occurrence
- Medical Malpractice – Claims Made
- Special Liability (e.g., ocean, aircraft)
- Other Liability – Occurrence
- Other Liability – Claims Made
- Special Property (e.g., inland marine, earthquake)
- Auto Physical Damage

EXHIBIT 12-13

Schedule P, Part 2, of the Annual Statement

SCHEDULE P — PART 2 — SUMMARY

Years In Which Losses Were Incurred	INCURRED NET LOSSES AND DEFENSE AND COST CONTAINMENT EXPENSES REPORTED AT YEAR END ($000 OMITTED)										DEVELOPMENT	
	1	2	3	4	5	6	7	8	9	10	11 One Year	12 Two Year
	1993	1994	1995	1996	1997	1998	1999	2000	2001	2002		
1. Prior												
2. 1993												
3. 1994	XXXX											
4. 1995	XXXX	XXXX										
5. 1996	XXXX	XXXX	XXXX									
6. 1997	XXXX	XXXX	XXXX	XXXX								
7. 1998	XXXX	XXXX	XXXX	XXXX	XXXX							
8. 1999	XXXX	XXXX	XXXX	XXXX	XXXX	XXXX						
9. 2000	XXXX	XXXX	XXXX	XXXX	XXXX	XXXX	XXXX					
10. 2001	XXXX	XXXX	XXXX	XXXX	XXXX	XXXX	XXXX	XXXX				XXXX
11. 2002	XXXX	XXXX	XXXX	XXXX	XXXX	XXXX	XXXX	XXXX	XXXX		XXXX	XXXX

12. Totals

SCHEDULE P — PART 3 — SUMMARY

Years In Which Losses Were Incurred	CUMULATIVE PAID NET LOSSES AND DEFENSE AND COST CONTAINMENT EXPENSES REPORTED AT YEAR END ($000 OMITTED)										11 Number of Claims Closed With Loss Payment	12 Number of Claims Closed Without Loss Payment
	1	2	3	4	5	6	7	8	9	10		
	1993	1994	1995	1996	1997	1998	1999	2000	2001	2002		
1. Prior	000										XXXX	XXXX
2. 1993											XXXX	XXXX
3. 1994	XXXX										XXXX	XXXX
4. 1995	XXXX	XXXX									XXXX	XXXX
5. 1996	XXXX	XXXX	XXXX								XXXX	XXXX
6. 1997	XXXX	XXXX	XXXX	XXXX							XXXX	XXXX
7. 1998	XXXX	XXXX	XXXX	XXXX	XXXX						XXXX	XXXX
8. 1999	XXXX	XXXX	XXXX	XXXX	XXXX	XXXX					XXXX	XXXX
9. 2000	XXXX	XXXX	XXXX	XXXX	XXXX	XXXX	XXXX				XXXX	XXXX
10. 2001	XXXX	XXXX	XXXX	XXXX	XXXX	XXXX	XXXX	XXXX			XXXX	XXXX
11. 2002	XXXX	XXXX	XXXX	XXXX	XXXX	XXXX	XXXX	XXXX	XXXX		XXXX	XXXX

SCHEDULE P — PART 4 — SUMMARY

Years In Which Losses Were Incurred	BULK AND IBNR RESERVES ON NET LOSSES AND DEFENSE AND COST CONTAINMENT EXPENSES REPORTED AT YEAR END ($000 OMITTED)									
	1	2	3	4	5	6	7	8	9	10
	1993	1994	1995	1996	1997	1998	1999	2000	2001	2002
1. Prior										
2. 1993										
3. 1994	XXXX									
4. 1995	XXXX	XXXX								
5. 1996	XXXX	XXXX	XXXX							
6. 1997	XXXX	XXXX	XXXX	XXXX						
7. 1998	XXXX	XXXX	XXXX	XXXX	XXXX					
8. 1999	XXXX	XXXX	XXXX	XXXX	XXXX	XXXX				
9. 2000	XXXX	XXXX	XXXX	XXXX	XXXX	XXXX	XXXX			
10. 2001	XXXX	XXXX	XXXX	XXXX	XXXX	XXXX	XXXX	XXXX		
11. 2002	XXXX	XXXX	XXXX	XXXX	XXXX	XXXX	XXXX	XXXX	XXXX	

Source: St Ives Burrups, "2002 Annual Statement Changes" (Marlton, N.J.: St Ives Burrups Insurance Division), 2002.

- Fidelity/Surety
- Other (e.g., accident and health)
- International
- Reinsurance – Nonproportional Assumed Property
- Reinsurance – Nonproportional Assumed Liability
- Reinsurance – Nonproportional Assumed Financial Lines
- Products Liability – Occurrence
- Products Liability – Claims-Made
- Financial Guarantee/Mortgage Guarantee

Schedule P also contains a Part 5 for each of these types of insurance, showing development of the number (rather than the dollar amount) of claims closed, the number of claims outstanding, and the number of claims reported. Schedule P has a Part 6 that shows development of earned premiums for certain long-tail types of insurance and a Part 7 that shows development under loss-sensitive policies.

Supplements to the Annual Statement

The Annual Statement is not the only financial statement that insurers must file with the state insurance departments or the NAIC.

Among the most important supplementary financial filings are the Insurance Expense Exhibit, the management discussions and analysis, and the statement of actuarial opinion.

Part 3 of the Annual Statement's Underwriting and Investment Exhibit already provides details about expenses, whether for loss adjustment, underwriting, investments, or other. The Insurance Expense Exhibit provides further detail and allocates all expenses to each type of insurance so that profit or loss for each type of insurance can be determined. Such reports of profit or loss include the investment returns allocated to each type of insurance by a mandated formula.[4]

A statement called "Management Discussion and Analysis" must be filed annually. This statement is a narrative intended to give regulators a better understanding of the reporting insurer's financial position and operations. In it, the insurer's management should explain all material changes in the insurer's financial reports, all material trends, and all material events known to management. For example, management should comment on material changes to the insurer's mix of business, or its invested asset mix, or its liquidity, or the status of its loss reserves, the collectability of reinsurance receivables, or any event not disclosed in the financial statements that is likely to have a material effect.

A "Statement of Actuarial Opinion" must accompany the filing of the Annual Statement. In it, an actuary appointed for this purpose by the reporting insurer's board must express his or her opinion about the loss and loss adjustment expense reserves of the reporting insurer. To qualify for this role, an actuary must be a member of the American Academy of Actuaries or the Casualty Actuarial Society, or must be someone whose demonstrated competence in loss reserving has been endorsed by a state insurance regulator. The actuary must comment on the actuarial methods, actuarial assumptions, and data used to determine reserves and must express an opinion about whether the reporting insurer's reserves (1) comply with state laws, (2) are determined according to accepted loss reserving methods, and (3) are sufficient to pay all outstanding loss and loss expense obligations.

Differences Between SAP and GAAP Accounting

Statutory accounting principles (SAP) differ from generally accepted accounting principles (GAAP) in significant ways. GAAP rules are promulgated by the Financial Accounting Standards Board and must be used by most businesses for most accounting purposes. For example, filings with the SEC must conform to GAAP, including filings from insurers.

Purpose

The first difference between SAP and GAAP is the purpose of the accounting principles. SAP rules serve a particular regulatory purpose. This difference in purpose is expressed by the NAIC as follows:

> The objectives of GAAP reporting differ from the objectives of SAP. GAAP is designed to meet the varying needs of the different users of financial statements. SAP is designed to address the concerns of regulators, who are the primary users of statutory financial statements. As a result, GAAP stresses measurement of emerging earnings of a business from period to period (i.e., matching revenue to expenses), while SAP stresses measurement of ability to pay claims in the future.[5]

Essentially, GAAP focuses on correctly measuring earnings, while SAP focuses on correctly measuring liquidation values. The "concerns of regulators" mentioned in the preceding quote are identified further in the same document:

> The primary responsibility of each state insurance department is to regulate insurance companies in accordance with state laws with an emphasis on solvency for the protection of policyholders. The ultimate objective of solvency regulation is to ensure that policyholder, contract holder and other legal obligations are met when they become due and that companies maintain capital and surplus at all times and in such forms as required by statute to provide an adequate margin of safety.[6]

Insurance regulators developed SAP to assure themselves that any insurer they regulate could stop business today and still have sufficient assets to pay all claims. SAP is part of the overall regulatory scheme for insurance that is designed to promote "solvency for the protection of policyholders." However, it is not a guarantee against insolvency. Insurers could still engage in poor underwriting, fail to set adequate reserves, and lose agents and customers once financial troubles become evident.

SAP is not fundamentally at odds with GAAP, and it is possible to overstate their differences. However, SAP takes precedence for insurers. GAAP applies to insurance regulatory financial reporting only as allowed. According to the NAIC:

> SAP utilizes the framework established by GAAP.... The NAIC's guidance on SAP is comprehensive for those principles that differ from GAAP.... Those GAAP pronouncements that are not applicable to insurance companies will not be adopted by the NAIC. For those principles that do not differ from GAAP, the NAIC may specifically adopt those GAAP Pronouncements to be included in statutory accounting. GAAP Pronouncements do not become part of SAP until and unless adopted by the NAIC.[7]

Many GAAP rules have been adopted by the NAIC, and many have been rejected as incompatible with SAP.

Nonadmitted Assets

The second difference between SAP and GAAP involves how SAP treats certain assets. SAP treats certain assets as valueless. These assets are assigned zero value on the SAP balance sheet, even though they would have some positive value under GAAP. An insurer that acquires such an asset will experience a direct reduction in its surplus when it trades cash, an **admitted asset**, for the **nonadmitted asset**. As explained by the NAIC:

> The ability to meet policyholder obligations is predicated on the existence of readily marketable assets available when both current and future obligations are due. Assets having economic value other than those that can be used to fulfill policyholder obligations, or those assets which are unavailable due to encumbrances or other third party interests should not be recognized on the balance sheet but rather should be charged against surplus when acquired or when availability otherwise becomes questionable.[8]

Virtually all of an insurer's tangible property, such as furniture, fixtures, leasehold improvements, office equipment, and vehicles, are nonadmitted assets worth nothing on the SAP balance sheet because these types of property cannot be liquidated readily to meet policyholder claims. However, EDP equipment and software (except nonoperating system software) are considered admitted assets but limited to three percent of the insurer's capital and surplus. (Statements of Statutory Accounting Principles [SSAP] No. 16)

Unsecured loans and cash advances (SSAP No. 20) and prepaid expenses (SSAP No. 29) are nonadmitted assets.

An important group of nonadmitted assets consists of certain receivables. Agents' balances and premium balances that are more than ninety days past due and bills receivable that are past due are nonadmitted assets (SSAP No. 6). Reinsurance recoverables are admitted assets unless they are deemed uncollectible or are due from an unauthorized reinsurer and are unsecured. (Indeed, there is no credit on a primary insurer's balance sheet

Admitted assets
Assets meeting minimum standards of liquidity that an insurer is allowed to report on its balance sheet in accordance with statutory accounting principles.

Nonadmitted assets
Assets that are not readily marketable and that are excluded from an insurer's balance sheet in accordance with statutory accounting principles.

for unsecured reinsurance from an unauthorized reinsurer—the primary insurer cannot net out its loss reserves or record recoverables as assets.)

Policy Acquisition Costs and Commissions

A third difference between SAP and GAAP requires that policy acquisition costs and commissions immediately be written off as expenses once incurred. In contrast, GAAP would allow these expenses to be capitalized and amortized over the policy's life. The effect of SAP is to create a loss, in an accounting sense, as each new policy is written because expenses are recognized immediately but premiums are earned incrementally over the term of the policy.

An insurer writing significant new business will experience a drain on its surplus because of this requirement. Eventually, over the life of the policies written, the insurer will experience the true economic results of these policies. But to offset the drain to its surplus as policies are written or as business is growing, an insurer might have to buy reinsurance to maintain the level of surplus needed to write the new business.

Bonds

A fourth difference between SAP and GAAP involves bonds. Bonds that trade are typically bought and sold at a premium or discount from the face amount that will be paid at the bond's maturity—that is, their market price might be greater or less than the face amount. And, until maturity, the market value of a bond will continue to fluctuate as interest rates fluctuate.

Under SAP, bonds are valued at amortized amounts. This means that the amount of premium or discount experienced when the bond is purchased is evenly amortized over the bond's remaining life so that, at its maturity, the bond's value is reported as equal to its face amount. This method of valuing bonds results in even appreciation or depreciation of a bond's value toward its face amount and prevents wide fluctuations in value. Exhibit 12-14 shows how market values for a bond are much more variable than are their amortized values.

Under GAAP, amortized bond valuation is permitted only if the insurer is able and intends to hold the bond to maturity. Otherwise, bond values must be reported at market values.

Subsidiaries, Affiliates, and Business Combinations

A fifth difference between SAP and GAAP involves subsidiaries, controlled, or affiliated entities (SCAs). These investments are considered admitted assets and must be shown on a parent company's balance sheet. Various rules are used for accounting for SCAs, depending on the particular circumstances. For example, if a subsidiary's stock trades publicly, the fair market value as determined in the market can be used. However, most subsidiary stock does not trade publicly. In such circumstances, parent companies might have to account for the equity in the SCA using statutory accounting, especially if the SCA is

EXHIBIT 12-14

Comparison of Market Values to Amortized Values of a $10,000 Bond Purchased at a Premium

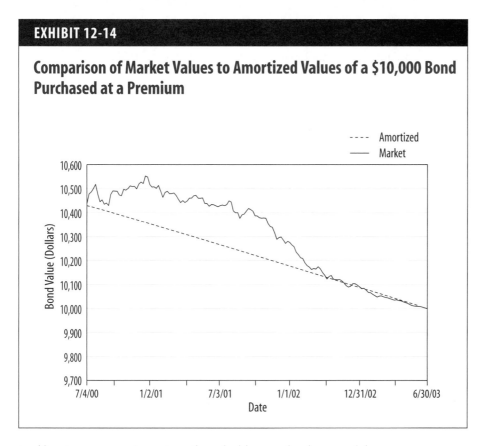

itself an insurer or exists primarily to hold assets for the use of the parent company. Under GAAP accounting, of course, statutory accounting principles would not be used to evaluate and record an SCA. Under GAAP, the financial statements of majority-owned subsidiaries are consolidated with the parent company's financial statements. There is no consolidation under statutory accounting.

Insurers might also purchase another entity or merge with another entity. Again, statutory accounting might require use of statutory principles to produce financial statements for the resulting organization, while GAAP, of course, would not.

Pensions

A sixth difference between SAP and GAAP involves statutory accounting for pensions. Statutory accounting for pensions considers only current retirees and employees who are fully vested. GAAP accounting requires provisions for all employees, both vested and non-vested.

Under statutory accounting for pensions, contributions made for non-vested employees under both defined-benefit plans and defined-contribution plans are not recognized when made and are therefore not a deductible expense on the income statement. Such contributions qualify as a prepaid expense but, under SAP, a prepaid expense is a nonadmitted asset. GAAP accounting recognizes expenses as incurred for all employees.

SUMMARY

Insurer financial statements have many unique characteristics compared to those of other businesses. As providers of financial services, insurers maintain a large portion of their assets in financial securities rather than in inventories or buildings and equipment. Insurance operations are also characterized by significant investment returns from cash flows generated from insurance sales.

Several parties have an interest in insurer financial statements. As with most other businesses, management reviews financial statements to monitor the insurer's overall performance and make operational decisions. Investors, rating services, and controlling owners also have an interest in an insurer's financial statements. Regulators are primarily interested in an insurer's financial strength to ensure that the insurer remains solvent and can meet its obligations to policyholders and claimants. Policyholders, producers, and risk managers are also interested in the financial strength of insurers.

The insurer's balance sheet includes many assets and liabilities unique to insurance operations. Assets consist primarily of bonds but might also include some stocks, cash, and cash equivalents. Important receivables on an insurer's balance sheet are the premiums due the insurer from its agents and funds due from reinsurers. On the liability side, the principal unique elements are unearned premium reserves and loss reserves. Unearned premium reserves are the money that has been received from policyholders but has not yet been earned. Loss reserves are those amounts held to pay for losses that have occurred but have not yet been paid. Also shown on the balance sheet is an amount for policyholders' surplus. This balance sheet element is equivalent to owner's equity on a non-insurer's balance sheet. It is called policyholders' surplus because all of an insurer's net worth is available to satisfy policyholders' claims before any owner is entitled to insurer funds.

The income statement for an insurer is similar in some respects to that of a non-insurer, and both serve the same basic purpose: to indicate net income over a period of time, after all expenses have been subtracted from revenues. Although the function is the same, the format and certain elements differ in the income statement for an insurer. For example, instead of net sales, an insurer reports earned premiums as its key revenue element. Also, because insurers do not make or sell a tangible good, there is no expense for cost of goods sold. Instead, incurred losses and loss adjustment expenses appear as the main expense elements. The income statement for an insurer also includes separate listings for both underwriting and investment operations because of the significance of an insurer's investment operations.

Insurers must file an Annual Statement with the insurance department of the state in which they are domiciled. The Annual Statement is based on a system of accounting known as statutory accounting principles (SAP) and consists of a balance sheet, an income statement, and supporting documentation and schedules. SAP rules differ from the GAAP rules that apply to other types of business operations. GAAP rules are promulgated by the Financial Accounting Standards Board and are designed to meet the divergent needs of different users of financial information. SAP addresses the specific concerns of regulators, who are the primary users of statutory financial statements. GAAP focuses on measuring the earnings from period to period, while SAP focuses on monitoring solvency and measuring an insurer's ability to pay claims into the future. Another difference between SAP and GAAP is the treatment of assets. Under SAP, assets are considered either admitted or nonadmitted. For an insurer, assets such as furniture, fixtures, supplies, automobiles, and accounts receivables over ninety days are all considered nonadmitted assets. As such, they are assigned a zero value on the SAP balance sheet because these assets cannot be liquated readily to meet policy-holder obligations. Also under SAP, all policy acquisition expenses and commissions must immediately be written off as expenses, so insurers that write considerable amounts of new business can experience an underwriting loss that results in a drain on surplus. Under GAAP, these types of expenses are amortized over the life of the policy.

Bonds under SAP are valued at amortized amounts, which prevents the wide fluctuations in bond values that can occur under GAAP. Additionally, subsidiaries, controlled, or affiliated entities (SCAs) are considered admitted assets under SAP and must be shown on a parent company's balance sheet. Under GAAP, financial statements of majority-owned subsidiaries are consolidated with the parent company's financial statements. Finally, the accounting for pensions is somewhat different under SAP than GAAP. SAP considers only current retirees and employees who are fully vested. Under GAAP, provisions are required for all employees, both vested and nonvested.

The next chapter continues the discussion of insurer financial statements and describes how the information contained in financial statements is interpreted and how to evaluate property-casualty insurers.

CHAPTER NOTES

1. National Association of Insurance Commissioners, *Accounting Practices and Procedures Manual* (Kansas City, Mo.: NAIC, March 2003), Statements of Statutory Accounting Principles, Preamble II, B. 8.

2. At the time of the original publication, aggregated industry results for the 2002 year were not available; therefore, 2001 data are used throughout this chapter.

3. "Statement of Principles Regarding Property and Casualty Loss and Loss Adjustment Expense Reserves," *ASTIN Bulletin*, 10, 1979, pp. 305–317.

4. Sholom Feldblum, "The Insurance Expense Exhibit and the Allocation of Investment Income," Casualty Actuarial Society, http://casact.org/library/study notes/feldblum7can3.pdf (accessed March 26, 2003).

5. *Accounting Practices and Procedures Manual*, March 2003, Statements of Statutory Accounting Principles, Preamble II, C. 10.

6. *Accounting Practices and Procedures Manual*, March 2003, Statements of Statutory Accounting Principles, Preamble III, 27.

7. *Accounting Practices and Procedures Manual*, March 2003, Statements of Statutory Accounting Principles, Preamble VII, 50.

8. *Accounting Practices and Procedures Manual*, March 2003, Statements of Statutory Accounting Principles, Preamble III, 33.

Appendix

Sources of Statutory Accounting

Codification

Until the 1990s, SAP evolved gradually from state laws and regulations and the NAIC's efforts to reconcile these sources. The NAIC produced manuals and standardized blank statements, but SAP did not exist as a single codified whole. During the 1990s, the NAIC created just such a single codified body of SAP. According to the NAIC:

> The purpose of the codification of statutory accounting principles (SAP) was to produce a comprehensive guide to SAP for use by insurance departments, insurers, and auditors. Statutory accounting principles, as they existed prior to codification, did not always provide a consistent and comprehensive basis of accounting and reporting. Insurance companies were sometimes uncertain about what rules to follow and regulators were sometimes unfamiliar with the accounting rules followed by insurers in other states. This was due to the fact that prior to codification, accounting guidance could be found in the NAIC Accounting Manual, Annual Statement Instructions, Examiners Handbook, and various states' laws and regulations. As a result, insurers' financial statements were not prepared on a comparable basis. (NAIC Policy Statement on Coordination of the *Accounting Practices and Procedures Manual* and the Annual Statement Blank)

The chief result of the codification project was a new *Accounting Practices and Procedures Manual*, effective January 1, 2001, described below. In addition, the NAIC created procedures and working groups for consideration of new or revised SAP.

The Preamble to the *Accounting Practices and Procedures Manual* codifies certain concepts as fundamental for all SAP. These are the concepts of conservatism, consistency, and recognition, which had long been principles of SAP but had not been codified before. The concept of conservatism recognizes that judgment is needed in estimating various accounting items. In such circumstances, SAP prefers the more conservative evaluations. The concept of consistency invokes one of the key motivations for the codification project—the need for comparable financial statements. Users and preparers of financial statements should work from consistent rules. The concept of recognition specifies that asset values, liabilities, revenue, and expenses should be recognized in a way that makes protection of policyholders the guiding principle.

The Preamble also acknowledges a hierarchy of SAP, with state laws and regulations being paramount. Next in the hierarchy are the Statements of Statutory Accounting Principles (SSAP) that constitute the bulk of the *Accounting Practices and Procedures Manual*. Next are other NAIC documents, such as the Annual Statement Instructions.

The Accounting Practices and Procedures Manual

The *Accounting Practices and Procedures Manual* is the heart of SAP, yet it does not set forth detailed instructions for completing financial statements. It consists of eighty-four (as of 2002) SSAPs that set forth the essential rules for dealing with accounting issues special to insurers, together with various background and supporting materials. SSAPs address the correct accounting approach for insurers to take with respect to various assets, liabilities, expenses, insurance products and contracts, affiliated entities, and preparation of financial statements. Most of the SSAPs are from one to several pages long, but the SSAPs concerning income taxes, derivatives, and property-casualty reinsurance are dozens of pages long. Exhibit 12A-1 shows one of the briefest SSAPs, No. 29, which identifies prepaid expenses as nonadmitted assets.

Other Sources of SAP

Several other sources supplement the *Accounting Practices and Procedures Manual* with respect to elaborating the details of SAP. The most important is the Annual Statement Instructions. The NAIC's Securities Valuation Office (SVO) publishes a manual called *Purposes and Procedures of the Securities Valuation Office*. The SVO establishes values for the securities owned by insurers. These are the values to be used in recording invested assets on insurer balance sheets. Many securities owned by insurers trade publicly, but many do not. Insurers are key buyers of limited offerings, issues of securities sold to few enough parties that SEC registration procedures may be avoided. SVO procedures ensure that all insurers place the same value on the same securities, thus enhancing consistency and compatibility of insurer financial statements.

The NAIC's *Financial Examiner's Handbook*, a guide for insurance department staff who conduct financial examinations of insurers, also helps document SAP.

EXHIBIT 12A-1

Statement of Statutory Accounting Principles No. 29

Prepaid Expenses

STATUS

Type of Issue:	Common Area
Issued:	Initial Draft
Effective Date:	January 1, 2001
Affects:	No other pronouncements
Affected by :	No other pronouncements
Interpreted by:	INT 00-29

SCOPE OF STATEMENT

1. This statement establishes statutory accounting principles for the accounting for prepaid expenses. This statement does not address accounting for deferred policy acquisition costs and other underwriting expenses, income taxes, and guaranty fund assessments.

SUMMARY CONCLUSION

2. A prepaid expense is an amount which has been paid in advance of receiving future economic benefits anticipated by the payment. Prepaid expenses generally meet the definition of assets in *SSAP No. 4—Assets and Nonadmitted Assets* (SSAP No. 4). Such expenditures also meet the criteria defining nonadmitted assets as specified in SSAP No. 4 (i.e., the assets are not readily available to satisfy policyholder obligations). Prepaid expenses shall be reported as nonadmitted assets and charged against unassigned funds (surplus). They shall be amortized against net income as the estimated economic benefit expires.

3. In accordance with the reporting entity's capitalization policy, immaterial prepaid expenses may be expensed when purchased.

Relevant Literature

4. This statement rejects *AICPA Practice Bulletin No. 13, Direct-Response Advertising and Probable Future Benefits, AICPA Statement of Position 93-7, Reporting on Advertising Costs* and *FASB Emerging Issues Task Force No. 88-23, Lump-Sum Payments Under Union Contracts.*

Effective Date and Transition

5. This statement is effective for years beginning January 1, 2001. A change resulting from the adoption of this statement shall be accounted for as a change in accounting principle in accordance with *SSAP No. 3—Accounting Changes and Corrections of Errors.*

RELEVANT ISSUE PAPERS

- Issue Paper No. 29—Prepaid Expenses (excluding Deferred Policy Acquisition Costs and other underwriting expenses, income taxes and Guaranty Fund Assessments)

Source: National Association of Insurance Commissioners, *Accounting Practices and Procedures Manual*, Vol. I (Kansas City, Mo.: NAIC, 2003), pp. 29-1 and 29-3.

Chapter 13

Direct Your Learning

Interpreting Insurer Financial Statements

After learning the content of this chapter, you should be able to:

■ Explain how the following types of ratios are used to evaluate property-casualty insurers:

  a. Capacity ratios

  b. Liquidity ratios

  c. Profitability ratios

■ Given a case situation, calculate the following ratios:

- Capacity ratio
- Liquidity ratio
- Loss ratio
- Financial basis expense ratio
- Financial basis combined ratio
- Trade basis expense ratio
- Trade basis combined ratio
- Operating ratio

■ Describe the quantitative and qualitative tests A.M. Best Company uses to rate insurers and what the tests measure.

■ Describe the components of the NAIC's IRIS system and what the components measure.

Develop Your Perspective

What are the main topics covered in the chapter?

This chapter discusses how insurer financial statements are used to evaluate insurers' financial strength, stability, and profitability.

Identify the ratios that can be used to analyze an insurer.

- What do these ratios measure?

- How can changes in the insurer's operations affect these ratios?

Why is it important to learn about these topics?

Ratios based on financial information assist in the evaluation of an insurer's financial condition. Standard ratings of insurers help outsiders to assess the insurer's ability to manage its finances.

Describe the standard ratings that are available for insurers.

- How are these ratings developed?

- How are these ratings used to evaluate the financial strength of an insurer?

How can you use what you will learn?

Analyze your own company's financial ratios and ratings.

- What do the results of these ratios tell you about your company's operation?

- What is the financial rating assigned to your company, and what does the rating mean?

Chapter 13

Interpreting Insurer Financial Statements

This chapter discusses how information contained in financial statements and Annual Statements can be interpreted to analyze the financial performance of insurers. The first section of this chapter describes the primary financial ratios used in the property-casualty insurance business. This is followed by a discussion of the tests A.M. Best Company (A.M. Best) uses to establish Best's Rating. Not only does A.M. Best assign ratings indicating the financial strength of individual insurers, it also provides a wealth of aggregated industry financial results. The chapter concludes by considering financial analysis from the regulator's perspective with a presentation of the financial ratios contained in the National Association of Insurance Commissioners' (NAIC) Insurance Regulatory Information System (IRIS).

In many ways, the financial condition of insurers is evaluated as it is for any other business. The financial measures of capacity, profitability, liquidity, and leverage are as important to the insurance industry as they are to other industries. The unique characteristics of insurance operations, however, require some modifications in how these financial measures are applied. Several primary financial ratios have been developed to analyze property-casualty insurers. However, those ratios have little meaning on their own and are only significant when compared to some standard or industry benchmark. Data developed from financial statements also become useful when compared to the data developed in previous years. Consequently, upward and downward trends become evident.

FINANCIAL RATIOS

Three categories of ratios are used to analyze the operations of property-casualty insurers: (1) capacity ratio, (2) liquidity ratio, and (3) profitability ratios. These financial ratios can be developed directly from income statements and balance sheets using statutory accounting principles (SAP). All comparisons of ratios among different insurers or over several time periods for a single insurer are based on an assumption that the underlying financial data from the balance sheet and income statement are accurate. For example, if loss reserves are inaccurate, so is reported policyholders' surplus, and any ratio developed from these data will also be inaccurate. These ratios are summarized in Exhibit 13A-1 at the end of this chapter.

Capacity Ratio

A capacity ratio measures the extent to which an insurer can issue policies for new business. The capacity ratio compares an insurer's net written premiums, which represent its exposure to potential claims, to its policyholders' surplus. The surplus represents the insurer's cushion for absorbing adverse operating results. If losses and loss adjustment expenses exceed earned premiums, the insurer must draw on its surplus to meet its obligations.

Rapid growth increases an insurer's premium-to-surplus ratio. Whenever an insurance policy is sold, acquisition expenses immediately reduce the insurer's surplus, but the surplus is replenished as premium is earned over time. An insurer that rapidly increases its written premiums might become technically insolvent, even if the new business is desirable from an underwriting standpoint.[1] Growth increases written premiums and reduces surplus to pay for immediate expenses. This effect creates a limit on the insurer's ability to expand and write new business because the insurer is required by state regulation to maintain minimum surplus.

New business is not the only factor affecting an insurer's capacity ratio. Changes in surplus caused by underwriting gains and losses, and capital gains and losses (both realized and unrealized), can also affect the premium-to-surplus ratio. Profitable but orderly growth permits additional expansion in subsequent years. Failure to successfully underwrite will produce losses that must be paid from surplus, thereby reducing the insurer's ability to write business in succeeding years.

Investment results also affect an insurer's capacity. Generally accepted accounting principles (GAAP) do not recognize investment gains and losses until they are realized when an asset is sold. SAP, however, require insurers to carry common stock on the balance sheet at market value (or association value) as of December 31. Changes in the value of securities are therefore reflected in the insurer's surplus even if the security is not sold.

> **Capacity or premium-to-surplus ratio**
>
> A ratio that measures the extent to which insurers can issue policies for new business by comparing an insurer's net written premiums to policyholders' surplus.

The **capacity ratio**, also called the **premium-to-surplus ratio**, is calculated as follows:

$$\text{Capacity ratio} = \frac{\text{Net written premiums}}{\text{Policyholders' surplus}}.$$

Generally, a ratio of 3 to 1 or less is considered an acceptable capacity ratio. The NAIC considers capacity ratios over 3 to 1 to be problematic.

Liquidity Ratio

> **Liquidity ratio**
>
> A ratio that measures the extent to which an insurer can meet its obligations as they come due and is the sum of cash plus invested assets (market value) divided by unearned premium reserve plus loss adjustment reserves.

A **liquidity ratio** measures the extent to which an insurer can meet its obligations as they come due. The ability to meet obligations depends on cash flow, the relationship between assets and liabilities, and the nature of assets available to discharge debt. Liquidity of specific assets is evaluated based on the time required to convert the asset to cash and the proportion of value expected when the asset is converted.

Almost all of an insurer's admitted assets are readily marketable. Insurer inventory consists of furniture, equipment, and operating supplies, which are not liquid (and, therefore, are nonadmitted assets). Agents' premium balances and uncollected premiums less than ninety days due to the insurer are analogous to accounts receivable in a noninsurance company. However, sales on credit are a relatively minor aspect of the insurance business compared to other businesses. These premium balances are customarily less than one-tenth of an insurer's assets. Because of the absence of significant investments in accounts receivable and inventory, typical turnover ratios (comparing cost of goods sold to inventories or sales to accounts receivable) are not relevant for insurer financial analysis.

The insurer's balance sheet liquidity can be measured by relating cash and the current value of invested assets to the insurer's policyholder obligations:

$$\text{Liquidity ratio} = \frac{\text{Cash} + \text{Invested assets (market value)}}{\text{Unearned premium reserve} + \text{Loss and Loss Adjustment Expense Reserves}}.$$

A ratio of less than 1 indicates an undesirable situation. Ratio values greater than 1 indicate that the insurer could cover the balance sheet values of its obligations to policyholders by converting invested assets to cash at current prices. Market values for most securities are listed in Schedule D of the Annual Statement and might also be included in notes to the general purpose financial statements.

Another aspect of liquidity is revealed by analyzing cash flows. Underwriting and investment operations provide cash through premiums, interest, dividends, rents, proceeds from the sale and maturity of investments, and the recapture of previously paid federal income taxes. Funds are applied to loss and loss adjustment expense payments, investment purchases, and dividends to policyholders and stockholders. Any remaining funds improve the insurer's cash position.

Companies that prepare audited GAAP financial reports issue a statement summarizing cash flows during the accounting period. The liquidity demands of underwriting operations can be determined by comparing the sources and uses of funds shown in the insurer's cash flow statement. For a growing insurer, underwriting operations should make a substantial net contribution to the insurer's cash reservoir.

Profitability Ratios

Profitability ratios measure the profitability of an individual insurer and of the industry as a whole. The ability of an insurer to operate profitably ultimately determines whether it grows and survives.

Several measures of profitability are used for property-casualty insurers. The most common ratio is the combined ratio. This ratio is important because it summarizes the underwriting performance of an individual insurer, or the industry as a whole, in a single number. Other profit measurements are determined by (1) combining underwriting and investment results; (2) relating profits to sales, assets, and net worth; and (3) expressing earnings on a per-share-of-stock basis.

Loss Ratio

The loss ratio can be calculated either with or without loss adjustment expenses. Most analysts and independent reporting services, such as A.M. Best, include loss adjustment expenses so that all expenses associated with losses are reflected in one ratio. The loss ratio is calculated from data on the income statement, as follows:

$$\text{Loss ratio} = \frac{\text{Incurred losses} + \text{Loss adjustment expenses}}{\text{Earned premiums}}.$$

Expense Ratio

Another important ratio that can be developed from the SAP income statement is the expense ratio. This ratio expresses the relationship between underwriting expenses and premiums. Expenses shown in the Underwriting and Investment Exhibit of the Annual Statement in Part 3 include acquisition costs, premium collection costs, and general expenses as well as taxes, licenses, and fees. Investment expenses are not included in the calculation of underwriting gain or loss. Loss adjustment expenses would also not be included in the expense ratio because they have already been included in the loss ratio.

The financial basis expense ratio is calculated as follows:

more conservative

$$\text{Expense ratio (financial basis)} = \frac{\text{Expenses incurred}}{\text{Earned premiums}}.$$

The trade basis expense ratio is calculated as follows:

$$\text{Expense ratio (trade basis)} = \frac{\text{Expenses incurred}}{\text{Net written premiums}}.$$

The reasons for using a financial basis expense ratio compared to a trade basis expense ratio are explained in the following section on combined ratio.

Combined Ratio

The combined ratio summarizes the insurer's underwriting performance during an accounting period. It expresses the percentage of the premium dollar paid for losses, loss adjustment expenses, acquisition expenses, and all underwriting expenses. For example, a combined ratio of 100 would mean the insurer pays every cent of the premium dollar for losses and expenses. Combined ratios can be over 100 or under 100. The combined ratio is useful for comparing results among various types of insurance and among insurers and for comparing the results of a single insurer over several accounting periods. This ratio is so called because it combines two ratios, the loss ratio and the expense ratio, each of which is also significant.

An insurer's loss ratio gives a general indication of the quality of business the insurer writes and might also provide insight into the adequacy of the insurer's rates. The expense ratio is a measurement of the insurer's efficiency and effectiveness. Comparing the expense ratios for successive time periods indicates overall expense trends and might highlight the need for increased expense controls.

The combined ratio is calculated by adding the loss ratio and the expense ratio. For a financial basis combined ratio, the financial expense ratio is added to the loss ratio. Conversely, for a trade basis combined ratio, the trade basis expense ratio is added to the loss ratio.

$$\text{Combined ratio} = \text{Loss ratio} + \text{Expense ratio}$$

Calculating a financial basis combined ratio using earned premiums rather than net written premiums produces a more meaningful measure of underwriting profit when premium volume is increasing or decreasing. The reason is that all losses and loss adjustment expenses and all acquisition and incurred underwriting expenses are related to earned premiums for that time period.

Although the financial basis combined ratio, when subtracted from 100 percent, accurately reflects the percentage profit margin on earned premiums, it fails to indicate considerable prepaid acquisition expenses. The financial basis approach, therefore, might improperly depress the results of underwriting operations. In the trade basis combined ratio, loss and loss adjustment expenses incurred are divided by earned premiums, but acquisition and underwriting expenses are divided by net written premiums. Exhibit 13-1 compares the calculation of combined ratios on a financial basis to the calculation on a trade basis. During successive periods of sales growth, the calculation on a trade basis results in a lower combined ratio by relating acquisition expenses to the corresponding premium for that period.

Operating Ratio

The **operating ratio** is calculated as follows:

$$\text{Operating ratio} = \text{Combined ratio} - \text{Investment income ratio.}$$

Investment Income Ratio

The investment income ratio is calculated as follows:

$$\text{Investment income ratio} = \frac{\text{Net investment income}}{\text{Earned premiums}}.$$

The operating ratio does not include other operating income or expenses, capital gains, or income taxes. The operating ratio is a measurement of a

Operating ratio
A ratio that measures an insurer's overall pretax operational profitability from underwriting and investment activities and is calculated by subtracting the investment income ratio from the combined ratio.

EXHIBIT 13-1

ABC Insurance Company

Financial Information
Year Ended 20XX
(000 omitted)

Net written premiums	$250,000
Earned premiums	200,000
Acquisition expenses incurred	75,000
Other underwriting expenses incurred	55,000
Loss and loss adjustment expenses incurred	100,000

$$\text{Combined ratio (financial basis)} = \frac{\$100,000 + \$75,000 + \$55,000}{\$200,000} = 1.15 \times 100 = 115.$$

$$\text{Combined ratio (trade basis)} = \frac{\$100,000}{\$200,000} + \frac{\$75,000 + \$55,000}{\$250,000} = (0.5 + 0.52) \times 100 = 102.$$

---

company's overall pretax operational profitability from underwriting and investment activities. When an insurer has an operating ratio of less than 100, this indicates that it is able to generate a profit from its core operations. Using the example from Exhibit 13-1, if ABC Insurance had an investment profit ratio of 8 percent for the year shown, the resulting operating ratio (using the trade basis combined ratio) would be 94 percent (102 – 8). The insurer's return on investments, therefore, offsets the unprofitable trade basis combined ratio. Using the financial basis combined ratio, the operating ratio remains over 100 percent (115 – 8) because this approach is more conservative.

Return on Invested Funds Ratio

Insurance reporting services use various measures of return on invested funds to evaluate the investment performance of property-casualty insurers. The **investment earnings ratio** shows the relationship between net investment income and average admitted assets:

Investment earnings ratio
A ratio that measures the return on invested funds by showing the relationship between net investment income and average admitted assets.

$$\text{Investment earnings ratio} = \frac{\text{Net investment income}}{\text{Average admitted assets}}.$$

Investment income includes interest, dividends, and real estate income, minus investment expenses but before federal income taxes. This ratio gives a narrowly defined measure of investment earnings.

Investment profit ratio
A ratio that measures the return on invested funds by dividing total investment profit (loss) by average admitted assets.

A broader rate of return figure for investment performance compares total *realized* investment profit or loss to average admitted assets:

$$\text{Investment profit ratio} = \frac{\text{Total investment profit (loss)}}{\text{Average admitted assets}}.$$

The numerator of the investment profit ratio adds realized capital gains (or losses) to investment income and produces an overall index of investment performance.

Return on Net Worth Ratio

The **return on net worth ratio** relates net income to the insurer's net worth (policyholders' surplus):

$$\text{Return on net worth ratio} = \frac{\text{Net income}}{\text{Policyholders surplus}}.$$

Return on net worth ratio
A ratio that relates net income to the insurer's net worth (policyholders' surplus).

Either SAP or GAAP data can be used in this calculation, but the result will be different based on the data used. If SAP results are being measured, net income includes underwriting gain or loss, investment income, and realized capital gains.

The rate of return on net worth is appropriate for comparisons among insurers. This ratio eliminates problems caused by differences in premium volume, underwriting results, and investment gains by summarizing overall operating success relative to the insurer's net resources.

Earnings per Share

Earnings per share (EPS) are determined as follows:

$$\text{Earnings per share} = \frac{\text{Net income}}{\substack{\text{Weighted average number of common} \\ \text{shares outstanding during the accounting period}}}.$$

Earnings per share (EPS)
A ratio that is calculated by dividing net income by the weighted average number of common shares outstanding during the accounting period.

Stock insurers can publish EPS figures based on SAP net income as well as on GAAP income. However, using SAP figures can result in profitability ratios that are significantly different from those calculated using GAAP figures. Many insurers reinvest most, if not all, of their earnings back into the insurer to enhance their value.

Several other per share ratios might be reported by stock insurers or calculated by the financial analyst and compared to EPS. The dividend paid per share of stock is of interest to investors who want to estimate the future dividend yield available from ownership of the insurer's stock. A comparison of EPS to dividends per share might indicate that the current dividend can be continued or might increase or decrease in the future.

The insurer's unassigned surplus per share indicates the insurer's ability to continue stockholder dividend payments even during a year in which EPS fall below the insurer's historical dividend per share payment. Unassigned surplus represents the maximum amount of accumulated earnings potentially available for distribution. Most insurers intend to retain unassigned surplus to support current obligations and to finance growth, but it can also be used to continue dividends.

A.M. BEST COMPANY'S PUBLISHED RATINGS

The A.M. Best Company (A.M. Best) has been in business for more than a century and has published financial-strength ratings of both life and property-casualty insurers during most of that time. Initially, its ratings were formulated only once each year, when insurers published financial statements. The ratings are now reviewed quarterly, although mergers, catastrophe losses, reinsurer insolvencies, or other unusual events might necessitate additional reviews.

Best's property-casualty insurer ratings and financial results for individual insurers are published annually in two books: *Best's Insurance Reports—Property/Casualty Edition* and *Best's Key Rating Guide*. Industry composite results are published annually in *Best's Aggregates and Averages*. The discussion that follows is based on the preface of the 2002 edition of *Best's Key Rating Guide* and on the "Users Guide for the Quantitative Analysis Reports" in *Best's Aggregates and Averages*.

Ratings that are changed (upgrades, downgrades, new assignments) during the year are reported online through *Best's Internet Services* or in *Best's Rating Monitor*, a special section of A.M. Best's newsletter *Best Week*. Selected changes in ratings and new ratings are reported monthly in *Best's Review* and sometimes in other insurance trade press or in the popular press, as well as on various online services. A.M. Best prepares reports and ratings for almost all significant insurers. Small insurers that are exempted from filing the NAIC Annual Statement form, the primary source of rating information, are one exception.

The sources of information for the ratings contained in the Best's guides are the NAIC Annual Statement and quarterly statement forms filed by the individual insurers listed. These resources may be supplemented by audit reports, SEC reports, reports of insurance department examinations, and internal insurer reports.

This chapter discusses two types of rating opinions published by A.M. Best: (1) a Best's Rating and (2) a Financial Size Category rating.

Best's Rating

The first type of rating opinion published by A.M. Best is a Best's Rating. When a person within the insurance industry refers to a Best's Rating without further qualification, he or she is most likely referring to the financial strength rating, officially called a Best's Rating by A.M. Best. The Best's Rating is generally considered to be the most important of the three ratings published for insurers. Best's states the objective of the rating system as follows:

> The objective of Best's rating system is to provide an opinion of an insurer's financial strength and ability to meet ongoing obligations to policyholders. The assigned Rating is derived from an in-depth evaluation of a company's balance sheet strength, operating performance and business profile as compared to Best's quantitative and qualitative standards.[2]

In addition, A.M. Best includes the following:

> While Best's Ratings reflect our *opinion* of a company's financial strength and ability to meet its ongoing obligations to policyholders, they are *not a warranty*, nor are they a recommendation of a specific policy form, contract, rate or claim practice (emphasis in original).[3]

As indicated, to determine a Best's Rating, A.M. Best uses a system that consists of a series of quantitative and qualitative tests described in the next sections.

Quantitative Tests

A.M. Best has more than 100 quantitative tests to rate insurers. This section focuses on tests of profitability, liquidity, leverage, loss reserves, and capital adequacy. The individual tests vary in importance by insurer, depending on the insurer's characteristics. Quantitative tests measure several financial characteristics of an insurer. The tests are based on the insurer's reported data for at least the past five years. An insurer's test results are evaluated by comparing them to its peer group as established by A.M. Best. The peer group standards are based on an analysis of the peer group's reported data for the past twenty years.

Profitability Tests

A.M. Best's first series of quantitative tests are profitability tests. Profitability indicates management's ability to operate the insurer in such a way as to generate or attract sufficient profit and capital to support its future operations and growth. The analysis of profitability encompasses underwriting profit or loss, investment profit or loss, and capital gains or losses. The magnitude and source of the insurer's profits and losses over the past five years are analyzed. Profits are strongly affected by operational changes, so trends in premium volume and premium distribution, investment income, net income, and surplus are analyzed.

The *Key Rating Guide* provides specific data for each insurer listed, related to the loss ratio, expense ratio, combined ratio, and operating ratio. Other key profitability tests are the pretax return on revenue, yield on invested assets, change in policyholders' surplus, and return on policyholders' surplus ratios.

Exhibit 13-2 is adapted from a Profitability Analysis chart from *Aggregates and Averages*. This exhibit shows the combined Underwriting and Operating Ratios for the five years from 1997 through 2001 for the entire industry. Where formulas apply, they are indicated by column numbers and shown at the bottom of the table.

EXHIBIT 13-2

Industry Composite (Excluding State Funds)
940 Property-Casualty Organizations (2,412 Companies) (in Millions of Dollars)

Profitability Analysis
Composition of Underwriting Earnings

Year	(1) Net Premiums Written	(2) Net Premiums Earned	(3) Pure Loss (%)	(4) LAE (%)	(5) Loss & LAE Incurred	(6) Commission Expense (%)	(7) Other Expenses (%)	(8) Underwtg. Expenses Incurred	(9) Policy-holder Dividends	(10) Net Underwtg. Income
1997	272,937	267,962	82.9	17.1	195,458	42.5	57.5	73,559	4,668	−5,723
1998	277,273	273,429	82.9	17.1	208,607	41.1	58.9	76,552	4,739	−16,469
1999	282,844	278,764	83.2	16.8	218,508	40.2	59.8	78,792	3,331	−21,868
2000	298,278	292,482	84.2	15.8	237,187	40.4	59.6	82,193	3,894	−30,792
2001	323,510	311,529	85.2	14.8	275,400	40.5	59.5	86,372	2,358	−52,602
Total	1,454,842	1,424,165	83.8	16.2	1,135,161	40.9	59.1	397,468	18,990	−127,454

Underwriting and Operating Ratios (%)

Year	(11) Pure Loss	(12) LAE	(13) Loss & LAE	(14) Commission Expense	(15) Other Exp.	(16) Total Underwtg. Expenses	(17) Combined Ratio B/Phds.	(18) Pol. Div.	(19) Combined Ratio A/Phds.	(20) Net Inv. Ratio	(21) Operating Ratio
1997	60.5	12.5	72.9	11.4	15.5	27.0	99.9	1.7	101.6	15.3	86.4
1998	63.2	13.1	76.3	11.3	16.3	27.6	103.9	1.7	105.6	14.4	91.2
1999	65.2	13.2	78.4	11.2	16.7	27.9	106.2	1.2	107.4	13.7	93.7
2000	68.3	12.8	81.1	11.1	16.4	27.6	108.7	1.3	110.0	13.9	96.1
2001	75.3	13.1	88.4	10.8	15.9	26.7	115.1	0.8	115.9	12.1	103.7
5 Yr. Avg.	66.8	12.9	79.7	11.2	16.1	27.3	107.0	1.3	108.4	13.8	94.5

Formulas

Column 3	=	Pure losses as a percentage of loss LAE incurred	
Column 4	=	LAE as a percentage of loss LAE incurred	
Column 6	=	Commission expense as a percentage of U/W expenses incurred	
Column 7	=	Other expenses as a percentage of U/W expenses incurred	
Column 10	=	Column 2 − Column 5 − Column 8 − Column 9	
Column 11	=	Pure losses as a percentage of Column 2	
Column 12	=	LAE as a percentage of loss LAE incurred	
Column 13	=	Column 11 and Column 12	
Column 14	=	Commission expense as a percentage of Column 1	
Column 15	=	Other expenses as a percentage of Column 1	
Column 16	=	Column 14 and Column 15	
Column 17	=	Column 13 + Column 16	
Column 18	=	Column 9 ÷ Column 2	
Column 19	=	Column 17 ÷ Column 18	
Column 20	=	Net investment income ÷ Column 2	
Column 21	=	Column 19 − Column 20	

Source: A.M. Best Company, *Best's Aggregates & Averages, Property/Casualty*, 2002 edition (Oldwick, N. J.: A.M. Best Company, 2002), p. 123.

Liquidity Tests

Liquidity tests measure an insurer's ability to meet claim obligations without selling long-term investments or fixed assets that might be saleable only at a substantial loss during unfavorable market conditions. The emphasis in the liquidity tests is on cash and short-term securities that can be converted to cash with little or no loss in all but the most severe market conditions. Best's Ratings include more than thirty liquidity tests. Five of the most useful liquidity tests are reviewed here:

1. Quick liquidity ratio
2. Current liquidity ratio
3. Overall liquidity ratio
4. Operating cash flow test
5. Class 3-6 bonds to PHS ratio

Quick Liquidity Ratio   The first liquidity test is the **quick liquidity ratio**, which evaluates the insurer's short-term liquidity by comparing quick assets to net liabilities. The quick assets used in the ratio are:

- Cash
- Short-term investments issued by companies not affiliated with the insurer
- Bonds maturing within one year and issued by companies not affiliated with the insurer
- Government bonds maturing within five years
- Eighty percent of common stocks issued by companies not affiliated with the insurer

Securities issued by companies affiliated with the insurer are excluded from quick assets regardless of their term or nature because they might not be marketable quickly without a substantial loss. A.M. Best Ratings considers a ratio of 30 percent to 50 percent for property insurers and of 20 percent to 30 percent for long-tailed liability insurers to be in the normal range.

Current Liquidity Ratio   The second liquidity test is the **current liquidity ratio**. This is the ratio of the sum of cash and all unaffiliated invested assets (excluding real estate) to net liabilities and ceded reinsurance balances payable, expressed as a percentage. If this ratio is less than 100 percent, the insurer might have to depend on the sale of its affiliated assets to cover its liabilities. A.M. Best Ratings consider a ratio of 120 percent to 140 percent for property insurers, or 100 percent to 120 percent for long-tailed liability insurers, to be in the normal range.

Overall Liquidity Ratio   The third liquidity test is the **overall liquidity ratio**. This ratio is the total admitted assets divided by total liabilities minus conditional reserves. It indicates an insurer's ability to pay net liabilities with total assets. This ratio does not address the quality and marketability of premium balances and investments in affiliates. A ratio of 140 percent to

Quick liquidity ratio
A ratio that measures short-term liquidity by comparing quick assets to net liabilities.

Current liquidity ratio
The ratio of the sum of all cash and all unaffiliated invested assets (excluding real estate) to net liabilities and ceded reinsurance balances payable, expressed as a percentage.

Overall liquidity ratio
A ratio that measures the ability to pay net liabilities with total assets and that is calculated by dividing total admitted assets by total liabilities minus conditional reserves.

180 percent for property insurers or 110 percent to 150 percent for long-tailed liability insurers is considered to be in the normal range.

Operating cash flow test
A measure of the ability to meet current obligations through internally generated funds.

Operating Cash Flow   The fourth liquidity test is the **operating cash flow test**. This test measures the insurer's ability to meet current obligations through internally generated funds. It includes all funds generated from insurance operations and invested assets attributable to underwriting activities, net investment income, and federal income taxes. Cash flows related to stockholder dividends, capital gains or losses, depreciation, amortization, or capital contributions are excluded. Negative results could indicate poor underwriting results, poor investment results, or both.

Class 3-6 Bonds to PHS ratio
The ratio of noninvestment grade bonds to policyholders' surplus.

Class 3-6 Bonds to PHS Ratio   The fifth liquidity test is the ratio of noninvestment grade bonds to policyholders' surplus (**Class 3-6 Bonds to PHS ratio**). The NAIC assigns a quality rating to all bonds held by insurers. The ratings range from 1 to 6, with 1 for bonds of the highest quality and 6 for bonds that are in or near default. Bonds rated 3, 4, 5, or 6 are considered below investment grade and carry higher default and liquidity risks.

Leverage Tests

An insurer's operating stability—that is, its ability to withstand losses from unfavorable underwriting results, catastrophes, poor management decisions, industry trends, and adverse economic developments—depends on its capital and leverage. An insurer's capital is its policyholders' surplus. Its leverage is the extent to which it uses funds from liabilities (that represent funds belonging to others) to supplement its capital in financing its operations. Leverage gained from loss reserves, unearned premium reserves, or other funds generated by insurance operations is common and likely to be substantial, especially for an insurer that writes a great deal of liability insurance. A.M. Best calls this form of leverage "underwriting leverage." Underwriting leverage increases as the insurer's written premiums increase.

A.M. Best includes more than forty tests for leverage; however, six tests are particularly useful in identifying areas that can affect an insurer's operating stability:

1. Change in net premiums written
2. Net premiums written to policyholders' surplus ratio
3. Net liabilities to policyholders' surplus ratio
4. Net leverage ratio
5. Ceded reinsurance leverage ratio
6. Gross leverage ratio

Change in net premiums written
A measure of the growth in an insurer's underwriting loss exposure.

Change in Net Premiums Written   The first leverage test is the percentage **change in net premiums written** (NPW). This indicates the growth in an insurer's underwriting exposure. A change in net written premiums greater than 10 percent is considered unfavorable because the insurer might be experiencing uncontrolled growth, which could negatively affect surplus levels. During periods characterized as a "soft market," when rates and policy terms and conditions are liberal, low growth in net premium rates is expected. "Hard market" conditions result in high rates of premium growth. A.M. Best indicates a range of 3 percent to 10 percent as acceptable for this leverage test.

Net Premiums Written to Policyholders' Surplus Ratio   The second leverage test is the ratio of **net premiums written to policyholders' surplus** (NPW to PHS), which measures leverage resulting from the insurer's current premium writings. Net written premiums are gross written premiums minus reinsurance premiums ceded and minus returned premiums. Some analysts calculate the premium-to-surplus ratio on the basis of SAP surplus, as reported in the NAIC Annual Statement. A.M. Best uses a modified surplus as regards policyholders, calculated by adjusting SAP surplus to reflect the equity in the unearned premium reserve, inadequacy or redundancy in loss reserves, the difference between the reported value and the market value of assets, and other relevant factors.[4] This ratio indicates the insurer's net exposure to pricing errors in its current book of business. A.M. Best considers an NPW to PHS ratio unfavorable if it exceeds 2.0.

Net Liabilities to Policyholders' Surplus Ratio   The third leverage test is the ratio of **net liabilities to policyholders' surplus**. This ratio determines the insurer's exposure to unpaid obligations, unearned premiums, and exposure to reserving errors. The net liabilities consist mostly of loss reserves and unearned premium reserves, which are adjusted to reflect relevant reinsurance transactions. The ratio measures the insurer's exposure to errors in estimating reserves (particularly loss reserves). By comparing liabilities to capital, this ratio is similar to traditional measures of financial leverage.

Net Leverage Ratio   The fourth leverage test is the **net leverage ratio**, which is the sum of the net premiums written and net liability leverage ratios. This ratio measures the insurer's exposures to both pricing errors and errors in estimating liabilities, after reinsurance, in relation to policyholders' surplus. A.M. Best considers a ratio of under 4.0 for property insurers and under 6.0 for long-tailed liability insurers acceptable.

Ceded Reinsurance Leverage Ratio   The fifth leverage test is the **ceded reinsurance leverage ratio**, which measures an insurer's dependence on reinsurers and its exposure to the possibility that it might be unable to collect amounts due from reinsurers. This ratio is the sum of reinsurance premiums ceded, plus reinsurance recoverables (paid and unpaid losses, IBNR, unearned premiums and commissions), minus funds held from reinsurers, divided by surplus. Reinsurance balances payable from U.S. affiliates are excluded so as not to distort results by including data associated with internal pooling or reinsurance agreements.

Gross Leverage Ratio   The sixth leverage test is the **gross leverage ratio**, which is the sum of the net leverage ratio and the ceded reinsurance ratio. This test measures an insurer's exposure caused by pricing errors in its current

Net premiums written to policyholders' surplus (net premiums written leverage ratio)
A ratio that measures leverage resulting from current premium writings.

Net liabilities to policyholders' surplus (net liability leverage ratio)
A ratio that determines an insurer's loss exposure to unpaid obligations, unearned premiums, and reserving errors.

Net leverage ratio
A ratio that measures an insurer's loss exposure to both pricing errors and errors in estimating liabilities, after reinsurance, in relation to policyholders' surplus.

Ceded reinsurance leverage ratio
A ratio that measures an insurer's dependence on reinsurers and its loss exposure to the possibility that it might be unable to collect amounts due from reinsurers; the sum of reinsurance premiums ceded plus reinsurance recoverables minus funds held from reinsurers, divided by surplus.

Gross leverage ratio
A ratio that measures an insurer's loss exposure caused by pricing errors in its current book of business, reserve estimation errors, and reinsurance exposure; the sum of the net leverage ratio and the ceded reinsurance leverage ratio.

book of business, reserve estimation errors, and reinsurance exposure. A.M. Best considers this ratio to be favorable when it is under 5.0 for property insurers and under 7.0 for long-tailed liability insurers.

Loss Reserve Tests

A.M. Best uses several tests to measure insurer loss reserves. It uses a proprietary model (details not disclosed) to measure the adequacy or inadequacy of the reserves. The needed reserves, as calculated by the model, are discounted for anticipated investment income to obtain an economic loss reserve figure. If the insurer's reported reserves are less than the calculated economic loss reserve, a deficiency in reserves is presumed to exist. If the reported reserves are greater than the economic reserve, a redundancy is presumed to exist. Any deficiency or redundancy is incorporated into the Best's Capital Adequacy Ratio (BCAR) model, discussed subsequently.

A.M. Best uses the ratio of reported loss reserves to policyholders' surplus (PHS), **loss reserves to PHS ratio**, to measure the trend and magnitude of an insurer's total loss reserves to surplus. A.M. Best considers 50 percent to 100 percent for property insurers and 200 percent to 300 percent for long-tailed liability insurers to be in the normal range.

Another test of loss reserves is the ratio of **loss development to policyholders' surplus** (Development to PHS). This ratio measures reserve deficiency or redundancy in relation to surplus and reveals the degree to which year-end surplus was either understated (–) or overstated (+) in each of the past several years. The development of loss reserves (increase or decrease from previously reported values) is shown in Schedule P of the NAIC Annual Statement. A.M. Best considers 0 percent to –25 percent (understatement up to 25 percent) to be in the normal range.

The ratio of **loss reserve development to net premiums earned** (Development to NPE) is also calculated. The loss reserve development figure used for this ratio is the same as that used for the Development to PHS. This ratio, like the other reserve tests, is calculated for the most recent five years. If a comparison over time shows that the ratio is falling, it could indicate that the insurer is not establishing adequate reserves. However, the Development to NPE ratios over time are affected by rapid growth (or shrinkage) of earned premiums and possibly by changes in the mix of business. Therefore, the ratio must be interpreted carefully.

Capital Adequacy Test

A.M. Best uses a proprietary model called Best's Capital Adequacy Ratio (BCAR) to measure the adequacy of the insurer's capital relative to the risks it assumes in its operations. The test compares actual surplus to a computed required amount of capital.

A.M. Best does not publish a detailed explanation of the BCAR calculation. Following is the explanation it provides:

Loss reserves to policyholders' surplus ratio

A ratio that measures the trend and magnitude of an insurer's total loss reserves to surplus.

Loss development to policyholders' surplus ratio

A measure of reserve deficiency or redundancy in relation to surplus that reveals the degree to which year-end surplus was either understated or overstated.

Loss reserve development to net premiums earned ratio

A ratio that is calculated for the most recent five years and measures the degree to which an insurer's loss reserves are keeping pace with its premium growth.

The BCAR ratio compares an insurer's adjusted surplus relative to the required capital necessary to support its operating and investment risks. Companies deemed to have 'adequate' balance sheet strength normally generate a BCAR score of over 100% and will usually carry a Secure Best's Rating. Companies deemed to have very strong balance sheet strength generate a BCAR score over 200%.[5]

Exhibit 13-3 provides a structural overview of Best's Capital Adequacy Ratio.

EXHIBIT 13-3

Structural Overview of Best's Capital Adequacy Ratio

$$BCAR = \frac{\text{Adjusted Surplus}}{\text{Net Required Capital}}$$

Adjusted Surplus Components	*Net Required Capital (NRC) Components*
	(B1) Fixed-Income Securities
Reported Surplus	(B2) Equity Securities
Equity Adjustments:	(B3) Interest Rate
Unearned Premiums	(B4) Credit
Assets	(B5) Loss and LAE Reserves
Loss Reserves	(B6) Net Written Premiums
Reinsurance	(B7) Off Balance Sheet
Debt Adjustments:	
Surplus Notes	
Debt Service Requirements	
Other Adjustments:	*Covariance*
Potential Catastrophe Losses	
Future Operating Losses	

$$NCR = \sqrt{(B1)^2 + (B2)^2 + (B3)^2 + (0.5*B4)^2 + \left[(0.5*B4) + B5\right]^2 + (B6)^2 + (B7)}$$

Source: Copyright 2001, A.M. Best Company, Inc.

Qualitative Tests

In addition to the series of quantitative tests to determine a Best's Rating, A.M. Best uses a series of qualitative tests to evaluate aspects of an insurer's operations, including the following:

- Capital structure of insurer holding companies
- Reinsurance agreement analysis
- Loss reserve adequacy
- Quality and diversity of investments
- Spread of risk
- Management
- Market position
- Surplus adequacy
- Event risk

Capital Structure of Insurer Holding Companies

The capital structure of the insurer and its holding company, if any, is analyzed to ensure that the capital structure is sound and the insurance subsidiary can meet its financial obligations. When a holding company exists, its associated capital structures can substantially influence the overall financial strength of an insurance company subsidiary. For example, if an insurer's holding company is heavily burdened by debt, the debt service costs might require large stockholder dividends from the insurer, thereby reducing the insurer's ability to accumulate surplus through retained earnings. In extreme cases, the dividend drain might hamper the insurer's efforts to provide efficient service to its policyholders.

Reinsurance Agreement Analysis

A.M. Best's reinsurance agreement analysis includes a review of the appropriateness of the reinsurance agreements purchased and the reinsurer's financial strength. The appropriateness of the reinsurance program depends on the insurer's underwriting practices, including the type of insurance written, the amount of coverage provided, territorial spread of risks, and catastrophe loss exposures, as well as its other financial resources. Reinsurance agreements are also reviewed to see whether they provide true risk financing or serve merely as loans or extensions of time for loss payments.

Loss Reserve Adequacy

Loss reserve analysis depends primarily on the quantitative tests previously discussed. However, qualitative tests also include an estimate of the uncertainty in loss reserve estimates. If the qualitative tests indicate that the estimated uncertainty is greater than any "equity" (redundancy) in the reserves as indicated by the quantitative tests, the insurer's rating might be adversely affected.

Quality and Diversity of Investments

A.M. Best carefully screens an insurer's invested assets to determine whether they could be sold quickly in an emergency with minimal market loss. Particular attention is given to large individual investments constituting 10 percent or more of the insurer's policyholders' surplus and to large investments in subsidiaries or affiliates. Lack of diversification by industry or by geographic area is also cause for concern.

Spread of Risk

The analysis of an insurer's spread of risk includes (1) the size of its premium volume, (2) the geographic spread of its business, (3) the diversity of types of insurance written, and (4) the marketing systems used. A.M. Best determines whether insurers have a sufficiently diverse book of business so that the loss ratio would not be excessively affected by natural catastrophes, adverse economic developments, or other factors that might apply to a limited geographic area or a limited class of business. An insurer that operates in a limited geographic area might also be exposed to adverse underwriting experience resulting from regulatory actions.

Management

Although the experience, capabilities, and integrity of management cannot be measured with mathematical precision, they are crucial factors in assessing an insurer's future prospects. Those factors are assessed based partly on the insurer's past success if the present management has been in place for several years. Otherwise, the assessment is based on past experience of the managers in other positions and on the raters' opinions of the managers, developed through periodic meetings with them.

Market Position

An insurer's market position depends on its ability to maintain or increase its market share. Maintaining and increasing market share, in turn, depends on having a low expense ratio, superior service, strong recognition by buyers and producers in the insurer's selected market, access to plentiful and affordable capital, and control over distribution channels.

Surplus Adequacy

An insurer's policyholders' surplus is a proxy for its financial strength. Surplus serves as a cushion should unexpected events occur. The adequacy of any insurer's surplus must be evaluated relative to other qualitative factors specific to that insurer, such as its investment portfolio, reinsurance program, uncertainty in loss reserve estimates, and the underwriting book of business.

Event Risk

Unexpected circumstances could also affect an insurer's financial strength and its Best's Rating. Such events include legislative or regulatory developments, changes in insurer management, significant litigation, adverse economic conditions, disruptions in financial markets, or catastrophic losses from unanticipated or unknown causes of loss.

Best's Rating Scale

The first type of rating opinion published by A.M. Best is based on the results of its quantitative and qualitative analysis. A.M. Best assigns a letter rating, called a Best's Rating, to almost all insurers licensed and operating within the U.S. The rating might be based on data from a single insurer and apply only to that insurer, or it might be based on the consolidated figures for several insurers operating under common ownership and management and apply to all insurers within the group. The fifteen letter ratings range downward from A++ to F. The rating of F is for insurers currently in liquidation.

A.M. Best assigns Not Rated (NR) to insurers that are too small to qualify for Best's Ratings or that cannot provide data for five representative years as required for a Best's Rating. The process for determining an NR is similar to that for obtaining a Best's Rating but is based on three years of data instead of five years. The NRs range from "NR 5" to "NR 1," all of which indicate that no Financial Performance Rating (FPR) is published. An insurer might not be rated because of limited financial information, small level of surplus, or lack of sufficient operating experience. An "NR-4" rating is assigned to insurers that have requested their ratings not be published because the insurer disagrees with A.M. Best's rating conclusions. Non-rated insurers constitute only about 2 percent of the entire industry's premium writings. Exhibit 13-4 shows all the Best's Ratings and FPRs along with a brief explanation of their meanings. It also shows the number of individual insurers that qualified for each rating as of June 2002. The bottom of Exhibit 13-4 indicates the means for all of A.M. Best "no rating opinion" levels.

Best's Ratings might be accompanied by one or more modifiers, indicated by lowercase letters. These modifiers are as follows:

- g—indicates that the rating is based on consolidated information for the rated insurer and one or more affiliated insurers under common ownership or management

- p—indicates a pooled rating based on data from two or more insurers operating under common ownership or management and pooling all of their business, with all premiums, expenses, and losses prorated among member insurers

- r—indicates that the rated insurer reinsures substantially all of its direct business with a single reinsurer and has been assigned the reinsurer's rating

- q—indicates a rating that has been qualified because the insurer's rating might be adversely affected by state legislation or losses from residual market programs

Exhibit 13-5 indicates the number of insurers to which the modifiers were assigned in 2002. As noted in Exhibit 13-5, two modifiers were assigned to the ratings of eighty-six insurers. The remaining ratings were subject to only one modifier each.

EXHIBIT 13-4

2002 Property-Casualty Rating Distribution Based on Individual Companies as of June 21, 2002

Best's	Rating Category	Number	Percent
	Secure Ratings		
A++	Superior	159	7.8%
A+	Superior	348	17.0
	Subtotal	507	24.8
A	Excellent	635	30.9
A−	Excellent	438	21.3
	Subtotal	1,073	52.2
B++	Very Good	169	8.2
B+	Very Good	127	6.2
	Subtotal	296	14.4
	Total—Secure Ratings	1,876	91.4%
	Vulnerable Ratings		
B	Fair	57	2.8%
B−	Fair	39	1.9
	Subtotal	96	4.7
C++	Marginal	14	0.7
C+	Marginal	9	0.4
	Subtotal	23	1.1
C	Weak	3	0.1
C−	Weak	0	0.0
	Subtotal	3	0.1
D	Poor	6	0.3
E	Under Regulatory Supervision	32	1.6
F	In Liquidation	17	0.8
	Subtotal	55	2.7
	Total—Vulnerable Ratings	177	8.6%
	Total—Rating Opinions	2,053	100.0%
	No Rating Opinions		
NR-1	Insufficient Data	447	55.5%
NR-2	Insufficient Size/Operating Experience	100	12.4
NR-3	Rating Procedure Inapplicable	202	25.1
NR-4	Company Request	36	4.4
NR-5	Not Formally Followed	21	2.6
	Total—No Rating Opinions	806	100.0%
	Total—Rated Companies	2,859	

EXHIBIT 13-5

Assignment of Rating Modifiers, 2002

Rating Modifier	Number of Companies
g – Group	474
p – Pooled	489
r – Reinsured	436
q – Qualified	0
u – Under review	102
Subtotal	**1,501**
Dual Assignments	**(86)**
Total Modified Ratings	**1,415**

© A.M. Best Company. Used with permission, *Best's Key Rating Guide®—Property-Casualty, United States,* 2002 Edition, p. xviii.

EXHIBIT 13-6

2002 Financial Size Category

Financial Size Category	Adjusted Policyholders' Surplus ($ Millions)	Number of Companies
Class I	0 to 1	125
Class II	1 to 2	154
Class III	2 to 5	298
Class IV	5 to 10	287
Class V	10 to 25	303
Class VI	25 to 50	213
Class VII	50 to 100	200
Class VIII	100 to 250	279
Class IX	250 to 500	204
Class X	500 to 750	77
Class XI	750 to 1,000	77
Class XII	1,000 to 1,250	54
Class XIII	1,250 to 1,500	50
Class XIV	1,500 to 2,000	79
Class XV	2,000 or greater	410
Total Companies		***2,810**

* Does not include 49 companies rated E and F.

© A.M. Best Company. Used with permission, *Best's Key Rating Guide®—Property-Casualty, United States,* 2002 Edition, p. xix.

Best's Financial Size Category

The second type of rating opinion published by A.M. Best is the Financial Size Category.

The Financial Size Category indicates the insurer's size as measured by its reported policyholders' surplus plus conditional reserves for contingencies. The fifteen financial size categories are indicated by Roman numerals. They range from Class I to Class XV, with Class I being the smallest insurers. Exhibit 13-6 indicates the categories and the number of insurers assigned to each class in 2002. Exhibit 13-6 does not include insurers with a Best's Rating of E or F.

The Financial Size Category is not a measure of the insurer's financial performance or financial strength. It is one measure of the insurer's capacity to handle large loss exposures in its insurance operation or large risks in its investment operations.

INSURANCE REGULATORY INFORMATION SYSTEM (IRIS)

IRIS was developed by the NAIC in the 1970s. It was originally known as the *Early Warning System*, a name that accurately indicates its original purpose. IRIS was developed to provide regulatory authorities with an early warning that an insurer might be experiencing financial difficulty. An early warning might enable the regulators to rehabilitate the insurer or, if rehabilitation is not practical, to minimize the losses resulting from liquidation.

IRIS consists of twelve tests and has two phases, statistical and analytical. In the statistical phase, financial ratios are first reviewed to verify that each ratio is relevant for solvency monitoring. Following this review, ratios are revised as needed.

For individual insurers, ratios that fall outside the "usual range" are not always a concern, but the reasons for any variances need to be determined. According to NAIC information, "approximately 14.9 percent of all property and casualty insurers fell outside the usual range on four or more ratios for 2001."[6] The ratios are, however, useful in identifying which insurers are more likely than others to experience financial difficulties.

In the analytical phase, an analyst team consisting of financial examiners and analysts from all zones of the NAIC meets annually to review IRIS results. Based on this review, each insurer is designated as either "Level A," "Level B," or "Reviewed—No Level." These levels help state insurance regulators to prioritize their workload. Potential problem insurers are handled first. A "Level A" designation indicates the highest review priority but does not necessarily mean that the insurer is financially unsound. "Level B" insurers might also have adverse financial results, but these insurers do not require as immediate a response as those with a "Level A" designation. For a "Level A" insurer, state regulators should perform a comprehensive analytical review of the insurer's financial condition to determine whether closer regulatory attention is required.[7]

Detailed instructions for calculating the IRIS test ratios and more detailed explanations of their interpretation are given in the NAIC's publication *Insurance Regulatory Information System, Property and Casualty Edition*, published annually. The twelve IRIS tests are:

- Ratio 1—Gross Premiums Written to Policyholders' Surplus Ratio
- Ratio 2—Net Premiums Written to Policyholders' Surplus Ratio
- Ratio 3—Change in Net Writings Ratio
- Ratio 4—Surplus Aid to Policyholders' Surplus Ratio
- Ratio 5—Two-Year Overall Operating Ratio
- Ratio 6—Investment Yield Ratio
- Ratio 7—Change in Policyholders' Surplus Ratio
- Ratio 8—Liabilities to Liquid Assets Ratio
- Ratio 9—Gross Agents' Balances to Policyholders' Surplus Ratio
- Ratio 10—One-Year Reserve Development to Policyholders' Surplus Ratio
- Ratio 11—Two-Year Reserve Development to Policyholders' Surplus Ratio
- Ratio 12—Estimated Current Reserve Deficiency to Policyholders' Surplus Ratio

Gross Premiums Written to Policyholders' Surplus Ratio

The first test in the IRIS system is the ratio of gross premiums written to policyholders' surplus, stated as a percent. This ratio is a measurement of the adequacy of the insurers' policyholders' surplus, which provides a degree of protection in absorbing above-average losses. It does not, however, consider the effect of ceded reinsurance. This ratio and the second one, net premiums written to policyholders' surplus ratio, can be reviewed together. Unusual differences between the two ratios could indicate that the insurer is relying heavily on reinsurance. The calculation for this ratio is shown in Exhibit 13-7. The NAIC specifies exactly where in the Annual Statement to obtain the data used to calculate each ratio.

For gross premiums written to policyholders' surplus, a result of 900 percent or less is considered acceptable. If this ratio is near 900 percent, it might be reviewed jointly with the net premiums written to policyholders' surplus, described next.

Net Premiums Written to Policyholders' Surplus Ratio

The second test in the IRIS system is the ratio of net premiums written to policyholders' surplus, stated as a percent. A ratio of 300 percent or less is considered acceptable. If this ratio is near 300 percent, it might be reviewed jointly with the ratio of surplus aid to policyholders' surplus, described subsequently, which shows the financial assistance provided to the insurer through its reinsurers.

EXHIBIT 13-7

Ratio 1
Gross Premiums Written to Policyholders' Surplus

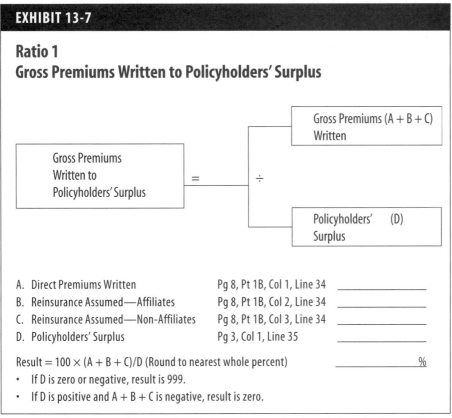

A. Direct Premiums Written   Pg 8, Pt 1B, Col 1, Line 34   _____
B. Reinsurance Assumed—Affiliates   Pg 8, Pt 1B, Col 2, Line 34   _____
C. Reinsurance Assumed—Non-Affiliates   Pg 8, Pt 1B, Col 3, Line 34   _____
D. Policyholders' Surplus   Pg 3, Col 1, Line 35   _____

Result = $100 \times (A + B + C)/D$ (Round to nearest whole percent)   _____ %
- If D is zero or negative, result is 999.
- If D is positive and A + B + C is negative, result is zero.

Source: National Association of Insurance Commissioners, *Insurance Regulatory Information System (IRIS)*, 2002 Property-Casualty Edition (Kansas City, Mo.: NAIC, 2002), p. 2.

Policyholders' surplus serves the important function of protecting an insurer from the effect of catastrophic losses or other higher-than-expected loss results. One consideration in comparing net written premiums to policyholders' surplus is the types of insurance an insurer writes. Insurers writing predominantly liability insurance should maintain a lower net premiums written to policyholders' surplus ratio than insurers concentrating in property insurance. This lower ratio is desirable because of the higher degree of uncertainty in projecting future loss for liability insurance and the relative instability of liability as compared with property insurance.

Change in Net Writings Ratio

The third test in the IRIS system is the percentage change in the insurer's net written premiums during the most recent year. Experience has shown that excessive growth in premium volume is frequently associated with financial problems. An increase or a decrease of 33 percent or less is considered acceptable for this ratio. The calculation for this ratio is shown in Exhibit 13-8.

EXHIBIT 13-8

Ratio 3
Change in Net Writings

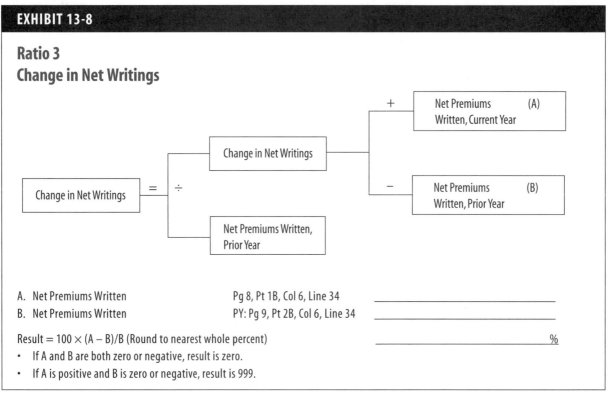

A. Net Premiums Written   Pg 8, Pt 1B, Col 6, Line 34   _____

B. Net Premiums Written   PY: Pg 9, Pt 2B, Col 6, Line 34   _____

Result = 100 × (A − B)/B (Round to nearest whole percent)   _____ %

•   If A and B are both zero or negative, result is zero.
•   If A is positive and B is zero or negative, result is 999.

Source: National Association of Insurance Commissioners, *Insurance Regulatory Information System (IRIS)*, 2002 Property-Casualty Edition (Kansas City, Mo.: NAIC, 2002), p. 2.

While insurers should generally show growth in written premiums, excessive growth is often achieved through inadequate pricing or underwriting. Wide variations between increases and decreases in written premiums would also be a concern. Such deviations indicate instability. Also, a sudden drop in written premiums could indicate that the insurer has withdrawn from a type of insurance or is facing substantial competition and losing market share.

Surplus Aid to Policyholders' Surplus Ratio

The fourth test in the IRIS system is the ratio of surplus aid to policyholders' surplus. Surplus aid is the extent of the insurer's policyholders' surplus that results from reinsurance purchases. The surplus aid is derived from ceding commissions on reinsurance ceded to nonaffiliated reinsurers. If the ratio exceeds 15 percent, it is considered unsatisfactory. If this ratio is above 15 percent, then regulators would be concerned about the quality of the insurer's reinsurance treaties and the threat to solvency if treaties are canceled.

Two-Year Overall Operating Ratio

The fifth test in the IRIS system is the insurer's two-year loss ratio plus its two-year expense ratio minus its two-year investment income ratio. The loss ratio is the ratio of incurred losses and loss adjustment expenses plus policyholder dividends to net earned premiums. The expense ratio is the ratio of underwriting expenses (all expenses except investment expenses) to net written premiums. The investment income ratio is the ratio of investment income to net earned premiums. A ratio of less than 100 percent is considered satisfactory.

As previously indicated, an insurer's operating ratio reflects the effect of investment returns on the combined ratio. If an insurer is being reviewed and this ratio exceeds 100 percent, regulators would concentrate their efforts on the individual components of the combined ratio. A high loss ratio, or a ratio that is increasing, could indicate large losses or possibly reserve strengthening on specific types of insurance, or it could indicate that the loss ratio is increasing because of increasing loss adjustment expenses. Underwriting expenses might increase because of a change in marketing systems, higher agent commissions, or operational inefficiencies. Low investment ratios might indicate poor performance of the insurer's investment portfolio or inadequate portfolio management.

Investment Yield Ratio

The sixth test in the IRIS system is the ratio of net investment income to the average cash and invested assets for the year, stated as a percent. A ratio greater than 4.5 percent but less than 10.0 currently is considered satisfactory. A low ratio might indicate that an insurer has made speculative investments intended to produce large capital over the long run, but that those investments are providing little income in the short term. A low ratio might also mean that the insurer is paying unusually high investment expenses that reduce the overall net investment yield. A high ratio might indicate investments in high-risk instruments or extraordinary dividend payments from subsidiaries to the parent company.

Change in Policyholders' Surplus Ratio

The seventh test in the IRIS system is the percentage change in adjusted policyholders' surplus during the year. Adjusted policyholders' surplus is the SAP policyholders' surplus (shown in the NAIC Annual Statement) plus equity in the unearned premium reserve (the amount of unearned premiums represented by already expensed acquisition costs). The ratio is considered to be in the usual range if it is between a decrease of 10 percent and an increase of 50 percent.

Large increases in policyholders' surplus might result from an increase in surplus aid from reinsurance, from a manipulation of loss reserves development, or from other undesirable accounting techniques. Of course, large increases can also result from favorable developments, such as the insurer's issuance and sale of additional capital stock. However, the reasons for any large change must be known and understood.

Liabilities to Liquid Assets Ratio

The eighth test in the IRIS system is the ratio of total liabilities to liquid assets. The calculation for this ratio is shown in Exhibit 13-9. The ratio is considered to be in the usual range if it is less than 105 percent.

It is important to review multiple years of ratios to note trends. NAIC analysis of insolvent insurers indicates that most such insurers reported increasing liabilities to liquid asset ratios in the years immediately before insolvency. When this ratio is above the satisfactory range, it could indicate that the

EXHIBIT 13-9

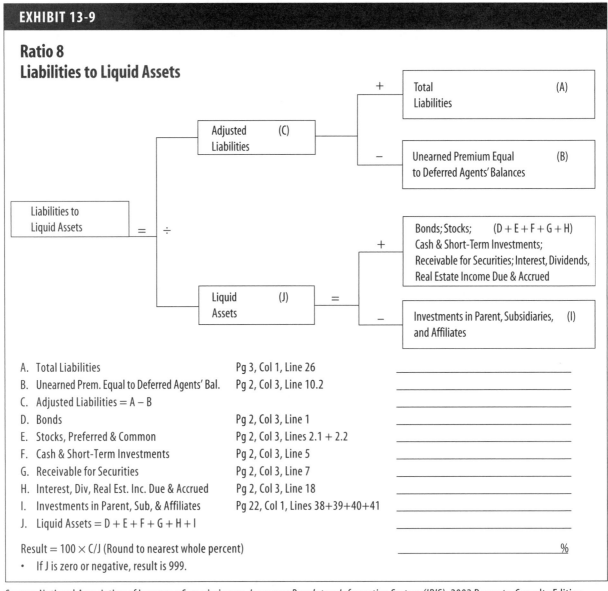

Ratio 8
Liabilities to Liquid Assets

A. Total Liabilities   Pg 3, Col 1, Line 26
B. Unearned Prem. Equal to Deferred Agents' Bal. Pg 2, Col 3, Line 10.2
C. Adjusted Liabilities = A − B
D. Bonds   Pg 2, Col 3, Line 1
E. Stocks, Preferred & Common   Pg 2, Col 3, Lines 2.1 + 2.2
F. Cash & Short-Term Investments   Pg 2, Col 3, Line 5
G. Receivable for Securities   Pg 2, Col 3, Line 7
H. Interest, Div, Real Est. Inc. Due & Accrued   Pg 2, Col 3, Line 18
I. Investments in Parent, Sub, & Affiliates   Pg 22, Col 1, Lines 38+39+40+41
J. Liquid Assets = D + E + F + G + H + I

Result = 100 × C/J (Round to nearest whole percent)   %
• If J is zero or negative, result is 999.

Source: National Association of Insurance Commissioners, *Insurance Regulatory Information System (IRIS)*, 2002 Property-Casualty Edition (Kansas City, Mo.: NAIC, 2002), p. 2.

insurer might face liquidity problems. A regulatory examiner would then focus on the adequacy of reserves, asset values, and the insurer's ability to meet its obligations to policyholders.

Gross Agents' Balances to Policyholders' Surplus Ratio

The ninth test in the IRIS system involves dividing agents' balances by policyholders' surplus, both as reported in the NAIC Annual Statement, with the result stated as a percent. A ratio of less than 40 percent is considered to be in the usual range.

One-Year Reserve Development to Policyholders' Surplus Ratio

The tenth test in the IRIS system is the ratio of loss development during the past year to the insurer's policyholders' surplus at the beginning of the year (or the end of the prior year). The loss development is (1) the incurred losses for all years reported at the end of the current year minus incurred losses for the latest accident year minus (2) the incurred losses for all years reported at the end of the prior year. This loss development figure is reported in Schedule P of the NAIC Annual Statement. The ratio is stated as a percent, and a ratio of less than 20 percent is considered to be in the usual range.

A high ratio on this test might indicate that the insurer's loss reserves are inadequate and that its surplus has consequently been overstated. The final two ratios also deal with the adequacy of loss reserves, indicating the importance attached to loss reserves as a factor in insurer insolvencies.

Two-Year Reserve Development to Policyholders' Surplus Ratio

The eleventh test in the IRIS system is a calculation done in the same manner as the tenth test, except the loss reserves and policyholders' surplus for the second prior year are used instead of those for the prior year. A ratio of less than 20 percent is also considered to be in the usual range.

Estimated Current Reserve Deficiency to Policyholders' Surplus Ratio

The twelfth test in the IRIS system is calculated by dividing the estimated current loss reserve deficiency by policyholders' surplus. The estimated reserve deficiency (or redundancy) is calculated by a complex formula based on the insurer's historical ratio of loss reserves to earned premiums.

A work sheet for the calculation is included in the NAIC's publication *Insurance Regulatory Information System*. This ratio is considered to be in the usual range if it is less than 25 percent.

SUMMARY

The information contained in corporate financial statements can provide invaluable insight into an insurer's operations and profitability. The primary financial ratios that property-casualty insurers use fall into the categories of capacity, liquidity, and profitability ratios.

A capacity ratio measures an insurer's ability to continue to write new policies. This ratio compares written premiums to policyholders' surplus. A liquidity ratio measures an insurer's ability to meet its obligations as they become due. The most widely used profitability ratio is the combined ratio. The components of this ratio include losses, premiums, and expenses. When an insurer's combined ratio is under 100, it indicates underwriting profitability.

The A.M. Best Company is one of the primary providers of financial analysis for the insurance industry. Best's uses numerous tests in its financial analysis, both quantitative and qualitative, to assign ratings to insurers. The results of these tests for individual companies are indicated in the *Best's Key Rating Guide*. Combined industry results can be found in *Best's Aggregates and Averages*. A.M. Best also makes available its Capital Adequacy Ratio (BCAR), which measures an insurer's capital relative to the loss exposure it assumes. Best's Ratings have been published for more than a century and are considered reliable indicators of an insurer's financial strength. A downgrade in an insurer's Best's Rating can have a substantial effect on that insurer's ability to market its products and services effectively.

Regulators are also concerned about the financial strength of insurers and particularly the solvency of insurers. The Insurance Regulatory Information System (IRIS) is a series of twelve financial tests. IRIS is not a rating system per se; rather, it is a tool designed to help regulators identify and prioritize which insurers should be reviewed further. Insurers that fall outside a usual range on three of the ratios are subject to scrutiny by state regulators. IRIS serves the public interest by helping regulators address insurers with financial problems before they impinge on the insolvent insurer's claim-paying ability.

This is the second of three chapters related to insurer financial analysis. The next chapter completes the discussion of the insurer financial topic by describing the investment strategy issues facing insurers.

CHAPTER NOTES

1. An insurer is considered to be "technically insolvent" any time its policyholders' surplus falls below minimum capitalization requirements set by the state, even though the insurer's net worth remains positive.

2. A.M. Best Company, *Best's Key Rating Guide, Property-Casualty*, United States, 2002 edition (Oldwick, N.J.: A.M. Best Company, 2002), p. viii.

3. *Best's Key Rating Guide, Property-Casualty*, United States, 2002 edition, p. viii.

4. Equity in the unearned premium reserve exists because insurers must count all written premiums as unearned *and* recognize all acquisition costs as an expense when a policy is written. The amount of acquisition expenses that are immediately recognized equals the "equity" in the unearned premium reserve.

5. *Best's Key Rating Guide, Property-Casualty*, United States, 2002 edition, p. xii.

6. National Association of Insurance Commissioners, *Insurance Regulatory Information System (IRIS)*, 2002 Property-Casualty Edition (Kansas City, Mo.: NAIC, 2002), p. 2.

7. *Insurance Regulatory Information System (IRIS)*, 2002 Property-Casualty Edition, p. 2.

EXHIBIT 13A-1

Summary of Financial Ratios

$$\text{Capacity ratio} = \frac{\text{Net written premiums}}{\text{Policyholders' surplus}}$$

$$\text{Liquidity ratio} = \frac{\text{Cash} + \text{invested assets (market value)}}{\text{Unearned premium reserve} + \text{Loss and loss adjustment reserves}}$$

Profitability Ratios

$$\text{Loss ratio} = \frac{\text{Incurred losses and loss adjustment expenses}}{\text{Earned premiums}}$$

$$\text{Expense ratio (Financial basis)} = \frac{\text{Expenses incurred}}{\text{Earned premiums}}$$

$$\text{Expense ratio (Trade basis)} = \frac{\text{Expenses incurred}}{\text{Written premiums}}$$

$$\text{Combined ratio (Financial basis)} = \text{Loss ratio} + \text{Expense ratio (financial basis)}$$

$$\text{Combined ratio (Trade basis)} = \text{Loss ratio} + \text{Expense ratio (trade basis)}$$

$$\text{Operating ratio} = \text{Combined ratio} - \text{Investment income ratio}$$

$$\text{Investment income ratio} = \frac{\text{Net investment income}}{\text{Earned premiums}}$$

$$\text{Investment earnings ratio} = \frac{\text{Net investment income}}{\text{Average admitted assets}}$$

$$\text{Investment profit ratio} = \frac{\text{Total investment profit (loss)}}{\text{Average admitted assets}}$$

$$\text{Return on net worth ratio} = \frac{\text{Net income}}{\text{Policyholders' surplus}}$$

$$\text{Earnings per share} = \frac{\text{Net income}}{\substack{\text{Weighted average no. of common shares} \\ \text{outstanding during the accounting period}}}$$

Chapter 14

Your Learning

Insurer Financial Management

After learning the content of this chapter, you should be able to:

- Describe the investment strategy issues faced by insurers.

- Describe the constraints imposed on insurer assets and investments.

- Describe the issues involved in managing an insurer's bond and underwriting portfolios.

- Explain how case reserves, as well as the IBNR reserve, are established.

- Describe the techniques used to analyze loss reserves.

- Explain how the NAIC's Risk-Based Capital system operates.

Develop Your Perspective

What are the main topics covered in the chapter?

This chapter describes the important financial management activities of insurers, including investment strategy, loss reserve analysis and verification, and the Risk-Based Capital requirements for insurers.

Consider the financial management activities of an insurer.

- What factors constrain insurer investments?

- What challenges do insurers face in managing bond and underwriting portfolios?

Why is it important to learn about these topics?

The financial management of an insurer is crucial to its ability to effectively pay claims and expenses, invest to build financial strength, provide a return to investors, and offer services to policyholders.

Evaluate the necessity of financial management activities as they are described in this chapter.

- What would the consequences be for an insurer if it failed to perform any of the activities?

- Why is accurate loss reserving an important component of insurer financial management?

How can you use what you will learn?

Judge your own company's financial management actions.

- What financial management activities and methods are applied?

- Who in the organization performs these activities?

Chapter 14

Insurer Financial Management

This chapter begins with a discussion of insurer investment strategy—in particular, the legal and business constraints insurers face in pursuing an investment strategy. In keeping with their conservative and consistent approach to protecting insurer solvency, regulators are the primary source of constraints imposed on insurer investment practices. These constraints take two main forms: asset restrictions and investment limitations. Insurers are permitted to show only certain assets on their balance sheets and are limited in the types of investments they can hold. To achieve diversification in insurer investment portfolios, regulators also restrict how much an insurer can hold in any single investment.

The chapter also reviews important issues regarding insurers' management of their bond and underwriting portfolios. Bonds are the preferred investment vehicle for insurers because most carry fixed maturity dates and fixed interest payment schedules that provide cash flows needed for loss payments. The maturity schedule and face amounts of bonds in the insurer's portfolio should be aligned with the insurer's expected cash flow needs.

Because loss reserves are usually the largest liabilities on an insurer's balance sheet, accurate loss reserving is critical. Therefore, this chapter also addresses how insurers evaluate their loss reserves. A discussion of accident-year, report-year, and loss ratio reserve analysis and verification techniques is provided.

The final section of this chapter reviews the National Association of Insurance Commissioners' risk-based capital requirements and the Risk-Based Capital (RBC) Model Act. Policyholders' surplus is assets minus liabilities, and regulatory requirements are imposed on policyholders' surplus. Insurers must maintain capital (surplus) at least equal to minimum prescribed levels that depend on how much risk they bear. The risk-based capital requirements consider not only underwriting risk, but also asset risk and reserve risk—that is, all potential effects on an insurer's policyholders' surplus.

INVESTMENT STRATEGY

Financial managers of insurers share many of the same concerns of financial managers of non-insurers. Both must create and monitor budgets, forecast cash and capital needs, pursue receivables, maintain bank relationships, meet payrolls, and file tax documents and payments. However, financial management of insurers is different because of admitted asset definitions and investment restrictions, as well as the risk-based capital requirements imposed by state regulation.

Below is an abstract balance sheet formula for an insurer:

Assets (primarily bonds and stocks) –

Liabilities (primarily loss reserves and unearned premiums) =

Policyholders' surplus.

This balance sheet formula indicates that, if all else is held equal, policyholders' surplus will shrink if assets shrink or if liabilities grow. Preserving and increasing policyholders' surplus is an important goal for every insurer. State regulations also impose requirements for policyholders' surplus levels. In addition, the goal of every business is to maximize the firm's value. Although the accounting item "policyholders' surplus" is not equivalent to an insurer's value, virtually any result that legitimately increases policyholders' surplus also increases its value.

Because the predominant assets for insurers are investment securities, investment strategy is essential to asset growth. Underwriting operations are an insurer's source of assets, along with paid-in and retained capital. Unearned premiums, which are readily determinable, are among the insurer's primary liabilities. Loss reserves are another primary liability; however, they are not readily determinable. In fact, they are the balance sheet item most subject to estimation error.

Insurance premiums provide immediate cash inflows to an insurer. In return for policyholders' paying those premiums, an insurer provides a financial guarantee to pay covered losses when they occur. The delay between the receipt of the premiums and the payment of losses gives insurers the opportunity to invest those cash inflows and earn a positive return. A sound investment strategy seeks to earn the highest possible return for a given level of risk or, alternatively, to minimize the risk associated with earning a given expected return. However, this strategy cannot be pursued in isolation. Rather, the investment strategy must support the needs of other functional areas, and it must explicitly recognize constraints imposed by shareholders, regulators, or other government authorities.

Integrating investment strategy with the strategies of other functional areas is particularly important for insurers. In addition to income, investment earnings are a primary source of funds available to insurers to pay losses. Therefore, the investment portfolio must be structured to provide sufficient earnings and cash flow to pay losses as they come due. Generally, property losses tend to be settled quickly, with most loss payments being made within two years. In contrast, some liability losses could be outstanding for ten or more years before they are fully settled. Consequently, an insurer's management strategy must coordinate investment and underwriting decisions.

Constraints on Insurer Investments

All states regulate insurer investments. This regulation helps to ensure insurer solvency and liquidity so that, ultimately, all policyholder claims can be paid. State regulation effectively mandates that insurers hold investment portfolios that are prudent (some would even say quite conservative) and well diversified.

Excerpts from the NAIC's Investments of Insurers Model (Defined Standards Version) are shown in Exhibit 14-1. This Model Act has *not* been enacted in most states because most states have similar laws that are more detailed and complex. Yet, the Model Act illustrates how state regulation promotes prudent and well-diversified portfolios, through asset restrictions and through investment limitations.

Asset Restrictions

While insurers can invest in a wide variety of assets, only certain assets are permitted to be included on an insurer's balance sheet. Any other investment by an insurer must be assigned zero value on the insurer's balance sheet, a more-than-sufficient incentive to avoid large investments in nonadmitted assets. Generally, permitted investments for insurers include money market instruments; high-quality investments that mature in less than one year, such as U.S. Treasury bills and commercial paper; bonds of investment grade or better (issued by the U.S. Treasury, state governments, certain municipalities, or credit-worthy private corporations); common stock; preferred stock; real estate loans (mortgages); and real estate. In many states, insurers must invest an amount equal to their required capital (or required capital plus certain other reserves) in an even narrower list of permitted investments.

Investment Restrictions

As previously mentioned, an insurer's investment strategy can be stated as seeking to earn the highest possible return for a given level of risk or, alternatively, to minimize the risk associated with earning a given expected return. Compared to undiversified portfolios (or insufficiently diversified portfolios), properly diversified portfolios can be expected to produce consistently higher returns for a given level of risk or lower risk for a given level of return. The mechanics of designing a properly diversified portfolio are beyond the scope of this text, but such a portfolio requires dozens of different investments.

EXHIBIT 14-1

Investments of Insurers Model Act (Defined Standards Version)

Section 7. Authorized Classes of Investments

The following classes of investments may be counted [as admitted assets] whether they are made directly or as a participant in a partnership, joint venture or limited liability company:

A. Cash in the direct possession of the insurer or on deposit with a financial institution regulated by any federal or state agency of the United States;

B. Bonds, debt-like preferred stock and other evidences of indebtedness of governmental units in the United States or Canada, or the instrumentalities of the governmental units, or private business entities domiciled in the United States or Canada, including asset-backed securities and SVO listed mutual funds;

C. Loans secured by mortgages, trust deeds, or other security interests in real property located in the United States or Canada or secured by insurance against default issued by a government insurance corporation of the United States or Canada or by an insurer authorized to do business in this state;

D. Common stock of equity-like preferred stock or equity interests in any United States or Canadian Business entity, or shares of mutual funds registered with the Securities and Exchange Commission of the United States under the Investment Company Act of 1940, other than Securities Valuation Office listed mutual funds;

E. Real property necessary for the convenient transaction of the insurer's business;

F. Real property, together with the fixtures, furniture, furnishings and equipment pertaining thereto in the United States or Canada, which produces or after suitable improvement can reasonably be expected to produce substantial income;

G. Loans, securities, or other investments of the types described in Subsections A to F of this section in countries other than the United States and Canada;

H. Bonds or other evidences of indebtedness of international development organizations of which the United States is a member;

I. Loans upon the security of the insurer's own policies in amounts that are adequately secured by the policies and that in no case exceed the surrender values of the policies;

J. Tangible personal property under contract of sale or lease under which contractual payments may reasonably be expected to return the principal of and provide earnings on the investment within its anticipated useful life;

K. Other investments the commissioner authorizes by regulation; and

L. Investments not otherwise permitted by this section, and not specifically prohibited by statute, to the extent of not more than five percent (5%) of the first $500,000,000 of the insurer's admitted assets plus ten percent (10%) of the insurer's admitted assets exceeding $500,000,000.

Section 8. Limitations Generally Applicable

A. Class Limitations. For the purposes of [determining admitted assets], the following limitations on classes of investments apply:

   (1) Investments authorized by Section 7B, and investments authorized by Section 7G that are of the types described in Section 7B;

      (a) The aggregate amount of medium and lower grade investments, twenty percent (20%) of its admitted assets;

      (b) The aggregate amount of lower grade investments, ten percent (10%) of its admitted assets;

      (c) The aggregate amount of investments rated 5 or 6 by the SVO, five percent (5%) of its admitted assets;

      (d) The aggregate amount of investments rated 6 by the SVO, one percent (1%) of its admitted assets; or

      (e) The aggregate amount of medium and lower grade investments that receive as cash income less than the equivalent yield for Treasury issues with a comparative average life, one percent (1%) of its admitted assets.

   (2) Investments authorized by Section 7C, forty-five percent (45%) of admitted assets in the case of life insurers and twenty-five percent (25%) of admitted assets in the case of non-life insurers;

   (3) Investments authorized by Section 7D, other than subsidiaries of the types authorized under [cite applicable provisions of holding company law] twenty percent (20%) of admitted assets in the case of life insurers and twenty-five percent (25%) of admitted assets in the case of non-life insurers;

   (4) Investments authorized by Section 7E, ten percent (10%) of admitted assets;

   (5) Investments authorized by Section 7F, twenty percent (20%) of admitted assets in the case of life insurers, and ten percent (10%) of admitted assets in the case of non-life insurers;

   (6) Investments authorized by Section 7G, twenty percent (20%) of admitted assets;

   (7) Investments authorized by Section 7H, two percent (2%) of admitted assets;

   (8) Investments authorized by Section 7J, two percent (2%) of admitted assets.

B. Individual limitations. For purposes of determining [admitted assets], securities of a single issuer and its affiliates, other than the government of the United States and subsidiaries authorized under [cite applicable provisions of holding company law], shall not exceed three percent (3%) of admitted assets in the case of life insurers, and five percent (5%) in the case of non-life insurers. Investments in the voting securities of a depository institution, or any company that controls a depository institution, shall not exceed five percent (5%) of the insurer's admitted assets.

Source: National Association of Insurance Commissioners' *Model Laws, Regulations, and Guidelines,* Vol. II (Minneapolis, Minn.: NIARS Corporation, 2003), pp. 283-7–283-8 and 283-9. Published by NIARS Corporation under the auspices of the National Association of Insurance Commissioners.

The primary goals of state regulation of insurer investments are to ensure liquidity and to ensure solvency for the sake of policyholders. Three investment restrictions help ensure that insurers have well-diversified portfolios that support the goals of liquidity and solvency:

1. Insurers can only invest up to a certain percentage of their assets in many of the permitted investments. For example, an insurer might be allowed to invest only up to 20 percent of its assets in common stocks. Any investment in common stock beyond such a restriction would result in the assets' being nonadmitted.

2. Insurers are typically restricted in how much of their assets can be invested in any single investment. For example, an insurer might be allowed to invest no more than 5 percent of its assets in a single investment, such as the AAA-rated bonds of the XYZ Corporation. No matter how high the quality of XYZ's bonds might be, an insurer cannot invest more than 5 percent of its assets in such a single investment.

3. Insurers are restricted in the percentage of another company's securities they can own. For example, insurers cannot own more than 5 percent of the common stock of any particular company (other than subsidiaries and affiliates). This last restriction ensures that insurers remain passive financial investors in companies in other industries and do not become active managers or owners.

The overall effect of the investment restrictions on insurers is to encourage predominant investment in high-quality bonds. As explained next, investment in bonds helps enable insurers to meet their cash needs to satisfy policyholder claims.

Issues in Managing Bond and Underwriting Portfolios

Bond portfolio management is particularly important for property-casualty insurers. Generally, investments in bonds account for more than 60 percent of insurers' admitted assets. Unlike equity investments in common or preferred stocks, bonds, which are debt securities, have a definite maturity date—a point in time when the issuer must repay the bond's principal (face) amount. Although paying cash dividends on stocks is at the discretion of the company's board of directors, interest payments on bonds are a contractual obligation that must be met according to a predetermined schedule. These two characteristics of debt securities, a fixed maturity date and a fixed interest payment schedule, are particularly valuable to insurers that rely on periodic and recurring cash inflows to pay losses.

An important goal of portfolio management in general and bond portfolio management in particular is to structure the portfolio so that the face amounts and maturity schedule of investment cash inflows correspond to the firm's expected cash outflows. For property-casualty insurers, the face amount and maturity schedule of expected cash outflows are determined largely by the composition of the underwriting portfolio. An insurer's underwriting portfolio is typically viewed as the collection of insurance policies issued by that insurer and currently in effect. Alternatively, the underwriting portfolio can be viewed as that collection of policies issued by the insurer that generate cash outlays in the future. This collection of policies consists primarily of current effective policies but also includes any past policies that will still generate claim payments. Because property losses tend to be settled relatively fast, short-term investments are needed to ensure that adequate funds are available when property claims must be settled. In contrast, some liability losses could be outstanding for many years before the claims are fully settled. Consequently, at least a portion of the insurer's assets can be invested in long-term securities that typically provide higher levels of investment earnings than do short-term securities.

Investing in bonds exposes an insurer to certain risks. The first source of risk is credit risk (also called repayment risk or default risk). **Credit risk** refers to the risk that customers or other creditors will fail to make promised payments as they come due. Obligations backed by the U.S. government are considered to have no default risk and are commonly referred to as "risk free." All debt issued by corporations has an element of default risk, though it might be small for well-established companies. Investors do, however, require a risk premium in the form of higher interest rates to hold these securities; the higher the risk of default, the higher the risk premium. Because this risk is specific to an individual investor, the risk can be minimized by diversifying the bond portfolio over a large number of bond issuers.

Credit risk
The risk that customers or other creditors will fail to make promised payments as they come due.

A second source of risk is interest rate risk. **Interest rate risk** refers to risk associated with the fluctuation of a security's value because of changes in market-determined interest rates. A debt security's market value is determined by the present value of the security's cash flows (interest and principal payments). As interest rates rise, a debt security's market value declines; as interest rates decline, a debt security's market value rises. Because of the effects of compound interest, the change in price (present value of the future cash flows) caused by a change in interest rates will be greater for long-term debt securities than for short-term debt securities. Consequently, long-term debt securities expose the holder to a greater degree of interest rate risk than do short-term securities. Moreover, when bonds have the same maturity date, the bonds paying lower interest rates are typically more sensitive to changes in market interest rates than are the bonds paying higher interest rates. Interest rate risk cannot be eliminated through diversification because changes in the level of interest rates affect the prices of *all* debt securities.

Interest rate risk
The risk that a security's future value will decline because of changes in interest rates.

Cash Matching and Interest Rate Risk

To illustrate the effects of interest rate risk, suppose that an insurer specializes in writing property insurance. Based on an analysis of its underwriting portfolio, the insurer expects to make a single $1 million loss payment at the end of the year. A conservative approach would be to "cash match" the investment and underwriting portfolios by using premium revenue to purchase a bond with a face amount of $1 million that would mature at the end of the year. For simplicity, assume that the bond pays no interest during the year (a security that pays only the face amount at maturity is called a "zero-coupon bond"). If the current market rate of interest is 8 percent, the insurer will pay $925,900 (rounded) to purchase the bond (the face amount of the bond × the present value of $1 due in 1 year at 8 percent = $1 million × 0.9259). When the bond matures, the insurer will receive the $1 million face amount from the issuer and can fully settle its claims.

The effect of interest rate risk can be seen by looking at the possibility of funding the same $1 million claim payment one year from now with a ten-year bond. A $2 million face amount ten-year zero-coupon bond could be bought for approximately $926,400 today (the rounded present value of $2 million discounted at 8 percent for ten years). If interest rates do not change in the next year, the same bond in one year would be worth approximately $1 million (the rounded present value of $2 million discounted at 8 percent for nine years is $1,000,500). However, what happens if interest rates go up? If interest rates increase to 10 percent, a zero-coupon bond with nine years to maturity is worth only about $848,200. The rise in interest rates would have two effects: (1) the necessary $1 million would not be available, and (2) the value of the investment would decline.

One approach to eliminating risk is **cash matching**, which is the process of matching an investment's maturity value with the amount of expected loss payments. Cash matching is a good way to eliminate interest rate risk because an insurer needs to hold the investment only until it matures. Changes in interest rates will not matter because the insurer will not want to sell the investment in the market before it matures. However, to be effective, this approach must meet two conditions:

1. The zero-coupon bonds' maturity dates and maturity values must precisely match the expected cash outflows from the underwriting portfolio.
2. The insurer must be able to purchase enough of each type of security to match its expected claims, assuming that such bonds are available.

Realistically, both of these conditions would rarely be met, and creating such a situation would be particularly difficult for insurers with very large underwriting portfolios. Moreover, management expectations about the future movement of interest rates might encourage an intentional mismatching of bond maturities with cash flow needs. In the example of the ten-year bond, if interest rates are expected to drop from 8 percent to 6 percent by the end of the first year, the long-term bond now with nine years to maturity would be worth about $1,216,000.

Matching Investment and Liability Duration

Another definition of interest rate risk refers to the risk presented by the mismatch of investment duration and liability duration. **Portfolio immunization** (also called **asset-liability matching**) is the process of matching investment and liability duration. In the real world, most bonds pay interest on a predetermined schedule (usually every six months). Insurance loss payments are spread throughout the year and could be paid out over several years. These circumstances seriously complicate the problems associated with managing investment and underwriting portfolios.

When an investor purchases bonds that pay interest, the investor must also consider what to do with those interest payments as they are received (assuming they will not be used to pay losses). If interest payments are going to be reinvested, the investor is now exposed to a second type of interest-related risk called reinvestment risk. **Reinvestment risk** refers to the uncertainty about the rate at which periodic interest payments can be reinvested over the life of the investment. To illustrate, consider an investor who purchases a $1,000 ten-year bond that pays 10 percent interest at the end of each year. If those interest payments can be invested to earn 10 percent, the balance in the investment account would be about $1,594 when the bond matures. The investor would then receive $1,000 from the issuer of the bond at maturity and also would have the $1,594 in the investment account. If, however, interest rates fell to 8 percent just after the bond was purchased, then the investment account would grow to only $1,448. When reinvesting periodic interest payments, the investor must not only worry about the interest rates available at the time the original investment is made, but also about the prevailing interest rates when each interest payment is received.

Reinvestment risk
The risk that the rate at which periodic interest payments can be reinvested over the life of the investment will be unfavorable.

Techniques have been developed to help portfolio managers control interest rate risk. Although an investment's maturity date gives some indication of its sensitivity to changes in interest rates (a change in market interest rates will have a greater effect the longer the term of the bond), duration is generally accepted as a better measure of interest rate sensitivity. **Duration** is a measure of a security's weighted average life. Bond duration measures the time it takes for the present value of the bond's cash inflows to equal the bond's price. Three important characteristics of duration should be noted:

Duration
A measure of a security's weighted average life.

1. The greater the duration, the more sensitive the security is to interest rate changes.
2. The duration of a zero-coupon bond is always equal to its time to maturity (when the face amount becomes due).
3. The duration of a bond that pays interest over its life will always be less than its time to maturity.

The concept of duration can also be applied to underwriting portfolios. The duration of an underwriting portfolio is the average time-weighted present value of the cash outlays that portfolio will require. By knowing the duration of the underwriting portfolio, a bond portfolio manager can either invest in one or more securities that have the same duration as the underwriting portfolio or combine several securities with different durations into a portfolio that has, in the aggregate, the same duration as the underwriting portfolio. When the durations of the underwriting and investment portfolio are matched, the portfolio is said to be *immunized* against changes in interest rates. (Note that another definition of interest rate risk is the risk presented by the mismatch of investment duration and liability duration.)

Unfortunately, matching the duration of the bond portfolio and the underwriting portfolio is a complex task. On the investment side, a change in interest rates affects the bond portfolio's duration. Theoretically, the composition of the bond portfolio should be changed every time interest rates change in order to keep the duration of the bond and underwriting portfolios properly matched. Furthermore, duration across assets (also liabilities) is not additive. A portfolio containing two bonds, each with a duration of twenty years, will not necessarily have a twenty-year duration.[1]

On the liability side, any changes in the insurer's mix of business would also indicate a need to rebalance the bond portfolio. For example, an increased emphasis on underwriting liability insurance would increase the duration of the underwriting portfolio.

Perfectly matching investments and liabilities on a continuous basis is not a realistic goal. Investments cannot be bought and sold without cost. The transactions costs associated with rebalancing a portfolio must be weighed against the risks of holding an imperfectly matched portfolio. Investment matching is especially challenging for insurers because the future cash outflows associated with the underwriting portfolio are not known with certainty and must be estimated. Nevertheless, insurers use the concept of duration to help coordinate asset and liability cash flows.

LOSS RESERVING

Loss reserves are generally the largest liability on the insurer's balance sheet and represent the amount the insurer would have to pay for all outstanding claims. Accurate loss reserving is crucial. Loss reserving consists of analyzing and verifying already established case reserves for losses that have been reported but not yet paid, and establishing reserves for losses that have been incurred but have not yet been reported (IBNR).

Case Reserves

Case reserves are amounts established that represent the estimated loss value of each individual reported claim. The claim department usually sets these reserves, but the actuarial department might assist with some complex claims. Three methods, with variations of each, are used to establish case reserves: (1) the average-value method, (2) the judgment method, and (3) the tabular method. These methods were discussed in a previous chapter.

Selecting the appropriate case reserving method depends primarily on the type of insurance. Sometimes, more than one method can be used for the same type of insurance. For example, some insurers might use an average value reserve to estimate the losses for liability claims when they are first reported. Insurers then adjust that reserve upward or downward, based on judgment or the tabular method, as more information becomes available.

IBNR Reserve

Insurers are required by law and good accounting practice to establish reserves for losses that reasonably can be assumed to have been incurred but not yet reported, the **IBNR reserve**. This reserve can have three components:

1. Reserves for unreported losses
2. Reserves for losses that have been reported but for which the established case reserves are inadequate
3. Reserves for losses that have been settled and then reopened

The sum of the first two reserve components is called the total IBNR reserve. Of course, analysts usually cannot identify the specific losses for which inadequate case reserves have been established or the settled losses that will be reopened, nor can they determine the amount of inadequacy for specific losses.

Because the insurer does not know either the number or the amount of such unreported losses or case reserve deficiencies, the IBNR reserve must be estimated. There are two possible approaches to such estimates. The estimating methods are:

1. Estimate the ultimate total amount of incurred losses for the period and subtract the paid losses and case reserves for reported losses. The remainder is the total IBNR reserve.
2. Estimate the pure IBNR reserve independently, without considering the case reserves. Then, separately calculate the reserve deficiencies to determine the total IBNR reserve. This method requires that historic loss data files include the loss's occurrence date and the claim's report date. Such data make it possible to determine the proportion of incurred losses, both in number and amount, reported after some specified cutoff date (such as December 31) in past years. A similar proportion of unreported losses for the year(s) in question is assumed. Of course, if environmental changes occur that could lengthen or shorten the reporting period, appropriate adjustments must be made. For example, enacting a shorter statute of limitations might cause some losses to be reported more quickly than indicated by historical data.

Some actuaries use both methods when sufficient data are available. If the two methods produce comparable total IBNR reserve estimates, then the level of confidence in those estimates is increased. If the estimates are not comparable, further analysis is needed to determine why and which estimate, if either, is more likely to be accurate.

For some types of insurance, the total IBNR reserve can be a substantial part of an insurer's total liabilities. Consequently, insurers should take great care in estimating the IBNR reserve.

IBNR reserve
A reserve established for losses that reasonably can be assumed to have been incurred but not yet reported.

Loss Reserve Analysis Techniques

Insurers maintain two loss reserving systems. The first reserving system is the case reserve system, which focuses on individual losses and which is primarily the claim department's responsibility. Ideally, the case reserving system should provide a reserve for each reported claim equal to the amount required to settle that claim. This ideal is seldom achieved and is probably impossible to achieve for most types of insurance.

The second reserving system is the actuarial reserving system or the bulk reserving system. Its principal purpose is to determine the insurer's claim liabilities for accounting purposes. This system is concerned with the insurer's total liability for all outstanding claims and not with the amount of reserve for individual claims.

The purpose of actuarial loss reserve analysis and verification is to determine whether the loss and loss adjustment expense reserves established by both these systems adequately cover the losses and loss adjustment expenses that have been incurred but have not yet been paid. Such analysis and verification might be undertaken by management as part of management control or by the insurer's auditors to determine whether the insurer's financial statements accurately indicate its financial condition and performance. It might also be undertaken to comply with regulatory requirements. The NAIC Annual Statement instructions require insurers to have their loss reserves certified by an actuary or another qualified person. Signing such opinions or certifications creates an exposure to potential professional liability claims. Consequently, such opinions or certifications ordinarily would not be provided without carefully analyzing the reserves.

Loss reserve review techniques analyze past patterns to estimate future case reserves. Consequently, a change in reserving practices, if it affects the pattern of case reserves, will result in an error in estimating future case reserves unless the change is detected and appropriate adjustments are made.

For example, a change in case reserving practices that increased case reserves could, if undetected, cause the analyst to assume that case reserves, having been inadequate in the past, are still inadequate. Actually, of course, the changed practices could result in reserves that are now adequate or even excessive.

This chapter describes two mathematical techniques for analyzing loss reserves: the accident-year loss analysis technique and the report-year loss analysis technique. However, the analysis is not an entirely mathematical process. The mathematical results must be evaluated carefully using nonmathematical information and common sense.

Accident-Year Loss Analysis Technique

The first technique for analyzing loss reserves is the accident-year loss analysis technique. This technique uses loss triangles (see Chapter 7,

Exhibit 7-8). Each line of data represents one accident year, with the entries read from left to right showing how losses for that accident year developed over time.

The number of accident years included in a loss development triangle for ratemaking purposes depends on the number of years in the experience period used for ratemaking purposes. One line appears for each year in the experience period. However, the number of lines in a triangle used for loss reserve analysis is determined primarily by the length of the delay between the occurrence of a loss and the time it is settled. Ideally, one line appears for each accident year for which one or more reported claims remain open or for which one or more unreported claims are expected to be reported.

As a practical matter, it might be necessary to combine very old years with very few claims outstanding into a single line in the triangle. For example, the triangle might include a separate line for each of the past ten accident years plus a single line containing the combined data for the eleventh year and all previous years.

Exhibit 14-2 shows the initial accident-year loss triangle used to analyze loss reserves for the period shown. The exhibit illustrates the dollar amount of incurred losses as reported for each accident year at various stages of development: twelve months, twenty-four months, and so on. Recall that incurred losses include both paid losses and case reserves. The losses are presumed to be fully developed at ninety-six months and do not change thereafter. Exhibit 14-2 differs from Exhibit 7-9 only in that it includes more accident years (ten plus a line for prior years instead of five years).

Exhibit 14-3 shows loss development multipliers calculated from the data in Exhibit 14-2. The multipliers for each accident year were calculated by dividing the amount of losses for one development period from Exhibit 14-2 by the amount of losses on the same line for the development period immediately prior. For example, the multiplier for development from twelve months to twenty-four months for 1997 was calculated by dividing the losses at twenty-four months of development ($66,968,794) by the losses reported at twelve months of development ($41,773,849). The resulting loss development multiplier is 1.603. The other multipliers were calculated similarly.

The figures on the line labeled "Mean" in Exhibit 14-3 are the means of the multipliers above them. The figures on the line labeled "Selected" are the ones chosen by the analyst to calculate the loss development factors on the line below. In this instance, the analyst has chosen to use the mean values without modification. In an actual analysis, the selected values might vary from the means. For example, if the accident-year multipliers indicated an increasing trend, the analyst might use selected values higher than the means. If the data were liability loss data from a state that had just shortened its statute of limitations, the analyst might use values higher than the average for previous years and lower than average values for later years, indicating that future losses are expected to be reported earlier than in previous years.

EXHIBIT 14-2

Loss Triangle: Reported Incurred Losses—Accident-Year Method Hypothetical Data

Accident Year	Months of Development							
	12	24	36	48	60	72	84	96
1992 & Prior	$279,554,361	$487,695,483	$498,712,348	$501,462,834	$507,832,541	$512,664,798	$515,447,632	$516,112,436
1993	26,443,738	44,658,934	46,112,869	47,355,873	48,586,914	48,967,324	49,116,736	49,214,873
1994	29,163,357	48,995,673	51,444,538	57,579,832	53,461,854	53,892,346	54,213,128	54,304,736
1995	32,561,477	54,564,783	52,668,598	58,234,768	58,977,654	59,541,632	59,843,486	59,925,726
1996	36,112,748	59,879,765	62,861,528	64,146,732	64,981,374	65,476,497	65,879,324	
1997	41,773,849	66,968,794	70,981,932	73,859,431	74,779,541	75,417,614		
1998	50,174,593	83,947,351	87,979,482	89,875,483	91,463,572			
1999	57,673,841	93,258,873	98,998,237	101,443,218				
2000	63,688,419	105,548,765	110,774,315					
2001	67,448,941	112,234,985						
2002	73,814,284							

EXHIBIT 14-3

Loss Triangle: Accident-Year Method
Hypothetical Data

	Months of Development						
Accident Year	12–24	24–36	36–48	48–60	60–72	72–84	84–96
1992 & Prior	1.745	1.023	1.006	1.013	1.010	1.005	1.001
1993	1.689	1.033	1.027	1.026	1.008	1.003	1.002
1994	1.680	1.050	1.022	1.017	1.008	1.006	1.002
1995	1.676	1.057	1.010	1.013	1.010	1.005	1.001
1996	1.658	1.050	1.020	1.013	1.008	1.006	
1997	1.603	1.060	1.041	1.012	1.009		
1998	1.673	1.048	1.022	1.018			
1999	1.617	1.062	1.025				
2000	1.657	1.050					
2001	1.664						
Mean	1.666	1.048	1.021	1.016	1.009	1.005	1.002
Selected	1.666	1.048	1.021	1.016	1.009	1.005	1.002
Ultimate	1.840	1.105	1.054	1.032	1.016	1.007	1.002

The ultimate development factors are shown on the bottom line of Exhibit 14-3. Ultimate development factors are factors that can be used to project immature loss data to full maturity. The ultimate development factors for months after ninety-six are not shown in Exhibit 14-3. However, all of those factors are 1.00, indicating that the losses are fully developed at ninety-six months, and no additional changes are expected subsequently. The ultimate development factor for eighty-four months of development (1.002) is simply the selected value from the previous line. For each of the other periods shown, the ultimate development factor was calculated by multiplying the selected value for that period by the ultimate development factor for the next period.

Exhibit 14-4 shows the ultimate development factor for each twelve-month period from twelve months to ninety-six months and later. Exhibit 14-5 shows the ultimate projected losses for each year in Exhibit 14-2. These projected ultimate losses were calculated by multiplying the reported amount of losses for the latest period in Exhibit 14-2 by the appropriate ultimate loss development factor from Exhibit 14-4.

EXHIBIT 14-4

Ultimate Loss Development Factors: Accident-Year Method Hypothetical Data

Accident Year	Ultimate Loss Development Factors
1992 & Prior	1.000
1993	1.000
1994	1.000
1995	1.000
1996	1.002
1997	1.007
1998	1.016
1999	1.032
2000	1.054
2001	1.105
2002	1.840

The projected ultimate losses in Exhibit 14-5 include both paid losses and reserves, including total IBNR reserves. The total loss reserve, including total IBNR, can be calculated by subtracting the total paid losses of $972,213,944 (not shown in the tables) from the total projected losses of $1,395,724,850, shown at the bottom of Exhibit 14-5.

The total IBNR reserve can be calculated by subtracting the total reported losses of $1,310,585,083 from the total projected ultimate losses of $1,395,724,850. Exhibit 14-5 shows this calculation along with the total IBNR for each of the accident years.

The loss triangles in this chapter include all reported claims, both closed and open. Some actuaries also use closed-claim loss triangles in loss reserve analysis. Closed-claim loss triangles are constructed and interpreted exactly as are open-claim loss triangles. The only difference is that closed-claim loss triangles use only data for closed claims, whereas the open-claim loss triangles also use data for open claims. Using closed-claim loss triangles eliminates the effects of errors in estimating case reserves. However, the delay between a loss occurrence and the closing of a claim can be substantially longer than the delay between a loss occurrence and the opening of a claim. Consequently, the number of months needed for finalizing ultimate loss development in closed-claim loss triangles is greater than in open-claim loss triangles. The extended period for finalizing ultimate loss development increases the chance of error in interpreting results.

EXHIBIT 14-5

Developed Losses: Accident-Year Method—Hypothetical Data

Accident Year	Reported Incurred Losses	Loss Development Factors	Projected Ultimate Losses	Total IBNR	IBNR as % of Total
1992 & Prior	$ 516,112,436	1.000	$ 516,112,436	$ 0	.000
1993	49,214,873	1.000	49,214,873	0	.000
1994	54,304,736	1.000	54,304,736	0	.000
1995	59,925,726	1.000	59,925,726	0	.000
1996	65,879,324	1.002	66,011,083	131,759	.200
1997	75,417,614	1.007	75,945,537	527,923	.695
1998	91,463,572	1.016	92,926,989	1,463,417	1.575
1999	101,443,218	1.032	104,689,401	3,246,183	3.101
2000	110,774,315	1.054	116,756,128	5,981,813	5.123
2001	112,234,985	1.105	124,019,658	11,784,673	9.502
2002	73,814,284	1.840	135,818,283	62,003,999	45.652
Totals	$1,310,585,083		$1,395,724,850	$85,139,767	6.100

Loss triangles for the number of claims are constructed similarly to loss triangles for loss amounts. The projected ultimate number of claims can then be cross-checked against the projected ultimate amount of losses to ensure consistency. Actuaries make many such cross-checks when certifying loss reserves.

Report-Year Loss Analysis Technique

The second technique for analyzing loss reserves is the report-year loss analysis technique. The loss triangles discussed to this point dealt with accident-year statistics. Loss data, either number of claims or dollar amount of losses, are grouped by accident year, the year in which the loss occurred. This section discusses a technique in which the loss data are grouped by report year, the year in which the loss was first reported to the insurer. This technique can be used to calculate the reserve for case reserve deficiencies.

For some types of property insurance, such as auto physical damage, a large majority of claims are reported in the same year in which the loss occurred. For those types of insurance, using the report-year technique for loss reserve analysis provides little additional information compared to the information provided by the accident-year loss analysis.

However, the majority of claims for long-tailed liability insurance, such as medical malpractice, could be reported to the insurer in years after the year in which the loss occurred. Reporting such claims to the insurer ten years or more after the loss occurred is not unusual. Claims included in *report-year* 2002, for example, would be quite different from those reported in *accident-year* 2002.

The report-year technique deals with a constant number of claims in the portfolio. The dollar amount of claims within the portfolio can change as claims are settled or case reserves are amended, and claims can move from being open to being closed. However, the total number of claims remains constant. Because only reported claims are considered, the exact number of claims in the portfolio is known on the last day of the report year and does not change thereafter.

Portfolio constancy is both a strength and a weakness of the report-year technique. The technique's strength is that it permits the analyst to follow the development of a specific group of claims and to test the accuracy of early case reserving. This is not possible with the accident-year technique because in that technique, new claims are added to the portfolio as they are reported to the insurer.

Portfolio constancy permits testing of only part of the total IBNR reserve: that part consisting of case reserve inadequacies for reported losses. However, the weakness of portfolio constancy is that it does not provide information needed to determine the amount of reserve required for losses that have been incurred but have not yet been reported to the insurer, the pure IBNR reserve. Consequently, the report-year technique cannot be used as the sole technique for loss reserve analysis. It can, however, be used as an important technique to supplement the insight gained from the accident-year technique.

Adequacy of Case Reserves

The adequacy of case reserves is sometimes difficult to determine, especially for a relatively new insurer writing long-tailed liability insurance. Because long-tail liability claims can have excessive reserves, this pattern of settlement that emerges can give the appearance that all case reserves are excessive, especially for an insurer that has not been in business long enough to settle a representative number of larger, more complex claims.

In several cases, this phenomenon has misled the management of new insurers into believing their reserves were adequate or even excessive when, in fact, they were grossly inadequate. The accident-year loss triangles, used alone, might not reveal this problem. Using the report-year technique can assist in preventing this problem if sufficient data are available.

Although the elements normally are not identified separately, the IBNR reserve reported in the NAIC Annual Statement includes two elements. The first element is claims incurred but not yet reported, the pure IBNR reserve. The second element is the deficiency (or perhaps redundancy) of the case reserves for reported claims. The report-year technique does not estimate the first of these elements of the IBNR reserve, only the second element.

Report-year triangles can be constructed using the number of claims as well as the amount of losses. However, such triangles are not as useful in the report-year technique as they are in the accident-year technique because the total number of claims for a given report year does not change in subsequent development. A triangle could be used to compile a distribution of lag times between reporting and settling claims.

The report-year technique alone is inadequate to analyze loss reserves. However, it is useful when combined with the accident-year technique. Because the report-year technique deals with a constant number of claims, it is an excellent technique for measuring the past performance of the case-reserving process. Judgment must be used to determine whether past performance indicates present performance.

RISK-BASED CAPITAL REQUIREMENTS

An insurer's surplus, or capital, provides a cushion that protects policyholders against an insurer's poor financial results. In the event of unexpectedly poor financial results, an insurer's capital enables it still to meet its obligations to policyholders and other claimants. How much capital should an insurer have? From the perspective of a policyholder or claimant, the more capital, the better. However, constant tension exists between the desire for ample capital and management's desire to minimize expenses.

Regulators specify how much capital is enough and how much is too little. Minimum capital requirements exist for starting an insurer. These requirements vary by type of insurance and by state. However, these requirements are too low for insurers writing any significant volume of business. Consequently, they serve only as bare minimums, not as benchmarks for sound, ongoing businesses.

Net-written-premiums-to-surplus requirements are one type of capital requirement. Prohibiting an insurer from writing more than $3 of premium for every $1 of policyholders' surplus is simultaneously a requirement to have at least $1 of surplus for every $3 of written premiums. Under this test, an insurer must have at least one-third the amount of its written premiums as capital. (Therefore, once written premiums become large enough, this test is more germane and the legal minimum-capital requirements for start-ups quickly become irrelevant.)

Nevertheless, the net-written-premiums-to-surplus requirement has limited value as a standard for capital adequacy for two reasons. First, writing more than $3 of premium for each $1 of surplus is not strictly prohibited. Second, the only type of risk to an insurer's financial strength that the requirement addresses is underwriting risk, the risk that premium will be insufficient to cover losses and expenses.

Risk-Based Capital System

The NAIC has developed a **risk-based capital (RBC) system** to determine the minimum amount of capital an insurer needs to support its operations, given the insurer's risk characteristics. Before implementing RBC, state laws that specified minimum capital requirements made little or no allowance for differences in risk characteristics among insurers. The NAIC RBC formula and the model law that authorizes it aim to make the minimum capital required for an insurer a function of the risks assumed by that insurer. The formula considers numerous risks beyond underwriting risk.

The Risk-Based Capital (RBC) for Insurers Model Act

For property-casualty insurers, the NAIC Model Law that created the RBC specifies the following:

> A property and casualty insurer's RBC shall be determined in accordance with the formula set forth in the RBC Instructions. The formula shall take into account (and may adjust for the covariance between):
>
> (1) Asset risk;
>
> (2) Credit risk;
>
> (3) Underwriting risk; and
>
> (4) All other business risks and such other relevant risks as are set forth in the RBC Instructions determined in each case by applying the factors in the manner set forth in the RBC Instructions[2]

This model law has been enacted in some form in all states. It broadly requires that capital requirements be based on all risks that insurers face.

Nondiscretionary Operation of RBC Requirements

The RBC model law enables insurance regulators to take regulatory action when warranted, before an insurer becomes too financially weak to be rehabilitated. Before the NAIC developed an RBC formula, state regulators were required to petition the courts and prove that the insurer was in financial difficulty before intervention was allowed, thereby subjecting the insurer to regulatory control. The NAIC RBC formula provides an objective test of the insurer's solvency and matches regulatory action to the level of solvency concern. For example, the first level of regulatory intervention is the Company Action Level. At this level, the insurer must submit a comprehensive financial plan that identifies the factors that caused the problem and proposes corrective action to solve the problem. At the fourth level of regulatory intervention, the Mandatory Control Level, the state regulators must seize control of the insurer.

The nondiscretionary operation of the RBC model has benefits for insurers, state regulators, and the insurance customers. State insurance departments do not have a choice about whether to implement the regulatory action specified; therefore, regulatory intervention is not arbitrary or motivated by political factors. State insurance regulators are given a clear mandate with RBC. Rehabilitation is no longer subject to delays caused by regulators' expectations that insurers will be able to solve their financial problems.

The RBC formula is complex but mechanical. Insurers can perform the RBC calculation themselves and know whether they will come under regulatory scrutiny. An insurer that has difficulty meeting RBC requirements can choose either, or both, of two options: (1) reduce the risks to which it is exposed or (2) increase its capital.

The RBC Standard

The specifics of the RBC formula are intricate, subject to change, and beyond the scope of this text. Generally, the RBC standard determines an acceptable level of capital for each insurer based on the risks that insurer faces. The insurer's actual capital is then compared to this acceptable level and, if found insufficient, various consequences result depending on the level of the insufficiency.

Although the main components of the NAIC RBC formula are well established, many of the factors used in the formula are regularly evaluated for their appropriateness and can change periodically. The NAIC formula was designed so that it could evolve into a more effective regulatory tool. Consequently, the following discussion addresses only the main components of the NAIC RBC formula, not the details that support it.

The NAIC RBC formula considers various forms of asset risk and underwriting risk. Included within these broad categories of risk are virtually all specific risks to which an insurer can be subject. Each component of the RBC formula weighs the risks assumed by an insurer, because those risks vary by insurer. For example, one insurer might invest solely in short-term government bonds, while another holds a large portfolio of common stocks. The components of the NAIC RBC formula attempt to evaluate these risks and consolidate them into a single index.

Because it is unlikely that all of the risks measured by the formula would befall an insurer simultaneously, the NAIC RBC formula adjusts the sum of the values assigned to each risk using a statistical technique called covariance. The covariance adjustment reduces the sum of the capital requirements indicated by the NAIC RBC formula. In other words, the capital required by each element of an insurer's risk need not be arithmetically summed.

The following section discusses the types of risks that the RBC formula considers.

Asset Risk

Asset risk
The risk that an asset's value will be lower than expected.

Asset risk is the risk that an asset's value will be lower than expected. Virtually all assets involve some such risk, though some assets are riskier than others. The RBC formula considers numerous categories of asset risk, including investments in subsidiaries, fixed income assets such as bonds and loans, and equity assets such as common and preferred stocks.

Under the RBC formula, riskier assets require more underlying capital than do less risky assets. The amount of capital required is determined by multiplying the NAIC Annual Statement value of the asset by a factor provided by the NAIC in the RBC booklet. U.S. government bonds, for example, have a factor of 0.000. This indicates that they are considered risk-free; no underlying capital is needed to support them. On the other hand, bonds in default require $3 of supporting capital for each $10 of reported value of the bonds.

To determine the amount of risk-based capital required to support its asset risks, an insurer multiplies the NAIC Annual Statement value of each asset by the appropriate risk factor and sums the resulting products. Additional RBC charges are imposed if the insurer's investments are concentrated in securities issued by a small number of issuers—that is, if investments are not sufficiently diversified.

Credit Risk

Credit risk reflects the possibility that the insurer will not be able to collect money owed to it. Although it is specifically mentioned in the RBC Model Law, credit risk is another type of asset risk. Receivables, the source of much credit risk, are money owed to and assets of an organization.

The most important credit risk is the chance that one or more of the insurer's reinsurers will not be able to pay amounts due under reinsurance agreements. Cessions to some reinsurers are not subject to the RBC charge. Such reinsurers include (1) state-mandated involuntary pools and federal insurance programs, (2) voluntary market mechanism pools that meet certain conditions specified in the RBC booklet, and (3) the insurer's U.S.-based affiliates, subsidiaries, and parents.

Other credit risks included in the RBC formula are (1) federal income tax recoverable; (2) interest, dividends, and real estate income due and accrued; (3) receivables from affiliates, subsidiaries, and parents; (4) amounts receivable relating to uninsured accident and health plans; and (5) aggregate write-ins for assets other than invested assets. For each of these, the value shown in the NAIC Annual Statement is multiplied by the appropriate RBC factor to determine the required RBC component for credit risk.

Underwriting Risk

The principal components of underwriting risk are premium risk and loss reserving risk, specifically the risks that both might be too low. Premiums can be inadequate for the losses they must cover. Loss reserving errors directly affect the amount of an insurer's capital. Inadequate reserves, as evidenced by excessive loss reserve development, indicate that capital might become impaired. The RBC formula applies different factors for each type of insurance to reflect the industry experience with the riskiness of each insurance type.

Another underwriting risk recognized in the RBC formula is excessive premium growth. A persistent concern exists that premium growth has been achieved by price cutting.

Action Levels

The RBC formula determines an "authorized control level" of capital for each insurer. When capital decreases to this level, the regulator may seize control of the insurer. Insurers should maintain capital at 200 percent of the authorized control level or more to avoid any regulatory action.

If an insurer's RBC does not exceed 200 percent of the authorized control level, various regulatory actions are triggered, as summarized in Exhibit 14-6.

EXHIBIT 14-6

Risk-Based Capital Levels

RBC Level	Percentage of Authorized Control Level (Minimum RBC)	Action Required
Company Action Level	200 percent	Insurer files comprehensive plan.
Regulatory Action Level	150 percent	Regulator conducts exam as necessary; insurer files comprehensive plan.
Authorized Control Level	100 percent	Regulator may seize control.
Mandatory Control Level	70 percent	Regulator required to place insurer under regulatory control.

Adapted from *NAIC Research Quarterly*, Vol. II, Issue 4 (Kansas City, Mo.: National Association of Insurance Commissioners, October 1996), p. 9. Used with permission.

• No Action Required: If the insurer's capitalization level is above the company action level (above 200 percent or more of the computed minimum RBC amount), no action is required by either the insurer or the regulator.

- Company Action Level: If the insurer's capitalization level falls between the regulatory action level and the company action level (between 150 and 200 percent of the computed minimum RBC amount), the insurer is required to submit a comprehensive financial plan to the regulator containing proposals to correct the insurer's financial problems.

- Regulatory Action Level: If the insurer's capitalization level falls between the authorized control level and the regulatory action level (between 100 and 150 percent of the computed minimum RBC amount), the regulator is required to conduct an examination or analysis as deemed necessary. The insurer is also required to file a comprehensive financial plan with the state insurance regulator.

- Authorized Control Level: If an insurer's capitalization level falls between the mandatory control level and the authorized control level (between 70 and 100 percent of the computed minimum RBC amount), the regulator *may* place the insurer under regulatory control but is not required to do so.

- Mandatory Control Level: If an insurer's capitalization level falls below 70 percent of the authorized control level (the computed minimum RBC amount), the insurance regulator is *required* to place the insurer under regulatory control.

SUMMARY

Financial management of an insurer involves using owner-supplied capital to generate cash flows from both underwriting and investment operations. Selling an insurance policy immediately creates a liability equal to the amount of the premium that will be earned ratably over the policy term. If losses occur and claims arise, another group of liabilities is created: loss reserves and loss adjustment expense reserves.

Liabilities are a source of funds for insurers. The most important liabilities of property-casualty insurers are the unearned premium reserve and reserves for losses and loss adjustment expenses. The amount of unearned premiums is fairly easy to establish. Estimating accurate loss reserves is more difficult but crucial. Loss reserves represent the insurer's largest source of funds. Loss reserves established for liability insurance are more uncertain than those established for property insurance. Most property claims are settled quickly, but liability claims might take years to settle. Because liability loss reserves remain outstanding for several years, they usually are much larger than property loss reserves relative to earned premiums. The critical importance of loss reserve analysis has grown as the product mix of the U.S. insurance industry has transitioned from a predominantly property insurance business to a predominantly liability insurance business.

Funds provided by underwriting operations must be held for the benefit of policyholders and other claimants until the protection offered by insurance policies has been provided and claims have been paid. Insurance company managers seek to maximize owners' net worth by investing cash flows from underwriting plus owner-supplied funds in income-producing assets. An insurer's investments in securities represent a significant portion of its overall assets. The investment strategy of an insurer is, therefore, a decisive factor in the insurer's overall profitability and growth. The types of investments an insurer can make are subject to regulatory and legal restrictions.

State laws impose specific requirements on the types of invested assets insurers can hold and percentage limitations on classes of investments. Generally, insurers can invest only in money market instruments, investment grade bonds, common and preferred stock, real estate loans, and real estate. The purposes of such requirements are to support diversification of the insurer's investment portfolio holdings and to ensure that funds will be available for policyholders and claimants.

The amount of owner-supplied and retained capital is also subject to regulatory guidelines. On one hand, public policy calls for more capital rather than less in order to make certain that an insurer will be able to fulfill its obligations. On the other hand, capital is supplied only at a cost, and management has the responsibility to reduce expenses to maximize the insurer's value. This natural tension between the calls for more or less capital is harmonized to some extent by state insurance regulation. Acting through the NAIC, state insurance regulators have developed several tools to assist in identifying financially weak insurers and initiating corrective action. The NAIC's Risk-Based Capital (RBC) formula considers an insurer's asset risk and underwriting risk and develops a minimum amount of capital each insurer should maintain. In this way, regulators seek to make the minimum capital required for an insurer a function of the risks it assumes. The RBC requirements also trigger mandatory regulatory consequences when an insurer's capital falls below prescribed levels.

This is the third and final chapter on financial topics. The next chapter illustrates the strategic management process and describes the considerations related to expanding insurer operations globally.

CHAPTER NOTES

1. Joan Lamm-Tennant, "Asset/Liability Management for the Life Insurer: Situation Analysis and Strategy Formulation," *The Journal of Risk and Insurance*, Vol. LVI, No. 3, September 1989, pp. 501–507.
2. National Association of Insurance Commissioners, *Model Laws, Regulations, and Guidelines*, Vol. II (Minneapolis, Minn.: NIARS Corporation, 2003), p. 312-3, Section 2.C. Published by NIARS Corporation under the auspices of the National Association of Insurance Commissioners.

Appendix

Report-Year Loss Analysis Example

Unlike accident-year loss triangles, which include loss data for several accident years, a report-year loss table includes data for only one report year.

Exhibit 14A-1 shows a report-year loss table, using hypothetical data. Several such tables, one for each report year, would be needed for a typical loss reserve analysis.

EXHIBIT 14A-1

Report-Year Loss Table for 1995—Hypothetical Data

Year	Closed Claims			Open Claims			All Claims		
	Number	Amount	Average	Number	Amount	Average	Number	Amount	Average
1995	1,451	$ 5,117,677	$3,527	9,122	$49,597,598	$ 5,437	10,573	$54,715,275	$5,175
1996	4,794	18,562,368	3,872	5,779	41,111,644	7,114	10,573	59,674,012	5,644
1997	6,579	30,862,089	4,691	3,994	30,122,975	7,542	10,573	60,985,064	5,768
1998	7,841	40,059,669	5,109	2,732	20,967,687	7,675	10,573	61,027,356	5,772
1999	8,987	49,635,201	5,523	1,586	12,882,948	8,123	10,573	62,518,149	5,913
2000	9,898	57,814,218	5,841	675	6,057,275	8,974	10,573	63,871,493	6,041
2001	10,570	64,762,390	6,127	3	282,706	94,235	10,573	65,045,096	6,152
2002	10,573	65,097,961	6,157	0	0	0	10,573	65,097,961	6,157

Several things should be noted about Exhibit 14A-1. First, at the end of the report year, all reported claims are known, so the number does not change thereafter. Claims move from the open column to the closed column when they are settled, even if they are settled without payment. Occasionally, a claim will move from the closed column back to the open column if it is reopened, but the total number of claims never changes. The total amount of losses does change, upward or downward, depending on an insurer's reserving practices. The change is always upward in Exhibit 14-5, indicating that, initially, the insurer's case reserves were substantially inadequate. Typically, the change will be upward in some years and downward in others.

EXHIBIT 14A-2

Report-Year Loss Table for 1998—Hypothetical Data

	Closed Claims			Open Claims			All Claims		
Year	Number	Amount	Average	Number	Amount	Average	Number	Amount	Average
1998	1,687	$ 6,677,146	$3,958	9,330	$57,474,845	$6,160	11,017	$64,151,991	$5,823
1999	5,135	24,139,635	4,701	5,882	43,559,830	7,406	11,017	67,699,465	6,145
2000	6,738	34,559,202	5,129	4,279	34,164,844	7,984	11,017	68,724,046	6,238
2001	7,953	43,590,393	5,481	3,064	26,653,999	8,699	11,017	70,244,392	6,376
2002	9,188	52,849,376	5,752	1,829	16,083,993	8,794	11,017	68,933,369	6,257

Both the average amount of a closed claim and the average amount of an open claim tend to increase as the claims mature. This results from the tendency of small claims to be settled first and large claims to take longer to settle. This increase in the average claim amount might not actually be as regular as it is depicted in Exhibit 14A-1. A year-to-year decrease might occasionally occur. However, such a decrease requires further checking for a data error or an anomaly.

The report-year loss table in Exhibit 14A-1 is for a *fully mature report year*, one for which all claims have been settled. Exhibit 14A-2 shows a similar table for a year not yet fully mature.

EXHIBIT 14A-3

Report-Year Method—Development Multipliers

Months of Development	Report Year			
	1995		1998	
	Amount	Multiplier	Amount	Multiplier
12	$54,715,275		$64,151,991	
24	59,674,012	1.091	67,699,465	1.055
36	60,985,064	1.022	68,724,046	1.015
48	61,027,356	1.001	70,244,392	1.022
60	62,518,149	1.024	68,933,369	.981
72	63,871,493	1.022		
84	65,045,096	1.018		
96	65,097,961	1.001		

A loss triangle similar to that used in accident-year analysis can be compiled from a series of report-year tables. The first step in compiling such a triangle is to calculate loss development multipliers from the total loss amount columns of the tables. Exhibit 14A-3 shows the calculation of such multipliers from Exhibits 14A-1 and 14A-2.

EXHIBIT 14A-4

Loss Triangle—Report-Year Method

	Months of Development						
Report Year	12–24	24–36	36–48	48–60	60–72	72–84	84–96
1994 & Prior	1.065	1.031	1.023	1.022	1.034	1.016	1.003
1995	1.091	1.022	1.001	1.024	1.022	1.018	1.001
1996	1.084	1.019	1.025	1.023	1.026	1.017	
1997	1.071	1.021	1.018	1.019	1.027		
1998	1.055	1.015	1.022	.981			
1999	1.063	1.024	1.019				
2000	1.073	1.020					
2001	1.059						
Mean	1.070	1.022	1.018	1.014	1.027	1.017	1.002
Selected	1.070	1.022	1.018	1.014	1.027	1.017	1.002
Development Factors	1.182	1.105	1.081	1.062	1.047	1.019	1.002

Exhibit 14A-4 shows a loss triangle using the data from Exhibits 14A-1 and 14A-2, along with additional data from other report years. The bottom line shows the ultimate development factors—that is, the factors that can be used to project immature loss data to full maturity. The various development factors in the next-to-last line of the table are the means of the multipliers above them for the report years. In actual practice, an analyst might select a value greater or lesser than the mean. Two reasons for such a selection might be because the data indicate an increasing or a decreasing trend in the multipliers or because case reserving practices have changed.

Exhibit 14A-5 shows the ultimate development factors alone. The losses for report year 1998, which are sixty months developed in Exhibit 14A-3, can be projected to ultimate value by multiplying by the ultimate development factor corresponding to sixty months, shown in Exhibit 14A-5 ($68,933,369 × 1.047 = $72,173,237).

The report-year triangle shows that the insurer in question has consistently established inadequate loss reserves during the period being analyzed. In the absence of an indication that reserving practices have changed, an analyst looking at these data would assume that current reserves are inadequate by approximately the same percentage as in previous years.

EXHIBIT 14A-5

**Report-Year Method
Ultimate Development Factors**

Months of Development	Ultimate Development Factor
12	1.182
24	1.105
36	1.081
48	1.062
60	1.047
72	1.019
84	1.002
96	1.000

The foregoing analysis is based solely on claims reported to the insurer in the report year in question. Those claims would include some that were incurred during the report year and some that were incurred in previous years. The data do not include any claims reported after the end of the report year, regardless of when they were incurred. Consequently, the claims projected to ultimate by this method do not include any amount for claims incurred but not reported. This part of the loss reserve must be computed separately when the report-year method is used.

Chapter 15

Direct Your Learning

Insurer Strategic Management and Global Operations

After learning the content of this chapter, you should be able to:

- Describe the strategic management process.

- Describe the Five Forces and SWOT methods of analyzing the environment.

- Explain how strategy is developed at the corporate, business, and functional levels.

- Explain how to implement strategy through organizational structure and organizational control.

- Explain how to analyze the global environment.

- Describe the methods used to enter global markets.

- Describe international loss exposures.

- Describe the advantages and disadvantages of admitted and nonadmitted insurance for multinational loss exposures.

Develop Your Perspective

What are the main topics covered in the chapter?

Companies follow the strategic management process to establish goals and to determine strategies to create a competitive advantage. Competing on a global basis requires understanding the culture, language, regulations, and laws in the countries where a company does business.

Consider the three levels within an organization at which strategy is formulated.

- What factors are involved at each level?
- Why is it important to integrate strategies at each level of the organization?

Why is it important to learn about these topics?

The strategic management process has two major components: strategy formulation and strategy implementation. Formulating strategy requires an assessment of the internal and external environments to identify factors that influence a company's competitive position.

Evaluate how a company analyzes its environment.

- What are the elements of the Five Forces Model, and how can they be used in an environmental analysis?
- What is the value of a SWOT analysis in evaluating a company's external environment?

How can you use what you will learn?

Review your organization's mission and value statements.

- Do these statements accurately reflect your company's operations and goals?
- How do these statements relate to your company's strategy?

Chapter 15

Insurer Strategic Management and Global Operations

Previous chapters discussed specific areas or functions within the insurance industry. This concluding chapter takes a broader view and examines the process that an organization, particularly an insurance operation, uses to formulate and implement its business strategy. This process is known as the **strategic management process**. The chapter also examines the global environment and considerations related to expanding an insurance operation internationally, a key strategic challenge for many insurers.

Strategic management process
The process an organization uses to formulate and implement its business strategies.

STRATEGIC MANAGEMENT PROCESS

The strategic management process is critical to an organization's success. At the heart of any successful strategy is the creation of a superior alignment between external factors and the organization's internal resources so as to create a sustainable competitive advantage. Organizations can be successful in the long term only when they have effective strategies that deploy resources in the most efficient manner. The strategic management process has two phases: strategy formulation and strategy implementation.

Strategy Formulation

Strategy formulation involves the following four steps:

1. Creating mission and vision statements.
2. Establishing organizational goals.
3. Analyzing the external and internal environments.
4. Determining strategy at different organizational levels.

Creating Mission and Vision Statements

The first step in strategy formulation is creating the company's mission and vision or value statements. The mission statement pinpoints what product or service the company provides, who its customers and other stakeholders are, and what is important to the organization. Mission statements frequently refer to customers, shareholders, employees, and other corporate stakeholders.

While broad in nature, the mission statement reflects the character and spirit of a company. For example:

- Kraft Foods's mission simply states, "Kraft's mission is to be widely recognized as the undisputed leader of the global food industry."[1]

- Southwest Airlines's mission reads, "The mission of Southwest Airlines is dedication to the highest quality of Customer Service delivered with a sense of warmth, friendliness, individual pride, and Company Spirit."[2]

- Microsoft's mission states, "To enable people and businesses throughout the world to realize their full potential."[3]

Mission statements are supplemented by vision or value statements that provide more details about how the company will achieve its mission.

Values such as integrity, honesty, customer focus, flexibility, and compassion are often included in these statements. Exhibit 15-1 shows some examples of mission and vision statements from several large commercial and personal insurers. Mission statements for insurance operations frequently mention policyholders and producers.

Establishing Organizational Goals

The second step in strategy formulation is establishing organizational goals. These goals are based on an organization's understanding of what its identity is, what customers it serves, and what its purpose is.

A company establishes organizational goals to set its direction. These goals clarify expectations, support the control function, and increase motivation within the organization.[4]

Organizational goals tend to be broad statements and are usually established by the CEO and executive team, sometimes with input from the board of directors or executives from the division level. Nationwide's values, shown in Exhibit 15-1, provide an example of such a statement. The statement indicates that the company seeks to provide advice and products to help customers protect and manage their most important assets. The company also focuses on "three core businesses, domestic property and casualty insurance, life insurance and retirement savings, and asset management."[5] How the company accomplishes these goals will differ at the division level and within local underwriting or claim departments. It is important, however, for the organization to coordinate activities so that each level in the hierarchy contributes to the overall success of the company.

Once organizational goals have been determined, the company can begin to build strategies at various organizational levels to meet those goals. These strategies are based on the company's core competencies, the competitive nature of the business, potential customer base, and other factors. To construct effective strategies, the organization should thoroughly assess its external and internal environments to determine its competitive position.

EXHIBIT 15-1

Examples of Insurer Mission/Vision Statements

STATE FARM:

Our Mission, Our Vision, and Our Shared Values

State Farm's mission is to help people manage the risks of everyday life, recover from the unexpected and realize their dreams.

We are people who make it our business to be like a good neighbor; who built a premier company by selling and keeping promises through our marketing partnership; who bring diverse talents and experiences to our work of serving the State Farm customer.

Our success is built on a foundation of shared values—quality service and relationships, mutual trust, integrity and financial strength.

Our vision for the future is to be the customer's first and best choice in the products and services we provide. We will continue to be the leader in the insurance industry and we will become a leader in the financial services arena. Our customers' needs will determine our path. Our values will guide us.

Source: http://www.statefarm.com/about/mission.htm (accessed January 14, 2003).

NATIONWIDE (Nationwide Mutual Insurance Co., Columbus, Ohio, U.S.A.):

Our Values

For more than 75 years, Nationwide has been on your side with high-quality insurance and financial services. Our mission is to provide advice and products that help our customers protect and manage the most important assets in their lives: their homes, their cars, their families and their incomes after they retire. By focusing on three core businesses, domestic property and casualty insurance, life insurance and retirement savings, and asset management, we remain committed to increasing the value our customers have come to expect from us. Our corporate values, and the investment we make to reinforce them, will enable us to be the great company we envision for tomorrow.

Performance Values	Core Values
We Have a Bias for Action and a Passion for Results	We Value People
We Act Accountably	We Are Customer Focused
We Value Coaching and Feedback	We Act With Honesty and Integrity
We Work as One Team	We Trust and Respect Each Other
We Have Fun	

Source: http://www.nationwide.com/about_us/our_values/index.htm (accessed August 8, 2003).

FIREMAN'S FUND:

Mission

Fireman's Fund's® mission is to be the premier provider of property and casualty insurance within our selected markets. We will strive to exceed customer expectations and deal honorably with our customers, producers and the general public.

Shared Values

Our people are our competitive advantage. We value and reward:

*   ACTION—We have a bias for action and a willingness to take risks that will allow for innovation and will make things happen. It is our responsibility to become involved and encourage others to use creativity to constantly search for a better way.

Continued on next page.

- COURAGE—We have the strength to confront the conventional, take risks, admit mistakes and carry out the hard decisions. With firmness of mind and will, we pursue excellence without compromising our values.

- TEAMWORK—We believe that teamwork can achieve what individuals cannot. The diversity of style, approach and skills available in our entire organization must be leveraged to achieve success. Essential to this is a mutual loyalty and respect and the need to both listen to and talk with each other. Success is everyone's responsibility.

- SENSITIVITY—We care about our customers, employees, producers and the communities in which we live and work. We treat others as we would want to be treated — with mutual respect, understanding and trust.

- HARD WORK—We value hard work as an important part of becoming the best. We recognize that success is earned through working smarter for continuous improvement. We look for opportunities to make work fun, enjoyable and to celebrate our successes.

- CLEAR THINKING—We acknowledge that ours is a complex and highly competitive industry in which the wisdom of decisions made today often cannot be evaluated for many years. We must consistently exercise the discipline of thinking things through, yet remain a Company of ideas, willing to take risks.

- COMPETITIVE SPIRIT—It takes competitive spirit to build a world-class organization. We have a passion for winning, a commitment to achieving our goals. We aggressively pursue that which provides us with a competitive advantage.

- HONESTY AND INTEGRITY—We maintain honesty and integrity in the achievement of success. Dealing with customers, employees, producers and the general public is done with the highest professional and personal standards. A well-founded reputation for honesty and integrity is itself a priceless asset.

- PROFESSIONALLY MINDED PEOPLE—Our strength is the talent, will and character of our people. We provide equal opportunity to grow and encourage continuing professional development. Enhancing expertise and skill-building are necessary ingredients in achieving and maintaining our objectives.

Source: http://www.ffic.com/careers/Values.html (accessed January 14, 2003. Used with permission of Fireman's Fund Insurer.

LIBERTY MUTUAL:

Creed

With our policyholders we are engaged in a great mutual enterprise. It is great because it seeks to prevent crippling injuries and death by removing the causes of home, highway, and work accidents. It is great because it deals in the relief of pain and sorrow and fear and loss. It is great because it works to preserve and protect the things people earn and build and own and cherish. Its true greatness will be measured by our power to help people live **safer, more secure lives.**

Source: http://www.libertymutual.com/omapps/ContentServer?pagename=Corporate Internet/Page/StandardTeal&cid=1003349317240&dir=/CorporateInternet/CorpHomePage/CorpAboutLibertyMutual/CorpCreed (accessed August 8, 2003).

Analyzing the Environment

The third step in strategy formulation is analyzing the environment. When conducting an external environmental analysis, managers consider factors in the general environment as well as in the task environment. The general environment affects all businesses regardless of the specific industry in which they operate. Conversely, the task environment deals with factors specific to the industry in which an organization competes. Analyzing factors in the general environment includes assessing demographic, sociocultural, legal, technological, economic, and global factors. An aging baby-boomer generation in the U.S., for example, is a demographic factor that could be considered when developing new insurance products and/or services. Sociocultural and legal factors created by an increasingly litigious society have led to substantial jury awards, insurance coverage modifications, and a debate over the need for tort reform. Factors in the task environment include customers, competitors, and suppliers. The next section of this chapter focuses on the task environment.

Many methods can be used to analyze the environment in which a company operates. Two commonly used methods, the Five Forces Model and SWOT analysis, are discussed here. Customers, competitors, and suppliers are analyzed in the Five Forces Model, which deals with the external environment.

The Five Forces Model

The first commonly used method of analyzing the competitive environment is the **Five Forces Model**. One of the leading experts in the field of competitive analysis is Michael E. Porter, a Harvard Business School professor who has been teaching and writing in this field for decades. Porter developed this widely used model, shown in Exhibit 15-2. Porter describes five forces that drive competition:

1. Threat of new entrants
2. Threat of substitute products or services
3. Bargaining power of buyers
4. Bargaining power of suppliers
5. Rivalry among existing firms[6]

By analyzing these forces and their effect on the organization, managers better understand their company's position in the industry. This increased understanding allows management to construct strategies that build a competitive advantage.

Five Forces Model
A method of evaluating the external environment in which a company operates. Involves assessing five forces that drive competition: threat of new entrants, threat of substitute products or services, bargaining power of buyers, bargaining power of suppliers, and rivalry among existing firms.

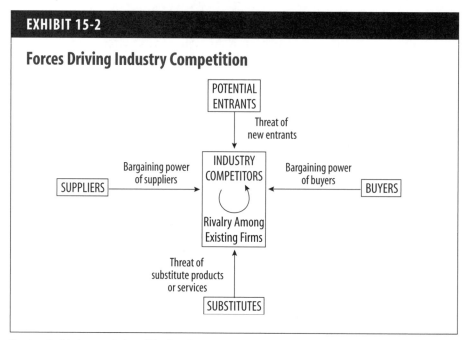

EXHIBIT 15-2

Forces Driving Industry Competition

Threat of New Entrants   One force that drives competition is the threat of new entrants in a market. This force depends on how difficult it is for outsiders to enter that market. Barriers to entry include economies of scale, which contribute to lower overall costs by decreasing the unit cost of products as volume increases. Personal insurers that write homeowners or personal auto policies have achieved economies of scale through technology. The standardized nature of these personal insurance policies allows automated processes to produce large numbers of policies with relatively low overhead costs. Insurers using these automated processes can charge premiums that are lower than those of insurers using more labor-intensive processes. Consequently, such personal insurers have gained a competitive advantage over other insurers and raised the barriers to entry for this market segment.

Companies can also raise barriers to entry by offering unique or customized products or services to their customers. These companies can build brand identification and increase customer loyalty, making it costly for competitors to gain market entry. For example, Chubb Insurance offers a variety of insurance programs designed for owners of high-value homes and for collectors of art, jewelry, wine, and other valuable items.[7] Progressive Insurance is particularly skilled at providing highly efficient, prompt claim adjusting. Many other insurers have found similar niches in which to build a competitive advantage based on products or services designed for a specific type of customer.

The ability to access distribution channels in a marketing system can also create barriers to entry and pose a competitive disadvantage for potential new entrants. For insurance products, the marketing system or distribution channel can be an important component of the overall marketing plan. These barriers might have been lowered because of the advent of new distribution channels, such as direct response and the Internet. On the other hand, having an established, long-term relationship with a group of producers or an exclusive agency arrangement could provide a competitive advantage for an insurer.

Government policy can also act as a barrier to entry and can deter new entrants from considering the highly regulated insurance industry. Generally, the barriers to entry into the insurance business are relatively low and consist primarily of the required human and financial capital to start an insurer. Regulatory requirements also govern the formation of new insurers. Regulations within a given jurisdiction can discourage some insurers from entering certain states. Many insurers have elected to stop writing auto coverage within a given jurisdiction because of restrictions on rate increases.

Other potential barriers to entry include the presence of switching costs, cost disadvantages independent of scale, and the need to invest large amounts of capital for production facilities or research and development.[8] All of these conditions would increase costs for potential entrants, raising the barriers for them.

Threat of Substitute Products or Services   A second force that drives competition is the threat of substitute products or services. This threat arises when products from one industry that are capable of performing the same function as those from another industry become widely available. This threat makes it difficult for any one seller to increase prices substantially and tends to hold down profits for all participants in the original industry. For example, malt-based wine cooler products manufactured by beer companies pose a threat as a substitute product to the wine industry and to nonalcoholic carbonated beverage processors.

The threat of substitute products or services is not a factor in the insurance industry to any great extent. If current plans for tort reforms or medical expense reimbursement programs were to develop in the future, they could pose the threat of substituting for traditional liability insurance coverages currently written by property-casualty insurers.

Bargaining Power of Buyers   A third force that drives competition is the bargaining power of buyers. When buyers have significant power, they can increase competition within an industry and can make ever-increasing demands for lower prices. According to Porter, "consumers tend to be more price sensitive if they are purchasing products that are undifferentiated, expensive relative to their incomes, or of a sort where quality is not particularly important to them."[9] This force affects the insurance industry, principally in the personal insurance market, in which customers have exerted great pressure on insurers to lower prices and increase availability, particularly for personal auto policies.

The cyclical nature of the insurance business also affects the bargaining power of customers. In a soft market, many insurers vie for business and provide undifferentiated products. Buyers have greater bargaining power and can negotiate for broader coverages at lower premiums. In a hard market, insurers limit capacity and raise prices, making it difficult for customers to bargain for reduced prices or broader coverage.

When formulating strategy, companies should consider customer buying power. Companies might decide not to enter certain markets because they feel pressure from buyer groups would inhibit their ability to be profitable.

Bargaining Power of Suppliers A fourth force that drives competition is the bargaining power of suppliers. In some industries, suppliers can exert power over companies by increasing price, restricting supply, or varying product quality. For example, in the energy industry, oil-producing countries can exercise tremendous power over the supply and price of petroleum products. By manipulating supply, the producers can directly affect price and the ultimate profitability of energy companies.

In the insurance industry, reinsurers are a supplier to primary insurers. Without access to reinsurance, many insurers would be constrained in the types and amounts of insurance they could profitably write. Depending on whether the market is hard or soft, reinsurers are in a position to control the price and amount of capacity they provide, as they did during the 2002 and 2003 renewal cycles. At that time, reinsurers initiated large price increases, in part to offset losses from September 11, 2001, and declines in returns from equity markets. These price increases constrained the amount of coverage that primary insurers could provide for their producers and customers.

Rivalry Among Existing Firms A fifth force that drives competition is the rivalry among existing firms. The rivalry among firms within an industry is reflected in pricing wars, aggressive advertising campaigns, and increased emphasis on customer service. Competitors are constantly striving to be at the top of their industry and to outperform other companies. Some industries, such as the personal computer (PC) segment of the technology sector, are more competitive than others. In the late 1990s, the struggle to be number one led to a spiraling price war primarily involving Dell Computers, Hewlett-Packard/Compaq Computer, and Gateway. Dell's approach was to eliminate costs in production and distribution in order to push its prices below its competitors' prices. This low-cost approach allowed Dell to become the PC segment leader on a volume basis. However, such pricing wars can erode overall profit potential within an industry and can lead to increased costs for advertising and other expenses for individual participants.

A high level of competition can be expected in industries having many companies, little product differentiation, or high exit costs. All of these characteristics are present in the insurance industry, making the market strongly competitive. While some insurers can use economies of scale to gain a competitive edge, no single insurer has been able to capitalize on such an advantage to block smaller, less efficient insurers from flourishing. Market leaders exist in the insurance industry, but the individual market share of insurers at the top of the market is still relatively small compared to that of other industries. No one insurer, therefore, has enough market share to dominate the overall property-casualty market. Exhibit 15-3 shows the top five property-casualty insurers based on net written premiums.

EXHIBIT 15-3

Leading Writers of Property-Casualty Insurance

Company/Group	2001 Net Written Premiums (Billions of Dollars)	Percentage Market Share
State Farm	$37.9	11.5%
Allstate	22.0	6.7
Zurich/Farmers	17.0	5.2
Amer. Int. Group	14.0	4.3
Berkshire Hathaway	11.7	3.5
Total P/C Industry Writings	$328.8	100.0%

© A.M. Best Company. Used with permission. *Best's Review*® (Oldwick, N.J.: A.M. Best Company, July 2002, p. 27.)

SWOT Analysis

The second commonly used method of analyzing the competitive environment is SWOT or situational analysis. **SWOT analysis** is used to assess the internal *strengths* and *weaknesses* of organizations as well as external *opportunities* and *threats* to which the organization is exposed.

Identifying internal strengths and weaknesses involves considering financial, physical, human, and organizational assets.[10] Managers use the SWOT analysis to determine the current state of their companies. Assets that management would consider include:

• Managerial expertise
• Available product lines
• Skill levels and competencies of staff
• Current strategies
• Customer loyalty
• Growth levels
• Organizational structure
• Distribution channels

SWOT analysis

A method of evaluating the internal and external environments by assessing an organization's internal strengths and weaknesses and its external opportunities and threats.

If an organization has an executive training program that is considered an industry standard, it would be a strength. If a company is having financial difficulty or is experiencing unfocused growth, it would be a weakness. In an insurance operation, an insurer that had been cutting prices to gain market share might identify a substantial weakness when an unanticipated rise in losses is projected as part of the SWOT analysis. Unfavorable loss results cause financial constraints. In the past few years, several major property-casualty insurers conducted studies to determine the accuracy of reserves for asbestos-related claims. As a result of these studies, many of these insurers were required to increase their reserves significantly. These increases had a negative effect on earnings and stock prices for the insurers involved and highlighted a key internal weakness for the insurers.

Managers also analyze the external environment to determine potential opportunities or threats. Both the general and task environment factors are considered as part of this analysis. Opportunities might be presented by new markets, possible acquisition targets, or a reduction in competition. Threats might include new competitors, an increase in competition levels, economic downturns, or changes in customer preferences.

Pearce and Robinson developed one approach to chart the results of a SWOT analysis using a graph with four quadrants that provides companies direction in choosing categories of strategies. Based on this graph, organizations that have numerous environmental opportunities but that also have critical internal weaknesses should consider strategies that are oriented toward turnaround. The best-positioned companies have substantial internal strengths combined with numerous environmental opportunities, which supports an aggressive strategic approach.[11] The SWOT Analysis Diagram is shown in Exhibit 15-4. The approach used by organizations varies based on each company's needs. A company should not only identify strengths, weaknesses, opportunities, and threats but should also thoroughly analyze how these affect its strategic plan.

Once the SWOT analysis has been completed, managers can develop strategies that position the company to gain a competitive advantage. This advantage is attained by leveraging organizational strengths while offsetting or reducing weaknesses. The company should also find ways to capitalize on identified opportunities and to neutralize existing threats.

Determining Strategy at Different Organizational Levels

The fourth step in strategy formulation is determining strategy at different organizational levels. Strategy is formulated at different levels throughout an organization, including the corporate level, the business level, and the functional level. In a single-business company, the corporate-level strategy and the business-level strategy are the same.

EXHIBIT 15-4

SWOT Analysis Diagram

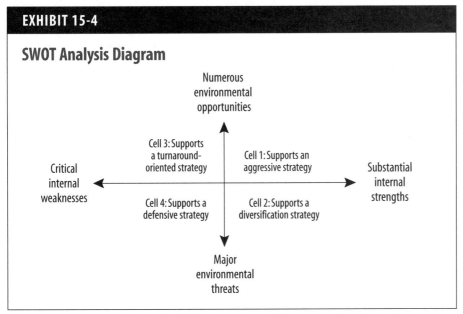

Source: John A. Pearce II and Richard B. Robinson, Jr., *Strategic Management: Formulation, Implementation, and Control,* 6th ed. (New York: Irwin/McGraw-Hill, 1997), p. 172.

Corporate-Level Strategies

Corporate-level strategies are formed by the CEO and the executive team. At the corporate level, executives are concerned about determining in what businesses the company should be involved, properly allocating organizational resources, and coordinating strategies at all company levels to maximize profits. Corporate-level strategies are relatively long term, established for a five-year period and beyond.

Competitive advantage is reinforced when each department or unit in an organization creates value for the customer and coordinates all activities toward this end. According to Porter, "Overall advantage or disadvantage results from all of a company's activities, not just a few."[12] In insurance operations, this means that the marketing, underwriting, claim, customer service, and other departments must all align to build value and to support corporate-level strategy in a continuous chain. Such alignment can also provide additional advantages in the form of reduced operating expenses or increased differentiation of products and services through the interaction of marketing, underwriting, and other departments.

Three generic corporate-level strategies are available for companies in a growth mode:

1. Single business
2. Vertical integration
3. Diversification

This section also includes corporate-level strategies for companies in a decline mode.

Concentration on a Single Business   The first corporate-level strategy is concentration on a single business. Based on an environmental assessment, a company might determine that the best corporate-level strategy is to confine its efforts to a single industry or market. By concentrating its resources on one industry or on one product, a company can build distinctive competencies and can gain a competitive advantage. Many property-casualty insurers are pursuing a single-business strategy, even though they write many types of insurance.

Several large companies, such as Sears and Coca-Cola, started as single businesses, experimented with diversification, and then returned to a core single business. Over the course of sixty years, Sears expanded its retail operation to include divisions such as Allstate Insurance, Dean Witter Reynolds, and Coldwell Banker. During the 1990s, however, Sears made the strategic decision to return to its retail roots and divested its varied financial services companies. Coca-Cola experienced a period of diversification during the 1960s and 1970s when its operations included water treatment, plastics, steam generators, and wine. In 1983, the company acquired Columbia Pictures and entered the entertainment industry. By the mid-1990s, however, the company changed strategies, refocused, and returned to producing only nonalcoholic beverages, primarily soft drinks and fruit juices.

Concentrating on a single business has some potential disadvantages. Most are related to missed opportunities to build a competitive advantage through either vertical integration or diversification into related areas.

Vertical Integration   The second corporate-level strategy is vertical integration. When a company pursues a **vertical integration strategy**, it either produces its own inputs (backward integration) or disposes of its own outputs (forward integration). In other words, the company either produces inputs that were previously provided by a supplier or distributes its own outputs instead of using a distributor, wholesaler, or retailer. When an organization produces inputs for processing, it is called backward integration. A pharmaceutical manufacturer that acquires its packaging provider to produce its drugs and medicines is using backward integration. When an organization sells its product directly to the customer rather than through a wholesaler, it is called forward integration. A food processor taking over the distribution of its finished products, eliminating a wholesaler or using a factory outlet, is using forward integration. By selling directly to customers, direct writer insurers are using forward integration.

Companies choose vertical integration to raise market-entry barriers, control the quality of goods, or use capital more efficiently. Some potential disadvantages include increased costs and lack of management expertise related to moving backward or forward through different stages of the production process.

Diversification   The third corporate-level strategy is diversification. Companies can pursue either related or unrelated diversification strategies. **Related diversification** expands business operations in areas similar to a company's existing operations. Property-casualty insurers that also provide

Vertical integration strategy
A corporate-level strategy through which a company either produces its own inputs or disposes of its own outputs.

Related diversification strategy
A corporate-level strategy through which a company expands its operations into areas that are similar to its existing operations.

life or health insurance are diversified into related areas. Related diversification allows companies to gain economies of scope by sharing resources, such as the same distribution system or research and development facilities. Another benefit of related diversification is the ability to leverage fixed expenses with additional revenues from diversified operations, resulting in a lower unit cost for each product or service offered. Several large brokers, primary insurers, and reinsurers entered into third-party administration of claims as their customers sought alternative risk financing approaches. This move is a form of related diversification that allowed insurers to use existing technology platforms, claim expertise, and other internal resources to build a competitive advantage and increase revenues.

Financial services modernization legislation led many banks to consider the insurance industry when looking for acquisition targets. Rather than following a related diversification strategy, however, most banks decided not to acquire insurance companies. Although the banks had expertise in the financial services area, many differences existed between banking operations and insurance operations. National banks are regulated at the federal level, while insurers are regulated at the state level. Different competencies are required for the two types of businesses. After completing their assessment, most banks made the strategic decision to enter into partnerships or strategic alliances with insurers to distribute products, such as annuities and life insurance. As an alternative to acquiring insurers, some banks acquired insurance agencies to use as a marketing system for various life insurance products. For example, in 2001, Wells Fargo acquired ACO Brokerage Corporation, the parent company of Acordia, the fifth largest insurance brokerage at the time. This acquisition made Wells Fargo's insurance agency network one of the biggest, with 176 offices operating in 38 states and with annual revenues of about $630 million.[13] Insurers made a different strategic decision. Several insurers applied for bank charters, once legally permitted to do so by the Gramm-Leach-Bliley Act. Instead of acquiring existing bank operations, major insurers such as State Farm and Allstate Insurance started their own banking operations. These are examples of insurers diversifying existing operations into the related banking field as part of a transformation to a broader financial services sector.

Unrelated diversification strategy, also referred to as *conglomerate diversification strategy*, involves acquiring companies that have no relationship to the existing business operations. Unrelated diversification is riskier than related diversification and should be undertaken only when there is significant potential for creating value for the company. Several companies, such as General Electric, Hitachi, Siemens, and Mitsubishi Corporation, have successfully followed an unrelated diversification strategy to increase profits. For example, General Electric (GE) holdings include such varied operations as appliances, lighting, jet engines, the NBC television network, and insurance operations within its GE Capital and Financial divisions. GE's insurance operations encompass Employers Reinsurance Corporation as well as GE Financial, which provides personal auto, home, life, health, and long-term care coverages, among others.

Unrelated diversification strategy
A corporate-level strategy through which a company expands its operations into areas that have no relation to its existing operations.

Some of the problems with unrelated diversification include the additional costs of coordinating divergent businesses. Often, companies overdiversify, which leads to a loss of synergy among business units and diminishing returns from any economies of scale or scope. Companies that have succeeded with an unrelated diversification strategy excel at making wise decisions about the right types of acquisitions. These companies have also developed strong structure and control mechanisms to offset some of the difficulties stemming from managing an extensive and varied group of profit centers.

Decline Mode Strategies   All of the strategies discussed to this point involve companies operating in markets that are growing. Some companies might not be growing or might be encountering substantial marketplace obstacles. These organizations might have numerous internal weaknesses and external threats. The problems that these companies encounter could include decreasing profits, loss of market share, or changing economic conditions. When a company is operating in a market in which demand for its products or services is decreasing, it is in a decline mode and its strategic options are different from those in a growth mode. Corporate-level strategies for such companies are defensive. In the worst-case scenario, the company might determine that the only option is bankruptcy or liquidation. In bankruptcy, companies seek court protection from creditors to reorganize and improve their financial standing. If a company cannot recover from bankruptcy, it is liquidated and any remaining proceeds are used to satisfy outstanding obligations.

Other corporate-level strategies that can be used in a decline mode include harvest, turnaround, and divestiture. Using a **harvest strategy**, a company seeks short-term profits while phasing out a particular product line or exiting the market. **Turnaround strategies**, on the other hand, are aimed at rebuilding organizational resources to return the company to profitable levels. When an organization decides the best approach is to sell off a portion of its operation, usually a division or profit center, it is following a **divestiture strategy**.

Citigroup, Inc., provides an excellent example of the use of a divestiture strategy. The merger of Citicorp and Travelers Insurance was touted as the largest such transaction in the financial services sector. In April 1998, the two companies announced the planned merger that would result in the largest financial services company in the world, to be named Citigroup. The strategic intent was to capitalize on pending financial overhaul legislation and to provide one-stop shopping for all of a customer's financial services needs. However, fewer than three years later, in late 2001, Citigroup stated its intent to spin off Travelers' property-casualty insurance units to focus more fully on its remaining financial services businesses. This spin-off was completed in 2002, with Travelers Property Casualty Corporation continuing as an independent company concentrating on non-life insurance.

Business-Level Strategies

Business-level strategies are developed at the business or division level by managers who are responsible for supporting the stated corporate-level

Harvest strategy
A corporate-level strategy through which a company seeks to gain short-term profits while phasing out a product line or exiting a market.

Turnaround strategy
A corporate-level strategy through which a company rebuilds organizational resources to return to profitable levels.

Divestiture strategy
A corporate-level strategy through which a company sells off a portion of an operation, usually a division or profit center that is not performing to expectations.

strategy. These managers must find ways for their business units to be competitive and to respond to changes in the external environment. Business-level management also budgets for needed resources and coordinates the functional-level strategy within the division. The time frame for business-level strategies, sometimes referred to as tactical strategies, is three to five years in most organizations. Porter's three business-level strategies are:

1. Cost leadership
2. Differentiation
3. Focus

Cost Leadership   The first business-level strategy is cost leadership. With a **cost leadership** strategy, companies seek to achieve cost efficiencies in all operational areas in order to charge a low price. This means eliminating costs in every aspect of the operation, from product development and design to processing to distribution and delivery. Cost leadership involves more than just charging the lowest price in the industry. Even when prices for similar products are comparable, the cost leader can earn higher overall profits than its competitors because of its lower costs. Cost leaders can also better withstand prolonged price wars. One requirement of a cost leadership strategy is that most products or services must be fairly standardized, because introducing varied types of products increases expenses and erodes any cost leadership advantages. Consequently, cost leaders are generally not first movers within an industry.

Cost leadership
A business-level strategy through which a company seeks cost efficiencies in all operational areas.

Airlines are a good example of companies that built competitive advantage by following a cost leadership strategy. As large hub-and-spoke carriers like U.S. Airways and United Airlines faced bankruptcy because of rising costs, small regional airlines gained market share. The best-known of these is Southwest Airlines, which saves costs by using only one type of aircraft, flying point to point, not providing in-flight meals, and turning flights around quickly. These cost savings allow the airline to gain customers by charging lower fares than the large national airlines. Southwest constantly faces competition in its market from other small airlines that are attempting to duplicate its success. Another frequently cited cost leader is in the retail industry. Wal-Mart has aggressively followed a cost leadership strategy that has affected not only other discount retailers, such as Kmart and Sears, but also grocery retailers. Wal-Mart reduces its overall cost of sales through inventory controls, warehousing, and product distribution. Individual store managers have access to inventory systems that provide detailed information on current stock and customer preferences as well as sales data. These controls and systems are difficult to imitate, strengthening Wal-Mart's competitive grip on the retail sector.

Competitors in other industries might use price cutting as part of a cost leadership strategy. For insurers, price cutting might be limited by regulatory constraints. Insurers must closely examine the three components of an insurance rate to determine where costs can be reduced. These three components are allowances for loss payments, expenses, and profit. When evaluating how to decrease costs, insurers consider reducing acquisition expenses by lowering agents' commissions, using a direct writer system for some or all of their marketing, and exploring alternative distribution channels.

Loss expenses can be reduced by streamlining claim adjusting processes, implementing cost containment practices for loss payments, and managing litigation expenses. Underwriting expenses can be reduced by using expert systems or changing underwriting guidelines. Technology can automate processes, improve interaction among departments, and speed policy processing times. All of these efforts combine to execute the cost leadership strategy.

Differentiation   The second business-level strategy is differentiation. A **differentiation strategy** requires the company to develop products or services that are distinct and for which customers will pay a higher price than that of the competition. Higher prices allow the company to enjoy higher profit margins. A successful differentiation strategy requires products and services that customers perceive as distinctive and that are difficult for rivals to imitate easily. Companies using this strategy must accurately determine customers' needs and preferences; otherwise, revenue and market share will be lost. Market share will also be lost quickly if competitors can match or exceed the product's unique features.

Insurers employing this strategy may choose to differentiate products or services to gain market share and to establish a competitive advantage. Insurers that offer special programs for commercial or homeowners insurance are an example. When an insurer writes only homeowners or personal auto insurance and targets multiple markets such as teachers, retired persons, and military personnel, it is following a differentiation strategy. If an insurer chooses instead to concentrate only on municipalities but offers a wide range of specialized coverages, it is following a focus strategy, described next.

Focus   The third business-level strategy is focus. A focus strategy involves using either a low-cost approach or a differentiation strategy, but only for a specific market segment. Focus companies concentrate on either a group of customers, a geographic area, or a narrow line of products or services. A **focused cost leadership strategy** centers on one group of customers and involves offering low-priced products or services. Conversely, a **focused differentiation strategy** also centers on one group of customers but involves offering unique or customized products or services. This uniqueness permits the company to charge a higher price for the product than that of the competition. Clothing retailer Gap Inc., for instance, follows a focused differentiation strategy in its Gap and Banana Republic stores and a focused cost leadership approach for its Old Navy stores. In this way, Gap Inc. chooses to focus on uniqueness, branding, and quality in its differentiated stores and price in its low-cost stores while still leveraging the value of the overall brand.

Many insurers follow a focus approach. Most niche marketing programs, which offer tailored coverages to specific groups of customers, are examples of

Differentiation strategy
A business-level strategy through which a company develops products or services that are distinct and for which customers will pay a higher price than that of the competition.

Focused cost leadership strategy
A business-level strategy through which a company focuses on one group of customers and offers a low-price product or service.

Focused differentiation strategy
A business-level strategy through which a company focuses on one group of customers and offers unique or customized products that permit it to charge a higher price than that of the competition.

focused differentiation. Using a focused cost leadership approach, a company would sell to a specific group of customers, such as retail hardware stores, and offer discounted commercial package or automobile policies using standard forms. This use of standard forms is an important consideration because any significant level of specialization increases costs and erodes profits.

Functional-Level Strategies

Functional-level strategies are the plans for managing a particular functional area and are sometimes called operational strategies. These strategies establish how functional departments support the organization's business- and corporate-level strategies. Functional areas include marketing, finance and accounting, human resources, and operations. In an insurer, underwriting, claims, actuarial, loss control, and premium audit are also functional areas. The time frame for these strategies is short term, usually one year.

When considering functional-level strategies, the idea of building value through the activities that are conducted at every organizational level is important. If customers value a company's product, they will be willing to purchase that product, which results in revenue for the organization.[14] All of a company's activities must provide value to allow the company to gain a competitive advantage. Companies build value and competitive advantage through efficiency, quality, customer responsiveness, and innovation.[15] For a company to pursue either a cost leadership or differentiation strategy at the business level, some combination of these factors must be incorporated into its activities at the functional or operational level. For example, without efficiency and innovation, cost leadership cannot be attained. Similarly, quality and customer responsiveness must be included in the development, production, and marketing functions for a company to execute a differentiation strategy effectively.

In insurance operations, functional-level strategies specify how the underwriting, claim, actuarial, and other departments advance business-level strategies. For an insurer to be successful at garnering market share using a cost leadership strategy, it must be a highly efficient organization. Specifically, human resources, in cooperation with the underwriting, claim, customer service, and marketing departments, must find ways to improve productivity. The information systems department must provide innovative technological solutions to lower overall production costs and to improve the speed of organizational communications, both internally and externally. Likewise, in a company that is pursuing a differentiation strategy, innovation and quality at all functional levels are critical to providing a distinctive product that meets the customer's needs.

Strategy Implementation

The second phase in the strategic management process is strategy implementation. A company cannot achieve its goals if its strategies are not implemented effectively. Strategy implementation involves:

•   Designing an effective organizational structure to support the strategy.

•   Implementing organizational strategic controls.

Strategies need to be continually assessed and modified based on market, economic, and competitive conditions.

Organizational Structure

The first consideration in strategy implementation is designing the structure of the organization. A company's strategic goals determine the most appropriate organizational structure. In a single-business company, a **functional structure** might be most suitable, with departments defined by the operation they perform; i.e., marketing, finance, research and development, and human resources, as shown in Exhibit 15-5. A diversified company is more likely to use a **multidivisional structure** to organize its operations and to segregate each division into separate profit centers. Exhibit 15-6 shows a multidivisional structure for an insurer using a related diversification strategy. Other structures organize company operations by region or type of product or customer. A food manufacturer, for example, might have separate departments for institutional customers, retail customers, and wholesale customers. This way, the expertise and technology required for specific customers is concentrated within the related department. Such an approach supports a differentiation strategy, in which the company seeks to provide unique products for specific market segments.

Functional structure
An organizational structure in which departments are defined by the operation they perform.

Multidivisional structure
An organizational structure in which divisions are organized into separate profit centers.

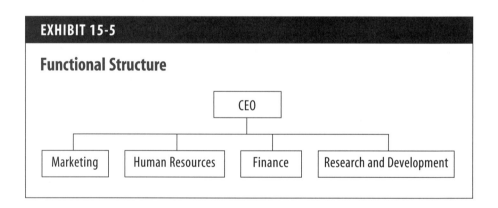

EXHIBIT 15-5

Functional Structure

Another decision about structure involves reporting relationships or the company's level of vertical differentiation. Some companies are tall organizations, with many levels ranging from executive through functional positions.

Conversely, a flat organization has fewer levels from the top of the organization to the bottom. When following a cost leadership strategy, a flat organization helps to eliminate costs related to maintaining multiple reporting relationships within the company.

EXHIBIT 15-6

Multidivisional Structure

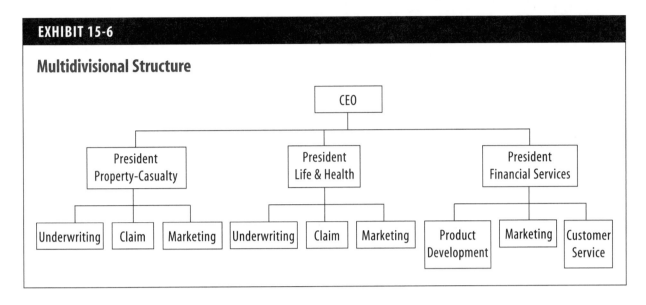

Companies should also decide what level of centralization is needed to operate efficiently and to meet organizational goals. Centralization involves whether authority is maintained at top levels of the organization or is delegated throughout headquarters, into regions, or even to the local level. For example, some insurers retain underwriting authority at the headquarters level, while others extend authority to local offices or to managing general agents. The claim department makes similar decisions about whether claim-settling authority resides with home office claim staff or is extended to regional claim managers or local company adjusters.

Organizational Control

The second consideration in strategy implementation is organizational control. Control mechanisms allow management at each level to integrate established strategies into the organization's activities. The control process also facilitates gauging the progress the organization is making toward achieving its goals. The four steps in the control process are:

1. Establish standards.
2. Create and apply measurements.
3. Compare actual results to standards.
4. Evaluate and implement corrective actions if goals are not met.

Following these steps provides a structured approach to strategy implementation. As an example, if a department has established a goal of increasing sales by 5 percent in a quarter, the next step would be to create and apply measurements. These measurements might consist of spreadsheets, sales reports, or similar metrics. At the end of the quarter, actual sales figures would be compiled and would be compared to those from the beginning of the quarter.

If sales increased by the established standard of 5 percent, the department met its goal. If sales increased by less than 5 percent, management would need to determine why the goal was not met and what changes need to made. Management's evaluation would examine all aspects of the sales process, including the product or service being provided, the customers for that product or service, the delivery process, and the performance of the employees in the department.

Controls can fall into several categories based on which goals are being monitored. The first category is financial controls. Financial controls include assessing the company's stock price or using a return on investment (ROI) formula for evaluating specific projects. ROI compares the income from a project or department to the capital invested in that project and can be used to compare the performance of one department to that of another. Budgets are used to allocate resources within the organization and can also be used as a control mechanism. Cost/benefit analysis is another frequently used financial control. Project benefits in the form of cost savings or additional revenues must exceed the cost of the project within a pre-determined time period, usually three years or fewer.

In the insurance industry, loss ratios, expense ratios, and combined ratios are financial controls that are used to evaluate not only overall corporate performance, but also the performance of business units, regional offices, and individual books of business. As an example, when applying the steps in the control process to an insurer's field office underwriting department, step one would involve establishing a combined ratio under 100 as the standard. Insurer combined ratios are usually readily available, which makes the ratio an appropriate and easily applied standard. Measurement would then consist of compiling all of the premium, expense, and loss data required to develop a combined-ratio figure for this individual office and determining a format for reporting these data. Motivating employees to meet the standard is an inherent part of this process, and managers need to communicate the importance of meeting this standard to all employees. These premium, expense, and loss reports would then be used in the third step of the process—in this case, comparing actual results to the established standard of a combined ratio under 100. If the standard has not been met, managers will need to determine the reason and then implement changes. Depending on the results of this comparison, these changes might involve training initiatives for employees, strengthening communications with producers, examining marketing activities, or taking other corrective actions. If the goal has been met, management should reward and recognize all employees involved, which can provide motivation to achieve future strategic goals.

Other categories of controls include operational or process controls that are used to monitor work flow, production processes, and customer service. In cost leadership companies, systems to track costs, sales data, and inventory are important in ensuring that expenses are being controlled. In an underwriting department, selection, pricing, and service standards serve as operational controls. For a claim department, such controls could include the average cost of settlement, average caseload per adjuster, or file turnover rates for individual claim adjusters.

Another important category of controls is human or behavior controls. This category includes rules, policies, and procedures that provide operating guidelines for employees within an organization, and it can be used to measure individual performance. The performance appraisal process is also a control device in which individual goals are established and assessed.

Reward systems are another form of control and can include profit-sharing programs, stock options plans, and other bonus arrangements. When developing such programs, rewards must be clearly linked to goal achievement.

GLOBAL OPERATIONS

A key strategic decision is whether an organization will operate solely on a domestic basis or will expand globally. The decision to operate globally involves many variables. Management needs to determine what products could be sold in other countries, what distribution channels should be used, and how regulations and government restrictions might affect global operations. Making these determinations is essential for an organization to decide whether operating globally would improve its competitive advantage. The remainder of this chapter discusses considerations related to operating on a global basis.

The pace of growth in global operations has increased rapidly over the past two decades. This growth is attributable to a reduction in national barriers as the result of decreased tariffs and quotas, as well as the activities of the World Trade Organization (WTO) and the growth of the European Union. Also, agreements such as the North American Free Trade Agreement (NAFTA), the ASEAN Free Trade Area (AFTA) in Southeast Asia, and the Caribbean Community and Common Market (CARICOM) have stimulated international trade. More than fifteen such trade agreements exist throughout the world. These agreements expand trade in specific regions of the world or between countries by lowering trade barriers.

Advances in technology and transportation have also fueled growth of global commerce by facilitating the movement of goods and information. The Internet has had an enormous effect on global commerce, not only by improving communication but also by promoting e-commerce worldwide.

Global Environment

When a company is considering global expansion, it must analyze the global environment in which it would be operating. This analysis is similar to the general environmental analysis performed for domestic operations. The factors to consider, however, change based on the country or countries in which the company would be doing business. Culture and language will usually differ from those of the U.S. Legal and regulatory requirements also change drastically from one country to another. And, in a rapidly changing world, political considerations are critical when investing in foreign operations. Stable governments and economies can deteriorate almost overnight because of political uprisings. Emerging markets can present tremendous opportunity but also tremendous risk because of volatile politics. All of these factors influence an organization's decision about global expansion.

Culture

Culture includes all of a society's values, beliefs, and customs and comprises the unwritten set of social rules that govern how members of a society behave toward one another. When meeting someone from another country, is it acceptable to shake hands? Is it customary to discuss business over a meal, or are business negotiations limited to office or business settings? Degree of formality is another aspect of culture. For example, in the U.S., most businesspeople use first names when addressing each other. In some parts of Europe or in Japan, the use of first names in business might be considered a sign of disrespect, and surnames are always used.

One important aspect of culture involves how individuals perceive time. In some parts of the world, such as the U.S., Great Britain, or Germany, meetings usually start on time and follow a prescribed agenda. In some Latin, Arab, or Asian cultures, the view of time is more fluid, and not as much emphasis is placed on punctuality. Meetings might not start on time, or they might last for many hours. These latter cultures emphasize personal relationships; therefore, business negotiations start by establishing a relationship before proceeding to business matters.

Some societies are individualist, while others lean toward collectivism. In individualistic cultures, such as those in the U.S., Canada, or Australia, the interests of the individual come first, and people tend to be more independent. In collectivist societies, such as in Japan, China, and some Latin American countries, the individual is part of a group, and the interests of the group or the family come first. Consequently, decisions take longer to make because collective cultures seek consensus. In an individualistic culture, one person might be empowered to make the final decision on a business deal. These differences mean that when a Canadian or U.S. company is negotiating with a Japanese company, frustration can arise on both sides. The Canadian or U.S. businesspeople might think that the discussions are proceeding too slowly and be eager to close the deal. The Japanese, however, might think that the discussion is proceeding too quickly.

Religious beliefs are also a part of any society's culture and can affect how and when business is conducted. In Islamic countries, religious influence can affect the role of women in the workplace. In other countries, prevailing religious beliefs can affect working hours, holidays, and other practices within local offices of a multinational company.

Companies that are considering global expansion need to be familiar with the cultures of countries in which they will be conducting business. Expatriate managers should receive cultural training, including how to deal appropriately with host-country customers and employees. The motivation, supervision, and assessment of employees varies by country based on cultural expectations.

Language

Language differences can be one of the greatest challenges in international business dealings. Although English is spoken in many countries, the native language is used in contracts, advertising, package information, and instructions for products sold in that country. To expedite hiring employees, purchasing raw materials, and entering into contracts, expatriate managers should be able to speak the language of the country in which they will be working.

Communication extends beyond spoken language to nonverbal communication, which can sometimes be complex. Nonverbal communication includes body language, eye contact, gestures, and even modes of dress. Silence, for example, means different things in different cultures. In the U.S., people tend to fill in periods of silence with additional information. In some Asian cultures, however, silence is a sign of respect and thoughtfulness. Nonverbal communication also includes physical touch. Care should be taken to determine whether a kiss on the cheek is appropriate or whether a handshake is a more proper greeting. In some cultures, the importance of maintaining eye contact in business dealings is stressed. In other cultures, such eye contact can be offensive or disrespectful.

Regulations

Companies in all industries should evaluate imports/exports and antitrust regulations before entering global markets. Several U.S. companies have had business ventures rejected by the European Union's Competition Committee based on antitrust concerns.[16] That committee also denied approval of the proposed merger between General Electric and Honeywell International, which had already been sanctioned by U.S. regulators.

For insurers, meeting regulatory requirements is even more important. As in the U.S., licensing of insurers, forms and rates, trade practices, and solvency are regulated in other countries. However, the degree of regulation varies, and specific requirements vary by jurisdiction.

In the European Union (EU), each country has its own set of insurance regulatory requirements, although the European Commission (EC) is continually working toward a European Single Market. The principles governing this movement to a single market are contained in the *EC Insurance Directives*. The following is an excerpt from the preface of the original printing of those directives:

> The objective, first is to allow insurers in one Member State to establish offices and undertake business in another member state, and, secondly, to allow insurers in one Member State to undertake business in another Member State without having to set up any form of local establishment.[17]

According to these directives, an insurer that is authorized to sell insurance in one EU member state can also sell insurance in other member states. Insurers wanting to sell insurance in member states other than their own must notify the regulators in their home country. A regulator in this home country completes a certificate indicating which types of insurance the company is authorized to write and that the regulator has no objections to the cross-border transactions.[18]

Asia has a wide range of markets and regulatory approaches. In Japan, insurance operations are regulated by the Ministry of Finance, which also regulates banking. The ministry controls the industry tightly and focuses on solvency and rate and form filings. In China, the insurance market is still heavily controlled by the state, although some foreign companies are making inroads. Although China joined the World Trade Organization in late 2001, regulators have been slow to adjust to market forces.[19]

Two organizations support regulatory activities. One is the National Association of Insurance Commissioners (NAIC), located in the United States. The NAIC assists state regulators in finding solutions for regulatory issues, including the formulation of model insurance acts. This association of state regulators facilitates the handling of regulatory issues but has no legislative authority.

The International Association of Insurance Supervisors (IAIS), headquartered in Switzerland, is similar to the NAIC but operates internationally. IAIS represents insurance regulators and sets international standards supervising insurance regulation. More than 100 IAIS members represent a wide range of jurisdictions, including the U.S., U.K., Singapore, Canada, Argentina, Fiji, and Denmark.

Laws

The written laws and regulations of a country are another aspect of its culture. Societies codify their values and beliefs in written laws or regulations, and culture has a critical effect on the concept of legal responsibility, legal process, and legal structure. As part of preparing to enter the global market, an organization must understand the laws to which the company will be subject in the international jurisdictions where it does business.

In some societies, the laws do not support the idea of risk transfer within the insurance mechanism. These laws would not allow an insurer to transfer to another the responsibility to pay for unintentional damage to property caused by the insured. The person who caused the damage is held responsible and must make reparation. For example, Japan adopted some aspects of the American legal system following World War II. Japanese companies involved in legal disputes, however, are still uncomfortable with litigating to solve disputes and seek compromise as part of their ingrained national culture. Additionally, far fewer attorneys practice in Japan than in the U.S., and a limited number of students are permitted to study law each year.[20] Also in Japan, the loser in a lawsuit is responsible for paying all expenses of both parties.

Economic Considerations

When a company is considering expanding into a foreign country, it must consider the country's economic environment. Factors to consider include the level of economic stability, monetary policies, the prevailing attitude toward foreign investors, and the potential for exchange-rate volatility. Other economic factors such as the country's gross domestic product or national income are also important. When making decisions on marketing to specific countries or regions, having information on personal income, wage levels, and individual disposable income is helpful.

Political Risks

Political risks are uncertainties faced by companies doing business in foreign countries that arise from the actions of host-country governments. These risks are greater in developing or emerging countries than in established countries with stable governments.

Of greatest concern is the potential for the confiscation of business assets by a foreign government or other interference with the rights of ownership of corporate assets, such as confiscation of inventory. Expropriation occurs when a foreign government takes property without compensating its owners. This occurred in Cuba during the 1960s when many U.S. firms had business properties and inventory expropriated as part of Cuba's regime change. Expropriation in Cuba started with U.S. sugar companies and led to the eventual nationalization of all foreign businesses in the country. Foreign governments might also nationalize a business and compensate the owners, usually at a lower rate than the market value of the assets. Companies are also concerned when countries treat local businesses more favorably than foreign businesses regarding taxes, government contracts, or access to required financing. Such discriminatory treatment can be subtle within some jurisdictions.

Another area of concern includes terrorism, civil unrest, and acts of war. Foreign nationals and their businesses can be at great risk in unsettled parts of the world.

Most of these loss exposures can be covered by political risk insurance, which is available from large insurers. This insurance can sometimes be extended to include kidnap and ransom and other related coverages. Companies can also work with consultants who provide country reports or political risk scores to determine what political risks are present and how dangerous those risks are for foreign businesses.

Global Market Entry

Once a decision has been made to operate globally, the choice of market entry must be made. A company can enter the global market using the following methods:

- Exporting
- International licensing
- Franchising
- Foreign direct investment

Insurers with customers that operate globally must understand the various loss exposures these customers acquire. In the insurance industry, insurers operating domestically might provide coverage for customers that have overseas operations. Other insurers might elect to open offices in foreign countries to provide coverage not only for customers in that nation but for multinational corporations (MNCs) that also have business locations there.

Exporting

The first method of expanding global operations is exporting. Exporting is the simplest mode of entry into global markets. It carries the lowest degree of risk because the exporting company is not physically located in another country. Exporting is also a cost-effective way to expand gradually into global operations. Much of the managerial responsibility for exporting can be contracted to an export broker. As an organization gains experience and becomes more familiar with foreign markets, it can assume more control over its export operations. Companies that engage in exporting must be knowledgeable about regulations, documentation procedures, packaging requirements, transportation, and export finance and accounting arrangements.

International Licensing

The second method of expanding global operations is international licensing. Licensing is another method of entering international markets without establishing a physical presence in a foreign country. Licensing involves a higher degree of risk than exporting goods to another country. A licensing arrangement is a contractual agreement allowing one party to use another party's distribution system or trademark. The risks involved include the potential for loss of control over the product or service, illegal use of the trademark, and possible conflicts with licensees. Licensing does, however, provide a cost-efficient method of accessing foreign markets and gaining the licensees' expertise in the local market.

Before entering into any agreement, the domestic company must assess the trustworthiness of the foreign company to which the license is being extended. The domestic company must also review the other company's financial condition and ability to meet the license agreement's financial requirements. Understanding the foreign legal environment regarding copyright, trademark, and patent protection within the applicable jurisdictions is also required.

Franchising

The third method of expanding global operations is franchising. In a franchise, one company, known as the franchiser, permits another party, known as a franchisee, to operate a business or provide a product under its name. A franchise is a contract entered into for a specific time period. The franchisee pays a fee or royalty to the franchiser for the contractual rights and provides its own capital for operation. The franchiser could provide training, technical assistance, specialized equipment, advertising services, and other support.

Much of the success of a franchise arrangement depends on the standardization of the company's product or services. Also important is how successful the franchiser has been domestically, how transferable that success is to foreign locations, and how many foreign investors are available to enter into a franchise agreement.[21]

As with licensing, franchising has the potential for loss of control of the franchiser's company name and the quality of the products and services provided by the franchisee. Some companies exercise control over the risk of improper use or poor quality by withholding vital technology or a component product. For example, hotels can maintain control of their reservation systems, and fast-food restaurants can maintain control of product formulas, recipes, or critical ingredients as part of the franchise agreement. The potential disadvantages of a franchise are disagreeing with a franchiser and creating a future competitor by providing the franchisee with expertise in the company's operation.

Despite these risks, many hotels and fast-food operations have been successful with international franchise agreements. Companies such as Holiday Inn, McDonald's, and KFC are all involved in worldwide franchise operations.

Foreign Direct Investment

The fourth method of expanding global operations is foreign direct investment. **Foreign direct investment (FDI)** is the most complex mode of entry into global markets and therefore carries the highest degree of risk. With FDI, the organization is involved in owning and controlling assets in a foreign country. FDI can take the form of strategic alliances, joint ventures, or wholly owned subsidiary operations.

> **Foreign direct investment**
> A global-market entry method involving owning or controlling assets in a foreign country.

Strategic Alliances

A **strategic alliance** is a form of foreign direct investment in which two organizations work together to achieve a common goal. The participants retain ownership of their individual companies. Strategic alliances have the advantage of bringing together separate areas of expertise and of gaining a host-country participant, who can access local markets and who is familiar with local laws, regulations, and customers. As with any other agreement, disagreements between participants might develop, and companies might not work together effectively to achieve intended goals. The benefit of a strategic alliance is that it provides a low-risk approach to quickly entering a new market.

> **Strategic alliance**
> An arrangement in which two companies work together to achieve a common goal.

Strategic alliances can take many forms and can be limited to financing, marketing, or research and development activities. According to a PricewaterhouseCoopers survey of 425 companies, 71 percent were involved in joint marketing and promotional arrangements, 58 percent had alliances for joint selling or distributing products, and 29 percent had research and development alliances.[22]

Joint Ventures

Joint venture
A specific type of strategic alliance in which companies share ownership, responsibilities, and management of a foreign venture.

Another form of foreign direct investment is a joint venture. A **joint venture** is a specific type of strategic alliance that involves shared ownership, shared responsibilities, and often joint management of the foreign venture. A joint-venture agreement brings together two companies to form a new organization that is legally separate and distinct from the parent companies. A joint venture has its own management and board of directors. The most common form of joint venture occurs when a domestic company joins with a company from the host country, the foreign location in which the operation is located. Joint ventures with governments or state-owned industries are also common, particularly in India, China, Russia, and the former Soviet republics. These joint ventures are referred to as *public-private ventures*. Less common are joint ventures of participants from two or more countries entering a third market and joint ventures of more than two or three participants.

Joint ventures allow companies to enter markets (both geographic and product markets) and acquire technology that would otherwise be beyond the reach of an individual company. However, joint ventures present an increased risk compared to exporting, franchising, or licensing and require a greater commitment of resources. For example, a joint venture requires the commitment of substantial managerial resources. A company might also have to make a substantial capital investment or share proprietary technology with its joint-venture partner. However, the costs of capital and of research and development could be shared among the participants.

One of the most important aspects of a joint venture is choosing the right participants. Companies must choose participants carefully and craft an equitable agreement for sharing resources, managerial responsibility, technology, and profits. Consequently, completing a joint-venture agreement to enter global markets might take considerably longer than completing a similar agreement in the domestic market.

Wholly Owned Subsidiaries

The last form of foreign direct investment is a wholly owned subsidiary. In a wholly owned subsidiary, the domestic company owns and controls assets in a foreign country. This form presents the highest degree of risk in entering global markets, including business, political, and economic risk. Operating a subsidiary in a foreign country requires more capital than exporting, licensing, or entering into a joint venture. A wholly owned subsidiary also gives the domestic company greater control over operations.

Companies considering this mode of entry into global markets must decide whether they want to begin a new operation or acquire an existing foreign company. The time required to enter global markets using subsidiary ownership varies depending on the decision that is made. Acquiring an existing foreign company could occur fairly quickly, whereas building a subsidiary from scratch could take a considerable amount of time. The latter approach, however, gives companies the greatest level of control over their foreign affiliates because the parent company makes decisions about management, distribution channels, product mix, and other organizational issues.

International Insurance Operations

Generally, global insurers are involved mostly with large commercial accounts. Personal insurance customers are more often serviced by domestic insurers. Reinsurance tends to be global and is dominated by international reinsurers.

Many domestic insurers become involved in global operations by providing coverage for incidental international loss exposures for their domestic insureds. Incidental international loss exposures include those arising from activities conducted outside the U.S., including the following:

- Overseas travel by company representatives, such as executives, salespersons, mechanics, and engineers
- Sales made in foreign countries either by direct sales or through an overseas distributor
- Participation in foreign trade shows or exhibits
- Small, pilot sales offices
- Imports from foreign countries

Global competition is now a factor in virtually every industry. As governments continue to deregulate industries, as more countries turn to market-based economies, and as trade barriers are lowered, global competition increases. Consequently, international mergers and acquisitions, both by U.S. insurers abroad and by those entering U.S. markets, have increased significantly in recent years. These developments have led many large insurers to expand their operations beyond covering only incidental loss exposures. As illustrated in Exhibit 15-7, world nonlife premiums grew 37.5 percent between 1991 and 2000.[23]

Some basic differences exist between types of insurance in the U.S. and in other parts of the world. In the U.S., insurers are categorized as either property-casualty or life and health companies. In most parts of the world, these categories are known as "life" or "nonlife." U.S. property-casualty companies are further categorized as providing either personal or commercial insurance. In most of the countries in the European Union, personal insurance is called "mass risks." Furthermore, in Great Britain, the equivalent of the U.S. property-casualty industry is called the general insurance sector of the nonlife business. Exhibit 15-8 shows the top ten global insurers based on 2001 revenue.

EXHIBIT 15-7

World Life and Nonlife Insurance Premiums, 1991–2000

(Direct written premiums, U.S. $ millions)

Year	Nonlife[1]	Life	Total
1991	$670,715	$ 743,648	$1,414,363
1992	697,503	768,436	1,465,939
1993	792,087	1,010,490	1,802,731
1994	846,600	1,121,186	1,967,787
1995	906,781	1,236,627	2,143,408
1996	909,100	1,196,736	2,105,838
1997	896,873	1,231,798	2,128,671
1998	891,352	1,275,053	2,166,405
1999	912,749	1,424,203	2,336,952
2000	922,420	1,521,253	2,443,673

[1] Includes accident and health insurance.

Source: Swiss Re, *sigma,* No. 6/2001.

Reprinted with permission from *The Fact Book 2003* (New York: Insurance Information Institute, 2003), p. 4.

EXHIBIT 15-8

Top Ten Global Property/Casualty Insurance Companies, by Revenue, 2001[1]

Rank	Company	Revenue[2] ($ millions)	Country
1	Allianz	$85,929	Germany
2	American International Group	62,402	U.S.
3	State Farm Insurance	46,705	U.S.
4	Munich Re Group	41,894	Germany
5	Zurich Financial Services	38,650	Switzerland
6	Berkshire Hathaway	37,668	U.S.
7	Allstate	28,865	U.S.
8	Royal & Sun Alliance	21,525	U.K.
9	Swiss Reinsurance	20,210	Switzerland
10	Loews (CNA Financial Corp.)	18,799	U.S.

[1] Includes stock and mutual companies. Based on an analysis of companies in the Global Fortune 500.

[2] Revenue includes premium and annuity income, investment income and capital gains or losses but excludes deposits; includes consolidated subsidiaries; excludes excise taxes.

Source: *Fortune*

Reprinted with permission from *The Fact Book 2003* (New York: Insurance Information Institute, 2003), p. 2.

Admitted Versus Nonadmitted Insurance for Multinational Loss Exposures

Insurers provide insurance for international loss exposures on one of three bases: admitted, nonadmitted, or a combination of the two. Multinational insurers must choose how to provide insurance for their international loss exposures and, accordingly, operate on either an admitted or a nonadmitted basis.

Admitted insurers are authorized (licensed) to conduct business in the country where they have operations. For example, in Nigeria, where nonadmitted insurance is prohibited, insurers must be licensed. Several countries have laws requiring insurance to be written by local insurers for designated classes of business.

Admitted insurance has the advantage of complying with local government laws and regulations. For example, having local government contracts or owning local real estate might require evidence of local insurance. If money is borrowed overseas, local insurance might be obligatory. Also, premiums and losses are paid in the local currency, minimizing any problems with currency restrictions or fluctuations. In some cases, local tax laws favor companies that purchase insurance through an admitted insurer. Additionally, when each affiliate of a multinational company pays its own premium, insurance costs reflect its loss exposures. Local management is more likely to be familiar with policy purchases, insurers, and local insurance nuances. When a local insurer provides insurance, loss settlements are more easily tailored to fit local needs, and loss control services might be superior to those provided from another country.

A multinational company encounters some disadvantages in purchasing insurance from an admitted insurer. The policy might be written in a foreign language, and it might be difficult to determine the solvency of the locally admitted insurer. Also, a U.S.-based company purchasing the insurance might be unable to adhere to its risk management philosophy. Locally admitted insurance often provides less-comprehensive coverage and contains more limitations than U.S. insurance. Also, obtaining high deductibles or partially self-insuring might be difficult or impossible if high deductible levels are unavailable or if deductible credit is significantly lower than in the home country.

Nonadmitted insurers are not authorized to write business in the particular country where the insured is located. To a multinational company, one advantage of purchasing nonadmitted insurance is that it might solve some of the language and currency problems related to purchasing admitted insurance. Insurance on a nonadmitted basis also facilitates a uniform risk management approach to policy provisions and can minimize coverage gaps. Also, nonadmitted insurance is not subject to override cost—an administrative fee for putting up admitted paper, issuing the policy, and arranging coverage.

Several disadvantages accompany nonadmitted insurance. In countries where nonadmitted insurance is not permitted, both the insurer and the insured could be subject to fines or penalties. Understanding local laws and regulations is important to prevent such fines or penalties. Also, the premiums under nonadmitted insurance might not be allowed as a deduction under local income tax. Premiums and losses might be difficult to allocate. Allocating premiums according to loss exposures is essential in encouraging the appropriate form of loss control. Without the advantage of admitted premiums, this process can be cumbersome. Claim handling can also be difficult with nonadmitted insurance because no local claim representation is available. Language and currency problems can also arise during claim settlement.

In some cases, admitted and nonadmitted insurance can be purchased in combination. To ensure proper coverage in such cases, however, provisions must be made to eliminate coverage gaps.

Exhibit 15-9 summarizes the advantages and disadvantages of admitted and nonadmitted coverages.

EXHIBIT 15-9

Admitted Versus Nonadmitted Insurance

Advantages of Admitted Insurance

- Favorable local tax laws
- Premiums and losses paid in the local currency
- Easier compliance with government laws and regulations
- Insurance costs reflected according to exposure

Disadvantages of Admitted Insurance

- Higher premiums required
- Policies might be written in a foreign language
- Risk management philosophy may be difficult to establish
- Solvency of locally admitted insurer might be difficult to determine

Advantages of Nonadmitted Insurance

- Currency and language problems minimized
- Risk management policy can be implemented
- Economies of multiple insurance uniformity
- Solvency problems minimized by centralized control
- No overrides to obtain local insurance
- Element of confidentiality

Disadvantages of Nonadmitted Insurance

- Insurer and insured subject to fines for noncompliance to local rules and laws
- Premiums might not be tax-deductible
- Premiums and losses are difficult to allocate
- Loss payments might be subject to local recapitalization taxes

SUMMARY

Formulating and implementing sound strategies is important for any organization. Doing so involves creating a mission and vision statement, identifying goals, analyzing the internal and external environments, and determining strategies. Well-formed strategies allow a company to meet goals and to build a competitive advantage in the marketplace.

The Five Forces Model can be used to thoroughly assess the organization's external environment by identifying factors related to customers, competitors, and suppliers. The five forces that drive competition are (1) the threat of new entrants, (2) the threat of substitute products or services, (3) bargaining power of buyers, (4) bargaining power of suppliers, and (5) rivalry among existing firms. Evaluating these forces also helps management to better understand the organization's position within its industry. A SWOT analysis can then be used to determine internal strengths and weaknesses related to the company's financial, physical, human, and organizational assets. An examination of the external environment would then be conducted to uncover opportunities and threats.

Strategy is planned and implemented at the organization's corporate, business, and functional levels. Corporate-level strategies in a growing company include concentration on a single business, vertical integration, and either related or unrelated diversification. When a company is encountering a decreasing market, corporate management is faced with a different set of strategies from those available to a growing company. For organizations in a decline mode, bankruptcy or liquidation may be undertaken as a last resort. Other available strategies include harvest, turnaround, or divestiture.

Business-level strategies are employed by divisional managers within the organization. These strategies include cost leadership, differentiation, and focus.

At the functional level, strategies focus on integrating efficiency, quality, customer responsiveness, and innovation in each functional process or operation. Insurer functional areas include the underwriting, claim, customer service, marketing, and other departments.

The chapter concludes with a discussion of global operations. When companies expand globally, management must carefully assess the global environment and decide on the best method for entering the global market. This assessment includes a consideration of the culture, regulations, language, laws, and economic conditions in the country or region into which the company will be expanding.

CHAPTER NOTES

1. Kraft Foods, Inc., "Investor Relations: Company Overview," http://164.109.67.247/investors/overview.html (accessed January 29, 2003).

2. The Mission of Southwest Airlines, http:// www.southwest.com/about_swa/ mission.html (accessed January 29, 2003).

3. Living Our Mission and Values, http://www.microsoft.com/mscorp/articles/ mission_values.asp (accessed January 29, 2003).

4. Kathryn M. Bartol and David C. Martin, *Management,* 3rd ed. (New York: McGraw-Hill Cos., Inc., 1998), pp. 192–193.

5. http://www.nationwide.com/about_us/our_values/index.htm (accessed January 14, 2003).

6. Michael E. Porter, *Competitive Strategy: Techniques for Analyzing Industries and Competitors* (New York: The Free Press, 1980), p. 4.

7. http://www.chubb.com/personal/homes (accessed August 6, 2002).

8. Porter, *Competitive Strategy,* pp. 9–12.

9. Porter, *Competitive Strategy,* p. 26.

10. Bartol and Martin, p. 228.

11. John A. Pearce II and Richard B. Robinson, Jr., *Strategic Management: Formulation, Implementation, and Control,* 6th ed. (New York: Irwin/McGraw-Hill, 1997), p. 172.

12. Michael E. Porter, "What Is Strategy?" *Harvard Business Review* (November/ December 1996), p. 62.

13. Irene Weber, "No Sale," *Best's Review* (May 2002), p. 51.

14. Michael E. Porter, *Competitive Advantage: Creating and Sustaining Superior Performances* (New York: The Free Press, 1985), pp. 36–39.

15. Charles W.L. Hill and Gareth R. Jones, *Strategic Management: An Integrated Approach,* 5th ed. (Boston: Houghton Mifflin Co., 2001), p. 126.

16. Stephen Baker, Gail Edmondson, and Dan Carney, "The World According to Monti," *Business Week* (March 25, 2002), p. 48.

17. Julian Maitland-Walker, *EC Insurance Directives* (London: LLP, 1992), p. vii.

18. Harold D. Skipper, ed., *International Risk and Insurance: An Environmental-Managerial Approach* (Boston: McGraw-Hill, 1998), p. 266.

19. David Pilla, "Going for the Gold," *Best's Review* (February 2003), p. 24.

20. Skipper, p. 213.

21. Ricky W. Griffin and Michael W. Pustay, *International Business: A Managerial Perspective,* 3rd ed. (Upper Saddle River, N.J.: Prentice Hall, 2002), p. 329.

22. "Strategic Alliances Give Big Revenue Boost to America's Fastest-Growing Companies," November 30, 2000, http://pwcglobal.com/extweb/ ncpressrelease.nsf (accessed February 10, 2003).

23. Insurance Information Institute, *The Fact Book 2003* (New York: Insurance Information Institute, 2003), p. 4.

Index

Page numbers in boldface refer to definitions of Key Words and Phrases.